Lecture Notes in Computer Science 3995

Commenced Publication in 1973
Founding and Former Series Editors:
Gerhard Goos, Juris Hartmanis, and Jan van Leeuwen

Günter Müller (Ed.)

Emerging Trends in Information and Communication Security

International Conference, ETRICS 2006
Freiburg, Germany, June 6-9, 2006
Proceedings

 Springer

Volume Editor

Günter Müller
Albert-Ludwigs-Universität Freiburg
Institut für Informatik und Gesellschaft, Abt. Telematik
Friedrichstr. 50, 79098 Freiburg, Germany
E-mail: guenter.mueller@iig.uni-freiburg.de

Library of Congress Control Number: 2006926426

CR Subject Classification (1998): E.3, C.2, D.4.6, H.3-4, K.4.4, K.6.5

LNCS Sublibrary: SL 4 – Security and Cryptology

ISSN	0302-9743
ISBN-10	3-540-34640-6 Springer Berlin Heidelberg New York
ISBN-13	978-3-540-34640-1 Springer Berlin Heidelberg New York

Springer is a part of Springer Science+Business Media

springer.com

© Springer-Verlag Berlin Heidelberg 2006
Printed in Germany

Typesetting: Camera-ready by author, data conversion by Scientific Publishing Services, Chennai, India
Printed on acid-free paper   SPIN: 11766155   06/3142   5 4 3 2 1 0

Preface

ETRICS: Security Remains a Moving Target

Günter Müller

Gerhard Schneider

Welcome to the proceedings of ETRICS 2006. Considering the progress of IT technologies, security is still one of the most vibrant and developing areas in computer science. ETRICS marks both the end of the six-year Priority Program (SPP 1079) of the German Research Foundation (DFG) and a call for intensified research on system-oriented security and privacy issues.

Protecting information and services from malicious use is essential for their deployment and acceptance. While the main protection goals denoting confidentiality, integrity and availability are of a general nature, their relevance, realization and enforcement vary depending upon the underlying architectures, technologies and applications. By categorizing the technological development according to "yesterday, today and tomorrow", three time spans result:

Yesterday, mainframe computing achieved security by means of mechanisms to prevent unauthorized access to data and thus safeguard confidentiality. The model of security mechanisms originated in the concept of a medieval castle, where the gate was the access point and the crest on the shield was the access credential. Security takes the form of physical and logical access control, where authentication is carried out by a firewall and achieved by, e.g., passwords and biometry. Authorization is even less sophisticated than in a castle and usually carried out by simple access control lists.

Today, with the dominance of the Internet, the protected space of the computing center has vanished. Instead, the connection of millions of computers combines many protected spaces, where the main challenge is the trustworthy proof of one's identity. Authorization depends on a statement of a certification authority about the relationship of the real identity and its digital representative. The authenticity is assured by a trusted third party and authentication is reduced to the application of the digital secret. Security of all nodes and even the whole network improves accountability, but since "the network is the computer", security mechanisms do not prevent privacy breaches.

Tomorrow, information systems will accommodate highly dynamic applications and build infrastructures with lots of mobile, autonomic nodes and ad hoc, structureless relationships between them. Human interaction assumes new forms and has to be pre-planned and expressed by means of rules that are part of security policies. To enforce security rules, not only context data, but also personal data is needed. In highly dynamic systems, security and privacy become mutually exclusive.

A program committee of 52 leading security researchers and practitioners, together with the help of many external expert reviewers, shaped the ETRICS 2006 scientific program. Only one-fifth of the submitted papers were accepted. ETRICS has promising research papers and keynotes covering the progress and changes in existing and future architectures and technologies. While the protection of data has reached a very encouraging level, malicious code is responsible for an exponential increase of errors and failures during the last decade, thus generating a back-door for security and privacy violations. In these proceedings, Trusted Computing approaches are discussed as a solution to prevent attackers from being able to deploy and execute malicious code. Other contributions go further by dissolving the black box paradigm of code. Data protection concentrating on mechanisms pursuing data economy, e.g., identity management, is shown to become obsolete for highly dynamic systems.

ETRICS is a conference based on and influenced by the efforts and contributions of scientists working together for many years on the SPP 1079 of the DFG. This Priority Program on security and privacy had, in addition to its scientific forums, many direct encounters with government and industry as well as standardization bodies. At the world's largest computing fair, CeBIT 2003, the German Ministry of Economics and Technology selected the results of the SPP 1079 to demonstrate the most advanced interplay of security and privacy mechanisms within a single, integrated, secure system platform. CeBIT 2003 gave us the incentive for ETRICS. We thank Dr. Gördeler and Dr. Glasmacher from the Ministry for venturing to give scientists a platform at a commercial fair.

ETRICS would not have happened and these proceedings would not have been completed without the help of so many. Markus Ruch, Stefan Sackmann, and Oliver Prokein took care of the organization. Lutz Lowis and Dirk von Suchodoletz organized the Web and managed the exhibition and infrastructure. Sven Wohlgemuth deserves special credit for the many versions of the program and the composition of these proceedings. In his position as the regional chair of the German Society for Computer Science (GI), he played a vital role in the assignment of ETRICS as part of the scientific year 2006, the "Informatics Year" in Germany. Without Rafael Accorsi and Moritz Strasser the review process and the complementary events such as workshops, the exhibition, tutorials, and excursions would not have been possible. Last but not least, we would like to thank Mrs. Julia Bär and our students Cathrin Christ, Christian Cordes, Felix Dorner, Johannes Glasmeyer, Benjamin Greschbach, Christoph Jasinski, Achilleas Karoulis, Angela Merkel, Fabian Preiß, Guido Roth and Arnt Syring.

We wish to encourage the authors, whether they present or do not present their work this year, to continue their efforts and remain an active part of the world's security community. We welcome all the participants, authors, exhibitors, presenters of "Best Practice Solutions" and tutorials, organizers of workshops and the keynote speakers to the University of Freiburg.

Freiburg, June 2006   Günter Müller, Chair of ETRICS,
                                       Gerhard Schneider, Co-Chair of ETRICS

German Federal Ministry of Education and Research

Annette Schavan

Information and communication technologies constitute the "nerve-system" of modern societies and the key to participating and succeeding in global economies. But in recent years the weaknesses of the Internet have also become obvious, and the damage resulting from misuse, cheating, theft, viruses and Trojan horses has become significant. Security has become a necessity to protect intellectual property and to preserve identity. In Germany, privacy is a constitutional right, and it is the blueprint of many privacy laws outside Germany. The Ministry of Education and Research (BMBF) was responsible for the beneficial law about digital signatures. The EC E-Commerce Directive acknowledged the crucial role of privacy and security for economic, technical and cultural progress.

The ETRICS conference is one step in a long lasting cooperation between the scientific and the political community. The organizer of ETRICS already cooperated with the Ministry of Education and Research to discuss the digital signature law and, influenced by this cooperation, it was a logical step to organize a six-year Priority Program on security under the auspices of the German Research Foundation (DFG). In 2003, this cooperation with Prof. Günter Müller continued with a joint series of talks in the "Future Parc" at the CeBIT fair about the chances and risks of the Internet and the role of privacy and security. The Priority Program scientists presented to the public the most complete secure platform to enable faster and safer application development.

I hope the participants of ETRICS take a lot of encouragement from the discussions with their international peers for their future work, and I hope that there is enough time to enjoy the natural and cultural treasures and traditions of the famous German university town of Freiburg. Together, both factors may lay the ground for exciting cooperation and progress.

Berlin, June 2006   Dr. Annette Schavan,
                    German Federal Ministry of Education and Research

Ministry of Science, Research and the Arts of Baden-Württemberg

Peter Frankenberg

The government of Baden-Württemberg is pleased to welcome ETRICS 2006 to Freiburg. Freiburg is not only surrounded by beautiful natural landscape at the border of the Black Forest and the Upper Rhine Valley, it is also embedded in one of Europe's leading research landscapes. Baden-Württemberg is home to several traditional universities, such as the Albert Ludwigs University of Freiburg. It is also home to two of the leading German technical universities, as well as universities of applied sciences, universities of cooperative education – which work closely together with industry – outstanding art academies and various other academic institutions.

Furthermore, many research institutes and centers, for example several Max-Planck and Fraunhofer Institutes and research centers of the Helmholtz Society, are located here. Very few countries, let alone states within countries, spend as much on research, proportionally, as Baden-Württemberg, in which 3.9 % of its GDP is devoted to research.

ETRICS 2006 is an event that is part of the Informatics Year 2006. But one "Informatics Year" is not sufficient for Baden-Württemberg. We pursue a long-term strategic research policy in which computer science and information and communication technologies have been specifically promoted and expanded since the 1990s in various programs.

The expansion of technological possibilities alone is not enough for I&C technologies. If the new technologies are to be used then this requires a high degree of acceptance on the part of the user. For this, we need to be able to rely on the security and reliability of I&C systems in which people place increasing trust. In their evaluation of research projects and plans, the experts pointed out that these security aspects and "human" aspects must be sufficiently taken into consideration.

This demonstrates the importance of the subjects being discussed here at ETRICS 2006 and the competences that the University of Freiburg has in this field. At the same time it shows that "accompanying research" on the security of I&C technologies, on their arrangement in a form that is accessible and on the prior assessment of their effects, must not be carried out in isolated "ivory towers" of meta information science. Instead, it is necessary to co-operate closely with the researchers who are responsible for progress in information and communication technologies.

Stuttgart, June 2006   Prof. Dr. Peter Frankenberg,
           Minister for Science, Research and the Arts of Baden-Württemberg

German Research Foundation

Ernst-Ludwig Winnacker

The year 2006 has been designated as the year of information technology. In various events scheduled throughout the year scientists will demonstrate how, and to what extent, this science influences our everyday lives. In particular, the exchange of electronic information and data – via computer, mobile phone or other devices – has increased dramatically in the recent past. Scientists help to ensure that the path through this information jungle remains safe. And, as we all know, the question of security is vital for money transfers and the exchange of personal data.

The DFG-funded Priority Program "Security in Information and Communication Technology" has been investigating this scientifically, economically and socially relevant subject since 1999. The Freiburg-based project has been instrumental in setting up an international platform, and it is due to its success that the 2006 International Conference on Emerging Trends in Information and Communication Security (ETRICS) will be hosted in Freiburg. Scientists from 18 universities and research institutes from all over Germany defined security for various underlying systems and combined single, tested components into safe frameworks. Increasing mobility and security requirements heightened the challenge during the course of the projects.

This program has made an essential contribution to the development of the emerging field of security research in information technology and to establishing a sustainable, nationwide cooperation network. My special thanks go to the coordinator of the Priority Program, Professor Günter Müller from Freiburg, who not only brought the right people together and managed the collaboration, but also increased public awareness and dialogue, for example by giving presentations at the CeBIT fair in Hannover.

The Priority Program has laid the groundwork for future research objectives, and it is my hope that other scientists will continue to pursue work in this rapidly growing field. I wish the participating scientists, as well as the coordinators and organizers, a successful meeting, and I look forward to the results of further research.

Bonn, June 2006

Professor Dr. Ernst-Ludwig Winnacker,
President Deutsche Forschungsgemeinschaft (DFG)

German Informatics Society

Matthias Jarke

With over 24.000 members, the German Informatics Society (GI) is the largest organization of computing specialists in the German-speaking countries. Security and privacy – being a critical success factor for the acceptance of information and communication technologies – have been among the most discussed topics within GI for many years, requiring continuous strategic attention. Besides a continuing advisory committee on security and privacy to the GI presidency, GI emphasized the importance of the field by bringing together all related activities in a new GI Security Division (Fachbereich) four years ago. We were also most happy to see the German Science Foundation DFG fund a six-year special research program in this area under the able coordination of Günter Müller.

However, the year 2006 does not only mark the end of this highly successful research program but has also been nominated by the German Federal Ministry of Research and Education (BMBF) as the "Informatics Year 2006". Informatics Year 2006 has three major aims: (a) increasing understanding and acceptance of the science and practice of Informatics in the overall society; (b) increasing the interest of the young generation (including girls) in choosing Informatics as a field of study; and (c) to improve further the position of Germany as a location for research and development in IT and its application through a re-focussing of the field. Several hundred partners, meetings and media events are contributing to Informatics Year 2006, coordinated by the BMBF, the organization "Science in Dialog", and the GI.

The ETRICS conference in Freiburg is the major security-related event of Informatics Year 2006, even though individual facets are of course also addressed elsewhere. Through discussion of leading international researchers and practitioners, it will promote all three above-mentioned goals and emphasize security not only as a necessity and problem, but also as an opportunity for fascinating R&D. In the name of GI, I would like to congratulate the organizers for setting up such an impressive program, and wish the conference every possible success.

Aachen and Bonn, June 2006

Matthias Jarke,
President, GI

Organization

General Chair

Günter Müller .... University of Freiburg, Germany

Program Chairs

Günter Müller .... University of Freiburg, Germany
Gerhard Schneider .... University of Freiburg, Germany

Organizing Committee

Markus Ruch .... Organization Chair
Stefan Sackmann .... Vice Organization Chair
Rafael Accorsi .... Workshops
Lutz Lowis .... Web
Oliver Prokein .... Finance
Moritz Strasser .... Exhibition and Events
Dirk von Suchodoletz .... Equipment and Infrastructure
Sven Wohlgemuth .... Program and Informatics Year 2006

Program Committee

Vijay Atluri .... Rutgers University, USA
Tuomas Aura .... Microsoft Research, Cambridge, UK
Elisa Bertino .... Purdue University, USA
Joachim Biskup .... University of Dortmund, Germany
Johannes Blömer .... University of Paderborn, Germany
Manfred Broy .... TU Munich, Germany
Jeremy Bryans .... University of Newcastle, UK
Jan Camenisch .... IBM Research, Switzerland
Clemens Cap .... University of Rostock, Germany
David Chadwick .... University of Kent, UK
Richard Clayton .... University of Cambridge, UK
Bruno Crispo .... VU Amsterdam, Netherlands
Frédéric Cuppens .... ENST de Bretagne, France
Mads Dam .... Swedish Institute of Computer Science, Sweden
Yves Deswarte .... LAAS-CNRS, France
Claudia Eckert .... TU Darmstadt, Germany

Simone Fischer-Huebner .... University of Karlstad, Sweden
Willi Geiselmann .... TU Karlsruhe, Germany
Dieter Gollmann .... TU Hamburg-Harburg, Germany
Dieter Hutter .... DFKI Saarbrücken, Germany
Sushil Jajodia .... George Mason University, USA
Jan Jürjens .... TU Munich, Germany
George Kesidis .... Pennsylvania State University, USA
Hiroaki Kikuchi .... Tokai University, Japan
Hartmut König .... BTU Cottbus, Germany
Kaoru Kurosawa .... Ibaraki University, Japan
Klaus-Peter Löhr .... FU Berlin, Germany
Norbert Luttenberger .... University of Kiel, Germany
Patrick McDaniel .... Pennsylvania State University, USA
Chris Mitchell .... Royal Holloway London, UK
Andreas Pfitzmann .... TU Dresden, Germany
Birgit Pfitzmann .... IBM Research, Switzerland
Reinhard Posch .... TU Graz, Austria
Kai Rannenberg .... University of Frankfurt, Germany
Erwin Rathgeb .... University of Duisburg-Essen, Germany
Wolfgang Reif .... University of Augsburg, Germany
Yves Roudier .... Eurécom Institute, France
Ryoichi Sasaki .... Tokyo Denki University, Japan
Andreas Schaad .... SAP, Germany
Christoph Schuba .... Linköpings University, Sweden
Wolfram Schulte .... Microsoft Research, USA
Rainer Steinwandt .... Florida Atlantic University, USA
Werner Stephan .... DFKI Saarbrücken, Germany
Stuart Stubblebine .... Stubblebine Consulting/Research Labs, USA
Joachim Swoboda .... TU Munich, Germany
Tsuyoshi Takagi .... FUN Hakodate, Japan
Kazuo Takaragi .... Hitachi, Japan
Masato Terada .... Hitachi, Japan
Dirk Timmermann .... University of Rostock, Germany
Anna Vaccarelli .... Italian National Research Council, Italy
Marianne Winslett .... University of Illinois, USA
Eric Yu .... University of Toronto, Canada
Alf Zugenmaier .... Docomo Euro-Labs, Germany

External Reviewers

Rafael Accorsi	Adolf Hohl	Lin Liu
Jens-M. Bohli	Sebastian Höhn	Lutz Lowis
Dubravko Culibrk	Zhihua Hu	Leonardo Martucci
Maike Gilliot	Martin Kähmer	Jörn Müller-Quade

Joon S. Park	Daniel Socek	Roland Vogt
Stefan Röhrich		Melanie Volkamer
Stefan Sackmann		

In Cooperation with

ACM Special Interest Group on Security, Audit and Control (SIGSAC), USA
Gesellschaft für Informatik e.V. (GI), Germany
German Research Foundation (DFG), Germany
IEEE Computer Society, USA

Sponsoring Institutions

DaimlerChrysler AG, Germany
Deutsche Bank AG, Germany
Deutsche Telekom AG, Germany
DoCoMo Communications Laboratories Europe GmbH, Germany
Endress+Hauser Metso AG, Switzerland
German Federal Ministry of Education and Research (BMBF), Germany
IBM Deutschland GmbH, Germany
Novartis AG, Switzerland
SAP AG, Germany
Siemens AG, Germany

Local Sponsors

Colombi Hotel, Freiburg, Germany
Sparkasse Freiburg Nördlicher Breisgau, Germany

Table of Contents

Multilateral Security

Security in Service-Oriented Computing

Secure Mobile Applications

Enterprise Privacy

Privacy, Identity, and Anonymity

Security Engineering

Perspectives of Cryptographic Security

Multilateral Security: Enabling Technologies and Their Evaluation*

Andreas Pfitzmann

TU Dresden, Department of Computer Science, 01062 Dresden, Germany
pfitza@inf.tu-dresden.de

Abstract. First, multilateral security and its potential are introduced. Then protection goals as well as their synergies and interferences are described. After pointing out some basic facts about security technology in general, a structured overview of technologies for multilateral security is given. An evaluation of the maturity and effectiveness of these technologies shows that some should be applied immediately, while others need quite a bit of further research and development. Finally, a vision for the future is given.

1   Introduction and Overview

Multilateral Security means providing security for all parties concerned, requiring each party to only minimally trust in the honesty of others:

- Each party has its particular *protection goals*.
- Each party can *formulate* its protection goals.
- Security conflicts are recognized and compromises *negotiated*.
- Each party can *enforce* its protection goals within the agreed compromise.

In the same way as enlightenment freed human beings from the suppression imposed by superstitious mental models and authoritarian political systems, technology for multilateral security has the potential to free users of IT systems from a lack of self-determination concerning their (in)security.

To set the tone, I begin with a rather comprehensive ensemble of protection goals, their synergies and interferences.

Thereafter, I state some basic facts about the constraints on security technology in general, and on multilateral security in particular. This helps to identify which technologies are particularly helpful, or even essential, for the construction, use, and maintenance of secure IT systems.

Some of these technologies can unilaterally be employed by various parties. To use others, bilateral cooperation is needed, e.g. the cooperation of both communication partners. For some, trilateral cooperation is required. An example are legally binding digital signatures which need not only cooperation of the at least two communicants, but additionally at least one somewhat trusted third party for the certification of public keys. For other technologies, even the

---

* Part of this work has been published in G. Müller, K. Rannenberg (Eds.): Multilateral Security in Communications, Addison-Wesley 1999; R. Wilhelm (Ed.): Informatics. 10 Years Back. 10 Years Ahead; LNCS 2000, pp. 50-62, 2001.

G. Müller (Ed.): ETRICS 2006, LNCS 3995, pp. 1–13, 2006.

Table 1. An ordered ensemble of protection goals

Protection of ╲ Threats	Content	Circumstances
unauthorized access to information	Confidentiality Hiding	Anonymity Unobservability
unauthorized modification of information	Integrity	Accountability
unauthorized impairment of functionality	Availability	Reachability Legal Enforceability

multilateral cooperation of a large number of independent parties is necessary. I use this distinction to structure a short overview of what is known about technology for (multilateral) security, providing pointers to the relevant literature.

In conclusion, I give an evaluation of the maturity and effectiveness of the different described technologies for (multilateral) security. This emphasizes which technologies should be introduced immediately in order to enhance existing IT systems or as a basis for new ones. Furthermore I give my opinion which technologies need quite a lot of further research and/or development.

Finally, I give my vision for the future of the field.

2 Protection Goals, Their Synergies and Interferences

Twenty-five years ago, security was nearly equated with *confidentiality*, e.g. in the Orange Book [13]. Twenty years ago, *integrity* of information and *availability* of functionality have been added, e.g. by Voydock and Kent [24] and in the European Security Evaluation Criteria [16]. Fifteen years ago, *accountability* has been added as a fourth protection goal, e.g. in the Canadian Criteria [12].

Outside the mainstream of government dominated security research, *anonymity* and *unobservability* became a big issue fifteen years ago [7, 20], when the technical advance of storage technology made it possible to store all person-related information forever nearly for free. In the last decade, attempts of governments to control the use of cryptography and the pressure of the music and film industries to develop digital copy protection technology, gave a big boost to steganography, i.e. the art of *hiding* information within other, unsuspicious data. Mobile networks, which technically allow people to be reached irrespective of where they are and what they do, gave rise to the protection goal *reachability*, i.e. to control who is able to reach whom under what circumstances by which media. Electronic-commerce caused attention to be given to *legal enforceability*, i.e. users have to fulfill their legal responsibilities within a reasonable period of time.

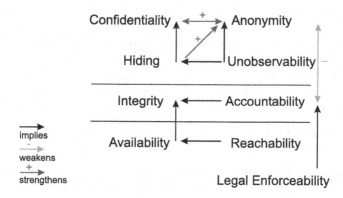

Fig. 1. Synergies and interferences between protection goals

To impose some order on this ensemble of protection goals in the context of communication over networks, it proves fruitful to discern between the content and the circumstances of communication [25], cf. Table 1.

Of course, there are quite a few synergies and interferences between these protection goals, which are explained in detail in [25] and depicted in Fig. 1.

In addition, it has to be expected that additional protection goals will be defined and will become important in the future.

3   Basic Facts

If the parties concerned, e.g. users, service providers and network operators, are unwilling or, perhaps even unable, to express the security properties they expect, it is unlikely that they will get what they require.

→ Users, service providers and network operators must be willing and able to formulate all the security properties they expect.

The security properties expected by different parties tend to be quite diverse in respect of applications and even transactions with different partners using the same application. Moreover, the security properties expected may change dramatically over time, e.g. as a result of negative personal experiences, or reports by the media.

→ Security properties have to be dynamically adaptable.

The security of a human user can only be as good as the security of the device he or she is directly interacting with.[1] (Whether the device is secure for other parties concerned, is only of secondary interest.)

---

[1] This is certainly true within the IT system. Outside the IT system, there may be compensation for security breaches. But this can work at best for those security properties where compensation is possible at all. Compensation is not possible for confidentiality properties – information which got public cannot be de-publicized –, but compensation is possible with regard to integrity and availability properties, e.g. accountability and legal enforceability, cf. [4].

→ Devices which are secure for their user(s) are needed.

If a user device is built to integrate more than one application, its security has to be adequate for its most demanding application. If a general purpose user device is built, its security has to be adequate for the most demanding application perceivable during its lifetime. If this is not achieved, the user device is clearly not general purpose – which applies to all Windows 98/ME/XP Home based PCs.

→ The security target of user devices is set by the most demanding application the device is intended to be used for.

If the designers are cautious, the security target will even be set by the most demanding application the device will ever be used for – and this application may not yet be known at the time the device is being designed.

→ User devices have to provide a very, very secure basis to bootstrap further security properties during their lifetime.

The erasure of data ever available in a globally networked IT system is by no reasonable means really to assure. In addition, the technical progress makes transfer, storage and usage of huge amounts of data very cheap. Therefore, wherever possible, the parties concerned have to be able to hinder even the ability to gather their data.

→ Data avoidance techniques for anonymity, unobservability, and un-linkability are needed. If accountability is required, a suitable form of pseudonymity should be used.[2]

4   Overview of Technologies for Security

Security technologies are mentioned and briefly explained in this section. It is structured according whether security technologies are uni-, bi-, tri-, or even multilateral.

4.1   Unilateral Technologies

Unilateral technologies can be decided on by each party for itself. Therefore, neither coordination nor negotiation is needed concerning their usage. Important unilateral technologies for multilateral security are:

Tools to help even inexperienced users to formulate all their protection goals, if necessary for each and every application or even each and every single action, cf. [22, 25]. Fig. 2 gives some examples.

(Portable) devices which are secure for their users in order to bootstrap se-curity. The devices need at least minimal *physical protection* comprising direct input/output with their users [21] and, if they are multi-purpose, an *operating*

---

[2] A structured explanation, definitions of and interrelationships between anonymity, unobservability, unlinkability, accountability, and pseudonymity can be found in [25, 18].

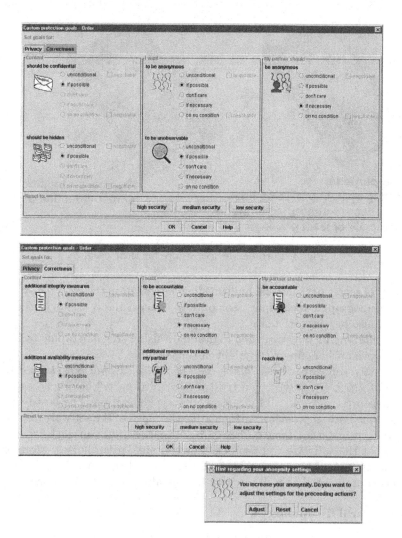

Fig. 2. User interface screen shots

system providing fine-grained access control and administration of rights for applications, adhering to the principle of least privilege, cf. Fig. 3. This is essential to limit the spread of Trojan horses, and can prevent computer viruses completely. For convenience, these devices might recognize their authorized user by biometrics.[3]

Encryption of local storage media to conceal and/or authenticate its contents.[4]

---

[3] Please note that this is the only place where biometrics is useful for multilateral security. And last but not least, this is the only place where biometrics does not pose unsolvable privacy and safety problems, cf. [19]

[4] Attempts to control the usage of encryption to conceal the contents of storage would be quite useless, since criminals might then employ steganography to do so.

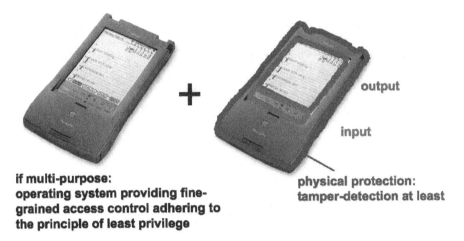

if multi-purpose:
operating system providing fine-
grained access control adhering to
the principle of least privilege

physical protection:
tamper-detection at least

Fig. 3. Portable devices secure for their users

Hiding of secret data in local multimedia contents or in the local file system [2] using steganographic techniques, not only to conceal the contents of the secret data, but also its very existence.[5]

Watermarking or *fingerprinting* digital data using steganographic techniques to help prove authorship or copyright infringements.

Using only *software* whose *source code is published and well checked* or the *security of which is certified* by a trustworthy third party[6] having access to the complete source code and all tools used for code generation. The best technique is to combine both approaches with regard to as much of the software as possible. It is only by using at least one of these two approaches that you can be reasonably certain that the software you use does not contain Trojan horses. More or less the same applies to hardware where all sources and tools used for design and production are needed as well to check for the absence of Trojan horses.[7]

4.2 Bilateral Technologies

Bilateral technologies can only be used if the communication partners cooperate. This means that some coordination and negotiation is needed concerning their usage.[8]

---

[5] Attempts to control the usage of steganography to hide the very existence of secret data in storage would be quite useless.

[6] In this case, other parties are involved than in the here presented uni-, bi-, and trilateral technologies where only the parties actively involved at the runtime of the IT system are taken into account. Of course these terms on laterality can be expanded to handle non-runtime situations as well, e.g. the preparation of communication or other circumstances like the software developing or testing process.

[7] Attempts to control thorough checking would be quite useless, since authorities need secure IT systems themselves.

[8] Note: the term "bilateral" does not necessarily mean that exactly two parties are involved, but there may be many communication partners, e.g. in a video conference,

Important bilateral technologies for multilateral security are:

Tools to negotiate bilateral protection goals and security mechanisms, cf. [22] and Fig. 4.

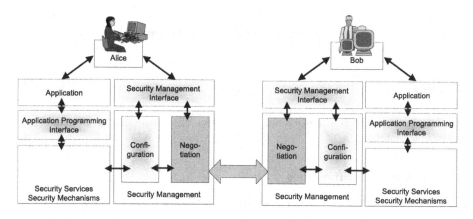

Fig. 4. Tools to negotiate

Cryptographic mechanisms[9] and *steganographic mechanisms*[10] to secure the communication content, cf. Figs. 5 and 6.

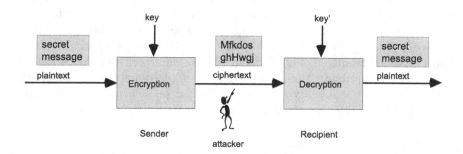

Fig. 5. Cryptography to achieve confidentiality and integrity of the communication contents

---

who may have differing interests. Nevertheless this is counted here as two sides (i.e. bilateral technologies): the user's side and the other side with at least one and perhaps more communication partners.

[9] Attempts to control the usage of encryption to conceal the contents of communication would be completely useless, since criminals might then employ steganography to do so.

[10] Attempts to control the usage of steganography to hide the very existence of secret data in communications would be completely useless.

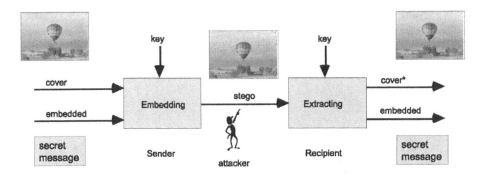

Fig. 6. Steganography to achieve hiding, i.e. secrecy of the confidentiality of the communication contents

4.3 Trilateral Technologies

Trilateral technologies can only be used if a third party is involved to fulfill a specific task for the other participating parties. This means that more coordination and negotiation is needed concerning their usage compared to unilateral - and in most cases as well bilateral - technologies. Important trilateral technologies for multilateral security are:

Tools to negotiate trilateral security mechanisms, e.g. for accountability.[11]

A *public-key infrastructure* (PKI) to provide users with certified public keys of other users to test their digital signatures and to give users the ability to revoke their own public key if the corresponding private key has been compromised.

Security gateways to bridge incompatibilities with regard to security mechanisms or their details, cf. Fig. 7. Security gateways work well concerning integrity and accountability mechanisms, but are of questionable value concerning confidentiality and anonymity mechanisms. Of course, security gateways cannot bridge incompatibilities concerning protection goals.

4.4 Multilateral Technologies

Multilateral technologies can only be used if a large number of independent parties cooperate. This means that coordination and negotiation are needed on a large scale. Important multilateral technologies for multilateral security are:

Tools to negotiate multilateral protection goals and security mechanisms, e.g. for anonymity, unobservability, unlinkability, and pseudonymity.[12]

---

[11] The negotiation process itself between the communication partners belongs to bilateral technologies, but as far as the negotiation is extended to include third parties in order to achieve accountability, it is a trilateral technology.

[12] The negotiation process itself between the communication partners belongs to bilateral technologies, but as far as the negotiation is extended to the necessary parties in order to achieve multilateral security goals, it is a multilateral technology.

Abstraction Layers:

Fig. 7. Security gateways

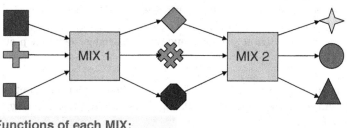

Functions of each MIX:
- batches
- discards repeats
- changes encoding (decryption)
- changes order

**-> hides relation between in-
and outgoing messages**

MIXes can be used to protect
- e-mail and Web-access,
  e.g. TOR and AN.ON, and
- mobile communications

Fig. 8. Anonymity, unobservability, and unlinkability for communication

Mechanisms to provide for *anonymity, unobservability,* and *unlinkability* with regard to

- communications,[13] i.e. protect who communicates when to whom from where to where [6, 7, 20, 11, 14, 17, 23, 15], cf. Fig. 8,
- payments, i.e. protect who pays what amount to whom and when [8, 1], and
- value exchange, i.e. protect electronic shopping from observation [5, 3], cf. Fig. 9,

without compromising integrity, availability, or accountability.

Mechanisms to provide for *digital pseudonyms*[14], i.e. a suitable combination of anonymity and accountability [6]. In particular, there are mechanisms to securely

---

[13] Data retention is quite useless, since criminals might employ e.g. public phones, prepaid mobiles bought by others, unprotected WLANs, or unprotected-bluetooth mobiles of others to avoid leaving traces.

[14] If we only consider the accountability aspect, digital pseudonyms are a trilateral technology. But taking into account anonymity as well, digital pseudonyms are clearly a multilateral technology.

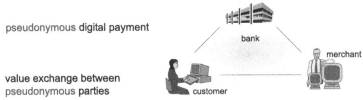

pseudonymity = digital signatures relative to a digital pseudonym
digital pseudonym = public key to test signatures

pseudonymous **digital payment**

value exchange between
pseudonymous **parties**

bank

merchant

customer

- identification in case of fraud (pseudonyms are certified and certification authority knows real identities): privacy cannot be checked by the pseudonymous parties
- use deposition of payment with an active trustee to prevent fraud (real identities behind pseudonyms are neither known to the other party nor to any third party): privacy can be checked by the pseudonymous parties

Fig. 9. Pseudonymous digital payment and value exchange between pseudonymous parties

transfer signatures (expressing authorizations, called credentials) between different pseudonyms of the same party [7, 9, 10]. This is called *transferring signatures between pseudonyms*.

5   Evaluation of Maturity and Effectiveness

Table 2 gives my evaluation of the maturity and effectiveness of the technologies for security mentioned in the last sections. Their sequence in the table is mainly bottom-up, i.e. a technology for security placed in a particular row is required before a technology listed below can be effective. In some places, examples are given following a semicolon.

As can be seen, the weakest link of the security chain today is the user device, in particular its physical protection and operating system. Much has to be done to improve both.

Obviously, security evaluation of software as well as IT and integration of security technologies are those challenges for research that have the most impact on IT security.

6   A Vision

Without multilateral security, e-commerce will be severely hindered and there will be definitely no e-democracy. Therefore, I expect that portable devices secure for their users will finally be developed and find their way into the mass market. The diverse projects to introduce secure and legally binding digital signatures are important first steps. Building on devices secure for their users, cryptography will prove as a very powerful enabling technology for all kinds of security services.

Of course, we will experience broad discussions (and at least some attempts of various secret services to achieve facts without any public discussion at all)

Table 2. Maturity and effectiveness of security technologies

	state of public research	demonstrators and prototypes	available products	products fielded on a large scale
physical protection	hardly any respectable publications	hard to assess	hard to assess; Me-chip	very poor; chipcards
security evaluation of software and IT	acceptable	hard to assess	hard to assess	hard to assess
security in operating systems	very good	good	poor; Windows NT, 2000, XP Professional, Linux, MacOS X	very poor; Windows ME, CE, Mobile, XP Home, MacOS 9, Symbian, PalmOS
cryptography	very good	good	good; PGP 2.6.x	acceptable; PGP 5.x, PGP 6.x
steganography	good	acceptable	very poor	very poor
public-key infrastructure	very good	good	hard to assess	hard to assess
security gateways	good	acceptable	-	-
mechanisms for anonymity, unobservability, and unlinkability	very good	good	acceptable; TOR, AN.ON	poor; proxies
digital pseudonyms	very good	good	good; PGP 2.6.x	acceptable; PGP 5.x, PGP 6.x
transferring signatures between pseudonyms	good	acceptable	-	-
tools to help even inexperienced users to formulate and negotiate	good	acceptable	-	-
integration of these technologies	acceptable	poor	poor	very poor

what the balance between electronic surveillance and digital privacy should be. In my opinion, we have to overcome 2001 to avoid 1984.

It is well known and agreed for at least three decades that nearly complete surveillance is possible by IT systems. I am happy that public research has shown in the last two decades that strong digital privacy is possible as well. So society is free to decide how we shall live in cyberspace – and beyond.

I am sure that multilateral security and privacy enhancing technologies are prerequisites for the long term acceptance of IT systems in general and for ubiquitous computing in particular in a democratic society as we know it.

Acknowledgements

Many thanx to my colleagues in general and Marit Hansen in particular for suggestions to improve this paper. In addition, Stefan Köpsell gave lots of technical support.

References

1. N. Asokan, Phillipe A. Janson, Michael Steiner, Michael Waidner: The State of the Art in Electronic Payment Systems; Computer 30/9 (1997) 28–35.
2. Ross Anderson, Roger Needham, Adi Shamir: The Steganographic File System; Information Hiding, 2nd Workshop, Portland, Oregon, LNCS 1525, Springer, Heidelberg 1998, 73–82.
3. N. Asokan, Matthias Schunter, Michael Waidner: Optimistic Protocols for Fair Exchange; 4th ACM Conference on Computer and Communications Security, Zürich, April 1997, 6-17.
4. Birgit Baum-Waidner: Ein Service zur Haftungsverteilung für kompromittierte digitale Signaturen; Verläßliche IT-Systeme, GI-Fachtagung VIS '99, DuD Fachbeiträge, Vieweg, Braunschweig 1999, 203–223.
5. Holger Bürk, Andreas Pfitzmann: Value Exchange Systems Enabling Security and Unobservability; Computers & Security 9/8 (1990) 715–721.
6. David Chaum: Untraceable Electronic Mail, Return Addresses, and Digital Pseudonyms; Communications of the ACM 24/2 (1981) 84–88.
7. David Chaum: Security without Identification: Transaction Systems to make Big Brother Obsolete; Communications of the ACM 28/10 (1985) 1030–1044.
8. David Chaum: Privacy Protected Payments - Unconditional Payer and/or Payee Untraceability; SMART CARD 2000: The Future of IC Cards, Proc. of the IFIP WG 11.6 Intern. Conference; Laxenburg (Austria), 1987, North-Holland, Amsterdam 1989, 69–93.
9. David Chaum: Showing credentials without identification: Transferring signatures between unconditionally unlinkable pseudonyms; Auscrypt '90, LNCS 453, Springer, Berlin 1990, 246–264.
10. David Chaum: Achieving Electronic Privacy; Scientific American (August 1992) 96–101.
11. David A. Cooper, Kenneth P. Birman: Preserving Privacy in a Network of Mobile Computers; 1995 IEEE Symposium on Research in Security and Privacy, IEEE Computer Society Press, Los Alamitos 1995, 26–38.

12. Canadian System Security Centre; Communications Security Establishment; Government of Canada: The Canadian Trusted Computer Product Evaluation Criteria; April 1992, Version 3.0e.
13. Department of Defense Standard: Department of Defense Trusted Computer System Evaluation Criteria; December 1985, DOD 5200.28-STD, Supersedes CSC-STD-001-83, dtd 15 Aug 83, Library No. S225,711.
14. Hannes Federrath, Anja Jerichow, Andreas Pfitzmann: Mixes in mobile communication systems: Location management with privacy; Information Hiding, 1st Workshop, Cambridge, UK, LNCS 1174, Springer, Heidelberg 1996, 121–135.
15. David Goldschlag, Michael Reed, Paul Syverson: Onion Routing for Anonymous and Private Internet Connections; Communications of the ACM 42/2 (1999) 39–41.
16. European Communities - Commission: ITSEC: Information Technology Security Evaluation Criteria; (Provisional Harmonised Criteria, Version 1.2, 28 June 1991) Office for Official Publications of the European Communities, Luxembourg 1991 (ISBN 92-826-3004-8).
17. Anja Jerichow, Jan Müller, Andreas Pfitzmann, Birgit Pfitzmann, Michael Waidner: Real-Time Mixes: A Bandwidth-Efficient Anonymity Protocol; IEEE Journal on Selected Areas in Communications 16/4 (May 1998) 495–509.
18. Andreas Pfitzmann, Marit Hansen: Anonymity, Unlinkability, Unobservability, Pseudonymity, and Identity Management – A Consolidated Proposal for Terminology; http://dud.inf.tu-dresden.de/Anon_Terminology.shtml.
19. Andreas Pfitzmann: Biometrie – wie einsetzen und wie nicht? Zum Umgang mit Sicherheitsproblemen von Biometrie und Sicherheits- und Datenschutzproblemen durch Biometrie; digma, Zeitschrift für Datenrecht und Informationssicherheit, Schulthess 5/4 (Dec. 2005) 154–157.
20. Andreas Pfitzmann, Michael Waidner: Networks without user observability; Computers & Security 6/2 (1987) 158–166.
21. Andreas Pfitzmann, Birgit Pfitzmann, Matthias Schunter, Michael Waidner: Trustworthy User Devices; in: G. Müller, K. Rannenberg (Eds.): Multilateral Security in Communications, Addison-Wesley 1999, 137–156.
22. Andreas Pfitzmann, Alexander Schill, Andreas Westfeld, Guntram Wicke, Gritta Wolf, Jan Zöllner: A Java-based distributed platform for multilateral security; IFIP/GI Working Conference "Trends in Electronic Commerce", Hamburg, LNCS 1402, Springer, Heidelberg 1998, 52–64.
23. Michael K. Reiter, Aviel D. Rubin: Anonymous Web Transactions with Crowds; Communications of the ACM 42/2 (1999) 32–38.
24. Victor L. Voydock, Stephen T. Kent: Security Mechanisms in High-Level Network Protocols; ACM Computing Surveys 15/2 (1983) 135–171.
25. Gritta Wolf, Andreas Pfitzmann: Properties of protection goals and their integration into a user interface; Computer Networks 32 (2000) 685–699.

Do You Trust Your Recommendations?
An Exploration of Security and Privacy Issues in
Recommender Systems

Shyong K. "Tony" Lam, Dan Frankowski, and John Riedl

GroupLens Research
Computer Science and Engineering
University of Minnesota
Minneapolis, MN 55455
{lam, dfrankow, riedl}@cs.umn.edu

Abstract. Recommender systems are widely used to help deal with the problem of information overload. However, recommenders raise serious privacy and security issues. The personal information collected by recommenders raises the risk of unwanted *exposure* of that information. Also, malicious users can *bias* or *sabotage* the recommendations that are provided to other users. This paper raises important research questions in three topics relating to exposure and bias in recommender systems: the value and risks of the preference information shared with a recommender, the effectiveness of shilling attacks designed to bias a recommender, and the issues involved in distributed or peer-to-peer recommenders. The goal of the paper is to bring these questions to the attention of the information and communication security community, to invite their expertise in addressing them.

1 Introduction

People are often overwhelmed with the number of options available to them. To combat this information overload, many have turned to *recommender systems*: tools that use a user's opinions about items in some information domain in order to recommend other items to that user. For example, Amazon.com uses a recommender system to make personalized recommendations suggesting products that a user might like based on the products she has purchased, expressed an opinion about, or viewed.

There are a wide variety of recommender systems in use today. Some, like Amazon.com, are automated and personalized to each user, while others, such as Epinions.com's review system, are non-personalized and "manually operated" in the sense that users need to read and evaluate the reviews published on the site to reach a conclusion about an item. In this paper, we focus on personalized recommender systems that use *automated collaborative filtering* algorithms [1, 2, 3], which generate recommendations on the basis that people who have expressed similar opinions in the past are likely to share opinions in the future.

G. Müller (Ed.): ETRICS 2006, LNCS 3995, pp. 14–29, 2006.

Such recommenders require personal information from a user, and in return give personalized predicted preferences, which we also call *recommendations*.

Recommender systems require two types of trust from their users. First, since the recommender must receive substantial information about the users in order to understand them well enough to make effective recommendations, they must trust that the system will protect their information appropriately. Second, automated recommender systems are often fairly opaque to their users. Although the algorithms used are easy to understand in principle, a user is usually not presented with sufficient information to know exactly how or why an item is being recommended to her. Thus, in order for a recommendation to be accepted, the user must trust that the recommendations are accurate.

Violations of user trust in a recommender come in three flavors:

Exposure. Undesired access to personal user information.

Bias. Manipulation of users' recommendations to inappropriately change the items that are recommended.

Sabotage. Intentionally reducing the recommendation accuracy of a recommender.

Exposure. There are many examples of exposure of private user data. In 2004, hackers accessed a University of California, Berkeley system containing the names and social security numbers of about 1.4 million Californians[1]. Identifying information is expected to be kept private, but so is preference information: during Robert Bork's confirmation hearings for the U.S. Supreme Court in 1987, his movie rental history was leaked to the press. In response, lawmakers passed the Video Privacy Protection Act of 1988 making it illegal to disclose personally identifiable rental information without consent. We do not yet know of recommender information being leaked or stolen – but many companies who own recommenders are not required to publicly report identity theft. A Harris poll in 2003 finds 90% of people are concerned about protecting themselves from misuse of their personal information[2]. Ackerman et al. found 83% of people more than marginally concerned about privacy [4].

What can be done about recommender system exposure? Can security techniques from other domains be applied in unique ways to recommender systems to make privacy violations difficult or impossible?

Bias. Bias may be to increase ("push") or decrease ("nuke") the visibility of other items. In 2002, Amazon.com's page for a spiritual guide by well-known Christian televangelist Pat Robertson included an automatically generated recommendation for "The Ultimate Guide to Anal Sex for Men". "Amazon conducted an investigation and determined these results were not that of hundreds of customers going to the same items while they were shopping on the site."[3] Instead, it is likely that a few motivated people accomplished this by repeatedly viewing the two items in sequence.

---

[1] http://www.securityfocus.com/news/9758

[2] http://harrisinteractive.com/harris_poll/index.asp?PID=365

[3] http://news.com.com/2100-1023-976435.html

In 2004, Amazon.com's Canadian site suddenly accidentally revealed the identities of thousands of people who had anonymously posted book reviews. It turned out that authors were praising their own books and trashing other authors' books. The New York Times reported that "many people say Amazon's pages have turned into what one writer called 'a rhetorical war,' where friends and family members are regularly corralled to write glowing reviews and each negative one is scrutinized for the digital fingerprints of known enemies."[4] To increase the credibility of some reviews, Amazon now has a "Real Name" badge applied to reviews written by customers who have verified their identity and agreed to publicly reveal that they wrote the review.

How can bias be limited in recommender systems? Can information-theoretic techniques be used to identify attempts to bias recommendations?

Sabotage. There are many examples of sabotage in web sites. The most common are denial of service attacks or defacement of the front page. Besides these and some of the bias attacks mentioned above, we know of no other direct sabotage attacks on recommender systems to date. We hypothesize that sabotage may become more prevalent in the future, as business competitors use recommenders as a key business advantage. For now, though, we recommend focusing research on the other types of attacks on recommender systems.

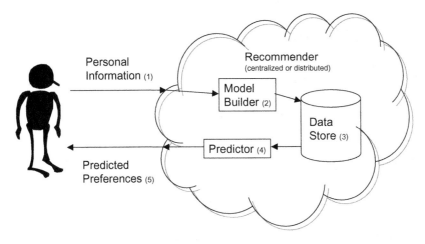

Fig. 1. Conceptual model of the interaction between a user and a recommender system

Figure 1 shows high-level data flow between a user and a recommender: the user gives personal information in return for predicted preferences. *Personal information* may be preferences or other identifying information such as name, zip code, age, gender, email, or account name. *Predicted preferences* may be a list of recommended items for the user to consider, or a predicted opinion for a given item or set of items.

---

[4] http://www.nytimes.com/2004/02/14/technology/14AMAZ.html

The recommender in figure 1 has internal structure. The *model builder* may select, combine, and compute a user model from personal information. The model builder may also be privacy-preserving if it discards or abstracts away from personal information. The *data store* holds the results of model building as well as any other information necessary for the application. The *predictor* uses the model to predict preferences. However, the figure is not intended to show concrete system architecture. For example, the TiVo TV show recommender puts the predictor on the user's machine, not a server [5]; peer-to-peer or distributed recommenders may distribute recommender components broadly.

Figure 1 is subject to many of the classic client-server security concerns: man-in-the-middle attacks, denial of service attacks, hacking into the recommender server(s), and so on. Such attacks are no different in the context of a recommender system than a standard client-server system, so they will not be considered in this paper. We instead focus on issues specific to recommenders.

Each of our research questions may be considered at several points along the flow of data. For example, predictions may be sabotaged or biased by users giving false information or misrepresenting their opinions (which we call *shilling*), or by the owner of a recommender altering the recommendations (e.g. to sell overstock or increase profit). Exposure may occur by looking for users' personal information directly or by trying to infer it from recommendations [6].

This paper is an extension of a workshop paper [7] that contains our thoughts about interesting research questions around privacy-preserving recommenders. In the present paper, we consider some topics that touch on these research questions: the prediction value and privacy cost of personal information (section 2), ways to bias prediction results (section 3), and distributed or peer-to-peer recommendations (section 4).

2   Value and Privacy Risks of Information

A personalized recommendation algorithm requires input from the user population in order to make recommendations. Providing more input potentially increases recommendation accuracy, but also increases the risk of unwanted exposure of personal information. Ideally, one would like to find a balance where the system is able to make good recommendations while not requiring users to give up too much information about themselves.

There is large body of prior work in this area. Many have looked at ways to preserve user privacy in recommender algorithms [8, 9] or datasets [10]. The data mining community has also become interested in privacy-preserving algorithms [11]. So far, they find that you can suppress, perturb, or generalize data with varying effects on algorithm outputs (such as recommendations) or dataset anonymity. Also, Ramakrishnan et al [6] describe a graph-theoretic model showing how information can be inferred about *straddlers* (users with eclectic tastes) by observing the recommendations made by a system.

When a user provides information to a recommender, two broad questions arise. 1) What value is gained? 2) What exposure is risked? We discuss value in 2.1 and exposure risk in section 2.2.

2.1   Value of Information

In this section, we discuss different ways of judging the value of preference information provided by the user. Value may take many forms: list-keeping, discussion, fun. For simplicity, we assume that value is increased prediction accuracy. The accuracy gained by providing information may be for the user who provided it ("value to self"), or for others using the recommender ("value to others").

There are many issues to consider. How to judge the value of information? How much data should the recommender solicit? Which data should it solicit? Should it keep all the data? What user interface should it use? How does changing the data available affect recommendation accuracy? We devote a sub-section to each question.

Metrics. The purpose of information collected by a recommender is to differentiate a user from her peers. Some pieces of data are inherently more valuable than others in an information-theoretic sense and thus, are better at differentiating among users. For instance, knowing that a user likes the universally-popular movie "Toy Story" reveals less than knowing that she likes "Fahrenheit 9/11," which has a higher level of diversity among users' opinions. This is the basis of an idea proposed by Pennock and Horvitz that says if one can calculate how useful a given piece of information is (a *value-of-information* or VOI metric), then one can tune a system to optimize its data collection process by soliciting user preferences on items that have the most value [12].

Such a metric has a variety of uses including judging whether the recommender has enough bits of data for a particular user or movie, or directing users to provide high-value information for others.

Amount of Data. How much data is needed from a user to make good recommendations to that user? Providing a recommender with data may produce diminishing returns. That is, perhaps once a certain amount is known about a user, obtaining further information is only marginally useful. Perhaps there is a "sweet spot" that maximizes the recommendation accuracy per unit of information known about the user.

How do we calculate the sweet spot? It is desirable for the recommender to know this so that it can stop soliciting data from a user once it has built a sufficiently good user model. With a VOI metric, it is possible to measure how much information is needed to make good recommendations, and then to stop collecting new information from the user once that point is reached. More generally, a recommender system might use VOI to bound the amount of information collected about a user to some optimal level with respect to both privacy and recommendation quality.

One issue is that how much information is useful may change over time. As the system or the user evolves, or as new items are introduced, will more information be needed to maintain high-quality recommendations?

Finally, suppose it would be useful for many other users if a particular user were to give more information than necessary for her own prediction accuracy? How do we appropriately balance these competing goals? Many users are probably willing to give value to others. Perhaps just ask?

Which Data to Solicit. Some people, particularly advertisers, seek to provide personalization based on a small amount of information. For instance, recommendations might be based on demographic data (e.g. *ZAG* — zip code, age, gender), or generalized preferences of attributes describing the items involved (in movies, this might mean the user's favorite genres). Even this seemingly-innocuous amount of information can have a striking effect on one's privacy. Sweeney showed that information *similar* to ZAG may be highly identifying: 87% of the people in the 1990 U.S. census are likely to be uniquely identified based on only zip code, *birthdate*, and gender [10].

Highly personalized recommenders, such as those based on automated collaborative filtering, require a far higher degree of personal preference information from the user. These requirements lead to even larger privacy concerns since this level of preference information may reveal substantial personal information about the user.

In past work we explored eliciting information from new users in the MovieLens movie recommender system in VOI-aware ways that optimize both the required user effort and initial recommendation accuracy [13, 14]. We built interfaces that successfully reduced the user effort needed to start receiving recommendations. Moreover, we found that people who used the VOI-aware interfaces received more accurate recommendations than people who were did not use the enhanced interfaces.

In the interest of user privacy, this kind of approach may be comforting to some users in that fewer discrete pieces of information (e.g. movie ratings) need to be provided before the system becomes accurate. However, since the recommendations are better, quite possibly the user has given up a greater amount of information about herself than she would have with an unoptimized approach.

Selectively Discarding Data. If a recommender knows "too much" about a user, which data should be kept? The answer to this question is not necessarily the information with the highest value. If "low-valued" information is discarded from many users' models, then perhaps that information is no longer low-valued since it has become more rare. Choosing an appropriate set of data that balances both the benefit to the overall community and the quality of each individual user model seems challenging.

User Interface. What should the user interface look like, especially after the system thinks it has learned enough about the user? What if the user *wants* to tell us more about herself? How does one present a privacy-preserving recommender system in an understandable way? In our experiences with MovieLens, we have found no shortage of people willing to provide hundreds and sometimes thousands of movie ratings. Indeed, user feedback from our periodic surveys reveals that rating movies is among the leading reasons people have for using the system! These observations that some users want to give up their information may make it tricky to create a usable interface that effectively conveys the privacy-preserving aspects of the recommender system.

Impact on CF Algorithms. How well do current collaborative filtering algorithms operate in reduced-data environments? Many different aspects of recommendation quality might be affected: accuracy, coverage, novelty, and so on. There is some evidence that it is possible to hide or change ratings and still have good recommendations. Berkovsky et. al. looked at the performance of distributed recommender algorithms when obfuscating (hiding) the ratings of users in a 100% dense subset of the Jester dataset of jokes [9]. Polat et. al. looked at the performance of collaborative filtering algorithms when randomly perturbing rating values in the Jester and MovieLens 100K datasets [8]. In both cases, the recommendations did become less accurate, but it is unclear whether the drop is noticeable to users.

Further practical privacy-preserving algorithms and tests on other datasets would be valuable. In particular, the highly dense Jester dataset may not reflect the results of most recommender systems, because usually a recommender is used when users cannot possibly rate all items, hence the data is very sparse. Some algorithms such as SVD seem more naturally suited for sparse data sets [15] — are they even better if given selectively chosen high-information data? Is this data inherently less noisy, and if so, could it even lead to *better* recommendations using specialized algorithms?

2.2   Exposure Risk

In this section, we discuss the potential risks to users who divulge personal information. There is the direct risk that someone will learn information that the user wished to keep private. For example, revealing identifying information could lead to identity theft. There are also indirect risks of *re-identification* — finding information about a user in one system that could identify her in another system [10]. The user may not have expected others to be able to "connect" her identities from the two systems (e.g. a personal webpage and a controversial blog written under a pseudonym).

Combinations of attributes may be highly identifying. Such combinations are sometimes called a *quasi-identifier* to differentiate them from directly identifying information like social security number. Our earlier example showed the combination of 5-digit zip code, birthdate, and gender to be a quasi-identifier. This was used to identify former Massachusetts governor William Weld in voter registration records, and then re-identify him in a supposedly anonymous medical records dataset given to researchers [10]!

Personal preferences like those expressed to many recommender systems may also turn out to be a quasi-identifier, especially if people express unusual preferences. That may allow undesired re-identification using only preference data. Furthermore, a centralized recommender system might be able to re-identify its users in locations those users did not expect. For example, perhaps Amazon.com could find former customers on a competitor's site and offer incentives to lure them away from the competitor.

Whether identification or re-identification is unwelcome is likely to vary by domain and by user. In some domains, such as music, some users may be open to sharing their tastes with others. In other domains, such as medical information, users may have serious concerns about sharing their preferences with anyone, because of the potential harm should the information leak to colleagues, employers, or insurers. In still other domains, such as scientific research papers, the sensitivity of the information may vary with time. While working on a paper, a researcher may not want others to know what related work she is studying; however, once the paper is published, the list of references is publicly available and no longer presents a privacy concern.

3   Recommender Algorithm Security

Now, we turn to another violation of trust — recommendation bias. There are many ways to bias a recommender system. Here, we ignore "typical" computer attacks such as breaking in to and directly modifying the system, and instead focus on ones specific to the recommender algorithm. In particular, we examine a *shilling attack*, which attempts to manipulate the system's recommendations for a particular item by submitting misrepresented opinions to the system. We discuss the motivation for shilling (3.1), research on specific attack types (3.2), defending against attacks (3.3), and open questions about how system modifications for privacy might affect vulnerability to shilling (3.4).

3.1   Motivation for Shilling Attacks

One of the primary uses for a recommender system is to help people make decisions. Naturally, this makes recommender systems very interesting to people with vested interests in what people choose. For instance, a restaurant owner would be more successful if more people ate at his establishment, so it is within his best interests to have it recommended often. One way to do this is to provide good service to garner a good reputation among restaurant diners. This would lead to more frequent recommendation as users express high opinions of the restaurant.

A more underhanded and perhaps cheaper way to increase recommendation frequency is to manipulate the system into doing so by executing a shilling attack. Alternatively, an attack could be used to reduce the recommendation frequency for a competitor's offering. In either case, the attacker will profit as the manipulated recommendations cause more people to choose what he wants. As noted in section 1, this actually happens: a number of book reviews published on Amazon.com are written by the author of the book being reviewed.

3.2   Known Attack Variants

A shilling attack may be executed by having a group of users (human or agent) provide specially crafted "opinions" to a recommender system that cause it behave as desired. Different attacks specify different ways to construct the users' opinions and have varying degrees of success depending on the collaborative filtering algorithm used by the targeted recommender system. Each attack has a cost, measured by the amount of knowledge required to execute it and the amount of work that needs to be done (e.g. number of new identities or new ratings needed).

Our previous work [16] describes two very simple attacks *RandomBot* and *AverageBot* that can be carried out with a small amount of information about the user and item population. When executed against the k-Nearest-Neighbor algorithms commonly in use today, these attacks are indeed effective in changing a target item's recommendation frequency. Moreover, the attacks are non-trivial to detect with typical measures of recommender system performance.

More recently, Mobasher, et al., show that the basic attacks described in [16] can be improved with a modicum of additional information about users and items. In particular, they find that it is possible to target an attack to strongly affect recommendations for a specific *segment* of the user population [17]. This focused attack has a lower cost per unit effect than the RandomBot or Average-Bot attacks, so they can be useful for adversaries who know what demographic of people they would like to target (i.e. targeted marketing campaigns) and who have limited resources to mount an attack with.

3.3   Defending Against Attacks

To formulate a response to shilling attacks, we examine a very similar attack faced by operators of reputation management and peer-to-peer systems, the *Sybil attack* [18]. In this type of attack, an attacker creates false identities that collude to achieve some objective such as increasing the reputation of an identity or increasing the influence of a node in a peer-to-peer network. For example, consider a dishonest seller on eBay who wishes to increase his feedback score. He could create a large number of identities and use them to leave himself positive feedback. This might increase the chances that a buyer will trust him and thus be tricked into purchasing an item from him.

Sybil attacks may be addressed by developing attack-resistant algorithms [19, 20], or increasing the cost of acquiring identities [21]. These ideas can be used to defend against shilling attacks as well. Work on shilling-resistant collaborative filtering algorithms is an active area of research. O'Donovan and Smyth show that an algorithm based on implicit trust scores that are computed from the accuracy of past recommendations can make shilling attacks less effective [22].

The other approach, making identities more expensive, is a simple-sounding solution that would prevent an attack from even reaching the recommender algorithm in the first place. However, the use of CAPTCHAs [23] or requiring some other non-trivial commitment of resources (e.g. monetary or computational) are believed to be either overly exclusive and unfair [21] or ineffective at preventing Sybil attacks due to unrealistic assumptions about users and attackers [18]. Thus, marginally increasing the cost of creating identities may be only a stopgap defense against shilling attacks.

There are more traditional cryptographic solutions of identity validation such as those described in [21] where the system uses a trusted third party to ensure that each person can only establish one identity. This can substantially raise the cost of an attack, but also raises privacy concerns as it requires that users reveal their identity to some entity just to use the system. Furthermore, if the trusted third party manages identities in multiple systems, it becomes possible to track one person across them, which increases the risk of re-identification.

3.4   Open Questions - Privacy and Shilling

The desire to preserve the privacy of users in a recommender system may confound the security problems. If we modify recommender systems to preserve user privacy, does that change how they are affected by shilling attacks? Likewise, as discussed above, defending against attacks may cause the loss of some privacy. What kinds of trade-offs between privacy and security might a recommender system operator need to make?

Attack Effectiveness. Do shilling attacks become more effective against privacy-preserving recommender systems? As additional privacy is introduced to a recommender system, the opportunities for attacks can increase considerably. Our work [16] shows that attacks that target recommendation frequency of low-information items (i.e. ones with few ratings) are more effective than attacks against high-information items.

In a system that tries to maintain a minimal amount of information about its members, it is possible that *every* item might have sufficiently few ratings to be vulnerable to highly-effective attacks.

Attack Difficulty. Are shilling attacks more or less difficult to mount against privacy-preserving recommender systems? As mentioned above, more individual items might become targets for effective attacks. On the other hand, if the recommender system only keeps a subset of data provided to it, an attack strategy will need to take that into consideration, both for the users being targeted and for the users introduced by the attack. This would require the attacker to know more about the system being attacked, thus increasing the cost of an attack.

Another possible impeding factor in an attack is the interface presented to users. A VOI-aware interface such as the ones used in our past work [13, 14] can control which items may be rated by a user in order to maximize the information gain per collected rating. This significantly constrains what an attacker can do and could make it more difficult to impact the system in precise ways.

Attack Detection. How does one detect shilling attacks? There are ways of detecting automated agents that are not specific to recommenders, such as noting patterns in account names, or the source or speed of account creation or opinion submission. Are there also robust ways of detecting profiles that differ significantly from normal, or that clearly affect particular items in unusual ways?

Moreover, in a privacy-preserving recommender system, is it easier or harder to detect an attack? One might theorize that in a low-data environment, it becomes easier to identify atypical patterns that are indicative of an attack. If true, this would certainly be a boon to recommender system operators. On the other hand, discarding some of the data entered by a shilling agent might leave the remaining data looking more like a human, and hence harder to detect.

4   Distributed Recommenders

4.1   Motivation

Users of MovieLens write to thank us for running a non-commercial recommender. They feel they can trust our recommendations because we do not have an external motivation to push them towards one movie or away from another.

Because traditional recommenders require large centralized resources, they must be run by some organization. That organization has control of the recommender cloud in figure 1: the data and algorithms used to form the recommendations, and even the user interface through which recommendations are presented. There are several reasons that users might wish to have more control over the recommendations. First, users might fear the centralized organization will expose their personal information. They might prefer to control their own data. Second, users might be concerned that the recommendations provided will be biased for the good of the organization rather than their own good. They might wish to have some assurances about the recommendation algorithm being used. They might even prefer to be able to select the recommendation algorithms by themselves, rather than have those algorithms chosen by someone else.

The high-level research question in this section is: can recommender systems be developed in which there is no centralized authority that can co-opt the recommendation process? A positive answer to this question might be based on developing a recommendation algorithm that has no centralized authority, limiting what the centralized authority can do, or verifying that the centralized authority is meeting certain standards of behavior in its actions. The first two approaches have been investigated in past research.

4.2   Prior Approaches

One such approach enables a community to build a shared view of a recommendation model, even though individuals only share cryptographically protected versions of their ratings vectors (preferences). Canny described a recommender system in which a centralized singular value decomposition model is built by a *tallier* combining encrypted ratings vectors from each user [24]. For security, there might be multiple, distributed talliers; indeed, each client might also be a tallier. Attackers cannot learn the original ratings vectors from the encrypted ratings vectors, but users can check that their uncorrupted ratings data is used in the model using a zero knowledge proof technique.

This approach protects against exposure of personal information, since no one can see the original ratings vectors. Canny also shows that the model-building algorithm protects against the model being unnoticeably corrupted if at least half the talliers are honest. Note that this does not protect against all forms of bias. For example, clients can still shill by providing false preferences in the correct protocol that is then dutifully incorporated into the model by talliers.

Miller et al. extends Canny's work by using Canny's approach to computation, but with an item-item recommendation algorithm [2, 25]. The idea is the same: encrypted ratings vectors are distributed by users; the vectors cannot be reverse-engineered to produce the original ratings; and a centralized model is built that can be used to produce individual recommendations [26]. The individual recommendations can be produced by a user by combining their own ratings with the model without sharing those ratings with anyone else.

One key advantage of Miller's algorithm is that it can produce models incrementally by collecting ratings vectors over time. In principle, each user could keep his own model, only sharing encrypted ratings data with others. Such a user might be satisfied with a partial model that was only suitable for making recommendations for himself, not for other users. Miller showed that these models are small, fast, and could easily be maintained on a personal workstation. Ratings could be distributed using a variety of well-known peer-to-peer approaches, such as those used in Gnutella[5], Freenet [27], or Chord [28].

In the extreme, the smaller model could be maintained on a mobile device. Distributing ratings to these devices would be more challenging, since they are only occasionally connected to the Internet. One radical idea is that the ratings might be distributed wirelessly using a personal-area network like Bluetooth. In this vision, the user walks around the world carrying her mobile device, which shares encrypted ratings vectors with nearby mobile devices. The encryption of the ratings vectors would protect privacy, while the resulting distributed recommendation model would provide accurate recommendations using a recommendation algorithm the user chose and maintained herself.

4.3   Open Questions

There are many open questions about the use of distributed recommenders that protect privacy or give individual control over the use of the ratings or recommender model. This section outlines some of the most important.

Practical Distributed Recommenders. Do distributed recommenders really work in practice? Do they lead to recommendations that are as accurate as those predicted by the analysis and offline experiments that have been performed? Actually implementing a distributed recommender system for a large user community, such as music or movie lovers, and solving the practical problems faced by such a system would be a substantial research contribution.

---

[5] http://rfc-gnutella.sourceforge.net/

An interesting area for experimentation is to investigate what would really happen with the distribution of ratings data over personal area networks such as Bluetooth. Would users be exposed to enough different types of people to get a wide variety of recommendations, or would there be too much similarity in the people they encounter on a day-to-day basis?

Integrity. Security attacks are especially of concern for distributed recommenders, because their ratings vectors would likely be shared openly through well-known protocols. (In principle the ratings vectors could be shared through a secure channel, but then only certified programs could participate in the recommendation process, a result that would be less satisfying to the peer-to-peer community, for example.) These ratings vectors could be destroyed or discarded as they are passed through the system. More simply, shilling attacks from robot "users" could be injected into the system as described in section 3. Since a distributed system makes it difficult to verify identity, these attacks would be challenging to thwart. What mechanisms could be developed to make shilling attacks more difficult in a distributed recommender system?

The bottom-line goal of the research questions in this section is to develop recommenders that are guaranteed to serve the needs of their end-users. What techniques other than those discussed here could provide such guarantees? Could certification techniques show with high probability that the recommendations are made honestly? Are there zero-knowledge proofs that show not only that the data used is the correct data, but also that the algorithms used have the desired properties? Research that could demonstrate properties of centralized recommender algorithms might be invaluable.

5   Conclusion

The issues of privacy and security in recommender systems is rich with important, unanswered research questions. Highly personalized recommender systems, like those discussed in this paper, collect large volumes of very personal data about their users. How can security techniques be used to guarantee that this personal data will never be leaked without the permission of its subject? Further, these recommender systems are increasingly important in guiding people's decisions about what they want to do, what they want to buy, even where they want to go. How can the users be sure that the recommendations they receive have not been inappropriately influenced or modified?

In this paper we explored three aspects of recommender systems that relate to these privacy and security questions: value and risks of personal information, shilling, and distributed recommenders. Previous work on value of information (VOI) shows that it can be used to more effectively collect information from new users. We believe it can similarly be used to determine when to stop collecting information to properly balance the privacy given up by users with the quality of the recommendations, and to intelligently choose which information to discard if "too much" is known about a user. The challenge of shilling is that the aforementioned privacy protections may make shilling easier, especially if they reduce the amount of information the recommender system keeps about each user. Past research in distributed recommenders has shown that security techniques such as cryptosystems and zero knowledge proofs can be used to provide recommenders with dramatically different security and privacy properties.

Rather than try to completely define the set of privacy and security issues involving recommenders, we have tried to outline some of the most important issues, and to identify some key research questions that may yield to the research techniques of the security community. We hope by raising these questions to inspire even more high quality research into the security and privacy implications of the increasingly important ubiquity of recommender systems.

Acknowledgments

Thanks to the participants of the 2005 User Modeling Workshop on Privacy-Enhanced Personalization for their helpful suggestions. Thanks also to members of GroupLens Research at the University of Minnesota for many exciting research collaborations, fruitful discussions, and overall fun. Particular thanks are due to our colleagues Al Mamunur Rashid, Istvan Albert, Dan Cosley, Sean M. McNee, and Joseph Konstan, our co-authors on the VOI research [13, 14], and to our colleagues Joseph Konstan and Brad Miller, our co-authors on the PocketLens research [26]. This work was supported by grants from the NSF (DGE 95-54517, IIS 96-13960, IIS 97-34442, IIS 99-78717, and IIS 01-02229).

References

1. Resnick, P., Iacovou, N., Suchak, M., Bergstrom, P., Riedl, J.: GroupLens: An open architecture for collaborative filtering of netnews. In: CSCW '94: Proceedings of the 1994 ACM Conference on Computer Supported Cooperative Work, Chapel Hill, North Carolina, United States, ACM Press (1994) 175–186
2. Sarwar, B., Karypis, G., Konstan, J., Riedl, J.: Item-based collaborative filtering recommendation algorithms. In: WWW '01: Proceedings of the 10th International Conference on World Wide Web, Hong Kong, ACM Press (2001) 285–295
3. Adomavicius, G., Tuzhilin, A.: Toward the next generation of recommender systems: A survey of the state-of-the-art and possible extensions. IEEE Transactions on Knowledge and Data Engineering (2005) 734–749
4. Ackerman, M.S., Cranor, L.F., Reagle, J.: Privacy in e-commerce: Examining user scenarios and privacy preferences. In: ACM Conference on Electronic Commerce. (1999) 1–8
5. Ali, K., van Stam, W.: TiVo: Making show recommendations using a distributed collaborative filtering architecture. In: KDD '04: Knowledge Discovery and Data Mining Conference, Seattle, Washington, USA (2004) 394 – 401
6. Ramakrishnan, N., Keller, B.J., Mirza, B.J., Grama, A., Karypis, G.: Privacy risks in recommender systems. IEEE Internet Computing **5** (2001) 54–62
7. Lam, S.K., Riedl, J.: Privacy, shilling, and the value of information in recommender systems. In: Proceedings of User Modeling Workshop on Privacy-Enhanced Personalization. (2005) 85–92

8. Polat, H., Du, W.: Privacy-preserving collaborative filtering using randomized perturbation techniques. In: ICDM '03: Proceedings of the Third IEEE International Conference on Data Mining. (2003)

9. Berkovsky, S., Eytani, Y., Kuflik, T., Ricci, F.: Privacy-enhanced collaborative filtering. In: Proceedings of User Modeling Workshop on Privacy-Enhanced Personalization. (2005) 75–83

10. Sweeney, L.: k-Anonymity: A model for protecting privacy. International Journal on Uncertainty, Fuzziness and Knowledge-based Systems (2002) 557–570

11. Verykios, V.S., Bertino, E., Fovino, I.N., Provenza, L.P., Aygin, Y., Theodoridis, Y.: State-of-the-art in privacy preserving data mining. In: SIGMOD '05: Proceedings of the Conference on the Management of Data. (2005)

12. Pennock, D.M., Horvitz, E., Lawrence, S., Giles, C.L.: Collaborative filtering by personality diagnosis: A hybrid memory and model-based approach. In: UAI '00: Proceedings of the 16th Conference on Uncertainty in Artificial Intelligence, Stanford, CA, Morgan Kaufmann Publishers Inc. (2000) 473–480

13. Rashid, A.M., Albert, I., Cosley, D., Lam, S.K., McNee, S., Konstan, J.A., Riedl, J.: Getting to know you: Learning new user preferences in recommender systems. In: Proceedings of the 2002 International Conference on Intelligent User Interfaces, San Francisco, CA (2002) 127–134

14. McNee, S.M., Lam, S.K., Konstan, J.A., Riedl, J.: Interfaces for eliciting new user preferences in recommender systems. In: User Modeling, Johnstown, PA, USA, Springer Verlag (2003) 178–187

15. Sarwar, B.M., Karypis, G., Konstan, J.A., Riedl, J.: Application of dimensionality reduction in recommender system – a case study. In: ACM WebKDD 2000 Web Mining for E-Commerce Workshop, Boston, MA, USA (2000)

16. Lam, S.K., Riedl, J.: Shilling recommender systems for fun and profit. In: WWW '04: Proceedings of the 13th International Conference on World Wide Web, New York, NY, USA, ACM Press (2004) 393–402

17. Burke, R., Mobasher, B., Zabicki, R., Bhaumik, R.: Identifying attack models for secure recommendation. In: ACM IUI Workshop: Beyond Personalization. (2005)

18. Douceur, J.: The Sybil attack. In: Proceedings of the 1st International Workshop on Peer-to-Peer Systems. (2002)

19. Dellarocas, C.: Immunizing online reputation reporting systems against unfair ratings and discriminatory behavior. In: ACM Conference on Electronic Commerce. (2000) 150–157

20. Kamvar, S.D., Schlosser, M.T., Garcia-Molina, H.: The Eigentrust algorithm for reputation management in P2P networks. In: WWW '03: Proceedings of the 12th International Conference on World Wide Web, New York, NY, USA, ACM Press (2003) 640–651

21. Friedman, E., Resnick, P.: The social cost of cheap pseudonyms. Journal of Economics and Management Strategy (1999)

22. O'Donovan, J., Smyth, B.: Is trust robust?: An analysis of trust-based recommendation. In: IUI '06: Proceedings of the 11th International Conference on Intelligent User Interfaces, New York, NY, USA, ACM Press (2006) 101–108

23. von Ahn, L., Blum, M., Hopper, N., Langford, J.: CAPTCHA: Using hard AI problems for security. In: Proceedings of Eurocrypt, 2003. (2003)

24. Canny, J.: Collaborative filtering with privacy via factor analysis. In: SIGIR '02: Proceedings of the 25th International ACM Conference on Research and Development in Information Retrieval, Tampere, Finland, ACM Press (2002) 238–245

25. Karypis, G.: Evaluation of item-based top-n recommendation algorithms. In: Proceedings of the 10th Conference of Information and Knowledge Management. (2001)

26. Miller, B.N., Konstan, J.A., Riedl, J.: Pocketlens: Toward a personal recommender system. ACM Transactions on Information Systems **22** (2004) 437–476

27. Clarke, I., Hong, T.W., Miller, S.G., Sandberg, O., Wiley, B.: Protecting free expression online with Freenet. IEEE Internet Computing (2002)

28. Stoica, I., Morris, R., Karger, D., Kaashoek, F., Balakrishnan, H.: Chord: A scalable Peer-To-Peer lookup service for internet applications. In: Proceedings of the 2001 ACM SIGCOMM Conference. (2001) 149–160

Optimized Workflow Authorization in Service Oriented Architectures

Martin Wimmer, Martina-Cezara Albutiu, and Alfons Kemper

Technische Universität München, 85748 Garching b. München, Germany
{wimmerma, albutiu, kemper}@in.tum.de

Abstract. Complex business processes are usually realized by specifying the integration and interaction of smaller modular software components. For example, hitherto monolithic enterprise resource planning systems (ERP) are decomposed into Web services which are then again orchestrated in terms of Web service workflows, bringing about higher levels of flexibility and adaptability. In general, such services constitute autonomous software components with their own dedicated security requirements. In this paper we present our approach for consolidating the access control of (Web service) workflows. The proposed security engineering method allows, first, to determine for whom workflows are executable from a privileges point of view, second, to assess compliance with the principle of least privilege, and, third, helps to reduce policy enforcement costs.

1 Introduction

The service oriented computing paradigm has introduced a change in the design of future large-scale enterprise applications. Monolithic software systems like classical enterprise resource planning systems (ERP) are increasingly replaced through Web services which provide the basic ERP functionality in the form of self-contained modules. As services constitute fine grained software components that can easily be linked due to a standardized interface description and communication protocol, complex business processes can be realized as service workflows. Though this architectural change brings about a plus of flexibility and adaptability, it poses new challenges in the area of administration, in particular w.r.t. security. Each Web service can pose individual security requirements, e.g., with respect to client authentication and authorization. Consider, for instance, the e-health workflow illustrated in Fig. 1. This simplified example workflow will be executed when a patient is transferred to the cardiology department of a hospital. Depending on the diagnostic findings, either an in-patient treatment is applied or an electrocardiogram (ECG) is made in order to acquire further expertise. Sub-activities of the workflow on the one hand represent practical activities that require human interaction like a medication. On the other hand, they stand for information processing tasks, like an update of the stock of pharmaceuticals in the database. In the following we concentrate on the technical aspects of the workflow and assume the subsequent access rules to be defined:

G. Müller (Ed.): ETRICS 2006, LNCS 3995, pp. 30–44, 2006.
© Springer-Verlag Berlin Heidelberg 2006

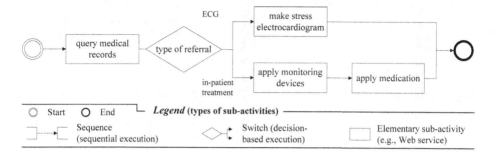

Fig. 1. Example for an e-health (Web service) workflow

- Health personnel with permanent employment and administrative employees are allowed to access the medical records of patients. These are stored in the table *MedicalRecordsTab* of the hospital's database (applies to *query medical records*).
- Nurses of the cardiology and internists are allowed to update medical records, e.g., by inserting ECG results (applies to *make stress electrocardiogram*).
- Internists are allowed to *apply monitoring devices* by marking them in the *DevicesTab* as *in use*.
- Nurses and physicians can *apply medications*, in case the patient is not allergic concerning the respective pharmaceutical.

Nowadays, access control is usually performed at the services' layer. This approach results from the mentioned autonomy of authorization but brings about two major shortcomings: First, security evaluations are performed redundantly. That is, authentication and authorization of the same client will be done repeatedly, which might be very costly considering for example certificate evaluation and verification. Second, further performance drawbacks can emerge, if services are needlessly invoked in cases when subjects lack privileges at later stages in the workflow. For instance, querying the medical records of a patient will be done unnecessarily, if the workflow is called by an administration employee that is neither able to pursue the *ECG-* nor the *in-patient-treatment*-branch of the workflow. Regarding Web service transactions even rollbacks or compensating actions can be required then. Therefore, at the time a workflow is designed, the following issues addressing access control arise:

1. *Who is allowed to execute the workflow?* We are interested in answering this question from the *single-user / single-role* perspective which applies to many business processes. Therefore, we determine the user profiles that grant workflow execution, without demanding for additional role activations or profile switches.
2. *What is the minimum set of required privileges?* This issue is also known as the *principle of least privilege* or the *need to know paradigm* which demand that subjects are only granted those privileges required to fulfill their tasks.

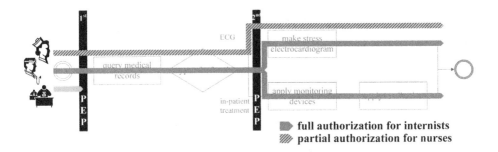

Fig. 2. Access control configurations

3. *Can policy evaluation be optimized?* At best, access control needs to be performed only once on top of the workflow layer, screening non-authorized requests and avoiding redundant policy evaluations at the services' layer.

Our contribution is a generic security engineering approach for (Web service) workflows that addresses these questions. It is based upon the consolidation of Web service policies that together define the access control settings of a workflow. That means, the minimum set of required privileges is derived from the privileges needed to execute the individual sub-activities. By means of a structural analysis it is analyzed whether subjects exist that are granted the necessary privileges to execute the workflow. In order to provide better scalability, role based access control can be employed. As we will show, our policy consolidation approach allows to determine the least-required roles that authorize the execution of the workflow.

To give an example, subjects being allowed to execute the *in-patient-treatment*-branch illustrated in Fig. 1 need to be granted privileges for the services *query medical records, apply monitoring devices,* and *apply medication.* Consequently, these subjects are in the intersection of the subjects authorized for the individual sub-activities. With regard to our informal policy specification, this applies to internists. As internists are also allowed to *make stress electrocardiograms,* they possess the privileges to invoke any branch within the workflow. We call this *full authorization.* On the contrary, nurses are granted *partial authorization,* as they are only allowed to execute the *ECG*-branch of the workflow. Other subjects, like administrative employees, – though being able to invoke *query medical records* – do not possess the required privileges to execute a complete branch and will be blocked right from the beginning. Fig. 2 illustrates the different access control configurations and shows how this information can be used to make access control more efficient. Instead of retaining access control at the services' layer and, thus, having to cope with the mentioned performance drawbacks, access control at the workflow layer can block unsuccessful execution at an early stage. To achieve this, policy enforcement points (PEP), i.e., points in the workflow where access control will be performed, are inserted at branches in the workflow. Moreover, if access control is constrained to *full authorization,* even one PEP (the first PEP in the figure) can be sufficient.

In this paper, we first introduce the underlying formal policy model in Sec. 2, which constitutes the basis for our policy consolidation approach that is described in Sec. 3. The different access control configurations and their impact on the complexity of the consolidation are discussed in Sec. 4. Finally, related work is presented in Sec. 5 before we conclude and sketch ongoing work in Sec. 6.

2 Policy Model

Our policy consolidation approach is based on a formal policy model supporting discretionary and role based access control (DAC and RBAC) schemes. The formal syntax and semantics of our policy model are based on those introduced by Bonatti et al. [1]. We adapted and extended this model where necessary, e.g., by introducing additional operators.

2.1 Syntax

Policies in our model are composed of individual access rules, i.e., a policy P is described through a set of rules $\{R_1, \ldots, R_n\}$. A rule $R = (S, O, A, c)$ assigns privileges specified by resource and action information (O and A) to subjects S. The assignment can further be restricted through a condition c. S represents a set of subjects sub_i and can be written as $S = \{sub_1, \ldots, sub_m\}$. For example, in the health service context, sub_i can stand for one individual nurse or physician. We call this the *set-based* representation of S. In comparison, the *attribute-based* description provides a higher level of expressiveness. Using *attribute-based* descriptions, subjects are specified through predicate conjunctions. A predicate is of the form (*attribute-identifier* ∘ *constant*). Depending on the attribute's domain, the comparison operator ∘ is in $\{<, \leq, =, \geq, >\}$ for totally ordered sets or in $\{\sqsubset, \sqsubseteq, =, \sqsupseteq, \sqsupset\}$ for partially ordered finite sets. A set of subjects S is represented as a disjunction of predicate conjunctions, i.e., $S \equiv (s_1 \vee \ldots \vee s_k)$, with $s_i = (s_{i,1} \wedge \ldots \wedge s_{i,l})$ (for $1 \leq i \leq k$). Thereby, $s_{i,d}$ represents a predicate conjunction that applies to one attribute. For instance, given the attribute identifiers *role* and *years of practice* (abbrev. *y-o-p*), the conjunction (role $\sqsupseteq$ Nurse $\wedge$ y-o-p ≥ 2) specifies users that are granted the role *Nurse* and have at least two years of operational experience.

Analogously, O and A are either described in the *set-based* or the *attribute-based* way. Subjects, resources, and actions are specified on disjoint sets of attribute identifiers, denoted as *S-Attr*, *O-Attr*, and *A-Attr*. S, O, and A are inequality-free, i.e., there is no predicate whose operator ∘ is $\neq$. The same does not hold for conditions, which are arbitrary Boolean formulae and can include user defined functions with Boolean codomain. Conditions are defined on environment attributes of *E-Attr*.

Projection-Operator. Given a rule $R = (S, O, A, c)$, the operator Π_S projects on the subjects-part of R, i.e., $\Pi_S(R) = S$. Similar operators are defined for projections on resources (Π_O), actions (Π_A), privileges ($\Pi_{O,A}$), and conditions (Π_C). Let $P = \{R_1, \ldots, R_n\}$ be a policy. $\Pi_S(P)$ is defined as:

$\Pi_{\mathcal{S}}(P) = \{\Pi_{\mathcal{S}}(R_1), \dots, \Pi_{\mathcal{S}}(R_n)\}$. Other projection operators on policies are defined in a similar way. We use the abbreviation $\mathcal{S}(P) = \bigcap_{1 \leq i \leq n} \Pi_{\mathcal{S}}(R_i)$ to denote those subjects that are granted all privileges defined in $\bar{P}$.

2.2 Semantics

An evaluation context $e \in \mathcal{E}$ is a partial mapping of the attributes in $S\text{-}Attr \cup O\text{-}Attr \cup A\text{-}Attr \cup E\text{-}Attr$. If $D_1, \dots, D_m$ are the distinguished attribute domains, then $\mathcal{E}$ is defined as $D_1^{\perp} \times \dots \times D_m^{\perp}$, with $D_j^{\perp} = D_j \cup \{\perp\}$ and $\perp$ representing an unspecified attribute value.

An evaluation context e is evaluated against the individual components of rules. A subject specification S applies to e, iff S maps to *true* w.r.t the attribute values of e. That is, $[\![S]\!]_e := S(e) = (true|false)$. Evaluating objects, actions and conditions is defined similarly. A rule R applies to e, iff $[\![R]\!]_e := [\![S]\!]_e \wedge [\![O]\!]_e \wedge [\![A]\!]_e \wedge [\![c]\!]_e$ maps to *true*.

Policies aggregate the access rights that specify the access control requirements of applications which are composed of individual sub-activities. The semantics of a policy P depends on the employed policy evaluation algorithm. If the access rules of the individual sub-activities are enforced successively, P applies to e, iff *any* of its rules apply. That is $[\![P]\!]_e^{pe\text{-}any} := \bigvee_{R \in P} [\![R]\!]_e$. In contrast to this, the policy evaluation algorithm *pe-all* can be used to statically enforce a policy before any sub-activity is invoked. It is defined as $[\![P]\!]_e^{pe\text{-}all} := \bigwedge_{R \in P} [\![R]\!]_e$.

2.3 Role Based Access Control

Policy administration can easily become unmanageable if privileges are independently assigned to each user. Better scalability is provided through role based access control (RBAC), which was introduced by Sandhu et. al. in 1996 [2] and for which the standard [3] has been released in 2004. Using RBAC, privileges that are required for performing a certain task are grouped by roles and users acquire these privileges via the indirection of being granted those roles. Consequently, roles play two parts in our policy model. On the one hand, roles act as subjects when being used to group privileges (*privilege-to-role* assignment). On the other hand, roles are objects when they are assigned to other subjects – which then could be a user or a further role (*role-to-subject* assignment). That way, roles can be organized in a hierarchy. As an example consider the role hierarchy for our e-health scenario which is shown in Fig. 3. Through the hierarchy a partial order on roles is defined: Senior roles, which are at higher levels in the hierarchy, are granted all privileges that are also granted to their junior roles. To give an example, the role *Internist* is senior to *Physician*, denoted as *Internist* $\sqsupseteq$ *Physician*. Accordingly, *Physician* is called junior role of *Internist*. All subjects that are granted the role *Physician* or any senior role of it are represented through the predicate (role $\sqsupseteq$ Physician).

With regard to workflow authorization we are interested in determining the *least-required roles*. For example, if the roles *Head Nurse* and *Nurse* authorize the execution of the workflow illustrated in Fig. 1, then the least-required role

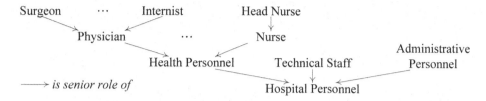

Fig. 3. Example role hierarchy for a hospital

with respect to the introduced role hierarchy is *Nurse*. If a role authorizes the execution of a workflow (or a workflow branch), we demand the role to authorize the execution of each sub-activity of the workflow (branch) without the activation of any further role. This *single-role*-approach is particularly relevant for ERP applications: Business processes like financial accounting or the admission of patients in our e-health scenario represent self-contained tasks that are to be performed by users that are granted business process specific roles, i.e., least-required roles in our terminology.

2.4 Example

According to the informal access rules stated in the introduction, we define the following policies: P_{MR} (applies to *query medical records*), P_{ECG} (*make stress electrocardiogram*), P_{App} (*apply monitoring devices*), and P_{Med} (*apply medication*). The attribute identifiers o and a represent resources and actions, *f-o-a* is the abbreviation for *field of activity*.

$$P_{MR} = \{(((\text{role} \sqsupseteq \text{Health Personnel} \land \text{employment} = \text{permanent}) \lor$$
$$(\text{role} \sqsupseteq \text{Administrative Personnel})),$$
$$(o = \text{MedicalRecordsTab}), (a = \text{select}), (\text{true}))\}$$
$$P_{ECG} = \{(((\text{role} \sqsupseteq \text{Nurse} \land \text{f-o-a} = \text{cardiology}) \lor \text{role} \sqsupseteq \text{Internist}),$$
$$(o = \text{MedicalRecordsTab}), (a = \text{select} \lor a = \text{update}), (\text{true}))\}$$
$$P_{App} = \{((\text{role} \sqsupseteq \text{Internist}), (o = \text{DevicesTab}), (a = \text{select} \lor a = \text{update}), (\text{true}))\}$$
$$P_{Med} = \{((\text{role} \sqsupseteq \text{Nurse} \lor \text{role} \sqsupseteq \text{Physician}), (o = \text{PharmaceuticalsTab}),$$
$$(a = \text{select} \lor a = \text{update}), (\textit{HighAnaphylaxisRisk}(\text{patient,drug}) = \text{false}))\}$$

3 Access Control for Web Service Workflows

3.1 Workflow Model

Workflows are used to model and realize complex (business) processes by specifying the invocation order of fine-grained sub-activities. BPEL4WS [4] will be widely used for defining Web service workflows. Currently it is revised by OASIS for standardization under the name WS-BPEL. It provides five control patterns, namely *flow*, *while*, *sequence*, *switch*, and *pick*. We refer to [4] for their specifications. The only aspect being of relevance for access control is, whether all or

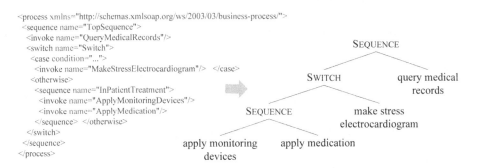

Fig. 4. BPEL4WS-extract and workflow tree for the e-health business process

only some of the sub-activities grouped by any of these control patterns have to be invoked. As the first three control patterns require all sub-activities to be executed[1], we group them together and represent them through the SEQUENCE-template. The remaining patterns specify that at most one sub-activity will be called, e.g., due to the evaluation of conditions or because of the arrival of certain events. We abstract from the respective flow specification and aggregate them together to the SWITCH-template. SEQUENCE and SWITCH are also sub-activities in the meaning of our workflow model.

A Web service choreography can be represented by a *workflow tree* as illustrated in Fig. 4 for our example business process. Inner nodes of such a tree either represent SEQUENCE- or SWITCH-nodes, while leaves represent Web services. In order to obtain a consolidated view onto the access control settings of a workflow, we perform a structural analysis of the workflow tree. This analysis offers possibilities for design-revision and optimization as described in Sec. 3.6.

3.2 Preliminary Remarks

As mentioned before, the leaves of a workflow tree represent Web services. In our setting, Web services are autonomous software components that can be supplied by varying service providers and that might be integral parts of varying workflows. This autonomy implies that in the general case the policy administration authorities vary. In order to be able to perform the intended policy analysis, we demand the following three conditions to hold:

1. Policies can be expressed in one common policy language and rely on DAC and RBAC models.
2. The access control specifications of the Web services fulfill the principle of least privilege.
3. The subject specifications are based on the same description language.

If condition 2 holds, we can infer the consolidated policies to comply with the principle of least privilege. The minimality criterion for Web services can

---

[1] We assume that sub-activities of *while*-patterns will be executed at least once.

often be automatically ensured, as we showed in [5] for database dependent Web services. The third assumption refers to the employed terminology. As one of our aims is to determine the set of subjects authorized for the workflow, we require subjects to be uniquely identifiable. If all policies belong to the same (intra-organizational) repository, this would typically be the case. With regard to distributed Web service invocations, access control usually relies on a federated identity management, e.g., realized via WS-Federation and SAML. In this case, identity mappings have to be resolved as a preliminary step. As mentioned in the introduction, our focus is on intra-organizational application integration like the service oriented implementation of ERP systems, where the three conditions are typically met.

3.3   Policy Consolidation

Through a bottom-up analysis, access control policies for higher levels of the workflow tree are iteratively determined and, finally, a consolidated policy for the complete workflow is inferred. Generating the policy for an inner node depends on the node's type, i.e., wether it is a SEQUENCE- or a SWITCH-node. In the following we consider a node NODE that has n child nodes. The child nodes are numbered from 1 to n and each of them represents a sub-activity, i.e., a further SEQUENCE- or SWITCH-node or an elementary service. For each sub-activity i, P_i represents the related policy.

Consolidating the policies of Sequence-nodes. A SEQUENCE node enforces the execution of all n sub-activities. Thus, each subject authorized for NODE must as well be authorized for each sub-activity. The consolidated policy for the SEQUENCE-node consists of all privileges that apply to the sub-activities and is restricted to the intersection of the subject specifications.

The set of subjects allowed to execute NODE is $S_{all} = \bigcap_{1 \leq i \leq n} \mathcal{S}(P_i)$. Consequently, the consolidated policy is constructed as follows:

$$P_{(all)}^{opt} = \{(S_{all}, \Pi_{\mathcal{O},\mathcal{A}}(R), \Pi_{\mathcal{C}}(R)) \mid R \in P_i, 1 \leq i \leq n\} \tag{1}$$

When aggregating the policies for a SEQUENCE-node, rules whose privileges are relaxed by another rule of $P_{(all)}^{opt}$ can be reduced by *AND*-ing the conditions, if the employed policy evaluation algorithm is *pe-all*. That is, given a partial order on policies, like the one we presented in [5], two rules (S_{all}, O_1, A_1, c_1) and (S_{all}, O_2, A_2, c_2) can be aggregated to $(S_{all}, O_2, A_2, c_1 \wedge c_2)$, in case $O_1 \subseteq O_2$ and $A_1 \subseteq A_2$. If $S_{all} \neq \emptyset$, the NODE is *subject-executable*. That means that there exists at least one subject or role that is granted the privileges to execute NODE.

Consolidating the policies of Switch-nodes. Identifying the policy for a SWITCH-node is more challenging, as the permission to execute the node depends on the user context and the history of previous execution steps. Users can be authorized to execute branches of the workflow but need not be privileged to perform all sub-activities. Thus, each subject defined in any sub-activity's policy is granted privileges for the SWITCH-node.

Again, let $S_{\text{all}} = \bigcap_{1 \leq i \leq n} \mathcal{S}(P_i)$ be the set of subjects authorized to execute all sub-activities. Then, all subjects defined in S_{all} are granted *full authorization* for the SWITCH-node. Thus, the applicable policy is $P_{(\text{all})}^{\text{opt}}$ as defined in equation (1).

On the opposite side, *partial-authorization* distinguishes the different execution paths. We obtain the following policy for the subjects that are authorized for the ith branch:

$$P_{(i)}^{\text{opt}} = \{(\mathcal{S}(P_i) - S_{\text{all}}, \Pi_{\mathcal{O},\mathcal{A}}(R), \Pi_C(R)) \mid R \in \mathcal{P}_i\} \tag{2}$$

Thus, if any of the delta sets $\mathcal{S}(P_i) - S_{\text{all}}$ are non-empty, policy analysis branches. Each of the up to $n + 1$ different cases are considered as virtual replications of the original workflow tree and analysis for them proceeds separately.

3.4   Computing Subject Intersections

In this section we discuss the computation of subject intersections, which is an integral part of the consolidation process presented in Sec. 3.3. As shown in Sec. 2, subjects (like resources and actions, too) are either described in the *set-based* or the *attribute-based* way. As the *attribute-based* description is more expressive, we assume this representation for explaining the computation of intersections.

Let S and S' be two subject sets. According to our policy model, both sets are represented in disjunctive normal form (DNF):

$$S \equiv s_1 \vee \ldots \vee s_k = (s_{1,1} \wedge \ldots \wedge s_{1,l}) \vee \ldots \vee (s_{k,1} \wedge \ldots \wedge s_{k,l}) \quad \text{and}$$
$$S' \equiv s'_1 \vee \ldots \vee s'_{k'} = (s'_{1,1} \wedge \ldots \wedge s'_{1,l}) \vee \ldots \vee (s'_{k',1} \wedge \ldots \wedge s'_{k',l})$$

S and S' are defined over attributes of *S-Attr*. The elements of *S-Attr* are also called the dimensions of a subject specification. We assume S and S' to be specified in each each dimension. If a conjunction s_i is not constrained in dimension d, the respective predicate $s_{i,d}$ represents the whole domain of d.

Alg. 1 gives a pseudo-code representation for computing the intersection of subject sets. We illustrate the computation of subject intersections by means of an example. Consider the following two subject descriptions:

$$S \equiv s_1 = (\text{role} \sqsupseteq \text{Nurse} \wedge \text{y-o-p} \geq 1)$$
$$S' \equiv s'_1 \vee s'_2 = (\text{role} \sqsupseteq \text{Admininistrative Personnel} \wedge \text{y-o-p} \geq 0) \vee$$
$$(\text{role} \sqsupseteq \text{Health Personnel} \wedge \text{y-o-p} \geq 2 \wedge \text{y-o-p} \leq 4)$$

S represents all subjects that are granted the *Nurse* role and that have at least one year of practice (*y-o-p*). S' represents administrative employees and all subjects that are granted senior roles of the *Health Personnel* role with at least two and at most four years of practice. Thus, the dimensions are *role* and *y-o-p*. While the domain of *role* is a finite lattice (defined by the role hierarchy shown in Fig. 3), the domain of *y-o-p* is $[0, +\infty[$.

s_1 and s'_1 represent disjoint sets. Both terms do not overlap in the *role* dimension as $s_{1,\text{role}} \equiv \{Nurse, Head Nurse\}$ and $s'_{1,\text{role}} \equiv \{Administrative Personnel\}$.

Algorithm 1. *intersect*(S, S'), with $S \equiv s_1 \vee \ldots \vee s_k$, and $S' \equiv s'_1 \vee \ldots \vee s'_{k'}$

1: Ψ = false
2: **for all** conjunctions s_i of S **do**
3:    **for all** conjunctions s'_j of S' **do**
4:       **for all** dimensions $d = 1 \ldots l$ **do**
5:          ψ_d = reduce$(s_{i,d} \wedge s'_{j,d})$
6:       **end for**
7:       $\Psi = \Psi \vee (\psi_1 \wedge \ldots \wedge \psi_l)$
8:    **end for**
9: **end for**
10: **return** Ψ

$$S \cap S' \equiv \Psi = \bigvee_{1 \leq i \leq k, 1 \leq j \leq k'} \left(\bigwedge_{1 \leq d \leq l} \left(s_{i,d} \wedge s'_{j,d} \right) \right)$$

That is, the intersection of both sets in this dimension is empty and ψ_{role} in line 5 of Alg. 1 is equivalent to *false*. Therefore, the overlap in the *y-o-p* dimension is ineffectual as the conjunctive add-on in line 7 evaluates to *false* and can be omitted.

In contrast to this, s_1 and s'_2 overlap in each dimension as illustrated in Fig. 5. The conjunction (y-o-p $\geq$ 1) $\wedge$ (y-o-p $\geq$ 2 $\wedge$ y-o-p $\leq$ 4) is reduced to (y-o-p $\geq$ 2 $\wedge$ y-o-p $\leq$ 4). In general, intersections of totally ordered sets are computed by comparing the respective lower and upper bounds. The predicates $s_{1,\text{role}}$ and $s'_{2,\text{role}}$ define the two finite sets $\Phi_1 = \{\text{Nurse, Head Nurse}\}$ and $\Phi'_2 = \{\text{Nurse, Head Nurse, Physician, Internist, Surgeon}\}$. Thus, $(s_{1,\text{role}} \wedge s'_{2,\text{role}})$ is equivalent to $\Phi_1 \cap \Phi'_2 = \{\text{Nurse, Head Nurse}\}$. The infimum of $\Phi_1 \cap \Phi'_2$ is the role *Nurse*. Therefore, $(s_{1,\text{role}} \wedge s'_{2,\text{role}})$ can be reduced to (role $\sqsupseteq$ Nurse) so that the intersection of S_1 and S_2 is equivalent to

(role $\sqsupseteq$ Nurse $\wedge$ y-o-p $\geq$ 2 $\wedge$ y-o-p $\leq$ 4)

That is, the intersection consists of those subjects that are granted the *Nurse* role and that have at least two and at most four years of practice.

3.5 Example

Performing the policy consolidation for our running example starts with analyzing the policies P_{App} and P_{Med} that apply to the activities *apply monitoring devices* and *apply medication* which are linked in sequence as illustrated in Fig. 1 and Fig. 4. The subjects allowed to execute both are those granted the *Internist* role. The consolidation process is continued by analyzing the SWITCH-node. The following cases have to be distinguished:

1. *Internists* are in the intersection of the subject sets that are allowed to execute both branches (*ECG* and *in-patient treatment*).
2. *Nurses* working at the cardiology are only granted privileges for the *ECG*-branch.

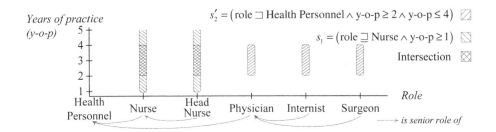

Fig. 5. Matching conjunctive terms

The last step is to analyze the top SEQUENCE-node for both cases that were derived in the previous step. We compute the intersection

$$(\text{role} \sqsupseteq \text{Health Personnel} \vee \text{role} \sqsupseteq \text{Administrative Pers.}) \wedge (\text{role} \sqsupseteq \text{Internist})$$
$$= (\text{role} \sqsupseteq \text{Internist})$$

Thus, subjects granted the *Internist* role are allowed to execute the complete workflow. The applicable consolidated policy is $P_{(\text{all})}^{\text{opt}}$ with

$$
\begin{aligned}
P_{(\text{all})}^{\text{opt}} = \{ & ((\text{role} \sqsupseteq \text{Internist} \wedge \text{employment} = \text{permanent}), (o = \text{MedicalRecordsTab}), \\
& (a = \text{select} \vee a = \text{update}), (\mathit{true})), \\
& ((\text{role} \sqsupseteq \text{Internist} \wedge \text{employment} = \text{permanent}), (o = \text{DevicesTab}), \\
& (a = \text{select} \vee a = \text{update}), (\text{true})), \\
& ((\text{role} \sqsupseteq \text{Internist} \wedge \text{employment} = \text{permanent}), (o = \text{PharmaceuticalsTab}), \\
& (a = \text{select} \vee a = \text{update}), (\mathit{HighAnaphylaxisRisk}(\text{patient},\text{drug}) = \text{false})))\}
\end{aligned}
$$

Analogously, according to the definition of P_{MR} and the role hierarchy depicted in Fig. 3, the subjects allowed to execute the *ECG*-branch are those that are granted the *Nurse* role. The consolidation for this branch results in

$$
\begin{aligned}
P_{(\text{ECG})}^{\text{opt}} = \{ & ((\text{role} \sqsupseteq \text{Nurse} \wedge \text{employment} = \text{permanent} \wedge \text{f-o-a} = \text{cardiology}), \\
& (o = \text{MedicalRecordsTab}), (a = \text{update} \vee a = \text{select}), (\text{true}))\}
\end{aligned}
$$

The conclusions to be drawn from the structural analysis are

1. The workflow is subject-executable for *Internists* that have full authorization and for *Nurses* that are only authorized for the *ECG*-branch. These two roles constitute least-required roles in the meaning of Sect. 2.3.
2. $\Pi_{\mathcal{O},\mathcal{A}}(P_{(\text{all})}^{\text{opt}})$ and $\Pi_{\mathcal{O},\mathcal{A}}(P_{(\text{ECG})}^{\text{opt}})$ entail the minimum sets of required privileges for *full* and *partial authorization*, respectively.
3. For *Internists*, the authorization decision can be made at the workflow layer, and access control costs for sub-activities can be reduced as discussed in the next section. For *Nurses*, access control has to be performed twice: On top of the workflow layer and when entering the *ECG*-branch. Other subjects, like those granted the *Administrative Personnel* role, can be blocked right from the beginning. Thus, access control can be optimized as illustrated in Fig. 2.

3.6   Interpretation

In this section we give a qualitative evaluation of the described consolidation approach with regard to the three objectives introduced in the beginning.

A workflow is subject-executable if the root node of the workflow tree has a non-empty policy that grants at least one subject the required privileges to execute a branch of the process. If the *full authorization*-approach is applied, subjects defined in the topmost policy are authorized to invoke any branch. The consolidation approach will also detect *dead paths* that are branches within the workflow which will never be subject-executable. Dead paths are identified via nodes with empty policies.

At the end of the policy consolidation process only those subjects and roles remain in the policy of the root node that are granted the required privileges to execute at least one branch of the workflow. If condition 2 of Sect. 3.2 holds, i.e., the Web services' policies fulfill the least-privilege criterion, then the principle of least privilege can be inferred for the complete workflow, too. By computing the infimum of authorized roles (see line 5 of Alg. 1 and Sect. 3.4) the least-required roles are determined. Providing workflow designers with this consolidated information, they can evaluate, whether only highly privileged users (or roles) remain – situations that are usually unintended and have to be revised.

The third objective is the reduction of access control costs. The described approach is a step towards saving recurrent policy enforcements, as those points in the control flow are determined, where policies have to be enforced at least. Without making use of this optimization, each Web service individually triggers policy evaluation. Using the *full authorization*-approach, the most costly part of access control will be processed on top of the workflow layer. If following the *partial authorization*-approach, intermediary policy enforcement points have to be realized for the SWITCH-nodes as shown in Fig. 2. As Web services are autonomous software components – a characteristics which will not be given up by our approach –, access control at the services' layer cannot be removed. Nevertheless, the enforcement costs can be reduced significantly by including workflow specific policies into the policies of the services. Instead of repeatedly initiating subject identification, only certain "pass-through"-credentials (e.g., realized as SAML assertions) are employed, allowing better performing security evaluation. Such "pass-through"- credentials are issued if access control at the workflow layer succeeds. This approach can be realized for intra-organizational business processes, when workflow architects have the possibility to optimize the Web services' policies4.

4   Complexity of Policy Consolidation

Policy Consolidation is performed at the time a workflow is designed and therefore is not as time critical as policy enforcement at runtime. The overall complexity is subdivided into the complexity for the calculation of subject intersections and the complexity for performing the structural analysis.

Computing the intersection of subject sets is needed to determine S_{all} in equations (1)–(2). Algorithm 1 is of polynomial complexity w.r.t. the number of conjunctions and number of dimensions. Furthermore, when following the *partial authorization* approach, also the difference of subject sets has to be computed (equation (2)). Using *set-based* descriptions this can be done in polynomial time w.r.t. set cardinalities. When employing *attribute-based* descriptions, computing the difference can be done by a modified implication test – instead of checking whether $\mathcal{S}(P_i) \Rightarrow S_{\text{all}}$ it is examined which predicates of $\mathcal{S}(P_i)$ are <u>not</u> subsumed by S_{all}. Due to space limitations we will not present further details of this algorithm. But, similar to the query subsumption problem [6], the complexity of such an algorithm is exponential in the worst case. This worst case arrives, if the conjunctive terms of $\mathcal{S}(P_i)$ overlap only partially with the conjunctions of S_{all} (and recursive iterations are necessary). Predicate conjunctions define subjects with similar characteristics (role attributes, age and so on). Thus, the likelihood of related subjects being described by different conjunctions within the same policy (which would be the reason for the worst case to occur) can be estimated to be quite low, so that the worst case is assumed to arise rarely.

The complexity for performing the structural analysis depends on whether the *full authorization*-approach is employed or not. In case of the *full authorization*-approach, the number of policy comparisons depends on the number of inner nodes of the workflow tree. Complexity can increase drastically, if *partial authorizations* should be determined. Then, if m represents the depth of the workflow tree and n its branching factor, up to $(n+1)^m$ cases have to be evaluated to derive the top level policy in the worst case. This worst case arises, if each inner node is a SWITCH-node, and for each such SWITCH-node the maximum number of subcases has to be considered. However, *partial authorization* is of minor practical relevance, if the top-level policies will reach an unmanageable size which reduces their interpretability by the process engineer. Thus, it is reasonable to consider *partial authorization* only if the workflow size and the number of switches are limited.

5   Related Work

Modeling processes as workflows is of importance for many applications, e.g., e-commerce, e-science or e-health. [7] gives an overview over approaches for defining Web service workflows also named Web service orchestrations or choreographies. In the course of this paper, we showed by use of an e-health example, how access rules for services determine the consolidated workflow policy. This example was simplified in order to keep the discussion concise. More details on access control for e-health scenarios are for instance provided by [8]. The authors of [9] present an approach to define and enforce conditions for the integration of Web services into workflows. [10, 11] describe architectures and algorithms for the enforcement of access control for workflows. [11] especially focuses on the enforcement of static and dynamic separation of duty. Therefore, they introduce a formalism that allows to specify and evaluate separation of duty constraints at the workflow level. In contrast to this, we concentrate on *single-user / single-role* execution schemes which we assume to be prevalent for most enterprise applications. Whether consolidated workflow policies have to be enforced successively (via *pe-any*) or can be evaluated statically (using *pe-all*), depends on whether dataflow and temporal interdependencies have to be taken into account or not [12].

Our consolidation approach is also related to work addressing access control for distributed and multi-layered applications [13, 14, 15] and the optimization of policies [16]. The authors of [16] show how policy sets can be optimized by detecting and resolving redundancies, which helps to reduce policy enforcement costs. [17] and [5] introduce partial orders on policies. These are useful for the consolidation of policies for application integration purposes, like the evaluation whether access control rules of dependent applications are compatible. We are addressing this issue in a larger context by evaluating the integrability of business services in workflows with the aim to optimize access control for complex business processes.

6   Conclusion and Future Work

The concise separation of security and business logic is a crucial aspect for the classical software engineering process. The same considerations apply to application integration and the design of business processes. We presented our approach to facilitate the reliable development of (Web service) workflows by providing consolidated views onto the access control requirements of workflows, which assists software engineers in revising business processes, determining whether or not processes are executable from a privileges point of view, and detecting possible security shortcomings like non-compliances with the principle of least privilege. Moreover, using our approach, policy enforcement for business processes can be optimized and unsuccessful invocations can be detected at an early stage, thus, avoiding unnecessary service executions and rollback costs or compensating actions. We realized a prototypical implementation of the presented consolidation technique, employing BPEL4WS as workflow specification language and XACML [18, 19] as policy language.

The described approach is particularly useful for intra-organizational workflows, where it is likely that access control policies rely on the same policy model. For distributed workflows, further preprocessing is required as mentioned before. Nevertheless, a comprehensive security engineering approach for the distributed case remains as future work.

References

1. P. Bonatti, S. De Capitani di Vimercati, and P. Samarati, "An Algebra for Composing Access Control Policies," *ACM Trans. Inf. Syst. Secur.*, vol. 5, no. 1, pp. 1–35, 2002.
2. R. S. Sandhu, E. J. Coyne, H. L. Feinstein, and C. E. Youman, "Role-Based Access Control Models," *IEEE Computer*, vol. 29, no. 2, pp. 38–47, 1996.
3. ANSI INCITS 359-2004, *Role Based Access Control.* American National Standards Institute, Inc. (ANSI), New York, NY, USA, Feb. 2004.

4. S. Thatte *et al.*, "Business Process Execution Language for Web Services version 1.1 (BPEL4WS 1.1)." `http://www-128.ibm.com/developerworks/library/specification/ws-bpel/`, May 2003.

5. M. Wimmer, D. Eberhardt, P. Ehrnlechner, and A. Kemper, "Reliable and Adaptable Security Engineering for Database-Web Services," in *Proceedings of the Fourth International Conference on Web Engineering*, vol. 3140 of *Lecture Notes in Computer Science (LNCS)*, (Munich, Germany), pp. 502–515, July 2004.

6. D. J. Rosenkrantz and H. B. Hunt, "Processing Conjunctive Predicates and Queries," in *Proc. of the Intl. Conf. on Very Large Data Bases (VLDB)*, (Montreal, Canada), pp. 64–72, Oct. 1980.

7. R. Khalaf and F. Leymann, "On Web Services Aggregation," in *Proceedings of the 4th International Workshop on Technologies for E-Services (TES 2003)*, vol. 2819 of *Lecture Notes in Computer Science (LNCS)*, (Berlin, Germany), pp. 1–13, Sept. 2003.

8. Deutsche Gesellschaft für Medizinische Informatik, Biometrie und Epidemiologie e.V., "AG Datenschutz in Gesundheitsinformationssystemen." `http://info.imsd.uni-mainz.de/AGDatenschutz/`.

9. M. Altunay, D. Brown, G. Byrd, and R. Dean, "Trust-Based Secure Workflow Path Construction," in *Proceedings of the 3rd International Conference on Service Oriented Computing*, vol. 3826 of *Lecture Notes in Computer Science (LNCS)*, (Amsterdam, The Netherlands), pp. 502–515, Dec. 2005.

10. W.-K. Huang and V. Atluri, "SecureFlow: a Secure Web-enabled Workflow Management System," in *RBAC '99: Proceedings of the 4th ACM Workshop on Role-based Access Control*, (New York, NY, USA), pp. 83–94, ACM Press, 1999.

11. E. Bertino, E. Ferrari, and V. Atluri, "The Specification and Enforcement of Authorization Constraints in Workflow Management Systems," *ACM Trans. Inf. Syst. Secur.*, vol. 2, pp. 65–104, Feb. 1999.

12. C. Bettini, X. S. Wang, and S. Jajodia, "Temporal Reasoning in Workflow Systems," *Distrib. Parallel Databases*, vol. 11, no. 3, pp. 269–306, 2002.

13. M. Rits, B. D. Boe, and A. Schaad, "Xact: a Bridge between Resource Management and Access Control in Multi-layered Applications," in *SESS '05: Proceedings of the 2005 Workshop on Software Engineering for Secure Systems*, (New York, NY, USA), pp. 1–7, ACM Press, 2005.

14. K. Rannenberg and G. Müller, *Security in Communications – Technology, Infrastructure, Economy*. Reading, MA, USA: Addison-Wesley, July 1999.

15. J. Biskup, T. Leineweber, and J. Parthe, "Administration Rights in the SDSD-System," in *Proceedings of the Seventeenth Annual Working Conference on Database and Application Security*, (Estes Park, Colorado, United States), Aug. 2003.

16. F. Rabitti, E. Bertino, W. Kim, and D. Woelk, "A Model of Authorization for Next-Generation Database Systems," *ACM Trans. Database Syst.*, vol. 16, no. 1, pp. 88–131, 1991.

17. E. B. Fernandez, E. Gudes, and H. Song, "A Model for Evaluation and Administration of Security in Object-Oriented Databases," *IEEE Transactions on Knowledge and Data Engineering*, vol. 6, no. 2, pp. 275–292, 1994.

18. T. Moses *et al.*, "eXtensible Access Control Markup Language (XACML) version 2.0." `http://www.oasis-open.org/committees/tc_home.php?wg_abbrev=xacml`, Feb. 2005.

19. A. Anderson, "Core and Hierarchical Role Based Access Control RBAC Profile of XACML version 2.0." `http://www.oasis-open.org/committees/tc_home.php?wg_abbrev=xacml`, Sept. 2004.

Dynamic Layer-2 VPN Services for Improving Security in the Grid Environment

Francesco Palmieri

Federico II University, Centro Servizi Didattico Scientifico, Via Cinthia 45,
80126 Napoli, Italy
fpalmieri@unina.it

Abstract. Pervasive and on-demand computing are now a reality, mainly in the scientific area, and the computational Grid concept is gaining popularity as a scalable way to deliver access to a wide range of distributed computing and data resources. But, as Grids move from an experimental phase to real production and their deployment in the Internet significantly increases, controlling the security of a Grid application becomes imperative. The most significant Grid security issue is that the different sites composing the Grid will generally be managed by different organizations each with their own security mechanisms and policies. This makes any communication security arrangement on the entities participating to the Grid generally more difficult than if they were on the same local area network. In this paper, we show how the security and privacy services offered by scalable on-demand layer-2 MPLS VPN services can be applied in large-scale Grid scenarios and propose a novel network resource abstraction for discovery and setup of on-demand layer-2 Virtual Private Networks. It has been implemented in a Grid Information Service prototype which was successfully tested on a dedicated testbed infrastructure.

Keywords: Grid computing, security, MPLS, Layer-2 VPN.

1 Introduction

The Grid technology is increasingly being looked upon as a natural application of the modern Internet for engaging in complex data processing tasks over resources which are distributed across the world. A typical Grid, consists of a large number of geographically distributed computing and storage resources, usually spanning multiple administrative domains, interconnected through an high performance network, to be shared amongst its users. Large computing endeavors (consisting of one or more "jobs") are then distributed over this network to these resources, and scheduled to fulfill requirements with the highest possible efficiency. A Grid offers a uniform and often transparent interface to its resources such that an unaware user can submit jobs to the Grid just as if he/she was handling a large virtual supercomputer. Recently, the Grid concept has been generalized to cover any virtual organization, defined as a dynamic collection of individuals and institutions which are required to share resources to achieve certain goals [1]. Thus the Grid will have applications in commerce and industry, supporting distributed collaborative design and engineering, or supporting

G. Müller (Ed.): ETRICS 2006, LNCS 3995, pp. 45–59, 2006.

distributed supply chains. Nevertheless, any distributed computing platform, including grids, needs to satisfy specific and often strict security demands. Without an adequate understanding of the security implications of a Grid, both the users and the system administrators who contributes with resources to a Grid can be subject to significant compromises. Thus the importance of data and application security issues assumes critical proportions as more and more industry and academic interests channelize their resources towards implementing such cross organizational computing infrastructures. However, existing approaches to security within distributed systems, usually based on access control policies enforced by firewalls or other kinds of packet filtering devices such as routers or layer-3 switches are stretched by the extreme conditions imposed by the modern Grids, and significant effort has been undertaken in, to provide support for secure use of resources without affecting the overall Grid functionality or computational efficiency. What clearly distinguishes grids from other platforms are its high dynamicity and complexity features, in terms of communication paradigms and protocols used, resulting in security requirements which cannot be addressed by existing access control technologies for distributed platforms. The elements of a grid are usually negotiated in a dynamic manner such that the trust relationship among these elements needs to be established during application execution time. There may not at all exist any direct security protocol among resources and processes which form this dynamic environment. Each resource belongs to a fixed administrative domain governed by its own security standards, policies and implementation within the domain. Grids that span several administrative sites and encourage the dynamic addition of resources are not likely to benefit from the security that static, centrally administered commercial firewalls or packet filtering routers provide. What is needed are some facilities that, while ensuring adequate end-to-end security features in terms of authentication, integrity and traffic isolation offer a totally dynamic and scalable "LAN extension" abstraction, so that as new resources are attached to the grid they can behave as belonging to the same LAN, without any apparent security concern. In this scenario, on-demand Layer-2 VPN technologies can be successfully applied to Grids, as they, offer all the above security features and can help to transparently bypass firewalls or any other filtering policy in order to prevent the performance and functionality penalties that may typically negatively affect high-end applications. Dynamic provisioning is needed in order to reduce management costs together with the number of Grid VPNs that the public networks have to support concurrently. The dynamicity relies on the availability of a suite of interfaces and protocols which perform discovery of available services, agreement negotiation and agreement establishment between initiators (the Grid user or proxy) and providers (e.g. Grid resource brokers). Of course, a control plane – capable of establishing, managing and tearing down services – is necessary for the actual provisioning of the service. Here Multi-Protocol Label Switching (MPLS), that has been now deployed to implement traffic engineering facilities on almost all the modern transport infrastructure making the Internet core, offers the essential features by providing the proper end-to-end label switched tunnels that will be useful to implement to the layer-2 VPNs. VPNs, can offer security and privacy to both Grid applications and data management services for large-scale Grid file transfers which rely on storage access protocols not providing security and privacy. In fact, VPNs can support confidentiality and integrity by means of data isolation, i.e. by separating in intermediate forwarding devices the forwarding control plane, the signaling and the routing information of each VPN. Layer-2 VPNs can also be used to dynamically cluster geographically dispersed resources belonging to the same Grid Virtual Organization. Clearly, in order to effectively use Layer-2 VPNs in large-scale Grids (e.g., to be capable to address an increasing number of users ubiquitously), stable and scalable VPN services are necessary. Accordingly, in this paper, we show how the security and privacy services offered by scalable on-demand layer-2 MPLS VPN services can be applied in large-scale Grid scenarios. We propose a novel network resource abstraction for discovery and setup of on-demand layer-2 Virtual Private Networks. It has been implemented in a Grid Information Service prototype which was successfully tested on a dedicated testbed infrastructure. The paper is organized as follows: section 2 briefly sketches the basic concepts behind the MPLS VPN architecture while section 3 presents the main security requirements in the Grid environment. The detailed components of the whole security proposal are described in section 4. Finally, section 5 is dedicated to conclusions and final remarks.

2 The Basic MPLS VPN Architecture

This section briefly introduces some of the basic concepts that will be useful to better explain the MPLS VPN framework, by presenting its architectural building blocks, ideology and the theory behind it.

2.1 The MPLS Paradigm

MPLS is a packet forwarding technique being standardized by IETF [2]. MPLS uses labels to make forwarding decisions at the network node level, in contrast to the traditional destination-based hop-by-hop forwarding in IP networks. The key idea of MPLS is a strict separation between control and forwarding planes in the network functions as well as in the software and hardware architecture of the routers. In MPLS, the space of all possible forwarding options in a network domain is partitioned into *"Forwarding Equivalence Classes" (FECs)*. For example, all the packets destined for a given egress may belong to the same FEC. The packets are labeled at the ingress depending on the FEC they belong to. Each of the intermediate nodes uses the label of incoming packet to determine its next hop, and also performs "label swapping," i.e., replaces the incoming label with the new outgoing label that identifies the respective FEC for the downstream node. Such a label-based forwarding technique reduces the processing overhead required for routing at the intermediate nodes, thereby improving their packet forwarding performance. Also, the label-merging procedure used by MPLS creates multipoint-to-point packet forwarding trees in contrast to a routing mesh in conventional network based on a similar paradigm such as ATM networks. This reduces considerably the size of forwarding table at the intermediate nodes, thereby improving their scalability. The MPLS encapsulation envelope is depicted in fig. 1.

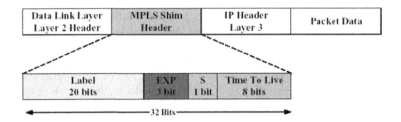

Fig. 1. MPLS shim header

While MPLS was originally conceived to improve the efficiency of packet forwarding in network equipments, it was soon realized that it could also provide other
advanced features, such as Traffic Engineering and Virtual Private Networks capabilities. Both these facilities need pre-determined paths to be established through the network to specific destinations. Once the paths, called *label switched paths* (LSPs),
have been created, traffic is mapped onto the them according to the dynamic needs of
the traffic and their capabilities.

2.2 Layer-2 VPN Services in the MPLS Environment

By pure definition, a virtual private network [3] is the interconnection of multiple
sites via a private backbone network, thereby skirting security and performance issues of the very public Internet. But this term has become muddled, and "VPN" has
been applied to virtual networks based on the public Internet for transmitting sensitive information. In a Grid scenario, a VPN can be better conceived as a service in
which customer connectivity amongst multiple sites is deployed on a shared infrastructure with the same access or security policies as a private network. The VPN
should be comparable to a private network in performance, reliability, management
security and Quality of Service (QoS). Customers of the VPN services use shared
facilities and equipment, which are managed, engineered and operated by a public
network operator, either totally or partly. Traditionally, the most common way for
cooperating organizations to build their own wide area networks was to set up a
private communication infrastructure on top of a number of point-to-point or point-
to-multipoint links (based on virtual circuits on a public switched communication
service such as Frame-Relay or ATM) provided by a service provider. This model
corresponds to what is usually known as *"layer 2 VPN"*. Although layer 2 VPNs
based on ATM or Frame Relay have been extensively deployed, several drawbacks
related to this kind of VPN can be identified. First, the service provider VPN infrastructure is dependent on a single layer 2 technology (e.g., ATM, Frame Relay). In
addition, the Internet infrastructure and the VPN infrastructure, even if they share the
same physical network, need separate administration and maintenance. Finally, provisioning is difficult – for example, adding a site to an existing VPN is usually a
complex task. Consequently, it can be easily seen that the above solution lacks of the
sufficient scalability that is an essential prerequisite for all the new-generation services offered on the modern Internet. Furthermore, to offer the abilities required to

establish a layer-2 virtual circuit between any two computers or clusters in a Grid environment, bandwidth allocation and management on the network must be dynamic. MPLS control-plane protocols allow large-scale transport networks to be created and enable these networks to respond to on-demand requests for rate-guaranteed connectivity between multiple points in the network. These features make MPLS-based networks well suited to serve Grids supporting the realization of bandwidth guaranteed on-demand VPNs. The idea of transporting generic Layer 2 protocols over MPLS backbones has introduced the concept of the so-called "Layer 2 VPN" over MPLS. An MPLS-based layer 2 VPN allows the use of a single MPLS-based network infrastructure to offer a wide range of services, including IP traffic, layer 2 VPNs, layer 3 VPNs, MPLS traffic engineering and DiffServ-based QoS control. Easy migration from traditional layer 2 VPNs is a significant advantage of this model, as the two VPN types are indistinguishable from the customer's point of view. Basically, in an MPLS-based Layer 2 VPN the service provider uses an MPLS network to provide layer 2 services to the customer. The interior of an MPLS infrastructure on which VPN services are offered is made up of MPLS-aware *provider (P)* router devices forming the MPLS core that are not directly connect to any VPN-terminating router. *Provider edge (PE)* routers that surround the core devices enable the VPN functions of an MPLS network. MPLS core and PE routers work as label switch routers (LSR) that are devices capable of switching packets based on their MPLS-imposed labels. The VPN-terminating router is referred to as a *customer edge* router *(CE)* and thus a VPN consists of a group of CE routers connected to the MPLS backbone PE routers [4]. Only the PE routers are aware of the VPN. The CE routers are not aware of the underlying network. The CE routers perceive that they are connected via a private network. From the customer's point of view, a layer 2 MPLS VPN is exactly the same as a layer 2 VPN, with layer 2 circuits interconnecting the various sites. For example, a customer CE device may be configured with a Frame-Relay Data Link Connection Identifier (DLCI) on which to transmit to other CEs through the provider network, which appears as a traditional layer 2 cloud to the customer. Within the service provider network, the layer 2 packets are transported in MPLS LSPs. The service provider does not participate in the customer's Layer 3 network routing. The establishment of emulated VCs, also called Virtual Leased Lines (VLL), or layer 2 point-to-point connectivity across an MPLS backbone is specified in the IETF drafts usually known as "drafts martini" [5] and [6]. These drafts define how MPLS can be used to support Layer 2 protocols such as Ethernet, Frame Relay or ATM. The first draft [5] concentrates on encapsulation methods, while the other [6] specifies signaling to set up point-to-point layer 2 circuits over an MPLS network. The following figure represents an example of an MPLS-based layer 2 VPN [7]. The connection between two customer's CE devices is composed of three segments: two CE-PE "attachment" VCs and one emulated VC in the core. The routing tables of the source CE router and the ingress and egress PE routers are indicated. Basically, the first CE router forwards the traffic to DLCIs 600 and 610 to sites B and C respectively, as in a normal Frame Relay network, whereas the ingress and egress PE routers perform the mapping between the DLCIs and the appropriate LSPs.

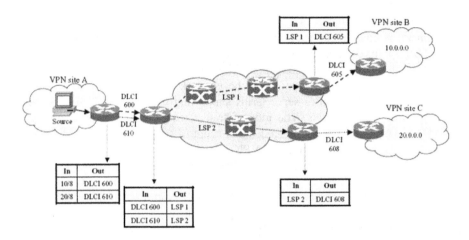

Fig. 2. The MPLS Layer-2 VPN paradigm

It should be noted that MPLS layer 2 VPNs make provisioning much easier in comparison to conventional layer 2 VPNs. In particular, adding a site to an existing VPN should simply require the configuration of the PE router connected to the new site, and not the reconfiguration of a high number of CEs. The IETF draft "An architecture for L2VPNs" [8], proposes a layer 2 VPN solution, which is based on the emulation of layer 2 circuits. In the service provider core, tunnels are established using a proper tunneling technology (usually MPLS, but L2TP or IPSec should also be possible) to emulate layer 2 VCs. This draft can be seen as an evolution of a previous draft, called "MPLS-based Layer 2 VPNs" [9], now obsolete, which originally described how to build layer 2 CE-to-CE VPNs using MPLS in the provider core. The draft [8] is based on the "drafts martini" indicated above for encapsulation of data frames and for the signaling used to setup and maintain the emulated VCs. The need to specify an auto-discovery mechanism is indicated but no solution is proposed for the time being. Recently, the PPVPN IETF group has reutilized the VPLS concept (Virtual Private LAN Service, following a term originally defined in RFC2764 [10]) as a layer 2 service that emulates a LAN across a WAN [11][12]. The basic purpose of a VPLS is to offer layer 2 connectivity to multiple customer sites in a manner that is transparent to the CE devices. The service provider is responsible for transporting customer Layer 2 frames and switching them across the service provider network between customer sites. From the customer's point of view the service is equivalent to connecting the CE devices via a switch, i.e., all in the same broadcast domain/LAN segment.

3 Security Requirements in the Grid Environment

Available Research and development efforts within the Grid community have produced protocols, services, and tools that address the challenges arising when we seek to build scalable virtual organizations. What distinguishes a virtual organization is that it may gather individuals and/or institutions that have agreed to share resources and otherwise collaborate on an ad-hoc, dynamic basis, while they continue to belong to different real organizations, each governed by their own set of internal rules and policies. This poses a challenge when combined with the fact that an individual or institution may be a member of several virtual organizations simultaneously. From a security point of view, one is thus confronted with protection domains that may superpose, straddle, and intersect one another in many different ways. Within this context, we require interoperability among domains while maintaining a clear separation of the security policies and mechanisms deployed by both virtual and real organizations.

3.1 The Main Challenges

The security challenges faced in a Grid environment can be grouped into four categories: dynamicity, integration with existing systems and technologies, interoperability with different "hosting environments" (e.g., J2EE servers, .NET servers, Linux/Unix systems), and trust relationships among interacting hosting environments.

3.1.1 Dynamicity

One of the aims of a grid is to enable the sharing of vast amounts of distributed resources within large, dynamic and distributed communities of users, where the availability of resources, membership of communities (or virtual organizations) and access rights are continually changing and evolving. A grid is expected to provide an architecture that enables such a dynamic structure. These changing patterns of use add considerably to the already great challenge of allowing controlled access to remote resources owned and managed by third parties: issues of trust and liability become very important.

3.1.2 Integration

For both technical and pragmatic reasons, it is unreasonable to expect that a single security technology can be defined that will both address all Grid security challenges and be adopted in every hosting environment. Existing security infrastructures cannot be replaced overnight. Each domain typically has its own authorization infrastructure that is deployed, managed and supported. It will not typically be acceptable to replace any of these technologies in favor of a single model or mechanism. Thus, to be successful, a Grid security architecture needs to step up to the challenge of integrating with existing security architectures and models across platforms and hosting environments. This means that the architecture must be implementation agnostic, so that it can be instantiated in terms of any existing security mechanisms (e.g., Kerberos, PKI); extensible, so that it can incorporate new security services as they become available; and integrable with existing security services.

3.1.3 Interoperability

Services that traverse multiple domains and hosting environments need to be able to interact with each other, thus introducing the need for interoperability at multiple levels:

– At the protocol level, we require mechanisms that allow domains to exchange messages. This can be achieved, for example, via SOAP/HTTP.

- At the policy level, secure interoperability requires that each party be able to specify any policy it may wish in order to engage in a secure conversation - and that policies expressed by different parties can be made mutually comprehensible. Only then can the parties attempt to establish a secure communication channel and security context upon mutual authentication, trust relationship, and adherence to each other's policy.
- At the identity level, we require mechanisms for identifying a user from one domain in another domain. This requirement goes beyond the need to define trust relationships and achieve federation between security mechanisms (e.g., from Kerberos tickets to X.509 certificates). Irrespective of the authentication and authorization model, which can be group-based, role-based or other attribute-based, many models rely on the notion of an identity for reasons including authorization and accountability. It would be nice if a given identity could be (pre)defined across all participating domains, but that is not realistic in practice. For any cross-domain invocation to succeed in a secure environment, mapping of identities and credentials must be made possible. This can be enforced at either end of a session through proxy servers or through trusted intermediaries acting as trust proxies.

3.1.4 The Trust Relationship

Grid service requests can span multiple security domains. Trust relationships among these domains play an important role in the outcome of such end-to-end traversals. A service needs to make its access requirements available to interested entities, so that they can request secure access to it. Trust between end points can be presumed, based on topological assumptions (e.g., in our case, a VPN), or explicit, specified as policies and enforced through exchange of some trust-forming credentials. In a Grid environment, presumed trust is rarely feasible due to the dynamic nature of the virtual organization relationships. Trust establishment may be a one-time activity per session or it may be evaluated dynamically on every request. The dynamic nature of the Grid in some cases can make it impossible to establish trust relationships among sites prior to application execution. Given that the participating domains may have different security technologies in their infrastructure (e.g., Kerberos, PKI) it then becomes necessary to realize the required trust relationships through some form of federation among the security mechanisms. The trust relationship problem is made more difficult in a Grid environment by the need to support the dynamic, user-controlled deployment and management of transient services. End users create such transient services to perform request-specific tasks, which may involve the execution of user code. For example, in a distributed data mining scenario, transient services may be created at various locations both to extract information from remote databases and to synthesize summary information.

4 The Architectural Framework

In our architecture, an application program running on a computer should be able to dynamically request via a web-service interface, a layer-2 circuit to a distant computer and have this request filled cooperatively by the network devices on the end-to-end path between these computers. Control-plane protocols define the procedures for the handling such on-demand calls, i.e., immediate requests for connectivity at a guaranteed rate. The adaptability/dynamicity feature of Grids makes support for immediate on-demand requests for bandwidth necessary in a suitable transport network, which may be a mesh of private or public shared networks, owned and managed by some cooperating service providers and/or enterprises. Anyway, the network must be a transparent cloud with respect to the Grid, so that all the necessary network operations have to be totally hidden to the customers.

4.1 Network Operations

First, the whole transport network involved in the implementation of the layer-2 VPN service must support MPLS to switch the traffic based in the MPLS labels. In most cases the customer service provider's sites will be located in different Autonomous Systems (ASes), different providers, so the VPN will transit through several domains (inter-domain MPLS VPN). There are no requirements for CE devices in order to map the logical connections to the remote sites - they have to be configured as if they were connected to a single bridged network or local area network. Also the Provider Routers, in the core do not have any information related to the VPN and only transfer the labeled packets from one PE to another in a transparent way. All the VPN intelligence is located in the PE. It is where the VPN connection originates and terminates, and where all the necessary tunnels are set up to connect to all the others PEs. As we already stated in section 2, there are several available strategies (expressed by different drafts) to implement layer-2 MPLS VPNs. The main difference between them is in the supported signaling protocol, that is vital to implement the label switched tunnels. The first one, (supported by Juniper Inc.) uses Border Gateway Protocol (BGP) while the other (supported by Cisco Systems Inc.) uses Label Distributed Protocol (LDP) for this purpose. Some of the benefits to use BGP as signaling protocol is that it allows for the auto-discovery of new sites, and is better supported at the inter-domain level. If we use BGP, when we add new sites we will only need to configure the PE connected to the new site. Moreover, BGP is a more scalable protocol, so we can use route reflectors or confederations to handle VPN deployment in complex inter-domain infrastructures. Anyway, they all, both solutions, have a common objective; to exchange VPN information generated inside an AS with the other remote ASes. The MAC addresses and connection ports of the users in the local sites will be known by the remote users. In our implementation we preferred the use of Multiprotocol Border Gateway Protocol-based (MP-BGP) signaling to distribute labeled VPN-IPv4 (Internet Protocol version 4) routes and VPN information between AS border or internal routers or router reflectors. We need to advertise the VPN information from one PE to the others, so we will configure one MP-BGP session from each PE to the rest of PEs. Note that some of these sessions will be external and others internal BGP sessions. Accordingly, we have to establish one internal MP-BGP session between the loopback addresses of all the PE routes belonging to an AS and configure Label Switching Paths (LSPs) between them. For this purpose, we need MPLS support and one signaling protocol, which can be LDP or RSVP. Clearly, we need a routing instance for each site we want to connect. To handle inter-domain connections, we could configure one normal BGP session between the AS border routers and extend the LSP from each PE to the others PEs through domains using LDP or RSVP, but there is another possible solution, this is, a new Network Layer Reachability Information (NLRI) family called labeled-unicast that results in labeled route exchanges between providers AS Border Routers (ASBRs) which establishes MPLS LSPs between the providers' PE routers. When the multipoint VPNs and the BGP sessions are established, the behavior of the final users will be as if they are in the same LAN and the transit networks from one user to others will be completely transparent.

4.2 Grid Service Interface

Our VPN-secured Grid network will result in an overlay communication facility on top of the existing underlying lower layer networks, whose configuration, security policies and functional behaviors are assumed to be totally independent. The overlay Grid communication facilities must be managed by a standardized middleware stratum, offering well-defined secure service interfaces to the Grid applications. The core middleware technologies that have been widely deployed in the Grid community already include security solutions that support management of credentials and policies, together with resource management protocols and services that support secure remote access to computing and data resources, when computations span multiple institutions. We developed our interfaces basing on the above technologies to ensure that each on-demand access to the secure layer-2 communication Grid will be preceded by the necessary identification, authentication and authorization activities.

4.2.1 Communication and Service Reference Model

Over the years, existing grid systems have stimulated a clear need for the existence of a well defined standard for possible protocols of secure communication between entities in a multi-enterprise grid system. Global Grid Forum (GGF) is the community involved actively in developing these standards and specifications for grid computing [13]. GGF has come up with a service oriented architecture which defines a set of basic capabilities and functionalities that address prime questions in grid systems that is known as Open Grid Services Architecture (OGSA). Industry efforts have rallied around Web services (WS) as an emerging architecture which has the ability to deliver integrated, interoperable solutions. A natural choice for implementing the VPN service interface on the Grid host sites is the Web Service Resource Framework (WSRF) [14] aiming at implementing some of the OGSA core services as Grid services, or better, web services enhanced for Grid applications. The implemented Web Service interfaces will be stateless and persistent, where data is not retained among invocations and services outlive their clients. They will also be compliant with the GGF's OGSA specification [15] and, in addition, conform to widely used Web Services standards (WSDL, SOAP, and XML). It is reasonable to expect that in the future all Grid applications will be required to be OGSA-compliant [14]. OGSA defines Grid services as special Web services [17] that provide a set of well-defined interfaces that follow specific conventions [18], usually coordinated, with delegated authentication credentials, in a virtual organization. In other words OGSA enhances Web Services to accommodate requirements of the Grid. The fundamental concept behind OGSA is that it is a service-oriented Grid architecture powered by Grid services [16]. Despite the fact that OGSA represents a long-overdue effort to define a Grid architecture, it is a relatively new standard [16]. The Open Grid Service Infrastructure (OGSI) was the first set of formal and technical specifications of the concepts described in OGSA, but many problems were reported regarding these. In order to circumvent the discrepancies in the OGSI specifications a new standard is emerging, which is called Web Services Resource Framework (WSRF) [19]. WSRF represents a refactoring and evolution of OGSI that delivers essentially the same capabilities in a manner that is more in alignment with the Web Services community [17]. As such, it represents an important next step towards the larger goal of a comprehensive Open Grid Services Architecture that supports on-demand, utility computing, collaborative and other Grid scenarios within a Web services setting. The most valuable aspect of WSRF is that it effectively completes the convergence of the Web services and Grid computing communities. WSRF specifications build directly on core Web services standards, in particular WSDL, SOAP and XML, and exploit capabilities provided by WS-Addressing [20]. Since the proposed architecture is Web Services based it can be integrated with anything based on WSRF standard. In our proposal we explicitly refer to the Globus Toolkit [21] that implements a subset of OGSA services based on WSRF and to the Grid Security Infrastructure (GSI) services [22] providing inter-domain security protocols that bridge the gap between the different local security solutions at a Grid's constituent sites, to address the unique security requirements that arise in Grid environments.

4.2.2 Interface Definitions

In the proposed architecture the transparent on-demand VPN security service provisioning is strictly related to basic connectivity services (like label switched path establishment) that should be hidden to the users. A fundamental construct underlying many of the required attributes of the Grid services architecture is that of service virtualization. It is virtualization of Grid services that underpins the ability to map common service semantic behavior seamlessly onto native platform facilities. For these reasons we proposed and developed a new service oriented abstraction that, based on the existing OGSA architecture and built on the Globus GSI toolkit, introduces a new secure connections layer, between the customers and the network infrastructure decoupling the connection service provisioning from the underlying network infrastructure implementation. On-demand allocation of VPN services requires on-line discovery of MPLS label-switched tunnel/path resource availability on the transport network to accommodate, if appropriate, new layer-2 VPN associations on existing LSPs between the terminating network elements or create, if needed new ones. Grid middleware supports this by relying on information models responsible for capturing structures and relationships of the involved entities. To cope with the heterogeneity of the network infrastructure resources when making advanced reservations or engineering, we proposed a new technology-independent network resource abstraction: the Traffic Engineered Tunnel, modeling the available PE-to-PE LSPs on the underlying networks that can be used from the Grid for VPN transport. A centralized *Tunnel Resource Broker* keeps track of all the above available resources and interfaces with the MPLS network elements to cope with all the necessary network operations needed for handling the VPN connection facilities. For example, a dedicated bandwidth may be reserved between cooperating Grid applications connected in a layer-2 VPN so that based on network condition, Grid middleware can request, through the Tunnel

Resource Broker, QoS or bandwidth constrained tunnels between relevant MPLS network elements. Once the service related tunnel resources are configured and provisioned, they have to be monitored from the performance and functionality point of views. Of course, this service too will be made available via the above resource broker. In detail, the proposed abstractions, supporting the VPN connectivity services concern:

- Connection Creation that allows a Layer-2 transparent connection with the specific attributes to be created between a pair of access points
- Connection deletion that allows an existing connection to be deleted
- Connection Status Enquiry that permits the status of certain connection parameters to be queried
- Connection Modification which allows parameters of an already established connection to be modified.

Each request to the Tunnel Resource Broker will be strongly authenticated against a Grid-wide PKI infrastructure through the GSI Generic Security Service (GSS) API [23] defining standard functions for verifying the identity of communicating parties, based on a Public Key Infrastructure where users authenticate to the grid using X.509 certificates. Thus the grid application or user must use its X.509 certificate provided in the GSI environment also to join to a layer-2 Grid association, identified by an existing VPN. The Grid Network Services interact with the Service Provider via the Grid User to Network Interface (GUNI) that implements the basic VPN functionalities and permits Grid applications to dynamic control and manage the underlying network resources according to the cooperation agreements stipulated between the Grid organization and the Service Providers owning the transport networks. Communication between the GRID applications and the GUNI top level service interface will take place via SOAP/HTTP (eventually secured by SSL) using well-defined extended WSDL Grid Web service interface. Requests and responses conform to Web Services specifications, i.e., they are SOAP messages, carried in HTTP envelopes and transported over TCP/IP connections. The GRID Service Interface can announce its services by means of a Universal data base Description, Discovery and Integration (UDDI). About the specific GUNI implementation, the Extensible Markup Language (XML) appears to be the best candidate thanks to its representation format which can be useful to describe and transmit management information and Grid and network resources. Each network resource or node can be described by a set of XML interface elements. The overlay VPN topology can be represented by mutually referencing node interfaces through the attributes of the VPN termination elements. Note that every Interface can be characterized by the virtual link or LSP tunnel (identified by the addresses engaged) that in turn is characterized by a set of attributes (Service class, Bandwidth available, and Bandwidth utilized). The ability of the Service Interface to hide the complexity of the service provisioning permits to define simple XML-based messages capable of supporting high level services. In particular we want to describe the messages exchanged through GUNI related to the Grid layer-2 connection service:

- *Create_L2_Grid (identifier)*: where an identifier uniquely associates to a new layer-2 VPN on a Grid. The details of VPN setup and configuration are totally hidden from the Grid applications and users.
- *Attach_L2_Grid (source, existing_VPN, bandwidth, Qos)*: a Grid site joins a VPN by establishing a transparent secure connection with the other nodes belonging to the secure Grid, with a guaranteed bandwidth and QoS service class such as Platinum, Gold, etc.
- *Leave_L2_Grid (source, existing_VPN)*: a Grid site leaves an existing VPN.
- *Modify_L2_Grid (source, existing_VPN, bandwidth, Qos)*: modifies the bandwidth and Qos parameters of an existing connection.
- *Query_L2_Grid (source, existing_VPN)*: query the status of an existing VPN connection.

Every basic service function is in turn mapped to a set of UNI primitives for network resource setting. Commercial routers are not yet provided with standard UNI but, in general, are equipped with an application programming interface (API) based on XML that routers use to exchange information with the Tunnel Resource Broker. Using this interface it is possible to manage and monitor the available LSPs and relative traffic and performance parameters. In order to validate the service, a very simple prototype testing scenario was created, with three PCs running Linux, used as three grid nodes, operating in the Globus environment and interconnected across an MPLS transport network made with five M10 Juniper routers. The signaling interface between the Tunnel Resource Broker and the network elements has been implemented by using XMLscript language via TCP socket. The JUNOScript eXtensible Markup Language (XML) API [24] is used to exchange configurations and operational data between the Tunnel resource broker and the JUNOScript agent on the router in a tagged format. The client-server communication is session-based. Data retrieved from the router can be recast in different formats through the Extensible Stylesheet Language Transformations (XSLT). The prototype of the Tunnel Resource Broker has been implemented on another Linux server which is responsible for the creation, modification and deletion of dynamic LSPs needed by the VPN services and is the only device talking with the Juniper routers. Proper configuration is needed when MPLS paths are requested to enable MPLS-based VPNs and set up a symmetric path from the destination to the source domain. All the LSPs are configured on the LSP head-end router, which is the gateway of the Grid host joining to the VPN. In order to identify the device to configure, the broker uses an internal topology database from which network devices and routing information can be accessed. Configuration requires the definition of the LSP name (according to some naming conventions), of the associated Exp-inferred class of service and, possibly, of some additional terms such as the LSP bandwidth. The setup of intermediate routers is done automatically by a MPLS signaling protocol (RSVP-TE or CR-LDP) that is supported by all the intermediate domains toward the destination. The interface architectural model is sketched in fig. 3.

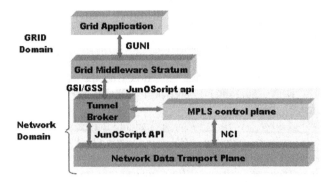

Fig. 3. The interface model

5 Conclusions

In this paper, we presented a service-oriented framework that allows distributed Grid applications to transparently control their private and dedicated transport networks, and communicate as they were on the same local area network independently from the security policies and access control mechanisms implemented on the sites which they belong to. The Grid "virtual organization" paradigm can be achieved at layer 2 and thus extensions to existing Grid services are provided to implement on-demand layer 2 VPN services in Grids. The proposed framework is based on the MPLS VPN, which is the most flexible and scalable between the available technologies to implement dynamic on-demand tunnels through which the VPN services are implemented. The layer-2 network partitions have been abstracted using a secure web service interface. We were able to demonstrate that the VPN services for Grids proposed here are viable, by transparently and dynamically configuring on the underlying transport network some test Grid nodes in a layer-2 VPN with different guaranteed bandwidth and packet forwarding behaviors.

References

1. Foster, I., Kesselman, C., Tuecke,S., The Anatomy of the Grid: Enabling Scalable Virtual Organization, *International Journal of Supercomputer Applications*, 2001.
2. Rosen, E., Viswanathan, A., Callon,R., Multiprotocol Label Switching Architecture, *IETF RFC 3031*, 2001
3. Ferguson, P., Huston, G., What is VPN, *The Internet Protocol Journal vol. 1 n. 1*, 1998.
4. Previdi, S., Introduction to MPLS-BGP-VPN, *Proceedings of MPLS Forum*, 2000.
5. Martini, L. et al., Encapsulation Methods for Transport of Layer 2 Frames Over IP and MPLS Networks, *IETF draft, draft-martini-l2circuit-encap-mpls-04.txt*, 2001.
6. Martini, L. et al., Transport of Layer 2 Frames Over MPLS, *IETF draft, draft-martini-l2circuit-trans-mpls-08.txt*, 2001.
7. Kompella, K. et al., MPLS-based Layer 2 Virtual Private Networks, http://www.juniper.net/techcenter/techpapers/200009.pdf, 2001.

8. Rosen, E. et al., An architecture for LSVPNs, *IETF draft, draft-ietfppvpn-l2vpn-00.txt*, July 2001.

9. Kompella, K. et al., MPLS-based Layer 2 VPNs , *IETF draft, draft-kompellampls-l2vpn-02.txt*, 2001.

10. Gleeson, B., Lin, A., Heinanen, J., Armitage, G., Malis, A.,A Framework for IP Based Virtual Private Networks, *IETF RFC 2764*, 2000.

11. Andersson, L. et al., PPVPN L2 Framework, *IETF draft, draft-andersson-ppvpn-l2-framework-01.txt*, 2002.

12. Agustyn, W. et al., Requirements for Virtual Private LAN Services (VPLS), *IETF draft, draft-augustyn-vpls-requirements-02.txt*, 2002.

13. Nagaratnam, N., Janson, P., Dayka, J., Nadalin, A., Siebenlist, F., Welch, V., Foster, I., Tuecke, S., The Security Architecture for Open Grid Services, http://www.cs.virginia.edu/~humphrey/ogsa-sec-wg/OGSA-SecArch-v1-07192002.pdf

14. Foster, I., What is the Grid? A Three Point Checklist, http://www-fp.mcs.anl.gov/~foster/Articles/WhatIsTheGrid. pdf, 2002

15. Foster, I. et. al., Open Grid Services Architecture, *GGF draft-ggf-ogsa-spec-014*, 2004.

16. Tuecke, S. et al, Open Grid Services Infrastructure (OGSI), *GGF Draft, GT3, Globus Toolkit 3*, 2003

17. Parastatidis, S., A Grid Application Framework based on Web Services Specifications and Practices, *Grid Application Framework White Paper*, http://www.neresc.ac.uk/projects/gaf/, 2003

18. Zhang, L. et al, Introduction of a Grid architecture and toolkit for building Grid solutions, *IBM developersWorks white paper*, 2002

19. Foster, I. et al, The WS-Resource Framework, http://www.globus.org/wsrf/

20. WS-Addressing, IBM technical note, http://www-106.ibm.com/developerworks/library/specification/ws-add/

21. The Globus Toolkit, http://www-unix.globus.org/toolkit/

22. Welch, V., Siebenlist, F., Foster, I., Bresnahan, J., Czajkowski, K., Gawor, J., Kesselman, C., Meder, S., Pearlman, L., Tuecke, S., Security for Grid Services, *Twelfth International Symposium on High Performance Distributed Computing (HPDC-12)*, 2003.

23. Linn, J., Generic Security Service Application Program Interface, Version 2, *IETF RFC 2078*, 1997.

24. The JUNOScript API software (http://www.juniper.net/support/junoscript/

A P2P Content Authentication Protocol Based on Byzantine Agreement

Esther Palomar, Juan M. Estevez-Tapiador,
Julio C. Hernandez-Castro, and Arturo Ribagorda

Computer Science Department – Carlos III University of Madrid
Avda. Universidad 30 – 28911, Leganes, Madrid
{epalomar, jestevez, jcesar, arturo}@inf.uc3m.es

Abstract. One of the main advantages of peer-to-peer (P2P) systems is their capability to offer replicas of the same content at various locations. This allows to access contents even when some nodes are disconnected. However, this high degree of redundancy implies that it is necessary to apply some security mechanisms in order to avoid attacks based on non-authorized content modification. In this paper, we propose a content authentication protocol for pure P2P systems. Under certain restrictions, our scheme provides guarantes that a content is authentic, i.e. it has not been altered, even if it is a replica of the original and the source has lost control over it. Our proposal relies on a set of peers playing the role of a certification authority, for it is unrealistic to assume that appropriate trusted third parties can be deployed in such environments. Finally, we discuss some of its security properties through several attack scenarios.

1 Introduction

In a peer-to-peer (P2P) network, peers communicate directly with each other to exchange information. One particular example of this information exchange, that has been rather successful and has attracted considerable attention in the last years, is file sharing. This kind of systems are typically made up of millions of dynamic peers involved in the process of sharing and collaboration without relying in central authorities. P2P systems are characterized by being extremely decentralized and self-organized. These properties are essential in collaborative and ad-hoc environments, in which dynamic and transient population prevails.

The popularity of these systems has motivated inspiring research lines in the application of distributed P2P computing. New approaches have also been presented, such as scalability, robustness and fault tolerance, organization and coordination, adaptability, distributed storage, location and retrieval, reputation, and security. In particular, security advances have focused on anonymity, access control, integrity, and availability. New areas are being explored, such as fairness and authentication [3].

G. Müller (Ed.): ETRICS 2006, LNCS 3995, pp. 60–72, 2006.

A significant part of the research on security in P2P systems intends to mitigate attacks against four main system properties: availability, authenticity, access control, and anonymity. Recent work primarily focus on addressing attacks against availability and authenticity [4]. For instance, some results already exist on the security of traditional Gnutella-like systems, in particular, concerning availability and authenticity [13]. Different authors have also studied how to use a P2P network to prevent DoS attacks on the Internet [8, 11]. On the other hand, works such as [2] study how to use P2P networks to provide user anonymity. Furthermore, current architectures for P2P networks are plagued with open and difficult issues in digital rights management and access control (e.g., [7] outlines some of the problems in this area).

Many of the network security services offered today rely in public key cryptography. One of the most important issues when dealing with public keys is ensuring their authenticity. In environments such as Internet, the classic solution relies on the existence of a Public Key Infrastructure (PKI). A hierarchy of Certificate Authorities (CA) can assure whether a public key belongs to someone or not. Nevertheless, it is not realistic to assume that trusted third parties (TTP) can be deployed in a P2P network, especially in the case of a mobile ad-hoc network, where there is a lack of fixed infrastructure [12].

A recent work addresses the issues related to this problem in P2P systems [14]. Authors introduce a scheme based on Byzantine agreement for authenticating public keys. The proposed mechanism is autonomous and does not require the existence of a trusted third party in charge of issuing certificates to ensure key authenticity. The key point is that the scheme works correctly if the number of honest peers in the network is above a certain threshold. Due to its relevance as an essential building block in the protocol proposed in this paper, we further elaborate on this proposal below.

An important issue in file sharing systems is to guarantee the authenticity of the shared resources, i.e. to ensure that distributed replicas have not been modified in a non-authorized way. A digital content is straightforwardly alterable; it can be manipulated, so that a binary stream looks like the original. If a public key can be securely associated to a party, the integrity of a content generated by her can be ensured as follows.

First, the source:

1. Computes a hash value from the content.
2. Encrypts the hash value with her private key, obtaining a digital signature.
3. The signature is enclosed together with the digital certificate which contains the user's public key.
4. A CA validates the sender's digital signature.

Then, the receiver:

1. Computes a hash value from the received content.
2. Decrypts the digital signature enclosed by using the public key certificate, thus generating a second hash value.
3. Compares both hash values to confirm the non-alteration of the content.

In this paper we concentrate in designing a secure content distribution protocol for P2P networks. For this, we rely on some results derived from well-studied problems such as those of reaching consensus in presence of traitors. Content authentication confirms non-alteration and source identification of the content, implemented through a digital content certificate. Our motivated scenarios are the implementation of these concepts in future P2P networks, in collaborative environments, and file sharing applications in order to make them more reliable and secure.

The rest of this paper is organized as follows. In Section 2, we briefly introduce the scheme suggested in Pathak and Iftode's paper [14] for public key authentication in P2P systems. Section 3 describes our proposal, while Section 4 is devoted to provide and informal security analysis through a number of attack scenarios. Finally, Section 5 concludes the paper and discuss some open issues and future work.

2   Public Key Cryptography for Pure P2P Systems

Since malicious attacks and dishonest peers can cause faulty nodes to exhibit Byzantine behavior, fault-tolerant algorithms are becoming increasingly important in many environments. The work described in [10] proposes a mechanism based on erasure coding for data durability, plus a Byzantine agreement protocol for consistency and update serialization. This technique is based on breaking the data into blocks and spreading them over many servers. The objects and their associated fragments are then named using a secure hash over the object contents, giving them globally unique identifiers. This provides data integrity by ensuring that a recovered file has not been corrupted (for a corrupted file would produce a different identifier). Blocks are dispersed with special care in order to avoid possible correlated failures, picking nodes in different geographic locations or administrative domains, or based on models of historical measurements.

Pathak and Iftode [14] apply the ideas presented in the Byzantine Generals Problem [9] for public key authentication in pure P2P systems. The Byzantine Generals Problem [9] consists in deciding if a group of distributed generals must "attack" or "retreat" the enemy. Each Byzantine army is camped around an enemy city. Each base communicates among each others sending conflict information, with the vulnerability of traitors and enemies who try to prevent the loyal generals from reaching a plan. Authors show that, using oral messages, this problem is solvable if and only if more than 2/3 of the generals are loyal, or it is the same, no solution with fewer than 3m+1 general can cope with m traitors; but with signed messages, the problem is solvable for any number of general and possible traitors.

In Pathak and Iftode's scheme, it is postulated that a correct authentication depends on an honest majority of a particular subgroup of the peers' community, labeled "trusted group". However, in P2P systems an authenticated peer could create multiple fake identities and act maliciously in the future (Sybil attack [6]).

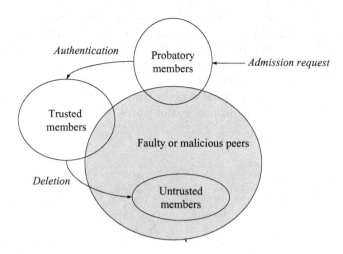

Fig. 1. Community structure according to the authentication state of each node

For this reason, the classification of the rest of the community maintained by each node (see Fig. 1) has to be proactive and should be periodically flushed. A periodic pruning of the trusted group will ensure honest majority. Thus, honest members from trusted groups are used to provide a functionality similar to that of the PKI through a consensus procedure.

The authentication protocol consists in the four phases that are briefly discussed below. Interested readers can find further details in [14].

1. **Admission request.** The protocol begins when B (Bob) run into a newly discovered peer A (Alice), which claims to be the owner of an unauthenticated public key K_A. Then, B asks to a subgroup of his trusted group for helping him in verifying the authenticity of K_A (Fig. 2, message 1). Finally, B sends K_A to those trusted peers that agree.

2. **Challenge response.** Each notified peer challenges Alice by sending a random nonce encrypted with Alice's supposed public key (Fig. 2, message 2). Alice is able to return each received nonce if and only if she holds the corresponding private key, K_A^{-1} (Fig. 2, messages 3). Each challenger checks if the received response is correct, thus obtaining a proof of possession of K_A.

3. **Distributed authentication.** Each peer helping Alice sends her proof of possession to Bob (Fig. 2, messages 4). If all peers are honest, then there will be a consensus, so Bob gets the authentication result: K_A belongs to Alice or not. However, some of the peers summoned by Bob could be malicious or faulty, which may result in Alice receiving different opinions about the authenticity of K_A. In this case, Bob must initiate the Byzantine agreement phase.

4. **Byzantine agreement.** First, Bob verifies if Alice is malicious by sending to her a proof request message. Alice must respond with all challenge messages received, and the respective responses sent by her (Fig. 2, message 5). If A

is honest, she can provide a correct response and also demonstrate her good behavior by sending to B the challenges she received and the corresponding responses. If A cannot be proved to be malicious, then some of the peers must be. At this stage, B announces a Byzantine fault to the group (Fig. 2, message 6). Each group member sends an agreement message to others. At the end of this phase, the honest peers will be able to recognize malicious peers causing the split in authentication votes.

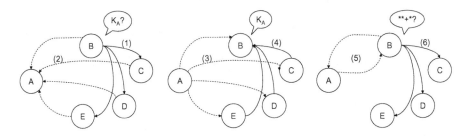

Fig. 2. Authentication protocol phases. Node A belongs to "others" group. Node B authenticates A using its trusted peers, and one of them turns malicious that tries to prevent authentication of A, C.

Successful authentication moves a peer to B's trusted group, while encountered malicious peers are moved to the untrusted group. Peers can be also deleted from trusted groups due to lack of liveliness and periodic pruning of the group.

The fundamental limit of this scheme is the following. Let N be the number of peers in the community; t the number of malicious or faulty peers; and ϕ a fraction of N, denoting that ϕN peers may not be reached during the protocol execution and another ϕN peers exhibit faulty behavior because the path between the source and them suffers a man-in-the-middle attack. Then, authors postulate that the community has honest majority if $t < \frac{1-6\phi}{3}N$. As the value of ϕ does not change the behavior of random selection, then we can consider that a group has honest majority with $3t + 1$ peers [14].

Summarizing, the previous protocol provides us with public key cryptography without relying in certification authorities. This can be viewed as an essential building block upon which more complex security schemes can be developed. As an example, Pathak and Iftode mention its application within an e-mail authentication system named SAM (Self Authenticating Mail).

3   A P2P Content Authentication Protocol

One of the most interesting aspects of P2P systems is the possibility of replicating the same content among different nodes. In many occasions, this task is not performed in a proactive way, but it is simply the result of the existence of a file sharing application. By using a search mechanism, users can locate a specific content and then download it from its source. Once a user gets the file, it is usual that a local copy will remain in the node, in such a way that future queries will identify the node as one of the various locations from which the content can be obtained.

This scheme presents some interesting properties. Faced with different locations of the same content, an application can grant priority to that which offers a less expensive path (e.g. in terms of bandwidth). To some extent, replication also guarantees some sort of fault tolerance, since information can be available even if some parts of the network are temporarily disconnected.

In a collaborative environment, previous features are highly desirable. However, it is unrealistic to assume that every integrating node will exhibit a honest behavior, even if they have always behaved correctly in the past. Once a content is replicated through different locations, the originator loses control over it. A malicious party can modify the replica according to several purposes:

- To claim ownership over the content.
- To insert malicious software into a highly demanded content. Not in vain, P2P networks are becoming an important medium to propagate recently developed viruses, spyware, etc.
- To boycott the system by offering fake contents. Eventually, this can generate distrust and bad reputation in the community.

In classic networking paradigms, guarantees of authenticity and integrity can be provided by digital signatures. If an authenticated user, A, wishes to offer a content m, she can rely on a CA to generate and sign an associated certificate, C_m, which can be checked by the rest of the community and also ensures that m has not been modified. Even tough the previous approach has been successfully applied in several domains (i.e. for public-key authentication), it requires the existence of trusted third parties. The reasons why A cannot sign her own certificates are simple. First, because she can misbehave, offering something different of what she announces. Furthermore, her signature alone does not prevent from manipulation. Suppose that A offers m in the form of a pair $< m, s_A(m) >$, being $s_A(m) = encryption(K_A^{-1}, h(m))$ the signature of A over m, and $h(m)$ any appropriate hash function. Once B obtains m, she can modify it and generate a new signature over the altered content. Moreover, even if B does not modify m, she can just remove $s_A(m)$ and add her own signature. As a result, several –and probably different– copies of m claimed by various parties may be circulating through the network.

As explained before, the key point is that assuming the existence of trusted third parties is an unrealistic hypothesis in P2P systems. Basically, the approach described in this paper relies on a honest majority of the nodes playing the role of a trusted CA. The owner of the content is responsible of generating a certificate containing the most important features of m, while a selected subset of the community signs it. Even though several signers do not constitute by themselves a proper "trusted third party", some security properties can be ensured if the group has honest majority.

3.1   Assumptions and Notation

Before presenting the details of this proposal, we assume the following five work-ing hypotheses:

1. Assured transactions without rejections. The absence of a message can be detected. This can be provided by using a scheme based on timeouts.
2. Identification of all participants is required through a unique pseudonym, the IP address, a network name, etc. Anonymity is not desired by now.
3. Identification of contents is also required. A unique name, which is also used for searching the content, is associated with the content.
4. Digital signatures cannot be forged unless the attacker get access to private keys.
5. Anyone can verify the authenticity of a node's signature by applying the Byzantine fault tolerant public key authentication protocol presented in [14].

Even though some terms have already been introduced, we summarize the notation that will be used throughout the paper:

- N is the number of network nodes.
- Each node is denoted by n_i. Eventually, specific nodes will be designated by capital letters: A, B, ...
- Each node n_i has a pair of public and private keys, denoted by K_i and K_i^{-1}, respectively.
- m denotes the content that nodes wish to publish.
- $h(x)$ represents a hash function on x.
- $s_i(x) = encryption(K_A^{-1}, h(x))$ is the signature of n_i over x.

3.2   Content Certificates

We are interested in avoiding non-authorized content alteration. For this, pre-viously to its diffusion, an entity A generates a certificate C_m for content m, containing:

- The identity of the originator, which ultimately establishes who has gener-ated the content and is its legitimate owner.
- The identity of the contents.
- A hash, $h(m)$, of m, assuring its integrity.
- An ordered list of signers (OLS) of the certificate. It contains the identity of $k + 1$ network nodes, denoted by $n_0, n_1, \ldots, n_k$, being $n_0 = A$ the content originator. The nodes are selected among A's trusted group.
- Finally, the previous items are recursively signed by the nodes listed in the OLS. First, A signs the certificate. The resulting signature is subsequently checked and signed by n_1, and so on.

The structure of the certificate is summarized in Fig. 3(a). Of course, this is just a functional description of the key elements contained in the certificate. In a real application, it would be necessary to include additional fields, such as

Content certificate C_m

Certificate C:
Originator: A
ID: I_m
Contents: $h(m)$
OLS: $A, n_1, \ldots, n_k$
Signatures:
$s_{n_k}(\cdots(s_{n_1}(s_A(C))))$

Table of signed certificates T_i

Date	Certificate received	Signature s_{n_i}
$Time_1$	C_{m_1}	s_{i1}
$\vdots$	$\vdots$	$\vdots$
$Time_n$	C_{m_n}	s_{in}

(a)   (b)

Fig. 3. (a) Content certificate; (b) local database maintained by each certification node

a code indicating the hash function which has been used, a timestamp and an expiration date, etc.

As it will be justified below, each node must maintain a local register with the certificates it has previously signed. Fig. 3(b) shows the fields that this table should store: a timestamp, the received certificate (including the signatures contained), and the signature generated by the node.

3.3 Certificate Generation

Before C_m can be used to ensure content authenticity and integrity, it must be progressively signed by the nodes included in the OLS. At each stage, the next node in the OLS adds its signature to the previous ones. Due to the structure of the chain of signatures, this task cannot be carried out in parallel. We will denote by $C_0, C_1, \ldots, C_k = C_m$ the successive versions of the certificate as it passes through the list of nodes.

The certificate is initialized by the originator, A, who selects an appropriate value for the number k of signing nodes and their identities (see discussion below). Next, A generates C_0 by providing the first signature and passes it to the next node in the OLS.

Local Verification. Each node n_i should perform a *local verification* stage when it receives certificate C_{i-1}. The purpose of this phase is to ensure the correctness of both the certificate and the previously added signatures. This consists in the following three steps:

- *Certificate verification.* Each peer verifies the correctness of the information received from the previous peer in the list of signers. This includes obtaining A's public key, computing $h(m)$ and comparing it with the value contained in the received certificate. The node must also check T_i and verify that no entries exist corresponding to the same content.
- *Signatures verification.* Each peer verifies the signatures contained in the received certificate according to the list order. If any public key is unknown, it can be acquired with an instance of Pathak and Iftode's public key authentication protocol.

- *Local management.* If previous verifications succeed, the node adds its signatures to C_{i-1}, thus creating C_i. Each peer stores separately C_{i-1} and the generated signature, $s_{n_i}(C_{i-1})$, in her local database T_i.

Signing the Certificate. We have identified two different ways in which the certificate can be signed by the nodes included in the OLS. Fig. 4 graphically illustrates both alternatives. The main differences are the following:

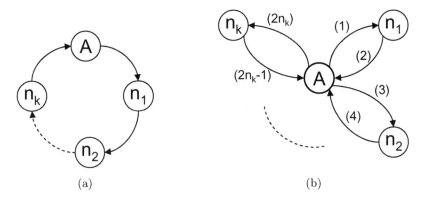

(a)   (b)

Fig. 4. Alternative procedures for certificate generation

- In the first one, illustrated in Fig. 4(a), each node is responsible of sending the signed certificate to the next node in the list. This way, A simply sends C_0 to n_1 and waits until C_m arrives. Although it is not explicitly pointed out in the figure, we assume that each peer must send a notification message to A when it passes the certificate to the next node. This, together with appropriate timeouts, allows A to be aware of the current state of the process.
- In the second alternative (Fig. 4(b)), A is responsible of sending C_{i-1} to each node and receiving C_i. Now, A can check whether the received certificate has been properly signed or not, thus having a higher level of control over the process. However, note that each node still has to perform its local verification stage in order to ensure that it is not being cheated on.

A more precise description for both alternatives is provided in Figs. 5 and 6.

3.4   Certificate Verification

Once obtained m, the certificate should be checked to ensure the authenticity and integrity of m. For this, a node B performs the following steps:

- *Step 1.* B computes $h(m)$ from m and compares the result with that included in the certificate. If both values differ, then either m has been altered or C_m is not an authentic certificate for m.

- *Step 2.* B obtains the public keys associated to each of the peers listed in the OLS. If any public key is unknown to B, it can be acquired by executing Pathak and Iftode's public key authentication protocol.
- *Step 3.* B verifies the chain of signatures by recursively encrypting C with the ordered list of public keys.

Protocol for distributed content certificate generation
(Note: $A = n_0$)

---

1. n_0 generates C and signs: $C_0 = < C, s_{n_0}(C) >$
2. n_0 sends (m, C_0) to n_1
3. For $i = 1$ to k
    (a) n_i performs the local verification stage on C_{i-1}
    (b) n_i adds its signature and generates C_i
    (c) n_i updates T_i with the tuple $< timestamp, C_{i-1}, s_{n_i}(C_{i-1}) >$
    (d) n_i sends (m, C_i) to $n_{i+1(mod\ k)}$
    (e) n_i sends a notification message to n_0

Fig. 5. Distributed content certificate generation

Protocol for centralized content certificate generation
(Note: $A = n_0$)

---

1. n_0 generates C and signs: $C_0 = < C, s_{n_0}(C) >$
2. For $i = 1$ to k
    (a) n_0 sends (m, C_{i-1}) to n_i
    (b) n_i performs the local verification stage on C_{i-1}
    (c) n_i adds its signature: $C_i = < C, s_{n_i}(C_{i-1}) >$
    (d) n_i sends C_i to n_0
    (e) n_i updates T_i with the tuple $< timestamp, C_{i-1}, s_{n_i}(C_{i-1}) >$
    (f) n_0 verifies the correctness of the signature of n_i

Fig. 6. Centralized content certificate generation

4   Security Analysis

In this section, we provide an informal analysis about the security of the proposed scheme. For this purpose, we discuss several attack scenarios and forms of malicious behavior which can occur during each phase of the protocol execution.

4.1   Content Authenticity

The protocol is initiated by n_0 and relies on her honesty. In case of n_0 being honest, we can assume that the original copy of m is authentic, the hash function is not manipulated, and the OLS contains A's trusted members. Therefore, the initial content certificate, C_0, is correct.

The originator might try to exhibit a malicious behavior. Any modification of the certificate fields will be eventually detected by, at least, one node in the OLS, since it is assumed honest majority, n_0 cannot collude with a sufficient number of traitors. This also prevents a group of malicious nodes to collude during the signing process in order to forge a false certificate. Suppose that a signer B, who belongs to the OLS, gets the pair $< m, C_m >$ and tries to generate a fake certificate, C'_m, as follows:

Certificate C':
   Originator: B
   ID: I_m
   Contents: $h(m)$
   OLS: $B, n_{1'}, \ldots, n_{k'}$
Signatures:
   $s_{n_{k'}}(\cdots(s_{n_{1'}}(s_B(C'))))$

This behavior will be detected by a subset of nodes in the OLS during the local verification stage, as at least one of them has previously signed C_m and will refuse to cooperate.

Note that this scheme does not prevent from B modifying m into m', changing the identifier I_m into I'_m, and subsequently executing another protocol instance with the aim of obtaining a different content certificate, C'_m. This kind of manipulation cannot be avoided exclusively by external means, but by inserting appropriate mechanisms *inside* m.

4.2   Local Verification

This phase can be attacked in a number of ways. *Assumption 5* assures that messages exchanged among trusted peers cannot be spoofed and man-in-the-middle attacks cannot be mounted, since they are signed by authenticated public keys. However, Pathak and Iftode's protocol can fail due to the impossibility of getting an honest majority. In this case, an adversary could convince a honest peer that the public key of a node is K_i when it is not. This kind of man-in-the-middle attack is detected if at least one peer (apart from A) is honest.

4.3   Incorrect Sending and Non-cooperation

A dishonest signer can delay the content authentication by not signing the certificate, not sending any message to the next node in the OLS, and/or not notifying anything to the originator A. Surely, this behavior will produce a kind of DoS attack [11], so A must check nodes' availability when this situation appears.

Each intermediate peer must ignore any messages that do not have the proper form of content and a signed certificate. Besides, peers know that the originator A is malicious if her signature is incorrect.

Furthermore, a dishonest signer could send its participation randomly or maliciously, instead of a properly constructed signature. Even though this fact can be trivially detected, in a sense it is a point of failure, since cooperation is required among the $k + 1$ nodes to achieve a successful execution of the protocol. In other words, the protocol allows to *detect* these forms of misbehavior and no cooperation, but it cannot enforce nodes to behave properly.

5   Conclusions and Future Work

Due to the very nature of P2P systems, it is usual that several copies of the same content exist at different network locations. Despite the advantages derived from replication, in general it is unrealistic to assume that every node will behave correctly. In this way, once a malicious node gets access to a content, its integrity can be compromised in several ways.

In this paper, we have proposed a content authentication protocol based on Byzantine agreement, especially oriented to pure P2P systems. This scheme allows for a secure content replication among peers, which is able to detect if non-authorized alterations have been made on the published contents. Furthermore, our proposal does not rely on the use of a trusted third party, an assumption that would be totally impractical for decentralized P2P environments.

Currently, we are working on statistically measuring how serious the problem of false content distribution is in real environments (e.g. eMule and BitTorrent). We are evaluating the level of boycott, mistrust, and bad reputation generated due to the distribution of forged contents. For this, we are studying several variables as: the download effort (time and bandwidth metrics), the user satisfaction degree, the content quality (especially relevant for multimedia contents), etc.

Future works will try to improve our protocol's efficiency, since it has not being our main objective in its conception. The large number of needed signers and the communication overhead could probably be improved with the use of other approaches, notably those based in multisignature schemes [1]. Additionally, we plan to include in C_m, as in most current digital certificates, two time parameters to specify when the certificate was generated and its expiration date. These fields, together with some additional information, could be added into the content certificate, for example as an agreed timestamp imposed from the source, and accepted and stored by each intermediate peer.

Finally, we are also studying the application of proof-of-work techniques for ensuring access control, for instance by using puzzles [5]. The use of Threshold Cryptography in P2P systems for reaching consensus is also an interesting research line that will be tackled in future works.

References

1. C. Boyd. "Digital multisignatures". In H. Baker and F. Piper (Eds.), *Cryptography and Coding*, pp. 241–246. Clarendon Press, 1989.
2. M. Conti, E. Gregori, and G. Turi. "Towards Scalable P2P Computing for Mobile Ad-Hoc Networks". In *Proceedings of the Second IEEE Annual Conference on Pervasive Computing and Communications Workshops (PERCOMW '04)*, Orlando, USA, pp. 109–113. March, 2004.

3. E. Damiani, S. De Capitani, S. Paraboschi, P. Samarati, and F.Violante. "A Reputation-Based Approach for Choosing Reliable Resources in Peer-to-Peer Networks". In *Proceedings of the 9th ACM Conference on Computer and Communications Security (CCS'02)*, Washington, USA, pp. 207–216. November, 2002.

4. N. Daswani, H. Garcia-Molina and B. Yang. "Open Problems in Data-sharing Peer-to-peer Systems". In *Proceedings of 9th International Conference on Database Theory*, Italy. January, 2003.

5. D. Dean and A. Stubblefield. "Using client puzzles to protect TLS". In *Proceedings of the 10th USENIX Security Symposium*. August, 2001.

6. J. Douceur. "The Sybil attack". In *Proceedings of 1st International Workshop on Peer-to-Peer Systems (IPTPS02) Workshop*, Cambridge, USA, pp. 251–260. March, 2002.

7. G. Fox. "Peer-to-Peer Networks". In *Computing in Science & Engineering, vol. 3, no. 3*. May, 2001.

8. A. Juels and J. Brainard. "Client puzzles: A cryptographic countermeasure against connection depletion attacks". In *Proceedings of the Network and Distributed Security Systems Symposium*, California , USA, pp. 151–165. February, 1999.

9. L. Lamport, R. Shostak and M. Pease. "The Byzantine General Problem". *ACM Transactions on Programming Languages and Systems, Vol. 4, No. 3*, pp. 382–401. July, 1982.

10. W. K. Lin, D. M. Chiu, Y. B. Lee. "Erasure Code Replication Revisited". In *Proceeding of the 4th IEEE International Conference on Peer-to-Peer Computing*. August, 2004.

11. P. Maniatis, T.J. Giuli, M. Roussopoulos, D.S.H. Rosenthal, and M. Baker. "Impeding Attrition Attacks in P2P Systems". In *Proceedings of the 11th ACM SIGOPS European Workshop*, Leuven, Belgium. September, 2004.

12. M. Oguchi, Y. Nakatsuka and C. Tomizawa. "A Proposal of User Authentication and a Content Distribution Mechanism using P2P Connection over a Mobile Ad Hoc Network". In *Proceedings of the IASTED International Conference on Communication Systems and Networks*, Marbella, Spain, pp. 65-69. September, 2004.

13. A. Oram, ed.: "Peer-to-Peer: Harnessing the Benefits of a Disruptive Technology". O'Reilly, Sebastopol (CA), 2001.

14. V. Pathak and L. Iftode. "Byzantine Fault Tolerant Public Key Authentication in Peer-to-Peer Systems". *Computer Networks, Vol. 50, No. 4*, pp. 579–596, March 2006. Elsevier.

Transitive Trust in Mobile Scenarios

Nicolai Kuntze and Andreas U. Schmidt

Fraunhofer Institute for Secure Information Technology SIT,
Rheinstrasse 75, 64295 Darmstadt, Germany
{Nicolai.Kuntze, Andreas.U.Schmidt}@sit.fraunhofer.de
www.sit.fraunhofer.de, www.math.uni-frankfurt.de/~aschmidt

Abstract. Horizontal integration of access technologies to networks and services should be accompanied by some kind of convergence of authentication technologies. The missing link for the federation of user identities across the technological boundaries separating authentication methods can be provided by trusted computing platforms. The concept of establishing transitive trust by trusted computing enables the desired cross-domain authentication functionality. The focus of target application scenarios lies in the realm of mobile networks and devices.

1 Introduction

Current information technology imposes on users a multitude of heterogeneous authentication mechanisms when they want to access networks, services, or content. The technical access channels to these desiderata are, however, undergoing a continual process of convergence. The mobile domain provides a striking example [1, 2]. The access to services through mobile devices shows a trend to become network-agnostic. Driven by the horizontal integration of technologies, users will soon be able to consume services seamlessly from a single device via a variety of channels and transport methods such as 2G, 3G, WLAN, Bluetooth, WiMAX, MobileIP, or the upcoming Zigbee. Accordingly, end users' attention will shift away from the pricing of bandwidth to that of content and services. Custom must then be attracted by offering applications and content with good price to quality ratio. Little room is left for returns generated by charging for network access and data transport. Business models necessarily undergo drastic changes, of which the mushrooming of virtual network operators is the salient epiphenomenon. Research has long foreseen this evolution toward 'value networks' [3, 4].

Thus, information networks are becoming ever more service oriented. On the application layer, identity management (IDM), as embodied, e.g., in the Liberty alliance standard suite, has proved to be a successful foundation for the user-centric integration of service access [5]. Mobile networks with millions of users and even more identities are already using IDM for essential services like roaming [6]. Yet, arguably, these top-level methods require infrastructural support of some kind [7]. In particular, it is desirable to overcome the boundaries between logically, technically, or even physically separated domains and their respective authentication methods. This signifies a second layer of technological

G. Müller (Ed.): ETRICS 2006, LNCS 3995, pp. 73–85, 2006.

convergence, namely convergence of authentication methods and the domains of trust defined by them. This is the subject matter of the present paper.

We argue that trusted computing (TC) can be a means to the above mentioned ends. In fact, two systems or devices can assure each other of their being in a trustworthy state through TC methods like direct attestation. If the devices carry credentials from various trust domains, they can then use TC-secured communication to exchange them. This assignment of credentials by trustworthy transmission between carriers yields *transitive trust relationships*. This allows for the mediation of trust between domains and user or device identities, and in fact, some of the concepts we present are rather similar to logical identity federation. However, transitive trust by TC enables the traversal of authentication domains hitherto separated by technical or even physical boundaries. The concept of transitivity of trust relationships was recently analysed in [8].

The paper is organised as follows. Section 2 explains the basic notions behind transitive trust, in particular the three most primitive operations supported by it. The exposition, while theoretical, is not completely formalised in view of the intended application scenarios. Three of the latter scenarios are described in ascending level of detail in Section 3.

Not by coincidence are these applications chosen from the mobile realm. In fact we show that mobile devices equipped with TC are not only good carriers for credentials but also excellent links between trust domains, when applying the methods of transitive trust. As will become clear from the few scenarios we consider, potential business models, enabled by transitive trust, abound. Needless to say, the newly conceived trust relationships that we describe in concrete business scenarios must be supported in the real world by contractual relationships.

2   Transitive Trust by Trusted Platforms

A completely formalised definition is outside of the scope of the present paper, since we aim at rather specific application scenarios. Nevertheless we want to provide a theoretical descriptions that allows to assess the generic character of the transitive trust relationships supported by trusted platforms, i.e., systems secured by TC as described below. A more formal treatment, e.g., along the lines of [8,9] or [10], is certainly possible. Yet, it would not contribute much to the present topic since we are more interested in pinpointing the properties and functionalities of trusted platforms involved in the establishment of transitive trust.

We use a simple model for actors in trust domains consisting of trust *principals* and *agents*. Trust principals are the subjects defining an authentication domain by issuing credentials to users or enrolling them to their devices. They control domain membership and applicable authentication methods, and therefore define a domain of trust like an identity provider. Trust principals are denoted by capital letters A, B, C, ... Agents asking for access to services provided in a certain domain are denoted by a, b, c, ... The notion of agent signifies *classes* of individuals, i.e., groups of agents who enjoy the same access rights in a certain application context when authenticated using their respective (individual) credentials. A subgroup of agents is written as $a' \subset a$ as usual. Our terminology is different from that in [9] in order to clearly separate the party issuing an authentication request (the agent) from the one answering it (the principal).

Credentials $\gamma_{a,A}$ are objects or data which authenticate agents a with respect to a principal A. We do not specify the particular kind of credentials used, nor the accompanying authentication methods. This notion is very generic and comprises classical examples like SIM/USIM, Hardware tokens, Smartcards, PKI-based certificates, PIN/TAN-based methods, or even personal credentials, e.g., Machine Readable Transfer Documents or a health (professional) card.

It should be clear that the overall security of the authentication assertions of transitive trust that are described below depend on the 'weakest link' in the trust chain. These assertions can in particular not be stronger than those provided by the original credentials. Furthermore, the trust scope implicated by a successful authentication, i.e., the specific type of trust assumed in a given principal-agent relationship, may vary from domain to domain. As already mentioned, risks arising from these complexities must be assessed and mitigated in the context of the specific application scenario at hand. Common instruments for that are contracts between principals and their agents and bridging contracts between principals.

2.1   Trust Credentials

Credentials that can be constructed basing on the functionalities of a trusted platform module (TPM [11]) play a special role in our concept. TPMs provide a number of features that can be used to securely operate a system. Methods for the secure generation, storage, and usage of asymmetric key pairs are the foundation for encrypted and authenticated operation and communication. Trust measurements on the system environment exerted at boot- and run-time allow for trustworthy assertions about the current system state and a re-tracing of how it was reached. The system state is securely stored in platform configuration registers (PCR) tamper-resistantly located inside the TPM. Memory curtaining and sealed storage spaces are enabled by pertinent TPM base functions. Trustworthy system and application software can build on this basis to establish authenticated communication with the exterior and transmit data maintaining integrity and confidentiality. In particular, Direct Anonymous Attestation (DAA), a method put forward in [12] and specified by the trusted computing group (TCG), enables the establishment of trust relationships of a trusted system with external entities. A central goal of DAA is to cover privacy issues related to previous versions of the standards [13].

Although certain flaws are known in the TCG standards (e.g. [14] points to a flaw in the OIA Protocol an authorisation protocol which represents one of the building blocks of the TPM) that exist currently future versions are likely to remedy them. We assume for the purport of our applications that the functions used are at least secured against common attack vectors in the scenarios below.

Using the described functionality, a trusted system, viewed as an agent a, can establish what we call a *trust credential* τ_a. Specifically, we assume that the trust credential can be used to attest the validity of three fundamental security assertions of a system to the exterior.

1. The presence of a live and unaltered TPM. This can for instance be carried out using a challenge-response method using the TPM's endorsement credential. Endorsement credentials are pre-installed by the TPM's manufacturer.
2. The integrity of the system and its components. This property is ascertained through trust measurements and communicated via DAA.
3. That an existing credential $\gamma_{a,A}$ is unaltered. This must be established by trusted system software and components used to access the credential's data. Again, this assertion is forwarded to other parties using direct attestation and secure communication channels established therewith.

These properties are not independent but build on each other, i.e, to prove 3. one needs first attestation of 2. and 1., etc. The TPM is capable of creating, managing, and transmitting own cryptographic credentials which can convey the described assertions 1.–3.

We now describe three basic, independent operations for creating trust between agents and principals. These methods represent the essence of transitive trust enabled by trusted platforms. They all rely on *referral trust* in the parlance of [8]. That is, on the ability of a trusted agent through assertions 1.–3., to make recommendations to trust another agent or even himself in a special, functional role.

2.2   Restriction

By the method of restriction, a subgroup of agents $a' \subset a$ belonging to the authentication domain of principal A can be defined. Agents of class a authenticate themselves in the conventional way associated to their credential $\gamma_{a,A}$. This establishes an authenticated channel, over which agents of subclass a' transmit an additional trust credential $\tau_{a'}$ identifying them as members of a'. Since by this method the trust and original credentials are used independently, only assertions 1. and 2. are needed.

The additional security and in effect higher trust in agents of a' provided by them allows to ascribe to a' more service access rights than to a-agents. In particular, the integrity of client software can be attested by 2. Those clients can access content or services only available to the privileged subgroup. This is in fact the classical scenario used to enforce copyright protection through digital rights management (DRM). A higher security level is provided by restriction in a very generic way. The possibility for A to check the consistency of the trust credential $\tau_{a'}$ with that of $\gamma_{a,A}$ makes at least the subclass a' more resilient against cloning attacks on the credential $\gamma_{a,A}$. This kind of attack is not uncommon in the mobile sector [15].

This raised resilience against cloning is the main reason why the usage of a trust credential is advantageous for the definition of the subclass a'. The latter definition can be implemented in various ways. The first-best approach is restriction under the authority of the principal. She can manage access control lists based on *individual* trust credentials identifying a single TPM. Or, e.g., she can use individual trust credentials to establish a secure channel with a'-agents and distribute a shared secret to them. This secret can reside in the part of the system protected by the TPM and thus become part of $\tau_{a'}$. In turn it may be used in subsequent authentication requests toward A, keeping an agent's individual identity secret.

A proper choice of enrolment method and time for the trust credential is essential for the validity of the additional trust provided by the restriction operation. If the credentials γ and τ are impressed on the agents independently of each other, i.e., not both under the control of the principal A, then, e.g., resilience against cloning attacks is restricted. Since A cannot associate the two credentials belonging to an individual agent, she can at best avoid to grant two agents with identical γ service access by using a first-come-first-served approach. It is possible to improve on this by forcing an activation of $\tau_{a'}$ at an early stage, e.g., the time of roll-out of a mobile device. Higher cloning-resilience can only be achieved if the principal individualises both credentials and controls their deployment to the agent.

It may be more the rule than the exception that the trust credential $\tau_{a'}$ provides stronger authentication than the original one $\gamma_{a' \subset a, A}$. Conventionally, τ would then be the preferable credential to authenticate agents of class a' with. It is essential for the understanding of the present concepts to notice that this is often not practical. Namely, the communication channel through which τ is conveyed to the principal is only available after authentication by γ. A paradigm is the access to mobile networks as described in section 3.1.

2.3 Subordination

By subordination an agent a in principal A's domain can enable the access to this domain, or certain services of it, for another agent a'. By this, a' is effectively included in A's domain of trust, respectively, A's domain is extended to a'. As for restriction, a authenticates himself using a generic credential $\gamma_{a,A}$ and then produces a specific trust credential σ_a identifying those agents of A's domain who are allowed to dominate certain other agents. The subordinated agent a' shows a trust credential $\sigma_{a'}$ to a, who in turn mediates the access to A's services, either by forwarding authorisation requests, or granting them himself. Furthermore, the authentication of a and a' can also be mutual rather than one-sided.

Implementation variants of this operation and authorisation based on it are manifold, despite its simplicity. The most restrictive approach would be to use the secure communication channels between a and a' (mutually authenticated by σ_a, $\sigma_{a'}$), and a and A to forward every single authorisation request from a' to A including the trust credential $\sigma_{a'}$. Independently of the degree to which A takes part in authorisation, the act of authentication for subordination is generically between a' and a. Nevertheless, in many scenarios $\sigma_{a'}$ is controlled and enrolled by A, and the principal can in implementation variants also partake in authentication, e.g., by facilitating steps in a challenge-response protocol.

If genuine trust credentials are used for subordination, the operation employs only TPM functions 1. and 2. above. TPMs provide user functions for the revocation of keys, which is a point of failure in this case. Thus one might use a dedicated credential $\gamma_{a',A}$ for subordination. Such a credential should then live in the trusted part of the subordinated system and be secured in the authentication by function 3. to mitigate forgery.

A subordination scenario is outlined in 3.2.

2.4 Transposition

Transposition operates between the trust domains of two principals A and B. The authentication of an agent b of B's domain is mediated by an agent a of A's domain and the principal A. This can make sense for instance if direct communication between b and B is not possible as in the scenario of Section 3.3.

We assume that authentication of a to A is done as above. Trust credentials τ_a and τ_b are used for (mutual) authentication of b to a (or between them). Here, the third TC function of τ_b is used to prove the integrity of a credential $\gamma_{b,B}$ with which b is ultimately authenticated with respect to B. The generic situation for the latter authentication is as follows. The credential $\gamma_{b,B}$ is forwarded to A. This bears the assurance that an authentic (by $\gamma_{a,A}$) and untampered (by τ_a) agent has handled the latter credential. In effect a establishes a trusted path for the transmission of $\gamma_{b,B}$. Whether or how $\gamma_{b,B}$ is transferred from A to B to finally authenticate b depends on communication means and contractual relations. The transposition concept leaves this open.

Again, transposition can be implemented in numerous variants. In particular, part or all of the functionality necessary for authentication of b can be deferred to A or a. From B's perspective, efficiency gains by such an outsourcing or even decentralised approach to authentication must be balanced with the protection of secrecy of his business data and processes, which, to a certain extent have to be turned over to A.

On the other hand, in the generic transposition operation where $\gamma_{b,B}$ is forwarded to B who in turn completely controls the authentication of b. Then, additional cryptographic means can be applied to render any sensitive information about the relationship of b and B inaccessible to a and A. In particular, B might want to keep his agents anonymous to A, and even the mere size of B's domain of trust might be an informational asset worth of protection.

3   Scenarios

This section outlines three concrete application scenarios of economical relevance, corresponding to the three operations explained above. The first two are sketched on a rather high level, while the third and most complex one is used to detail processes and protocols. A detailed description of the first two scenarios would be very similar.

3.1 Functional Discrimination of Mobile Devices

As already said, the paradigm for restriction scenarios is DRM. We want to pursue a slightly different direction and take a look at the relationship between network operator and customer in the mobile domain. The standard form of customer retention exerted by the mobile network operator (MNO) is SIM-lock, a crude form of functional restriction of mobile devices bonding mobile devices to SIMs of a certain MNO. Based on transitive trust restriction, a finer grained functional discrimination of mobile devices becomes possible. Depending on the device vendor's and MNO's business models, various client functions of the device can be restricted to certain, more or less privileged customer groups. The management of mobile devices, of which functional discrimination is an important instance is viewed by the industry as a fundamental application area of TC [16].

A multitude of benefits accrue to MNO and customer in this kind of scenario. First, it is cost-efficient to produce a single product line with many appearances to the end-user, rather than marketing a multitude of makes and models as customary today. Second, the up- and downgrading of functionalities can be implemented dynamically, without physical access to the device. To the user, the relative seamlessness with which device control operates is an ergonomic benefit and allows for better customisation and even personalisation.

The efficient means to implement functional restrictions of mobile devices is provided by the trusted boot process and operating system of the trusted platform it represents. Thereby, the trust credential can attest two properties via DAA. First, that the device belongs to a certain, restricted group defined explicitly or implicitly by a list of enabled functions. Second, that the device actually is in a state where only the allowed functions are enabled. The set of functions to be managed could be pre-configured and the dynamic control effected via simple changes of parameters, e.g., for values in PCRs.

The enforcement level of this approach is stronger as compared to SIM-lock precisely because the trusted platform's base operation software is tamper resistant. Based on this assurance, the MNO can deliver specific services or content only to the restricted group privy to it. Thus functional restriction provides the foundation on the client side for further service discrimination, policy enforcement, and DRM proper.

As a simple instance using the transitive trust restriction operation, a prepaid mobile phone can be implemented. The phone carries in its trusted storage area a running total which is decremented by a trusted software. While the initial access to the mobile network is still established using SIM authentication, DAA and the trust credential then yield assurance to the MNO that the running total is nonzero, upon which access to the network's communication services can be granted. This releases the MNO from operating (or paying for) a centralised accounting.

3.2 Bonding of Mobile Accessories

For the mobile domain, an application of subordination which suggests itself is to extend the authentication of devices toward an MNO to devices not equipped with SIM cards or even physical access to the mobile network. A commercial application is the extension of SIM-lock to such devices. For the purpose of customer retention, such a scheme can for instance be combined with loyalty programmes. Just as SIM-locked mobile phones are highly subsidised, an MNO can give away technical accessories such as digital cameras, media players, or high quality headsets. The functioning of those subordinated devices is then dependent on authentication toward a mobile device or any device in a specific MNO's network.

In effect, the accessories can be given away for a very low price or even for free on the condition that they work only within the subsidising MNO's network. The devices are bonded to the MNO. As an additional benefit for the MNO, the traffic generated by subordinated devices is bound to his own network (as traffic volume is a traditional economic value indicator for MNO businesses). Of course, advanced service provisioning can be based on accessory bonding, e.g., the MNO or another provider can offer storage, organisation, and printing services for photographs taken with a bonded camera.

3.3 Point of Sales

We now come to scenarios employing the transposition operation, and here present the related technical processes and communication protocols in some detail.

A user with a TPM-equipped mobile device wants to purchase a soft drink from a likewise trust-enabled vending machine, the point of sales (POS). While the user still makes up her mind on her taste preferences, device and POS initiate a trusted communication session using DAA and transport layer encryption. Device and POS thus achieve mutual assurance that they are in an unaltered, trustworthy state, and begin to exchange price lists and payment modalities. After the user selects a good and confirms his choice at his device, signed price and payment processing information is transferred to the MNO. After verifying the signatures and optionally informing the good's vendor and a payment service provider, the MNO sends a signed acknowledgement to the mobile device, which relays it to the POS, where it is verified and the good is delivered.

The benefits for the vendor that arise in this scenario basically stem from the transitivetrustrelationship that is mediated between MNO and POS by the mobile device. That it is economically attractive is a view shared by prominent market researchers [1]. The scenario entails in particular that no network communication is required during the initiation of a trusted session, that no transaction data needs to be stored in the POS, and that, ultimately, the POS does not need

---

[1] As John Curtis, head of the department Information, Communications & Entertainment of KPMG Germany put it: "Doch permanent subventionierte Handys auf den Markt zu werfen, bringt langfristig keinen Geschäftserfolg. Sinnvoller ist es, sich mit Hilfe attraktiver konvergenter Dienstleistungen [. . .] eine stabile und loyale Kundenbasis aufzubauen. Damit wird man für Werbekunden und Partner im digitalen Handel attraktiv und eröffnet sich neue Einnahmequellen [. . .] Verrechnungsmanagement wird deshalb künftig zu einer Schlüsselkompetenz." (Throwing subsidised handsets on the market is not a sustainable strategy for success. It makes more sense to build a stable and loyal customer base with attractive and convergent services [. . .]. In this way, new revenue sources open up and attractiveness for advertising customers and partners in digital trade is increased [. . .] Charging management will therefore be a future key competency). [KPMG Germany press release, 19th March 2006. http://www.kpmg.de/about/press_office/13609.htm]

to be equipped with networking capabilities — at least for the sales process. In this way the MNO provides payment services as well as authorisation control for the vendor. This requires little more than a TPM and a short-range communication module in the vending machine. In extended service scenarios, the customer's mobile devices can as well be utilised to transfer valuable information to the POS, e.g., updated price and commodity lists, or firmware.

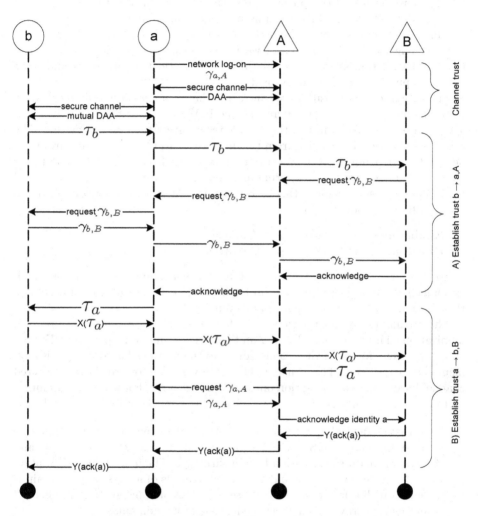

Fig. 1. Sequence diagram for the transposition operation from POS b via mobile device a, MNO A, to POS owner B. The notation $X(\cdot)$, $Y(\cdot)$ means protection by secrets X, Y shared between b and B.

A similar example regards home automation and lets a user and her mobile device become part of the maintenance service of, say, the heating system of her home. Based again on their respective TPMs, heating system and mobile device establish a secure communication channel to exchange maintenance data, or data used for metering. This can be done both at specific user requests or even seamlessly during normal operation of device and heating system, every time the machine-to-machine communication module of the device gets in the range of the one in the heating system. In this way, the mobile device can notify user and a maintenance chain about necessary repairs and also support accounting and billing. Here, a trusted computing approach not only ensures the protection of personal data, it also enables a simple means of remote maintenance and home automation in non-networked homes by efficiently utilising the mobile network.

Returning to the POS scenario, we now describe one possible implementation in more detail. We concentrate on the authentication processes and leave selection, purchase, and payment aside.

The variant of transposition we consider is that of *maximal mutual trust*. That is, both principals A, the MNO, and B, the POS' owner, can trust the involved agent of the other domain, i.e., the POS b, respectively the mobile device a. The raised level of security ensuing from this may be desirable in particular from B's perspective, depending on the sensitivity of business data handled by a and A as mediators, for instance if accounting and charging services of B are transferred to A. The process to achieve this kind of transposition can be divided into two principally independent steps.

A) Establishment of trust of a and A in agent b.
B) Establishment of trust of b and B in agent a.

These two steps are in fact equivalent to two subordination operations with exchanged roles. A sequence diagram for both steps is shown in Figure 1. Note that A) and B) can be interchanged or even overlap.

The two main steps must both be preceded by an establishment of a secure communication channel between b and a and between a and A, respectively. For the latter, the usual log-on of the mobile device to the network based on $\gamma_{a,A}$ is augmented by attestation of the trusted platform a via DAA toward A over a secured channel based on, say, encryption on the transport layer. For the former, mutual platform attestation over an encrypted channel is carried out between b and a.

A) The trust credential τ_b of b is passed on to B, attesting to B that there is one of his untampered POS down the communication line. B then requests and receives proper authentication from b with $\gamma_{b,B}$. The underlying assumption that B can associate trust and generic credentials of agents in his domain is a central anchor for trust in the present variant of transposition. In effect B is an identity provider for trust credentials of his domain.

 B acknowledges successful authentication of b to A who passes it on to a. The trust relationship between the two principals and A and his agent a assures the latter two actor of the authenticity of b.

B) Agent a initiates his authentication toward B and b by handing his trust credential to b. This credential cannot be utilised by b directly to authenticate a, but is rather used as a pledge which is then redeemed by b at the principals. To that end, b uses some secret X he shares with his principal to protect τ_a. X can for instance be established using the Diffie-Hellman method [17]. The protection of τ_a by X prevents a and A from tampering with the authentication request that is embodied in the message $X(\tau_a)$ passed on to B.

It should be noted that, apart from transport and addressing information, a and A need not know for which of A's agents authentication is requested, if X comprises encryption. Thus, the identity of the authenticated agent a could be kept secret from A in an advanced scenario. This could be used to protect the privacy of agents in the domain of A, e.g., with respect to their purchasing patterns.

B sends τ_a to A and with that requests from A the authentication of it. If A does not have a registry of all valid trust credentials in his domain or any other means of authenticating them then A has to exert a secondary authentication of a by the generic credential $\gamma_{a,A}$ (again assuming that association of τ_a to γ_a is possible). A acknowledges the identity of a to B. This acknowledgement is passed on from B to b, again protected by a shared secret Y to prevent tampering with it on its way.

4   Conclusions

We introduced the notion of transitive trust for a pragmatic purport. It is intended as a conceptual blueprint for the systematic construction of concrete, TC-based application scenarios. The examples exhibited show that transitive trust has a potential to be a fertile concept to that end. In particular, new application and business scenarios are enabled by transitive trust as well as more efficient and/or more secure implementations of old ones. Protection of privacy is not in opposition to the use of TC in those scenarios. It can, on the contrary, be supported in carefully constructed implementation variants of transitive trust.

Returning to the possibility of formalising our concepts, let us briefly sketch how they relate to those of [9, Sections 2 and 3]. Firstly, for a full treatment not only principals and agents must be taken into account, but also the trusted computing base (TCB) which can issue the assertions 1.–3. about an agent. That is, in every of the three operations the agent speaks for its TCB in transmitting, as a channel, the trust credential and the assertions to the principal. In this way the TCB *hands off* authority to the agent to speak on its behalf. It must then be shown that this procedure establishes a credential (in the sense of [9]) for the agent. The joint authentication with respect to the agent's principal using the ordinary and the trust credential is stronger than the original one. In the case of subordination for instance, it allows a secondary hand-off from the subordinated to the subordinating agent, allowing the principal to infer the authenticity of the former. This proceeding would establish a formal description of the most basic technical operation used in all three transitive trust operations. It must be accompanied and complemented by a formalisation of transitivity *per se* on a higher conceptual level, as in [8]. Both formal levels must be coherently interweaved to produce a full formalisation of our concepts. This task, which is well beyond the scope of the present paper, should be treated elsewhere.

Economically the prospect to federate the identities of millions of subscribers of mobile networks with other providers of goods and services, is rather attractive. As said, transitive trust is very similar to identity federation, but TC has additional application potential due to the possibility to transgress boundaries of authentication domains that are closed to IDM on the application layer. The standard way of remote attestation using trusted computing [11] is analogous to classical ID federation in that every TPM is assigned to the domain of trust of its manufacturer *and* the device vendor *viz* OEM via the platform endorsement keys. Thus every TPM-equipped device has an unique identity which can be resolved by these principals who in turn can act as identity providers. Demand for provisioning of identity federations in the mobile domain is confirmed by the recent market survey [1, Section 6] — whether MNOs or other parties are ready to take on that role remains to be seen.

While this way of TC-based remote attestation does not provide for anonymity the novel feature DAA in the TCG specification version 1.2 is qualitatively very different. Resting on involved methods of zero-knowledge proofs [13] it enables a trusted platform in principle to convince the outside world of any of the assertions 1.–3. without revealing its identity, with cryptographic security. In particular, this could be used to issue trustworthy assertions about the membership of a trusted device in a certain domain while staying fully anonymous. Namely, the system state asserted by DAA can include information about the presence of a generic domain credential on the device, without revealing it. This potentially opens up a new area of research and applications centred around methods of anonymous, privacy-protecting, methods for the establishment of trust.

A particular trait of transitive trust mentioned above is the enabling of de-centralised authentication through the trusted agents. A benefit of such approaches can be enhanced resilience and availability of service access. They can also be a base for de-centralised authorisation and ultimately de-centralised business models, such as super-distribution of virtual goods from agent to agent, cf. [18, 19, 20].

As a further example, in an advanced scenario for the restriction operation, it can be envisaged that a group of agents defines itself in a manner similar to building a web of trust [21] of which PGP is a well-known instance [22]. To that end, the transposition operation could be used to establish mutual trust between agents, extend it to trust paths in a community, and eventually define the subgroup as the resulting web of trust.

References

1. KPMG:Consumers and Convergence - Challenges and opportunities in meeting next generation customer need. 2006. `http://www.kpmg.de/about/press_office/13611.htm`
2. Marhöfer, M., Schmidt, A. U.: Trusted Integration of Mobile Platforms into Service-oriented Networks. Contribution to the 11th German-Japanese Symposium "Security, Privacy and Safety in the Information Society" of the Mnchner Kreis, Tokio, Japan, 13th-16th September 2005

3. Li, F., Whalley, J.: Deconstruction of the telecommunications industry: from value chains to value networks. Telecommunications Policy **26** (2002) 451–472
4. Ulset, S.: Mobile virtual network operators: a strategic transaction cost analysis of preliminary experiences. Telecommunications Policy **26** (2002) 537–549
5. Clauß, S., Köhntopp, M.: Identity management and its support of multilateral security. Computer Networks **37** (2001) 205–219
6. Rannenberg, K.: Identity management in mobile cellular networks and related applications. Information Security Technical Report **9** (2004) 77–85
7. Lopez, J., Oppliger, R., Pernul, G.: Authentication and authorization infrastructures (AAIs): a comparative survey. Computers & Security **23** (2004) 578–590
8. Jsang, A., Gray, E., Kinateder, M.: Simplification and Analysis of Transitive Trust Networks. Web Intelligence and Agent Systems, to appear. http://security.dstc.edu.au/papers/JGK2005-WIAS.pdf
9. Lampson, B., Abadi, M., Burrows, M., Wobber, E.: Authentication in distributed systems: theory and practice, ACM Transactions on Computer Systems (TOCS) **10** (1992) 265 - 310
10. Maurer, U.: Modelling a Public-Key Infrastructure In: Proc. 1196 Symposium on Research in Computer Security (ESORICS' 96), E. Bertino (Ed.), Lecture Notes in Computer Science, vol. 1146, Berlin: Springer-Verlag, 1996, pp. 325–350
11. Trusted Computing Group: TPM Specification Version 1.2 Revision 85. February 2005. www.trustedcomputinggroup.org
12. Brickell, E., Camenisch, J., Chen, L.: Direct anonymous attestation. In: Proc. 10th ACM Conference on Computer and Communications Security, Washington DC, ACM Press, 2004
13. Camenisch, J.: Better Privacy for Trusted Computing Platforms. In: Proc. 9th European Symposium On Research in Computer Security (ESORICS 2004), Sophia Antipolis, France, September 13-15, 2004, Springer-Verlag, 2004, pp. 73–88
14. Bruschi, D., Cavallaro, L., Lanzi, A., Monga, M.: Attacking a Trusted Computing Platform. Improving the Security of the TCG Specification. Technical Report RT 05-05, Dipartimento di Informatica e Comunicazione, Universitï¿½degli Studi di Milano, Italy, 2005
15. Cheney, P.: How a terror group cloned Ted Rogers' cellphone. The Globe and Mail, Toronto, Canada, December 17, 2005
16. NTT DoCoMo, IBM, Intel Corporation: Trusted Mobile Platform Protocol Specification Document — Revision 1.00. 04/05/2004. http://www.trusted-mobile.org
17. Diffie, W., Hellman, M. E.: New Directions in Cryptography. IEEE Transactions on Information Theory **22** (1976) 644–654
18. Schmidt, A.: Incentive Systems in Multi-Level Markets for Virtual Goods. In: [23] 134–141
19. Schmucker, M., Ebinger, P.: Alternative Distribution Models based on P2P. In: [23] 142–149
20. Rajasekaran, H.: An Incentive Based Distribution System for DRM Protected Content Using Peer-to-Peer Networks. In: [23] 150–156
21. Khare, R., Rifkin, A.: Weaving a web of trust, World Wide Web Journal **2** (1997) 77–112
22. Zimmermann, P.: The PGP user's guide, the International PGP Home Page, October 1994. www.pgpi.org
23. Nesi, P., Ng, K., Delgado J. (Eds.): Axmedis 2005, Proceedings of the 1st International Conference on Automated Production of Cross Media Content for Multi-Channel Distribution, Volume for Workshops, Industrial, and Application Sessions, Firenze University Press, 2005.

An Open, PKI-Based Mobile Payment System

Marko Hassinen, Konstantin Hyppönen, and Keijo Haataja

University of Kuopio, Department of Computer Science
POB 1627, FIN-70211, Kuopio, Finland
{Marko.Hassinen, Konstantin.Hypponen, Keijo.Haataja}@uku.fi

Abstract. Most mobile commerce applications require a secure mobile payment solution for performing financial transactions. However, it is difficult to strongly authenticate users remotely and provide non-repudiation of transactions. In this paper, we present a novel mobile payment scheme which supports both virtual point-of-sale (POS) and real POS transactions. For user authentication, our scheme uses PKI-SIM cards. In virtual POS payments, the mobile phone communicates with a service provider through SMS messaging or IP-based data transfer (e.g. GPRS). In real POS payments, Bluetooth is used as the communication channel. Communication with a bank is done using either SMS messaging or IP-based data transfer. The system is open to any mobile network operator, any merchant, and any financial institution.

1   Introduction

Mobile payment (MP) is a potential killer application in future mobile networks. Active development efforts in the mobile payment domain are boosted by tough competition between mobile network operators, financial institutes, and payment service providers. The common goal is enhancing customer service by providing new payment solutions, with the hope to grow the customer base and, ultimately, increase revenues.

In the third quarter of year 2005 there were 2.03 billion mobile phone users globally [1]. In many countries it is more common for people to have a mobile phone than to have a credit card. Considering vending machine payments, it is often easier for a user to have their mobile phone in a pocket, rather than a suitable set of coins or banknotes. Mobile payment is therefore an attractive service for many mobile network users. Moreover, in some cases switching to mobile payments provides benefits not only to customers, but also to the service providers. For example, vending machines that accept cash or credit cards have moving parts and thus require regular maintenance. Besides that, someone has to remove money from the machine regularly.

Various mobile payment scenarios have been devised (see [2] for a survey), and many of them are now in active commercial use. However, expectations that exist among participants of an MP service are rather divergent, and meeting them have proved to be difficult. It is very often, for instance, that an MP solution deals only with micro-payments or mini-payments (less than $20). Services that can process

G. Müller (Ed.): ETRICS 2006, LNCS 3995, pp. 86–100, 2006.

macro-payments usually involve independent MP providers that act as mediators between mobile network operators and credit companies. This increases the cost of a payment, and makes the system less transparent from the user's perspective, decreasing trust. Moreover, most of the solutions support only virtual point-of-sale (POS) transactions, while customers expect them to work at a real POS. Many payment models rely on the traditional Short Message Service (SMS) as the carrier of payment-related data. However, SMS messages can be forged [3], potentially making the MP solution untrustworthy and insecure.

Our results: This paper describes a mobile payment scheme that is based on a governmental Public Key Infrastructure (PKI). The scheme does not involve any MP mediator. Two mobile payment protocols are presented: a protocol for virtual POS payments, and a protocol for real POS (or vending machine) payments.

Before proceeding with more detailed description of our MP scheme, we give an overview of existing MP solutions. We concentrate in more detail on a few examples of schemes that either provide the same functionality, or use similar ideas in their implementation.

1.1 Related Work

The simplest mobile payment schemes are based on calling a premium phone number or sending a premium SMS message. The amount of payment is then charged on the phone bill. A drawback of this approach is that there is no possibility to authenticate the phone user. This creates a problem for instance in the case when a phone gets stolen. Since the system does not provide any kind of non-repudiation, users may argue that they have not used their phones for making payments. Because of this particular reason current systems have been limited to products with small monetary value, such as newspapers, candies or lemonade.

The risks related to poor authentication and non-repudiation are mitigated in many schemes by introducing an extra MP provider that takes care of them. Users sign up for the MP services and either establish a pre-paid account within the MP provider system, or register a debit/credit card to be charged for future payments. In addition to better support for macro-payments, this solution provides flexibility: users of different mobile networks and even from different countries can use the same MP provider company. A drawback of such schemes is that payment mediators charge an extra premium, making use of the system more expensive. Moreover, handling pre-paid accounts used in many schemes and controlling balance on them is an extra burden placed on users of the system.

Mobipay[1] is a typical example of a payment mediator. It works currently in Spain, and is expected to be introduced in other countries in the future. Mobipay works for both virtual and real POS payments. In a real POS payment the merchant enters the user's identifier (their phone number or alias), or scans the barcode attached to the user's phone. Details of the payment, such as the price of purchased products and the name of the shop, are then sent to the user's phone. USSD (Unstructured Supplementary Service Data, a session-oriented version of

---

[1] http://www.mobipay.com

SMS) is used as the channel for sending this message. The user confirms the payment by entering their PIN code associated with Mobipay.

In a virtual POS payment on the Internet, the customer gets the reference number that has to be entered at the mobile phone along with the PIN code. The user sends the message to Mobipay, after which both the user and the merchant receive a confirmation of the payment.

Mobipay can also handle vending machine and invoice payments, which are performed in a similar way. Payments are charged to a debit or credit card, or to the user's pre-paid account.

In Mobipay, the network operator is a trusted party. However, it does not produce sufficient evidence for later adjudication in case if a dispute arises. Users can theoretically repudiate transactions, claiming that they never entered the PIN code, and that everything was generated by the network operator. This problem must be solved by additional security measures, for example, by introducing a reliable storage for transaction logs on the network operator side, and keeping it under control of a trusted auditor.

MP schemes that use extra PIN codes for confirmation of payments provide better authentication than those based on simple SMS messaging. Stolen or lost mobile phone is not a problem in these systems. An exception, however, is the case when the attacker first learns the PIN code for mobile payments by shoulder surfing, and then steals the phone.

To provide stronger authentication and non-repudiation, some systems use mobile PKI. Several smart card vendors manufacture SIM cards with PKI capabilities, providing an off-the-shelf solution for mobile network operators. Mobile PKI can be used as a way to strongly authenticate a user in numerous mobile applications [4]. A message with a valid digital signature can be used to show commitment, and it can provide non-repudiation. Confidentiality of the communication can be also guaranteed.

SmartPay (MobilHandel)[2] is an MP scheme developed by Telenor, a Norwegian mobile operator. SmartPay uses mobile PKI for authentication and non-repudiation. The certificate of each user is stored in their SIM card, in a PKI application implemented as a SIM toolkit applet. SmartPay can handle virtual POS payments of orders created by SMS messages or by browsing the merchant's WAP pages. When the merchant receives an order, it sends a request to Telenor mCommerce PKI-server to confirm the payment. The user is identified by their mobile phone number. The PKI-server generates an SMS request with a transaction value for the payment and sends it to the user's phone. In the phone the request is forwarded to the PKI application. At this step the user can choose the means of payment: phone bill or a credit card registered in the system. The transaction value is signed using the user's private key and sent back to the mCommerce PKI-server. Upon successful verification of the signature, the server sends confirmations of the payment to both the merchant and the user.

In some MP schemes not only the GSM functionality of the mobile phone is used, but also other communication technologies that are implemented in either the

---

[2] http://telenormobil.no/mobilhandel

phone or the SIM card. Short-range communication channels are used for payments at a cash register or for exchange of electronic cash between two mobile phones. An incomplete list of these channels contains Bluetooth, infrared ports (IrDA), and direct wireless connection to the SIM card. Other prominent technologies are RFID and NFC; however, we are not aware of any current MP schemes that use them.

An example of such systems is *Beamtrust*[3], an MP system developed in Denmark. It supports in-store payments and allows to withdraw money from ATMs. The mobile phone uses Bluetooth or infrared link for communication with the cash register or the ATM. In the case of an in-store payment, the user brings their mobile phone in a close proximity to the payment terminal. The total price of purchased goods is transmitted to the phone via Bluetooth or IrDA and shown on the screen. The user accepts the payment by entering their PIN code.

Although functionality of our system is similar to that of Mobipay, and the use of mobile PKI corresponds to that in SmartPay, the ideology of our MP scheme is rather different. Instead of relying on independent payment processing companies or on agreements between mobile network operators and credit card companies, our system uses governmentally controlled PKI. The SIM card contains a certificate issued by the Population Register Centre (PRC) of Finland. The certificate database maintained by PRC is freely accessible to everybody. Therefore, our system is open to any mobile network operator, any merchant, and any credit card company.

The rest of the paper is organized as follows. Section 2 gives a short introduction to the technologies used in our MP scheme. Section 3 provides an overview of the mobile payment model and describes two protocols for mobile payments: one for virtual POS payments, and another one for real POS payments. We further discuss the protocols and provide their security and privacy analysis in Sect. 4. Finally, Sect. 5 summarizes our conclusions.

2   Underlying Technologies

This section gives an overview of technologies used in the design of our MP system. We describe the public key infrastructure, communication technologies, and issues related to certificate validity assurance.

2.1   FINEID

For authentication of users, we use PKI provided by the Finnish Population Register Centre [5]. The centre issues electronic identity cards that contain three certificates:

1. Card holder's authentication and encryption certificate;
2. Card holder's non-repudiation certificate;
   (The key usage objects of these two certificates define different key usage policies; otherwise certificates are technically the same.)
3. Population Register Centre's own Certification Authority (CA) certificate.

---

[3] http://www.beamtrust.com

The card holder's private keys are stored in the memory of this tamper resistant card. There are no other copies of these keys, and it is practically impossible to manufacture duplicates of the card. This suits perfectly our requirements for authentication and non-repudiation.

Finnish Electronic Identification (FINEID) [5] application manages the contents of the electronic identity card and provides a command interface for performing private key operations. The card authenticates its user by a PIN code.

Population Register Centre maintains an online certificate directory (FINEID directory). Each registered individual gets a unique Finnish Electronic User ID (FINUID). Public keys of each user can be downloaded upon a search with appropriate criteria. Besides that, revocation list of invalid certificates is available from the FINEID directory.

Recently, it has become possible to include the FINEID functionality on SIM cards for mobile phones. In our MP scheme SIM cards perform digital signature and decryption operations, whereas encryption and signature verification are done by the mobile phone. Validity of certificates used in the MP scheme is checked upon the FINEID directory.

2.2   Bluetooth and NFC

Bluetooth [6] is a technology for short range wireless data and two-way voice transfer providing data rates up to 3 Mb/s. It operates at 2.4 GHz frequency in the free ISM-band (Industrial Scientific Medicine) using frequency hopping, and is supported by a wide range of various devices. The price of a Bluetooth chip has become reasonable and it is very common in modern mobile phones. In our MP scheme, Bluetooth is used as a communication channel in vending machine payments.

Although all data exchanged via Bluetooth is encrypted using built-in encryption with 128-bit keys, we use Bluetooth as an untrusted transport media. All sensitive data is encrypted on the application level. Integrity and freshness of messages is ensured by digital signatures, timestamps, and nonces.

In real POS payments, Near Field Communication (NFC) could be used instead of Bluetooth or in addition to it. The benefit of using NFC is its shorter working distance (about 20 cm). In places where POS terminals are placed close to each other NFC provides an easier way for ensuring that a proper terminal is contacted. NFC can be also used to initiate and configure the Bluetooth communication. The drawback, however, is that NFC is still supported only by a few devices, whereas Bluetooth is already widespread.

2.3   J2ME and SATSA

We propose to use Java 2 Micro Edition (J2ME) [7] as the programming platform for implementing the mobile phone part of the MP application. Theoretically, other platforms could also be used, as long as they provide a way to access extended features of the SIM card (the FINEID application). In J2ME, this is achieved by an optional package, *The Security and Trust Services API* (SATSA) [8]. Among other features, the SATSA specification defines methods for communication with applications on the SIM card, by exchanging messages in the APDU format [9].

A number of new mobile phones support features defined by the SATSA specification. Expectedly, this number will grow in the near future.

2.4   Secure Message Exchange

To provide confidentiality, authentication and non-repudiation of messages that constitute a payment transaction, messages are encrypted and signed. Figure 1 depicts the secure message exchange scheme, showing the process of delivering a message from the vending machine to the mobile phone. The same scheme is used also if a message is sent from the bank; however, SMS or IP-based data transfer is used instead of Bluetooth in this case. Operations with the private key of the mobile user are performed on the SIM card. If a message is originating from the mobile phone, FINEID application on the SIM card signs the message.

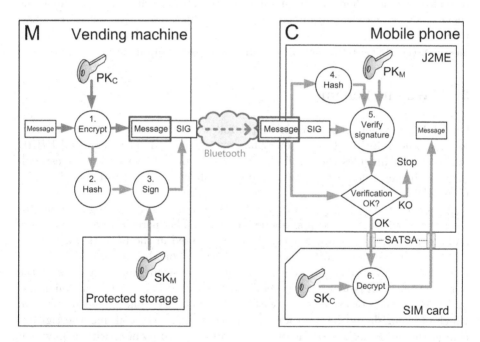

Fig. 1. An example of secure message exchange. SMS or IP-based data transfer can be used instead of Bluetooth.

2.5   Certificate Validity Assurance

With mobile devices, one clear restriction is the amount of available permanent storage. With the traditional certificate revocation list (CRL) approach we have to download the full CRL to the client, and the amount of storage needed for this may be too big for a mobile device. Moreover, downloading the full list to a mobile device can be rather slow and expensive to the user.

Protocols such as OCSP (Online Certificate Status Protocol) [10] and DPV (Delegated Path Validation) [11] can be used to offload most of the validation process from the client to a server. These protocols relieve the client from downloading the bulky CRL. However, as in some cases a POS terminal does not have a connection to the Internet, it cannot use the abovementioned protocols. We propose a solution where clients (mobile phones) provide proofs of the validity of their certificates. The client can request such for their certificate from the OCSP server. The proof contains the status of the certificate and it is digitally signed (see 2.2 in [10]). The POS terminal can then verify this signature and be confident that the certificate had the stated status at the time the proof was issued.

One problem still remains, since the POS terminal cannot get a current timestamp from the OCSP server. This means that it might be possible for a client to replay an old OCSP token in a fresh message. To avoid this we use a challenge-response scheme, where the terminal sends the client a challenge for which the client has to show a timestamped response by the same OCSP server. For simplicity we propose to have one signature which ties together the response, the message, the timestamp, and the certificate validity statement.

3   Payment Scheme

Our mobile payment scheme includes the following parties. A *customer* is a user of a hand-held device. The customer has received a SIM card with the FINEID applet, which includes the public key certificate of the user and a corresponding private key. Identity of the customer is their Finnish Electronic User ID (FINUID).

A *merchant* is an owner of a point-of-sale terminal (or a vending machine) or a service provider that accepts mobile payments. The merchant has a secret key and a corresponding public key certificate registered in the FINEID system.

A *bank* or another credit organization like VISA or MasterCard is a financial institution that acts as a payment processor. The customer has an account in the bank, or has been issued with a credit card operated by it. If the customer has multiple accounts or credit cards within the bank, the bank has been informed which of them should be used for mobile payments. The bank has the right to charge the customer's account or credit card when presented with a payment order signed by the customer's private key.

In this section we describe two mobile payment protocols: one for a virtual POS payment, and another for a real POS (vending machine) payment. The following notation is used in the description: C is a customer, M is a merchant, and B is a bank. ID_X is the identity of subject X. SK_X is the secret RSA key of subject X, and PK_X is the corresponding public key. Cert_X is the public key certificate of subject X. $\{m\}_K$ denotes RSA encryption of the message m under the key K. SIG_{XY} is a digital signature generated by X, intended to be verified by Y. H is a hash function; we use SHA-1 in our protocol.

3.1   Virtual POS Payment

Our protocol for a virtual POS payment contains the following steps (Fig. 2):

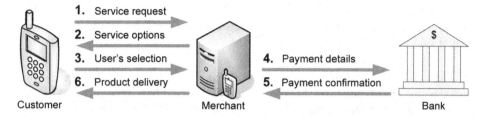

Fig. 2. Virtual POS Payment Model

1. Service request. In phase 1, the customer initiates the protocol with the merchant by requesting product options. The request may contain information which limits possible options.

$$C \xrightarrow{\text{Service request}} M$$

2. Service options. In phase 2, the merchant sends a list of options to the mobile device. The list includes short descriptions of products and pricing information. The merchant also attaches its certificate to the list of options.

$$M \xrightarrow{\text{Service options}|\text{Cert}_M} C$$

3. Product selection. In phase 3, the customer is prompted by the mobile device to select a product from the list. The information on the customer selection is sent to the merchant. The selection is signed using the private key of the customer. The message is

$$C \xrightarrow[\text{SIG}_{C_B} = \{H(TS_C|ID_M|AM)|H(PD|N_C)\}_{SK_C}]{\text{MSG} = \left\{PD|N_C|TS_C|\{H(PD|TS_C)\}_{SK_C}|ID_B|\text{SIG}_{C_B}\right\}_{PK_M}} M$$

where N_C and TS_C are a random nonce and a timestamp generated by the customer C, AM is the amount of money the purchase will cost and PD is a string that describes product details.

4. Payment request. Phase 4 of the protocol includes the merchant sending the payment details to the credit company. This payment information is signed using the merchant's private key and encrypted using the public key of the credit company. The message in phase 4 includes merchant's details and payment details, such as amount, id of the customer and the signed message received in phase 3.

$$M \xrightarrow[\text{SIG}_{M_B} = \{H(ID_M|ID_C|TS_C|AM|H(PD|N_C))\}_{SK_M}]{\text{MSG} = \left\{ID_M|ID_C|TS_C|AM|H(PD|N_C)|\text{SIG}_{M_B}|\text{SIG}_{C_B}\right\}_{PK_B}} B$$

In this message SIG_{C_B} is the same signature as in phase 3. After receiving this message the credit company B checks that the timestamp TS_C is newer than the timestamp of the previous communication to detect any replay attacks.

It is possible for the merchant to sign a contract for processing mobile payments with a single acquiring bank. In this case M sends the message to the acquirer. The acquirer has to pass the message to B, receive the payment confirmation (see step 5) and forward it to M.

5. Payment confirmation. The indicated amount of money is transferred from the account of the buyer to the account of the seller. Phase 5 is initiated by the credit company if this transaction can be processed and finalized. The credit company sends a confirmation message to the merchant. The message is signed using the private key of the credit company.

$$B \xrightarrow{\text{MSG=}\{H(ID_M|ID_C|TS_C|AM|H(PD|N_C))\}_{SK_B}} M$$

From this message the merchant can check that the payment was made with the agreed amount AM from the account of C to the account of M. The hash value $H(PD|N_C)$ is meant for the customer to make sure that the merchant can not claim that the customer bought something else than the original product.

6. Product delivery. Finally, in phase 6, the merchant checks the message received in phase 5. If the message is valid and the payment has been done, the merchant delivers the product to the customer. The merchant also sends the customer a message stating that the payment has been made and the product has been delivered.

$$M \xrightarrow{\text{MSG=}\{H(ID_M|ID_C|TS_C|AM|H(PD|N_C))\}_{SK_B}} C$$

The customer can check that the amount of money AM, product details PD, the nonce N_C and the timestamp all match the original values to be sure that the correct amount was paid for the correct product.

3.2   Real POS (Vending Machine) Payment

Our protocol for a secure vending machine payment contains the following steps (see Fig. 3):

1. Initiation. The customer C initiates the protocol with the merchant M by choosing a product. In case the vending machine supports several ways of payment, the user may need to explicitly select the mobile payment option. Optionally, the protocol can be initiated by the vending machine, which detects the device when it comes in the range of the Bluetooth communication. No messages are sent in this phase.

2. Bluetooth pairing. To enable exchange of messages, Bluetooth pairing must be performed between the vending machine and the mobile phone. If several Bluetooth devices are in the range, the machine can use a random PIN code for pairing and show this PIN on its display. User must enter this PIN code in the mobile phone.

3. Product offer. If the user has not selected a product yet, the vending machine sends a message with information about available products and their prices. In case phase 1 was initiated by the user, and the product is already selected, the list of products contains only the selected item. In addition to this data, the vending machine sends its own certificate $Cert_M$ and a random nonce N_M.

$$M \xrightarrow{\text{MSG=Cert}_M|N_M|\texttt{List of products}} C$$

After receiving the message, C extracts M's certificate and checks its validity.

4. Product selection. The user is prompted by the mobile device for selection of a product, unless it has already been selected. The information on the user selection is sent to the vending machine. Also, the customer's certificate $Cert_C$ is included in the message.

The mobile phone must store the price AM of the selected product, as it will be needed later on for payment.

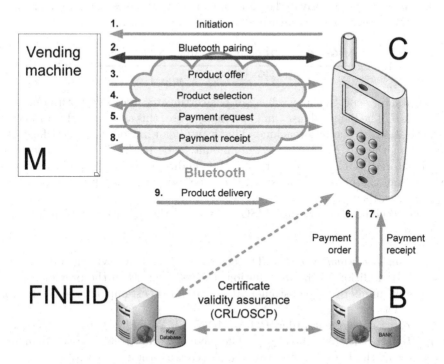

Fig. 3. A Mobile Payment Protocol for Vending Machines

The message in phase 4 consists of three parts. The first part is the user's selection S, and a nonce N_C generated by the mobile device. This part of the message is encrypted with the vending machine's public key PK_M. Second, the user's certificate Cert_C is appended to this message. The last part of the message is a signature $\text{SIG} = \{H(S|N_M|N_C)\}_{SK_C}$.

$$C \xrightarrow[\text{SIG}=\{H(S|N_M|N_C)\}_{SK_C}]{\text{MSG}=\{S|N_C\}_{PK_M}|\text{Cert}_C|\text{SIG}} M$$

After receiving the message, M extracts C's certificate and verifies it. After this M decrypts the message MSG obtaining S and N_C. To conclude, M verifies the signature SIG using the customer's public key. The vending machine could also check the certificate revocation list to see that the user certificate has not been revoked, but this checking can also be made responsibility of the bank.

5. *Payment request.* The vending machine sends a payment request to the mobile device. The request is signed using the vending machine's private key SK_M.

The payment details include the account number ACN_M, and a reference id of the vending machine ID_M. Note that the price of the product is not sent with the payment details, since C already knows it. However, it is included in a hash in the second part of the message. Namely, C's certificate, price of the product AM, and two nonces N_M and N_C are concatenated, hashed, signed with the vending machine's private key and appended to the message MSG. The last part of the message is a signature $\text{SIG} = \{H(\text{MSG})\}_{SK_M}$.

$$M \xrightarrow[\text{SIG}=\{H(\text{MSG})\}_{SK_M}]{\text{MSG}=ACN_M|ID_M|\{H(\text{Cert}_C|AM|N_M|N_C)\}_{SK_M}|\text{SIG}} C$$

C will later send the signed hash of C's certificate, price and both nonces to the bank B. The bank will use (and optionally store) this as a proof of transaction authorization by vending machine. This way C can not offer one certificate to M and another to B, or change the amount to be paid. The signed hash can also be stored by C as a receipt from the vending machine. Combined with a receipt from the bank (see phase 7), it can be used later as a proof of purchase if a dispute arises.

After receiving the message MSG, C verifies the signature SIG using M's public key.

6. *Creation of a payment order.* The customer C sends a payment order to the bank B. In addition to the information received from M in the previous steps, an account number of the customer ACN_C and a timestamp TS are needed for the transaction.

C creates a payment order $PO = ACN_C|ACN_M|ID_C|ID_M|AM|N_M|N_C|$ $|TS|\{H(\text{Cert}_C|AM|N_M|N_C)\}_{SK_M}$. The payment order is sent to the bank encrypted with the bank's public key and signed with the C's private key.

$$C \xrightarrow{\begin{array}{c} PO=ACN_C|ACN_M|ID_C|ID_M|AM|TS|\{H(\mathrm{Cert}_C|AM|N_M|N_C))\}_{SK_M} \\ \hline \mathrm{MSG}=\{PO\}_{PK_B}|SIG; \ SIG=\{H(PO)\}_{SK_C} \end{array}} B$$

In this message everything except C's account number ACN_C was received from M in the previous stage. The bank B is obviously the one where the mobile phone user has an account.

Here we assume that the mobile device already has the public key of the bank. Certificates of participating banks can be installed into the device when the software is installed. We can also include a procedure for importing a certificate of a bank which has joined the protocol after the software was installed.

7. Payment processing. After receiving and decrypting the payment order, the bank verifies C's signature attached to it. For this, the bank retrieves C's certificate from the FINEID directory; ID_C is used as the search key. In the same way B gets M's certificate in order to verify the signature $\{H(\mathrm{Cert}_C|N_M|N_C))\}_{SK_M}$. This is done to make sure that the same certificate and nonces were used in communication between C and M. In addition, the bank checks that both certificates are not on the revocation list. The bank also compares the timestamp TS to the stored timestamp of the previous payment order received from C (if any) to defeat replay attacks. Upon successful pass of all checks, the bank transfers the amount of money from C's account to M's account. In case M's account is in another bank, usual interbank procedures are used for crediting money to M. If the transaction can be processed and finalized, the bank sends a confirmation message (receipt) to the mobile phone.

The receipt provides a proof that the payment has been made. The bank account number of the vending machine, amount of money and nonces N_M and N_C are hashed and signed using the bank's private key:

$$B \xrightarrow{\mathrm{MSG}=\{H(ACN_M|AM|N_M|N_C)\}_{SK_B}} C$$

C has all information needed for calculation of the same hash and verification of the bank's signature.

8. Proof of payment. In phase 8, the mobile phone forwards the bank receipt to the vending machine. In order to specify which bank's public key must be used for verification of the receipt, the bank's id ID_B is included in the message.

$$C \xrightarrow{\mathrm{MSG}=ID_B|\{H(ACN_M|AM|N_M|N_C)\}_{SK_B}} M$$

We assume that the vending machine already has certificates of participating banks. Therefore, the vending machine can decrypt the receipt using the bank's public key. The vending machine then calculates hash $H(ACN_M|AM|N_M|N_C)$ and verifies that its value is the same as in the receipt.

The vending machine must have a list of valid public keys of different banks. In case the vending machine does not have a network connection, updating and revoking bank certificates may be cumbersome. The protocol may be extended to check the validity of bank certificates by forwarding Online Certificate Status Protocol (OCSP) requests through the mobile phone to a trusted server (see 2.5 for more details).

4 Security and Privacy

The mobile payment scheme described in this paper satisfies the following security and privacy requirements. In the description, we follow the list of requirements given in [12].

Bank requirements. *Proof of transaction authorization by customer.* Customer signs the payment order that includes id of the vendor, amount of money to be paid, and a timestamp. The signature provides an undeniable proof that the customer has authorized the payment. Signatures are protected against replay attacks by timestamps. Due to their legal acceptance, signatures can be used to resolve possible disputes between the customer and the bank.

Proof of transaction authorization by vendor. Payment requests are signed by the vendor using its private key. Payment requests are not replayable neither by an external adversary nor by the customer due to use of timestamps (in the virtual POS payment) or nonces (in the real POS payment).

Merchant requirements. *Proof of transaction authorization by customer.* The mobile user signs the selection of product or service using their private key. The signature is an unforgeable proof that the customer has authenticated the transaction.

Proof of transaction authorization by bank. If the bank transaction is successfully processed, the bank generates and signes a receipt which is delivered to the merchant. If the merchant does not receive the receipt, or if verification of the signature fails, product is not delivered to the customer. The merchant can store the receipt as a proof of transaction authorization by the bank. Replaying of bank receipts is prevented by the use of timestamps and nonces.

Customer requirements. *Unauthorized payment is impossible.* It is not possible to produce valid signatures, unless one possesses a practically unforgeable token (FINEID card) of the customer and knows the PIN code corresponding to it. The security level is thus comparable to that of ATM cards.

Proof of transaction authorization by bank. In both protocols the customer receives a signed receipt from the bank. In case of a virtual POS payment, the receipt is forwarded by the merchant to the customer. In a real POS payment, the receipt is sent by the bank directly to the customer. Bank receipts are protected against replays by inclusion of timestamps and nonces.

Certification and authentication of merchant. In our MP scheme, the customer receives merchant's certificate directly from the merchant. The customer can check the validity of the certificate by submitting a query to the FINEID directory. Messages that contain product selections are encrypted under the merchant's public key. Nonces are included in these messages, to enable challenge-response authentication of the merchant. Unless the merchant possesses the secret key associated with the public key in the certificate, it cannot proceed with the payment protocol.

Receipt from merchant. In virtual POS payment the merchant forwards a signed bank receipt to the customer. The receipt states that the bank has authorized the payment, which in turn means that the merchant had asked for a payment and thus agreed to deliver the product or service. It must be noted that the merchant can always refuse forwarding the bank receipt to the customer. However, in this case the customer can use the next bank statement as a proof of purchase. In real POS payment, the customer receives two receipts: one from the vending machine as an authorization of transaction, and another one from the bank as a proof of payment.

Privacy. In an ideal payment system, merchants should not learn identities of their customers, and banks should not receive any information about the products that their customers purchase. Clearly, confidentiality of order and payment details should be protected from eavesdropping. Our MP scheme does partially satisfy these requirements. The customer sends product selection details to the merchant in encrypted form, preventing eavesdropping. Messages with payment details are also encrypted. The bank does not receive any information about the purchase except its price, and identities of the customer and the merchant. Note that although in a virtual POS payment the bank receives a hash $H(PD|N_M)$, where PD is a description of the product, a nonce N_M prevents the bank from guessing PD. The merchant learns the identity of their customer, and in a real POS payment also the name of the bank used by the customer. These are the same details as in a credit card payment.

Implementation note. The protocols, clearly, do not guarantee that there are no delays or errors in delivery of messages. There is a number of implementation details to be considered, for example, error handling. They are, however, out of scope of this paper.

5   Conclusions

In this paper we gave a short survey of current mobile payment methods and proposed a novel mobile payment scheme. The scheme can be used in real POS (Point-Of-Sale) as well as in virtual POS. The main advantage of our system is that it does not require any mediator. This reduces the total cost of a payment. We also described two protocols, one for virtual POS and another one for real POS.

The system described in this paper utilizes a governmental PKI infrastructure, namely the FINEID, making it an affordable solution since administration of the system is provided by the government. Furthermore, as citizens have adopted this system for secure electronic transactions, it has a high level of trustworthiness. Our system is built using Java to gain the best possible portability across device platforms.

The proposed mobile payment solution provides strong authentication of communicating parties, integrity of data, non-repudiation of transactions, and confidentiality of communication. Based on governmental PKI, the system is open to all merchants, financial institutions and mobile users.

References

1. GSM Association statistics, Q3 2005. http://www.gsmworld.com
2. Karnouskos, S.: Mobile Payment: A Journey through Existing Procedures and Standardization Initiatives. IEEE Communications Surveys & Tutorials, vol. **6**, no. 4, Oct. 2004.
3. Risks and Threats Analysis and Security Best Practices. Mobile Payment Forum, http://www.mobilepaymentforum.org/pdfs/MPF_Security_Best_Practices.pdf, May 2003.
4. Hassinen, M., Hyppönen, K.: Strong Mobile Authentication. Proceedings of the 2nd International Symposium on Wireless Communication Systems, pp. 96–100, Sept. 2005.
5. Finnish Population Register Centre: FINEID S1 Electronic ID Application. http://www.fineid.fi
6. Bluetooth SIG: Bluetooth specifications 1.0, 1.1, 1.2 and 2.0+EDR. Technical specifications, 1999-2004. https://www.bluetooth.org
7. Sun Microsystems, Inc.: Java 2 Platform, Micro Edition (J2ME). http://java.sun.com/j2me/
8. Java Community Process: JSR-000177 Security and Trust Services API for J2ME. http://jcp.org/aboutJava/communityprocess/final/jsr177/
9. ISO/IEC 7816-4:1995. Integrated circuit(s) cards with contacts. Part 4: Interindustry commands for interchange.
10. Myers M., Ankney R., Malpani A., Galperin S., and Adams C.: X.509 Internet Public Key Infrastructure Online Certificate Status Protocol - OCSP. RFC 2560, June 1999.
11. Pinkas D. and Housley R.: Delegated Path Validation and Delegated Path Discovery Protocol Requirements. RFC 3379, Sept. 2002.
12. Bellare, M., Garay, J., Hauser, R., Herberg, A., Krawczyk, H., Steiner, M., Tsudik, G., and Waidner, M.: iKP – a family of secure electronic payment protocols. In Proceedings of the 1st USENIX Workshop on Electronic Commerce, July 1995.

Secure Rejoining Scheme
for Dynamic Sensor Networks

Young-Sik Hwang[1,2], Seung-Wan Han[1], and Taek-Yong Nam[1]

[1] Privacy Protection Research Division,
Electronics and Telecommunications Research Institute,
161 Gajeong-dong Yusung-gu Daejeon, South Korea
{yshwang, hansw, tynam}@etri.re.kr
[2] University of Science & Technology,
52 Yeoeun-dong Yusung-gu Daejeon, South Korea

Abstract. The establishment of cryptography keys is one of the challenging problems in the sensor networks. *Key Infection* [1] is a promising model to solve this problem on the commodity sensor networks without complex mechanism. This model, however, does not consider the mobility of sensors, so if sensor nodes move out of initial communication range, then they cannot rejoin the network. So, key infection model has been limited to the static sensor network. To be applied on the dynamic sensor network, therefore, key infection model has to be extended to handle node's rejoining. In this paper, we propose secure rejoining scheme for dynamic sensor networks and verify the proposed scheme formally. Our scheme is secure, since it uses old pair-wise key information to verify sensor node's rejoining. Furthermore, our scheme does not require additional verification information and maintains the reasonable number of links.

1 Introduction

The sensor network is a promising approach for a variety of applications, such as military surveillance, habitat monitoring [7], and environment monitoring. Sensor networks will also play an essential role in the upcoming age of ubiquitous computing. However, due to sensor's constraints in computation, memory, and power resources, possibility to physical capture, and use of wireless communications, security is a challenge in the sensor network fields [8].

The establishment of cryptography keys is important primitive in security, since all secure mechanisms depend on key's security. So far, many key establishment schemes have been proposed in the traditional network fields. For example, public key cryptography make key establishment phase easy by removing complex key establishment processes [9]. In the sensor network, however, public key cryptography is not suitable, since it requires powerful computation, many memories and much energy resources. However, sensor nodes do not fully serve these requirements due to sensor's constraints mentioned above. Therefore, other key establishment schemes that are different from traditional key establishment schemes should be researched for the sensor networks. Recently, many researches have investigated and many new key establishment schemes have been proposed for the sensor networks [1, 2, 3, 4, 6].

G. Müller (Ed.): ETRICS 2006, LNCS 3995, pp. 101–114, 2006.

Most of the proposed key establishment schemes are based on symmetric cryptography, since symmetric cryptography requires low computation. In the sensor networks, one of the prevailing scheme using symmetric cryptography is *Random Key Pre-distribution* [2, 3, 4], which uses pre-loaded keys on the sensor's memory, and establishes secure connection based on probability that each other sensor nodes have the common shared keys. To maintain high probability, however, each sensor node requires many memories to store pre-loaded keys. To cope with this problem, R. Anderson et al. proposed another scheme that does not need pre-distributed key set, which is *Key Infection* [1].

Key infection model assumed an environment with a partially present passive adversary. And, the time while the nodes are doing key information exchange may last only several seconds. In this environment, it is almost impossible that adversary knows where or when sensors are deployed. Also, it is not likely that adversary has pre-compromised sensor in advance to attack sensor networks at key establishment time. With these assumptions, key infection model serves more simple and efficient key establishment than the previous probability based random key pre-distribution schemes. Although key infection model is a promising technique in commodity sensor networks, it is not considering a sensor's mobility. Therefore, key infection model's application range is limited to the static sensor network fields. In this paper, we suggest extended key infection model supporting sensor node's rejoining. This extended scheme is suitable for dynamic sensor network fields, since it allows an incoming node to rejoin networks.

The remainder of this paper is organized as follows. We describe background for this paper in Section. 2. We propose a secure rejoining scheme for key infection, which supports dynamic sensor networks that provide sensor node's mobility in Section. 3. We then analyze security and performance of the proposed scheme in Section. 4 and Section. 5. Finally, we conclude our results in Section. 6.

2 Background

In this section, we will introduce some background for this paper. We first review random key pre-distribution schemes for sensor networks [2, 3, 4]. These are representative key establishment schemes in the sensor networks. Second, we overview key infection scheme that we are based on throughout this paper. And then, we introduce key infection's drawback not supporting incoming sensor node's rejoining on the dynamic sensor networks and finish this section with an example of key infection's communication fail state on the dynamic sensor networks.

2.1 Random Key Pre-distribution Scheme

Recently, many key establishment researches are proposed and one of the active researches is random key pre-distribution scheme. In general, random key pre-distribution scheme uses symmetric cryptography that is more efficient than asymmetric cryptography, so it is suitable for the sensor node's constraints.

L. Eschenauer et al. [2] (called *EG* for simplicity) first proposed key pre-distribution scheme. In EG scheme, each node randomly selects subset keys called *key ring* from *key pool* and tries to find neighbor sensor nodes that have common shared key. If neighbor sensor node that shares same key exists, then they establish a secure connection by using the common shared key. In EG scheme, however, each node needs to pre-load enough key ring size to establish a secure connection with neighbor nodes.

Based on EG scheme, H. Chan et al. [3] (called *CPS* for simplicity) introduced the extended EG scheme and developed two key pre-distribution techniques. These are *q-composite key pre-distribution* and *random pair-wise keys*. The difference of q-composite scheme from EG scheme is that CPS requires any two nodes to share at least q common shared keys to establish a secure connection. q-composite key pre-distribution serves the sensor networks with enhanced resilience against small size attack. In CPS scheme, random pair-wise keys scheme is that each node randomly picks subset keys from key pool that consists of $n-1$ pre-generated pair-wise keys and stores subset keys with identity m that is used to distinguish pair-wise keys in the key ring. Using key ring, each node tries to find neighbor nodes that shared common pair-wise keys and to establish a secure connection by using the shared common pair-wise keys. Random pair-wise keys scheme is modification of traditional pair-wise key scheme. So, random pair-wise keys scheme provides much improved security, since it has traditional pair-wise scheme's security advantage.

W. Du et al. (called *DDHV* for simplicity) [4] presented another scheme that extended *Blom's key management scheme* [5]. Blom's scheme allows any pair of $n-1$ nodes to find a secret pair-wise key. However, Blom's scheme is not perfectly resilient against node capture attack in the sensor networks. If an adversary captures over some ratio nodes, then all nodes in the sensor networks have became insecure state. To prevent this case, DDHV scheme extended Blom's single key space to τ spaces, this extension serves sensor network with high security against the node capture attack.

All of the schemes mentioned above are promising techniques, but they do not guarantee all secure connections with all neighbor nodes not only guarantee n secure connection with probability p, but also they require many memories that store pre-distrusted keys (e.g., EG scheme's key ring, CPS scheme's key ring and DDHV scheme's key space). It means that all of mentioned schemes are not suitable for the sensor node's constraints and should need to reduce the stored pre-distributed key size. J. M. Hwang et al. [6] have researched this problem and have developed some methods that give an opportunity to reduce the pre-distributed key size.

2.2 Key Infection

R. Anderson et al. [1] proposed simple key establishment scheme called key infection for the commodity sensor networks. At economic aspects, the commodity sensor networks do not require high secure mechanism. When considering this matter, they introduced a *real attack model* that is the new type attack on the commodity sensor networks and developed *Secrecy Amplification* for enhanced security level.

The authors first defined the real attack model. The real attack model assumed the environment with a partially present the passive adversary. And also, time when the nodes exchange key information may last only several seconds in the real world. Therefore, an adversary does not know where or when sensors are deployed. And it is not likely that the adversary has the pre-compromised sensor in advance to attack the sensor network at initial key establishment time. With these assumptions, at initial key establishment time, key infection model's each node i sends key information K_i to neighbor nodes in plain text. And then receiver node j resends a pair-wise key information $\{j,K_{ij}\}_{Ki}$ to sender node i. Using this pair-wise key K_{ij}, these two nodes once establish a secure connection at initial key establishment time. Second, the authors developed secrecy amplification that reinforces the pair-wise key's security and gives security improvement to key infection model. After initial key establishment time, secrecy amplification is processed by exchanging new key information that used to reinforce initial pair-wise key through common mediator nodes.

Key infection model does not store pre-distributed keys, and it needs only key information to create pair-wise keys at key establishment time. Furthermore, key establishment process at initial key establishment time is simples, since almost of the key information is exchanged in plaintext. At the result, key infection model was suitable for commodity sensor networks and it offered simple key establishment processing.

2.3 Key Infection's Drawback on the Dynamic Sensor Network

The key infection model is a promising one in the commodity sensor networks, but it is not considering a sensor's mobility. Therefore, in key infection model, once key establishment is performed at initial key establishment time, additional key establishment process does not exist. It means that there is no rejoining scheme for incoming nodes that need new pair-wise key to communicate with networks. That is key infection's drawback when key infection model is applied on the dynamic sensor networks. This drawback leads key infection model's application range to be limited on the static sensor network fields. There are specific examples when key infection model was applied on the dynamic sensor networks (See Fig. 1, Fig. 2).

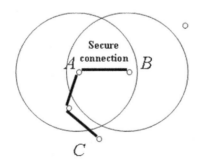

—— : Secure connection with pair-wise key

o   : Sensor node

Fig. 1. State that all sensor nodes established secure connection using the pair-wise key in key infection model. Solid line is a secure connection using pair-wise key. Small circle is a sensor node. Big circle is a sensor node's maximum communication range.

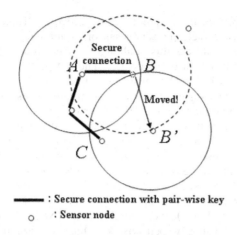

—— : Secure connection with pair-wise key

○   : Sensor node

Fig. 2. State that one sensor node moved out of neighbor node's range and this node cannot communicate with the networks, since it does not have new pair-wise key in the key infection model. Solid line is a secure connection using pair-wise key. Small circle is a sensor node. Small dashed circle is a node's position before movement. Big circle is a sensor node's maximum communication range. Big dashed circle is a old maximum communication range. Arrow means that sensor node moves from *B* to *B`*.

After initial key establishment by using key infection's key establishment scheme (See Fig. 1), in the dynamic sensor networks, if one sensor moved out of other sensors' communication range like Fig. 2, then this node cannot communicate with the networks any more, since incoming node only has old pair-wise key that can be used to securely communicate with old neighbor node (Node *A*). Therefore, incoming node requires a new pair-wise key to securely communicate with new neighbor node (Node *C*). A case like Fig. 2 frequently takes place in the dynamic sensor networks, since all sensor nodes can move on the sensor networks. When considering sensor's mobility, we need to solve this communication fail state of incoming node and to suggest secure rejoining scheme for incoming node. Otherwise the secure connection is almost disconnected on the dynamic sensor networks and almost all sensors cannot communication with the whole networks due to low secure connection degree. Therefore, we present our secure rejoining scheme for supporting sensor's mobility on the dynamic sensor networks in detail in Section 3.

3 Secure Rejoining Scheme

In this section, we present a concept of design for solving key infection model's drawback. This proposed scheme allows disconnected sensors to rejoin networks. After introducing the concept of design, we finish this section with by presenting the proposed protocol that treats the sensor's secure rejoining.

3.1 The Concept of Design

When one sensor moved out of other sensors' communication range in key infection model, it cannot communicate with networks (See Fig. 2). This is a big problem when considering applications on the dynamic sensor networks. Therefore, we need new concept that solves this obstacle and serves sensor's rejoining.

The main concept to address this challenge is using incoming node's old pair-wise key information to rejoin the networks. The old pair-wise key information is useful, when verifying whether the sensor node that wants to rejoin the networks is appropriate node or not. Since all of the appropriate nodes maintain pairs about pair-wise key information– [*Node id, Pair-wise key*] – after initial key establishment time in key infection model. It means that the appropriate pairs can be used to identity appropriate nodes. This is our main concept for secure rejoining scheme for dynamic sensor networks. With our concept, we simply present the rejoining process for incoming node and extended key infection model. The simple cases are as follows.

Using our concept, first, when one sensor (Node *B*) moved out of the secure communicate range (See Fig 2), the incoming node (Node *B'*) finds new neighbor node (Node *C*) to establish new pair-wise key that is required to maintain secure communication with the networks (See Fig. 3). Once incoming node finds new neighbor node, and then it asks new neighbor node to establish a secure connection by sending old pair-wise key information used to verify node's rejoining (See Fig. 4). After this process, new neighbor node asks old node (Node *A*) that is matched pair's node *id* field whether or not to know the incoming node (See Fig. 5). If old node knows the incoming node, then verification result message is delivered to new neighbor node through secure channel. After receipt of this message, new neighbor node decides the incoming node's rejoining. If new neighbor node received appropriate message from the old node, then new neighbor node accepts the incoming node's rejoining. Finally, the incoming node can maintain secure connection with the

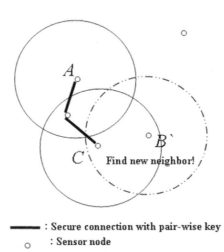

——— : Secure connection with pair-wise key

○   : Sensor node

Fig. 3. State that an incoming node finds new neighbor to establish new secure connection. Solid line is a secure connection using pair-wise key. Small circle is a sensor node. Big circle is a sensor node's maximum communication range. Dashed circle is an incoming node's maximum communication range.

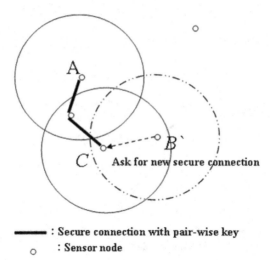

Ask for new secure connection

━━━ : Secure connection with pair-wise key
○   : Sensor node

Fig. 4. State that an incoming node asks new neighbor node to establish a secure connection. Solid line is a secure connection using pair-wise key. Small circle is a sensor node. Big circle is a sensor node's maximum communication range. Dashed circle is an incoming node's maximum communication range. Dashed arrow is a message flow using insecure channel.

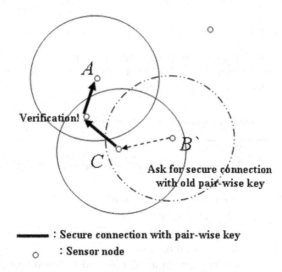

Verification!

Ask for secure connection
with old pair-wise key

━━━ : Secure connection with pair-wise key
○   : Sensor node

Fig. 5. State that a new neighbor node verifies incoming node using incoming node's old pair-wise key. Small circle is a sensor node. Big circle is a sensor node's maximum communication range. Dashed circle is an incoming node's maximum communication range. Dashed arrow is a message flow using insecure channel. Bold arrow is a message flow using secure channel.

networks (See Fig. 6.). When considering these all of the mentioned processes, the sensor's rejoining and verification are simply addressed by using old pair-wise key information over our extended key infection model.

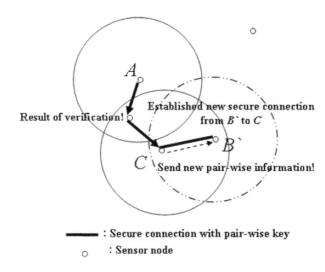

: Secure connection with pair-wise key

o   : Sensor node

Fig. 6. State that the new secure connection for incoming node is established with new pair-wise key. Solid line is a secure connection using pair-wise key. Small circle is a sensor node. Big circle is a sensor node's maximum communication range. Dashed circle is an incoming node's maximum communication range. Dashed arrow is a message flow using insecure channel. Bold arrow is a message flow using secure channel.

3.2   Detailed Protocol

In this section, we will present protocol mentioned in Section 3.1 in detail. This protocol serves secure rejoining scheme on the dynamic sensor networks. We first define and list the notations in the paper below:

Table 1. Notation used our proposed protocol

Notation	Description
Ask	The request for establishing secure connection
Ack	Acknowledgement
Yes	The result of verification
ID_i	i-th node's identification
T_i	Time information field made by node i
N	The value of nance
R	The random value that is used for challenge and response verification
S	The seed value that is used for making new pair-wise key
$old\_pairwise\_key$	The key value that incoming node has before movement
$\parallel$	Concatenation operator
$\oplus$	Exclusive or operator
K_{ij}	Pair-wise key between node i and node j
$H(.)$	One way hash function
$\{.\}_{Kij}$	Symmetric encryption function using key K_{ij}

The proposed protocol is based on the scenario mentioned at Section 2.3 and 3.1. (1) Incoming node (Node B') first finds new neighbor node (Node C) to establish new secure connection. (2) If new neighbor node is detected, then incoming node sends message $Ask \parallel ID_{b'} \parallel ID_a \parallel \{H(old\_pairwise\_key), T_b, N\}_{Kab'}$ to old node (Node A). $old\_pairwise\_key$ field is the key value that is used for secure connection before incoming node's movement, so it can be used to verify node's identity. (3) New neighbor node analyzes whether same id ($ID_{b'}$) exists in the network. (4) If same id dose not exist in the network, by using $ID_a \parallel ID_{b'}$ field, new neighbor node finds old node, and then sends $ID_a \parallel ID_b$ fields to old node. (5) Old node analyzes whether incoming node exists in its communication range. (6) If incoming does not exist, old node sends Ack message to new neighbor node. (7) After received Ack message, new neighbor node sends $\{ID_{b'}, \{H(old\_pairwise\_key), T_b, N\}K_{ab'}\}K_{ac}$ message that is used to verify incoming node's identity by old node. (8) And then, old node sends $\{Yes \parallel old\_pairwise\_key \parallel T_b+1 \parallel N\}_{Kac}$ message after $H(old\_pairwise\_key)$ message has been verified by old node. (9) If new neighbor node receives the result of verification from old node, then new node sends Ack message to old node. (10) Old node deletes old pair-wise key after receiving Ack message, since old pair-wise key value is already forwarded at the new neighbor node. (11) Once new neighbor node receives $old\_pairwise\_key$ field, by using this field and S field that generated by new neighbor node, new neighbor node calculates a new pair-wise key that is used to establish new secure connection with the incoming node. (12) After the calculation of the new pair-wise key, new neighbor node sends encrypted S field to incoming node. (13) Incoming node either calculates the new pair-wise key by using received S field. (14) After all of the processes mentioned above, the new pair-wise key is established between incoming

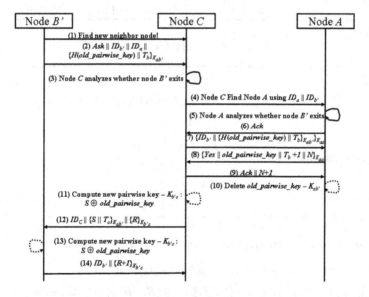

Fig. 7. Proposed protocol that processes sensor's rejoining is based on the scenario mentioned at Section 2.3. Arrow is a message flow. Dashed curve arrow is an internal process. Solid curve arrow is an external process.

node and new neighbor node. Finally, incoming node and new neighbor node verify the secure connection by using *challenge and response method*. Fig. 7 depicts this process.

4 Formal Verification

In this section, we use *BAN* logic [10] to verify our proposed protocol formally and mechanically. The BAN logic formulae and rules, which we used, are listed in Table 2 and Table 3. Since proposed protocol was extended from key infection model, we assume that the parts related to key infection model is secure. Therefore, we do not verify the whole protocol, but we only verify parts related to new pair-wise key establishment. Additionally, people who are not familiar with BAN logic refer to [10, 11] to easily understand this section.

Table 2. Common BAN logic formulae

Symbol	Denotation
$A \models X$	A *believes* X; A believes X is true.
$A \Rightarrow X$	A has *jurisdiction* over X; A is trusted on the truth of X.
$A \triangleleft X$	A *sees* X; A has received a message from which X can read.
$A \mid\sim X$	A *said* X; A has sent (or uttered) a message containing X.
$\#(X)$	X is *fresh*; X has not been sent previous to the current protocol run.
$\{X\}_K$	X is encrypted using key K.
$A_{\underline{K}}B$	A and B shares a key K which is *good* in the sense that it remains confidential to A, B and principals trusted by either A or B.

Table 3. Common BAN logic rules

Rules	Denotation
Message-meaning	$$\frac{A \models A_{\underline{K}}B, A \triangleleft \{X\}_K}{A \models B \mid\sim X}$$
Nonce-verification	$$\frac{A \models \#(X), A \models B \mid\sim X}{A \models B \models X}$$
Jurisdiction	$$\frac{A \models B \Rightarrow X, A \models B \models X}{A \models X}$$

We first can idealize our proposed protocol (See Fig. 7) as follows:

Message (8) $A \rightarrow C$: $\{old\_pairwise\_key \parallel T_b \parallel N\}_{Kac}$.

Message (12) $C \rightarrow B'$: $\{S \parallel T_c\}K_{ab'} \parallel \{R \parallel B'_{\underline{Kb'c}}C\}K_{b'c}\ from\ C$.

Message (14) $B' \rightarrow C$: $\{R \parallel B'_{\underline{Kb'c}}C\}K_{b'c}\ from\ B'$.

To analyze our proposed protocol, we give the following assumptions:

$$B' \models A \underset{K_{ab'}}{\leftrightarrow} B', \ C \models A \underset{K_{ac}}{\leftrightarrow} C, \ A \models A \underset{K_{ab'}}{\leftrightarrow} B', \ A \models A \underset{K_{ac}}{\leftrightarrow} C, \ A \models B' \underset{Kb'c}{\leftrightarrow} C$$

$$B' \models (A \Rightarrow B' \underset{K}{\leftrightarrow} C), \ C \models (A \Rightarrow B' \underset{K}{\leftrightarrow} C), \ C \models \#(N), \ C \models \#(R),$$

$$B' \models \#(T_c), \ B' \models \#(R).$$

C receives message (8), and *old_pairwise_key* is $B' \underset{Kb'c}{\leftrightarrow} C$. Therefore, the annotation rules yield $C \triangleleft \{B' \underset{Kb'c}{\leftrightarrow} C \parallel N\}_{K_{ac}}$. Since we have the hypothesis that is $C \models A \underset{K_{ac}}{\leftrightarrow} C$, the message-meaning rule for shared keys can apply and yield $C \models A \vdash (B' \underset{Kb'c}{\leftrightarrow} C \parallel N)$. And then, since we also have the hypothesis that is $C \models \#(N)$, the nonce-verification rule can apply and yield $C \models A \models (B' \underset{Kb'c}{\leftrightarrow} C \parallel N)$. Again, we break a conjunction to obtain $C \models A \models B' \underset{Kb'c}{\leftrightarrow} C$. Then, we instantiate K to $K_{b'c}$ in the hypothesis $C \models A \Rightarrow B' \underset{K}{\leftrightarrow} C$. We can derive the more concrete one that is $C \models A \Rightarrow B' \underset{Kb'c}{\leftrightarrow} C$.

Finally, the jurisdiction rule applies, and yields the following:

$$C \models B' \underset{Kb'c}{\leftrightarrow} C \tag{1}$$

This concludes the analysis of message (8).

B' receives $\{S \parallel T_c\}K_{ab'}$ that is a part of message (12), and S is $B' \underset{Kb'c}{\leftrightarrow} C$ in our protocol. Therefore, the annotation rules yield $B' \triangleleft \{B' \underset{Kb'c}{\leftrightarrow} C \parallel T_c\}_{K_{ab'}}$. Since we have the hypothesis that is $B' \models A \underset{K_{ab'}}{\leftrightarrow} B'$, The message-meaning rule for shared keys can apply and yield $B' \models A \vdash (B' \underset{Kb'c}{\leftrightarrow} C \parallel T_c)$. And then, since we also have the hypothesis that is $B' \models \#(T_c)$, The nonce-verification rule can apply and yield $B' \models A \models (B' \underset{Kb'c}{\leftrightarrow} C \parallel T_c)$. Again, we break a conjunction to obtain $B' \models A \models B' \underset{Kb'c}{\leftrightarrow} C$. Then, we instantiate K to $K_{b'c}$ in the hypothesis $B' \models A \Rightarrow B' \underset{K}{\leftrightarrow} C$. We can derive the more concrete one that is $B' \models A \Rightarrow B' \underset{Kb'c}{\leftrightarrow} C$

Finally, the jurisdiction rule applies, and yields the following:

$$B' \models B' \underset{Kb'c}{\leftrightarrow} C \tag{2}$$

The rest of message (12) is $\{R \parallel B' \underset{Kb'c}{\leftrightarrow} C\}K_{b'c}$. Therefore, the annotation rules yield $B' \triangleleft \{R \parallel B' \underset{Kb'c}{\leftrightarrow} C\}_{K_{b'c}}$. Since we have the equation (2) that is $B' \models B' \underset{Kb'c}{\leftrightarrow} C$, the message-meaning rule for shared keys can apply and yield $B' \models C \vdash (R \parallel B' \underset{Kb'c}{\leftrightarrow} C)$. And then, since we also have the hypothesis that is $B' \models \#(R)$, the nonce-verification rule can apply and yield $B' \models C \models (R \parallel B' \underset{Kb'c}{\leftrightarrow} C)$.

Finally, we break a conjunction to obtain the following:

$$B' \mid\equiv C \mid\equiv B'_{\underline{Kb'c}} C \qquad (3)$$

Equation (2) and (3) conclude the analysis of message (12)

C receives message (14). The annotation rules yield $C \triangleleft \{R \parallel B'_{\underline{Kb'c}} C\}_{K_{b'c}}$. Since

we have the equation (1) that is $C \mid\equiv B'_{\underline{Kb'c}} C$, the message-meaning rule for shared

keys can apply and yield $C \mid\equiv B \mid\sim (R \parallel B'_{\underline{Kb'c}} C)$. Since we also have the hypothesis

that is $C \mid\equiv \#(R)$. The nonce-verification rule can apply and yield

$C \mid\equiv B \mid\equiv (R \parallel B'_{\underline{Kb'c}} C)$.

Finally, we break a conjunction to obtain the following:

$$C \mid\equiv B \mid\equiv B'_{\underline{Kb'c}} C \qquad (4)$$

This concludes the analysis of Message (14).

Through equation (1) ~ (4), the final result is as follows:

$$B' \mid\equiv B'_{\underline{Kb'c}} C, B' \mid\equiv C \mid\equiv B'_{\underline{Kb'c}} C, C \mid\equiv B'_{\underline{Kb'c}} C, C \mid\equiv B \mid\equiv B'_{\underline{Kb'c}} C \qquad (5)$$

Equation (5) means that the key $K_{b'c}$ is securely established between node B' and node C. Therefore, our rejoining protocol is secure, since it has been formally verified by BAN logic.

5   Simulation

We use a simulation to investigate the effect of our proposed scheme on the dynamic sensor networks. The simulation is conducted by software program made by C language. Since the objective of this simulation is comparison between key infection and our scheme in the dynamic sensor networks, we only devise software program for application layer for key infection and our scheme. Three simulations are conducted: (a) key infection at initial key establishment time, (b) key infection scheme in the dynamic sensor networks and (c) our rejoining scheme in the dynamic sensor networks.

The simulation conditions are as follows; (1) One hundred sensor nodes are randomly deployed at restricted deployment area. (2) Sensor node's deployment area size is $80m \times 80m$. (3) Each sensor node's maximum communication range is $10m$. (4) One hundred simulations are conducted for each case. (5) In all of three cases, each node tries to establish links between all neighbors involved its maximum communication range. (6) Since initial key establishment time may last only several seconds, we assumed that the sensor node does not move at initial key establishment time. (7) We defined a dynamic sensor network's environment as follows: all of the nodes randomly move $10m$ from their position maximum 100 times in the restricted deployment area.

The simulation result of case (a), key infection scheme at initial key establishment time, shows that each node has almost 4.34 links. After initial key establishment time, since we assumed the dynamic sensor network's environment, each node can move in the deployment area with having initial pair-wise keys. In this dynamic sensor networks environment, the simulation result of case (b) shows that each node only has almost 0.38 links. It means that key infection scheme cannot maintain node's links and cannot communicate each sensor nodes due to low link's degree. Therefore, key infection scheme is not suitable for the dynamic sensor networks. Otherwise, in the same environment above, the simulation result of case (c) shows that each node has almost 3.38 links. Case (c) nearly maintained the node's links that are created at initial key establishment time. Our scheme has been developed to support sensor node's rejoining, so nodes that moved out of initial communication range can rejoin networks and maintain the node's links. When comparing case (a) to case (c), there is some reduction. This reduction is generated by the reason that our rejoining scheme has used initial pair-wise key information to rejoin to the networks. So, in our scheme, if one node has four pair-wise key after initial key establishment time, then incoming node can maintain less than four links (See Fig. 8).

All simulation results show that our rejoining scheme reasonably maintained the number of links in the dynamic sensor networks. Therefore, our scheme can be applied for the dynamic sensor networks environment. The detail simulation result is depicted on Fig. 8.

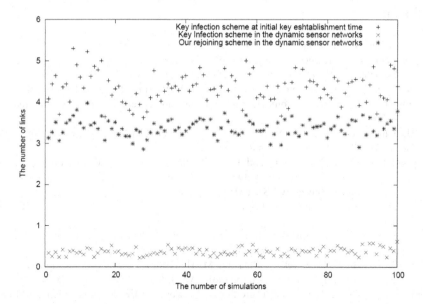

Fig. 8. Comparison of the simulation results of three cases: (a) Key infection scheme at initial key establishment time, (b) key infection scheme in the dynamic sensor networks and (c) our rejoining scheme in the dynamic sensor networks

6 Conclusions

We have presented the secure rejoining scheme for dynamic sensor networks. This considered the node's mobility characteristics like a *MANET*. Our scheme solves the sensor node's rejoining problem when node moved out of established secure communication range in the key infection. To solve this problem, we have used old pair-wise key information to verify incoming node's identity and securely extended key infection model. This old pair-wise key information has been made for secure connection before node's movement or at initial secure connection establishment time. So, only appropriate sensor nodes can have this key information in key infection model. Using these facts, we have proposed detailed protocol. It verifies incoming node's identity and accepts sensor's rejoining. Solving sensor's rejoining problem, in difference of previous key infection model that is limited on static sensor networks field, our proposed model can be used at the dynamic sensor networks field and then can be applied various applications (e.g., habitat monitoring).

We have analyzed our proposed protocol's security formally and mechanically, and also compared its performance with key infection scheme in the dynamic sensor networks by the simulation. The results of verification and simulation showed that our scheme guarantees secure rejoining and maintains the reasonable number of node's links in the dynamic sensor network. Furthermore, our proposed protocol only uses symmetric cryptography and hash function, and our scheme is suitable for the sensor network when considering sensor's constraints.

References

1. R. Anderson, H. Chan, A. Perrig, "Key Infection: Smart Trust for Smart", IEEE International Conference on Network Protocols (ICNP 2004), 2004
2. L. Eschenauer, V. D. Gligor, "A Key-Management Scheme for Distributed Sensor Networks", Conference on Computer and Communications Security. Proceedings of the 9th ACM conference on Computer and communications security 2002. Washington, DC, USA. 2002
3. H. Chan, A. Perrig, D. Song, "Random Key Predistribution Schemes for Sensor Networks", IEEE Symposium on Research and Privacy, 2003
4. W. Du, J. Deng, Y. S. Han, and P. K. Varshney, "A Pairwise Key Pre-Distribution Scheme for wireless sensor networks", In ACM conference on Computer and Communications Security (CCS), 2003
5. R. Blom, "An Optimal Class of Symmetric Key Generation Systems", In EUROCRYPT 84, 1985
6. J. M. Hwang, Y. D. Kim, "Revisiting Random Key Pre-distribution Schemes for Wireless Sensor Networks", SASN'04, Washington, DC, USA, October, 2004
7. R. Szewxzyk, E. Osterwell, J. Polastre, M. Hamiltom, A. Mainwaring, and D. Estrin, "Habitat Monitoring", Communication of the ACM, Vol. 47, No. 6, June, 2004
8. E. Shi, A. Perrig, "Designing Secure Sensor Networks. IEEE Wireless Communications", December, 2004
9. W. Diffle, M. E. Hellman, "New Directions in Cryptography", IEEE Transactions on Information Theory, Vol. IT-22, No. 6, November, 1976
10. M. Burrows, M. Abadi, and R. Needham, "A Logic of Authentication", ACM Transactions Computer Systems, February 1990
11. C. Boyd, A. Mathuira, Protocols for Authentication and Key Establishment, Springer-Verlag, 2003, 59–62

Developing Provable Secure M-Commerce Applications

Holger Grandy, Dominik Haneberg, Wolfgang Reif, and Kurt Stenzel

Lehrstuhl für Softwaretechnik und Programmiersprachen
Institut für Informatik, Universität Augsburg
86135 Augsburg Germany
{grandy, haneberg, reif, stenzel}@informatik.uni-augsburg.de

Abstract. We present a modeling framework and a verification technique for m-commerce applications[1]. Our approach supports the development of secure communication protocols for such applications as well as the refinement of the abstract protocol descriptions into executable Java code without any gap. The technique is explained using an interesting m-commerce application, an electronic ticketing system for cinema tickets. The verification has been done with KIV [BRS+00].

1 Introduction

Many m-commerce applications (e.g. electronic ticketing) transmit and store confidential user data and digital data that represents business goods. Data that is transmitted or stored is subject to modification or duplication. This poses a threat to the applications because it may lead to fraud, therefore such problems must be ruled out in order to offer a secure application. One major problem are design errors in the security protocols, another are programming errors in the protocol implementation.

Many cryptographic protocols initially had weaknesses or serious errors (see, e.g. [AN95] [WS96] [BGW01]). Different approaches have been proposed to verify the protocols, e.g. model checking based approaches [Low96] [BMV03], specialized logics of belief [BAN89], interactive theorem proving [Pau98] [HRS02] and specialized protocol analyzers [Mea96]. To cope with the problem of erroneous implementations the generic techniques for program verification can be used, but must be adapted.

This paper presents an interesting m-commerce application called Cindy for buying cinema tickets using mobile phones. It is modeled and formally analyzed using Abstract State Machines (ASM). We deal with the formal verification of the security protocols and verify a refinement step to a Java implementation. While not highly security critical, the Cindy application is simple to understand and serves to illustrate the relevant issues.

The usual verification of cryptographic protocols is focused on proving standard properties like secrecy or authenticity. We, however, focus on application

---

[1] This work is supported by the Deutsche Forschungsgemeinschaft.

G. Müller (Ed.): ETRICS 2006, LNCS 3995, pp. 115–129, 2006.

specific properties. We also do not use the common Dolev-Yao attacker model [DY83]. Instead the abilities of our attacker are tailored to realistically represent the application scenario. Additionally, the properties that must be proved are more complicated than the standard properties. Secrecy or authenticity of data is just the basis for proving the properties we are interested in, e.g. 'only tickets issued by the cinema permit entry to it'. An especially important difference to the usual protocol analysis is that we also deal with availability properties that are of interest to the customer and prove such properties without using a temporal logic.

This paper is structured as follows: Section 2 introduces the example application Cindy. In section 3 the formal application model is described, followed by the refinement to Java (section 4). Section 5 presents the security properties and their proofs, and section 6 contains a conclusion.

2   The Cindy Application

Cindy introduces electronic tickets for a cinema. A ticket is stored on the visitor's mobile phone and displayed for inspection. The service works as follows (see Fig. 1): The user orders a ticket in advance, either by Internet or with an application running on a mobile phone. Payment is handled either by credit card number or by the usual phone bill. Then the ticket is sent to the phone as a MMS (Multimedia Messaging Service) message. It contains the ticket data and

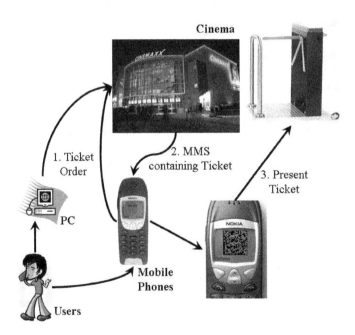

Fig. 1. The Cindy Application

an image that is unique for this ticket. On entry this image is scanned from the phone's display. This can be done automatically using a special entrance with a turnstile.[2] The application exists in the Netherlands for seven cinemas [Bee]; the authors are not aware of any other deployments in Europe.

Electronic tickets are attractive for customers because the typical moviegoer has a mobile phone, and can buy the ticket everywhere, any time without a PC and without waiting in a queue. The cinema, on the other hand, can reduce the ticket sales staff, and save on specialized paper and ink for printing tickets.

One important question for the cinema is, of course, how to avoid fraud. The idea is simple: Every ticket contains a nonce, a unique random number that is too long to guess. Therefore, it is virtually impossible to 'forge' a ticket. This nonce is displayed as a data matrix code, a two-dimensional matrix bar code that can be scanned from a handheld's display. The scanner must be connected to a server that keeps track of issued and presented tickets. It is possible to copy a ticket: A user can buy one ticket and send it to his friends. However, this is easy to detect. On entry, the server must check if this number was already presented. If this was the case the second visitor is not admitted.

The more interesting question in the context of this paper is: What can be guaranteed for the user of the service? The user must register in advance and provide payment information. Then tickets can be ordered either with a PC by Internet (with a password and using a standard SSL (Secure Sockets Layer) connection) or with a mobile phone. The ticket can be sent to an arbitrary phone number, for example as a gift. Furthermore, it is possible to pass on a ticket from one phone to another (e.g. one person buys the tickets for a group of people). We will assume that the cinema is honest, but the user should be secure from third-party attacks. We want to guarantee (and formally prove) the following properties:

1. If the user orders a ticket he will eventually receive it.
2. If the user is charged for a ticket he ordered it.
3. If the user has a ticket and presents it at the turnstile, then he will be admitted.

These properties are quite natural, and describe what one would expect. However, they do not hold in this general form. They all have preconditions, for example concerning the user's behavior: If a user sends the ticket to another phone, another person has access to the ticket and could pass the turnstile *before* the user, who then will be rejected.

(Maybe not) surprisingly, these properties are usually not considered in the world of formal (cryptographic) protocol verification. First, they do not deal with confidentiality, but rather with availability, or with things that can or will happen. This, however, is usually difficult to express formally unless temporal logic is used. Second, the usual attacker in formal protocol verification is a Dolev-Yao attacker that may analyze, modify, or suppress any protocol message between

---

[2] However, this is not unique to electronic tickets, but could be done with paper tickets as well.

any participants in real time. But if any message concerning our user is suppressed he will not be admitted to the cinema. Due to that we model a limited attacker, that cannot manipulate all communication channels.

Going to the movies requires three 'messages': 1. the ticket order (by PC or by SMS), 2. delivery of the ticket (by MMS), 3. ticket inspection at the turnstile (by visual scan). In principle, all three messages can be suppressed by an attacker. However, suppressing, manipulating, or faking the originator of a GSM (Global System for Mobile Communications) message requires either insider access or sophisticated equipment, and is out of proportion for this application. It is also very difficult to eavesdrop on a GSM connection. Suppression of the ticket presentation at the turnstile requires physical force, and can also be discounted for protocol verification purposes. The PC/Internet connection, on the other hand, can be suppressed or manipulated, but can be considered confidential if we assume that an underlying SSL protocol is secure enough. To summarize, even though the application does not actually use cryptography, it is an interesting m-commerce application with several features that are usually not considered in formal protocol verification.

3   The Abstract Model of Cindy

The formal model of the Cindy application uses a combination of Abstract State Machines (ASM) and algebraic specifications. The algebraic part contains the necessary information on the participants of the application (the so-called agents), the communication between the agents, the abilities of the attacker and so on. The dynamic aspects of the application, i.e. the possible actions of the agents, are described by the rules of the ASM. ASMs are an abstract specification formalism [BS03] [Gur95] that has a programming language-like syntax and an exact semantics. ASMs can be used for a variety of specification tasks, from programming language semantics to distributed systems. The protocol ASM describes the possible traces of the application. In this context the term 'trace' designates a possible run of the application. A trace is a list of events that may happen within the application, e.g. an activity by the attacker or a protocol step consisting of receiving some input and sending an output.

3.1   The Formal Application Model

The formal application model consists of two parts. The first part is an algebraic specification and the second part is the protocol ASM. The algebraic specification defines the used data types (e.g. the messages that are exchanged between the agents are represented by the freely generated data type **Document**, cf. [HGRS05]) and describes the communication structure of the application and how the attacker can influence the communication. The protocol ASM is a set of rules each describing a step possible for one agent type. These include, of course, the actual protocol steps by the different systems appearing in the application, but also steps that represent actions of the attacker or steps of the infrastructure representing the environment in which the application is operating, e.g. changes to the established connections. The agents consist of the users, their mobile phones, the PCs, the cinema, and the attackers. In the Cindy application we must consider attacks that involve several people, e.g. one person buys a ticket and all his buddies are admitted to the cinema as well.

3.2   Communication in the Cindy Application

The Cindy application uses different communication techniques each with very specific features. The most important ones are:

- The usage of MMS to send tickets. The GSM network guarantees[3] that a transmitted MMS cannot be manipulated and the attackers cannot eavesdrop into the communication. Also important is that the receiver of a MMS is determined uniquely (by the phone number to which the MMS is sent) and that the sender of a MMS is known to the receiver (because the phone number of the sender is contained in the MMS).
- A SSL connection between the Internet PC and the cinema. The attackers cannot eavesdrop on or manipulate the data transmitted using the SSL connection. Additionally, the user can identify the cinema as his communication partner (by checking the SSL certificate) but the cinema cannot directly identify the Internet PC.
- The visual scan of the ticket at the turnstile. We assume that the attacker can eavesdrop on the presentation of the ticket (e.g. taking a photo of the data matrix code on the customer's mobile phone display) but he cannot manipulate the presentation of the ticket. (Something that is shown on a display should never be considered secret.)

All these communication techniques are different from the Internet-like communication assumed in the formal analysis of cryptographic protocols which uses an attacker model based on the Dolev-Yao attacker [DY83]. The Dolev-Yao attacker has access to all communication, and the infrastructure does not guarantee the identity of sender and receiver. This is inadequate for the Cindy application.

All the specific features of the communication must be specified in the formal model, because they are essential for the security of the application (otherwise the security goals would not be provable). For example, the algebraic specification of the infrastructure ensures that the sender of a MMS cannot be forged by the attackers.

3.3   State of an Agent

The state of an agent is defined by the values that are currently contained in the fields of the agent (this is an object-oriented view of the agents). Therefore

---

[3] Although this is not entirely true, for the scope of this application an attack against the infrastructure seems unlikely.

the content of the fields of all agents must be stored. This is done using dynamic functions, as usual in ASM.

The state of the attackers and the users only consists of sets of documents (containing data) that they may use to generate new documents. Each user knows his personal login secret for Internet orders. The attackers initially have an empty knowledge. Since in the worst case all attackers cooperate they share a common knowledge. The state of a mobile phone consists of three lists of documents, one for the tickets stored on the cell-phone (*tickets*), one for the tickets that were passed on to another mobile phone (*passedOn*) and one for the bookings that were done by the phone (*booked*). The cinema state contains one list of documents containing the issued tickets (*issued*), all the nonces that were presented at the turnstile (*presented*), the ones that were rejected (*rejected*) and those that were accepted (*accepted*). In order to express a specific security property the information which visitor was admitted for a given ticket is stored, too (*accepted-with-presenter*). A PC stores all the ticket orders it sends to the cinema in the list *booked*.

3.4   The Protocol ASM

The protocol ASM is a nondeterministic machine built in a modular way. The ASM on top-level only chooses nondeterministically the agent that should perform its next protocol step. The nondeterministic selections ensure that the ASM can construct all possible traces of the application. On the agent level of the ASM there is a rule for each type of agent that exists in the application. After the agent was chosen the protocol ASM branches into the ASM rule that describes its behavior. All these rules consist of a case statement that tests the applicability conditions of all protocol steps specified for this type of agent until the first condition is found that holds in the current state. Then the protocol step that belongs to this condition is executed.

```
 . . .
1) if    is-comdoc(indoc) ∧ indoc.inst = loadTicket
2)     ∧ inport = 2 ∧ is-doclist(indoc.data)
3)     ∧ # indoc.data.list = 2 ∧ is-intdoc(get-part(indoc.data, 1))
4)     ∧ is-noncedoc(get-part(indoc.data, 2))
5)     ∧ #(tickets)(agent) < MAX-NO-TICKETS
6) then tickets(agent) := tickets(agent) + inmsg '
 . . .
```

Fig. 2. ASM rule for receiving tickets

For example, the protocol step that is performed by a mobile phone after it received a MMS containing a new ticket is on described in figure 2. The condition part (lines 1 to 5) states that this step will be performed only if the message that is processed is a command to load a new ticket (line 1 to 4), is-comdoc(*doc*) is a predicate that is true if *doc* has a certain form. Basically, the condition means that the data part of the MMS is well-formed, i.e. it contains an encoded ticket in a format that is accepted by the mobile phone. Line 5 demands that the list of tickets stored in the mobile phone has not yet reached its maximal accepted length. The change of the internal state for this protocol step is limited to extracting the new ticket from the MMS and appending it to the list of already stored tickets. This is done in line 6. The new ticket is represented by the variable *inmsg* which contains the message that is currently processed by the agent.

4   Refinement

Refinement is a well-established method for proving concrete implementations correct with respect to an abstract specification [HHS86] [BDW99] [WD96] [dRE98] [DB01]. When the concrete implementation adheres to certain rules, all properties of the abstract specification (especially security properties in our case) are automatically satisfied by the concrete implementation.

Refinement is difficult because when writing the specification on the abstract level, one usually does not consider how things should be implemented later. For example, when specifying a list of tickets for the mobile phone, the first thought on the abstract level would be to use an algebraically specified list of arbitrary length. To permit a later refinement and an implementation, the writer of the abstract specification has to keep such things in mind. Additionally, the encoding of certain types is different on the abstract and on the concrete level.

4.1   Refining a Protocol ASM

After specifying the protocol on an abstract level and proving security we now verify that the real implementation running on a mobile phone is correct with respect to the abstract specification. For this purpose we developed a refinement method for ASM protocol specifications. In our approach the concrete implementation contains the Java source code for the real application. In the Cindy scenario this implementation is based on the Java Micro Edition [Sun].

The KIV system supports the verification of Java source code. It includes a calculus and semantics for sequential Java [Ste04] [Ste05]. The calculus has been proven correct regarding the semantics. Verification support has been tested and improved in many case studies.

Additionally, we use a verification kernel approach [GSR05]. Verification kernels allow to extract the security relevant part of the Java source code running on the mobile phone, thereby separating e.g. the GUI (Graphical User Interface) or the Communication subsystem without losing security properties.

The general idea of the refinement approach is to combine the Java calculus with the ASM methodology in KIV. The protocol ASM is refined to another ASM in which the Java source code running in the real application is embedded. Due to the modular specification on the abstract level it is possible to do a stepwise refinement and substitute the abstract protocol part of one agent after another by a Java implementation.

The Java calculus in KIV uses a store st, which contains all the information relevant for the behavior of a certain piece of Java source code. E.g. all the Java objects of the program with their actual field values are inside the store. Basically, the store can be seen as the heap together with the internal state of the Java Virtual Machine. This store st is now part of the state of the ASM on the concrete level.

The refinement is based on Downward Simulation, which has been adapted to ASM [Sch01] [Bör03] [Sch05]. We use the following notations:

- st is the Java store
- as is the state of the abstract ASM, cs is the state of the concrete ASM, both given by the state functions (the fields of the agents)
- $step_a$ is the relation of type $as \times as$ describing one step of the abstract ASM, and $step_c$ of type $(cs \times st) \times (cs \times st)$ the one for the concrete ASM
- $init_a$ is the initialization condition on as, $init_c$ the one for $cs \times st$
- fin_a is the finalization condition (condition for termination of the ASM) on as, fin_c the one for $cs \times st$
- R with type $as \times (cs \times st)$ is the retrieve relation between the states

Figure 3 shows the relation between the abstract protocol ASM and the concrete one in the Cindy scenario.

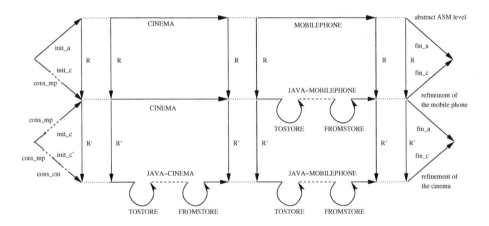

Fig. 3. Refinement Diagram

Figure 3 shows two subsequent refinements. All Java parts are shown as dashed lines. *CINEMA* and *MOBILEPHONE* are two of the possible abstract steps ($step_a$). *JAVA-MOBILEPHONE* and *JAVA-CINEMA* are possible concrete steps ($step_c$). The upper layer describes the abstract protocol specification. The middle layer represents the first refinement, in which the abstract mobile phone specification is replaced by a Java implementation. The third layer additionally contains a refinement of the cinema.

For this paper we refine the mobile phone which means that the following explains the upper two layers of figure 3.

4.2   The Cindy Implementation

The concrete ASM specification is an extension of the abstract specification, since all the agents that are not refined work as on the abstract level. What is added is the Java implementation for the phone.

As an example, the mobile phone implementation of Cindy is partially listed below:

```
public class Cindy {
    private CommInterface comm;
    private static Protocol theinstance;
    private Doclist tickets;

    public Cindy(CommInterface comm){  ... }

    public void step(){
        if(comm.available()){
            Document inmsg = comm.receive();
            phoneStep(inmsg);
        } else {  ... } }

    private void phoneStep(Document inmsg) {
        Document originator = inmsg.getPart(1);
        inmsg = inmsg.getPart(2);
        Doclist ticket = getTicket(inmsg, originator);
        if(ticket != null && tickets.len() < MAXTICKETLEN){
            tickets = tickets.attach(ticket);} }
    ...}
```

The class Cindy is responsible for executing the protocol steps. Communication with other participants is handled by the CommInterface comm, which is a field of class Protocol. The CommInterface implements a mechanism for sending and receiving objects of the class Document, which is the Java counterpart for the abstract **Document** type used in the protocol ASM. For every abstract document there exists one Java class which represents this document. The source code above is the main skeleton for receiving a ticket from the cinema. The method step() first tests whether a MMS message is available in the phone (comm.available()). Afterwards the incoming MMS is received and converted to a Java Document (inmsg = comm.receive()). The method phonestep(inmsg) extracts the ticket from this message and stores it in the local ticket store (tickets.attach(ticket)). This implementation is closely related to the abstract ASM rule for receiving a ticket, but has to deal with Java specific details like Nullpointer Exceptions.

During the initialization step of the concrete ASM the Java constructor of the Cindy class is called. In figure 3 this is shown by the Java step $cons_{mp}$ for the mobile phone and $cons_{cin}$ for a further refinement of the cinema's server application. The object resulting from the constructor call is assigned to the static field theinstance of the Cindy class. All further method calls are done on this object.

5   Proving Properties

For Cindy we consider two different kinds of security properties. Two security properties for the cinema are formalized and proved within the model, but we chose the customer's point of view as a main focus of the analysis of the Cindy application. Therefore we formalized and proved three properties that a user of the service will expect (cf. section 2). All formal specifications, theorems and proofs can be inspected on our project web page [KIV].

5.1   Security Properties of the Cinema

The following two important security properties are proven for the cinema:

1. Only tickets (i.e. nonces) issued by the cinema are accepted at the turnstile.
2. Each ticket is accepted at most once.

Given the representation of the state of the cinema (cf. section 3.3) the properties can be expressed as follows:

1. $\forall$ *ticket. ticket* $\in$ accepted(cinema) $\rightarrow$ *ticket* $\in$ issued(cinema)
2. $\neg$ duplicates(accepted(cinema))

If these two properties hold in every state that can be reached by the agent representing the cinema the corresponding security property holds at any time. Proving that these properties hold in every state is quite simple. It is just proved that the properties are invariant with respect to the protocol ASM. This is done by symbolic execution. The proof contains one branch for each possible step of the ASM and in each branch (i.e. after each protocol step) it must be proved that the property holds in the modified state given it was in the initial state. The KIV verification systems achieves a high degree of automation in the proofs (approximately 80 percent). E.g. the proof obligation for the second property is:

> **tickets-accepted-only-once:**
> $\neg$ duplicates(accepted(cinema))
> $\rightarrow$ [CINDY-STEP(as)] $\neg$ duplicates(accepted(cinema))

This theorem uses as as abbreviation for the complete state of the ASM. It states that if the accepted tickets initially had no duplicates then it holds that after all possible steps[4] of the protocol ASM the list still contains no duplicates. The proof of this property is done by symbolic execution of the ASM and almost automatic (317 proof steps and 2 interactions).

5.2   Security Properties of the Customer

In section 2 three properties that the customers of the service would expect were introduced. Formulating these security properties is not straightforward

---

[4] This is expressed using the box-operator of Dynamic Logic [HKT00]. $[\alpha] \varphi$ states that after all terminating runs of program α the property φ holds.

because they deal with availability and we do not use a temporal logic that offers operators like *eventually*. Instead, the look ahead contained in formulations like 'he will eventually receive it' is replaced by a backward analysis of all traces of the application that end in a well-formed final state. The well-formedness condition wfc(*as*) of the final state is used as termination criteria for the ASM, i.e. when the ASM terminates, the state is well-formed. In the Cindy scenario the termination condition demands that all the tickets that were issued by the cinema (and that were not lost because they were sent to a phone number that does not exist or to a phone that has no space left) were presented at the turnstile and that there are no more unprocessed messages. This can be seen as the closing of the cinema at the end of the day, when all shows are finished and all tickets were presented[5].

The properties from section 2 have the following formal representations:

1. ∀ *agent.*   mobile-phone?(*agent*)
   → ∀ *ticket.*   ordered-for(*ticket, agent,* booked)
   → *ticket* ∈ tickets(*agent*)
   (If the user orders a ticket he will eventually receive it)
2. ∀ *agent.*   user?(*agent*)
   → # bill(*agent,* issued) ≤ # booked(*agent,* booked)
   (If the user is charged for a ticket he ordered it.)
3. ∀ *ticket, agent.* owner-accepted(*ticket, agent,* tickets, passedOn,
   presented, accepted-with-presenter, inputs)
   (If the user has a ticket and presents it at the turnstile, then he will be admitted.)

The definitions given above are, of course, just a snippet of the real properties. E.g. the predicate *owner-accepted* used in property 3 has the following definition which states that each ticket that is stored in a mobile phone, and that was not passed on to another phone, and that was received from the cinema, and that was presented at the turnstile was accepted. The definition of *owner-accepted* is:

owner-accepted(*ticket, agent,* tickets, passedOn, presented,
   accepted-with-presenter, inputs)
↔   mobile-phone?(*agent*)
∧ cinema-ticket-tickets(*ticket,* tickets(*agent*))
∧ ¬ ticket-forwarded(*ticket, agent,* passedOn)
∧ *ticket* ∈ presented(cinema)
→   doclist(intdoc(*agent*.no) + noncedoc(*ticket*))
∈ accepted-with-presenter(cinema)

However, to actually prove the invariance of one of the security properties a lot of additional information is necessary. To prove property three more than 10 additional preconditions are necessary, e.g. stating that certain parts of the agent's states are well-formed. Additionally, the history of each ticket must be represented in the invariant. Basically this means that for all tickets stored in

---

[5] We assume that anybody who has a cinema ticket actually comes to see the movie.

a mobile phone their complete life-cycle must be expressed. In total, the state invariant contains almost 30 predicates, each describing a different aspect of the state of the application.

5.3 Correctness of the Refinement

In general we show that for every concrete step $\mathbf{step_c}$ starting in a state cs that corresponds to an abstract state as via the retrieve relation $\mathbf{R}$ there exists an abstract step $\mathbf{step_a}$ whose result state also corresponds to the concrete result state via the retrieve relation. The ASM refinement methodology leads to the following proof obligation:

$$\forall as, cs, cs', st, st' \; .$$
$$as \; \mathbf{R} \; (cs \times st) \wedge$$
$$(cs \times st) \; \mathbf{step_c} \; (cs' \times st') \rightarrow$$
$$\exists \; as'. \; as \; \mathbf{step_a} \; as' \wedge as' \; \mathbf{R} \; (cs' \times st')$$

Additionally, it must be proven that the initialization and finalization steps are correct:

$$\forall as, cs, st \; . \; \mathbf{init_c}(cs, st) \wedge as \; \mathbf{R} \; (cs \times st) \rightarrow \mathbf{init_a}(as)$$
$$\forall as, cs, st \; . \; as \; \mathbf{R} \; (cs \times st) \wedge \mathbf{fin_c}(cs, st) \rightarrow \mathbf{fin_a}(as)$$

To prove these obligations we need a model in which the Java implementation can interact and communicate with the other agents in the scenario that are still specified by the rules of the protocol ASM and working on a state given by state functions. The following code snippet is taken from the ASM rule for the mobile phone on the concrete level:

> . . .
> **if**($agent$ = mobile-phone) **then** //rule for Java part
>   TOSTORE(cs, st);
>   **choose** st_1 **with** ⟨st; Cindy.theinstance.step(); ⟩ ($st = st_1$) **in**
>   FROMSTORE(st_1, cs)
> **else** . . . // rules for other agents

If the agent is the mobile phone, a Java step is done. Otherwise, the rule for the agent is specified as on the abstract level. The Java step requires the store for the concrete Java method call of the mobile phone implementation. For this, the refined ASM also contains the state of the mobile phone given by state functions. Before calling a Java method, the current abstract state is converted into Java objects and put into the store (TOSTORE(cs, st)). The Java method works on this converted state by executing the Java protocol step (Cindy.theinstance.step();). Afterwards the state of the refined agent is extracted from the store and transformed back into the state functions (FROMSTORE(st_1, cs)).

For the refinement we need the retrieve relation which links abstract and concrete state. With the integration mechanism for Java described above, this relation is quite simple:

$$as \; \mathbf{R} \; cs \times st \leftrightarrow as = cs \wedge \mathrm{INV}(st) \wedge \mathrm{INV}(as)$$

Since the refined ASM is an extension of the protocol ASM, the states of the agents have to be the same. Additionally, we need some technical invariants on the Java store and an invariant on the abstract state. The invariant on the Java store basically says that the objects in the store are well-formed, meaning that e.g. the list of tickets is not **null** and contains no other documents than tickets. The invariant on the abstract state as is used e.g. to express that messages are always well-formed (e.g. every MMS received by the phone contains the originator's phone number).

The proofs of the refinement properties pose some difficulties. One major problem is the encoding of the abstract state into Java objects and the corresponding backward transformation. Many lemmas are needed that are used during the proofs to close side goals. Additionally, a quite complex invariant about the concrete Java store is needed to ensure that the pointer structures and types of objects are all correct.

An example of a typical problem of this type of refinement is the encoding of abstract documents. It is fairly straightforward to write an encode-function that transforms instances of the abstract data type **Document** into Java objects. This means that an abstract data type is implemented by a Java pointer structure. But on the concrete level, more pointer structures are possible than abstract documents. Those are e.g. pointer structures containing null pointers or cyclic pointers. These are valid Java objects, but have no abstract data type counterpart. However, they can be constructed by an attacker in the real application and are a typical reason for errors in the implementations. As a consequence the refinement has to treat those documents during the step of the refined agent. Since they can occur in reality, they must be legal inputs for the refined agent. This is achieved by integrating them in the *TOSTORE* rule. The implementation has to ensure that those undesired pointer structures are treated with an error handling mechanism without crashing.

Since many of the problems during refinement do not depend on the particular application we have a library of reusable functions and predicates for those aspects of the refinement proof. The automation of the proofs is enhanced with every case study.

6   Conclusion

We presented an approach for the development of secure m-commerce applications. Electronic cinema tickets were used as an example. The approach supports the full development process starting from specification and continuing down to an implementation. The approach supports different means of communication and different attacker models. In the example, we considered availability properties instead of the standard confidentiality or authentication properties.

We start with the specification of the security protocol as an ASM, and prove application specific security properties. The proof method uses symbolic execution of the ASM and invariants over the possible traces. Additionally, we refine the abstract specification into real Java source code and verify that this code is a correct implementation of the security protocol. This is not trivial: It is very easy to make the protocol specification too abstract (so it cannot be implemented). The refinement is based on the ASM refinement method, which is a well-known and established technique for the stepwise development of concrete implementations. The whole method is fully supported by the KIV system [BRS⁺00], our interactive theorem prover. All specifications and proofs can be found on our webpage [KIV].

References

[AN95]   R. Anderson and R. Needham. Programming Satan's Computer. In J. van Leeuwen, editor, *Computer Science Today: Recent Trends and Developments.* Springer LNCS 1000, 1995.

[BAN89]   M. Burrows, M. Abadi, and R. Needham. A logic of authentication. *Proceedings of the Royal Society of London,* (Series A, 426, 1871), 1989.

[BDW99]   C. Bolton, J. Davies, and J.C.P. Woodcock. On the refinement and simulation of data types and processes. In K. Araki, A. Galloway, and K. Taguchi, editors, *Proceedings of the International conference of Integrated Formal Methods (IFM),* pages 273–292. Springer, 1999.

[Bee]   *Tickets on your Mobile.* URL: http://www.beep.nl [last seen 2006-03-16].

[BGW01]   Nikita Borisov, Ian Goldberg, and David Wagner. Intercepting Mobile Mommunications: The Insecurity of 802.11. In *MobiCom '01: Proceedings of the 7th annual international conference on Mobile computing and networking,* pages 180–189, New York, NY, USA, 2001. ACM Press.

[BMV03]   David Basin, Sebastian Mödersheim, and Luca Viganò. An On-The-Fly Model-Checker for Security Protocol Analysis. In *Proceedings of Esorics'03,* LNCS 2808, pages 253–270. Springer-Verlag, Heidelberg, 2003.

[Bör03]   E. Börger. The ASM Refinement Method. *Formal Aspects of Computing,* 15 (1–2):237–257, November 2003.

[BRS⁺00]   M. Balser, W. Reif, G. Schellhorn, K. Stenzel, and A. Thums. Formal system development with KIV. In T. Maibaum, editor, *Fundamental Approaches to Software Engineering,* number 1783 in LNCS. Springer-Verlag, 2000.

[BS03]   E. Börger and R. F. Stärk. *Abstract State Machines—A Method for High-Level System Design and Analysis.* Springer-Verlag, 2003.

[DB01]   J. Derrick and E. Boiten. *Refinement in Z and in Object-Z : Foundations and Advanced Applications.* FACIT. Springer, 2001.

[dRE98]   W. de Roever and K. Engelhardt. *Data Refinement: Model-Oriented Proof Methods and their Comparison,* volume 47 of *Cambridge Tracts in Theoretical Computer Science.* Cambridge University Press, 1998.

[DY83]   D. Dolev and A. Yao. On the security of public key protocols. In *IEEE Transactions on Information Theory,* volume 29, 1983.

[GSR05]   H. Grandy, K. Stenzel, and W. Reif. Object-Oriented Verification Kernels for Secure Java Applications. In B. Aichering and B. Beckert, editors, *SEFM 2005 – 3rd IEEE International Conference on Software Engineering and Formal Methods.* IEEE Press, 2005.

[Gur95]   M. Gurevich. Evolving algebras 1993: Lipari guide. In E. Börger, editor, *Specification and Validation Methods*, pages 9 – 36. Oxford University Press, 1995.

[HGRS05]   D. Haneberg, H. Grandy, W. Reif, and G. Schellhorn. Verifying Security Protocols: An ASM Approach. In D. Beauquier, E. Börger, and A. Slissenko, editors, *12th Int. Workshop on Abstract State Machines, ASM 05*. University Paris 12 – Val de Marne, Créteil, France, March 2005.

[HHS86]   He Jifeng, C. A. R. Hoare, and J. W. Sanders. Data refinement refined. In B. Robinet and R. Wilhelm, editors, *Proc. ESOP 86*, volume 213 of *Lecture Notes in Computer Science*, pages 187–196. Springer-Verlag, 1986.

[HKT00]   D. Harel, D. Kozen, and J. Tiuryn. *Dynamic Logic*. MIT Press, 2000.

[HRS02]   D. Haneberg, W. Reif, and K. Stenzel. A Method for Secure Smartcard Applications. In H. Kirchner and C. Ringeissen, editors, *Algebraic Methodology and Software Technology, Proceedings AMAST 2002*. Springer LNCS 2422, 2002.

[KIV]   Web presentation of KIV projects. URL: http://www.informatik.uni-augsburg.de/swt/projects/.

[Low96]   G. Lowe. Breaking and fixing the Needham-Schroeder public-key protocol using FDR. In *Tools and Algorithms for the Construction and Analysis of Systems (TACAS)*, volume 1055, pages 147–166. Springer-Verlag, 1996.

[Mea96]   Catherine Meadows. The NRL protocol analyzer: An overview. *Journal of Logic Programming*, 26(2):113–131, 1996.

[Pau98]   Lawrence C. Paulson. The inductive approach to verifying cryptographic protocols. *Journal of Computer Security*, 6:85–128, 1998.

[Sch01]   G. Schellhorn. Verification of ASM Refinements Using Generalized Forward Simulation. *Journal of Universal Computer Science (J.UCS)*, 7(11):952–979, 2001. URL: http://hyperg.iicm.tu-graz.ac.at/jucs/.

[Sch05]   G. Schellhorn. ASM Refinement and Generalizations of Forward Simulation in Data Refinement: A Comparison. *Journal of Theoretical Computer Science*, vol. 336, no. 2-3:403–435, May 2005.

[Ste04]   K. Stenzel. A formally verified calculus for full Java Card. In C. Rattray, S. Maharaj, and C. Shankland, editors, *Algebraic Methodology and Software Technology (AMAST) 2004, Proceedings*, Stirling Scotland, July 2004. Springer LNCS 3116.

[Ste05]   Kurt Stenzel. *Verification of Java Card Programs*. PhD thesis, Universität Augsburg, Fakultät für Angewandte Informatik, URL: http://www.opus-bayern.de/uni-augsburg/volltexte/2005/122/, 2005.

[Sun]   Sun Microsystems Inc. Java Micro Edition. URL: http://java.sun.com/j2me/index.jsp.

[WD96]   J. C. P. Woodcock and J. Davies. *Using Z: Specification, Proof and Refinement*. Prentice Hall International Series in Computer Science, 1996.

[WS96]   David Wagner and Bruce Schneier. Analysis of the SSL 3.0 protocol. In *2nd USENIX Workshop on Electronic Commerce*, November 1996. A revised version is available at http://www.schneier.com/paper-ssl.html.

An Algebra for Enterprise Privacy Policies Closed Under Composition and Conjunction

Dominik Raub[1] and Rainer Steinwandt[2]

[1] Department of Computer Science,
ETH Zurich, CH-8092 Zurich, Switzerland
[2] Department of Mathematical Sciences, Florida Atlantic University,
777 Glades Road, Boca Raton, FL 33431, USA

Abstract. A prerequisite for processing privacy-sensitive data with automatic tools is a fine-grained formalization of privacy policies along with appropriate operators to manipulate such policies. The most promising results for the formalization of privacy policies so far have been achieved with the language EPAL resp. its academic counterpart E-P3P.

As shown at ESORICS 2004, in the existing form E-P3P has fundamental limitations in the expressability of composed policies as desired in projects involving multiple departments or enterprises. We describe a Novel Algebraic Privacy Specification (NAPS) which addresses these problems by offering conjunction, composition and scoping operators, which are defined analogously to those known from E-P3P, but exhibit desirable algebraic properties. Most notably NAPS is, in contrast to E-P3P, closed under all of these operators. Also, we show how existing E-P3P policies fit into the NAPS framework.

1 Introduction

The processing of privacy-sensitive data is accompanied by increasingly complex regulations that have to be taken into account. Hence research on formal models for privacy policies and (semi-)automatic tools for processing these policies is gaining attention in academic and industrial research. Compared to access control, the available tools for managing privacy policies are far from being satisfactory, and even the formalization of privacy policies is not solved in a satisfactory manner yet. The association of purposes and obligations with data access, as needed for privacy policies, complicates the application of access control tools significantly and motivates the development of specific tools for expressing and processing privacy policies. Here it is useful to differentiate between i) the "simple" requirements needed to deal with privacy issues relating enterprise and private users and ii) the fine-grained tools needed for handling privacy-sensitive data in enterprise-to-enterprise relations. For handling privacy policies in the latter context, the currently most promising approach is the Enterprise Privacy Authorization Language (EPAL) resp. its academic abstraction E-P3P (see [1, 17, 5, 4]).

Having in mind large projects, possibly involving several enterprises, the question for a modular construction of privacy policies naturally arises. Based on EPAL resp. E-P3P an interesting first step in this direction has been presented by Backes et al. at ES-ORICS 2003 [5]. Albeit being of great value, the operator for ordered composition discussed therein does not offer the desired flexibility for composing privacy policies yet.

G. Müller (Ed.): ETRICS 2006, LNCS 3995, pp. 130–144, 2006.

Thus, motivated by well-known algebraic tools from access control [9, 24, 10, 25], at ESORICS 2004 Backes et al. put forward an *algebra for composing enterprise privacy policies* [4]. Next to the ordered composition of privacy policies formulated in E-P3P, here also conjunction and disjunction operators are introduced, thereby allowing for more flexibility in deriving new privacy policies from existing ones in a modular way. Unfortunately, the algebra in [4] suffers from fundamental limitations in the expressiveness of EPAL resp. E-P3P, which prohibit an intuitive definition of policy conjunction and disjunction as would be desirable. To cope with this problem, [4] introduces a class of *well-founded* privacy policies, for which a comparatively convenient algebraic treatment is possible. However, this policy class is not closed under ordered composition, which makes the combination of different policy operators quite inconvenient. Also, with regard to the operator semantics some aspects are not fully satisfactory at the moment. E. g., i) incorporation of the default ruling into the policy, as proposed before the definition of ordered composition in [4], makes ordered composition trivial for any but a "don't care" default ruling. The default ruling of the first—higher priority—policy, now incorporated in the ruleset, will treat all queries, and leave none to be treated by the second—lower priority—policy; ii) the fact that in E-P3P obligations on, say, a department are always at least as strict as obligations imposed on members of the department makes the definition of minimum requirements on a department somewhat cumbersome; iii) restricting rulings to "allow", "deny" and "don't care" (plus obligations) as in E-P3P is not really suited to differentiate between "access can be allowed" and "access must not be denied". When dealing with privacy-sensitive data, a convenient way to express these different types of "allow" is desirable: While accessing a data item for marketing purposes may be acceptable, legal regulations may impose that a client may never be denied access to her personal data.

The Novel Algebraic Pricavy Specification (NAPS) framework described below addresses these issues, thereby overcoming some limitations of E-P3P. The semantics of NAPS is more or less straightforward, defined by simply evaluating rules by descending priority. Definition of minimal requirements, say in the privacy policy of a company, is well supported by NAPS and the refinement of these to department or workgroup policies can be achieved through ordered composition. NAPS allows the separate specification of obligations both for the case when access to a data item is denied or granted. Furthermore NAPS is closed under its operators, including conjunction, ordered composition, and scoping. Also the handling of partial or missing information about privacy relevant data (such as age of a customer) is taken into account.

Despite these attractive features it would certainly not be justified to claim NAPS to be a totally superior substitute for E-P3P. E. g., so far no automatic tools for processing NAPS policies exist, while for E-P3P resp. EPAL progress in the development of such tools has been made already (cf. [3, 2]). Thus, much work remains to be done to explore the practical value of NAPS, but we think the results achieved so far certainly justify further research in this direction.

Further related work. The starting point to develop NAPS was the E-P3P based algebra to compose enterprise privacy policies presented in [4] and building on [5]. In particular, NAPS keeps the established approaches to formulate purpose-specific requests and obligations associated with data accesses. Individual privacy-specific aspects of data processing have been discussed already in [15, 6, 8, 21], for instance. E-P3P resp. EPAL offers one of the most elaborated frameworks in this context and getting rid of limitations in policy composition of these frameworks without giving up E-P3P's resp. EPAL's merits is indeed desirable.

Policy composition has been explored in various contexts already (cf., e. g., [19, 23, 14, 12]), particularly in access control [11, 16, 9, 27, 10], and—as already mentioned in [4]—existing algebraic tools for access control [9, 10, 24, 25] are a key motivation to establish algebraic tools for the treatment of privacy policies.

2 Basic Definitions

Statements to be captured by privacy policies typically have a form like "*John Doe* from *sales* may *read customer data* for *marketing* purposes, if the *customer has consented*, with the *obligation to notify the customer*." To formalize such statements we follow the established approach of using hierarchies to represent users, data, actions, and purposes (cf. [5, 4]). Also for expressing obligations, we mainly adopt the modelling from [4]. For expressing conditions and rulings of policies, our approach deviates from E-P3P and we refer to Section 2.4 for a discussion of how to embed E-P3P policies into the NAPS framework.

2.1 Hierarchies, Obligations, and Conditions

As in E-P3P we use hierarchies to model users, data, purposes and actions. This in particular enables the specification of policies applying to entire subhierarchies, e. g. all users within ("$\leq$") the sales department. Unlike [5, 4] we do not require hierarchies to have unique predecessors:

Definition 1 (Hierarchy). *A hierarchy $(H, \leq_H)$ is an ordered[1], finite set. A hierarchy $(H, \leq_H)$ is a* subhierarchy *of a hierarchy $(G, \leq_G)$, written $(H, \leq_H) \subseteq (G, \leq_G)$, iff $(H \subseteq G)$ and $(\leq_H \subseteq \leq_G)$. We set $(H, \leq_H) \cup (G, \leq_G) := (H \cup G, (\leq_H \cup \leq_G)^*)$ with $*$ denoting reflexive, transitive closure. Note that $(H, \leq_H) \cup (G, \leq_G)$ is only a hierachy if $(\leq_H \cup \leq_G)^*$ is an order, in which case we call H and G* compatible.

A privacy policy not only regulates access to data, but can impose *obligations* like "delete this data set within two weeks" or "notify the customer". Analogously as in [4], it is convenient to impose some algebraic structure on the set of obligations:

Definition 2 (Obligation Model). *An* obligation model *$(O, \leq, \wedge, \top, \bot)$ is a meet-semilattice (a commutative, idempotent monoid) [7, 26] with maximal element $\top$, the empty obligation or no obligation, and minimal element $\bot$, the unfulfillable obligation. In keeping with the definition of a semilattice we have $\forall o, p \in O : o \leq p : \iff o \wedge p = o$.*

We assume that all occurring obligation models $(O, \leq)$ are subsets of a fixed (super) obligation model $(\mathcal{O}, \leq_{\mathcal{O}})$ such that $\leq$ is the restriction of $\leq_{\mathcal{O}}$ to $O \times O$.

Imposing the obligation $\bot$ indicates, that an action must not be performed. Imposing $\top$ signifies, that an action may be performed without restriction.

---

[1] We use order and partial order synonymously. Total orders are explicitly called so.

Remark 1 (Standard Obligation Model). For most purposes it will suffice to imagine a powerset lattice $(\mathfrak{P}(\tilde{O}), \supseteq)$ over a set of elementary obligations $\tilde{O}$ (like the ones stated above) with the set union $\cup$ as conjunction $\wedge$, $\top := \emptyset$, $\bot := \tilde{O}$ and for $A, B \in \mathfrak{P}(\tilde{O})$: $A \leq B \iff A \supseteq B$.

We want to enable policy specifications, making no final decision upon granting access or not, but still providing an obligation for either case. This allows to defer the final decision of granting or denying access to another policy or to an access control system (in the simplest case just granting (or denying) access by default). Therefore, we design NAPS rules to yield a pair of obligations $r = (o^+, o^-)$ as ruling, where o^+ is the obligation to be imposed if access to the data is later granted whereas o^- is the obligation to be imposed if access to the data is later denied. A rule may impose the obligation $o^+ = \bot$, meaning access must not be granted, or it may impose $o^- = \bot$, meaning access must not be denied. The ruling $o^+ = \bot$, $o^- = \bot$ is contradictory and used as an error state.

Definition 3 (Ruling). *Let O be an obligation model. A ruling r is a pair of obligations $r = (o^+, o^-) \in O \times O$ where o^+ is the obligation imposed on granting access to a data element and o^- is the obligation imposed on denying access to a data element. Defining the operation $\wedge$ elementwise on the pairs (o^+, o^-), we obtain a semilattice of rulings $(O \times O, \leq, \wedge, (\top, \top), (\bot, \bot))$ with minimal element $(\bot, \bot)$ and maximal element $(\top, \top)$. Keeping with the definition of a semilattice, for all $r_1 = (o_1^+, o_1^-), r_2 = (o_2^+, o_2^-) \in O \times O$ we have $r_1 \leq r_2 : \iff r_1 \wedge r_2 = r_1 \iff (o_1^+ \wedge o_2^+, o_1^- \wedge o_2^-) = (o_1^+, o_1^-) \iff o_1^+ \leq o_2^+$ and $o_1^- \leq o_2^-$.*

Privacy related regulations often depend on context information; e. g., accessing the data of under age customers for marketing purposes may require the consent of a legal guardian. Hence "age of customer" and "consent of legal guardian" are variables that have to be considered in the evaluation of privacy policies. Restrictions of the type in this example are captured by a 3-valued, many sorted *condition logic*, which is defined over the following *condition vocabulary*.

Definition 4 (Condition Vocabulary). *A condition vocabulary (S, X, Σ, ρ) consists of (adapted from [13, Chapter 10]) i) a finite set $S \dot{\cup} \{l_3\}$ of sorts (or types) such that S is nonempty; ii) logical connectives $\wedge$, $\vee$ of rank $(l_3, l_3; l_3)$, $\neg$, $\sim$ of rank $(l_3; l_3)$, 0, u, 1 of rank $(\varepsilon; l_3)$; iii) for every sort $s \in S$ the equality symbol $\dot{=}_s$ of rank $(s, s; l_3)$; iv) for every sort $s \in S$ a finite set $X_s = \{x_{s0}, x_{s1}, x_{s2}, \ldots\}$ of variables, each variable x_{si} being of rank $(\varepsilon; s)$; we define the family of sets $\mathbf{X} := \{X_s \mid s \in S\}$ and $X := \bigcup_{s \in S} X_s$ the set of all variables; v) auxiliary symbols "(" and ")"; vi) a finite $(S \dot{\cup} \{l_3\})$-ranked alphabet (Σ, ρ) with rank function $\rho : \Sigma \rightarrow S^* \times (S \dot{\cup} \{l_3\})$ of nonlogical symbols consisting of:*

- *A finite set $\Sigma_F := \{f \in \Sigma \mid (t; s) := \rho(f) \in S^+ \times S\}$ of function symbols. The string t is called arity of f and the symbol s sort (or type) of f.*
- *For each sort $s \in S$ a finite set $\Sigma_C^s := \{c \in \Sigma \mid \rho(f) = (\varepsilon; s)\}$ of constants. The family of sets Σ_C^s is denoted by Σ_C.*
- *A finite set $\Sigma_P := \{P \in \Sigma \mid (t; l_3) := \rho(P) \in S^* \times \{l_3\}\}$ of predicate symbols. The string t is the arity of P, if $t = \varepsilon$, P is a propositional letter.*

We call a condition vocabulary with set of nonlogical symbols Σ a vocabulary Σ.

Having defined a vocabulary for a condition logic, we next define models, the many-sorted algebras, for this logic.

Definition 5 (Many-sorted Algebra). *Given an S-ranked alphabet Σ, a many-sorted Σ-algebra M is a pair (M, I) with $M = (M_s)_{s \in S}$ an S-indexed finite family of finite sets $M_s \neq \emptyset$, the carriers of sort s, and I an interpretation function $I : \Sigma \to \bigcup_{n \in \mathbb{N}} \bigcup_{s, s_1 \ldots s_n \in S} M_s^{M_{s_1} \times \ldots \times M_{s_n}}$ s. t.: $\forall f \in \Sigma : \rho(f) = (s_1 \ldots s_n, s) \implies I(f) \in M_s^{M_{s_1} \times \ldots \times M_{s_n}}$ and $\forall c \in \Sigma : \rho(c) = (\varepsilon, s) \implies I(c) \in M_s$.*

Now we can define terms, formulas, models and semantic for our condition logic.

Definition 6 (Condition Language). *Let (S, X, Σ, ρ) be a condition vocabulary. The condition language $C(S, X, \Sigma, \rho)$ is the set of correctly typed formulas over (S, X, Σ, ρ). Formulas are defined recursively as usual for predicate logic (see [13, Ch. 10]). The free variables of a formula $c \in C$ are denoted by free(c). As the condition logic has no quantifiers, these are all variables of c. The semantics of C formulas is defined as usual for the 3-valued Lukasiewicz logic L_3 (cf., e. g., [18, 13, 22]), using the following two definitions.*

Definition 7 (Admissible Model). *A many-sorted Σ-structure (M, I) is a many-sorted Σ-algebra, where for all $s \in S$ the symbol for "unknown" $\oslash \in M_s$ and $M_{l_3} = \{0, u, 1\}$. A structure (M, I) is called admissible or admissible model for a condition language C, provided that $I|_{\Sigma_C} : \Sigma_C \to \bigcup_{s \in S} M_s$ is a surjective map, i. e. there is a constant for every possible data item in the structure M. If a fixed admissible structure is given, we will usually choose one of these constants and use it and the data item interchangibly.*

Definition 8 (Variable Assignment). *An assignment of sort s of the variables is a function $\alpha_s \in M_s^{V_s}$. An assignment $\alpha = (\alpha_s)_{s \in S}$ is an S-indexed family of assignments of sort s. The set of all assignments for a set of variables X and a structure M is written $\mathfrak{Ass}(X, M)$. An assignment α is partial if $\alpha(x) = \oslash$ for some $x \in X$ and complete if this is not the case. For the set of complete assignments we write $\mathfrak{Ass}^*(X, M)$. To allow a uniform treatment of policies defined over different vocabularies, we assume a set $\mathcal{X}$ all variables and a set $\mathcal{M}$ all values are taken from. Typically these are sets of strings over a given alphabet, e. g. valid XML expressions; we define the set of assignments $\mathfrak{Ass} := \mathcal{M}^{\mathcal{X}}$.*

2.2 Syntax of NAPS Policies

Having described the basic components of NAPS policies, we now collect them into a vocabulary.

Definition 9 (NAPS Vocabulary). *A (NAPS) vocabulary V consists of hierarchies (ordered sets) U, D, P, and A, called user, data, purpose, and action hierarchy, respectively; a condition language C, an admissible structure (M, I) for C and an obligation model O: $V = (U, D, P, A, C(S, X, \Sigma, \rho), (M, I), O)$*

Given two vocabularies V and V' we write $V \subseteq V'$ iff $U \subseteq U'$, $D \subseteq D'$, $P \subseteq P'$, $A \subseteq A'$, $S \subseteq S'$, $\Sigma \subseteq \Sigma'$, $O \subseteq O'$, $\forall s \in S : X_s \subseteq X'_s$, $\forall s \in S : M_s \subseteq M'_s$, $\rho = \rho'|_\Sigma$, $I = I'|_{\Sigma, M}$, where $\forall f \in \Sigma : I'|_{\Sigma, M}(f) := I'(f)|_M$.

As a naming convention, we assume that the components of a vocabulary V are always called as in Definition 9 except if explicitly stated otherwise. In a vocabulary V_i all components also get a subscript i, and similarly for superscripts.

As indicated before, privacy policies make statements about *users* performing an *action* on *data* with a specific *purpose*. Accordingly, a NAPS query is a tuple (u, d, p, a) in the query set $Q(V) := U \times D \times P \times A$ for the given vocabulary V. NAPS queries are not restricted to minimal elements in the hierarchies. This facilitates the handling of policies in scenarios, where a coarse policy, say a company policy referring only to departments, is refined, say to a department policy making statements about workgroups or individuals. In such a scenario elements that are initially minimal may later get children: User John Doe my not be mentioned in the company policy, but may very well appear in a department policy. Also, it may still be of interest to query the company policy with a department, to find out about the (minimum) restrictions for that department.

To be able to treat policies defined on different vocabularies in a uniform manner, we define the semantics for queries outside the given vocabulary. We assume a superset $\mathcal{H}$, in which all hierarchy sets are embedded; in practice it is typically a set of strings or valid XML expressions.

Definition 10 (Query). *For a vocubulary V, we call $Q(V) = U \times D \times P \times A$ the* query vocabulary *associated with V and define an order $\leq$ on $Q(V)$ as follows. For queries $(u, d, p, a), (u', d', p', a') \in Q(V)$ we set $(u, d, p, a) \leq (u', d', p', a') : \iff (u \leq_U u') \wedge (d \leq_D d') \wedge (p \leq_P p') \wedge (a \leq_A a')$. Given a superset $\mathcal{H}$ of the sets U, D, P, A of all considered vocabularies, the set of* all queries *is $Q := \mathcal{H}^4$.*

Whether a rule in a privacy policy applies to a query $q \in Q(V)$ is determined by evaluating a logical expression or guard over the predicate $\leq$. These logical expressions are taken from the query or guard logic.

Definition 11 (Query or Guard Logic). *The* query *or* guard logic G *for a vocabulary V is a boolean predicate logic without quantifiers over i) the* vocabulary *consisting of the binary predicate "$\leq$" and constants $C_G := Q(V)$; ii) the* set of variables $\{p\}$; *iii) operators $\wedge$, $\vee$, $\neg$, 1, 0; iv) auxiliary symbols "(", ")".*

We fix a model $M_G := Q(V)$ for G with the interpretation $I_G(\leq) :=\leq (on\ Q(V))$ and for $q \in C_G$: $I_G(q) := q \in Q(V)$. The semantics are as usual for a boolean predicate logic and we set $g(q) := \mathrm{eval}_{I_G, M_G, \alpha_G : p \mapsto q}\ g$.

Given the definitions above we can now define NAPS policies. Each NAPS policy is defined over a vocabulary V and consists of a ruleset as its central component and a default ruling. The ruleset states how requests are to be treated, while the default ruling provides a safe default behavior for queries that are not (yet) handled by a rule in the ruleset.

Definition 12 (Ruleset and Privacy Policy). *A ruleset R over a vocabulary V is a subset of $\mathbb{Z} \times G \times C \times O \times O$. A rule $(i, g, c, r) \in R$ consists of a* priority $i \in \mathbb{Z}$, *a* guard $g \in G$ (the guard logic), *a* condition $c \in C$ (the condition logic) *and a* ruling $r \in O \times O$. *A* privacy *or* NAPS policy $\mathcal{P} = (V, R, dr)$ *is a triple of a vocabulary V,* *a rule-set R over V, and a* default ruling $dr \in O \times O$. *We call the set of these policies* NAPS *and the subset for a given vocabulary* $\mathrm{NAPS}(V)$.

As a naming convention, we assume that the components of a privacy policy called $\mathcal{P}$ are always called as in Def. 12, and if $\mathcal{P}$ has a sub- or superscript, then so do the components.

2.3 Semantics of NAPS Policies

The *Chief Privacy Officer* (CPO) of a company should be able to define a binding set of base regulations for the departments of a company, that can in turn be refined by the departments. One goal of NAPS is to improve the control over the refinement of rules versus E-P3P, and to facilitate the intuitive handling of partial knowledge, i. e. partial variable assignments α for the condition logic C. Because of that NAPS uses a 3-valued condition logic C. As in E-P3P a condition evaluating to "0" means that a rule does not apply and a condition evaluating to "1" states that the rule applies and terminates evaluation. The third logical value "u" signifies that a rule applies, but evaluation is to proceed. This way we can treat rules that, due to a partial assignment, might (or might not) apply by applying their obligation conjunctively and proceeding with evaluation, yielding a ruling that might be more restrictive than necessary, but never too lenient. The distinction between "u" and "1" can also be used to mark certain rules as "amendable" by lower priority rules or as "final". Hence we speak of *amendable, final* and *semi-amendable rules*. Amendable rules can be refined by lower priority rules, while final rules terminate the evaluation of the policy if they apply and can thus not be refined. Semi-amendable rules can be refined in some cases, depending on the variable assignment α for the condition logic C.

Definition 13 (Amendable, Final, Semi-Amendable Rules). *Let* $\mathcal{P} = (V, R, dr)$ *be a policy. Then a rule* $(i, g, c, r) \in R$ *is* amendable *iff* $\forall \alpha \in \mathfrak{Ass}(X, M) : \mathrm{eval}_\alpha(c) \in \{0, u\}$. *Similarly, a rule* $(i, g, c, r) \in R$ *is* final *iff* $\forall \alpha \in \mathfrak{Ass}(X, M) : \mathrm{eval}_\alpha(c) \in \{0, 1\}$. *A rule that is neither amendable nor final is called* semi-amendable.

A rule $(i, g, c, r) \in R$ *is called* strongly amendable *iff* $\exists c' \in C : c = c' \wedge u$, *and a rule* $(i, g, c, r) \in R$ *is called* strongly final *iff* $\exists c' \in C : c =\sim\sim c'$, *with* $=$ *meaning equality up to equivalence transformations of the underlying* L_3 *logic [18, 22].*

Remark 2. Clearly strongly amendable rules are amendable and strongly final rules are final over each vocabulary, over which their symbols are defined.

The terms above describe a rule as such, independent of a specific query $q \in Q(V)$ or assignment $\alpha \in \mathfrak{Ass}(X, M)$. Given a specific query $q \in Q(V)$ and assignment $\alpha \in \mathfrak{Ass}(X, M)$, we may distinguish *applicable*, *terminal* and *non-applicable* rules under q and α. A rule is not applicable under q and α if either the guard or the condition evaluate to 0, if both guard and condition evaluate to 1, we call a rule terminal under q and α, if they evaluate to 1 and u or 1 respectively, the rule is called applicable under q and α. Therefore, while final rules are either terminal under q and α or not applicable, amendable rules are never terminal.

Definition 14 (Applicable and Terminal Rules). *Let a privacy policy* $\mathcal{P} = (V, R, dr)$, *a query* $q \in Q(V)$, *and an assignment* $\alpha \in \mathfrak{Ass}(X, M)$ *be given.*

Then a rule $(i, g, c, r) \in R$ *is* applicable *iff* $g(q) = 1$ *and* $\text{eval}_\alpha(c) \in \{u, 1\}$; *the rule* $(i, g, c, r) \in R$ *is* terminal *iff* $g(q) = 1$ *and* $\text{eval}_\alpha(c) = 1$.

By $R_A(\mathcal{P}, q, i, \alpha) := \{(i, g, c, r) \in R \mid g(q) = 1 \text{ and } \text{eval}_\alpha(c) \in \{u, 1\}\}$ *we denote the set of applicable rules for priority* i. *We define the set of terminal rules for priority* i *as* $R_T(\mathcal{P}, q, i, \alpha) := \{(i, g, c, r) \in R \mid g(q) = 1 \text{ and } \text{eval}_\alpha(c) = 1\}$.

Definition 15 (Precedence Range). *For a privacy policy* $\mathcal{P} = (V, R, dr)$ *and* op $\in \{\max, \min\}$, *let* $\text{op}(\mathcal{P}) := \text{op}(R) := \text{op}(\{i \mid \exists (i, g, c, r) \in R\})$.

The semantics of a NAPS policy, i. e. the result of a query given an assignment, is given by Alg. 2.1. A policy is evaluated by simply collecting the obligations of all applicable rules for the given query and assignment conjunctively, descending by priority until a terminal rule is found. Should no rule apply, the default ruling is returned, and should query or assignment be out of vocabulary, an error is returned. In addition to a ruling, the policy evaluation returns a tag $v \in \{\mathsf{f}, \mathsf{a}, \mathsf{d}\}$ stating how policy evaluation terminated: f (final) indicates, that the evaluation terminated with a terminal rule, a (amendable) states, that no terminal rule was found, but a rule was applicable, d indicates that the default rule was applied. These evaluation tags are helpful in defining useful notions of policy refinement, composition and conjunction, purely on the level of evaluations without regard to the internal structure of a policy.

Definition 16 (Semantics). *Let a privacy policy* $\mathcal{P} = (V, R, dr)$, $q \in Q$, *and* $\alpha \in \mathfrak{Ass}$ *be given. We define the set of possible* evaluation results *or* evaluations $E(V) := O \times O \times \{\mathsf{f}, \mathsf{a}, \mathsf{d}\} \subseteq \mathcal{E} := \mathcal{O} \times \mathcal{O} \times \{\mathsf{f}, \mathsf{a}, \mathsf{d}\}$. *The* evaluation result $e = (r, v) := \text{eval}_\alpha(\mathcal{P}, q) \in E(V)$ *of policy* $\mathcal{P}$ *for query* q *and assignment* α *is defined by Alg. 2.1, where "*return*" returns its argument and terminates the algorithm. The* evaluation tag $v \in \{\mathsf{f}, \mathsf{a}, \mathsf{d}\}$ *states if the evalation was terminated by a terminal rule, found non-terminal rules only or if the default rule was applied.*

From the definition of the semantics of a NAPS policy the benefits of a 3-valued condition logic are apparent. The purpose of the logical value u as result of a condition c is as such twofold: i) u may indicate that due to incomplete information (a partial variable assignment with too many $\oslash$'s) one cannot determine if the rule is to be applied. In this

Algorithm 2.1. Policy Evaluation

Input: policy $\mathcal{P}$, assignment $\alpha \in \mathfrak{Ass}$, query $q \in \mathcal{Q}$.
Output: NAPS evaluation $e \in E(V)$.

```
if  q ∉ Q(V)  or  α|ₓ ∉ 𝔄𝔰𝔰(X,M):  return e := ((⊥,⊥),f);  //  invalid input
r := (⊤,⊤);
for  i := max(P) downto min(P):  //  descend by priority i ...
      r := r ∧ ⋀(i,g,c,r')∈R_A(P,q,i,α) r';  //  ... picking up the rulings
      if  R_T(P,q,i,α) ≠ ∅:  return e := (r,f);  //  ... terminating, if needed
if  ∀i ∈ ℤ: R_A(P,q,i,α) = ∅:  return e := (dr,d);  //  no applicable rule
return e := (r,a);  //  applicable rule(s) but no final rule found
```

case the rule is applied and the obligations are imposed to guarantee correct treatment of data, should it turn out later that the rule was to be applied. Then evaluation proceeds to look for other rules that might also match the incomplete data; ii) u may indicate that a rule is amendable. An amendable rule has a condition always returning u instead of 1, so that evaluation continues and picks up further rules concerning the query.

A final rule is, if applicable, automatically terminal, i.e. its condition c returns 1. In that case the evaluation stops at the priority level of the rule in question and the obligations accumulated up to and including that level are returned.

Remark 3 (Interdependence of Query and Assignment). In general we expect the variable assignment to be determined by the requested data object. Variables not being fixed by the requested data object are, if not determined globally, set to unknown ("$\oslash$"). A variable "age of customer", e. g., should be set to the age entry in the customer dataset. For corporate customers "age of customer" makes no sense and is hence set to unknown ("$\oslash$"). The same is true if the age of a customer is simply unknown. As a dataset may in principle induce an arbitrary assignment, NAPS views query and assignment as independent and does not model the connection just explained.

2.4   Embedding E-P3P Policies into the NAPS Framework

A privacy policy can be regarded as description of a function mapping a query q and an assignment α to an evaluation e. Each such function can be represented by a NAPS policy. To prove this, an algorithm creating the policy in question can be constructed. However, due to the page limit here we omit the proof.

Theorem 1 (Functional Completeness of NAPS). *The set of NAPS policies is functionally complete in the sense that, for an arbitrary but fixed $dr \in O \times O$, we may describe an arbitrary function $f \in (O \times O \times \{\mathsf{a},\mathsf{f}\} \cup (dr, \mathsf{d}))^{Q(V) \times \mathfrak{Ass}(X,M)}$ through a NAPS policy $\mathcal{P}$.*

In particular, every E-P3P policy defined over an obligation model, that can be turned into a meet-semilattice, can be transformed into an equivalent NAPS policy, using the map $(+, o^+) \mapsto (o^+, \bot, \mathsf{f})$, $(-, o^-) \mapsto (\bot, o^-, \mathsf{f})$, $\circ \mapsto (\top, \top, \mathsf{d})$ from E-P3P rulings to NAPS evaluations.

2.5   Refinement and Equivalence of Privacy Policies

It is of interest to determine, if a policy is more specific or restrictive than another. Department policies should be more specific or restrictive than the minimum requirements set in a company policy and it might be important to know if a policy is at least as restrictive than applicable law or a treaty requirement, so that the company fulfills its legal obligations. To be able to state what it means that a policy is more restrictive than another, we first define in which case we consider an evaluation more restrictive or a *refinement* of another.

Definition 17 (Refinement of Evaluations). *Given two evaluations $e_i = (r_i, v_i) \in E(V_i) \subseteq \mathcal{E}$ for $i = 1, 2$, we say that e_2 functionally refines e_1, written $e_2 \preceq e_1$, iff*

$r_2 \leq r_1$. *We say that* e_2 *weakly refines* e_1, *written* $e_2 \precsim e_1$, *iff* $(v_1 = \mathsf{d}$ *and* $v_2 \neq \mathsf{d})$ *or* $(r_2 \leq r_1$ *and* $(v_1 = \mathsf{d}$ *or* $v_2 \neq \mathsf{d}))$. *Finally, defining* $\mathsf{f} \leq \mathsf{a} \leq \mathsf{d}$, *we say that* e_2 *refines* e_1,

$$e_2 \leq e_1 : \iff (v_1 = \mathsf{d} \text{ and } v_2 \neq \mathsf{d}) \text{ or } (v_2 \leq v_1 \text{ and } r_2 \leq r_1). \tag{1}$$

Remark 4 (Refinement of Evaluations). The functional refinement relation $\preceq$ and the weak refinement relation $\precsim$ on evaluations are reflexive and transitive, as $\leq$ is an order on the rulings. The refinement relation $\leq$ is even an order on the evaluations and we have $e_2 \leq e_1 \implies e_2 \precsim e_1$.

Note the special treatment of the default ruling in the definitions of weak refinement and refinement. The default ruling is to describe some safe (possibly very restrictive) behavior until an actual rule has been implemented ("stub behavior"). As we expect a refinement to be more specific, refinement may replace the default ruling on some query with a (possibly less restrictive) non-default ruling. Otherwise we demand a refinement to be more restrictive, imposing stronger obligations or turning amendable rulings into final ones.

From evaluations we now extend the notion of refinement to policies. As with evaluations, functional refinement only captures the notion "more restrictive", whereas (weak) refinement states if a policy is more specific than another, taking into account the special semantics of the default ruling and the vocabulary. Since policies are not uniquely determined by their functional behavior, we collect them into equivalence classes and distinguish i) *functionally equivalent* policies, that generate matching rulings for each query and assignment; ii) *equivalent* policies, that have the same vocabulary and generate matching evaluations for each query and assignment; iii) *strongly equivalent* policies, that have the same vocabulary and generate matching evaluations under each vocabulary extension (see Def. 19) for each query and assignment.

Definition 18 (Refinement and Equivalence of Policies). *A policy $\mathcal{P}'$ is called* functional refinement *of a policy $\mathcal{P}$, written $\mathcal{P}' \preceq \mathcal{P}$, iff $\forall q \in Q, \alpha \in \mathfrak{Ass}$* : $\mathrm{eval}_\alpha(\mathcal{P}', q) \preceq \mathrm{eval}_\alpha(\mathcal{P}, q)$. *A policy $\mathcal{P}'$ is called* refinement *of a policy $\mathcal{P}$,*

$$\mathcal{P}' \leq \mathcal{P} : \iff (\forall q \in Q(V), \alpha \in \{\beta \in \mathfrak{Ass}(X', M') \mid \beta|_X \in \mathfrak{Ass}(X, M)\} : \tag{2}$$
$$\mathrm{eval}_\alpha(\mathcal{P}', q) \leq \mathrm{eval}_\alpha(\mathcal{P}, q)) \text{ and } V \subseteq V'.$$

Policy $\mathcal{P}'$ is a weak refinement *of policy $\mathcal{P}$, written $\mathcal{P}' \precsim \mathcal{P}$, iff $V \subseteq V'$ and $\forall q \in Q(V), \alpha \in \{\beta \in \mathfrak{Ass}(X', M') \mid \beta|_X \in \mathfrak{Ass}(X, M)\}$: $\mathrm{eval}_\alpha(\mathcal{P}', q) \precsim \mathrm{eval}_\alpha(\mathcal{P}, q)$.*

Finally, two policies $\mathcal{P}$ and $\mathcal{P}'$ are called i) functionally equivalent, *written $\mathcal{P}' \approx \mathcal{P}$, iff $\mathcal{P}' \preceq \mathcal{P}$ and $\mathcal{P} \preceq \mathcal{P}'$, ii)* equivalent, *written $\mathcal{P}' \cong \mathcal{P}$, iff $\mathcal{P}' \leq \mathcal{P}$ and $\mathcal{P} \leq \mathcal{P}'$, iii)* strongly equivalent, *written $\mathcal{P}' \equiv \mathcal{P}$, iff $V = V'$ and $\forall W \supseteq V : \mathcal{P}' \uparrow_W \cong \mathcal{P} \uparrow_W$ (regarding $\uparrow$ see Def. 19).*

Remark 5 (Refinement and Equivalence of Policies). The refinement relations $\preceq, \precsim, \leq$ just defined are reflexive and transitive and we have $\mathcal{P}' \leq \mathcal{P} \implies \mathcal{P}' \precsim \mathcal{P}$. Moreover, the relations $\approx, \cong, \equiv$ are equivalence relations and we have $\mathcal{P}' = \mathcal{P} \implies \mathcal{P}' \equiv \mathcal{P} \implies \mathcal{P}' \cong \mathcal{P} \implies \mathcal{P}' \approx \mathcal{P}$.

3   NAPS Operators

Having presented the basic definitions of the NAPS framework, we now turn to defining operators. Since the legal requirements and the structures within a company are subject to change we first define a *vocabulary extension* or *up-scoping* operator, that extends the vocabulary over which a policy is defined, e. g. by adding new users, departments, data types or variables.

Definition 19 (Vocabulary Extension, Up-Scoping). *Let* $\mathcal{P} = (V, R, dr)$ *be a privacy policy over the vocabulary* V *and let* V' *be a vocabulary such that* $V \subseteq V'$. *Then* $\mathcal{P} \uparrow_{V'} := (V', R, dr)$ *is the* up-scoping *of* $\mathcal{P}$ *w. r. t.* V'.

In a similar fashion we can define a *down-scoping* operator $\downarrow_{V'}$, that restricts a policy $\mathcal{P}$ to a policy $\mathcal{P} \downarrow_{V'}$ over a smaller vocabulary $V' \subseteq V$. The down-scoping operator is useful to extract department relevant data from a company policy or to discard entitites that are no longer of concern.

Due to space limitations we omit a precise definition of the down-scoping operator and refer the interested reader to the full version of this paper [20]. Note however, that down-scoping only makes sense if i) $\leq_{H'} = \leq_H \cap (H' \times H')$ for $H \in \{U, D, P, A\}$; ii) R contains no symbol in $\Sigma \setminus \Sigma'$; and iii) R and dr contain no obligation in $O \setminus O'$. In the sequel, if we make statements about $\mathcal{P} \downarrow_W$ for a vocabulary $W \subset V$, these are to be understood to apply only for vocabularies W, that fulfill the requirements above. In the full paper [20] we also define *ruleset* and *policy reduction* operators "reduce", that remove redundant terms from a ruleset, thereby possibly enlarging the number of vocabularies suitable for down-scoping.

Often scoping leads to a refinement or at least functional refinement of a policy. E. g., extending the vocabulary will generally lead to a refinement (the policy becomes more comprehensive), while restricting it (such that nothing changes on the remaining items) will lead to a functional refinement (the policy will behave the same on the smaller vocabulary, but produce error states otherwise).

Lemma 1 (Refinement Properties of Scoping Operators). *Given a privacy policy* $\mathcal{P} = (V, R, dr)$ *and vocabularies* V', V'', *s. t.* $V' \subseteq V \subseteq V''$, $\leq_{H'} = \leq_H \cap (H' \times H')$ *and* $\leq_H = \leq_{H''} \cap (H \times H)$ *for* $H \in \{U, D, P, A\}$, *we have* $\mathcal{P} \uparrow_{V''} \leq \mathcal{P}$, $\mathcal{P} \preceq \mathcal{P} \uparrow_{V''}$ *and* $\mathcal{P} \uparrow_{V''} \downarrow_V = \mathcal{P}$.

Furthermore, if the symbols in $\Sigma \setminus \Sigma'$ *and in* $X \setminus X'$ *do* not *occur in the ruleset* R, *we have* $\mathcal{P} \downarrow_{V'} \preceq \mathcal{P}$ *and* $\mathcal{P} \leq \mathcal{P} \downarrow_{V'}$. *But in general* $\mathcal{P} \downarrow_{V'} \uparrow_V \not\approx \mathcal{P}$.

Analogously as for E-P3P, we define precedence shifts:

Definition 20 (Precedence Shift). *Let* $\mathcal{P} = (V, R, dr)$ *be a privacy policy and* $j \in \mathbb{Z}$. *Then* $\mathcal{P} + j := (V, R + j, dr)$ *with* $R + j := \{(i + j, g, c, r) \mid (i, g, c, r) \in R\}$ *is called the* precedence shift *of* $\mathcal{P}$ *by* j. *We define* $\mathcal{P} - j := \mathcal{P} + (-j)$.

Remark 6 (Precedence Shift). Clearly $\forall j \in \mathbb{Z} : \mathcal{P} \equiv \mathcal{P} + j$.

3.1   Composition of Policies

A framework for privacy policies should allow to start, say, from a company policy, stating some minimal requirements, and then to add new rules, collected in another policy, to refine the company policy to a department policy. NAPS supports this through the *composition* operator, that refines its first argument by adding the rules of its second argument with lower priority.

Definition 21 (Composition). *Let* $\mathcal{P}_1 = (V, R_1, dr_1)$, $\mathcal{P}_2 = (V, R'_2, dr_2)$ *be privacy policies over a vocabulary* V, $R'_2 := R_2 - \max(R_2) + \min(R_1) - 1$. *Then* $\mathcal{P}_1 \parallel \mathcal{P}_2 :=$ $(V, R_1 \cup R'_2, dr_1 \wedge dr_2)$ *is the (ordered)* composition *of* $\mathcal{P}_2$ *under* $\mathcal{P}_1$.

Composition can also be defined functionally, pointwise on the evaluations of two policies. Differing from E-P3P this is possible, due to the introduction of the evaluation tag $v \in \{\mathsf{f},\mathsf{a},\mathsf{d}\}$. From Def. 21 (Composition) we get

Lemma 2 (Functional Definition of Composition). *For policies* $\mathcal{P}_1$, $\mathcal{P}_2$ *over the same vocabulary* V *define the composition* $e_1 \parallel e_2$ *on evaluations* $e_1 = (r_1, v_1), e_2 = (r_2, v_2) \in E(V)$ *as in Table 1. Then for all* $q \in Q(V)$ *and* $\alpha \in \mathfrak{Ass}(X, M)$, *we have* $\mathrm{eval}_\alpha(\mathcal{P}_1 \parallel \mathcal{P}_2, q) = \mathrm{eval}_\alpha(\mathcal{P}_1, q) \parallel \mathrm{eval}_\alpha(\mathcal{P}_2, q)$.

Table 1. Ordered Composition

$\parallel$	(r_2, f)	(r_2, a)	(r_2, d)
(r_1, f)	(r_1, f)	(r_1, f)	(r_1, f)
(r_1, a)	$(r_1 \wedge r_2, \mathsf{f})$	$(r_1 \wedge r_2, \mathsf{a})$	(r_1, a)
(r_1, d)	(r_2, f)	(r_2, a)	$(r_1 \wedge r_2, \mathsf{d})$

Table 2. Conjunction

$\wedge$	(r_2, f)	(r_2, a)	(r_2, d)
(r_1, f)	$(r_1 \wedge r_2, \mathsf{f})$	$(r_1 \wedge r_2, \mathsf{a})$	(r_1, a)
(r_1, a)	$(r_1 \wedge r_2, \mathsf{a})$	$(r_1 \wedge r_2, \mathsf{a})$	(r_1, a)
(r_1, d)	(r_2, a)	(r_2, a)	$(r_1 \wedge r_2, \mathsf{d})$

By construction, the composition of two policies refines the first policy. Namely, from Eq. (2), (1) and Lemma 2 we obtain

Lemma 3. *For policies* $\mathcal{P}_1$ *and* $\mathcal{P}_2$ *over the same vocabulary, we have* $\mathcal{P}_1 \parallel \mathcal{P}_2 \leq \mathcal{P}_1$.

3.2   Policy Normalization

Each NAPS policy can be normalized, i. e. transformed into a strongly equivalent policy, that has only strongly final and strongly amendable rules and only one rule per priority level, where all final rules are of lower priority than any amendable rule.

Definition 22 (Normalization). *A ruleset* R *over the vocabulary* V *is called* normalized *iff i)* $R = R^A \cup R^F$; *ii) all rules* $(i, g, c, r) \in R^A$ *are strongly amendable; iii) all rules* $(i, g, c, r) \in R^F$ *are strongly final and* $r = (\top, \top)$; *iv)* $\max(R) = 0$; *v)* $\forall i$ *s. t.* $\min(R) \leq i \leq 0$ *there is exactly one rule of priority* i *in* R *denoted by* $R(i)$; *and vi)* $\forall (i, g, c, r) \in R^A \; \forall (i', g', c', r') \in R^F : i' < i$.

A policy $\mathcal{P} = (V, R, dr)$ *is called* normalized, *iff the ruleset* R *is normalized.*

We always write R^A for the subset of strongly amendable rules of a ruleset R, and R^F for the subset of strongly final rules of a ruleset R. If R carries a sub- or a superscript, so does R^A, R^F. Due to the page limit we omit the proof of

Lemma 4 (Ruleset & Policy Normalization). *There is an algorithm that given a rule-set R over the vocabulary V generates a normalized ruleset $\mathrm{norm}(R)$. From a policy $\mathcal{P} = (V, R, dr)$ we can generate a normalized policy $\mathrm{norm}(\mathcal{P}) := (V, \mathrm{norm}(R), dr)$ such that $\mathrm{norm}(\mathcal{P}) \equiv \mathcal{P}$.*

3.3 Conjunction of Privacy Policies

If two companies A and B cooperate, it may be necessary to apply the privacy policies of A *and* of B with equal priority. Unlike composition, which regards its first argument as being of higher priority—and thus in general does not refine its second argument—conjunction combines two policies in equal right and returns a result that weakly refines both. Specifying the conjunction of two policies such that up-scoping, down-scoping and composition distribute requires careful consideration of the inner workings of the policies involved, as up-scoping may introduce new vocabulary items, on which the effect of the conjunction policy cannot be determined by the functional properties of the original policies alone.

Definition 23 (Policy Conjunction). *Let $\mathcal{P}_1$, $\mathcal{P}_2$ be privacy policies over a vocabulary V. The conjunction $\mathcal{P} = \mathcal{P}_1 \wedge \mathcal{P}_2$ of $\mathcal{P}_1$, $\mathcal{P}_2$ is the output of Alg. 3.1.*

Algorithm 3.1. Policy Conjunction

```
Input:   policies P1 = (V, R1, dr1), P2 = (V, R2, dr2)
Output: conjunction policy P = P1 ∧ P2
```

```
for i = 1,2: if Ri not normalized: Ri := norm(Ri);
dr := dr1 ∧ dr2;
R := R1^A ∪ (R2^A + min(R1^A) − max(R2^A) − 1);  // "union" of amendable parts
i := min(R) − 1;
for j := max(R1^F) downto min(R1^F):
    (j,g1,c1,r1) := R1^F(j);
    for k := max(R2^F) downto min(R2^F):
        (k,g2,c2,r2) := R2(k);
        R := R ∪ {(i, g1 ∧ g2, c1 ∧ c2, (⊤,⊤))};  // "pairwise final conjunction"
        i := i − 1;
return P = (V, R, dr)
```

Although being defined on policies, policy conjunction exhibits the intuitively desired property that the evaluation of $\mathcal{P}_1 \wedge \mathcal{P}_2$ can be derived pointwise from the evaluations of $\mathcal{P}_1$, $\mathcal{P}_2$. Due to the page limit we omit the proof of

Lemma 5 (Functional Properties of Policy Conjunction). *For privacy policies $\mathcal{P}_1$, $\mathcal{P}_2$ over the same vocabulary V define the conjunction $\wedge$ on evaluations $e_1 = (r_1, v_1)$, $e_2 = (r_2, v_2) \in E(V)$ as in Table 2. Then for all $q \in Q(V)$ and all $\alpha \in \mathfrak{Ass}(X, M)$ we have $\mathrm{eval}_\alpha(\mathcal{P}_1 \wedge \mathcal{P}_2, q) = \mathrm{eval}_\alpha(\mathcal{P}_1, q) \wedge \mathrm{eval}_\alpha(\mathcal{P}_2, q)$.*

A Note on Disjunction. Adding a meaningful disjunction operation to NAPS is possible (without losing closedness). Few use cases impose a disjunctive composition of privacy policies, however. So here we do not discuss policy disjunction.

4   Algebraic Properties of Operators

Now we can prove intuitive algebraic properties, the NAPS operators were designed towards, but due to the page limit we must omit the actual proof of

Theorem 2 (Operator Laws). *Let* $\mathcal{P}_1$, $\mathcal{P}_2$ *be privacy policies on a vocabulary* V *and let* V', V'' *be vocabularies s. t.* $V' \subseteq V \subseteq V''$. *Then* $\mathcal{P}_1 \wedge \mathcal{P}_1 \equiv \mathcal{P}_1$, $\mathcal{P}_1 \wedge \mathcal{P}_2 \equiv \mathcal{P}_2 \wedge \mathcal{P}_1$, $(\mathcal{P}_1 \wedge \mathcal{P}_2) \wedge \mathcal{P}_3 \equiv \mathcal{P}_1 \wedge (\mathcal{P}_2 \wedge \mathcal{P}_3)$, $\mathcal{P}_1 \parallel \mathcal{P}_1 = \mathcal{P}_1$, $(\mathcal{P}_1 \parallel \mathcal{P}_2) \parallel \mathcal{P}_3 = \mathcal{P}_1 \parallel (\mathcal{P}_2 \parallel \mathcal{P}_3)$, $(\mathcal{P}_1 \wedge \mathcal{P}_2) \parallel \mathcal{P}_3 \equiv (\mathcal{P}_1 \parallel \mathcal{P}_3) \wedge (\mathcal{P}_2 \parallel \mathcal{P}_3)$, $(\mathcal{P}_1 \wedge \mathcal{P}_2) \uparrow_{V''} = (\mathcal{P}_1 \uparrow_{V''}) \wedge (\mathcal{P}_2 \uparrow_{V''})$, $(\mathcal{P}_1 \wedge \mathcal{P}_2) \downarrow_{V'} = (\mathcal{P}_1 \downarrow_{V'}) \wedge (\mathcal{P}_2 \downarrow_{V'})$, $(\mathcal{P}_1 \parallel \mathcal{P}_2) \uparrow_{V''} = (\mathcal{P}_1 \uparrow_{V''}) \parallel (\mathcal{P}_2 \uparrow_{V''})$, $(\mathcal{P}_1 \parallel \mathcal{P}_2) \downarrow_{V'} = (\mathcal{P}_1 \downarrow_{V'}) \parallel (\mathcal{P}_2 \downarrow_{V'})$, $\mathcal{P}_1 \wedge \mathcal{P}_2 \lesssim \mathcal{P}_1$, $\mathcal{P}_1 \parallel \mathcal{P}_2 \leq \mathcal{P}_1$, $\mathcal{P}_1 \wedge \mathcal{P}_2 \lesssim \mathcal{P}_1 \parallel \mathcal{P}_2$, $\mathrm{norm}(\mathcal{P}_1) \equiv \mathcal{P}_1$ *and* $\mathrm{reduce}(\mathcal{P}_1) \equiv \mathcal{P}_1$.

The next lemma, the proof of which we also omit due to the page limit, shows strong equivalence to have the desired property, that strongly equivalent policies remain strongly equivalent (and thereby also equivalent, i. e. same output under all assignments and queries) under all operators.

Lemma 6 (Properties of Strong Equivalence). *Let* $\mathcal{P}_1 \equiv \mathcal{P}_1'$, $\mathcal{P}_2 \equiv \mathcal{P}_2'$ *policies over* V *and let* $V' \subset V \subset V''$ *then we have* $\mathcal{P}_1 \uparrow_{V''} \equiv \mathcal{P}_1' \uparrow_{V''}$, $\mathcal{P}_1 \downarrow_{V'} \equiv \mathcal{P}_1' \downarrow_{V'}$, $\mathcal{P}_1 \wedge \mathcal{P}_2 \equiv \mathcal{P}_1' \wedge \mathcal{P}_2'$ *and* $\mathcal{P}_1 \parallel \mathcal{P}_2 \equiv \mathcal{P}_1' \parallel \mathcal{P}_2'$.

5   Conclusions

NAPS provides a powerful tool to operate on and reason about privacy policies by providing useful operators along with intuitive algebraic relations. Compared to E-P3P, constructing policies seems less involved, as in E-P3P policy evaluation involves a more complicated preprocessing of rulesets ("rule unfolding") [5, 4]. E-P3P rulings can be mapped to NAPS evaluations, opening a possibility to embed E-P3P policies into NAPS. Still NAPS' usefulness remains to be proved: a prototype implementation with an experimental deployment of such a system has to be done to explore practical strengths and weaknesses. We think the already achieved results justify research in this direction.

References

1. P. Ashley et al. E-P3P privacy policies and privacy authorization. In *WPES-02*, pp. 103–109, ACM Press, 2002.
2. M. Backes et al. Efficient Comparison of Enterprise Priv. Policies. In *SAC'04*, pp. 375–382. ACM Press, 2004.
3. M. Backes et al. Unification in Priv. Policy Evaluation – Translating EPAL into Prolog. In *POLICY'04*. IEEE Comp. Soc., 2004.
4. M. Backes et al. An Algebra for Composing Enterprise Priv. Policies. In *ESORICS 2004*, vol. 3193 of *LNCS*, pp. 33–52. Springer, 2004.
5. M. Backes et al. A Toolkit for Managing Enterprise Priv. Policies. In *ESORICS 2003*, vol. 2808 of *LNCS*, pp. 162–180. Springer, 2003.

6. C. Bettini et al. Obligation monitoring in policy management. In *POLICY 2002*, pp. 2–12, 2002.

7. G. Birkhoff. *Lattice Theory*, vol. 25 of *AMS. Colloquium Publications*. AMS, Providence, Rhode Island, 1973.

8. P. A. Bonatti et al. A Component-Based Architecture for Secure Data Publication. In *ACSAC 2001*, pp. 309–318, 2001.

9. P. A. Bonatti et al. A modular approach to composing access control policies. In *CCS-00*, pp. 164–173, ACM Press, 2000.

10. P. A. Bonatti et al. An algebra for composing access control policies. *ACM Trans. on Inf. and Syst. Sec.*, 5(1):1–35, Feb. 2002.

11. S. D. C. di Vimercati and P. Samarati. An authorization model for federated systems. In *ESORICS 1996*, vol. 1146 of LNCS, pp. 99–117. Springer, 1996.

12. Z. Fu et al. IPSec/VPN security policy: Correctness, conflict detection and resolution. In *IEEE Policy 2001*, vol. 1995 of *LNCS*, pp. 39–56. Springer, 2001.

13. J. H. Gallier. *Logic for Comp. Science: Found. of Automatic Theorem Proving*, Ch. 2.5 and 10, pp. 448–456, 483–488. John Wiley & Sons, 1986, http://www.cis.upenn.edu/~jean/gbooks/logic.html.

14. V. D. Gligor et al. On the Formal Definition of Separation-of-Duty Policies and their Composition. In *Proc. 19th IEEE Symp. on Sec. & Priv.*, pp. 172–183, 1998.

15. S. Jajodia et al. Provisional authorization. In *Proc. of the E-commerce Sec. and Priv.*, pp. 133–159. Kluwer Academic Publishers, 2001.

16. S. Jajodia et al. Flexible support for multiple access control policies. *ACM Trans. on Database Syst.*, 26(2):214–260, June 2001.

17. G. Karjoth et al. The platform for enterprise privacy practices – privacy-enabled management of customer data. In *CSFW 2002*, vol. 2482 of *LNCS*, pp. 69–84. Springer, 2002.

18. J. Łukasiewicz. Philosophische Bemerkungen zu mehrwertigen Systemen des Aussagenkalküls. *C. R. Soc. Sc. Varsovie*, 23:51–77, 1931.

19. J. D. Moffett and M. S. Sloman. Policy hierarchies for distributed systems management. *IEEE JSAC Special Issue on Network Manag.*, 11(9):1404–1414, 1993.

20. D. Raub and R. Steinwandt. An Algebra for Enterprise Privacy Policies Closed Under Composition and Conjunction. Full Version, 2006, http://www.crypto.ethz.ch/~raub/publications.html.

21. C. N. Ribeiro et al. SPL: An access control language for security policies and complex constraints. In *NDSS 2001*, pp. 89–107, Internet Soc., 2001, http://www.gsd.inesc-id.pt/~avz/pubs/SPL.pdf.

22. P. H. Schmitt. Nichtklassische Logiken. Script, Universität Karlsruhe, 2004, http://i12www.ira.uka.de/studium.htm.

23. R. T. Simon and M. E. Zurko. Separation of Duty in Role-based Environments. In *CSFW 1997*, pp. 183–194, 1997.

24. D. Wijesekera and S. Jajodia. Policy algebras for access control: the propositional case. In *CCS 2001*, pp. 38–47, ACM Press, 2001.

25. D. Wijesekera and S. Jajodia. A propositional policy algebra for access control. *ACM Trans. on Inf. and Syst. Sec.*, 6(2):286–325, 2003.

26. Semilattice. Wikipedia, the free encyclopedia, http://en.wikipedia.org/wiki/Semilattice.

27. eXtensible Access Control Markup Language (XACML). OASIS Committee Specification 1.0, Dec. 2002, http://www.oasis-open.org/committees/xacml.

Privacy-Preserving Decision Tree Mining Based on Random Substitutions*

Jim Dowd, Shouhuai Xu, and Weining Zhang

Department of Computer Science, University of Texas at San Antonio
{jdowd, shxu, wzhang}@cs.utsa.edu

Abstract. Privacy-preserving decision tree mining is an important problem that has yet to be thoroughly understood. In fact, the privacy-preserving decision tree mining method explored in the pioneer paper [1] was recently showed to be completely broken, because its data perturbation technique is fundamentally flawed [2]. However, since the general framework presented in [1] has some nice and useful features in practice, it is natural to ask if it is possible to rescue the framework by, say, utilizing a different data perturbation technique. In this paper, we answer this question affirmatively by presenting such a data perturbation technique based on *random substitutions*. We show that the resulting privacy-preserving decision tree mining method is immune to attacks (including the one introduced in [2]) that are seemingly relevant. Systematic experiments show that it is also effective.

Keywords: Privacy-preservation, decision tree, data mining, perturbation, matrix.

1 Introduction

Protection of privacy has become an important issue in data mining research. A fundamental requirement of privacy-preserving data mining is to protect the input data, yet still allow data miners to extract useful knowledge models. A number of privacy-preserving data mining methods have recently been proposed [3, 4, 1, 5, 6], which take either a cryptographic or a statistical approach. The cryptographic approach [7] ensures strong privacy and accuracy via a secure multi-party computation, but typically suffers from its poor performance. The statistical approach has been used to mine decision trees [1], association rules [4, 6, 8, 9], and clustering [10], and is popular mainly because of its high performance. This paper focuses on the statistical approach to privacy-preserving decision tree mining.

The notion of privacy-preserving decision tree mining was introduced in the seminal paper [1]. However, the problem of privacy-preserving decision tree mining has yet to be thoroughly understood. In fact, the privacy-preserving decision tree mining method explored in [1] was recently showed to be completely broken, meaning that an adversary can recover the original data from the perturbed (and public) one. The reason for the attack to be so powerful was that the adopted

---

* This work was supported in part by US NFS grant IIS-0524612.

G. Müller (Ed.): ETRICS 2006, LNCS 3995, pp. 145–159, 2006.

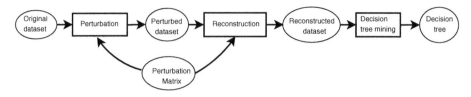

Fig. 1. A Framework of Privacy-Preserving Decision Tree Mining

data perturbation technique, called *noise-adding*, turned out to be fundamentally flawed [2].

In spite of aforementioned attack, the framework introduced in [1] (shown in Fig. 1) has a nice and useful feature: the perturbed data can be analyzed by arbitrarily many data miners using conventional mining algorithms. On one hand, an owner can protect its data by releasing only the perturbed version. On the other hand, a miner equipped with a specification of the perturbation technique can derive a decision tree that is quite accurate, compared to the one derived from the original data. We believe that this feature makes the framework a good-fit for many real-life applications. Therefore, it is natural to ask if the framework can be rescued by, say, utilizing some other data perturbation technique.

This paper makes several contributions towards privacy-preserving decision tree mining. What is perhaps the most important is that the framework introduced in [1] can be rescued by a new data perturbation technique based on *random substitutions*. This perturbation technique is similar to the randomization techniques used in the context of statistical disclosure control [11, 12], but is based on a different privacy measure called ρ_1-to-ρ_2 privacy breaching[1] [6] and a special type of perturbation matrix called the γ-diagonal matrix [4]. This utilization of both ρ_1-to-ρ_2 privacy breaching and γ-diagonal matrix seems to be new. This is because both [6] and [4] were explored in the context of privacy-preserving association rule mining. Further, it was even explicitly considered as an open problem in [4] to extend the results therein to other data mining tasks such as decision tree mining. For example, the integration of the perturbation matrix of [4] is non-trivial, because we need to make it work with continuous-valued attributes. As a consequence, we need to analyze the effect of the dimension size of the matrix with respect to the accuracy of decision trees and the performance of the system. To this end, we introduce a novel error-reduction technique for our data reconstruction, so that it not only prevents a critical problem caused by a large perturbation matrix, but also guarantees a strictly better accuracy (see Section 3.3 for a theoretic treatment and Section 5.1 for experimental results).

In addition, we show that the resulting privacy-preserving decision tree mining method has the following properties.

---

[1] Roughly, a perturbation technique prevents a ρ_1-to-ρ_2 privacy breaching if the adversary has an a prior probability about some private information in the original data no more than ρ_1, she can derive a posterior probability about the same private information no more than ρ_2.

- It is immune to the relevant *data-recovery* and *repeated-perturbation* attacks. The data-recovery attack was introduced in [2] (and further explored in [13]) to recover the original data from a given perturbed dataset. Our method is immune to this attack because the random substitution technique is fundamentally different from the noise-adding one [1]. Specifically, noise-adding technique draws noises from a *single* probabilistic distribution, but the random substitution draws noises from *many different* distributions, even if it is "artificially and mechanically" viewed as a kind of noise-adding. This suffices to defeat the data-recovery attack, which crucially relies on that the noises are drawn from the *same* distribution. The repeated-perturbation attack is introduced in this paper based on the observation that an adversary may repeatedly perturb the data with the hope to recover the original data. This attack can be effective if the perturbation technique can be viewed as a function f that has the property $f(...f(f(x))) = x$, where x is an original dataset and f is known to the adversary (or a data miner). Fortunately, we are able to show rigorously that our method is also immune to this attack. While our perturbation technique may have inherited the privacy assurance guarantee of [6], the *data-recovery* and *repeated-perturbation* attacks were not accommodated in the model of [6].
- It ensures that the decision trees learned from the perturbed data are quite accurate compared with those learned from the original data. Furthermore, a small number of parameters are seemingly sufficient for capturing some important trade-offs in practice. The parameters include: (1) the privacy assurance metric γ, (2) the dimension size N of perturbation matrix, which affects the accuracy of reconstructed data as well as performance, and (3) the entropy of a perturbation matrix, which, to some extent, can encompass the effect of both γ and N. Systematic experiments show that there is a strong correlation between entropy of the perturbation matrix and accuracy of the resulting decision tree. As a result, both γ and accuracy can be used to select N. Furthermore, it is showed that by selecting an appropriate N, one can achieve the desired trade-off between accuracy, privacy, and performance.

The rest of the paper is organized as follows. In Section 2, we present random substitution perturbation algorithm and analyze its immunity to the data-recovery attack. In Section 3, we present the reconstruction algorithm with heuristic methods for reducing estimation error of original data distributions. In Section 4, we analyze the effect of perturbation matrix parameters and the immunity to the repeated-perturbation attack. In Section 5, we present results from our experiments. In Section 6, we discuss how to select perturbation matrix parameters in practice. Section 7 concludes the paper.

2 Random Substitution Perturbation and Analysis

In the following, we assume that data records have attributes $A_1, \ldots, A_q$, with discrete- or continuous-valued domains. Without loss of generality, we consider the perturbation of a single discrete- or continuous-valued attribute, because it is straightforward to extend the method to perturb a set of attributes together.

2.1   Perturb a Discrete-Valued Attribute

The basic idea is to replace the value of each data record under the attribute by another value that is chosen randomly from the attribute domain according to a probabilistic model. The general algorithm is given in Algorithm 1 and explained in the following.

Algorithm 1. Random Substitution Perturbation (RSP)

Input: a dataset $\mathcal{O}$ of n records, an attribute A with domain $\mathcal{U} = \{u_1, \ldots, u_N\}$, and a perturbation matrix $\mathbf{M}$ for $\mathcal{U}$.
Output: the perturbed dataset $\mathcal{P}$.
Method:

    $\mathcal{P} = \emptyset$;
    for each $o \in \mathcal{O}$ begin
    1. $k = getIndex(o[A])$;
    2. $p = o$;
    3. obtain a random number r from a uniform distribution over $(0, 1]$;
    4. find an integer $1 \leq h \leq N$ such that $\sum_{i=1}^{h-1} m_{i,k} < r \leq \sum_{i=1}^{h} m_{i,k}$;
    5. set $p[A] = getValue(h)$;
    6. add p to $\mathcal{P}$;
    return $\mathcal{P}$;

To perturb a set of data records $\mathcal{O} = \{o_1, \ldots, o_n\}$ on an attribute A, we create a perturbation matrix $\mathbf{M}$ for the attribute domain $\mathcal{U} = \{u_1, \ldots, u_N\}$. For each $u_k \in \mathcal{U}$, $p(k \rightarrow h) = \Pr(u_k \rightarrow u_h)$ denotes the (transition) probability that u_k is replaced by $u_h \in \mathcal{U}$. The perturbation matrix is then defined as $\mathbf{M} = [m_{h,k}]_{N \times N}$, where $m_{h,k} = p(k \rightarrow h)$. Since each value must be replaced by a value in $\mathcal{U}$, $\sum_{h=1}^{N} m_{h,k} = 1$, for $1 \leq k \leq N$. Therefore, each column k of $\mathbf{M}$ defines a probability mass function, that is, $p(h) = m_{h,k}$ for $1 \leq h \leq N$, and a cumulative probability function $F(a) = \sum_{h=1}^{a} m_{h,k}$, where $1 \leq a \leq N$. The choice of probabilities in the perturbation matrix is an important issue (in particular, it is related to the privacy assurance guarantee) that will be described in Section 4.

We associate two functions with the attribute domain: function $getIndex(u)$, which returns index of value u (that is i if $u = u_i$), and function $getValue(i)$, which returns the ith value in $\mathcal{U}$ (that is u_i). Naturally, we call $\mathcal{O}$ and $\mathcal{P}$ the original and the perturbed dataset and the records in them the original and perturbed records, respectively.

We now explain steps of algorithm RSP. In step 1, we obtain the index of domain value $o[A]$. Step 2 initializes the perturbed data record. Steps 3 and

4 determine the index of the replacement (or perturbed) value using the perturbation matrix. Notice that we can always find the index h that satisfies the condition of Step 4. Step 5 replaces the original value by the value chosen in Step 4. Finally, the perturbed record is added to the perturbed dataset in Step 6. The time complexity of Algorithm RSP is $O(n \cdot N)$.

2.2   Perturb a Continuous-Valued Attribute

One way to apply RSP to a continuous-valued attribute is to discretize the attribute domain into intervals $I_1, \ldots, I_N$ for some given N, and to define the perturbation matrix over the discretized domain $\mathcal{U} = \{I_1, \ldots, I_N\}$. As a result, each element $m_{h,k}$ of the perturbation matrix is now interpreted as the probability that a value in I_k is replaced by a value in I_h. To maintain consistent semantics, each interval is represented by a value that is contained in it. This value can be either a fixed value, such as the center or an endpoint of the interval, or a randomly selected value. Thus, in this case, the function $getIndex(u)$ returns index i, such that $u \in I_i$ and function $getValue(i)$ returns the representative value of I_i. In our experiments, the representative value of an interval is its center.

Many discretization methods are known. We use a simple equi-width binning method in our experiments. Without loss of generality, let the attribute domain be an interval of real numbers with finite endpoints (for simplicity), that is $[l, u) \subset \mathbf{R}$, where $-\infty < l < u < \infty$. With a user-specified parameter $N > 1$, the discretization method partitions the domain into N intervals (also called bins) $I_i = [l_i, u_i)$, such that, $l_1 = l$, $u_N = u$, $u_i = l_{i+1}$ for $1 < i < N$, and $u_i - l_i = \frac{u-l}{N}$. The choice of N has an impact on performance and will be further explored in Sections 4 and 6.

2.3   Why Is Random Substitution Fundamentally Different from Adding Noise?

The adding noise perturbation method introduced in [1] is subject to what we call *data-recovery* attacks [2, 13], which can accurately derive the original data from the perturbed data. It is natural to ask if these attacks will also be effective against the random substitution perturbation method. In this section, we show that the answer to this question is negative. These attacks are based on, among other things, a crucial assumption that the noises are independently drawn from a single distribution and the noise variance σ^2 is known. While this assumption is certainly valid for adding noise perturbation of [1] due to its very design, we show that this assumption is no longer valid for the random substitution perturbation. Thus, the random substitution perturbation method is immune to the attacks explored in [2, 13].

The basic idea is to view the random substitution perturbation as a special adding noise perturbation and show that the added noises must be drawn from *different* probabilistic distributions that depend on the original data.

Let $\mathcal{O} = \{o_1, \ldots, o_n\}$ be a set of original data and $\mathcal{P} = \{p_1, \ldots, p_n\}$ be a set of perturbed data that are obtained using the random substitution perturbation. The original data can be viewed as a realization of a set $O = \{O_1, \ldots, O_n\}$ of independent, identically distributed random variables, and the perturbed data as a realization of another set $P = \{P_1, \ldots, P_n\}$ of random variables. By the design of the random substitution perturbation, all these random variables have the same domain, which is assumed without loss of generality to be a set $D = [a, b]$ of integers where $a < b$.

The random substitution perturbation can be viewed as a special case of adding noise perturbation: for each original data o_i, it draws a noise r randomly from the interval $[-(b - a), (b - a)]$ with a probability

$$\Pr[r \mid o_i] = \begin{cases} m_{k,o_i}, & \text{if } a \leq k = o_i + r \leq b; \\ 0, & \text{otherwise.} \end{cases}$$

and generates a perturbed data $p_i = o_i + r$. It is easy to verify that this special adding noise perturbation is indeed equivalent to the random substitution perturbation. The following theorem[2] indicates that for this special adding noise perturbation, if the perturbation matrix allows any domain value to be perturbed into a different value, the probability distribution of the noise given an original data can be different from that given another original data, therefore, the noises must not be drawn from the same distribution.

Theorem 1. *If some non-diagonal element of the perturbation matrix is positive, that is, $m_{k,h} > 0$, for $k \neq h$, then $\exists o_i, o_j \in [a, b]$, $o_i \neq o_j$ and $\exists r \in [-(b - a), +(b - a)]$, such that $\Pr[r \mid o_i] \neq \Pr[r \mid o_j]$.*

3   Generating Reconstructed Dataset

3.1   A Reconstruction Algorithm

The purpose of creating a reconstructed dataset is to allow the data miner to learn decision trees using existing decision tree mining algorithms. We emphasize that while it can be used to learn accurate decision trees, a reconstructed dataset is not the original dataset and will not violate the privacy guarantee.

Algorithm 2 is the matrix-based reconstruction (MR) algorithm that we use to create the reconstructed dataset, which is based on a heuristic method of [1]. Using function $estimate(\mathcal{P}, \mathbf{M})$ (whose detail is given in Section 3.2 below), it first estimates the data distribution of the attribute that we want to reconstruct, and sort the perturbed records on that attribute. Next, it heuristically assigns the attribute values to perturbed data records according to the estimated data distribution. For example, if the estimated distribution predicts that for $1 \leq i \leq N$, $Dist[i]$ original records have value $getValue(i)$ in attribute A, we assign $getValue(1)$ to the first $Dist[1]$ perturbed records, $getValue(2)$ to the next $Dist[2]$ perturbed records, and so on. If multiple attributes need to be reconstructed, we apply MR to one attribute at a time.

---

[2] Due to space limitation, proofs of all results of this paper have been omitted. The readers are referred to [14] for the proofs.

Algorithm 2. Matrix-based Reconstruction (MR)

Input: a perturbed dataset $\mathcal{P}$, an attributes A and an $N \times N$ perturbation matrix $\mathbf{M}$ of A.
Output: a reconstructed dataset $\mathcal{R}$.
Method:

```
R = ∅;
Dist = estimate(P, M);
sort P on A in ascending order;
next = 1;
for i = 1 to N do begin
  for j = 1 to Dist[i] do begin
    r = p_next;
    next = next + 1;
    r[A] = getValue(i);
  end
end
return R;
```

3.2   Estimating Original Data Distributions

We now briefly describe a simple method for estimating original data distribution [4]. Let $\mathcal{U}$ be the domain of a discrete-valued attribute containing N values. Recall that $\mathcal{O}$ and $\mathcal{P}$ are the original and perturbed datasets of n records, respectively. Let $\mathbf{M}$ be the perturbation matrix defined for $\mathcal{U}$. For each value $u_i \in \mathcal{U}$, let Y_i be the count (that is, total number) of u_i in a perturbed dataset generated from a given original dataset and let X_i be the count of u_i in the original dataset. Since from the data miner's point of view, $\mathcal{O}$ is unknown and many $\mathcal{P}$ can be randomly generated from a given $\mathcal{O}$, both X_i and Y_i, for $1 \leq i \leq N$, are random variables. Let $X = [X_1, \ldots, X_N]^T$ and $Y = [Y_1, \ldots, Y_N]^T$ be the (column) vector of counts of the original and the perturbed datasets, respectively. For a given $\mathcal{O}$, we have

$$E(Y) = [E(Y_1), \ldots, E(Y_N)]^T = \mathbf{M}X$$

where $E(Y_h) = \sum_{k=1}^{N} m_{h,k} X_k = \sum_{k=1}^{N} p(k \rightarrow h) X_k$ is the expected number of u_h in any $\mathcal{P}$ perturbed from $\mathcal{O}$ and $p(k \rightarrow h) X_k$ is the expected number of u_h due to the perturbation of u_k. If $\mathbf{M}$ is invertible and $E(Y)$ is known, we can obtain X by solving the following equation

$$X = \mathbf{M}^{-1} E(Y)$$

However, since $E(Y)$ is unknown, we estimate X by $\hat{X}$ with the following formula

$$\hat{X} = [\hat{X}_1, \ldots, \hat{X}_N]^T = \mathbf{M}^{-1} \mathbf{y} \tag{1}$$

where $\mathbf{y} = [y_1, \ldots, y_N]$ is the number of u_k in the observed perturbed dataset $\mathcal{P}$. Notice that this method can be applied directly to estimate interval distribution of a discretized domain of an attribute.

3.3   Reducing Estimation Errors

A problem of the distribution estimation method is that $\hat{X}$ often contains an estimation error. For small N, such as that considered in [4], the error can be undetected, but for larger N, the error may cause some $\hat{X}_i$ to become negative, which can in turn cause the failure of the reconstruction. To resolve this problem, let us explore the estimation error.

Let $\hat{X} = X + \Delta$, where $\Delta = [\delta_1, \ldots, \delta_N]^T$ is a vector of errors. It is obvious that if the 1-norm $||\Delta||_1 = \sum_{i=1}^{N} |\delta_i| = 0$, the estimate is accurate. Since neither X nor Δ is known, in general, we may not even know whether $\hat{X}$ contains an error. Fortunately, if the estimate $\hat{X}$ is accurate, it must satisfy the following constraints **C1** and **C2**.

C1: The 1-norm of $\hat{X}$ should be equal to n. This can be shown by the following Lemma.

Lemma 1. *For any set of n perturbed data, $||\hat{X}||_1 \geq n$, and furthermore, if $\hat{X} = X$, $||\hat{X}||_1 = n$.*

C2:$\hat{X}$ contains no negative element. This is because it is the estimated counts and if it contains a negative count, it must has an estimation error.

While **C1** can be used to detect an estimation error, the following proposition indicates that **C2** can also be used to reduce an estimation error in $\hat{X}$, and therefore lead to a useful heuristic (adopted in our experiments).

Proposition 1. *If $\hat{X}$ contains any negative element, setting the negative element to zero strictly reduces the estimation error.*

4   Perturbation Matrix and Analysis

Given that the privacy is measured by the (ρ_1-to-ρ_2) privacy requirement (as defined in [6]) and the accuracy is measured by the condition number, [4] showed that for a given $\gamma \leq \frac{\rho_2(1-\rho_1)}{\rho_1(1-\rho_2)}$, the optimal perturbation matrix is the gamma diagonal matrix $\mathbf{M} = x\mathbf{G}$, where $x = \frac{1}{\gamma+N-1}$, and

$$\mathbf{G} = \begin{bmatrix} \gamma & 1 & 1 & \cdots \\ 1 & \gamma & 1 & \cdots \\ 1 & 1 & \gamma & \cdots \\ \vdots & \vdots & \vdots & \ddots \end{bmatrix}$$

which guarantees γ and has a minimum condition number.

Now we investigate some important aspects of perturbation matrix that are relevant to privacy-preserving decision tree mining.

Diagonal vs Off-diagonal Elements. We observe that both *privacy* and *accuracy* are affected by the ratio of diagonal and off-diagonal elements in the perturbation matrix. As a starting point, consider the gamma diagonal matrix and let $\gamma = \infty$. In this case, $\mathbf{M}$ essentially becomes the identity matrix $\mathbf{I}$. It provides the maximum accuracy, since each original value is perturbed into itself, therefore, $E(Y) = X = Y$. But it also provides the minimum privacy guarantee, since $\gamma = \infty$ implies $\rho_1 = 0$ and $\rho_2 = 1$, that is, the perturbed data discloses the private information completely.

As γ reduces, diagonal elements $\frac{\gamma}{\gamma+N-1}$ will be smaller and off-diagonal elements $\frac{1}{\gamma+N-1}$ larger. As a result, each domain value is more likely to be perturbed into other values during the perturbation. Thus, the privacy guarantee is improved due to reduced γ and the estimation accuracy is reduced because the increased randomness in the perturbation matrix makes accurate estimation more difficult. As γ approaches 1, both diagonal and off-diagonal elements will converge to $\frac{1}{N}$, that is, the probability distribution of each column approaches the uniform distribution. This is the case of the maximum privacy guarantee and the minimum estimation accuracy. However, for practical reason, $\gamma = 1$ is not allowed. Otherwise, $\mathbf{M}$ becomes singular, and the estimation method is invalid since $\mathbf{M}^{-1}$ no longer exists.

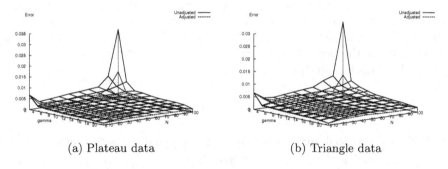

(a) Plateau data   (b) Triangle data

Fig. 2. Estimation Errors of Two Original Data Distributions

The Dimension of Perturbation Matrix. In the previous analysis , we assume that the dimension N of $\mathbf{M}$ is fixed. What if N can also vary? Previous work has not considered the effect of N. In [6], the amplification factor concerns only the ratios between transition probabilities and does not care how many such probabilities there are. In [4], N is treated as a constant. In our work, when a continuous-valued (and maybe also some discrete-valued) attribute domain is discretized into N intervals, we need to decide what the N should be. Ideally, we should choose N to improve privacy guarantee and estimation accuracy.

Let us consider the ratio of the diagonal element to the sum of off-diagonal elements in a single row, which is the likelihood that a domain value is perturbed into itself. This is given by $\frac{\gamma}{N-1}$. Let us assume a fixed γ and a varying N. If $N = \infty$ or $N = 1$, we have a singular matrix, and both perturbation and distribution estimation are impossible. So, assume $1 < N < \infty$. As N increases, the likelihood decreases that a domain value will be perturbed into itself, since the diagonal elements are reduced. But, at the same time, the probability is also reduced that the domain value is perturbed into any other specific domain value, since non-diagonal elements also become much smaller. Thus it is more likely for the estimated counts of domain values to be negative, which will increase the estimation error.

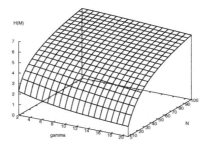

Fig. 3. Entropy of some perturbation matrices

The Entropy of Perturbation Matrix. So far, we analyzed how γ and N individually affect privacy and accuracy. But, it is also important to know how γ and N collectively affect these measures, particularly if we need to determine these parameters for a given dataset. Ideally, a single "metric" that can "abstract" both γ and N could simplify this task. To study this problem, we introduce a new measure of the perturbation matrix, namely, the entropy of perturbation matrix $\mathbf{M}$, which is defined as

$$H(\mathbf{M}) = \sum_{j=1}^{N} P_j H(j)$$

where P_j is the probability of value u_j in the original dataset, which captures the prior knowledge of the adversary, and $H(j) = -\sum_{i=1}^{N} m_{i,j} \log_2 m_{i,j}$ is the entropy of column j of the perturbation matrix. Since we do not have any prior knowledge about the original dataset, we assume that $P_j = \frac{1}{N}$, and therefore, $H(j) = -\frac{\gamma}{\gamma+N-1} \log_2 \frac{\gamma}{\gamma+N-1} - \sum_{i=1}^{N-1} \frac{1}{\gamma+N-1} \log_2 \frac{1}{\gamma+N-1}$, for any column j, and $H(\mathbf{M}) = -\frac{\gamma}{\gamma+N-1} \log_2 \frac{\gamma}{\gamma+N-1} - \frac{N-1}{\gamma+N-1} \log_2 \frac{1}{\gamma+N-1}$. Figure 3 shows the graph of $H(\mathbf{M})$ over a range of $2 \le \gamma \le 21$ and $5 \le N \le 100$. It is easy to see that for a given γ, the entropy increases as N increases, which indicates a decrease of estimation accuracy, and for a given N, the entropy increases as γ decreases, which indicates a increase of privacy guarantee. In Section 6, we will show that the entropy is a very useful instrument to give an insight of how γ and N affect the accuracy of decision tree.

Security Against the Repeated-Perturbation Attack. The random substitution perturbation described in Section 2 can be viewed as a two-step Markov chain with a specific N-state Markov matrix, namely, the gamma diagonal matrix.

This Markov chain is irreducible and ergodic since all the states communicate with each other and have period 1. An interesting question about this perturbation method is whether an adversary can gain any additional information by repeatedly perturbing the original dataset using the given perturbation matrix. We call this attack *repeated-perturbation*. In the following, we show that the effect of such a repeated perturbation will converge to the effect of a single perturbation using a perturbation matrix with the maximum entropy. Therefore, the adversary can *not* gain any additional information by repeatedly perturbing the perturbed dataset.

Assume that we apply the perturbation t times using the given perturbation matrix $\mathbf{M}$, the process is a Markov chain of $t+1$ steps. The t-step transition probability that u_j is replaced by u_i after the tth step is $m_{i,j}^t = \Pr[u_j \xrightarrow{t} u_i]$, which is the (i,j)th element of the t-step transition matrix $\mathbf{M}^t = \prod_{i=1}^{t} \mathbf{M}$. The following theorem says that the transition probabilities in $\mathbf{M}^t$ strictly converges to a uniform distribution as t approaches ∞, which implies that $\mathbf{M}^t$ has the maximum entropy (for the given N).

Theorem 2. *For any integer $t > 1$, $m_{i,i}^t > m_{i,i}^{t+1}$ and $m_{i,j}^t < m_{i,j}^{t+1}$, and $\lim_{t \to \infty} m_{i,j}^t = \frac{1}{N}$ for $1 \le i, j \le N$.*

5   Experiments

We performed extensive experiments to study the impact of perturbation matrix on the reconstruction of original data distribution and on the accuracy of decision trees. These experiments were run on a Pentium 4 PC with all algorithms implemented in Java.

5.1   Estimation Error of Data Distribution

In this experiment, we study how perturbation parameters affect the estimation error of original data distribution. We consider two (single-attribute) numerical datasets similar to those studied in [1]. The domain of these datasets is the integers between 1 and 200. We consider perturbation matrices with integer γ that varies from 2 to 21 and N that takes values 5, 10, 15, 20, 30, 40, ..., and 100. These give 240 combinations of γ and N (or different perturbation matrices). For each dataset and each combination of γ and N, we first discretize the domain into N equi-width intervals and create the perturbation matrix. We then repeat the following steps five times: perturbing the dataset, reconstruct the data distribution, measure the estimation error using

$$E = \frac{\sum_{i=1}^{N} |\hat{X}_i - X_i|}{\sum_{i=1}^{N} X_i}.$$

To reduce the randomness of the result, we report the average error over the five runs (see Fig. 2). To show the effects of the heuristic error reduction technique, we included errors both with and without applying the heuristic error reduction.

As shown in Fig. 2, the error surfaces of the two different data distributions are almost identical. This indicates that the estimation procedure is independent of data distributions and only depends on the perturbation parameters γ and N. Also, the error surfaces of the heuristically adjusted estimation are under that of unadjusted estimation. Thus, the heuristic error adjustment is effective. In fact, for most combinations of γ and N, the heuristic is able to reduce estimation error by 50%.

5.2   Decision Tree Accuracy

In this experiment, we study how perturbation matrix parameters affect decision tree accuracy (measured against testing sets). We considered 5 synthetic datasets that were studied in [1] and 2 datasets from the UCI Machine Learning Repository [15]. Again, we consider perturbation matrices based on the same 240 combinations of γ and N.

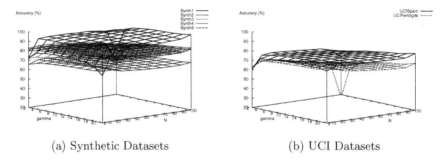

(a) Synthetic Datasets   (b) UCI Datasets

Fig. 4. Accuracy of decision trees learned from reconstructed data

Each dataset consists of a training set and a testing set. For each training set and each combination of γ and N, we discretize the domain and create the perturbation matrix as explained before. We then perturb the dataset, generate the reconstructed dataset, mine a decision tree, and measure the classification accuracy using the corresponding testing set. This process is repeated five times and the decision tree accuracy averaged over the 5 runs is reported here. The decision tree mining algorithm used is a version of C4.5 [16] implemented in Java.

Figure 4 shows the accuracy of decision trees for various combinations of γ and N. Notice that the accuracy surfaces for all datasets are lower than the accuracies of decision trees learned from original datasets. This confirms our intuition that decision trees learned from reconstructed datasets are less accurate than those learned from the original datasets. However, the overall accuracy is still reasonably high (about 80-85% for synthetic datasets and 75-80% for UCI datasets).

To illustrate the relationships among γ, N, and decision tree accuracies, we take the average of accuracies of decision trees that are learned from the 7 datasets on each combination of γ and N, and plot this average accuracy together with γ and N against the entropy of perturbation matrix. This is given in Fig. 5, which shows incredibly clear an insight into how γ and N affect the decision tree accuracy, therefore illustrates the usefulness of the entropy measure.

As shown in Fig. 5, accuracies in various intervals of entropy form bands of points that have dropping tails. As the entropy increases, the tails of bands drop increasingly earlier and deeper. It clearly shows that each band corresponds to a single N and include a point for every value of γ. In general, the entropy increases as N gets larger. Within a band, the accuracy decreases as γ decreases and the degree of the decrease depends on the corresponding N. When N is small, a small decrease of γ causes a small decrease of accuracy. But when N is large, a small decrease of γ can cause a large decrease of accuracy. This is because that for a given N, γ determines the probability that a data is perturbed into itself (that is, element $m_{i,i}$ of the perturbation matrix). That is the higher the γ is, the more likely the data is perturbed into itself. As γ decreases, the probability for a data to be perturbed into other values increases and that for it to be perturbed into itself decreases. This not only increases privacy but also increases the estimation error of data distribution, and therefore, reduces the accuracy of decision trees. This effect is compounded when N gets larger. This is because that the number of data records having a given value for a large N is lower than that for a small N. Thus, the estimation error of data distribution is larger for larger N than for small N. Thus, the effect of N is to intensify the effect of γ.

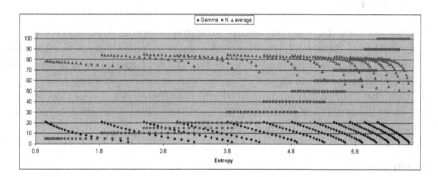

Fig. 5. Entropy vs. γ, N, and Average Accuracy . Notice that the vertical axis has **three** meanings: for γ (represented by diamonds), it is integer between 2 and 21 (i.e., on the bottom of the chart); for N (represented by squares), it is integer between 5 and 100 (i.e., scattered from bottom left to top right); for average accuracy (represented by triangles), it is percentage between 0% and 100% (the actual values are always above 50% and typically above 70%). This further shows the usefulness of the newly introduced notion of *entropy*, because it provides a "platform" to unify accuracy, privacy and performance.

On the other hand, when N is very small, each interval (resulted from discretization) will contain many distinct values of the domain. The reconstructed data distribution becomes very different from that of the original dataset, which explains why the accuracies at the low end of the entropy (for example, $N = 5$) in Fig. 5 are lower than those in some other intervals of entropy.

6   A Guide to Select Parameters in Practice: Putting the Pieces Together

Figure 5 (or any such figure obtained from representative domain datasets) can be used as a useful guide for data owners to determine the parameters of a perturbation matrix.

For example, given a dataset, the data owner can first determine the maximum of tolerable γ based on the ρ_1-to-ρ_2 privacy breaching measure. In practice, since large γ provides a poor protection of privacy and small γ reduces the accuracy, we suggest that a reasonable range of γ should be $5 \leq \gamma \leq 12$.

For a given set of γ (say $5 \leq \gamma \leq 12$), the data owner can find the highest accuracy from Fig. 5 for each γ in the set, and determine the N that corresponds to this accuracy. This will result in a set of combinations of γ and N among which the combination with the smallest N will be the best choice, since it will result in the smallest perturbation matrix and therefore reduces the computational as well as storage complexity of perturbation and distribution reconstruction. We notice that if the domain of an attribute has only $d \leq N$ distinct values, it is wise to choose $N = d$ for the perturbation matrix of that attribute. In this case, there is no need for discretization. Further discussion can be found in [14].

7   Conclusion

Inspired by the fact that the pioneering privacy-preserving decision tree mining method of [1] was flawed [2], we explored a random substitution perturbation technique for privacy-preserving decision tree mining methods. The resulting method is showed to be immune to two relevant attacks (including that of [2]). In addition, we thoroughly investigated the parameter selections that are important in guiding privacy-preserving decision tree mining practice. Systematic experiments show that our method is effective.

References

1. R. Agrawal and R. Srikant. Privacy-preserving data mining. In *ACM SIGMOD International Conference on Management of Data*, pages 439–450. ACM, 2000.
2. Hillol Kargupta, Souptik Datta, Qi Wang, and Krishnamoorthy Sivakumar. On the privacy preserving properties of random data perturbation techniques. In *IEEE International Conference on Data Mining*, 2003.
3. Dakshi Agrawal and Charu C. Aggrawal. On the design and quantification of privacy preserving data mining algorithms. In *ACM Symposium on Principles of Database Systems*, 2001.
4. Shipra Agrawal and Jayant R. Haritsa. A framework for high-accuracy privacy-preserving mining. In *IEEE International Conference on Data Engineering*, 2005.
5. Cynthia Dwork and Kobbi Nissim. Privacy–preserving datamining on vertically partitioned databases. Microsoft Research, 2004.
6. A. Evfimievski, J. Gehrke, and R. Srikant. Limiting privacy breaching in privacy preserving data mining. In *ACM Symposium on Principles of Database Systems*, pages 211–222. ACM, 2003.

7. Y. Lindell and B. Pinkas. Privacy preserving data mining. In M. Bellare, editor, *Advances in Cryptology – Crypto 2000*, pages 36–54. Springer, 2000. Lecture Notes in Computer Science No. 1880.
8. A. Evmievski, R. Srikant, R. Agrawal, and J. Gehrke. Privacy preserving mining of association rules. In *International Conference on Knowledge Discovery and Data Mining*, 2002.
9. Shariq J. Rizvi and Jayant R. Haritsa. Maintaining data privacy in association rule mining. In *International Conference on Very Large Data Bases*, 2002.
10. Srujana Merugu and Joydeep Ghosh. Privacy-preserving distributed clustering using generative models. In *IEEE International Conference on Data Mining*, 2003.
11. S. L. Warner. Randomized response: A survey technique for eliminating evasive answer bias. *Journal of American Statistical Association*, 57:622–627, 1965.
12. Leon Willenborg and Ton de Waal. *Elements of Statistical Disclosure Control*. Springer, 2001.
13. Zhengli Huang, Wenliang Du, and Biao Chen. Deriving private informaiton from randomized data. In *ACM SIGMOD International Conference on Management of Data*, pages 37–47, 2005.
14. Jim Dowd, Shouhuai Xu, and Weining Zhang. Privacy-preserving decision tree mining based on random substitutions. Technical report, Department of Computer Science, University of Texas at San Antonio, 2005.
15. The UCI machine learning repository. http://www.ics.uci.edu/ mlearn/databases/.
16. J. Ross Quinlan. *C4.5: Programs for Machine Learning*. Morgan Kaufmann, San Mateo, CA, 1993.

Policy-Based Integration of User and Provider-Sided Identity Management

Wolfgang Hommel

Munich Network Management Team
Leibniz Supercomputing Center Munich
hommel@lrz.de

Abstract. Depending on whether the users or the providers are performing it, Identity Management (IM) traditionally has different meanings. For users, IM means to choose between one's own identities and roles, in order to make selected personal information available to providers under privacy aspects. For providers, IM typically consists of centralized identity data repositories and their use by the offered services. Methods and tools for both aspects of IM have developed almost orthogonally, failing to consider their interoperability and complementary purposes. We analyze the similarities between both IM aspects and demonstrate how both sides can benefit from the use of a common policy language for personal information release and service provisioning. We derive criteria for this common policy language, demonstrate XACML's suitability and discuss our prototype for the Shibboleth IM system.

1 Introduction and Problem Statement

Identity management (IM) has turned into a double-edged term over the past few years. From the user's point of view, managing her identities is comprised of registering different subsets of her personal information at service providers and subsequently selecting and using these different profiles appropriately [1, 2]. Also, many research projects focus on the privacy issues of this aspect of IM, often closely related to anonymous service usage [3, 4]. On the other hand, major software vendors sell *identity & access management* software to enterprises; its purpose is to centrally acquire the relevant identity information and make it available to the local systems and services, which is referred to as *provisioning*. Concerning privacy, typically the conformity with laws, user acceptance, long-term data retention and other obligations are the primary issues [5, 6, 7].

Methods and tools for these related, yet different aspects of IM have been developed independent of each other; thus, many of them are suffering from interoperability deficiencies and the lack of fulfilling some of other side's elementary requirements. For some branches, approaches to privacy-aware IM have been mutually agreed on by both sides, e.g. regarding e-commerce [8, 9, 10]. However, standards such as P3P are limited to their respective domain and cannot be used in other types of identity federations in general. For application areas such as Grid computing [11], e-learning [12] and business-to-business (B2B) outsourcing [13], dedicated solutions are required and actually being developed.

G. Müller (Ed.): ETRICS 2006, LNCS 3995, pp. 160–174, 2006.

In this paper, we demonstrate the role of user-sided Attribute Release Policies and provider-sided Attribute Acceptance Policies for privacy-aware IM and present an integrated approach, which applies the policy language XACML successfully for both purposes. In section 2, we analyze the requirements on both ends and give an overview of the currently existing solutions. We discuss in section 3 how ARPs and AAPs fit together and why a common policy language should be used. The use of XACML for this approach is specified in section 4, which focusses on the service provider side, complementing our earlier work regarding the user side. In section 5, we share our preliminary experiences with this approach, and also discuss its present limitations. An outlook to our next research activities concludes this paper.

Throughout this paper, we use the following terms and acronyms:

Service Provider (SP). A real or virtual organization which offers one or more services to users based on arbitrary conditions; the primary condition we consider in this paper is that the SP acquires sufficient information about a potential user from a *trusted* data source.

Identity Provider (IDP). For our discussion, we define an IDP as entity which stores personal information about one or more users. Atomic elements of this information are called **attributes**. The two most common IDP types are a) a software or hardware device which the user runs locally, which we call a **local wallet**, and b) an organization which offers this functionality as a service. Typically, in the latter case, the organization will verify the data before storing it, and vouch for its correctness afterwards.

Identity Federation (IF). A set of SPs and IDPs with established trust relationships; thus, SPs can rely on the correctness of the data retrieved from IDPs in the same IF. Examples for IFs are the *Circles of Trust* as suggested by the Liberty Alliance [14]. The term **Federated Identity Management (FIM)** refers to technical and organizational measures as well as legal aspects within IFs; its most widely adopted industrial and academic approaches are SAML, Liberty Alliance, WS-Federation and Shibboleth.

Attribute Release Policies (ARPs). As detailed in section 2, releasing personal information to SPs is based on rules and criteria specified by each user, which we model and enforce as policies; the term ARP for these policies has been coined by Shibboleth [15], which is based on SAML.

Attribute Acceptance Policies (AAPs). SPs will accept users for each service only if sufficient information about them is available under acceptable conditions, e.g. regarding data handling and retention limitations, and the values of the retrieved attributes fulfill arbitrary criteria, e.g. for access control. These criteria are formulated as AAPs.

2 Requirements Analysis and State of the Art

Obviously, in order to successfully build an integrated, common solution for both sides, the requirements and goals of the users as well as the SPs must be considered. We analyze these requirements and refer to previous approaches on the user side in section 2.1 and on the provider side in section 2.2; we then discuss their similarities and derive consequences for an integrated approach in section 2.3.

2.1   User-Sided Requirements and Solutions

From the user perspective, we have to distinguish four aspects of identity management, which are also shown in figure 1:

1. Which identity data does the SP need? Three main types of services are presently being offered:
   - Services that can be used anonymously, i.e. do not require any information about the user at all, or only collect data, which does not make the user distinguishable from a sufficiently large set of other users (called *anonymity set* [1]).
   - Services that can be used pseudonymously, i.e. they utilize profiles to identify their users individually, without necessarily acquiring any personally identifying information (PII), e.g. internet discussion forums.
   - Services that users must be personally known to, e.g. online banking.
   These categories are also known as "nymity levels" [16]: Services may allow users to select their preferred level, depending on how much information they want to reveal, e.g. in order to benefit from website personalization [17].
2. Which identity and role is the user acting in? Users may want to use different identities, e.g. for professional and private activities, which in turn may be divided into several roles, e.g. being a lecturer, researcher and dean at a university. For example, using different email addresses for each of these roles will result in different attribute values stored in each profile.
3. Where is the identity data stored? As a general principle of identity federations and single sign-on systems, manually registering the data at each SP is not desired, which basically leaves two options [18]:
   - The data is stored locally on the user side, i.e. in a software or hardware device, which, for example, automatically fills out the SP's HTML formulars and manages the user's login names and passwords. While such a *local wallet* approach gives the user full control over her data [19], additional measures are necessary in order to enable the SP to verify the authenticity of this data. Attribute certificates, which are signed by a trusted authority, could be used for this purpose, but turned out to be hard to handle on the user side in practice [20].
   - The data is stored by an organization, which is trusted by both the user and the SPs which request the data from it. As centralized approaches, such as Microsoft Passport, have failed, modern FIM architectures are decentralized and allow an arbitrary number of IDPs within IFs. However, this complicates the trust relationships between the providers, which today are mostly based on contracts that have been made out-of-band a priori.
4. How is the identity data being used? For example, is it only being used locally by the SP for service provisioning, or will the data be released to third parties, and how long will it be retained?

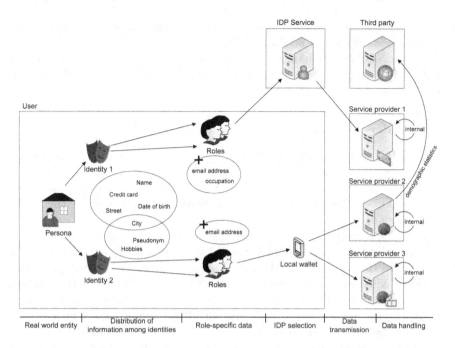

Fig. 1. User-sided aspects of Identity Management

Traditionally, users had to study the services' terms and conditions and privacy statements in detail before deciding which information they sign up with. Thus, any automation of this process must be flexible enough to capture and express the rationale behind these decisions.

For mere web sites, various *local wallet* implementations exist, with P3P [8] being a profound standard with the highest adoption rate: P3P-enabled browsers fetch the web sites' P3P privacy statements, parse and compare them to the user's preferences and can fill out HTML forms automatically or warn the user about conflicts.

However, P3P and the other implementations are limited to web sites, a pre-defined user data schema, and are not interoperable with the modern FIM protocols, as we have discussed in previous work [21].

Consequently, users need a more generic way to specify

- which identity and role to use for
- which service provider and service,
- which information (attributes) to release
- under which conditions (e.g., release the credit card number only if actually placing an order, not when just browsing for information), and
- under which obligations (e.g., delete the data after 90 days of inactivity).

Additionally, in many situations, such as B2B cooperations, users cannot freely choose which information may be released about them; thus, there must be a way for administrators to specify defaults, which may either be refined by the users or override the users' settings [13].

In the terms of Shibboleth, such specifications are called Attribute Release Policies (ARPs). While there is no policy language standard for ARPs yet, various prototypes for the diverse FIM approaches exist [22, 23, 24, 15, 25, 26].

2.2 Provider-Sided Requirements and Solutions

Obviously, IM requirements increase with the types and number of services offered by an SP. In our analysis we assume that the SP is an enterprise offering multiple services, which require different subsets of the user's identity data over a longer period of time, as this imposes the hardest requirements on the implemented IM system.

Historically, the services or their administrators had to acquire and maintain the identity data themselves, which has led to redundant work, data inconsistencies within the enterprise, and thus a higher total cost of ownership.

Identity & Access Management (I&AM) systems, as presently available from several major software vendors, recentralize an enterprise's identity data management processes, typically by storing all user information in a central relational database management system or an LDAP-based directory service. The services then either directly access this central identity repository or are being fed by it.

Dedicated management frontends for administrators and self service web interfaces for users exist to maintain the data. However, the current FIM protocols, such as SAML, are not sufficiently integrated with I&AM software yet; instead, they are intended to directly feed the services with identity data, effectively bypassing the I&AM software and its central identity repository. While this may be sufficient for SPs which only offer a single service, e.g. an e-commerce website, it is counterproductive for larger enterprises which already have an I&AM infrastructure deployed.

Concerning the information, which is requested about users, SPs distinguish between

- identity data that must be known for service provisioning, e.g. for accounting and billing purposes. Unless this data is available and valid, the service cannot be used.
- additional data that can improve the user experience, e.g. through personalization.
- additional data that can be used for other purposes, e.g. data mining for long-term service improvement.

Additionally, parts of this data must be or could be given to third parties; for example, an e-commerce web site might use an external service for credit card billing and has to give the user's shipping address to a courier or postal service.

Regarding privacy, enterprises are bound to laws as well as to user acceptance issues; we distinguish between

- the acquisition or collection of data, which can be based on
  - information provided by the user or IDP, e.g. during signing up for the service, and
  - information collected during service usage, e.g. analyzing the user's click-stream on web sites [24],
- data handling policies, e.g. making data available to third parties [7].
- data protection measures, e.g. encryption or auditing to prevent internal abuse, as well as the enforcement of the stated privacy practices [5].
- data retention policies, e.g. logfiles are deleted after a fixed period of time [27].

In this paper, we focus on the acquisition and maintenance of information provided by the user's IDP. To this extent, SPs have to specify which data they acquire for which purposes, e.g. in their privacy statements; while P3P can be used for single web sites, no such standards exist yet for IFs and generic FIM.

Some implementations, such as Shibboleth [28], support the specification of AAPs based on simple proprietary policy languages. They can be used by the service administrators to specify which user attributes shall be requested from the IDP, and to formulate simple conditions on their values. In practice, only simple access control mechanisms are implemented this way, which have to be maintained separately and are not integrated into the SP's I&AM system.

The use of AAPs in IFs and their integration into I&AM systems has not been researched in detail yet; in section 4 we demonstrate the suitability of the policy language XACML for AAPs.

2.3   Similarities and Synergies

ARPs and AAPs have been treated isolated of each other in most previous research and implementations. In the above sections, we summarized the necessity of both types of policies, making obvious how they complement each other. Consequently, we belief that ARPs and AAPs must be discussed in unity to achieve interoperability in FIM and a seamless integration into the SP's I&AM system.

Policy-based management provides useful formal methods and tools to model and enforce these information release and acceptance decisions, and the similar structure and content of ARPs and AAPs, which we detail in the next section, can be exploited by the use of a common policy language for both types.

3   Policies for Privacy Management and Service Provisioning

We subsequently demonstrate that a policy based management approach fulfills the requirements discussed above. Again, we first discuss the user and the SP sides separately and then point out their commonalities. This section is explicitely independent of any concrete policy language; whereas several existing policy languages could be used for the purposes described below, or a new dedicated language could be created, our prototype is based on XACML as described in section 4.

3.1 User or IDP-Sided Attribute Release Policies

In order to use policies as a formal base of automated attribute release decisions, we define the content of each policy and discuss how multiple policies can be combined and work together.

To meet the criteria laid out in section 2.1, an ARP must provide syntactical elements for the following tasks:

- Naming the user attributes, e.g. the user's given name, which are stored in an IDP database. A data schema, such as P3P's, defines which attributes a user object may have; in general, not all SPs and IDPs will use the same data schema, but on-the-fly conversion mechanisms that work with FIM protocols exist [13].

  As the values of attributes may vary with the selected identity and role of the user (which are known to the IDP, and optionally to the SP), we use URIs in the format `https://address.of.idp/identity/role/attributename` to name attributes. Furthermore, attributes may be grouped for user convenience, so for example the shipping address of a user, consisting of full name, street, ZIP code and city name, can be referred to as a single attribute when specifying release policies.
- Naming SPs, services and request purposes. This distinction is necessarily hierarchical, as one SP may offer multiple services and each service may request information for various purposes (e.g., personalized browsing vs. handling an actual order). Again, URIs in the format `https://address.of.sp/service` can be used as identifiers for tuples of SPs and services, and a common terminology for purpose specifications must be established in the IF (see also [22]).
- Specifying the type of access allowed on the data. Presently, we distinguish between a one-time read access to the data and subscribing to the attribute; in the latter case, changes in the attribute may be made available to the SP after service usage, in order to avoid data inconsistencies between IDP and SP. In the future, also write access may be grantable to SPs; however, current FIM protocols do not support this operation yet. Each request must provide the tuple *(access type, purpose)*.
- Formulation of conditions. For example, the release of an attribute may depend on its current value, the release of other attributes, or the presence of certain criteria in the SP's privacy statement.
- Specification of obligations on both the IDP and the SP side. As a typical obligation that has to be fulfilled by the IDP, users want to be notified when an SP attempts to access certain sensitive attributes. SP-sided obligations may include restrictions on the maximum data retention time or the opt-out of giving the data to third parties.

For each user, an arbitrary number ARPs can be specified; typically, there will be:

- One default ARP, which is used if no other ARP matches a request. Usually, this default ARP will deny the release of any attribute.
- Any number of SP-specific ARPs set by the user according to her preferences, either a priori, or at run-time if the used FIM protocol allows suitable interaction mechanisms (such as BBAE [29] or Liberty [30]).
- Any number of SP-specific ARPs set by the IDP administrators, e.g. according to B2B contracts.

Policies, which refer to the same SP, service, and purpose, may cause policy evaluation conflicts, e.g. if one policy allows the release of an attribute while the other policy denies it. While a lot of research on policy based management suggests various sophisticated conflict avoidance, detection and resolving techniques, we presently make use of a simple priority-based policy combination workflow: Depending on which priorities users are allowed to assign to their policies, user settings may override administrator settings or vice versa.

3.2 Attribute Acceptance Policies for Service Providers

In analogy to ARPs on the user side, SPs specify in an AAP:

- Which services the AAP applies to, also identified by URIs as in the ARPs described above. This allows to manage multiple services through a single AAP, in contrast to existing implementations, in which each service requires a dedicated AAP, whose content then is possibly redundant.
- Which IDPs and requested user attributes this policy applies to (policy target specification). The list of trusted IDPs is typically derived from federation meta-data; the data schema and conversion issues discussed in the previous section also apply here. The currently selected identity and role of the user do not have to be known.
- Which purpose the data is being requested for. This field is intended to hold the identifier of a machine or human readable section of a privacy statement in which the data handling, protection and retention practices are stated; it thus complements, and does not replace, existing mechanisms like P3P.
- Conditions on the availibility and values of attributes. For example, a credit card number might not be accepted unless also the expiry date is provided, or the number of an already expired credit card may be rejected.
- Obligations for SP-sided policy evaluation, such as keeping logfiles of denied transactions. Other obligations, e.g. for data handling, protection, and retention, could be specified here as well; however, in this paper we focus on the data acquisition only and will investigate the integration of complementary methods, such as EPAL [5], in our further research.

An arbitrary number of AAPs can be combined with each other, e.g. in order to specify enterprise-wide defaults and service-specific refinements thereof. In analogy to ARPs, using a priority-based policy combination algorithm to re-solve potential policy conflicts allows a fine-grained identity data provisioning configuration for each service and enables decentralized service-specific administration.

3.3 Using a Common Policy Language

Unlike existing approaches to ARPs and AAPs [15, 25, 31, 10], we suggest to use a common language for both types of policies due to their structural similarity and their complementary contents.

Furthermore, using a common language for both ARPs and AAPs brings several practical advantages, such as lower implementation overhead for both IDP and SP software, as well as the possibility to use the same or at least similar tools and graphical user interfaces to maintain the policies.

A policy language must be able to specify the following elements to be suitable for the purposes discussed above, which are also shown in figure 2:

- Subjects, i.e. services which request attributes (in ARPs), and users which want to use services (in AAPs).
- Objects, such as the protected user attributes (in ARPs) and services (in AAPs).
- Actions, such as reading an attribute for a certain purpose (in ARPs) or using a certain functionality of a service, which relates to the purpose of an attribute request (in AAPs).
- Conditions, which decide whether the subjects are allowed to perform the actions on the objects.
- Obligations, which have to be fulfilled or queued for later fulfillment during policy enforcement.

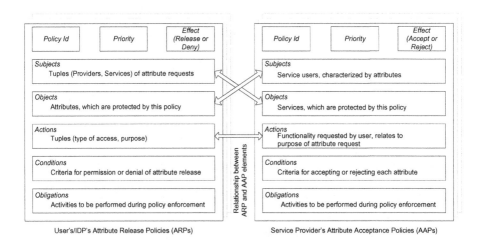

Fig. 2. Common structure of ARPs and AAPs

As further requirements, it must be possible to combine multiple distributed policies, e.g. ARPs specified by the administrator and by the user, and to efficiently decide whether a policy is relevant for an actual request or can be safely ignored. The necessary policy elements lead to access control specific policy languages. We subsequently discuss the policy evaluation workflow and present the use of XACML as policy language for ARPs and AAPs in section 4.

3.4   Policy Evaluation Workflow

A Policy Decision Point (PDP) is used to evaluate the policies, whereas the consequences are taken by the Policy Enforcement Point (PEP), which is

- the FIM component, which replies to attribute requests, in the case of ARPs on the IDP side
- the service, which the user wants to use, or a component delivering the data to it, in the AAP case.

As the PDP may need to evaluate multiple policies in order to decide, and the policies may be arbitrarily distributed, there must be a database or registry service which lists all policies that have been set up for a user (IDP-sided) or service (SP-sided). Out of all policies related to a user or service, the ones, which are relevant for a request, can be selected based on their target specifications:

- For ARPs, all policies that match the *(SP, service)* and *(access type, purpose)* tuples of the attribute request must be considered.
- For AAPs, those policies must be combined, which match the *(IDP, user attributes, purpose)* triple of an attribute response.

After the relevant policies have been identified this way, they need to be combined into a single so-called policy set, i.e. a sequence of policies, which the PDP can evaluate in one logical step.

As discussed in the previous section, we are presently using a simple priority-based policy combination algorithm, i.e. a different priority is assigned to each policy, and the policy set is ordered by the descending priority of the contained policies. While this is sufficient for the small amount of policies we are currently working with, clearly more sophisticated policy conflict detection and avoidance approaches will have to be used in larger scale environments.

The created policy set is then evaluated by a PDP to decide

- whether a user attribute may be released to an SP (on the IDP side)
- whether the attribute, its origin, value and associated obligations are acceptable for the service (on the SP side).

The PDP's decision is sent to the PEP, along with the list of optional obligations. The PEP has to fulfill these obligations, or trigger their later fulfillment, e.g. by setting a date for data deletion to enforce retention obligations.

4   XACML as ARP and AAP Policy Language

We have analyzed existing FIM-specific approaches and concluded that most of them fail short of fulfilling the core requirements of ARPs in previous work [32], thus they are also unsuitable for the modelling and enforcement of AAPs, especially as they have not been designed for this purpose.

However, various more generic policy languages exist and are suitable for both ARPs and AAPs, e.g. PERMIS' policy language [33], Ponder [34], XrML [35] and XACML [36]. Out of those, XACML excels as most frequently used policy language in the areas of FIM and distributed access control (for an overview, see [37]; details can be found in [38, 39, 40, 41]).

We have detailed how XACML can be used for ARPs in previous work [26]; subsequently, we specify how AAPs can be modeled in XACML, and discuss the evaluation and enforcement workflows.

4.1   Modeling AAPs with XACML

In analogy to the specification in section 3.2, we use XACML policy elements as follows for AAPs:

- The services, which the policy applies to, are the `Resources` in XACML terms. Multiple services can be specified by URIs, optionally using wildcards, regular expressions or the XACML `AnyResource` element.
- The URIs of the requested user attributes and optionally the trusted IDPs are specified as XACML `Subjects`, i.e. consecutive XACML `SubjectMatches`. The restriction to certain IDPs, which could for example be derived from a federation member list, is only necessary if the used FIM software does not communicate with trusted IDPs only anyway, or if different trust levels have to be supported.
- Request purposes are related to the service functionality, which the user has requested, and they point to sections of privacy statements and policies. We store identifiers of the different functionalities as XACML `Actions` and the pointers as XML attributes of `Action` elements in the URI format. Multiple actions can be specified in a single AAP if the same user attributes are requested for different purposes, depending on the used service functionality.
- A XACML `Condition` element can be used for the formulation of acceptance conditions; XACML offers a variety of statements and functions, which can be used to create arbitrary complex conditions, e.g. based on the user attributes' values or environmental data such as the current date and time.
- XACML `Obligation` elements are used to specify short- or long-term obligations. Currently, XACML only supports sending emails and writing to logfiles as standardized obligations, but arbitrary obligations can be specified as long as the PEP knows how to interpret them.

The above elements are used within XACML `Rules`; each AAP may contain any number of rules and must specify a rule combination algorithm, such as "first-applicable" or "deny-overrides", and optionally have a description, which can be used to document its purpose. Additionally, we assign a priority to each AAP to control the policy set combination.

4.2   Evaluation and Enforcement of XACML AAPs

To create the XACML `PolicySet`, the relevant AAPs are chosen by matching their subjects, actions and objects against the current user attribute response sent by the IDP and the context of the current request. We had to implement the priority-based policy combination algorithm as it is not part of the XACML standard yet, which however allows the definition of custom policy combiners.

The resulting `PolicySet` can be evaluated by any standard-compliant XACML PDP, such as Sun's reference implementation [42]. Presently, we have to trigger the PDP for each user attribute separately and cannot evaluate all user attributes at once, because XACML results can contain only one decision, but we need to be able to accept some user attributes, even if others are not accepted. The performance drawback is discussed in section 5.

The PDP's decision is enforced by the PEP, which is either the service itself or a component which delivers the user attributes to the service; it also has to fulfill the obligations, which are part of the PDP's decision. Guaranteeing the enforcement of obligations, which have been stated in human- or machine-readable privacy policies external to the AAPs, is outside the scope of our work, but our AAPs provide the interface to complementary components such as those described in EPAL and TPM-related work [43].

5   Preliminary Experiences

We have extended our XACML ARP prototype for Shibboleth, which we described in previous work [26], to also support XACML AAPs on the SP side. Although this prototype is not yet made available to our users, implementing and testing it revealed promising preliminary experiences and leads to further tasks:

- Adapting Shibboleth to XACML AAPs by using Sun's reference XACML PDP implementation is straight-forward, as only the AAP fetching and evaluation Java methods have to be replaced.
- Existing Shibboleth AAPs, which are based on a simple XML files, can automatically be converted to XACML AAPs via an XSLT stylesheet.
- Evaluating and enforcing XACML AAPs has a noticeable performance impact; basic instrumentation of our code revealed that evaluating the AAPs for each requested attribute leads to overhead, which we will investigate to eliminate by caching the compiled XACML PolicySets in our future work.
- Due to the lack of a dedicated graphical user interface, we currently have to set up and maintain the XACML AAPs manually, which is tedious and error-prone. A web-based GUI for intuitive ARP and AAP configuration will be developed as part of a student project. Clearly, such an interface must be available to hide the underlying complexity from the users before we can switch to production use.

Furthermore, our web portal already allowed to specify basic ARPs, which were not based on XACML yet. The usage of this functionality has shown that less than ten percent of all users have modified their ARP settings. As a consequence, we belief that

- users have to be sensitized for privacy aspects and made aware of their rights and options.
- defaults, which are suitable for most users, have to be set up.
- intuitive and well-documented GUIs must be available, which allow setting up, maintaining, test and comprehend these policies.

We will contribute future versions of our implementation and tools to the Shibboleth project.

6   Conclusion and Outlook

In this paper, we have argued for an integrated approach to privacy-aware identity management on both the user and the service provider side. Based on the need to automate the decision making about information release and acceptance, we derived the suitability of policy-based management from a discussion of requirements on both sides. The novelty of our approach lies in the use of a common policy language for both Attribute Release and Attribute Acceptance Policies. We specified the required policy elements and the evaluation workflow in general and extended a prototype developed in previous work, which now allows us to use the standard XACML policy language for ARPs and AAPs within the Shibboleth software framework. Finally, we shared some preliminary experiences and outlined our next steps concerning the enhancement of performance and usability aspects.

Our future research will focus on the Service Provider side; especially, we will analyze the interface of AAPs to identity & access management systems in order to seamlessly integrate FIM workflows into the local business processes, and strive for a tighter coupling of AAPs with privacy policy enforcement frameworks presented in related work.

Acknowledgment

The authors wish to thank the members of the Munich Network Management (MNM) Team for helpful discussions and valuable comments on previous versions of the paper. The MNM Team directed by Prof. Dr. Heinz-Gerd Hegering is a group of researchers of the University of Munich, the Munich University of Technology, and the Leibniz Supercomputing Center of the Bavarian Academy of Sciences. The web server of the MNM Team is located at http://www.mnm-team.org/.

References

1. Pfitzmann, A., Köhntopp, M.: Anonymity, unobservability, pseudonymity, and identity management – a proposal for terminology. In: Lecture Notes in Computer Science, Volume 2009, Springer (2000) 1–9
2. Bonatti, P.A., Samarati, P.: Regulating Service Access and Information Release on the Web. In: Proceedings of CCS 2000, Athens, ACM Press (2000)
3. Camenisch, J., Shelat, A., Sommer, D., Fischer-Hübner, S., Hansen, M., Krasemann, H., Lacoste, G., Leenes, R., Tseng, J.: Privacy and identity management for everyone. In: 1st conference on Digital Identity Management, ACM Press (2005)
4. Bhargav-Spantzel, A., Squicciarini, A., Bertino, E.: Establishing and protecting digital identity in federation systems. TR 2005-48, Purdue University (2005)
5. Powers, C., Schunter, M.: Enterprise Privacy Authorization Language, W3C submission. http://www.w3.org/Submission/2003/SUBM-EPAL-20031110/ (2003)
6. Karjoth, G., Schunter, M., Waidner, M.: The Platform for Enterprise Privacy Practices — Privacy-enabled Management of Customer Data. In: Proceedings of the Workshop on Privacy Enhancing Technologies, Springer (2002)
7. Mont, M.: Dealing with privacy obligations in enterprises. Technical Report HPL-2004-109, HP Laboratories Bristol (2004)
8. Reagle, J., Cranor, L.F.: The Platform for Privacy Preferences. In: Communications of the ACM. Volume 42., ACM Press (1999) 48–55
9. Langheinrich, M. (Ed.): A P3P Preference Exchange Language — APPEL 1.0. http://www.w3.org/TR/P3P-preferences/ (2002)
10. Damiani, E., di Vimercati, S.D.C., Fugazza, C., Samarati, P.: Semantics-aware privacy and access control: Motivation and preliminary results. In: Proceedings of 1st Italian Semantic Web Workshop. (2004)
11. Baker, M., Apon, A., Ferner, C., Brown, J.: Emerging grid standards. IEEE Computer Journal (2005) 43–50
12. Allison, C., et al.: Integrated user management in the european learning grid. http://www.hlrs.de/publications/ (2005)
13. Hommel, W., Reiser, H.: Federated Identity Management in B2B Outsourcing. In: Proceedings of the 12th Annual Workshop of the HP OpenView University Association (HPOVUA 2005), Porto, Portugal, ISBN 972-9171-48-3 (2005)
14. Linn, J. (Ed.): Liberty Trust Models Guidelines (2003)
15. Cantor, S.: Shibboleth v1.2 Attribute Release Policies. http://shibboleth.internet2.edu/guides/deploy-guide-origin1.2.html#2.e. (2004)
16. Goldberg, I.: A Pseudonymous Communications Infrastructure for the Internet. PhD thesis, University of California, Berkeley (2000)
17. Koch, M.: Global identity management to boost personalization. In: 9th Research Symposium on Emerging Electronic Markets. (2002) 137–147
18. Pashalidis, A., Mitchell, C.: A taxonomy of single sign-on systems. In: Lecture Notes in Computer Science, Volume 2727, Springer (2003)
19. Pfitzmann, B.: Privacy in browser-based attribute exchange. In: ACM Workshop on Privacy in Electronic Society (WPES 2002), ACM Press (2002) 52–62
20. Josang, A., Pope, S.: User Centric Identity Management. In: Proceedings of AusCERT 2005. (2005)
21. Hommel, W.: An Architecture for Privacy-aware Inter-domain Identity Management. In: Proceedings of the 16th IFIP/IEEE Distributed Systems: Operations and Management (DSOM 2005), Barcelona, Spain (2005)

22. Aarts, R., et al.: Liberty architecture framework for supporting Privacy Preference Expression Languages (PPELs). Liberty Alliance White Paper (2003)

23. Ahn, G.J., Lam, J.: Managing Privacy Preferences for Federated Identity Management. In: 1st Workshop on Digital Identity Management, ACM Press (2005)

24. Koch, M., Möslein, K.: Identities management for e-commerce and collaboration applications. International Journal of Electronic Commerce (IJEC) (2005)

25. Nazareth, S., Smith, S.: Using SPKI/SDSI for Distributed Maintenance of Attribute Release Policies in Shibboleth. Technical Report TR2004-485, Department of Computer Science, Dartmouth College, Hanover, HN 03744 USA (2004)

26. Hommel, W.: Using XACML for Privacy Control in SAML-based Identity Federations. In: Proceedings of the 9th Conference on Communications and Multimedia Security (CMS 2005), Salzburg, Austria (2005)

27. Mont, M., Thyne, R., Bramhall, P.: Privacy Enforcement with HP Select Access for Regulatory Compliance. Technical Report HPL-2005-10, HP Bristol (2005)

28. Cantor, S., Carmody, S., Erdos, M., Hazelton, K., Hoehn, W., Morgan, B.: Shibboleth Architecture, working draft 09. http://shibboleth.internet2.edu/ (2005)

29. Pfitzmann, B., Waidner, M.: BBAE — a general protocol for browser-based attribute exchange. Technical Report RZ 3455, IBM Research, Zürich (2002)

30. Aarts, R. (Ed.): Liberty ID-WSF Interaction Service Specification (2004)

31. Choi, H.C., et al.: A privacy protection model in id management using access control. In: Proceedings of ICCSA 2005, Springer (2005) 82–91

32. Hommel, W., Reiser, H.: Federated Identity Management: Shortcomings of existing standards. In: Proceedings of the 9th IFIP/IEEE International Symposium on Integrated Management (IM 2005), Nice, France, IEEE Press (2005)

33. Chadwick, D., Otenko, A.: The PERMIS X.509 Role Based Privilege Management Infrastructure. In: 7th ACM SACMAT, ACM Press (2002)

34. Damianou, N., Dulay, N., Lupu, E., Sloman, M.: The ponder policy specification language. In: Lecture Notes in Computer Science, Volume 1995. (2001)

35. ContentGuard Holdings Inc.: XrML 2.0 Technical Overview. http://www.xrml.org/reference/XrMLTechnicalOverviewV1.pdf (2002)

36. Moses, T. (Ed.): OASIS eXtensible Access Control Markup Language 2.0, core specification. OASIS XACML Technical Committee Standard (2005)

37. Lorch, M., Proctor, S., Lepro, R., Kafura, D., Shah, S.: First Experiences Using XACML for Access Control in Distributed Systems. In: Proceedings of the ACM Workshop on XML Security, ACM Press (2003)

38. Lorch, M., Kafura, D., Shah, S.: An XACML-based Policy Management and Authorization Service for Globus Research Resources Work in Progress Draft Paper. Department of Computer Science, Virginia Tech (2004)

39. Wu, J., Periorellis, P.: Authorization-Authentication Using XACML and SAML. TR CS-TR-907, University of Newcastle, UK (2005)

40. Vullings, E., Buchhorn, M., Dalziel, J.: Secure Federated Access to GRID applications using SAML/XACML. Tr, Macquarie University, Sydney (2005)

41. Lopez, G., Gomez, A., Marin, R., Canovas, O.: A Network Access Control Approach Based on the AAA Architecture and Authorization Attributes. In: 19th IEEE Int. Parallel and Distributed Processing Symposium, IEEE Press (2005)

42. Proctor, S.: Sun's XACML implementation. http://sunxacml.sf.net/ (2004)

43. Crane, S., Mont, M., Pearson, S.: On helping individuals to manage privacy and trust. Technical Report HPL-2005-53, HP Laboratories Bristol (2005)

Privacy with Delegation of Rights by Identity Management

Sven Wohlgemuth and Günter Müller

Institute of Computer Science and Social Studies
Department of Telematics
Albert-Ludwig University Freiburg, Germany
{wohlgemuth, mueller}@iig.uni-freiburg.de

Abstract. Privacy in business processes with proxies is not possible. Users need to share attributes with their proxies which leads to "Big Brothers". This is the reason why identity management systems such as Liberty Alliance and Microsoft .NET Passport are not successful. We propose a generic privacy-preserving protocol for sharing identifying attributes as credentials with others. This delegation protocol extends current identity management systems.

1 Introduction

E-Commerce shows two trends: personalized services and automatization of business processes [1, 2, 3]. Personalized services are adapted to users' attributes to address them among others according to their interests and to offer them individual prices. Automatization of business processes is realized by coupling autonomous services, e.g. web services, to establish an information system for the purpose of a business process. If personalized services are combined in a business process, some services act on behalf of a user. A user delegates some personal attributes to his proxy so that this proxy is able to use subordinate services according to user's interests. These attributes are used as an authorization for using subordinate services, so disclosing attributes is thereby a delegation of access rights. A profile of this user arises at his proxy. The user cannot be sure whether his proxy follows its agreement according to the use of these attributes.

To prevent misuse, one can either focus on existing profiles or on the collection of attributes. Preventing misuse by looking at existing profiles means either to enable a user to control the use of disclosed attributes or to identify misuse and penalize the corresponding service provider afterwards. Both approaches requires user's knowledge of service's behavior which cannot be assumed in general.

Regarding the collection of user's attributes means to prevent or to minimize profiling. Anonymity services prevent profiling based upon connection data [4]. However, they are not suitable for personalized services. Profiles can be minimized by using identity management. Identity management empowers a user to control the disclosure of his attributes [5]. However, current identity management systems do not data economy in business processes with proxies. If current

G. Müller (Ed.): ETRICS 2006, LNCS 3995, pp. 175–190, 2006.
© Springer-Verlag Berlin Heidelberg 2006

identity management systems are used, a proxy gets access to user's identity and becomes a "Big Brother". The challenge is to control the disclosure of attributes to personalized services via a proxy and at the same time prevent undesired collection and use of user's attributes by a proxy.

Our contribution is a general privacy-preserving protocol for the delegation of user's attributes as credentials. This delegation protocol prevents identification of the user, linkability of his transactions, and misuse of disclosed attributes as credentials. Our idea is to use a credential-based access control on disclosed attributes by means of a credential similar to Kerberos V5 [6]. It makes use of the identity manager *iManager* [7] and of the anonymous credential system *IBM idemix* [8].

This paper is structured as follows: Section 2 investigates on privacy in business processes without proxies and derives criteria for privacy with respect to data economy. Section 3 focuses on business processes with proxies and shows that "Big Brothers" arise at a proxy, if current identity management systems are used. This section extends the privacy criteria for a privacy-aware delegation of attributes as credentials. Section 4 introduces our generic delegation protocol for identity management. Section 5 shows its privacy properties. Section 6 compares our approach with credential-based authentication systems considering a delegation of rights. Section 7 concludes this work and gives an outlook to on-going work.

2   Privacy by Identity Management

Alan F. Westin defines privacy as *"the claim of individuals, groups and institutions to determine for themselves, when, how and to what extent information about them is communicated to others"* [9]. The judgment of the German Federal Constitutional Court relating to the census in Germany in 1983 extends Westin's definition and takes up the use of disclosed identifying attributes [10]. It defines informational self-determination as the right of every individual to decide on the disclosure and use of identifying attributes which is only restricted in exceptional cases. Relating to informational self-determination, we investigate on identity management and show whether current identity management systems achieve it.

2.1   Scenario: Personalized Services

Suppose the following scenario for personalized services. A user wants to travel by train and rent a car at his travel destination. At an electronic ticket machine, he gets a discount by using his digital railway loyalty card. The web-based car rental service needs to know whether its customer has a driving license as an authorization to rent the desired type of car. According to the situation, the user shows his digital railway loyalty card and his digital driving license. Both is technically realized by an attribute certificate also known as a credential [11]. After proving these credentials, the electronic ticket machine returns the electronic railway ticket and the web-based car rental service returns a confirmation.

While using personalized service, a user leaves data traces. In our example, both service providers get identifying attributes of the user which are part of his credentials: the digital railway loyalty card and the digital driving license. Furthermore, they get to know the characteristics of user's device, e.g. the IP address.

2.2 Attacker Model

Our attacker model takes untrustworthy service providers into account. We omit eavesdroppers of user's network traffic as attackers, since linkability based on user's communication data can be prevented by using anonymity services. We assume that an attacker cannot break cryptographic primitives and does not control the communication network. Untrustworthy service providers aim to identify and trace a user as well as to misuse his attributes, e.g. for undesired advertisement or to impersonate him.

2.3 Privacy Criteria for User-Controlled Disclosure of Attributes

Identity management empowers a user to control the disclosure of his attributes and thereby to minimize data traces. The security interests of service providers with respect to accountability of a user are also considered [5]. Our privacy analysis embraces the authentication protocols of respectively for identity management systems *Microsoft .NET Passport* [12], *Shibboleth* [13], *Liberty Alliance* [14], *iManager* [7], and *IBM idemix* [8].

Microsoft .NET Passport does not prevent their users against undesired identification and profiling. Although its specification is not completely published, it can be derived from the review guide [12] that every user has a global identifier and each service may get every attribute of a user. *Shibboleth* and *Liberty Alliance* are identity management systems with an identity provider. The role of an identity provider is to certify user's identity and to manage user's attributes. This implies two different trust models. Firstly, an identity provider is a certification authority (*CA*) and so service providers as well as users trust in her that she certifies identities according to her certification policy. This is the usual trust model as it is used in public-key infrastructures [15]. Secondly, since an identity provider manages user's attributes such as his pseudonyms, an identity provider is able to trace a user. It follows that a user has to trust his identity provider that she uses the user's attributes according to the agreed privacy policy. This is the difference to a CA, so we call an identity provider with these trust relationships a *Privacy-CA*. The identity manager *iManager* focuses on the usability of identity management for security novices as managing the identity of its user by partial identities and self-signed credentials. *IBM idemix* is the latest anonymous credential system extending anonymous credential by Stefan Brands [16]. Anonymous credentials do not need a Privacy-CA. *Shibboleth, Liberty Alliance, iManager,* and *IBM idemix* have the following five properties with respect to privacy in common.

Showing attributes depending on service: A user is able to choose which attributes he wants to disclose with respect to the given service provider and the service. *Shibboleth* and *Liberty Alliance* identify the service by its uniform resource locator (URL) and disclose user's attributes according to his policy. If an attribute request needs the real-time decision of a user, the user will be asked. *iManager* uses pre-defined partial identities which are a subset of user's attributes for a particular role of the user. A user chooses a partial identity according to the service provider and service. By *IBM idemix* a user is able to show certain attributes without revealing them and to decide which attribute he wants to disclose towards a service provider.

Non-linkability of transactions: Identity management systems offer a user to act with pseudonyms instead of his real name. Non-linkability of transactions is achieved, if a user uses a pseudonym only for one particular transaction. *Shibboleth* and *Liberty Alliance* manages the pseudonyms of their users by an identity provider. *iManager* and *IBM idemix* enables a user to manage his pseudonyms without such a *Privacy-CA*.

Authentication without revealing identifying attributes: A user is able to show a certain property of his attributes instead of revealing the corresponding attributes. This is either done by an identity provider or by a zero-knowledge proof. Regarding showing a credential by a zero-knowledge proof, a CA certifies user's attributes by issuing a credential with respect to a pseudonym and secret key k_{User} of the user. When showing a credential, the user shows by a zero-knowledge proof that he knows k_{User}.

Non-repudiation of user's transactions: A service provider gets a proof by the authentication protocol that a particular transaction has been conducted by a particular user. Either an identity provider vouches for the identity of a user by issuing a credential within an authentication or the user shows the relationship between an anonymous credentials and his secret key by a zero-knowledge proof.

De-anonymizing criminal users: The anonymity of a user can be revealed under certain conditions. Since identity providers know the identity and transactions of their users, they are able to reveal the identity of a criminal user. When using anonymous credentials, a third party is able to reveal the identity either according to a particular credential or to all credentials of a user. The user has to trust this de-anonymization party regarding the enforcement of their de-anonymization policy.

3   Business Processes and Privacy

We extend our scenario by the ticket machine as a proxy for the user. Suppose that each train is equipped with a electronic ticket machine supporting wireless connectivity and that the user has a mobile device. The user is able to connect to this ticket machine within the train and buys there his electronic railway ticket. Unfortunately, the user is not able to connect to the Internet and use a web-based car rental service. But, the ticket machine offers him the service to rent a car on his behalf. Therefore, the ticket machine needs the digital driving license of the user. The user delegates it to this ticket machine and the ticket machine chooses a car rental service and rents a car for the user at his travel destination. It follows that the user shares the attributes of his digital driving license with this ticket machine. Figure 1 shows the information flow about the user in this exemplary scenario.

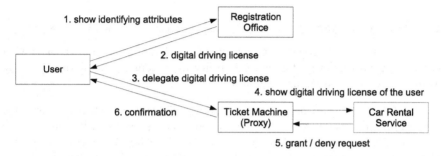

Fig. 1. Flow of user's attributes in business processes with a proxy

We see two cases for the role of a proxy. First, the proxy offers the user a collection of possible service providers for the subordinate services and the user chooses the service provider. Second, the user does not know anything about the subordinate services and his proxy decides which service provider is used on behalf of the user. Latter is not possible, if a credential link user's attributes to a particular service provider. According to the accountability interests of service providers, the user and his proxy must be distinguishable.

3.1   Attacker Model

The attacker model is extended by untrustworthy proxies. A proxy is a man-in-the-middle between the user and subordinate service providers. An untrustworthy proxy aims to trace a user and to impersonate him without his consent. The following privacy threats arise by an untrustworthy proxy.

Identifying a user: Business processes require for authentication purposes the property of user's attributes and not the identifying attributes. If identifying attributes of a user are disclosed, proxies and end service providers are able to identify the user.

Tracing a user: If a user delegates the same identifying attribute to different proxies, these transactions can be linked by them. We do not consider unlinkability of transactions which belong to the same instance of a business process with a proxy, since this proxy is involved in these transactions. So, the relationship of these transactions is implicitly known by this proxy.

Impersonation of a user contrary to the purpose of a delegation: A proxy gets some attributes of a user in order to act on his behalf. However, this proxy is now able to use these attributes for his own purposes, e.g. to use the service of a patent office for his own but with the attributes of the user.

Re-delegation of disclosed attributes: An untrustworthy proxy delegates attributes of a user to other service providers. It follows that a user does not control the disclosure of his attributes anymore and every recipient of his attributes is able to impersonate him.

3.2   Identity Management and Business Processes with Proxies

We apply identity management on our scenario with a proxy and focus on the two kinds of authentication protocols for identity management: (a) with a Privacy-CA and (b) with anonymous credentials.

Privacy-CA: A user authenticates towards a Privacy-CA with his secret token or password and optionally decides in real-time whether certain attributes will be disclosed [17]. If a proxy needs user's attributes for using a subordinate service, he must have access to these at the corresponding Privacy-CA. *Shibboleth* and the first phase of *Liberty Alliance* do not consider proxies. A user would have to disclose his password respectively security token to his proxy. This means that a proxy would have access to the complete identity of the user: a proxy becomes a "Big Brother" and is able to use his attributes for own purposes. The user does not control his identity anymore. *Liberty Alliance Phase 2* extends their authorization model by proxies as specified in the draft [18]. But, a delegation of attributes or their properties is not considered. Furthermore, a delegated credential is not linked to the purpose of the delegation so that a proxy is able to use a credential with respect to user's attributes for his own purposes at the given service.

Anonymous credentials: Anonymous credentials and pseudonyms of a user are based on his secret key k_{User}. If a user delegates a credential, he needs to give k_{User} to his proxy. The anonymous credential system *IBM idemix* prevents explicitly sharing of credentials by two non-transferability mechanisms in order to prevent misuse: PKI-based and all-or-nothing non-transferability [19]. By PKI-based non-transferability, the relationship between user's real name and his asymmetric cryptographic key pair (pk_{User}, sk_{User}) is certified by a conventional CA. The user gives sk_{User} encrypted with k_{User} to the CA which publishes the encrypted sk_{User}. Whenever a user shares k_{User} with a proxy, this proxy is able to decrypt sk_{User} and to know user's name as well as to impersonate him in the conventional PKI. By all-or-nothing non-transferability, all credentials and pseudonyms of a user are based on a single secret key k_{User}. A credential-issuing organization publishes the pseudonym and credential of a user. This means the user needs to give only k_{User} to his proxy in order to use his credential. But, if a user gives k_{User} to a proxy, the proxy is able to use all published pseudonyms and credentials of this user. The user will also lose control over his identity. Additionally, an untrustworthy proxy is able to fake a criminal use of user's credential in order to convince the responsible de-anonymization organization to reveal the identity of this user.

We see, that privacy is not possible by identity management in business processes with proxies. But business processes needs the disclosure of user's attributes, so we derive criteria for a secure delegation of attributes as credentials.

3.3   Criteria for a Privacy-Preserving Delegation of Rights

We extend the criteria for identity management for a controllable use of disclosed attributes as credentials by the following four criteria.

Delegating least privilege: Proxies may request more attributes and so more rights of the user as it is necessary for the purpose of their service. A user must be able to control the disclosure of his credentials so that only credentials relating to the purpose of a delegation are given to a proxy and thereby controlling the disclosure of his attributes as credentials.

Delegated credentials are only valid for particular purposes: The use of a delegated credential should be bound to the purpose of the corresponding business process. Since business processes are conducted by autonomous services, we define the purpose by the participants, necessary operations and user's attributes for a particular transaction. This means that a purpose is defined by the identity of the proxy, the identity of the subordinate services or their type to which this proxy is allowed to show the credential, the allowed interface call or its type, the validity of a delegated credential, and the allowed number of usage. A delegated credential should only be accepted, if it is used according to the purpose of a given delegation.

Restricting re-delegation of a credential: A re-delegated credential should only be valid if the user has given his consent to the re-delegation. This should be verifiable.

Revoking a delegated credential: A user must be able to revoke a delegated credential, if the delegation purpose has finished earlier than expected, the certified statement is no longer valid, or a proxy has been shaped up as an attacker.

If a proxy is free in his choice, a delegated credential is not bound to the purpose and a proxy would be able to misuse it. Due to binding delegated credentials to the purpose of the corresponding transaction, a proxy is not free with respect to his choice of subordinate service providers. A user decides which subordinate service provider his proxy is allowed to use.

4   DREISAM: Secure Delegation of Rights by Anonymous Credentials

We propose a privacy-preserving delegation protocol called *DREISAM*. It combines anonymous credentials for authentication with a credential-based access control on disclosed attributes as anonymous credentials. The added value of our protocol is that it does not need a Privacy-CA. We use the identity manager *iManager* in combination with the anonymous credential system *IBM idemix*.

We act on the assumptions, that the channels between the user and the service providers are completely anonymous. Furthermore, we assume that the participants in a protocol run authenticates one another and establish secure channels which means that the communication is confidential, of integrity, and accountable. If one participants detects an error in the protocol run, he will immediately inform his communication partner about this error and the protocol run will be canceled.

4.1   Overview

DREISAM is realized by four phases shown in figure 2. Phase A considers the request of user's attributes as a credential. Phases B and C realize a secure delegation by a credential-based access control on anonymous credentials. The goal of phase B is the delegation of the requested attributes to a proxy without sharing k_{User}. Instead of sharing k_{User}, the user delegates an authorization by a proxy credential for using these attributes. A proxy credential is similar to proxy tokens of [20], but without disclosing any personal attributes. The goal of phase C is to issue an anonymous credential for the proxy with respect to a proxy credential. The goal of phase D is to follow user's restrictions on the use of his delegated credentials. The protocol phases A and D use for the user interface and disclosure of attributes the identity manager *iManager* and for the establishment of pseudonyms and anonymous credentials the anonymous credential system *IBM idemix*.

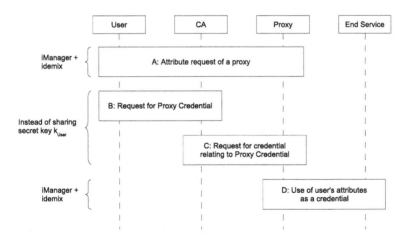

Fig. 2. Protocol phases of a privacy-preserving delegation of credentials by DREISAM

4.2   The Delegation Protocol

Phase A is realized by steps 1-3. In step 1, a user requests a service from a proxy and establishes a pseudonym *pseudonym(user,proxy)*. In step 2, this proxy requests certain attributes from the user in order to get access to certain subordinate services. The requests consists also of the privacy policy of the proxy, e.g, for which purposes the requestes attributes will be used. Of course, knowing the privacy policy of a requesting service provider does not guarantee privacy, if a user is not able to control the enforcement of this policy or gets evidences from a trusted third party. In our model, we omit a trusted third party with respect to privacy. We make use of the trust relationships with respect to access control in credential-based access control systems [21] in order to realize the interests of users with respect to the use of delegated credentials. In step 3, the user decides whether he wants to disclose them. Since the user is not in general an expert for every business process, he does not know which personal data is at least necessary for the proxy. Therefore, the user discloses the property of his attributes instead of the attributes themselves by using anonymous credentials. Figure 3 shows this protocol phase.

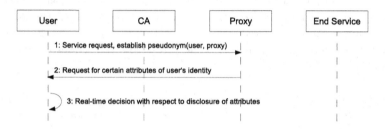

Fig. 3. Phase A: Attribute request by a proxy

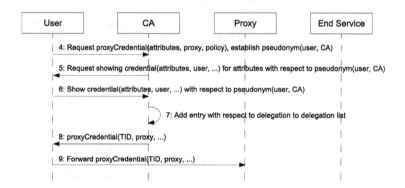

Fig. 4. Phase B: Request for a proxy credential by the user

Phase B is realized by steps 4-9 as shown in figure 4. In step 4, the user inquires the CA to issue a proxy credential. The interests of a user relating to the use of these attributes are specified in his policy which is part of the request. Since we set up on anonymous credentials of [19], the user establishes a pseudonym *pseudonym(user, CA)* with the CA so that the CA is able to verify the corresponding credential of the user. In step 5, the CA requires the user to prove that these attributes are related to him. In step 6, the user proves this assumption by showing his corresponding credential. The CA verifies this credential and whether the user is allowed to delegate these attributes. If the verification is successful, the CA adds an entry in his delegation list in step 7. This list is used as an access control list for issuing credentials for proxies. These access rights correspond to user's policy. In step 8, the CA issues a proxy credential for this proxy and sends it as an acknowledgment to the user. In step 9, the user forwards this proxy credential to the proxy.

Phase C is realized by steps 10-14 and shown in figure 5. In step 10, the proxy requests a user's credential. In step 11, the CA asks the proxy to prove his authorization by showing his proxy credential. This is done in step 12. Additionally, the proxy establishes a pseudonym *pseudonym(proxy, CA)* which is a premise for issuing an anonymous credential [19]. In step 13, the CA verifies the proxy credential of the proxy and checks whether his request is permitted according to user's policy. If so, the CA logs this delegation in the delegation list and issues a one-show credential for the proxy. The use of this one-show credential is specified by restrictions. The proxy gets the requested anonymous credential in step 14.

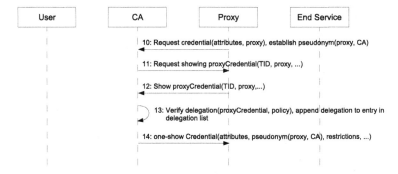

Fig. 5. Phase C: Request for a credential relating to a proxy credential by a proxy

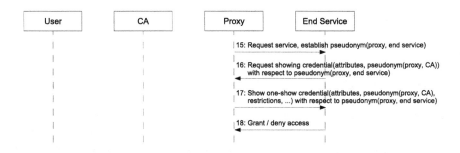

Fig. 6. Phase D: Showing an anonymous one-show credential by a proxy

Phase D is realized by steps 15-18. In step 15, the proxy requests a service of the end service provider and establishes a pseudonym *pseudonym(proxy,end service provider)* in order to link an anonymous credential to his own identity. In step 16, an end service provider asks the proxy to show the necessary attributes in order to get access to this service. In step 17, the proxy shows these attributes respectively their property by the corresponding anonymous credential. In step 18, the end service provider grants access to the proxy according to his request, if his credential is valid, otherwise the end service provider denies the access. Figure 6 shows this last part of *DREISAM*.

4.3 User's Policy for Using Disclosed Attributes

A user defines the permitted use of his delegated credential according to the purpose of a delegation by a policy. This policy represents an access control list for use of the disclosed attributes respectively their property as credentials. A policy considers the following interests of a user with respect to the use of disclosed attributes as credentials:

- **Proxy:** Only particular proxies are allowed to use the attributes of the user. The user defines a list of them as subjects of an access control list.
- **End service provider:** A proxy is allowed to show the credential of user's disclosed attributes only to particular end service provider. The user restricts the use of this credential by naming these end service providers.
- **Service:** We assume that an end service provider offers different services. If a credential is not restricted to a specific service, a proxy is able to call functions which are not needed for the purpose of the transaction, e.g. a proxy should be able to read but not to modify data at the service provider. The user names the permitted services for a proxy.
- **Number of credential usage:** The user specifies the number of times a proxy is allowed to use a credential with user's attributes.
- **Re-delegation:** The user specifies whether a proxy is allowed to further disclose user's attributes as a credential and to whom.
- **Validity:** A credential with user's attributes is only valid for the period of the corresponding business process. The user defines this period by its start and end date.

4.4 Proxy Credential as Authorization for Using Delegated Attributes

A user is not able to request an anonymous credential for the proxy, since this requires proxy's secret key k_{Proxy}. If a user issues proxy credentials, his transactions are linkable by the digital signature of this user. Hence, a CA replaces the user in a certification chain and issues proxy credentials on his behalf. A CA proves on behalf of end service providers whether the user has got the claimed attributes and is allowed to delegate them.

A proxy credential is similar to a Ticket Granting Ticket of Kerberos, but it does not contain any personal information about the user. It consists of the name of the proxy, e.g. his public key pk_{Proxy} which the user has received during the authentication of this proxy, the unique transaction identifier (TID) of user's entry in the delegation list, so that the CA is able to refer to the attributes and policy of the user, a timestamp of the CA, the validity of a proxy credential by a start and end date, and an unambiguously serial number which is needed for revocation. These attributes are digital signed by the CA. A proxy credential is implemented by means of a X.509 attribute certificate [22].

4.5   Using Disclosed Attributes on Behalf of a User

If a CA issues credentials for a proxy with respect to user's attributes, an untrustworthy proxy is not barred from misusing it. It is possible for a proxy to use an anonymous credential unlimited times and for arbitrary purposes if the policy of a user is not considered when issuing and using anonymous credentials for a proxy. A user and a CA are not able to enforce user's policy, since they do not control the information system of this proxy. In order to prevent unlimited use, a CA issues anonymous one-show credentials [19], if a credential is requested with a proxy credential. A CA is not able to recognize whether a proxy has already got this credential, hence she uses a delegation list for logging every issue of an anonymous credential for a proxy.

An entry of a delegation list refers to one particular delegation requests of an user. An entry consists of a unique TID, the pseudonym *pseudonym(user,CA)* of the user, his attributes to be delegated, his anonymous credential *credential(attributes,user)*, his policy according to an issue and use of corresponding anonymous one-show credentials, the name of proxies who have already got such credentials, and for each proxy the number of issued anonymous one-show credentials with respect to these attributes. A delegation lists is also been used in disputes for distinguishing users and proxies.

An anonymous one-show credential gives an incentive for a proxy not to use it twice. Some valuable information about the proxy are encrypted within a one-show credential, e.g. his signature key [19]. If a proxy uses an anonymous one-show credential twice, these encrypted information will be revealed. The end service provider recognizes this double-spending and rejects his request. Additionally, the CA embeds restrictions according to the desired use in an anonymous one-show credential.

4.6   Revocation of Delegated Credentials

If a credential of a user has expired or revoked, the purpose of a delegation has finished earlier than expected, or a proxy has been shown to be an attacker, the delegated credential of this proxy must be revoked. This affects his proxy credential and anonymous credentials. Since a proxy credential is an X.509 attribute certificate, the revocation mechanisms of a PKI, e.g. a certificate revocation list and an on-line verification protocol can be used [15].

These mechanisms cannot be used for anonymous credentials, since they require a credential to be unambiguously identifiable and so transactions which made use of an anonymous credential would be linkable. Anonymous credentials are revoked by using an accumulator which summarizes the valid credentials issued by a particular CA within one value [23]. Each credential has a witness value which is added to the accumulator of a CA and removed if a credential is revoked. Whenever a credential is revoked, the CA has to update her accumulator. A user shows that his credential is not revoked by showing that the corresponding witness is part of the accumulator. This is done by a zero-knowledge proof so that the user does not reveal any identifying attributes. We re-use this kind of revocation for revoking anonymous one-show credentials of a proxy.

5   Privacy Evaluation of DREISAM

We have to show that using *DREISAM* (a) does not reveal any personal attributes of the user, (b) the transactions of a user cannot be linked, and (c) a proxy is only able to use user's attributes as a credential according to the purpose of the corresponding business process. Cases (a) and (b) refer to a controlled disclosure of attributes, case (c) refers to a prevention of misuse. Additionally, disputes must be resolvable to clarify liability.

5.1   Controlling Disclosure of Attributes

Since *DREISAM* makes uses of the identity manager *iManager*, a user is able to disclose his attributes as partial identities relating to the service provider and the service. Linkability of transactions is achieved by using a pseudonym only for one transaction and by using anonymous credentials. Non-repudiation of a delegation is achieved by the log in the delegation list of the corresponding CA. Non-repudiation of a service use is achieved by showing a credential and by the access log of the corresponding service provider. As we have seen that a delegation of anonymous credentials implies that a user lose control about his identity, *DREISAM* enables a user to delegate specific attributes as a credential to a proxy by using proxy credentials. This empowers a user to delegate least attributes necessary for the purpose of a proxy. We re-use the de-anonymization mechanism of *IBM idemix* [19] for revealing the identity of a criminal user.

5.2   Preventing Misuse of Disclosed Attributes as Credentials

If a service provider grants access to his service to a proxy whose credential is not specified for this service, the service provider would grant access to an unauthorized party. This contradicts with the security interests of service providers and his motivation to use an access control. From this contradiction it follows that service providers will follow the restrictions of an anonymous one-show credential. Double-spending of a one-show credential is detected, if the end service provider checks on-line with a CA whether the shown credential has already been used [19]. In the off-line case, such a double-spending cannot be prevented but it can be detected afterwards by the same way as in the on-line case. With respect to undesired re-delegation of a proxy's credential, the CA would issue an anonymous credential for another party which neither mentioned in user's policy nor this policy allows a re-delegation. It follows that this CA does not follow her certification policy and is not trustworthy. This contradicts our assumption of a trustworthy CA.

5.3 Solving Disputes

Disputes between a user and a proxy relating to the use of a credential may occur in two cases. A proxy uses a delegated credential of the user and denies its use or a criminal user uses a credential in the name of a proxy and denies its use. A dispute is solved by a CA based on the log of a delegation transaction and the log of the corresponding end service provider with respect to the access queries. The CA compares the log of the credential use with the log of issued credentials to identify the identity of the cheater.

6 Discussion

Credential-based authentication systems such as Kerberos V5 [6], SPKI [24], and X.509 Proxy Certificates [25] support a delegation of rights by credentials. A user is able to delegate his attributes to proxies either via a third party [6] or immediately by issuing a credential for the proxy [24, 25]. Regarding the role of a proxy, these systems support a proxy to be able to choose subordinate service providers without asking the user, e.g. Kerberos defines a forwardable ticket granting ticket for this purpose. A restricted delegation with SPKI is possible, if the user is also the owner of the resource which should be accessed by a proxy with user's attributes [24]. By X.509 Proxy Certificates a user is able to delegate a policy with a proxy certificate with respect to its use to realize a delegation of least privilege [25].

Regarding privacy, these systems do not consider a controlled disclosure of attributes. Transactions of a user are linkable by his communication partners. Kerberos uses the name of the user in ticket granting tickets and service tickets which can be seen by their recipients and the key distribution center. SPKI and X.509 bind user's attributes to his public key. Attributes of SPKI and X.509 certificates can be read by anyone.

7 Conclusion

Privacy is nowadays achieved by a user-controlled disclosure of attributes with identity management systems. However, business processes with intermediate services acting on behalf of a user need the disclosure of attributes to these proxies. Then, a user is not able to control the disclosure and use of his attributes anymore by using current identity management systems. They have not only to realize the principle of data economy, but also the control about the use of disclosed attributes to prevent or at least to detect misuse of disclosed attributes.

By our generic delegation protocol delegating personal attributes as access rights by means of anonymous credentials, we have introduced an extension for identity management which controls the use of delegated credentials to one proxy. Thereby, a user does not have to trust any service provider relating to non-linkability. Misuse is prevented by a credential-based access control on credentials for a proxy. Although the user has to trust a CA and end service providers that they follow user's restrictions regarding the use of delegated credentials. But this assumption overlaps with the security interests of these parties without conflicting with the assumption of untrustworthy service providers regarding profiling and is therefore realistic. We see further work in a permitted transitive re-delegation of delegated, anonymous credentials by a proxy to subordinate proxies on behalf of the user.

Acknowledgment

This work was funded by the German Research Foundation (DFG) within the priority programme "Security in the Information and Communication Technology" (SPP 1079).

References

1. Müller, G., Eymann, T., Kreutzer, M.: Telematik- und Kommunikationssysteme in der vernetzten Wirtschaft. Oldenbourg (2003)
2. Sackmann, S., Strüker, J.:Electronic Commerce Enquête 2005 - 10 Jahre Electronic Commerce: Eine stille Revolution in deutschen Unternehmen. Institut für Informatik und Gesellschaft, Telematik, Freiburg i.Br., Germany (2005)
3. Huhns, M., Singh, M.: Service-Oriented Computing: Key Concepts and Principles. IEEE Internet Computing 49(1) (2005) 75–81
4. Chaum, D.: Untraceable Electronic Mail, Return Addresses, and Digital Pseudonyms. In: Communications of the ACM 24(3), ACM Press, New York, NY (1981) 84–88
5. Clauß, S., Köhntopp, M.: Identity management and its support of multilateral security. In: Computer Networks 37(2), Elsevier (2001) 205–219
6. Kohl, J., Neumann, C.: The Kerberos Network Authentication Service V5. Request for Comments 1510. Network Working Group (1993)
7. Jendricke, U., Gerd tom Markotten, D.: Identitätsmanagement: Einheiten und Systemarchitektur. In: Fox, D., Köhntopp, M., Pfitzmann, A. (eds.): Verlässliche IT-Systeme – Sicherheit in komplexen Infrastrukturen. Vieweg, Wiesbaden, Germany (2001) 77–85
8. Camenisch, J., Van Herreweghen, E.: Design and Implementation of the idemix Anonymous Credential System. In: Proceedings of the 9th ACM Conference on Computer and Communications Security. ACM Press, Washington, DC (2002) 21–30
9. Westin, A.: Privacy and Freedom. Atheneum, New York, NY (1967)
10. Bundesverfassungsgericht: Volkszählungsurteil. In: Entscheidungen des Bundesverfassungsgerichts, Urteil vom 15.12.1983; Az.: 1 BvR 209/83; NJW 84, 419 (1983)

11. Chaum, D.: Security without Identification: Transaction Systems to make Big Brother Obsolete. In: Communications of the ACM 28(10), ACM Press, New York, NY (1985) 1030–1077

12. Microsoft Corporation: Microsoft .NET Passport Review Guide, http://www.microsoft.com/net/services/passport/review_guide.asp, accessed December 2003 (2003)

13. Erdos, M., Cantor, S.: Shibboleth-Architecture DRAFT v05.http://shibboleth.internet2.edu/docs/draft-internet2-shibboleth-arch-v05.pdf, accessed July 2004 (2004)

14. Wason, T. (ed.): Liberty ID-FF Architecture Overview Version: 1.2. Liberty Alliance Project. http://www.projectliberty.org/specs/liberty-idff-arch-overview-v1.2.pdf, accessed at July 2004 (2004)

15. Ford, W., Baum, M.: Secure Electronic Commerce. Prentice-Hall, New Jersey (1997)

16. Brands, S.: Rethinking Public Key Infrastructures and Digital Certificates: Building in Privacy. MIT Press (2000)

17. Pfitzmann, B., Waidner, M.: Federated Identity-Management Protocols – Where User Authentication Protocols May Go. In: 11th International Workshop on Security Protocols (Cambridge 2003), LNCS, Vol. 3364, Springer-Verlag, Berlin (2005) 153–174

18. Ellison, G. (ed.): Liberty ID-WSF Security Mechanisms Version: 1.2. Liberty Alliance Project. http://www.projectliberty.org/specs/liberty-idwsf-security-mechanisms-v1.2.pdf, accessed at August 2005 (2005)

19. Camenisch, J., Lysyanskaya, A.: Efficient non-transferable anonymous multi-show credential system with optional anonymity revocation. In: Advances in Cryptology – EUROCRYPT 2001, International Conference on the Theory and Application of Cryptographic Techniques (Innsbruck 2001). LNCS, Vol. 2045, Springer-Verlag, Berlin (2001) 91–118

20. Neuman, C.: Proxy-Based Authorization and Accounting for Distributed Systems. In: 13th International Conference on Distributed Computing Systems (Pittsburgh) (1993) 283–291

21. Aura, T.: Distributed Access-Rights Managements with Delegations Certificates. In: Secure Internet Programming. LNCS, Vol. 1603, Springer-Verlag, Berlin (1999) 211-235

22. Farrell, S., Housley, R.: An Internet Attribute Certificate Profile for Authorization. Request for Comments 3281. Network Working Group (2002)

23. Camenisch, J., Lysysanskaya, A.: Dynamic Accumulators and Application to Efficient Revocation of Anonymous Credentials. In: Advances in Cryptology – CRYPTO 2002, 22nd Annual International Cryptology Conference (Santa Barbara 2002). LNCS, Vol. 2442, Springer, Berlin (2002) 61–76

24. Ellison, E., Frantz, B., Lampson, B., Rivest, R., Thomas, B., Ylonen, T.: SPKI Certificate Theory. Request for Comments 2963. Network Working Group (1999)

25. Welch, V., Foster, I., Kesselmann, C., Mulmo, O., Pearlman, L., Tuecke, S., Gawor, J., Meder, S., Siebenlist, F.: X.509 Proxy Certificates for Dynamic Delegation. In: 3rd Annual PKI R&D Workshop. http://www.globus.org/Security/papers/pki04-welch-proxy-cert-final.pdf, accessed June 2004 (2004)

A Framework for Quantification of Linkability Within a Privacy-Enhancing Identity Management System⋆

Sebastian Clauß

TU Dresden, Germany
Sebastian.Clauss@tu-dresden.de

Abstract. Within a privacy-enhancing identity management system, among other sources of information, knowledge about current anonymity and about linkability of user's actions should be available, so that each user is enabled to make educated decisions about performing actions and disclosing PII (personal identifiable information).

In this paper I describe a framework for quantification of anonymity and linkability of a user's actions for use within a privacy-enhancing identity management system. Therefore, I define a model of user's PII and actions as well as an attacker model. Based thereon, I describe an approach to quantify anonymity and linkability of actions. Regarding practical applicability, a third party service for linkability quantification is discussed.

1 Introduction

A privacy-enhancing identity management system[1] shall assist a user in using services (on the Internet) in a least privacy invading way. A basic technique for this is to be initially anonymous, e.g. by using an anonymity service at the network layer. So, in principle a user can control that only information required to perform services is disclosed. Depending on the service, such required information restricts privacy of the user to some extent.

Within a privacy-enhancing identity management system, a user needs to get reasonable information about his privacy status in order to make educated decisions about performing actions and disclosing PII (personal identifiable information). Among other sources of information, knowledge about current anonymity or about linkability of certain actions can help a user to assess his privacy.

In this paper a framework for quantification of anonymity and linkability of a user's actions is described, with the perspective of using such quantification within a privacy-enhancing identity management. After outlining related work on anonymity and linkability measurements in Section 2, a model for users and actions with regard to transferring PII is introduced in Section 3. Further, an

---

⋆ Parts of this work have been supported by the Project FIDIS, a Network of Excellence within the EU's 6th Framework Programme.

[1] See e.g. [1] for details on functionality of a privacy-enhancing identity management system.

G. Müller (Ed.): ETRICS 2006, LNCS 3995, pp. 191–205, 2006.

attacker model is defined in Section 4. Based on these models, an approach for quantifying user's anonymity and linkability between actions is described in Section 5. Therefore, the problem of getting information needed for such quantification is discussed in Section 5.1. The basic model does not incorporate the time aspect, i.e. that user's attributes may change over time. An enhancement regarding this issue is discussed in Section 5.5. As quantification of anonymity and linkability of actions is a highly resource consuming calculation, in Section 5.6 possibilities to make use of third parties for this task are discussed.

2   Related Work

Over the years aspects of anonymity and (un-)linkability evaluation have been researched mainly with respect to evaluation of anonymity providing services on the network layer, e.g., mixes [2].

Regarding the connection layer, methods for anonymity evaluation have been described by Díaz et al. [3] and Serjantov and Danezis [4]. They describe properties of anonymity services and derive methods for measuring anonymity. The scenario used there is not directly comparable with the one I use. Their approach differs in that they consider a known set of users, whereas in our model the number of entities (users) is only restricted by the possibility to distinguish entities by their attributes[2]. Another difference is the main objective: these authors define a measure of anonymity based on prior knowledge, whereas they do not define how such knowledge is gathered and organised. Similar to these papers, I use entropy based measures for anonymity.

Based on [3] and [4], Steinbrecher and Köpsell [5] describe a general information-theoretic model for (un-)linkability of similar items (e.g., subjects, messages, events, actions, etc.) within a system. This model is consistent with ours. In Section 5.4 I apply methods for linkability measurement described in this paper.

Regarding the application layer, Díaz et al. [6] describe how entropy can be used to measure anonymity, but similar to [3], they assume that the number of users is known. They also assume that the attacker does get more information about a message than just the data in it, e.g. he can also see which user sends at a given time. In our model, the attacker only gets to know properties of the user (entity). Such properties may also be used to model information gained on the connection level, but our system abstracts from this by only talking of entities' attributes which can have different values. Similarly to the other papers referenced above, they also do not describe how exactly the attacker gains information, and how this information is aggregated.

Besides the information theoretic approaches discussed above, Hughes and Shmatikov [7] describe the partial knowledge of a function based on a mathematical abstraction. They specify anonymity properties using a modular approach. Their approach can be used independent of the underlying algebra or logic. In contrast to our approach, their approach is not probabilistic, i.e. items of interest are considered either fully linkable or not linkable at all.

---

[2] See Definition 6, *observer state*.

3   Modelling Users and Actions

In this section I define a model with regards to the entities involved, actions, data flow and the modelling of the data.

Within the model there is a finite set $\mathcal{E}$ of *entities*[3] $e \in \mathcal{E}$. An entity represents a subject out of the real life, like a real person or an artificial person (e.g., legal person). Entities are considered to be able to communicate by means of computer networks, mainly the internet. Further, entities have properties, by which entities can be classified into different subsets of $\mathcal{E}$. For each entity $e \in \mathcal{E}$ there exists at least one set of properties by which it can be identified within $\mathcal{E}$. These properties are also called personal identifiable information (PII).

Actions take place in form of communication between entities. Thereby, a single action takes place between exactly two entities e_m and e_n. In an action at least one of the communicating entities transmits data to the other one. Data transmitted during an action is considered to *belong together*. Further, these data can contain properties of the originating entity.

3.1   Attributes and Digital Identities

In order to structure the properties of entities transmitted during actions, data can be modelled as *attributes* and their *values*. These terms are defined as follows:

Definition 1 (Attribute Value). *An* attribute value *is a property of an entity.*

Definition 2 (Attribute). *An* attribute $\mathcal{A}$ *is a finite set of values* $a \in \mathcal{A}$, *and a special value "not applicable"* $\ominus$.

For example, the attribute "gender" consists of two attribute values "male" and "female". In case also legal persons or machines are considered as entities, the attribute "gender" would get the value "not applicable".

In addition to information from the content of messages, knowledge gained at the connection layer can also be modelled by means of attributes.

Within the model, I assume a finite set of attributes. Based on the attributes, the *digital identity* can be defined corresponding to the definition in [8].

Definition 3 (Digital Identity). *A digital identity is a complete bundle of attribute values. Thereby "complete bundle" means, that a digital identity comprises one value of every attribute.*

An entity has at least one digital identity. In case multiple values of an attribute are properties of one entity e, this entity has multiple digital identities.

Example 1. In Figure 1 relations between attributes, their values and a digital identity are shown by a concrete example.

---

[3] For reasons of intuitive understanding, I often speak about *users* throughout this paper. Regarding the model defined here, a *user* is an *entity*.

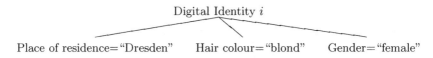

Digital Identity i

Place of residence= "Dresden"   Hair colour= "blond"   Gender= "female"

Fig. 1. Attributes with values assigned to a digital identity

The above definition is static, i.e. attribute values within a digital identity cannot change[4].

For describing a general framework for anonymity and linkability quantification within the next sections, this static model will be used. In Section 5.5 an approach for incorporating time properties will be described.

In this model values of attributes are assumed to be discrete. So the model does not directly consider attributes, where values can be continuous. But to use such values in the digital world, they must be measured and thereby (considering a certain fuzziness of the measurement) are transformed into discrete values, which then are covered by the model given[5].

4   Attacker Model

Generally, an entity's security goal is to find out, whether and to what extent the disclosure of a set of PII items (values of attributes) helps an attacker to link the current action to other actions of the entity, or to identify[6] the entity. To clarify this, the attacker and the success criterion of an attack, i.e. *linkability of actions* or *identification*, must be defined.

With respect to privacy-enhancing identity management, the attacker is assumed to be a set of service providers, with which users perform actions. More formally, the attacker is characterised by the following assumptions with respect to an entity e:

- The attacker controls one or more communication partners of e, i.e. gets to know data disclosed by e during actions with these communication partners.
- The attacker has general knowledge about attributes of entities, i.e. has access to public information services, e.g., phonebook entries, statistical offices.

Using this information, the attacker tries to identify entities, and tries to find out, whether different actions can be linked.

---

[4] I.e., with this definition a change of an attribute value of an entity means that the entity switches to another digital identity.

[5] An observer may nevertheless make a difference between attributes resulting from measurements and attributes defined in a discrete space, e.g., authorisation tokens. I discuss this issue in Section 5.2 with respect to matching functions for attribute values.

[6] Throughout this document, the term "identified" is used as the opposite of "anonymous".

Regarding the model defined in Section 3.1 two goals can be specified:

- Observing an action, an attacker wants to find out the digital identity this action belongs to.
- Observing two actions, an attacker wants to find out whether they originate from the same digital identity.

In order to quantify anonymity and unlinkability of *entities*, we need to specify the relation between entities and digital identities. In order to identify entities, the set of attributes considered within the system must contain a subset which is sufficient to identify entities (in the physical world[7]). Under this assumption, two cases need to be considered regarding the relation between entities and digital identities. Either, attributes are defined in a way that an entity has only one digital identity. In this case, identifying a digital identity means identifying an entity. In case an entity may have more than one digital identity, the attacker needs to group digital identities by data identifying the entity (in the physical world). (See Section 5.3 and 5.4 on how this influences measurements.)

5 Quantification of Anonymity and Linkability

A user wants to know, how his current privacy status is, or how it will be regarding actions planned given the current circumstances. The focus of this document is technical. So, privacy is seen here from a technical point of view, i.e. it is interpreted as degree of anonymity or linkability.

According to [8], unlinkability of actions can defined as follows:

Definition 4 (Unlinkability). Unlinkability *of two or more actions means that within the system, from the attacker's perspective, these actions are no more and no less related after his observation than they are related concerning his a-priori knowledge.*

In the scope of this section, "related" means the grade of certainty of the attacker, that these actions originate from the same entity. Measuring linkability means determining this certainty.

Anonymity can be defined as follows [8]:

Definition 5 (Anonymity). Anonymity *is the state of being not identifiable within a set of subjects, the anonymity set.*

For quantifying anonymity, the information gained from action c needs to be compared to the information needed to identify a certain entity out of a given set of entities (the anonymity set).

Within this section I first deal with anonymity and unlinkability with respect to digital identities as defined in Section 3.1. After that, I discuss anonymity and unlinkability with respect to entities under the assumption that a set of data sufficient for identification of entities in the physical world is known.

---

[7] This paper does not aim at defining, which data is sufficient for this purpose. Here, possibly legal definitions may suffice, but it may vary depending on the attackers context.

5.1   Sources of Information

Quantification of privacy is not possible without information from outside the user's domain. In other words, the user needs to know what an assumed attacker knows, in order to quantify information contained in disclosed data against this knowledge. The following example illustrates this:

Example 2. Let's assume a user disclosing his surname "Sebastian". Within the system, there may be many users named "Sebastian", but this name could also be unique. Only with knowledge about the other users it is possible to quantify, how much information is contained in this name.

Privacy quantification would be easy, if there was a "Big Brother"-like source of information [9], which has all knowledge available within the system. But such a source of information does not exist in today's internet[8].

So, multiple sources of information need to be taken into account, each having different partial knowledge about the system. Sources of information can be distinguished into the following categories:

- The user himself, i.e., the user who wants to quantify his privacy in a certain situation. The main source of information the user has itself is the history of data disclosed in past actions.
- Other users. Information from other users can be parts of their disclosure history.
- Public parties, e.g., public statistical offices, or special services supporting anonymity and linkability quantification by aggregating data about users in order to generate specific statistics regarding service providers considered as attackers.
- Service providers. Usually, it seems strange to assume service providers to be sources of information, because they are rather seen as the attackers on privacy, which a user wants to defend against. But the goal of a service provider can be seen differentiated. On the one hand, his goal is to find out as much as possible about profiles of users in order to optimise his services etc. On the other hand, some of the profiled information can be published for marketing or corporate image purposes, e.g., the total number of users may be a criterion to decide on the acceptance of a service for users, so it could be published by the service. There could also be privacy certificates for which service providers can apply, which are only issued in case certain information important for user's anonymity and linkability quantification is provided.

In order to utilise sources of information for evaluating the privacy situation, they need to be trusted regarding *correctness* of information. This also includes that information needs to be up to date.

In this paper, I will not go into detail how trust in sources of information may be established. Possibilities here are trust because of legal regulations, because of personal or third party evaluations, reputation systems, etc.

---

[8] Even that it would make privacy quantification easy, it would also be a perfect attacker on privacy.

Correctness of Information. In order to make use of information for evaluation of the privacy situation of a user, the information needs to be correct regarding the following aspects:

- the scope of the information, i.e., it must be clear, about which number, kind etc. of people a statistic contains information,
- the validity period of the information.

As noted above, there is no general master source of information. So, verification of correctness of data is not generally possible. The only possibility for verification is to have multiple sources of information about the same items of interest, which can be compared against each other. Then, techniques known from research on fault tolerance, e.g., majority voting, can be used to decide on the correct information.

Summary. The above sections make clear, that evaluation of a user's privacy exclusively bases on sources of information, which can be more or less trusted by the user. In this context, the evaluation can never be objective and universal. It will always be a subjective view, and under realistic circumstances, it will nearly never be possible to exactly get to the same results as an (assumed) attacker.

As a consequence of this, a technical evaluation of privacy should not be used as a automatic criterion to base decisions about actions on, but it can give hints.

5.2   A Method for Calculation

In this section, a method for calculation of anonymity and linkability measures is described in order to show, how information from the different sources could be aggregated. Further, this method forms the basis for enhancements described in Section 5.5.

Aggregating Input Data. The mathematical model sketched here enables to use entropy metrics for determining an anonymity set size for a given set of disclosed data items. Here, only the aspects of the model are described, which are needed to describe the calculation anonymity and linkability metrics. A more detailed description can be found in [10]. This model operates on static digital identities as defined in Section 3.

By observing actions an observer gets a limited insight into user's PII and into relations between PII items. The observer can collect this information, and conduct any desired statistical analysis on them. With a growing number of observations the information on probability distributions of the digital identities gets more exact[9]. I define the knowledge of an attacker which he gained by observations in form of the *observer state*:

Definition 6 (Observer State). *The State $Z^{\mathcal{X}}$ of an observer $\mathcal{X}$ is a triple $(\mathcal{I}, h, g)$, where:*

---

[9] "exact" here means exact with respect to the observation. Observations may nevertheless yield incorrect information (see Section 5.1).

- $\mathcal{I}$ is the set of all digital identities possible.

$$\mathcal{I} = \mathcal{A}_1 \times \mathcal{A}_2 \times \ldots \times \mathcal{A}_n$$

- $h : \mathcal{I} \mapsto \mathbb{R}$ is a function, which assigns a probability to every digital identity, i.e., $(\forall i \in \mathcal{I}.0 \leq h(i) \leq 1)$
- g is the number of observations leading to this state.
- the sum of all probabilities is 1.

$$\sum_{(\mathcal{I})} h(i) = 1$$

$h(i)$ denotes the probability that within the set $\mathcal{I}$ of all possible identities the identity i is observed by the attacker. When the attacker observes an action of a user, the probability of the identities matching to the observation (i.e., the suspects with respect to the observation) is raised, whereas the probability of all other identities is lowered. After defining observations, I specify a method for matching identities and observations.

Definition 7 (Observation). *An* observation *is a (possibly incomplete) bundle of attribute values. Such a bundle contains at most one value per attribute. The set $\mathcal{B}$ of all possible* observations *is the cross product of all attributes with an additional element "not observed" $\bot$.*

$$\mathcal{B} = (\mathcal{A}_1 \cup \bot) \times (\mathcal{A}_2 \cup \bot) \times \ldots \times (\mathcal{A}_n \cup \bot)$$

Intuitively, this means that during actions a user discloses PII. The observer *observes* this PII and gets a more and more refined view on the digital identities and by that on the users.

Within the set of all possible digital identities an observer can separate suspect digital identities with respect to an observation from non-suspect digital identities. The set of *suspects* related to an observation can be defined as follows:

Definition 8 (Suspects). *The set of* suspects *$\mathcal{V}_b$ related to an observation $b = (x_1, .., x_n)$ contains all digital identities $i = (x'_1, .., x'_n)$, whose attribute values are either equal to attribute values of b or are not contained in b.*[10]

$$\mathcal{V}_b = \{i | x_k \in \{x'_k, \bot\}, k = 1, .., n\} \tag{1}$$

As stated above, the observer "learns" by observations. The following definition formalises this learning process:

---

[10] The matching function "equality" used here is a simple example. This makes only sense, if attribute values are discrete and not related to each other. If this is not the case, e.g., if measuring faults for originally continuous attribute values (see Section 3.1) need to be taken into account, other matching functions should be used which reflect such properties of attributes.

Definition 9 (Observer State Update). *Let* $b \in \mathcal{B}$ *be an observation and* $\mathcal{Z}$ *a set of observer states. An observer state update* $\delta : \mathcal{Z} \times \mathcal{B} \rightarrow \mathcal{Z}$ *constructs a new observer state from a given state and an observation.*

These definitions are a framework for formalising concrete observations and statistical analysis based on digital identities. In order to not restrict this model to passive (observing only) attackers, it is intentionally not defined how an observation is done. So, an attacker may observe messages, but may also actively insert or fake messages in order to observe users' reactions.

Based on the above definitions a statistical observer model is defined as follows:

Definition 10 (Statistical Observer Model). *A* statistical observer model *of an observer* $\mathcal{X}$ *comprises a set* $\mathcal{I}$ *of digital identities, a set of observations* $\mathcal{B}$, *a set* $\mathcal{Z}^{\mathcal{X}}$ *of observer states and a function* δ, *which derives new observer states from previous states and observations.*

The statistical observer model specifies the observer's knowledge in form of statistics about digital identities together with a method for aggregating newly gained knowledge. This is an abstract definition, as it leaves open how actually the aggregation of new observations influences the probabilities of digital identities.

In order to actually perform calculations within this framework model, a concrete model can be defined as follows[11]:

Let $\mathcal{I}$ be a set of digital identities and $\mathcal{B}$ the set of all observations possible. The set of states $\mathcal{Z}$ is defined inductively. First, I define the initial state, in which the attacker did not do any observations. For the initial state $Z_0 = (\mathcal{I}, h, g)$ it shall hold, that $g = 0$ and $(\forall i \in \mathcal{I}.h(i) = \frac{1}{|\mathcal{I}|})$.

Now I specify how an observation actually changes the probabilities of the digital identities. A function $\delta : \mathcal{Z} \times \mathcal{B} \rightarrow \mathcal{Z}$ derives a new state $Z_{k+1} = (\mathcal{I}, h_{k+1}, g_{k+1})$ from a previous state $Z_k = (\mathcal{I}, h_k, g_k)$ and an observation $b \in \mathcal{B}$ as follows:

$$h_{k+1} : i \mapsto \frac{h_k(i) * g_k + x}{g_k + 1} \tag{2}$$

$$x = \begin{cases} \frac{1}{|\mathcal{V}_b|} & \text{iff } i \in \mathcal{V}_b \\ 0 & \text{otherwise} \end{cases}$$

$$g_{k+1} = g_k + 1 \tag{3}$$

This intuitively means, that first each observation gets an equal "weight" 1. Then, this "weight" is divided by the number of suspects of this observation. By doing that, more significant observations (i.e., observations containing values of more attributes) get a bigger influence on the probability of the suspect identities

---

[11] The concrete model described here is an example, in order to show a possibility how observations can be aggregated in a meaningful way into a *statistical observer model*. There may exist other concrete models.

than less significant ones. Further, the "weight" of the observation is set into relation to the number of observations already aggregated, so that every observation already aggregated has the same overall influence on the probabilities.

In fact, the observer model defined above sums up relative frequencies. With a growing number of observations, it can be assumed that the relative frequencies converge to probabilities. By induction over g, it can be shown, that function h always has the properties of a probability distribution, i.e., $\sum_{(i \in \mathcal{I})} h(i) = 1$ and $h(i)$ is not negative[12].

A useful feature of this observer model is the fact, that two observer states can be aggregated without the need to add every single observation of one state to the other. So, observer states of different sources of information can be aggregated easily into a general state:

Definition 11 (State Aggregation). *Two states* $Z^A = (\mathcal{I}, h^A, g^A)$ *and* $Z^B = (\mathcal{I}, h^B, g^B)$ *based on the same set of digital identities are aggregated to a new state* $Z^A \cup Z^B = (\mathcal{I}, h^C, g^C)$ *as follows:*

$$g^C = g^A + g^B \tag{4}$$

$$h^C : i \mapsto \frac{g^A h^A(i) + g^B h^B(i)}{g^C} \tag{5}$$

For a proof the correctness of state aggregation see [10].

5.3   Quantifying Anonymity

As described in Section 2, Shannon entropy [11] is often used as a metric for anonymity. Given an observer state Z, the Shannon entropy $H_\varnothing$ of an information b can be computed.

Definition 12 (Shannon entropy). *Let* b *be an observation and* $\mathcal{V}_b$ *a set of suspects related to observation* b. *The Shannon entropy of* b *related to a state* Z *is the Shannon entropy of the suspects* $\mathcal{V}_b$.

$$H_\varnothing = - \sum_{(v \in \mathcal{V}_b)} p(v|b) \log_2 p(v|b) \tag{6}$$

$$p(v|b) = \frac{p(v \wedge (\bigvee_{(w \in \mathcal{V}_b)} w))}{p(\bigvee_{(w \in \mathcal{V}_b)} w)} \tag{7}$$

$$= \frac{h(v)}{\sum_{(i \in \mathcal{V}_b)} h(i)} \tag{8}$$

Thereby, $h(i)$ *denotes the probability of the identity* i *within the observer state* Z.

---

[12] See [10] for the proof.

Given a Shannon entropy $|\mathcal{S}| = 2^{H_{\varnothing}}$ denotes the equivalent size of a uniformly distributed anonymity set $\mathcal{S}$.

I first evaluate the case that a user has only one digital identity. The Shannon entropy $H_{\varnothing}$ specifies the average amount of information needed in addition to b in order to uniquely identify a digital identity. In case of a user evaluating his anonymity, he usually knows his digital identity. So, it may be more useful for him to compute the amount of information needed to identify him, i.e., his digital identity. This so called "individual anonymity" can be computed as follows:

$$H(i) = \log_2 p(i|b) \tag{9}$$

From the viewpoint of a single user, $individual\ anonymity$ is the most accurate anonymity measure.

In case a user has multiple digital identities, this measure can also be used, but before calculating entropy all suspect digital identities belonging to the same user need to be grouped into one "personal" digital identity. This grouping is done by summing up their probabilities. This grouping needs to be done by information considered to be sufficient to identify users (in the physical world.)[13] The entropy is then calculated based on the "personal" digital identities.

5.4   Quantifying Linkability of Actions

Regarding linkability, it is interesting for a user, to what extent it can be determined that actions have been done by the same user. More formally, there are two actions c_1 and c_2 which have been observed in the form of observations b_1 and b_2.

According to [5], linkability of items of interest can be measured regarding equivalence classes, for which (after observations) an attacker has partial knowledge about which items of interest belong to which class.

Applied to the model used here, the equivalence classes are the digital identities. By an observation of an action, suspect digital identities can be determined corresponding to the observation of this action (see Definition 8), i.e., information about association of items of interest (actions) to equivalence classes (digital identities) is gained.

Regarding observations b_1 and b_2, the suspect sets are $\mathcal{V}_{b_1}$ resp. $\mathcal{V}_{b_2}$. Within a set of suspects, a digital identity has the probability $p(v|b)$, which is derived from the current observer state as shown in equations (7) and (8).

The probability p_r, that actions c_1 and c_2 belong to the same digital identities, can be computed as follows:

$$p_r = \sum_{(v \in \mathcal{V}_{b_1 \cup b_2})} p(v|b_1) \cdot p(v|b_2)$$

Thereby, $\mathcal{V}_{b_1 \cup b_2}$ denotes the set of digital identities, which are contained in both sets $\mathcal{V}_{b_1}$ and $\mathcal{V}_{b_2}$. According to [5], the probability $p_{\neg r}$, that the actions c_1 and c_2 do not belong to the same digital identity is $1 - p_r$.

---

[13] See also Section 4.

From probabilities p_r and $p_{\neg r}$ a degree of linkability d can be computed by using the Shannon entropy [5]:

$$d := H(p_r, p_{\neg r}) = -p_r \cdot \log_2 p_r - p_{\neg r} \cdot \log_2 p_{\neg r}$$

The degree of linkability d specifies, how much an observer has learnt about the relation between c_1 and c_2 from observations V_{b_1} and V_{b_2}, taking also into account the a-priori knowledge about the digital identities derived from the current observer state.

If $p_r > p_{\neg r}$, the degree denotes the certainty of the observer, that actions c_1 and c_2 *belong to the same digital identity*, otherwise it denotes the certainty of the observer that the actions do *not belong to the same digital identity*.

In case a user has only one digital identity, linkability related to a digital identity is the same as linkability related to a user. In case a user may have more than one digital identity, before actually calculating linkability the suspect digital identities belonging to the same user first need to be grouped into "personal" digital identities, as described in Section 5.3 for the same purpose. Then, the calculation of linkability can be performed as shown above, but based on the "personal" digital identities.

5.5   Incorporating Time

As described in Section 3.1, the above model does not consider changes of attribute values of users. But for a system more closely modelling the real world this is an important feature, because many attributes of users can be subject to change over time, e.g., the family name may be changed by marriage.

In order to also consider timely changes of attributes within a digital identity, I define the *dynamic digital identity* as follows:

Definition 13 (Dynamic Digital Identity). *A* dynamic digital identity *is a bundle of functions $f_A(t) : f(t) \rightarrow a$ for each attribute A. This means, that for each attribute a function exists, which determines the value of the attribute at a given point in time t.*

A (static) digital identity can be seen as a snapshot at a point in time t of a dynamic digital identity. At a given point in time, the digital identity of an entity comprises all information, which can be transmitted by the entity during an action, so (regarding data to be possibly communicated to other entities) an entity can be seen as an incarnation of a particular digital identity.

For an observer, this means that observations "grow older", i.e., an observation matches a set of digital identities only at the time of the observation. For the knowledge base of the observer, the observer state, this means that probabilities of digital identities need to be adjusted according to time by using the functions $f_A(t)$ of the digital identity. In most cases, the observer will not fully know this function, so he needs to estimate it. This leads to growing uncertainty with regards to older information.

As this "ageing" does not change the structure of the observer state, quantification of anonymity and linkability of actions can be performed in the same way as described above for the static model.

So, in general the observer state model described in Section 5.2 can be enhanced to incorporate time. For use for anonymity and linkability quantification within a real system, specific time dependent functions need to be defined for the single attributes.

5.6   Linkability Quantification Service

Despite getting enough and reliable information[14], the major problem with linkability quantification is resource usage. Detailed quantification needs a major amount of storage as well as computing power, depending on the number of attributes and attribute values to consider. Especially if considering e.g., mobile phones or PDAs as devices of the user, both storage and computing power are very much limited. Even if calculation within the general observer model described above could be optimised to some extent, this will usually exceed resources available on such smaller devices.

A usual way to address such a problem would be to introduce a third party linkability quantification service (LQS), which could compute anonymity and linkability quantification on behalf of users.

In the following I will go in some more detail about intended functionality of such a service, and especially on privacy and security risks introduced by an LQS and possibilities to solve them.

Basic Functionality. Basically, the service has two functions:

- Answering user requests for linkability computation.
- Gathering base data needed for linkability computation, i.e. the data described in Section 5.1. This data can be aggregated to an observer state as described in Section 5.2.

The first function is processed in the following way:

Input: The user inputs a request for (pre-)computation of measurements of his anonymity or linkability of actions. Such a request consists of one or more sets of data to be disclosed or already disclosed, relative to which anonymity or linkability can be quantified.
Processing: Measurements are computed using the base data aggregated from sources of information.
Output: The service outputs the measurement results, together with an arbitrary set of details regarding the computation, e.g., a description of the sources of information used.

In general, a LQS is just a linkability quantification done by a TTP. For the linkability quantification calculation, in terms of input and output, it is rather straight forward to compute it remote instead of local, but as the TTP running the LQS is not under the user's control, security and privacy issues arise.

---

[14] See Section 5.1 for details.

Security and Privacy Issues. Without countermeasures, the user needs to trust in the LQS for the following reasons:

1. Users need to trust for correct computation of linkability measurements by the LQS.
2. Users need to trust, that the LQS does not disclose their action data to third parties. This is a rather important issue, as the LQS essentially aggregates the user profiles, which should be prevented from being known to the attacker. Additionally the LQS gets to know data, which a user will potentially not disclose to the attacker. It is only input to LQS for computing linkability measures for the potential case of a disclosure. So, the LQS is a major goal for attackers which want to get user profiles.

The first problem can be solved by using redundant LQS' in order to detect wrong computation by techniques known from research on fault tolerance, e.g., majority voting.

For solving the second problem technically, an approach would be needed, so that the LQS can compute linkability metrics without getting knowledge of the input data. Basically, a secure-function-evaluation[15]-like approach using multiple instances (i.e., no single instance alone has enough knowledge to reconstruct the user profiles) could help, but this is a rather theoretic approach, as this adds a huge amount of extra resource usage to the service.

Besides this, legal regulations could help to restrict misuse, but on the other hand, to avoid the need to utilise such regulations is a goal of linkability computation at the user's side.

So, even if such a service would be desirable to save resources at the user's device, more research needs to be done on possibilities to implement desired security features to it.

6   Summary

In this paper I describe a framework to quantify anonymity and linkability of actions for use within a privacy-enhancing identity management. An appropriate attacker model is defined, and an approach for computing such quantification based on observations of user's actions is proposed. Further, I discuss an enhancement to the basic approach regarding time dependency of observations. The problem of getting enough information to do the quantification is analysed. Regarding the problem of high resource consumption for quantification computations, I analyse possibilities for utilising third party services especially with respect to privacy and security requirements.

Further research needs to be done regarding optimising computations with respect to resource consumption and regarding matching functions for attribute values depending on attribute characteristics. Another topic for further research is how to secure privacy of PII when using third party services for quantification of anonymity and linkability.

---

[15] e.g. [12].

Acknowledgement. I want to thank Sandra Steinbrecher and Stefan Schiffner for valuable discussions and hints during creation of this work.

References

1. Clauß, S., Köhntopp, M.: Identity management and its support of multilateral security. Computer Networks, Special Issue on Electronic Business Systems (37) (2001) 205–219 Elsevier, North-Holland.
2. Chaum, D.: Untraceable electronic mail, return addresses, and digital pseudonyms. Communications of the ACM **4**(2) (1981) 84–88
3. Díaz, C., Seys, S., Claessens, J., Preneel, B.: Towards measuring anonymity. In Dingledine, R., Syverson, P., eds.: Proceedings of Privacy Enhancing Technologies Workshop (PET 2002). Number 2482 in LNCS, Springer-Verlag (2002) 54–68
4. Serjantov, A., Danezis, G.: Towards an information theoretic metric for anonymity. In Dingledine, R., Syverson, P., eds.: Proceedings of Privacy Enhancing Technologies Workshop (PET 2002). Number 2482 in LNCS, Springer-Verlag (2002) 41–53
5. Steinbrecher, S., Köpsell, S.: Modelling unlinkability. In Dingledine, R., ed.: Proceedings of Privacy Enhancing Technologies workshop (PET 2003). Number 2760 in LNCS, Springer-Verlag (2003) 32–47
6. Díaz, C., Claessens, J., Seys, S., Preneel, B.: Information theory and anonymity. In: Proceedings of the 23rd Symposium on Information Theory in the Benelux, May 29-31, 2002, Louvain la Neuve, Belgium, Werkgemeenschap voor Informatie en Communicatietheorie (2002)
7. Hughes, D., Shmatikov, V.: Information hiding, anonymity and privacy: A modular approach. Journal of Computer Security **12**(1) (2004) 3–36
8. Pfitzmann, A., Hansen, M.: Anonymity, unlinkability, unobservability, pseudonymity and identity management - a consolidated proposal for terminology. Version 0.27 at   `http://dud.inf.tu-dresden.de/literatur/Anon_Terminology_v0.27.pdf` (2005) Version 0.8 in: Hannes Federrath (Ed.): Designing Privacy Enhancing Technologies; Proc. Workshop on Design Issues in Anonymity and Unobservability; LNCS 2009; 2001; 1-9.
9. Orwell, G.: Nineteen Eighty-Four. Martin Secker & Warburg (1949)
10. Clauß, S., Schiffner, S.: Anonymität auf Anwendungsebene. In Dittmann, J., ed.: Proceedings of Sicherheit 2006. Volume P-77 of Lecture Notes in Informatics., Bonn, GI (2006) 171–182 (german).
11. Shannon, C.: A mathematical theory of communication. The Bell System Technical Journal **27** (1948) 379–423
12. Micali, S., Rogaway, P.: Secure computation. In: Crypto '91. Number 576 in LNCS, Springer Verlag (1992) 392–404

Revocable Anonymity

Stefan Köpsell[1], Rolf Wendolsky[2], and Hannes Federrath[2]

[1] Dresden University of Technology
`sk13@inf.tu-dresden.de`
[2] University of Regensburg
{`rolf.wendolsky, hannes.federrath`}`@wiwi.uni-regensburg.de`

Abstract. Anonymity services in the EU may be forced by the new EU data retention directive to collect connection data and deanonymise some of their users in case of serious crimes. For this purpose, we propose a new privacy-friendly solution for incorporating revocation in an anonymous communication system. In contrast to other known methods, our scheme does not reveal the identity of a user to any other entity involved in the revocation procedure but the law enforcement agency. Another advantage is, that no user will need to provide more identifying information than his connection (IP) address, that is what he needs to communicate with the system anyway. The proposed scheme is based mainly on threshold group signatures and threshold atomic proxy re-encryption.

1 Introduction

On december 14, 2005, the EU parliament has passed a data retention directive that forces all EU telecommunication providers to store the connection data of their users for at least six months. The goal is to use the data "for the prevention, investigation, detection and prosecution of serious criminal offences" [EP05]. Unfortunately, this act gives the member states' legislature the possibility, almost at its will, to raise the retention interval and to define the type of crimes that allow the local law enforcement agencies to request the connection data.

If running in the EU, even anonymity services are forced to obey the act mentioned, and non-EU countries will adapt to this directive with a high possibility, too. In Germany, for example, even without this new law anonymity providers are, in certain cases, obliged to release connection data to law enforcement agencies [FeGo04]. Therefore, sooner or later, a deanonymisation protocol is needed for all anonymity systems that are not of pure theoretical nature.

In this paper we propose a new scheme that - in case of a court order - allows for deanonymisation without weakening the general trust model of an anonymity service. Moreover, the revocation of anonymity should preserve the privacy of all lawful users, especially without the need of logging all communication data.

The paper is structured as follows: In the next section we describe our requirements for revocation and deduce the general attributes of our scheme. Section 3 gives an overview of related work. Section 4 describes the basic idea and recalls properties of cryptographic primitives used. Section 5 describes our scheme in detail and Section 6 analyses the security of the scheme.

G. Müller (Ed.): ETRICS 2006, LNCS 3995, pp. 206–220, 2006.

2   Revocation Requirements

The scenario we have in mind is pictured in Figure 1. Some users want to access the Internet anonymously and therefore use an anonymity service C. This service is based on n intermediary servers. We will call such a server *Anonymiser*.

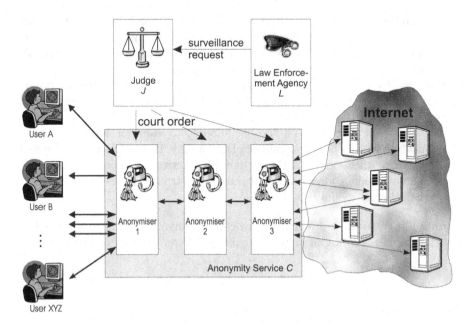

Fig. 1. Anonymous communication system

As the revocation scheme should not depend on a certain anonymity mechanism it does not matter how the anonymity service works in detail. In practice the anonymity service could be based on Mix cascades [Chau81], DC-nets [Chau88], threshold-mixes [Jak99a] etc.

The only assumption on the type of service is that the service offers unconditional anonymity as long as not at least k of the n servers collude (e.g. k=n for Mixes). Note that this assumption defines the trust model of the anonymity service: a user has to trust that the number of colluding servers is less than k. Otherwise the service will not provide any anonymity at all.

To depict law enforcement processes, two extra parties are added to the basic system: A law enforcement agency L that wants to observe certain communication relations, and a judge J that may confirm this request by a court order O. If this order is obligatory for the operators of all Anonymisers, the supervision has to be done.

We want to stress these facts, as it turns out that many people have some "back-doored" system in mind if they think about revocable anonymous communication. The term "back-doored" is misleading for various reasons:

- It suggests the existence of a hidden and undocumented functionality within the system – our approach, in contrast, is well documented and especially communicated to the users of the anonymity service.
- It suggests that a single centralised entity has the possibility to deanonymise every arbitrary communication – in contrast, the approach described in this paper needs the cooperation of different entities to deanonymise a certain communication relation. In addition, only a well defined subset of these entities will learn something about the identity of the communication partners.
- It implies that there is an automatic procedure that allows deanonymisation without human interaction. Although the proposed protocol may work in this way, too, our suggestion is that only human representatives of the organisations that run the Anonymisers may trigger "deanonymisation events" (see chapter 6).[1]
- It implies that there exists a "no-back-doored" system for anonymous communication which offers unconditional anonymity. But to our knowledge such a system neither exists in theory nor in practice – due to the fact that deanonymisation is always possible if more or stronger parties than specified by the attacker model collude.

Figure 2 illustrates that designs for revocable anonymity are not only black or white solutions regarding privacy, but exist in different shapes of grey:

privacy ignoring
(e.g. logging and publishing
all communication)

privacy respecting
(our approach)

privacy guaranteeing
(i.e. unconditional privacy;
does not exist)

Fig. 2. Designs for revocable anonymity exist in different shapes of grey

As we know from a practical system, law enforcement agencies do typically not observe certain users, but usually just want to know the IP address of the sender of a certain message [KöMi05]. The IP address contains information regarding the ISP, who will, after a court order, provide the law enforcement agency with the name, address etc. of the corresponding user. Therefore, the proposed scheme is desinged to reveal the connection data of an observed user request only, but may of course be easily extended to provide more identifying information.

---

[1] In the following it is assumed that each Anonymiser is run by an independent organisation. Therefore "Anonymiser" is used as synonym for "organisation", too.

In the following, the messages requested by L are called "suspicious". The decision which messages are "suspicious" is either based on the recipient's address (IP-address, URL etc.) or on the message content. The procedure how to identify "suspicious" messages is independent of the deanonymisation protocol and is beyond the scope of this paper.

The following requirements summarise the required attributes *Full Traceability* (1,2,3) and *Full Anonymity* (4,5):

1. It has to be feasible to disclose the identity of the sender of any given "suspicious" message. There must be no need to rely on the help of the sender.
2. Revocation should only deanonymise a single user *ID*, but should not affect the anonymity of other users (besides that the size of the anonymity set decreases by one).
3. Based on the link between a user *ID* and a requested "suspicious" message, it must be impossible for any entity (the user itself or entities involved in the revocation process) to lie on the *ID*.
4. For privacy reasons, the link between the *ID* and the "suspicious" message must not be revealed to any other entity than L. In particular, the Anonymisers must not learn anything about *ID*.
5. The revocation scheme has to be compatible with the trust model of the anonymity service, that means at least k of the n Anonymisers have to cooperate to deanonymise a certain user and less than k of them are malicious.

3   Related Work

[Golle04] describes a method for Mix networks that allows a Mix to prove that he is not the sender of a given "suspicious" message. The procedure is based on blind signatures and does not offer the possibility to identify the real sender of the "suspicious" message.

The ticket-based authentication system described in [BeFK01] is also based on blind signatures. Its goal is to protect against flooding attacks. A user has to pseudonymously register with all Mixes and gets so-called tickets (credentials) valid for a short period of time and allowing him to anonymously send messages. The user has to send a valid ticket with every message.

This original method does not offer the option to link a certain message to its sender by means of the tickets. [ClDí03] is an extension of [BeFK01] where this linkage is possible. This is achieved by using fair blind signatures instead of blind signatures. From a privacy point of view a disadvantage of [ClDí03] is, that besides the law enforcement agency also other entities involved in the revocation procedure learn the identity of the sender. Another disadvantage is, that the user needs to request a new ticket for every message he wants to send.

[BaNe99] explains how payment for an anonymity service could be done by the means of anonymous digital cash. The main idea is that every message contains a digital coin which the Mix will get for processing the message. If we used a fair anonymous digital cash system, then the fairness property could be used to reveal the spender (sender) of the digital coin. But as there are no such payment schemes in practice this does not solve the problem.

4 Preliminaries: Basic Idea and Cryptographic Primitives

The basic idea of our revocation scheme is similar to the one proposed in [ClDí03]: Any request (message) that should reach its recipient has to be signed pseudonymously. A verifier V sitting between the last Anonymiser and the recipients will check this. V will drop any unsigned message. If V detects a "suspicious" request, he demands the disclosure of the true identity of the pseudonym.

Note that this scheme allows sending of revocable and unconditional anonymous messages using the same anonymity service at the same time without changing the anonymity protocol etc. This is achieved by instructing V not to check any signature if the request is for certain recipients (for instance a voting machine), which are allowed to receive anonymous requests unconditionally.

Cryptographic Primitives

In order to explain our solution in detail, we first recall properties of the cryptographic primitives used in the revocation scheme.[2] These building blocks are: *threshold group signatures*, *blind signatures* and *threshold atomic proxy re-encryption*.

Recall the following properties of a threshold group signature scheme that provides *Full Anonymity* and *Full Traceability* [CaGJ99, CaGr04, CaLy04]:

- *Full Anonymity* allows group members to anonymously sign messages. Anyone who knows the public group key can check signatures done by a group member but cannot link a signature to the group member by whom it was created.
- To join the group, a user creates a pseudonym Y and performs the Join(Y) operation with the help of GM. As a result, the user learns his secret group key sk_Y and may now forge signatures that are verifiable with the public group key.
- *Full Traceability* means that without the secret key of a group member it is infeasible to create a valid signature that could be linked to this member. Note that this holds even if the secret key of GM is exposed, so that GM in particular cannot generate signatures that are linkable to this group member.
- The group manager GM can revoke the anonymity of a given signature. This will reveal the pseudonym Y under which the signer is known to the group manager.[3]

---

[2] A security discussion of these primitives is beyond the scope of this paper. They are used as basic building blocks only.

[3] Note that GM does not necessarily get to know the true identity ID of Y and that the anonymity revocation capability could be separated from the member management capability.

- *Threshold* means that the group manager *GM* is distributed on n parties and that at least k of these parties are needed to revoke the anonymity of a group member.

Recall the following properties of a blind signature scheme [CaKW04] that provides *Unforgeability* and a *Partial Message Proof* [Rab78]:

- $\text{Sig}_E(m)$ denotes a signature on m done by the entity E.
- *Blindness* allows a user U to get a signature $\text{Sig}_E(m)$ on a message m from a signer E by interacting with E, whereas E does not know the message content and is not able to link $\text{Sig}_E(m)$ with the protocol session during which $\text{Sig}_E(m)$ was created, or with the user that sent the message and received the signature, respective.
- *Unforgeability* means that after k runs of the protocol with the signer, the user cannot obtain strictly more than k valid message-signature pairs.
- $[m]$ denotes a blinded version of m.
- $\text{Sig}_E^{\text{blind}}([m])$ denotes a blind signature on m which after unblinding leads to $\text{Sig}_E(m)$.
- *Partial Message Proof* means that the signer E only signs a message m blindly if he can previously verify a part p_m of the message m. This could be achieved using cut-and-choose protocols or by selecting a blind signature scheme that incorporates zero-knowledge proofs on p_m. In a (simple) cut-and-choose protocol, for example, U sends many blinded versions of the message m that must all contain a valid p_m to E. E selects all but one of them which U has to unblind so that E can read them. E signs the remaining blinded message m if all unblinded messages contain a valid p_m.

Recall the following properties of a threshold atomic proxy re-encryption scheme [Jak99b]:

- A (k, n)-threshold atomic proxy re-encryption scheme allows any k members of a group of n entities to re-encrypt an encrypted message m which is encrypted with the public key of the group. The result of the re-encryption is the message m encrypted with another public key, whereas m is not revealed.
- $\text{Enc}_y(m)$ denotes an encryption of m done with the public key y.
- $\text{Enc}_{y_1}(m) \underset{P}{\rightarrow} \text{Enc}_{y_2}(m)$ denotes a re-encryption from the public key y_1 to the public key y_2. This will lead to a proof P, showing that both encryptions decrypt to the same message m. Any third party can verify this proof.

5   The Revocation Scheme

This section describes the revocation scheme in detail. We revise our basic idea introducing some new parties and describe the different protocol steps in detail.

The pseudonymous signatures mentioned in the basic idea are in fact group signatures. If V detects a "suspicious" message, the group manager GM will revoke the anonymity of the signature. This leads to the pseudonym Y and a certificate issued by a third party I. This certificate links Y to an encrypted identity $\text{Enc}_{y_C}(ID)$. This encryption is done with the public key y_C of the anonymity service. The Anonymisers will jointly proxy re-encrypt ID to the public key y_L of the law enforcement agency $L : \text{Enc}_{y_C}(ID) \underset{\text{P}}{\rightarrow} \text{Enc}_{y_L}(ID)$. L can finally decrypt this to ID. Figure 3 illustrates this.

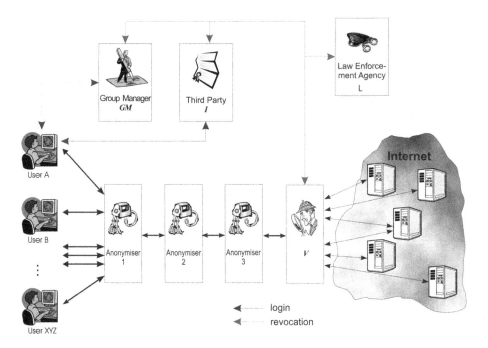

Fig. 3. Overview of the revocation scheme and the involved parties

General Setup

The Anonymisers $A_1, \dots, A_n$ jointly generate a public key y_C of a (k, n)-threshold atomic proxy re-encryption scheme and the public group verification key y_{GM} of a (k, n)-threshold group signature scheme. They are thus commonly seen as the group manger GM.[4] The party I publishes the public verification key y_I of its blind signature scheme.

User Login Procedure

In order to use the anonymity service each user has to login to it first. Besides the necessary key exchange to encrypt a message according to the Anonymiser protocol, the login procedure comprises the following steps:

1. A user U creates a self-signed certificate that includes his current connection address ID as attribute (e.g. his IP address).

---

[4] For simplification, the group manager will be seen as separate entity in most cases.

2. He non-anonymously connects to the Anonymiser that may grant access to the anonymity service to let his certificate get signed by him. The certificate will get a timestamp and may only be used for requesting a group signature key as long as the connection to the access-granting Anonymiser is held.[5]

3. U selects a random pseudonym Y.

4. Now the user U contacts the third party I and requests a blind signature
$$c = (Y, \mathrm{Enc}_{y_C}\,(ID, \mathrm{Sig}_{ID}(Y, ID)))$$
$$U \longrightarrow I : [c], \mathrm{Sig}_{ID}([c])$$

5. I issues the blind signature, but only if I is confident that she really signs an encryption of the right ID with respect to U (partial message proof). If this is done by cut-and-choose, U has to reveal Y and $\mathrm{Sig}_{ID}(Y, ID)$ several times so that I can do the encryption $\mathrm{Enc}_{y_C}\,(ID, \mathrm{Sig}_{ID}(Y, ID))$ to verify the unblinded messages. Therefore, for each blinded message, U has to choose another pseudonym Y_i and re-encrypt $\mathrm{Enc}_{y_C}\,(ID, \mathrm{Sig}_{ID}(Y_i, ID))$. Otherwise I would know Y and the encrpytion of the corresponding $\mathrm{Sig}_{ID}(Y, ID)$ and could, in collusion with one of the other parties, get the ID of the sender of a malicious message m.
$$I \longrightarrow U : \mathrm{Sig}_I^{\mathrm{blind}}([c])$$

6. U unblinds the signature and gets $cert = \mathrm{Sig}_I\,(Y, \mathrm{Enc}_{y_C}\,(ID, \mathrm{Sig}_{ID}(Y, ID)))$

7. U becomes a group member by performing the Join() operation with the group manager using the pseudonym Y. U also sends $cert$ to GM. Note that all communication with GM is done unconditional anonymously using the anonymity service C. Otherwise he would get the connection address and therefore, in the end, the real identity of U.
$$U \longrightarrow GM : \mathrm{Join}(Y), cert$$

8. Now the user may connect to the anonymiser service using his group signature key for authentication.

Sending Messages Anonymously

U can now send messages anonymously according to the Anonymiser protocol. The additional step he has to do is to sign the messages with his secret group signature key sgk_Y. V will check for every message whether it is signed and verifies the signature with y_{GM}. If the signature is OK and the message is "good", it will be forwarded to the requested resource. If m does not have a valid signature, the message is dropped.

Revoking Anonymity

The prerequisite for revoking anonymity is that V gets a court order O. O contains a public key y_L of the law enforcement agency L and a relation R, which says for every message m if m is "suspicious" or "good"; $R : \{m\} \rightarrow \{$"good", "suspicious"$\}$.

---

[5] Note that this temporary certificate may be replaced by a real one if a PKI with trusted authorities exists. This certificate could contain much more information than only the connection address at a certain time and would therefore tend to be less privacy-friendly but far more accountable.

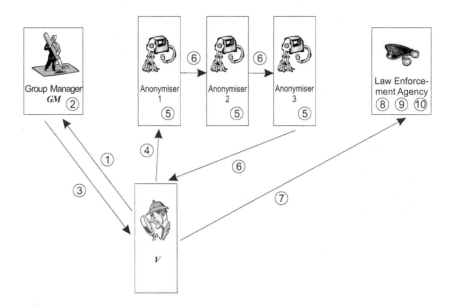

Fig. 4. The revocation procedure

If V detects a "suspicious" message m, revealing the identity of the sender works as follows (cf. Fig. 4):[6]

1. V shows m, $\text{Sig}(m)$ and O to GM.
2. GM checks that $R(m) =$ "suspicious" and verifies $\text{Sig}(m)$.
3. GM reveals $cert = \text{Sig}_I\left(Y, \text{Enc}_{y_C}\left(ID, \text{Sig}_{ID}(Y, ID)\right)\right)$ and a proof Pr that $\text{Sig}(m)$ was done by Y.
4. V verifies $cert$ and Pr and shows m, $\text{Sig}(m)$, O, $cert$ and Pr to k of the Anonymisers $A_1, \ldots, A_n$.
5. Each Anonymiser A_i of these k Anonymisers checks that $R(m) =$ "suspicious" and verifies $\text{Sig}(m)$, $cert$ and Pr.
6. The k Anonymisers jointly proxy re-encrypt $\text{Enc}_{y_C}\left(ID, \text{Sig}_{ID}(Y, ID)\right)$:
   $\text{Enc}_{y_C}\left(ID, \text{Sig}_{ID}(Y, ID)\right) \underset{P}{\rightarrow} \text{Enc}_{y_L}\left(ID, \text{Sig}_{ID}(Y, ID)\right)$
   One of the k Anonymisers sends $\text{Enc}_{y_L}\left(ID, \text{Sig}_{ID}(Y, ID)\right)$ and the proof P that both encryptions decrypt to same content to V.
7. V verifies P and sends m, $\text{Sig}(m)$, $cert$, Pr, $\text{Enc}_{y_L}\left(ID, \text{Sig}_{ID}(Y, ID)\right)$ and P to L.
8. L checks that $R(m) =$ "suspicious" and verifies $\text{Sig}(m)$, $cert$, Pr and P.
9. L decrypts $\text{Enc}_{y_L}\left(ID, \text{Sig}_{ID}(Y, ID)\right)$ to ID and $\text{Sig}_{ID}(Y, ID)$.
10. L verifies $\text{Sig}_{ID}(Y, ID)$.

---

[6] We assume that every non malicious party will only proceed if the checks she has to do are successful.

Efficiency Remarks

In practical systems performance is crucial. Especially when no revocation takes place - that is the case most of the time the system is running - the performance of the underlying anonymity service should be affected as little as possible.

The overhead introduced arises from the group signature check that V has to perform for every message. In case the scheme described in [CaGr04] is used, the verification of a single signature takes about three times as long as the verification of an RSA signature with comparable security parameters. If the anonymity service introduces linkability between messages by the means of anonymous communication *channels*, then V only needs to check one signature per channel instead of one per message. Additionally, if the anonymity service concurrently outputs a bunch of messages, a group signature scheme should be used where verifying x messages at once is less expensive than verifying x times a single message [BeGR98]. This is appropriate for instance for anonymity services based on Mixes working in batch mode.

6   Security Analysis

As defined in section 2, the revocation scheme should provide the two properties *Full Traceability* and *Anonymity*:

1. *Full Traceability* means that without the secret key of a user it is infeasible to create a valid revocation that wrongly leads to this user (or more informally: it is impossible for a given message m sent by the user ID to convince L that m was sent by another user ID'.)

2. *Anonymity* means that without the help of k colluding Anonymisers or all but one users it should hold that:

   A1 besides L and the sender U no other party learns the identity ID of the sender U of a given "suspicious" message m

   A2 in case no revocation takes place the system should provide the same anonymity as the underlying anonymity service would provide without the revocation scheme. Informally that means that the existence of the revocation scheme does not influence the anonymity of "good" messages.

Full Traceability

This property deduces from the properties of the chosen signature schemes. In order to analyse if the proposed scheme offers *Full Traceability*, we have to look at steps 2 and 8 of the login procedure and at the checks done by L in the steps 8 and 10 of the revocation procedure.

(1) In step 8 of the login procedure, the user U has to authenticate himself at the anonymity service with his group signature key that, in the end, leads to his current connection address (identity) ID. If the user does not collude with the Anonymiser that grants access to the service or with the third party I, he has no chance to cheat by presenting another certificate or by choosing another address, as the Anonymiser has signed the certificate in step 2, both can compare the ID attribute and the user's current address, and the blind and group signature keys are replaced within short time periods.

(2) If U colludes with the Anonymiser that grants access, he may lie on his real address. But without this protocol, and if all connection addresses simply had to be logged and given to the law enforcement agency instead (worst case for privacy), the problem would be the same if these parties colluded. This is therefore no weakness of the revocation protocol[7].

(3) In step 10 L verifies the signature $Sig_{ID}(Y, ID)$, which in fact is a statement given by the user with ID that he is responsible for all messages signed by the pseudonym Y. As the signature scheme itself complies with unforgeability, it is impossible for an attacker to generate a signature $Sig_{ID'}(Y, ID')$ without the help of ID'.

(4) In step 8 L verifies $Sig_Y(m)$ and Pr, where Pr is a proof that $Sig_Y(m)$ was done by Y. This is in fact a check that GM has revealed the right Y. Due to the *Full Traceability* property of the group signature scheme, an attacker could not create a valid signature that frames Y without knowing the secret key of Y. Note that this holds even if the group manager colludes with the attacker.

As shown in (1), (3) and (4) the attacker can neither manipulate $Sig_Y(m)$ nor $Sig_{ID}(Y, ID)$. Therefore m has to be sent by ID. In case of (2), the manipulation is not in the scope of this scheme, but of the law enforcement agencies and the attacking Anonymiser that will be punished if caught.

Anonymity

Note that, according to the assumptions made in section 2, regardless of the revocation scheme the anonymity service will not provide any anonymity if at least k Anonymisers collude.

(1) A1 and A2 hold as long as the group manager does not collude with the attacker. This derives from the facts that
  – the GM is the only one that can reveal the pseudonym of a given sender that is needed to get his ID (satisfies A1) and
  – the only change made to the underlying anonymity service was adding a group signature and this scheme offers full-anonymity (satisfies A2).

(2) In order to break A1, the attacker has to learn the true identity ID of the owner of Y. GM himself does not know ID because during the Join() operation (step 7 of the login procedure) the communication with the user was done by means of an unconditional anonymity service. Also colluding with I would not help, because the linkage between Y and ID by means of the signature issued by I on *cert* is impossible due to the blindness property of the signature scheme.

(3) If it is possible for the attacker to reveal the pseudonym Y of the sender of a given message m, A2 would be broken as the attacker could link messages which are sent by the same sender and therefore has at least a higher chance of intersection attacks. But as less than k Anonymisers collude with the attacker, GM cannot reveal Y.

---

[7] If a PKI with trusted authorities is available, these temporary certificates may be replaced by real ones with high accountability but less privacy-friendliness.

This makes clear that the anonymity of the system is not tampered by this scheme apart from the fact that, of course, the anonymity set is decreased by one member for each "suspicious" message.[8]

Additional Remarks

It is not possible to simplify the revocation scheme by omitting the blind signature from party I and just using the identity ID of U as pseudonym Y for the threshold group signature scheme. This would mean that, in the revocation process, all k revoking group managers or Anonymisers, respective, would learn both ID and m and may easily link them. The benefit of the revocation scheme would be at least very questionable, and virtually no benefit would remain if $k = n$.

If V is "malicious" with respect to the law enforcement agency L, he could ignore and, in order not to make himself "suspicious", block all "suspicious" messages. In this case, no revocation is done at all. This behaviour of V is not preventable in general, but could be detected later on if m is not blocked and leads to an incident detectable by L. Otherwise, if a revocation takes place, the procedure either reveals the identity of the sender of the "suspicious" message or identifies a malicious party (V, GM, I, A_i).

Identifying Malicious Parties

If V tries to revoke the anonymity of a "good" message m, he has to prove that he has shown m, $\text{Sig}(m)$ and O to GM. As V is not able to do this, he is detected as malicious party and the revocation procedure fails.

If the user U colludes with I and uses a faked ID certificate, I would get exposed as malicious party as the ID certificate has to be signed by the access-granting Anonymiser[9] and the timestamp in the certificate would not fit to the validity of the blind signature key of I.

If GM can't reveal the pseudonym Y of the group member who signed m or can't show a valid $cert$ then GM is malicious. If the proof Pr does not hold then some Anonymisers cheat during the re-encryption. The re-encryption scheme reveals which Anonymisers are malicious. If L can't decrypt what he gets to a valid signature $\text{Sig}_{ID}(Y, ID)$ then I is malicious.

Recommendations for Combining Entities

The revocation scheme introduces a lot of new entities: I, J, V, L, and GM. The security discussion has made clear that a collusion between these entities does not lead to the deanonymisation of a message m without the help of at least k Anonymisers or will at least expose the malicious parties. It is therefore allowed to simplify the organisational structure and combine these entities among each other and with the Anonymisers. These combinations may influence the general performance of the protocol and, in a small manner, security and trust aspects.

---

[8] Even this is not the case for more than one "suspicious" messages that are sent by the same sender.

[9] Note again that these temporary certificates may be replaced by real ones.

Generally, the more entities are combined, the more trust must be set in single entities by the system users.

Combining J with other entities does not make sense, as, in this context, judges won't do any other work than creating court orders for L and, on the other hand, must be independent from other entities by law.

I could be integrated in all Anonymisers that grant access to the anonymity service, for example in the first Mix of a Mix cascade. The creation of the temporary certificate may be thus combined with the creation of the blind signature.

V may be operated by L. This would mean that all "suspicious" messages that are not blocked by the last Anonymiser will surely be deanonymised. On the other hand, overeager officers could try to block some "good" messages. Therefore, a better choice would be to let the last Anonymiser in the cascade run V, as he has the power to block (and thus hide) messages anyway.

For the reason that an Anonymiser run by a police authority will diminish the general user trust in the whole service greatly, L should never be combined with an Anonymiser. Even if combined with V, it may be realised by the users as part of the system. Combining it with another entity does not make sense, either, as law enforcement agencies won't do any work that is not directly useful for crime detection, prevention and prosecution.

Last but not least GM is, as defined before, integrated in the n Anonymisers.

7   Conclusion

We have proposed a new scheme for incorporating revocation in an anonymous communication system. In contrast to known methods, our scheme is zero-knowledge with respect to any entity involved in the revocation procedure but the law enforcement agency. Another advantage is, that the user needs to authenticate himself only once to anonymously send as many messages as he wants. Moreover, the very privacy-friendly user identification by his connection address may be sufficient for his authentication, as the responsibility to find the real identity behind the address may be assigned to the law enforcement agency.

This scheme is sufficient to serve the type of surveillance requests currently launched by law enforcement agencies, namely to revoke the anonymity of the sender of a certain request. A subsequent work could be to design schemes that allow for the uncovering of all requests of a certain user, while diminishing the privacy of the other anonymity group members as little as possible. As stated before, this kind of revocation is not yet needed in practical systems, but could be of interest in the future.

Acknowledgement

First we wish to thank Julius Mittenzwei who asked the question: "How can revocation be done so that I as a Mix operator could not learn anything about the sender of a 'suspicious' message?". Thanks also to Jan Camenisch for helping to find and understand the right cryptographic primitives. Moreover, we wish to thank the members of the research group in Dresden, namely Mike Bergmann, Rainer Böhme, Sebastian Clauß, Thomas Kriegelstein, Andreas Pfitzmann, Sandra Steinbrecher and Andreas Westfeld. The discussions with them helped a lot in developing the revocation scheme.

References

[BaNe99]   Matthias Baumgart, Heike Neumann: Bezahlen von Mix-Netz-Diensten. Verläßliche IT-Systeme - VIS 1999, Vieweg, 1999.

[BeFK01]   Oliver Berthold, Hannes Federrath, Stefan Köpsell: Praktischer Schutz vor Flooding-Angriffen bei Chaumschen Mixen. in: Patrick Horster (Hrsg.): Kommunikationssicherheit im Zeichen des Internet. DuD-Fachbeiträge, Vieweg, 2001, 235–249.

[BeGR98]   Mihir Bellare, Juan A. Garay, Tal Rabin: Fast Batch Verification for Modular Exponentiation and Digital Signatures. Advances in Cryptology — EUROCRYPT '98, LNCS 1403, Springer, 1998, 236–250.

[CaGJ99]   Ran Canetti, Rosario Gennaro, Stanislaw Jarecki: Adaptive Security for Threshold Cryptosystems. Advances in Cryptology — CRYPTO '99, LNCS 1666, Springer, 1999, 98–115.

[CaGr04]   Jan Camenisch, Jens Groth: Group Signatures: Better Efficiency and New Theoretical Aspects. in: Proc. of Security in Communication Networks (SCN 2004), LNCS 3352, Springer, 2004, 120–133.

[CaKW04]   Jan Camenisch, Maciej Koprowski, Bogdan Warinschi: Efficient Blind Signatures without Random Oracles. in: Proc. of Security in Communication Networks (SCN 2004), LNCS 3352, Springer, 2004, 134–148.

[CaLy04]   Jan Camenisch, Lysyanskaya: Signature Schemes and Anonymous Credentials from Bilinear Maps. Advances in Cryptology — CRYPTO 2004, LNCS 3152, Springer, 2004, 56–72.

[Chau81]   David Chaum: Untraceable Electronic Mail, Return Addresses, and Digital Pseudonyms. Communications of the ACM 24/2, 1981, 84–88.

[Chau88]   David Chaum: The dining cryptographers problem: Unconditional sender and recipient untraceability. Journal of Cryptology, 1(1), 1988, 65–75.

[ClDí03]   Joris Claessens, Claudia Díaz, et al.: APES, Anonymity and Privacy in Electronic Services, Deliverable 10, Technologies for controlled anonymity, 2003, https://www.cosic.esat.kuleuven.ac.be/apes/docs/APES_d10.pdf, 34–40.

[EP05]   European Parliament: European Parliament legislative resolution on the proposal for a directive of the European Parliament and of the Council on the retention of data processed in connection with the provision of public electronic communication services and amending Directive 2002/58/EC (COM(2005)0438 C6-0293/2005 2005/0182(COD)), 2005

[FeGo04]   Hannes Federrath, Claudia Golembiewski: Speicherung von Nutzungsdaten durch Anonymisierungdienste im Internet. Datenschutz und Datensicherheit DuD 28/8, 2004, 486–490.

[Golle04]   Philippe Golle: Reputable Mix Networks. in Proc. of Privacy Enhancing Technologies workshop (PET 2004), 2004, LNCS, Springer

[Jak99a]   Markus Jakobsson: Flash mixing. in Proc. of 1999 ACM Symposium on Principles of Distributed Computing (PODC), 1999, 83–89.

[Jak99b]   Markus Jakobsson: On Quorum Controlled Asymmetric Proxy Re-encryption. in Proc. of the Second International Workshop on Practice and Theory in Public Key Cryptography, LNCS 1560, Springer, 1999, 112–121.

[KöMi05]   Stefan Köpsell, Tobias Miosga: Strafverfolgung trotz Anonymität - Rechtliche Reahmenbedingungen und technische Umsetzung, DuD Datenschutz und Datensicherheit, Heft 7, Vieweg, 2005, 403–409

[Rab78]   M. Rabin: Digital signatures. in: Foundations of Secure Computation, R. DeMillo, D. Dobkin, A.Jones and R.Lipton (editors), Academic Press, 1978, 155–168.

Low Latency Anonymous Communication –
How Long Are Users Willing to Wait?

Stefan Köpsell

Dresden University of Technology
sk13@inf.tu-dresden.de

Abstract. One of the heavily discussed design questions for low latency
anonymity systems is: "How much additional anonymity will the system
provide by adding a certain amount of delay?" But current research on
this topic ignores an important aspect of this question – the influence of
the delay on the number of users and by this means on the anonymity
provided. This paper shows some first experimental results in this area.
Hopefully, it supports better design decisions for low latency anonymity
systems.

1 Introduction

In the last two decades a lot of research was done in the field of anonymous
communication using computer networks. This comprises the design and development of anonymity systems as well as analysing and attacking them. Most
of these systems have in common, that the messages between senders and recipients are redirected to some servers which form the anonymity system. One
important open research question is: "How much additional anonymity will the
system provide by adding a certain amount of delay?"[Ding05]. This paper tries
to give some part of the answer with the goal to support better design decisions.

The following definitions are taken from [PfHa05]:

Definition 1. *Anonymity is the state of being not identifiable within a set of
subjects, the anonymity set.*

Definition 2. *All other things being equal, anonymity is the stronger, the larger
the respective anonymity set is and the more evenly distributed the sending or
receiving, respectively, of the subjects within that set is.*

The first systems (like the Mixes described in Chaum's seminal paper 1981
[Chau81]) were designed for so called "high latency" communication like e-mail.
Here "high latency anonymity system" means that latency introduced by the
anonymity system has only negligible influence on the quality of service of the
communication service used by the end-users. Anonymous e-mail is one example for this. Practical systems like the anonymous remailers or the Mixminion
system [DaDM03] delay e-mails for several hours in order to achieve reasonable
anonymity properties. But as long as the end-user does not use e-mail as replacement for instant messaging this delay is acceptable for mail communication.

G. Müller (Ed.): ETRICS 2006, LNCS 3995, pp. 221–237, 2006.
© Springer-Verlag Berlin Heidelberg 2006

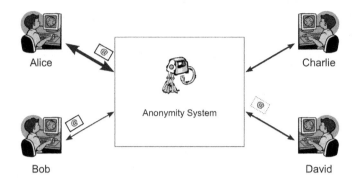

Fig. 1. Delay of messages may be necessary to achieve anonymity

Current research on designing anonymous communication systems focuses on so called "low latency anonymity systems" for the Internet. Here "low latency" means that the latency introduced by the anonymity system has *strong* influence on the quality of service of the communication service as perceived by the end-user. Surfing the Web is one example for this. Recent research shows that the amount of delay is crucial for the user's satisfaction with a web-site and his intention to return [Nah04, GHCP04]. Therefore the design of low latency anonymity systems has to balance the delay so that both the quality of service and the provided level of anonymity are acceptable by the users.

Naturally it would be best if low latency anonymity systems would introduce *zero* additional delay. But as stated above the modern systems uses the Internet as transport medium. Due to the fact that the Internet will not offer reasonable quality-of-service guarantees in terms of latency and throughput it seems to be impossible to build such nearly-zero-latency anonymity systems. On the other hand if the characteristics of the transport medium changes, nearly-zero-latency anonymity systems are feasible. A good example for this is the Telephone-Mix design [PfPW91] which uses ISDN for data transmission. In contrast to the Internet the ISDN offers reliable nearly-zero-latency isochronous transport of data.

Recent designs for low latency anonymity systems like *AN.ON* [BeFK00] or *Tor* [DiMS04] are as well based on the ideas of the Chaumian Mixes. That means that each message is redirected through several servers before it reaches its final destination. Each of these servers "processes" each message. Here "processes" mainly means to do some cryptographic operation (decryption etc.) on each message. Summarising this, there exist two fundamental reasons for the delay of a message:

1. The latency of the communication network which connects the users to the anonymity servers and the servers with each other.
2. The time a server needs to process a message (according to the anonymity protocol and the resources of the servers)

Processing messages as soon as possible is not the best strategy for anonymous communication as Figure 1 illustrates. Imagine that there are some Alice and Bob who want to communicate anonymously with Charlie and David. Alice has a high speed connection to the anonymity system (which is drawn as "black box" in the picture) whereas Bob has only a modem line. Both want to sent an e-mail which is padded to 10 kbyte to make them look similar. As a result the e-mail Alice sends will be received by the anonymity service early compared with the one Bob sends. If now the anonymity system processes Alice's message as fast as possible and forwards them to David just before Bob's message was received completely then an attacker who eavesdrops the lines will learn that Alice is communicating to David. Therefore in this scenario it would be best if the anonymity system delays Alice's message until it has also received Bob's message.

The Batch Mix design [Chau81], the Pool Mix design [MöCo00] and the "Stop-and-Go" Mix design [KeEB98] are some examples on how to deal with this problem.

Although a lot of research exist on the measurement of anonymity and the design of anonymity systems it is still an open question how the function F_{AD} which describes the relation between delay and anonymity looks like. Moreover all research done so fare just analyses runs of the anonymity system with different delays but assumes *a fixed number of users*. The proposed assumption is that in this case F_{AD} is monotonically increasing with increasing delay. The function may look like the one shown in Figure 2(a).

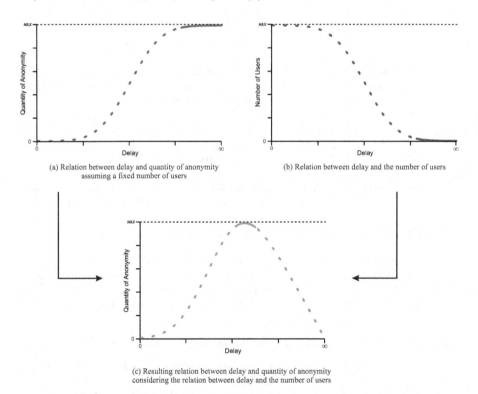

(a) Relation between delay and quantity of anonymity
assuming a fixed number of users

(b) Relation between delay and the number of users

(c) Resulting relation between delay and quantity of anonymity
considering the relation between delay and the number of users

Fig. 2. Relation between delay and quantity of anonymity

The function depicted in 2(a) gives only a incomplete view on the relation between the amount of anonymity the system offers and the delay – it hides the fact that with increasing delay the users become frustrated and will leave (see Figure 2(b)). According to Definition 2 this results in decreasing anonymity. Therefore the real graph of F_{AD} may more look like the one shown in Figure 2(c).

This paper describes some experimental results regarding the proportion of decrease of the number of users and delay. Designers of low latency anonymity protocols can use these results as one input on finding the right delay for optimal anonymity.

In the next section we will summarise some related work. Section 3 describes our experiments and the anonymity system used. Section 4 analyses the measurements and finally Section 5 draws some conclusions.

Table 1. Summary of studies of users' tolerable waiting time [GHCP04, Nah04]

Time (Seconds)	Year	Author	Remarks
0.1	1993	Nielsen	perceived as instantaneous access
1	1993	Nielsen	limit for users' flow of thought to stay uninterrupted
2	1968	Miller	interference with short-term memory occurs
2	1984	Schneidermann	response to simple commands becomes unacceptable
2	2004	Nah	tolerable waiting time for information retrieval
4	2004	Galletta et al.	decreases in performance and behavioural intentions begin to flatten
8	1999	Zona Research	
8	2004	Galletta et al.	attitudes flatten
10	1993	Nielsen	limit for keeping users' attention
10	1997	Nielsen	
10	≤2003	IBM Web Guidelines	user should have a sense of the page content or be able to navigate off the page within 10 seconds of download
12	2000	Hoxmeider, DiCesare	satisfaction decreases
15	1995,1996	Nielsen	users have been "trained to endure"
30	1999	Selvidge	cut-off based on users' performance and frustration
41	1998	Ramsay et al.	cut-off for long delays based on users' perceptions
1,10,20	1999	Selvidge	no statistical difference in both performance and frustration
5,30	2001	Rose, Straub	e-commerce: negative attitudes do not carry over to retailer

2   Related Work

There exists a lot of research on a variety of issues related to delays and their effects on users – in the general field of Human-Computer Interaction as well as in the special field of Web browsing. Table 1 summarises some of these investigations. Good surveys about the research in that field can be found in [GHCP04] and [Nah04].

As Table 1 shows there exists a great variety on "magic numbers" related to the tolerable waiting time (TWT). It even shows that there exist contradictory results on the amount of delay which will be accepted by the users. And finally it is unclear if the presented results can simply be used as a basis for design decisions related to low latency anonymity systems. The users will get additional benefit from being anonymous and therefore may be willing to accept longer waiting times.

To the best of our knowledge there exist no literature which studies the influence of delay on users' behaviour in case of anonymous communication.

3   Research Model, Methodology and Task

In contrast to many of the cited studies above we did not perform some laboratory experiments where some students have to fulfil some tasks. Instead we used a real world anonymity system (which we have developed over the past five years) for our measurements. The anonymity system (called AN.ON) is publicly available since September 2000. The main purpose of AN.ON is to allow users to browse the Web anonymously. Interested users have to download a client software called JAP, as it is the necessary component which connects the users' browser with the AN.ON servers.

Conceptual the AN.ON servers are connected in fixed sequences, which are called cascades. The user can choose the cascade he wants to use. The user's JAP establishes one and only one TCP/IP-connection with the first Mix of the cascade. Over this TCP/IP-connection the user can establish many so called *anonymous communication channels*. Each channel can be seen as an anonymous end-to-end TCP/IP-connection. In the case of Web browsing, each URL is typically requested using a separate channel.

In order to measure the number of users of a cascade, we count the number of TCP/IP connections to the first Mix and assume that this number is equal to the number of users of that cascade.

There exist different cascades operated by the AN.ON project itself and by project partners. The main difference between these cascades is the quality of service (in terms of latency and throughput) offered to the users – whereas we assume that the *perceived* quantity of anonymity is nearly the same among the cascades. The later assumption arises from the following three facts:

1. The *actual* quantity of anonymity is nearly the same among the cascades.
2. The feedback component of the JAP, which informs a user about the "measured" quantity of anonymity typically shows a value between "low" and "fair".

3. In order to make a strategic decision for a certain cascade regarding the quantity of anonymity it provides, a users needs a good understanding of how the system works. But from the frequently asked questions we got the impression, that most of our users do not have this knowledge.

For our experiments we used two cascades:

DD-cascade The servers of this cascade are situated in the computer centre of the computer science department of the Dresden University of Technology. The cascade offers poor quality of service, mainly because the network connectivity is restricted to a 10 Mbit/s ethernet link. The DD-cascade is the default cascade which is selected if a users starts the JAP for the first time. Therefore the number of users of this cascade is high, leading to an overload of the 10 Mbit/s ethernet link decreasing the quality of service even more.

HE-cascade The servers of this cascade are hosted by an Internet Service Provider (ISP). They are connected with a 100 Mbit/s link to the backbone of the ISP. This leads to a much better quality of service.

Table 2. Comparison of roughly estimated parameters of the DD-cascade with the HE-cascade

Parameter	DD-cascade	HE-cascade
Mean number of users	1150	325
Throughput [bytes/s per channel]	5000-10000	> 50000
Additional Latency	2-5 seconds	< 1 second

Table 2 compares some of the interesting parameters roughly estimated for both cascades.

Most of the time during the experiments there existed two additional cascades operated by project partners. The servers belonging to that cascades are also hosted by ISPs leading to good quality of service.

The Experiments

The general idea of the experiments is that we gave "shocks" (add some artificial delay) to the cascades and then we measured the resulting changes in the number of users.

Some early experiments were organised as follows:

1. A shock was done by adding an additional delay of t_d seconds to each anonymous communication channel. This means that the last Mix of the cascade waits t_d seconds before it starts to send bytes down the cascade to the user. As the main purpose of AN.ON is to browse the Web anonymously it implies that after the user requested a certain Web page (URL) he has to wait at least t_d seconds before he will receive the first bytes of the requested item.

2. Each shock lasted 15 minutes. Then the cascade returns to normal operation ($t_d = 0$) for 105 minutes. Note that this does not mean that the delay becomes close to zero, as depending on the quality of service a certain cascade offers, there still existed some noticeable delay (see Table 2).
3. The procedure described above is repeated for a whole day. The first shock of a day started at 01:00 a.m. German local time (CEST,CET).
4. The shocks occurred only on odd days whereas on even days the cascade operated normal.

After the first round of experiments the setting was changed in the following way:

1. The periodicity was changed from 120 minutes to 109 minutes. That means that after 15 minutes of shock the cascade returns to normal operation for 94 minutes.
2. The procedure repeated continuously for a whole month. There were no longer periods of normal operation any more (like the even days in the setting above).
3. The first shock occurred at 00:00 a.m. on the first day of the month.

These changes were done mainly for the following reasons:

- We wanted to make the times of shocks less predictable for the users.
- We wanted to shorten the overall time needed for our experiments.

Each single experiment lasted for at least two days. Preliminary experiments showed that the results become indefinite for a shorter duration. On the other hand it turned out that prolonging an experiment has only negligible influence on the calculated result D_{ar}.

During the experiments the total number of users of the cascade was stored into a database every minute. Additionally the number of users *per country* was logged. In order to assign a country to a user the source IP-address of his connection from JAP to the first Mix in conjunction with free GeoIP database of MaxMind LLC [MaxMind05] was used.

4   Results and Interpretation

The general idea behind the analysis of the measured data is to estimate the normal curve of the number of users (assuming that the shock did not happen) and compare it with the actual curve of the number of users (Fig. 3). The problem is that the number of users is a time series and comprises at least of the tree components: trend, season and remainder.

We need to know the values of these three components for our analysis e.g. to be sure that the decrease of the number of users is not explained by the normal daily trend. Therefore we have to decompose the data.

We use *STL* [CCMT90] for analysing our measurements. STL is a filtering procedure for decomposing a time series of N values Y_i into trend T_i, seasonal

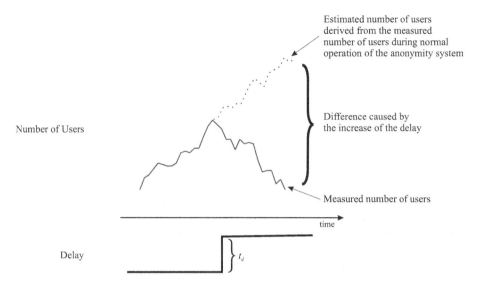

Fig. 3. Estimation of the decrease of the number of users

S_i and remainder R_i components: $Y_i = T_i + S_i + R_i$ ($i = 1$ to N). STL consists of a sequence of smoothing operations, which uses locally weighted regression (loess) for smoothing.

In our case Y_i is the number of users at time i. The period of each time series was set according to the period of the experiments (120 minutes or 109 minutes respectively). Afterwards S_i^* was calculated as the percentage of S_i on the mean $\bar{Y}$ of number of users:

$$\bar{Y} = 1/N \cdot \sum Y_i$$
$$S_i^* = S_i \cdot 100.0/\bar{Y}$$

Finally $D_{ar} = \max(S_i^*) - \min(S_i^*)$ was calculated as the number describing the average relative decrease of users during a certain experiment.

All computations were done using the R environment for statistical computing [R]. The stl() function of the "stats" package was used with the following parameters:

- s.window="periodic" - The seasonal component is found by taking the mean of each sub-series instead of loess smoothing them.
- robust=TRUE - The number of passes through the inner loop is set to 1 ($n_{(i)} = 1$) and the number of robustness iterations of the outer loop is set to 15 ($n_{(o)} = 15$).

Figure 4 shows an example of a STL decomposition. It can be seen that the trend component shows the daily trend of the number of users.

STL decomposition results for some experiments can be found in the appendix.

Figure 5 depicts the D_{ar} values for the different experiments and the linear regression curves. It clearly shows the expected result that with increasing delay

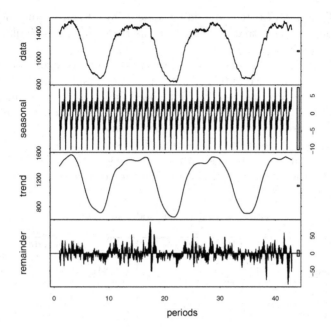

Fig. 4. Example of STL decomposition (DD-cascade, 20 seconds additional delay)

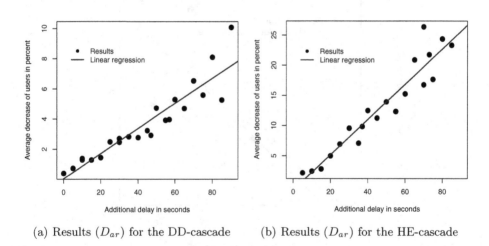

(a) Results (D_{ar}) for the DD-cascade   (b) Results (D_{ar}) for the HE-cascade

Fig. 5. Relation between additional delay and drop-out rate of users

the percentage of users which leave the cascade also increases. Moreover it shows that the relationship is linear – at least for the most interesting values where the additional delay is less than 60 seconds.

Figure 7 (Appendix A) shows the curves of various experiments with different additional delay for the DD-cascade. In addition, Figure 8 shows the curves of experiments where the throughput of the anonymous communication channels was artificially limited (instead of adding some delay). Figure 7 and Figure 8 validate the educated guess that a decrease of the throughput has similar influence as increasing the delay.

There exist a lot of factors which were beyond our control during the experiments which may have influenced the measured results: users' expectations of delay (e.g. dial-up connection vs. high-speed DSL) users' goals, incentives or rewards for using the anonymity service, demographics of users (e.g. experience, age, gender, culture), availability of alternative anonymity services, time pressure, environmental factors etc. Moreover it is possible that some of the counted users are not actual human beings but machines (e.g. download scripts or robots) or that some of the users just idle during the time of the experiments.

Table 3. Regression model summary

	DD-cascade			HE-cascade		
	Estimate	Std. Error	p-value	Estimate	Std. Error	p-value
Intercept	0.040012	0.368424	0.915	-0.67841	1.18100	0.573
x	0.083305	0.007263	0.000	0.29162	0.02227	0.000
Adjusted R^2	0.8558			0.8997		

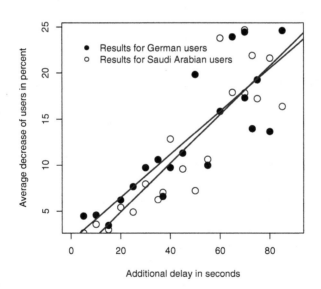

Fig. 6. Comparison of the results for Germans and Saudi-Arabians (HE-cascade)

Interestingly enough the influence of these factors may not be as high as one may expect. Comparing the results for German users with the results for Saudi-Arabians our expectation was, that the Saudi-Arabians are willing to accept a longer delay:

- [RoES03] showed that subjects from polychronic cultures (Saudi-Arabia) were significantly less concerned with delays than subjects in monochronic cultures (Germany).
- Due to censorship in Saudi-Arabia [RSF] we assume that the Saudi-Arabian users use the anonymity service to circumvent this censorship. Therefore they may have higher incentives to use the service than the German users.

On the other hand Figure 6 shows that there is no considerable difference between the results for German users and Saudi-Arabians (see also Section B in the Appendix).

Therefore the primary result of our study is not the actual number of calculated decrease of number of users for a certain amount of delay but the fact that the relation between the increase of delay and the decrease of the number of users is linear.

5 Conclusions

As expected, the experiments show that with increasing delay the number of users of the anonymity system decreases. This decrease of the number of users has in general negative impact on the quantity of anonymity the system provides. As providing anonymity is the main purpose of an anonymity system, designers of such systems have to pay attention to this fact.

The main result of our experiments is that the relationship between the increase of delay and the drop-out-rate of users is linear. The designers can take this result to take care that the decrease of the number of users will not overrule the positive effects (regarding anonymity) an increase of delay may have.

Acknowledgment

I want to thank my colleges of the Dresden research group for the open-minded discussions, advises and careful reviews of my work. Especially I thank Andreas Pfitzmann for pushing me to perform these experiments – even though I believed that the achieved results would be questionable at best. Andreas Westfeld and Rainer Böhme helped me a lot with the statistical analysis of the data. Finally I thank Professor Maurílio Coutinho at UNIFEI, Itajubá, Brazil for offering me undisturbed working conditions in his office. May the Brazilian sun had inspired this work...

References

[BeFK00]   Oliver Berthold, Hannes Federrath, Stefan Köpsell: Web MIXes: A system for anonymous and unobservable Internet access. in Proc. of Designing Privacy Enhancing Technologies: Workshop on Design Issues in Anonymity and Unobservability, Springer Verlag, LNCS 2009, July 2000, 115-129.

[CCMT90]   Robert B. Cleveland, William S. Cleveland, Jean E. McRae, Irma Terpenning: STL: A Sesonal-Trend Decomposition Procedure Based on Loess. Journal of Official Statistics Vol. 6 No. 1, 1990, 3–73.

[Chau81]   David Chaum: Untraceable Electronic Mail, Return Addresses, and Digital Pseudonyms. Communications of the ACM 24/2 (1981) 84–88.

[DaDM03]   George Danezis, Roger Dingledine, Nick Mathewson: Mixminion: Design of a Type III Anonymous Remailer Protocol. in Proc. of the 2003 IEEE Symposium on Security and Privacy, May 2003.

[DiMS04]   Roger Dingledine, Nick Mathewson, Paul Syverson: Tor: The Second-Generation Onion Router. in Proc. of the 13th USENIX Security Symposium, August 2004.

[Ding05]   Roger   Dingledine: Research   question   for   Tor. http://freehaven.net/%7Earma/slides-dagstuhl05.pdf, Dagstuhl Seminar 05411: Anonymous Communication and its Applications. Schloss Dagstuhl, Germany, October, 2005.

[GHCP04]   Dennis F. Galletta, Raymond Henry, Scott McCoy, Peter Polak: Web Site Delays: How Tolerant are Users? Journal of the Association for Information Systems Vol. 5 No. 1, January 2004, 1–28.

[HoDi00]   J. A. Hoxmeier, C. DiCesare: System response time and user satisfaction: An experimental study of browser-based applications. in. Proc. of the Association of Information Systems Americas Conference, Long Beach California, August 2000, 140–145.

[IBM03]   International   Business   Maschines: Final   Testing.   2003, http://www-3.ibm.com/ibm/easy/eou_ext.nsf/Publish/609

[KeEB98]   Dogan Kesdogan, Jan Egner, Roland Büschkes: Stop-and-Go MIXes: Providing Probabilistic Anonymity in an Open System. in Proc. of Information Hiding Workshop (IH 1998), Springer Verlag, LNCS 1525, 1998.

[MaxMind05]   Web-Site of MaxMind LLC. http://www.maxmind.com/, 2005.

[Mill68]   R. B. Miller: Response time in man-computer conversational transaction. in Proc. of AFIPS Fall Joint Computer conference, 33, 1968, 267-277.

[MöCo00]   Ulf   Möller,   Lance   Cottrell: Mixmaster   Protocol   –   Version   2.   Unfinished   draft,   January   2000, http://www.eskimo.com/%7Erowdenw/crypt/Mix/draft-moeller-mixmaster2-protocol-00.txt

[Nah04]   F. Nah: A study on tolerable waiting time: how long are Web users willing to wait? Behaviour & Information Technology, Special Issue on HCI in MIS Vol. 23, 2004.

[Niel93]   J. Nielsen: Response times: the three important limits. in Usability Engineering, Chapter 5, Academic Press, 1993.

[Niel95]   J.   Nielsen: Guidelines   for   multimedia   on   the   web. Jakob   Nielsen's   Alertbox   for   December   1995,   1995, http://www.useit.com/alertbox/9512.html

[Niel96]   J. Nielsen: Top ten mistakes in Web design. Jakob Nielsen's Alertbox for May 1996, 1996, http://www.useit.com/alertbox/9605.html

[Niel97]   gJ. Nielsen: The need for speed. Jakob Nielsen's Alertbox for March 1997, March 1997, http://www.useit.com/alterbox/9703a.html

[PfHa05]   Andreas Pfitzmann, Marit Hansen: Anonymity, Unlinkability, Unobservability, Pseudonymity, and Identity Management – A Consolidated Proposal for Terminology. http://dud.inf.tu-dresden.de/Anon_Terminology.shtml, November 2005.

[PfPW91]   Andreas Pfitzmann, Birgit Pfitzmann, Michael Waidner: ISDN-mixes:
             Untraceable communication with very small bandwidth overhead. in
             Proc. of the GI/ITG Conference on Communication in Distributed
             Systems, February 1991, 451–463.

[R]   R Development Core Team (2005): R: A language and environment
             for statistical computing. R Foundation for Statistical Computing,
             Vienna, Austria. ISBN 3-900051-07-0, http://www.R-project.org/.

[RaBP98]   J. Ramsay, A. Barbesi, J. Preece: A psychological investigation of long
             retrieval times on the world wide web. Interacting with Computers,
             10(1), 1998, 77–86.

[RoES03]   G. M. Rose, R. Evaristo, D. W. Straub: Culture and Consumer Re-
             sponses to Web download Time: A Four-Continent Study of Mono
             and Polychronism, IEEE Transactions on Engineering Management,
             50(1), 2003, 31–44.

[RoSt01]   G. M. Rose, D. W. Straub: The effect of download time on consumer
             attitude toward the e-service retailer. e-Service Journal, 1, 2001, 55–76.

[RSF]   Reporters without borders: Saudi Arabia - 2005 annual report.
             http://www.rsf.org/article.php3?id_article=13312, 2005.

[Selv99]   P. Selvidge: How long is too long for a website to load? Us-
             ability News, 1(2), 1999, http://psychology.witchita.edu/surl/
             usabilitynews/1s/time_delay.htm

[Shne84]   B. Shneidermann: Response time and display rate in human perfor-
             mance with computers. Computing Surveys,16, 1984, 265–285.

[Zona]   Zona Research Inc.: The Economic Impacts of Unacceptable Web-Site
             Download Speeds., April 1999.

A   Results for the DD-Cascade

The following diagrams show the evaluation of results for some experiments with different additional delay. Each curve shows one period of the seasonal component calculated by the STL decomposition of the measured number of users. The shown values of the seasonal component were normalised to the mean of the number of users during each experiment. The grey bars indicate the times were the additional delay was added (i.e. the shock occurred).

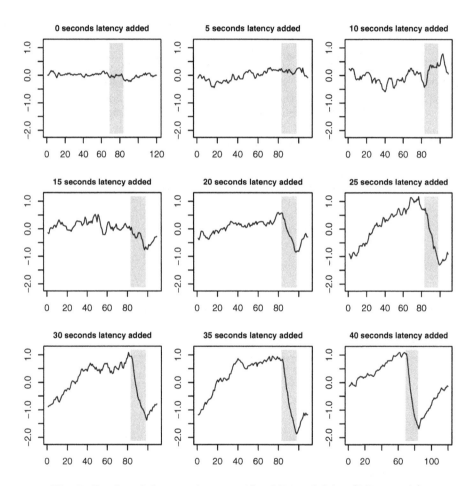

Fig. 7. Results of the experiments with additional delay (DD-cascade)

Instead of adding some additional delay the following diagrams show the evaluation of results for some experiments where the throughput per channel was artificially limited.

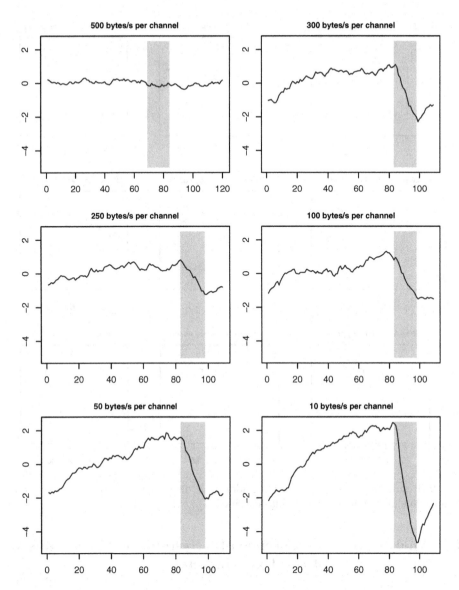

Fig. 8. Results of the experiments with throughput limitation (DD-cascade)

B   Comparison of the Results for Germans and Saudi-Arabians (HE-cascade)

The following diagrams show the evaluation of the results for German and Saudi-Arabian users of the HE-cascade. As stated in Section 4 it does not show a considerable difference between them.

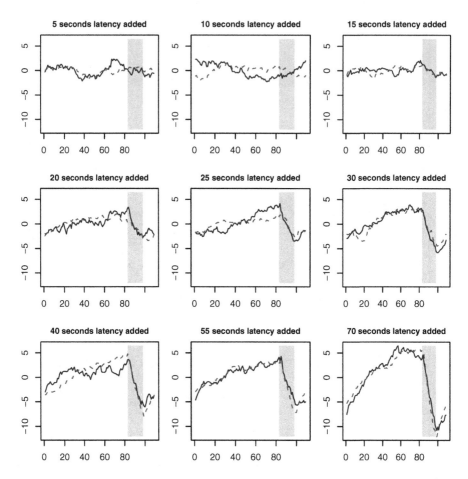

Fig. 9. Results of the experiments with additional delay (HE-cascade, Germans [continuous line] and Saudi-Arabians [dashed line]).

C   Analysis of the Existence of a Systematic Error Caused by the Dates of the Experiments

As stated in Section 4 there exist a variety of factors which may have influenced the measured results. One of these factors is the date on which each experiment was done. It may be possible that the composition of the user group of each cascade or the attitude to wait of the users changes for instance from workdays to weekends. In addition public holidays or religious celebrations may have influenced the experimental results.

A simple check to test if this systematic error exists is to look at the residuals of the linear regression computed in Section 4 ordered by the dates of the experiments. These residuals are shown in Figure 10(a) for the DD-cascade and Figure 10(b) for the HE-cascade.

Because no conspicuous pattern can be seen it seems that the dates do not have a considerable influence on the results of the experiments. Obviously for more sound statements better statistical analyses involving more experiments have to be done. But this would overload the available time frame of this work.

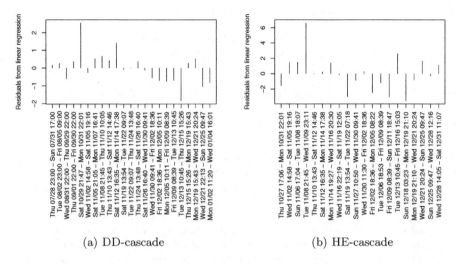

(a) DD-cascade   (b) HE-cascade

Fig. 10. Residuals of the linear regression ordered by the dates of the experiments

Security Engineering Using Problem Frames

Denis Hatebur[1,2], Maritta Heisel[2], and Holger Schmidt[2]

[1] Institut für technische Systeme GmbH, Germany
d.hatebur@itesys.de
[2] University Duisburg-Essen, Faculty of Engineering,
Department of Computer Science,
Workgroup Software Engineering, Germany
{denis.hatebur, maritta.heisel,
holger.schmidt}@uni-duisburg-essen.de

Abstract. We present a method for security engineering, which is based on two special kinds of problem frames that serve to structure, characterize, analyze, and finally solve software development problems in the area of software and system security. Both kinds of problem frames constitute *patterns* for representing security problems, variants of which occur frequently in practice. We present *security problem frames*, which are instantiated in the initial step of our method. They explicitly distinguish security problems from their solutions. To prepare the solution of the security problems in the next step, we employ *concretized security problem frames* capturing known approaches to achieve security. Finally, the last step of our method results in a specification of the system to be implemented given by concrete security mechanisms and instantiated *generic sequence diagrams*. We illustrate our approach by the example of a secure remote display system.

1 Introduction

Security engineering [1] is a discipline concerned with building secure systems to remain dependable in the face of malice, error and mischance. Tools, processes, and methods are needed to analyze, design, implement, and test secure systems, and to evolve existing systems as their environment evolves. *Security engineers* must be cross-disciplinary experts in cryptography, computer security, formal methods, and software engineering, and they must have knowledge about applied psychology, the law, organizational and audit methods.

Knowing that building security-critical systems is a highly sensitive process, it is important to reuse the experience of commonly encountered challenges in this field. This idea of using *patterns* has proved to be of value in software engineering, and it is also a promising approach in security engineering.

Patterns are a means to reuse software development knowledge on different levels of abstraction. They classify sets of software development problems or solutions that share the same structure. Patterns are defined for different activities at different stages of the software life cycle. *Problem frames* [10] are patterns that classify software development *problems*. *Architectural styles* are patterns that characterize software architectures [2].

G. Müller (Ed.): ETRICS 2006, LNCS 3995, pp. 238–253, 2006.

Design patterns [5] are used for finer-grained software design[1], while *idioms* are low-level patterns related to specific programming languages [4].

Using patterns, we can hope to construct software in a systematic way, making use of a body of accumulated knowledge, instead of starting from scratch each time. The problem frames defined by Jackson [10] cover a large number of software development problems, because they are quite general in nature. Their support is of great value in the area of software engineering for years. To support software development in more specific areas such as security engineering, however, specialized problem frames are needed. Jackson [10] states: "If you find the problem frame approach helpful you may want to find more frames to add to your personal repertoire. There are several situations that may suggest new problem frames."

In this paper, we show how to use the problem frames approach in the area of security engineering. We first introduce Jackson's problem frames in Section 2. Then we discuss a special security problem frame in Section 3 that captures authentication, a software development problem occurring frequently in the area of security engineering. Furthermore, we define a concretized security problem frame in Section 4, that captures known approaches to achieve authentication. We present a *generic security protocol* represented by generic sequence diagrams as a basis for a more concrete specification in Section 5.

We propose a method tailor-made for security engineering using security problem frames, their concretized counterparts, and generic security protocols to proceed from a security problem towards a solution. Initially, a security engineer must describe a security problem by an instantiated security problem frame. Then, concretized security problem frames must be employed to derive a specification given by concrete security mechanisms and instantiated generic sequence diagrams. Section 6 gives an overview of this method.

We illustrate our approach by developing a secure remote display system in Section 7. Section 8 discusses related work, and we conclude in Section 9.

2   Problem Frames

Problem frames are a means to describe software development problems. They were invented by Michael Jackson [10], who describes them as follows: "A problem frame is a kind of pattern. It defines an intuitively identifiable problem class in terms of its context and the characteristics of its domains, interfaces and requirement." Problem frames are described by *frame diagrams*, which basically consist of rectangles and links between these (see Fig. 1). The task is to construct a *machine* that improves the behavior of the environment it is integrated in.

Plain rectangles denote *application domains* (that already exist), a rectangle with a single vertical stripe denotes a *designed domain* physically representing some information, a rectangle with a double vertical stripe denotes the machine to be developed, and *requirements* are denoted with a dashed oval. The connecting lines represent interfaces that consist of *shared phenomena*. A dashed line represents a requirements reference, and the arrow shows that it is a *constraining* reference.

---

[1] Design patterns for security have also been defined, see Section 8.

Furthermore, Jackson distinguishes *causal* domains that comply with some physical laws, *lexical* domains that are data representations, and *biddable* domains that are usually people. *Connection domains* connect two other domains. They represent a communication medium between these domains. Examples are devices that measure vital factors of patients, or a keyboard that is used to type user input. Connection domains have to be considered if connections are unreliable, introduce delays that are an essential part of the problem, convert phenomena, or if they are mentioned in the requirements.

In the frame diagram of Fig. 1, the "X" indicates that the corresponding domain is a lexical domain. The notation "AS!Y1" means that the phenomena *Y1* are controlled by the biddable domain *Authentic subject*, which is indicated by "B".

Problem frames greatly support developers in analyzing problems to be solved. They show what domains have to be considered, and what knowledge must be described and reasoned about when analyzing the problem in depth. Developers must elicit, examine, and describe the relevant properties of each domain. These descriptions form the *domain knowledge*, which can be explained essentially in the following way [10]: "These descriptions are *indicative* – they indicate the objective truth about the domains, what's true regardless of the machine's behaviour."

Requirements describe the environment, the way it should be, after the machine is integrated. *Assumptions* are conditions that are needed, so that the requirements are accomplishable. Usually, they describe required user behavior. For example, we cannot distinguish a fake user from an authentic user if both have the same credentials. Hence, we must assume that only the authentic user knows the credentials. In contrast to the requirements, the *specification* of the machine gives an answer to the question: "How should the machine act, so that the system fulfills the requirements?" Specifications are descriptions that are sufficient for building the machine. They are implementable requirements. For the correctness of a specification S, it must be demonstrated that S, the domain knowledge D, and the assumptions A imply the requirements R ($A \wedge D \wedge S \Rightarrow R$, where $A \wedge D \wedge S$ must be non-contradictory).

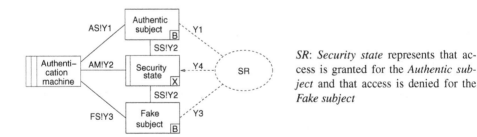

SR: *Security state* represents that access is granted for the *Authentic subject* and that access is denied for the *Fake subject*

Fig. 1. Authentication frame diagram

Software development with problem frames proceeds as follows: first, the environment in which the machine will operate is represented by a *context diagram* (see upper left-hand side of Fig. 4). Like a frame diagram, a context diagram consists of domains and interfaces. However, a context diagram contains no requirements, and it is not shown who is in control of the shared phenomena. Then, the problem is decomposed into subproblems. If ever possible, the decomposition is done in such a way that the subproblems fit to given problem frames. To fit a subproblem to a problem frame, one must instantiate its frame diagram, i.e., provide instances for its domains, phenomena, interfaces and requirements. The instantiated frame diagram is called a *problem diagram*. Since the requirements refer to the environment in which the machine must operate, the next step consists in deriving a specification for the machine (see [11] for details). The specification is the starting point for the development of the machine.

Successfully fitting a problem to a given problem frame means that the concrete problem indeed exhibits the properties that are characteristic for the problem class defined by the problem frame. Since all problems fitting to a problem frame share the same characteristic properties, their solutions will have common characteristic properties, too. Therefore, it is worthwhile to look for solution structures that match the problem structures defined by problem frames.

3   Security Problem Frames

To meet the special demands of software development problems occurring in the area of security engineering, we developed three security problem frames considering the security problems of authentication, confidentiality, and integrity. For reasons of space, we only present the security problem frame for authentication in this paper. The security problem frames for confidentiality and integrity are presented in [7].

Security problem frames consider *security requirements*. The goal is the construction of a machine that fulfills the security requirements. The security problem frames we have developed strictly refer to the *problems* concerning security. They do not anticipate a solution. For example, we may require the confidential transmission of data without being obliged to mention encryption, which is a means to achieve confidentiality.

Solving a security problem is achieved by choosing generic security mechanisms (e.g., encryption to keep data confidential), thereby transforming security requirements into *concretized security requirements* (see Section 4 for details). The benefit of considering security requirements without reference to potential solutions is the clear separation of problems from their solutions, which leads to a better understanding of the problems and supports the reusability of the security problem frames.

In contrast to Jacksons' problem frames, security problem frames and also their concretized counterparts contain patterns for the security requirements, they explicitly involve and describe a potential attacker (threat model), they integrate assumptions, and they also consider non-functional requirements (such as condidentiality).

Security Problem Frame for Authentication

Authentication of users and other systems is an important issue in many security-critical systems. Authentication is the problem to verify a claimed identity that is necessary to control access to data. Accessing data includes not only reading data, but also writing data, executing programs, and creating new data.

The frame diagram in Fig. 1 depicts this security problem. The domain *Authentic subject* in the frame diagram represents an authentic user or another authentic system. In contrast, the domain *Fake subject* represents a fake user or another fake system. The domain *Security state* represents the fact that access is granted to the *Authentic subject* domain and denied to the *Fake subject* domain. The *Security state* domain is externally visible, because the subject must be at least implicitly informed whether the access is granted or denied. The security requirement *SR* is stated according to this description.

4   Concretized Security Problem Frames

Security requirements are often difficult to address. Our approach for dealing with security requirements is to transform them into *concretized security requirements*, which take the functional aspects of a security problem into account (e.g., using a common secret to distinguish an authentic subject from a fake subject). For this purpose, we concretize the security problem frame introduced in Section 3, using generic security mechanisms.

For transforming security requirements into concretized security requirements, it is important to consider some basic properties of the involved domains, e.g., that the domain representing an authentic subject differs from the domain representing a fake subject. We call this kind of domain knowledge *basic domain knowledge* (D_{Basic}).

In transforming a security requirement SR into a concretized security requirement CSR, new concretized security problem frames evolve from the security problem frames. A detailed description of the transformation process can be found in [7], Section 4.

We must explicitly describe any assumptions made (denoted by A). Especially the strength of potential attackers must be characterized. The assumptions are necessary to check if the implication $A \wedge D_{Basic} \wedge CSR \Rightarrow SR$ is fulfilled. By proving this implication, we demonstrate that the concretized security problem frame is sufficient for the security problem frame under the assumptions A.

The security problem frame and its concretized counterpart presented in this paper and the frames considering confidentiality and integrity introduced in [7] are intended to be the first in a more complete collection. To consider other security problems such as availability or non-repudiation, it is necessary to integrate additional security problem frames and concretized security problem frames into the collection. Once a (relatively) complete collection is defined, it will be of considerable help for security engineers. For a new security-critical system to be constructed, the catalogue can be inspected in order to find the frames that apply for the given problem. Thus, such a catalogue helps to avoid omissions and to cover all security aspects that are relevant for the given problem.

Concretized Security Problem Frame for Authentication

The concretized security problem frame for authentication is shown on the left-hand side of Fig. 2. In the course of transforming the security requirement for authentication into a concretized security requirement, we introduce a designed domain *Credentials*, which makes it possible to distinguish between the domains *Authentic subject* and *Fake subject*. The *Credentials* domain must be known by the domain *Authentication machine*.

We introduce an additional domain *Trusted subject* that distributes the credentials to the machine and to the domain *Authentic subject* in the concretized security problem frame. That domain represents trusted subjects such as a system administrator for password-based authentication or a trust center in a public key infrastructure. It ensures that only the domain *Authentic subject* gets the credentials. Hence, we can state the assumption that the credentials distributed to the *Authentic subject* are represented by the phenomenon *CredentialsAS*, whereas a potential attacker represented by the domain *Fake subject* does not know these credentials. Therefore, we assume that it can only submit *CredentialsFS* to the machine. Depending on who generates the credentials represented by the symbolic phenomena *CredentialsTS1* and *CredentialsTS2*, the control direction of the interfaces *e* and *f* must be assigned during instantiation of this concretized security problem frame. In a password-based system, we can decide to let an authentic user (instance of the domain *Authentic subject*) choose a password (instance of the domain *Credentials*), or we can decide to let an administrator (instance of the domain *Trusted subject*) choose a password. In the first case, the authentic user controls the phenomenon and in the second case, the administrator controls the phenomenon.

For the authentication problem, we assume *trusted paths* for the interfaces of the domain *Trusted subject* to prevent replay attacks. Trusted paths are confidentiality- and integrity-preserving paths. To distinguish between trusted paths and other paths, trusted paths are depicted as two parallel lines in the frame diagrams.

The security requirement is transformed into a concretized security requirement *CSR* on the basis of the assumption that the domain *Fake subject* has no *CredentialsAS*. If and only if the phenomenon *CredentialsAS* conforms to the domain *Credentials*, the considered subject is an *Authentic subject*.

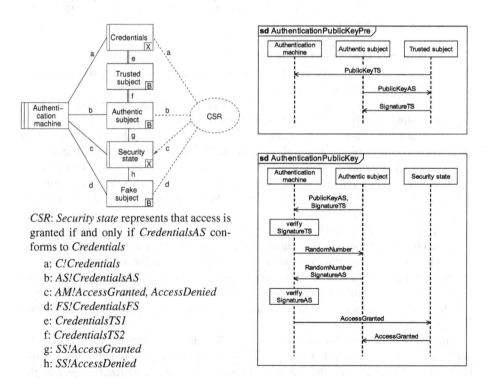

CSR: Security state represents that access is granted if and only if *CredentialsAS* conforms to *Credentials*

    a: *C!Credentials*
    b: *AS!CredentialsAS*
    c: *AM!AccessGranted, AccessDenied*
    d: *FS!CredentialsFS*
    e: *CredentialsTS1*
    f: *CredentialsTS2*
    g: *SS!AccessGranted*
    h: *SS!AccessDenied*

Fig. 2. Concretized security problem frame for authentication and generic sequence diagrams for public-key-based authentication

5   Generic Sequence Diagrams

The generic security mechanisms introduced in the concretized security problem frame only work if certain *generic security protocols* are adhered to. Hence, the concretized security problem frame must be equipped with at least one generic security protocol. We represent such (existing) protocols by generic sequence diagrams. The generic security protocols in this section and in [7], Section 5, are intended to be the first in a more complete collection. Once a (relatively) complete collection is defined, it helps security engineers to find suitable generic security protocols for the described security problems.

UML sequence diagrams [15] can be used to express interactions between the different domains occurring in problem diagrams. The shared phenomena are represented by messages, while the involved domains are represented by processes or objects in the sequence diagram. The security protocol and the sequence diagrams presented in this section are called *generic*, because they must be instantiated with the concrete domains and concrete messages between the domains.

The messages in the generic sequence diagrams cannot fit exactly to the symbolic phenomena of the concretized security problem frames of Section 4, because the generic security protocol descriptions require a more detailed view on the communication. The instances of a concretized security problem frame and a generic sequence diagram, however, should use the same names for the shared phenomena and the messages in the generic sequence diagram.

Generic Sequence Diagrams for Authentication

Different generic security protocols for authentication are possible, e.g., biometric protocols, passwords, or public key protocols.

The generic sequence diagrams on the right-hand side of Fig. 2 show authentication sequences using a public-key-based protocol. For reasons of simplicity, we only present one-sided authentication. The presented generic security protocol does not require a trusted connection between *Authentic subject* and *Authentication machine*, because replay attacks and man in the middle attacks respectively are excluded by using random numbers. However, a *Trusted subject* is necessary, and the *Authentic subject* must be able to create a digital signature. The *Trusted subject* must be a trusted third party that can sign the public key of *Authentic subject*. With this signature, the *Authentic subject* can be distuingished from fake subjects. For example, the *Trusted subject* could be instantiated by a *Trust center*. The *Trusted subject* also distributes its own public key to those who want to verify the subjects known by the *Trusted subject*.

The generic sequence diagram on the upper right-hand side of Fig. 2 shows the distribution of the public key (*PublicKeyTS*) of the *Trusted subject*, the public key (*PublicKeyAS*) of the *Authentic subject*, and the signature (*SignatureTS*) of the *Trusted subject*.

After distributing and signing the keys, the following authentication sequence can be performed (see lower right-hand side of Fig. 2). The *Authentic subject* sends its public key (*PublicKeyAS*) and the signature (*SignatureTS*) of the *Trusted subject* to the *Authentication machine*. The *Authentication machine* verifies the signature using the

the public key (*PublicKeyTS*) of the *Trusted subject*, which was already distributed (see upper right-hand side of Fig. 2). In case of a valid signature, it sends a random number (*RandomNumber*) to the *Authentic subject*, which uses its private key to calculate a signature *RandomNumberSignatureAS* of the random number that is sent back to the machine. The machine can verify the signature using the public key (*PublicKeyAS*) of the *Authentic subject* that was sent as the first message in the authentication sequence. If the signature is valid, then access is granted (*AccessGranted*). Otherwise, access is denied (not shown in Fig. 2).

If a fake subject sends its public key without a valid signature, access will be denied. If it sends a public key of another subject with the corresponding signature, it will not be able to calculate the signature of the random number without having the corresponding private key.

The strength of such an authentication protocol depends on the size and quality of the random number, the used keys, and algorithms for signing and verifying the signature. RSA (Rivest, Shamir, Adleman, based on factorization of prime numbers), DSA (Digital Signature Algorithm, based on discrete logarithm) or algorithms based on elliptic curves can be used for signing and verifying (see [13], Chapter 10, page 678).

6 Method for Security Engineering Using Problem Frames

In order to give concrete guidance to security engineers in using the concepts introduced so far, we propose a method to proceed from a software development problem in the area of software and system security towards a solution. The presented method constitutes a tailor-made security engineering method using security problem frames, their concretized counterparts, and generic security protocols. Figure 3 shows an overview of that method, which consists of three steps. These are presented one by one in the following. Instantiating security problem frames is the first step of our method, which is presented in Section 6.1. It is followed in the second step by instantiating concretized security problem frames introduced in Section 6.2, and it is completed in the third step presented in Section 6.3 by instantiating generic sequence diagrams and validating the specification with concrete security mechanisms. For the practical relevance of our method it is important that we also support the development of documentation for the *Common Criteria certification process* [8]. This issue is discussed in [7], Section 6.

6.1 Instantiation of Security Problem Frames (First Step)

According to our method, security engineers start their job by bounding security-critical problems, using context diagrams which show the machines to be developed and their environments. Then, the security-critical problems must be decomposed into subproblems, and these must be fitted to given security problem frames. Successfully fitting a security problem to a given security problem frame means that the security engineer will then be guided by our method to a specification of an appropriate solution.

Instantiating the security problem frames results in security problem diagrams and textual descriptions of the assumptions and domain knowledge. In the area of software and system security, it is very important to analyze security problems using a *threat model* (see [1], Chapter 10.2). Security engineers must assume a certain level of skill, equipment, and determination that a potential attacker might have. The assumptions concerning biddable domains (e.g., instances of the domain *Fake subject*) are used to integrate threat models into this step. Threat models are important for scaling the strength of a security mechanism with the strength of a potential attacker. One method to describe an attacker is proposed in the *Common Evaluation Methodology* (see [9], Annex B.8). It gives an approach to calculate the attack potential on the basis of a function of expertise, resources, and motivation of the attacker.

Other biddable domains (e.g., *Authentic subject*) must also be described in detail. The corresponding assumptions $A_{Biddable}$ possibly constrain the generic security mechanisms and the generic security protocols to be chosen in the subsequent steps of our method. If we choose a password-based authentication mechanism, then the assumptions made for the *Authentic subject* domain can require us to use a password with, e.g., a good memorability.

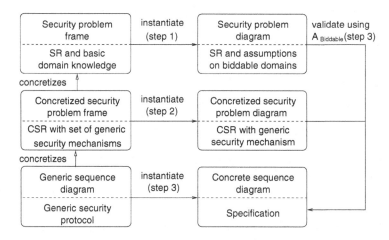

Fig. 3. Overview of our security engineering method

6.2   Instantiation of Concretized Security Problem Frames (Second Step)

Concretized security problem frames (as presented in Section 4) constitute the basis for the second step of our method. Such a frame contains a concretized security requirement, which defines a possible generic security mechanism, e.g., asymmetric or symmetric encryption mechanisms. It does not describe the concrete security mechanism, such as DES or AES.

Instantiating the concretized security problem frames is the second step of our method. For instantiating the concretized security problem frames, the same procedure as described in Section 6.1 is applied. In addition to providing instances for domains, phenomena, and interfaces, a security engineer must choose a generic security mechanism. The security engineer must decide if, e.g., a symmetric or an asymmetric mechanism should be used, or which kind of authentication is appropriate for the given context. The domain knowledge and especially the assumptions on the biddable domains, $A_{Biddable}$, gained in the first step of our method are preserved and can completely be reused.

6.3   Instantiation of Generic Sequence Diagrams and Derivation of a Specification with Concrete Security Mechanisms (Third Step)

Instantiating the generic security mechanism and the generic security protocol represented by generic sequence diagrams is the third step of our method. Here we use the assumptions concerning the biddable domains $A_{Biddable}$ gained in the first step, the domain knowledge D (including the basic domain knowledge D_{Basic} described in Section 4, which is used to transform security requirements into concretized security requirements), the instances of the concretized security requirements CSR, and the generic security mechanisms selected in the second step to derive a specification S. The specification S of the machine to be developed must solve the initially given security problem. It consists of a set of concrete sequence diagrams and concrete security mechanisms. This specification must be validated by demonstrating the following implication: $A_{Biddable} \wedge D \wedge S \Rightarrow CSR$, where $A_{Biddable} \wedge D \wedge S$ must be non-contradictory. The concrete security mechanisms must be chosen by a security engineer according to the following principles:

1. The concrete mechanisms must take assumptions (especially the assumptions about the biddable domains $A_{Biddable}$) and domain knowledge into account.
2. Relative to the domain knowledge and the assumptions, the concrete mechanisms must fulfill the concretized security requirement.
3. The concrete mechanisms must be available at the interface of the machine to be developed.

The procedures of instantiating a generic security protocol and instantiating a generic security mechanism must be performed in parallel. When instantiating the generic sequence diagrams, generic mechanisms like symmetric encryption must be replaced by concrete mechanisms, such as DES or AES. For password-based authentication, e.g., the minimal length of a password must be specified. After that, the instantiated sequence diagrams must be composed. To avoid composing incompatible solutions, we use the concept of expressing dependencies between the different security problem frames. (As it is beyond the scope of this paper, this issue will not be discussed further.)

7   Case Study

We illustrate our method by developing a secure remote display system, which allows its users to view and control a computing desktop environment not only on the desktop computer where it is running, but also from a *PDA* (Personal Digital Assistant) over a Bluetooth connection. After successfully establishing a connection between the PDA and the desktop computer, the desktop computer and the user must both be authenticated. In addition, any data transferred between the PDA and the desktop computer must be kept confidential and must not be modified. We now carry out the steps of our method for this problem.

7.1   Instantiating Security Problem Frames (First Step)

Figure 4 shows on the upper left-hand side the environment in which our machine must operate, expressed as a context diagram. The machine to be developed is called *Desktop,*

PDA, bluetooth network. The context diagram also contains a *Malicious user* domain and a *Malicious subject* domain. They represent potential attackers, which must be described in detail. We use the method proposed in the Common Evaluation Methodology [9] for that description. The domain *Malicious user* represents an attacker who wants to make the machine believe that the domain *Malicious user* is the domain *Authentic user*. The domain *Malicious subject* represents another computer that tries to act as an authentic desktop or to intercept and modify the communication.

The Common Evaluation Methodology defines the attack potential or the strength of a potential attacker as a function of time, expertise, knowledge, and equipment. It also identifies two numeric values for each of these factors. The first value is for identifying and the second one is for exploiting a *vulnerability*. In our system (named as *TOE* (Target of Evaluation)), we must consider the vulnerabilities of authentication, confidentiality, and integrity. For reasons of simplicity and instead of calculating three (possibly different) vulnerabilities, we only calculate one vulnerability and use the resulting value for all vulnerabilities to be considered. We assume that a potential attacker needs less than one day for exploiting a vulnerability, a proficient expertise of the attacker, a public known TOE, less than one day access to the TOE, and standard attack equipment. Using Table 3 in the Common Evaluation Methodology [9], we look up the corresponding numeric values for the domains *Malicious user* and *Malicious subject*, as shown in Table 1. Thus, we derive from the sum 22 of the ten values that the attack potential is rated as "Moderate".

Table 1. Example calculation of the attack potential according to the Common Evaluation Methodology [9]

Factor	Identification value	Exploit value	Sum
Elapsed time ($<$ **1 day**)	2	3	5
Expertise (Proficient)	2	2	4
Knowledge of TOE (Public)	2	2	4
Access to TOE ($<$ **1 day**)	2	4	6
Equipment (Standard)	1	2	3
Sum	9	13	**22**

After the context is described, the problem must be decomposed into subproblems, instantiating the appropriate security problem frames. The machine to be developed has to solve a *user authentication subproblem*, a *desktop authentication subproblem*, a *confidentiality subproblem for the user input*, a *confidentiality subproblem for the screen content*, an *integrity subproblem for the user input*, and an *integrity subproblem for the screen content*.

For reasons of space, we concentrate on the *desktop authentication subproblem*. The diagrams for the other subproblems are given in [7].

The security problem diagram for desktop authentication is shown on the right-hand side of Fig. 4. We instantiate the authentication frame (see Fig. 1) using the domain instances *Desktop, Desktop auth machine, PDA security state*, and *Malicious Subject*. These domain instances are also used to instantiate the security requirement SR.

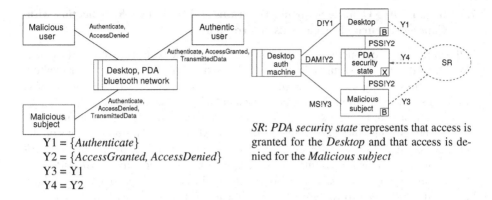

Y1 = {Authenticate}
Y2 = {AccessGranted, AccessDenied}
Y3 = Y1
Y4 = Y2

SR: *PDA security state* represents that access is granted for the *Desktop* and that access is denied for the *Malicious subject*

Fig. 4. Context diagram of a secure remote display system and security problem diagram for desktop authentication

7.2 Instantiating Concretized Security Problem Frames (Second Step)

In this step, we must choose appropriate generic security mechanisms, and we must instantiate the corresponding concretized security problem frames.

For the desktop authentication, we choose a public-key-based mechanism. Therefore, we must instantiate the concretized security problem frame for authentication (see left-hand side of Fig. 2). We reuse the domain instances introduced in the first step of our method, and we must additionally introduce the domain instances *Trust Center* and *Public key of trust center*. For the instantiation of the *CSR*, we assume that the *Malicious subject* cannot send *SignatureD*. Instead, it sends a *SignatureMS*. The phenomena *SignatureD*, *SignatureMS*, and *SignatureTC* represent the usage of the private keys for creating digital signatures. The usage of the public keys is represented by the domain *Public key of trust center* and the phenomena *PublicKeyD*, *PublicKeyMS*, and *PublicKeyTC*. Figure 5 shows on the left-hand side the concretized security problem diagram for desktop authentication.

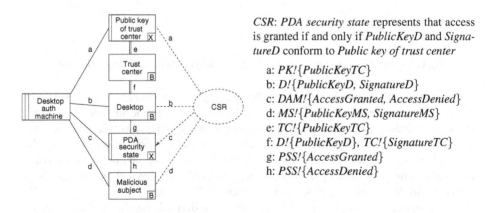

CSR: *PDA security state* represents that access is granted if and only if *PublicKeyD* and *SignatureD* conform to *Public key of trust center*

a: *PK!{PublicKeyTC}*
b: *D!{PublicKeyD, SignatureD}*
c: *DAM!{AccessGranted, AccessDenied}*
d: *MS!{PublicKeyMS, SignatureMS}*
e: *TC!{PublicKeyTC}*
f: *D!{PublicKeyD}, TC!{SignatureTC}*
g: *PSS!{AccessGranted}*
h: *PSS!{AccessDenied}*

Fig. 5. Concretized security problem diagram for desktop authentication

7.3 Instantiating Generic Sequence Diagrams and Deriving a Specification with Concrete Security Mechanisms (Third Step)

In the third step of our method, we must instantiate generic security protocols (see Section 5) and the generic security mechanisms chosen in the second step of our method. The concrete security mechanisms should be selected in such a way that the CSR is fulfilled using the assumptions concerning the biddable domains $A_{Biddable}$.

We calculated in the first step of our method (see Section 7.1) that the assumed attack potential of the *Malicious subject* is rated as "Moderate". The assumptions on the biddable domains $A_{Biddable}$ are represented by this attack potential of the domain *Malicious subject*, whereas the assumptions on the other biddable domains *Trust center* and *Desktop* are neglected for reasons of simplicity. In the second step, we chose a public-key-based mechanism for the desktop authentication. For the *Desktop auth machine*, we conclude in this step that the public-key-based mechanism RSA (see [14], Chapter 4.3 for details) with 768 bits is appropriate according to the assumptions concerning the biddable domains $A_{Biddable}$. Furthermore, we use the generic sequence diagrams *AuthenticationPublicKeyPre* and *AuthenticationPublicKey* on the right-hand side of Fig. 2 as patterns. The domains in the generic sequence diagrams are instantiated as described in Section 7.2. The instantiated sequence diagrams for public-key-based desktop authentication are shown in Fig. 6.

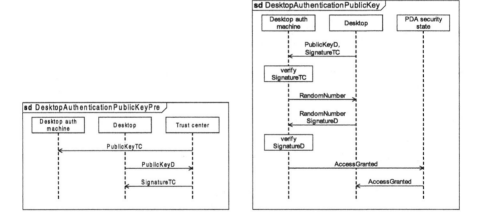

Fig. 6. Instantiated sequence diagrams for public-key-based desktop authentication

It is improbable that the *Malicious subject* can guess or calculate *SignatureD* and *RandomNumberSignatureD*. RSA is based on factorization of prime numbers. Until now, nobody succeeded in factorizing a prime number with a length greater than 576 bit (see [16] for details). Therefore, the 768 bit RSA used in our example is secure (not only for attackers of moderate strength) until further notice. Thus, we have demonstrated that the specification S (defined by the instantiated sequence diagrams and the 768 bit RSA) suffices to fulfill the concretized security requirement CSR: $A_{Biddable} \land D \land S \Rightarrow CSR$.

Hence, our original problem will be solved if the derived specification is correctly implemented.

8   Related Work

In the first step of our method, security requirements must be expressed, using a threat model. Lin et al. [12] take a different approach to use the ideas underlying problem frames in security. They define so-called anti-requirements and the corresponding *abuse frames*. An anti-requirement expresses the intentions of a malicious user, and an abuse frame represents a security threat. The purpose of anti-requirements and abuse frames is to analyze security threats and derive security requirements. Hence, abuse frames and security problem frames complement each other.

Seperating security problem frames and concretized security problem frames enhances the so-called security frames introduced in [6]. We now carefully distinguish the problem description using security problem frames and the preparation of a solution using concretized security problem frames.

Security patterns [3] are applied later, in the phase of detailed design. The relation between our concretized security problem frames, which still express problems, and security patterns is much the same as the relation between problem frames and design patterns: the frames describe problems, whereas the design/security patterns describe solutions on a fairly detailed level of abstraction. Moreover, design and security patterns are applicable only in an object-oriented setting, while problem frames and our security problem frames are independent of a particular programming paradigm.

9   Conclusions and Future Work

In this paper, we have presented new kinds of problem frames tailored for representing security problems, called security problem frames and concretized security problem frames. They are patterns for software development problems occurring frequently when security-critical software has to be developed.

Security problem frames consider security requirements in order to increase the potential for reuse by carefully distinguishing security problems from their solutions. The security requirements are stated as patterns to be instantiated. In transforming security requirements into concretized security requirements, new concretized security problem frames evolve from the security problem frames. The concretized security problem frames introduce generic security mechanisms, which only work if certain generic security protocols are adhered to. Hence, we equip each of the concretized security problem frames with such generic security protocols, described by generic sequence diagrams. The instances of generic security protocols are *solutions* to the initially given security problems.

Both kinds of security problem frames and the generic security protocols presented in this paper are intended to be the first in a more complete collection. Once a (relatively) complete collection is defined, it is of considerable help for security engineers. For a new security-critical system to be constructed, the catalogue can be inspected in order to find the frames and protocols that apply for the given problem. Thus, such a catalogue helps to avoid omissions and to cover all security aspects that are relevant for the given problem.

While the frames themselves "only" help to comprehend, locate and represent problems, our method supports security engineers to *solve* the problems fitted to security problem frames step-by-step. The instantiation of the security problem frames is the first step. Here, we gain important information about the problem environment. Moreover, a threat model is defined about the assumed capabilities on potential attackers. The method proceeds in the second step with the instantiation of concretized security problem frames. In this step, the principles of the envisaged solution are fixed. The third step consists of selecting concrete security mechanisms and deriving a specification of the security-critical system on the basis of instantiated generic security protocols represented by sequence diagrams.

With the concept of security problem frames and the associated method based on concretized security problem frames and generic sequence diagrams (in addition to security patterns), security engineers can hope to cover large parts of the development of security-critical systems with a pattern-based approach.

In the future, we intend to extend this work by formalizing assumptions, domain knowledge, and requirements. Second, the compositionality of the security problem frames will be considered in more detail, by performing interaction analyses. Third, we intend to elaborate more on the later phases of software development. For example, we want to investigate how to integrate component technology in the development process.

References

[1] R. Anderson. *Security Engineering*. Wiley, 2001.

[2] L. Bass, P. Clements, and R. Kazman. *Software Architecture in Practice*. Addison-Wesley, 1998.

[3] B. Blakley and C. Heath. *Technical Guide: Security Design Patterns*. The Open Group, April 2004. http://www.opengroup.org/publications/catalog/g031.htm.

[4] F. Buschmann, R. Meunier, H. Rohnert, P. Sommerlad, and M. Stal. *Pattern-Oriented Software Architecture: A System of Patterns*. John Wiley & Sons, 1996.

[5] E. Gamma, R. Helm, R. Johnson, and J. Vlissides. *Design Patterns – Elements of Reusable Object-Oriented Software*. Addison Wesley, Reading, 1995.

[6] D. Hatebur and M. Heisel. Problem frames and architectures for security problems. In B. A. Gran, R. Winter, and G. Dahll, editors, *Proceedings of the 24th International Conference on Computer Safety, Reliability and Security (SAFECOMP)*, LNCS 3688, pages 390–404. Springer-Verlag, 2005.

[7] D. Hatebur, M. Heisel, and H. Schmidt. Using problem frames for security engineering. Technical report, Universität Duisburg-Essen, 2006. http://swe.uni-duisburg-essen.de/intern/seceng06.pdf.

[8] International Organization for Standardization (ISO) and International Electrotechnical Commission (IEC). Common criteria 2.3. ISO/IEC 15408, 2005. http://www.commoncriteriaportal.org.

[9] International Organization for Standardization (ISO) and International Electrotechnical Commission (IEC). Common evaluation methodology 2.3. ISO/IEC 18405, 2005. http://www.commoncriteriaportal.org.

[10] M. Jackson. *Problem Frames. Analyzing and structuring software development problems*. Addison-Wesley, 2001.

[11] M. Jackson and P. Zave. Deriving specifications from requirements: an example. In *Proceedings 17th Int. Conf. on Software Engineering, Seattle, USA*, pages 15–24. ACM Press, 1995.

[12] L. Lin, B. Nuseibeh, D. Ince, M. Jackson, and J. Moffett. Introducing abuse frames for analysing security requirements. In *Proceedings of 11th IEEE International Requirements Engineering Conference (RE'03)*, pages 371–372, 2003. Poster Paper.

[13] C. P. Pfleeger. *Security in Computing*. Prentice Hall, third edition, 2003.

[14] G. Schäfer. *Security in Fixed and Wireless Networks*. John Wiley & Sons, Ltd, Chichester, 2003.

[15] UML Revision Task Force. *OMG Unified Modeling Language: Superstructure*, August 2005. http://www.uml.org.

[16] E. W. Weisstein. RSA-576 factored. *MathWorld Headline News*, 2003. http://mathworld.wolfram.com/news/2003-12-05/rsa/.

SecTOOL – Supporting Requirements Engineering for Access Control

Steffen Kolarczyk, Manuel Koch, Klaus-Peter Löhr, and Karl Pauls

Freie Universität Berlin
Institut für Informatik
Takustr. 9, D–14195 Berlin, Germany
{kolarczy, mkoch, lohr, pauls}@inf.fu-berlin.de

Abstract. SecTOOL is a case tool for security engineering. It comes as an extension to traditional UML tools, taking into account *access control requirements*. In particular, it supports the developer in eliciting access control information from UML diagrams for the early phases, starting with *requirements analysis* and use case diagrams. *Access control policies* coded in VPL or XACML are generated from the diagrams; vice versa, textually coded policies can be *visualized* in UML diagrams. Design and usage of the tool are described, emphasizing its *platform independence* through XACML.

1 Introduction

For a long time, security has been seen as a possible add-on to software systems, a non-functional property to be considered in the late phases of system development, if at all. A long series of security disasters, often continuing after "refitting" systems with security patches, has led to a rethinking and has given rise to the notion of *security engineering*: security aspects are now seen as an integral part of a software system, to be considered right from the early phases of development and to be implemented throughout the software life cycle.

This paper deals with taking into account *access control* requirements in UML-based software development. We take the view that these requirements can naturally be expressed as additions to several UML diagrams, starting with the use case diagram. Early work on this approach has been reported in [7]. Other authors have adopted similar approaches. Model-driven development has been extended to cover access control, resulting in *SecureUML* for J2EE applications [12], and methods for dealing with object-oriented access control have been applied to web services [8, 1]. Information flow and multi-level security is the subject of [10], and a comprehensive treatment of UML-based security engineering is given in [9].

While methodologies for access control engineering in the context of model-driven development are emerging, tools support and enforcement infrastructures are lagging behind. To improve this situation, we have developed SecTOOL, a plugin for the *Rational* UML case tool for supporting the early development phases. SecTOOL has been developed in the context of the RACCOON project

G. Müller (Ed.): ETRICS 2006, LNCS 3995, pp. 254–267, 2006.

[5, 6] and reflects RACCOON's approach to access control management: object-oriented access control policies are specified in a formal policy language; access protection according to a given policy is enforced through an appropriate infrastructure (originally for CORBA objects, using CORBA middleware); the application software has no built-in protection, and the policy to be applied can be modified without modifying any application code.

The implications for SECTOOL are as follows: both access control requirements and functional requirements *are* specified in an integrated fashion; *however*, the policies resulting from the access control requirements are not enforced by the application code derived from the diagrams but by an independent security infrastructure. In this respect, SECTOOL is similar to the SecureUML plugin for the *ArcStyler* tool [13]. There are three differences, though: first, SECTOOL covers all the *early development steps*, beginning with requirements analysis and use case diagrams; secondly, it supports the specification of *dynamic* modifications of privileges; and third, its design is *platform-independent* (*XACML* code can be generated).

The contribution of SECTOOL to security is seen in the enhanced reliability in handling all phases of access control engineering: requirements, design, implementation, management and maintenance. This is the heritage from the RACCOON approach to access control management, in particular from its *View Policy Language* (VPL) [4, 5]. A short introduction to VPL is given in section 2. How SECTOOL is used in specifying a first approximation to the access rights to be granted is described in section 3. Refining this according to the principle of least privilege is the subject of section 4. Section 5 presents a comprehensive view of the tool's features, and section 6 explains how an access control policy is actually enforced. The paper ends with a discussion of related work and a conclusion. A running example - a *conference management system* - is used throughout the paper.

2   VPL Revisited

2.1   View-Based Access Control

View-Based Access Control (VBAC) [6] is an object-oriented version of *Role-Based Access Control (RBAC)*, or more precisely, of a restricted version of RBAC3. VBAC policies were originally introduced to overcome weaknesses in the standard CORBA security model. Aiming at improved manageability of application-specific access control, VBAC uses grouping mechanisms such as *roles* (for subjects), *types* (for objects) and *views* (for operations). A *view* is basically a subset of the set of operations of an interface (originally an IDL-coded interface) and may contain additional information related to access control. (Note that there is no relation to the notion of "view" as known from database systems.)

Views on types are assigned to roles statically, but views on objects or types can also be assigned to or removed from subjects or roles in a dynamic fashion. Assigning a view on an object to a subject is tantamount to passing a capability for that object to the subject.

2.2   Static Policies

VBAC policies are coded in *VPL (View Policy Language)*, a simple language for specifying roles, views and view assignments/removals. VPL has no type system of its own: a VPL text refers to interfaces specified in a suitable typed language, e.g., IDL or UML. A simple text fragment should suffice for getting a first impression of VPL. The reader is referred to [4, 6] for a more detailed description of the language and its semantics.

```
policy conference {
    roles Author
              holds Submitting
          Reviewer
              holds BrowsingPapers
          Chair: Reviewer
              holds Steering
              maxcard 1
              excludes Author

    view BrowsingPapers controls Conference {
          allow listPapers, getPaper
    }
    ...
}
```

This example alludes to the conference management system that will be introduced in section 3. Three roles are declared: Author, Reviewer, Chair. The role Chair is declared to extend, or *dominate*, the role Reviewer, according to the RBAC₃ model. This role is restricted to at most one subject, and the roles Chair and Author exclude each other.

The holds clauses specify the initial views held by the roles. An extended role inherits the views of the dominated role, so the role Chair holds two views, BrowsingPapers and Steering. Views are tied to interfaces, as mentioned before. The view BrowsingPapers is tied to the interface Conference (shown in the appendix); it includes the operations listPapers and getPaper.

2.3   Dynamic Policies

VPL supports the dynamic modification of the application's protection status: execution of an operation can be specified to cause *assignment or removal of views* to roles or subjects. For instance, the right to select a paper for reviewing will be granted to a PC member only when the PC chair executes the operation submissionDeadline. This is specified in the VPL policy by a construct known as *schema*: assign or remove clauses are attached to the relevant operations, as shown here:

```
policy conference {
    ...
    schema SteeringSchema observes Conference {
        submissionDeadline
            remove Submitting from Author
            assign ChoosingPapers to Reviewer
        decide
            remove ChoosingPapers from Reviewer
    }
    schema ReviewSchema observes Review {
        submit ...
    }
    ...
}
```

The schema `SteeringSchema` refers to the `Conference` interface which includes operations `submissionDeadline` and `decide` (see appendix).

3   Identifying Required Privileges

SecTOOL supports the design of VPL-coded access control policies, exploiting information inherent in several types of UML diagrams for the early phases of software development. The first step in acquiring access control information involves the use case diagram, the class diagram and several sequence diagrams. This step produces an approximation to the access privileges to be granted to roles. The privileges are then refined in a second step (to be described in section 4).

The operating mode of SecTOOL is best explained through a running example: we use a simplified version of a *conference management system*.

3.1   A Conference Management System

This system is to support the program committee, and in particular the PC chair, in preparing the conference program. (The organization committee's work is *not* supported.) The requirements are as follows:

- The preparation of the conference program goes through several *phases*: paper submission, reviewing, acceptance/rejection decision, submission of final versions. The end of each phase is marked by a certain *deadline*.
- An author may submit more than one paper. PC members - except the PC chair - may submit papers as well. All PC members, including the chair, act as reviewers.
- The PC members can inspect the submissions. After the submission deadline, they can choose (in FCFS fashion) the papers they want to review. Blind reviewing is put into practice: the reviewers do not learn the names of the authors. For n PC members and x papers, each PC member should choose at least $3^*x/n$ papers (resulting in a total of 3 reviews per paper).

– A PC member may inspect all reviews for a paper *as soon as* she has submitted her own review for that paper. She may then decide to modify her review.
– When reviewing is finished, the PC decides about acceptance and rejection, and the PC chair sends notifications to the authors. The authors of accepted papers modify their papers and submit the final versions.

3.2 Use Case Diagrams Contain Role Information

The written requirements give rise to a UML use case diagram where authors, reviewers and the PC chair appear as actors. Use cases include the phases mentioned above, plus the *steering* done by the chair. The use case diagram is shown in Figure 1.

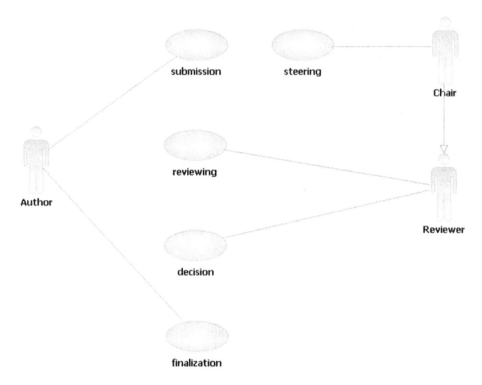

Fig. 1. Use case diagram

An *actor* in a use case diagram can be identified with a *role* in role-based access control. Note the inheritance relation between Chair and Reviewer - so Chair *dominates* Reviewer. Deriving an initial fragment of VPL text from the diagram can obviously be left to a tool - and this is where working with SECTOOL begins: a policy skeleton is generated that introduces role declarations as shown in section 2.2, but without mentioning any views. The views refer to the objects involved, so they cannot be derived from the use case diagram. A class diagram has to be designed.

3.3   Class Diagrams Contain Interface Information

According to the requirements, the system deals with objects such as *papers, reviews* and the singleton *conference*. The class diagram shown in Figure 2 contains the appropriate interfaces, plus empty interfaces for the roles mentioned above.

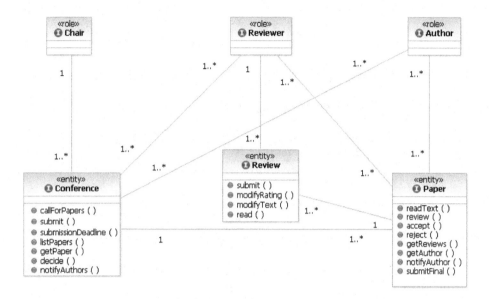

Fig. 2. Class diagram

The detailed specification of the operations is omitted, as the reader will be able to infer the semantics from the signatures (see Appendix A). For instance, the `readText` operation will deliver just the text of a paper, not its author and neither its status.

The access control policy has to restrict the permissions granted to roles to certain confined views on the interfaces of the objects. For instance, only the PC chair should be allowed to issue the `accept/reject` operations on `Paper` objects. So the question arises whether there is a systematic way of assigning proper views to roles or subjects.

3.4   Sequence Diagrams Contain View Information

A UML *sequence diagram* augments the information given in the use case diagram and the class diagram by indicating the operations actually executed for a certain use case. Figure 3 shows a diagram for the use case `Reviewing`. Similar diagrams for other use cases are not shown here.

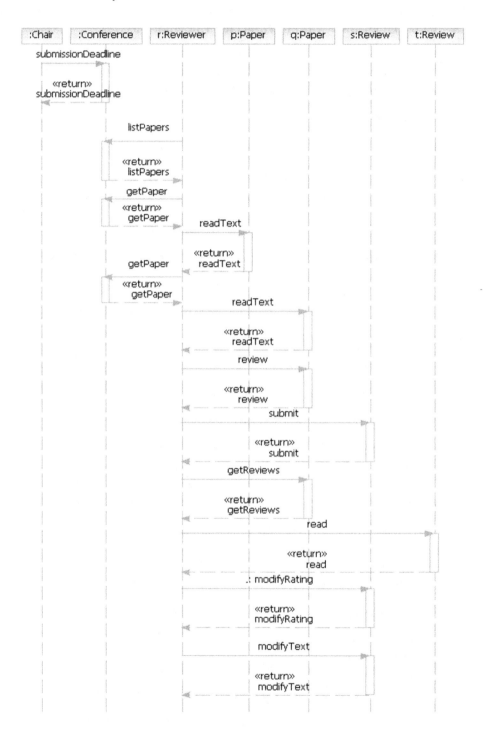

Fig. 3. Sequence diagram

Without SecTOOL, the human reader would derive the following views, written in VPL, from the sequence diagram:

```
view BrowsingPapers controls Conference {
      allow listPapers, getPaper
}
view HandlingPapers controls Paper {
      allow readText, review, getReviews
}
view Reviewing controls Review {
      allow submit, read, modifyRating, modifyText
}
```

SecTOOL automates this, adds the views to the VPL text *and* produces a graphical version: given the sequence diagram from Figure 3, the *view diagram* shown in Figure 4 is generated. The names of the views are chosen by the tool in a standard fashion. They are less distinctive than the names chosen above, but they do reflect the interfaces they refer to.

It is now the designer's task to decide about initial view assignment (**holds** clause) and dynamic assignment and removal (**schema** clause). For instance, the designer would append **holds BrowsingPapers** to the declaration of **Reviewer** in the VPL text. SecTOOL knows about the association between **BrowsingPapers** and **Reviewer**, and would refuse an accidental introduction of, say, **Author holds BrowsingPapers**.

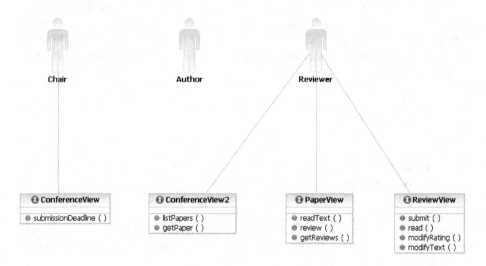

Fig. 4. View diagram

4 Refining the Privileges

The view diagram generated by SECTOOL lacks precision, in particular with respect to dynamic policies. First, the specific sequencing of invocations, as given in the sequence diagrams, is not taken into account; for instance, a PC member must get permission to choose papers for reviewing only when the chair has signalled the submission deadline. Secondly, certain permissions pertain to specific subjects and objects, not just to roles and object types; for instance, a reviewer may modify his or her own review, but not the reviews of others. And there is a third aspect that has to be considered: it must be possible to specify *denials* (negative permissions), in order to account for exceptions to general permissions. For instance, if a PC member has submitted a paper, she must not act as a reviewer *for that paper*.

4.1 Specifying Capability Assignment and Removal

In addition to supporting round-trip security engineering using diagrams, the ultimate goal of SECTOOL is the generation of complete access control policies, coded in VPL. So it is natural to use the *schema* construct of VPL for textual amendments to diagrams: they specify the dynamic assignment and removal of views on objects (i.e., capabilities) to and from subjects or roles.

A VPL schema for the operations of an interface can be attached as a UML pop-up *note* to the interface in the class diagram. SECTOOL understands this kind of decoration, ensures that consistency requirements are met, and integrates the assign/remove clauses into the final access control policy.

An example `schema SteeringSchema observes Conference` was given in the VPL introduction, section 2.3. Another schema would state that a reviewer gets permission to inspect all reviews for a paper as soon as she has submitted her own review. The schema refers to a view `getReviews` that has to be introduced manually:

```
view GetReviews controls Paper {
    allow getReviews
}
 schema ReviewSchema observes Review {
    submit
        assign GetReviews on result to caller
}
```

`result` is a reserved identifier, denoting the result of the operation `submit` (which is the associated `Paper` object). `caller` is another reserved identifier, denoting the invoking subject.

Note that singling out the `getReviews` operation from `PaperView` (see Figure 3) requires a modification of that view (viz., removal of `getReviews`). The modified view is the one that was called `ChoosingPapers` in the introductory section 2.3.

4.2   Negative Permissions

A VPL view may contain both positive and negative permissions. A negative permission is specified using the keyword deny; it overrides any related positive permissions (allow).

When working on a view diagram with SECTOOL, the developer can explicitly add views with negative permissions. While positive permissions are marked with a green bullet, negative permissions are marked with a red square. Figure 5 shows a variant of the earlier view diagram (Figure 4).

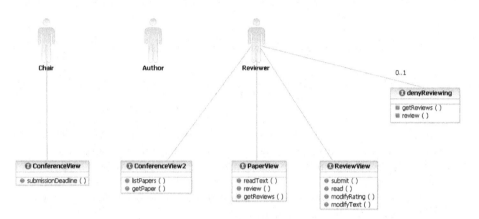

Fig. 5. Variant of view diagram

A negative view, denyReviewing, has been added to the diagram manually. This view reflects the requirement that a PC member must not review his or her own paper (if any). Note, however, that the new view diagram itself does not ensure this. The following clause can be added to the schema SteeringSchema given in section 2.3:

```
submit
    assign denyReviewing on result to caller
```

This overrides the general permission given by submissionDeadline in the original schema (assignment of ChoosingPapers).

5   SECTOOL in Action

5.1   Development

A graphical overview of SECTOOL-based development is given in Figure 6. SECTOOL cooperates with the typical UML tools, generating VPL policies from UML diagrams and, vice versa, visualizing VPL texts as UML diagrams. Manual modification of generated VPL text is possible as desired. So the tool supports round-trip engineering of access control policies in a comfortable manner, adding safety to the complex process of security engineering.

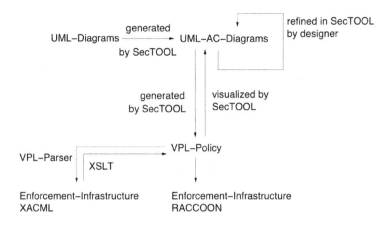

Fig. 6. SecTOOL in action

As explained earlier, the generation of VPL code describing a first version of a policy starts from a use case diagram, a class diagram and several sequence diagrams. A view diagram is created as an intermediate product. The developer may want to extend this diagram, e.g., to prepare for any denials that might be required. The view diagram, plus the schema information in the class diagram, are used as input to the VPL generation.

The name of the *policy* (in this case `Conference`) can be given by the designer or can be derived from the UML project name. The *roles* are derived from the actors in the use case diagram, as mentioned in section 3.2: each actor defines a role (here `Author`, `Reviewer` and `Chair`). Specialization between actors defines role inheritance; as `Chair` specializes `Reviewer` we have `Chair: Reviewer`.

Views are derived as follows: for each view in the view diagram with name `V` a VPL view clause `view V on I ...` is generated, where `I` is the interface name as found in the sequence diagram. The (positive) permissions, listed after the keyword `allow`, are given by the operations of the view in the view diagram. The VPL *schema* is generated by combining the schema information given in the notes in the class diagram.

The actual output of SecTOOL, as generated from the internal XML representation of VPL, is a specially formatted version of the VPL code shown earlier. Importing VPL code into SecTOOL for visualization as UML diagrams is also possible. This is useful if VPL is used for a system where UML-based documentation is not available, or in the case of round-trip engineering. Changes in the VPL specification are then reflected in the model, and consistency between model and implementation is preserved.

5.2 Maintenance

SecTOOL's separation of concerns – application logic vs. access control policy – is of great value during operation and maintenance of a developed system. In addition to the flexibility given by the role concept, the security administrator enjoys the freedom to modify the security policy without touching the application logic.

We have to keep in mind, of course, that the user interface will often be designed in such a way that certain operations are *a priori* impossible. For instance, an author will never encounter a Web interface that would give him the choice to inspect reviews meant for other authors. In general, however, modifying a policy will frequently make sense, in some cases even without adapting the user interface.

Consider the following example. The PC members should be allowed to check submitted papers only *after* the submission deadline. The policy is adapted to this changed requirement just by removing holds BrowsingPapers from the declaration of role Reviewer and by adapting the schema SteeringSchema as follows:

```
schema SteeringSchema observes Conference {
      submissionDeadline
         remove Submitting from Author
         assign BrowsingPapers, ChoosingPapers to Reviewer
      ...
}
```

6   Enforcement Infrastructure

The deployment and management infrastructure designed for VPL policies is called RACCOON [4, 5]. A deployment tool processes VPL policies and stores view and role definitions in repositories that can be managed using graphical management tools. At runtime, role membership is represented by digital certificates issued by a role server. Access decisions are made by intercepting operation accesses which are forwarded in the case of a permitted access and blocked in the case of a denied access. Whether an intercepted access is permitted or denied depends on the policy information that is supplied by policy servers, which rely on the deployed policy information.

The RACCOON infrastructure is based on CORBA and IDL specifications. The presented access control modeling process, however, is independent of the RACCOON infrastructure. Therefore, generated VPL policies should be available in any distributed system without requiring the RACCOON infrastructure. VPL policies should be presented in a platform-independent standard format. The OASIS has defined an XML standard for the specification of access control policies, called *eXtensible Access Control Markup Language* (XACML), together with an enforcement infrastructure specification. We have implemented a VPL parser which transforms VPL policies into XACML policies (XSL is used for transforming an XACML text back into VPL). This allows us to use SecTOOL for any platform that includes a standard XACML enforcement infrastructure.

7   Related Work

Work related to our approach to security engineering is presented in [2]. Basin et al. describe SecureUML, a model–driven approach to developing role-based

access control policies for J2EE applications. A formal basis allows the designer
to reason about access control properties; tool support is given by an integration
of SecureUML into the ArcStyler tool [13]. In contrast to our approach, however, the analysis stage of the software process is not considered. ArcStyler is a
CASE tool for UML 2.0 and MDA–based modeling. The SecureUML extension
is realized via plugins that allow to refine SecureUML–enhanced models towards
different platform–specific security constraints (support currently includes J2EE
and .NET). This is similar to our integration of SECTOOL as a plugin for Rational. It should be noted that the SecureUML meta–model is more expressive than
the security model of the target platforms. Hence, not all parts of a model can
be expressed declaratively. SECTOOL generates model–equivalent policies only.

Another approach to integrating security into UML has been described by
Jürjens [9]. He shows how to model several security aspects by UML model
elements such as, for example, stereotypes or tagged values. His approach is more
general than ours since it is not restricted to access control; security protocols are
considered as well. In contrast to our approach and [2], Jürjens does not provide
tool support or an infrastructure to generate security policies from UML models
or to enforce security policies.

In [1, 3], approaches to UML–based access control integration are given, focusing on a OCL–related workflow control language. High level security aspects as
part of UML models, specified using OCL, are refined down to code or platform–
independent XACML policies. As already mentioned above, we believe that visual modeling support should be provided to the developer.

8   Conclusion and Future Work

We have presented a tool for eliciting access control requirements from UML diagrams. Our approach is integrated into the UML software process and presents
a UML representation of an access control policy. SECTOOL generates a basic
access control model from UML diagrams and allows the designer to refine this
model. Access control deployment files can be generated. The generated policies
can be transformed into XACML policies, thus achieving platform independence.

Future work will be concerned with a more detailed investigation of the refinement of the generated view diagram: how does the designer arrive at a final
access control policy? We would like to find out how this refinement process can
be methodologically supported. Formal results [11] based on graph transformations look promising. It remains to be seen how they can be brought to fruition
in future versions of SECTOOL.

References

1. M. Alam, R. Breu, and M. Breu. Model–Driven Security for Web Services. In
   Proceedings of the 8th Int. Multi-Topic Conference, pages 498–505. IEEE, 2004.
2. D. Basin, J. Doser, and T. Lodderstedt. Model–Driven Security: from UML Models to Access Control Infrastructures. *Journal of ACM Transactions on Software
   Engineering and Methodology*, 2005.

3. R. Breu, M. Hafner, B. Weber, M. Alam, and M. Breu. Towards Model Driven Security of Inter-Organizational Workflows. In *Proceedings of the Workshops on Specification and Automated Processing of Security Requirements*, pages 255–267, 2004.
4. G. Brose. *Access Control Management in Distributed Object Systems*. PhD thesis, Freie Universität Berlin, 2001.
5. G. Brose. Raccoon — An Infrastructure for Managing Access Control in CORBA. In *Proc. Int. Conference on Distributed Applications and Interoperable Systems (DAIS)*. Kluwer, 2001.
6. G. Brose. Manageable Access Control for CORBA. *Journal of Computer Security*, 4:301–337, 2002.
7. G. Brose, M. Koch, and K.-P.Löhr. Integrating Access Control Design into the Software Development Process. In *Proc. of 6th Int. Conference on Integrated Design and Process Technology (IDPT)*, 2002.
8. T. Fink, M. Koch, and C. Oancea. Specification and Enforcement of Access Control in Heterogeneous Distributed Applications. In *Proc. of Int. Conference on Web Services - Europe 2003 (ICWS-Europe'03)*, 2003.
9. J. Jürjens. *Secure Systems Development with UML*. Springer, 2005.
10. Jan Jürjens. Towards Development of Secure Systems Using UMLsec. In H. Hussmann, editor, *Proc. of Fundamental Approaches to Software Engineering (FASE'01)*, number 2029 in LNCS, pages 187–200. Springer, 2001.
11. M. Koch, L.V. Mancini, and F. Parisi-Presicce. Foundations for a Graph-based Approach to the Specification of Access Control Policies. In F.Honsell and M.Miculan, editors, *Proc. of Foundations of Software Science and Computation Structures (FoSSaCS 2001)*, Lect. Notes in Comp. Sci. Springer, March 2001.
12. T. Lodderstedt, D. Basin, and J. Doser. SecureUML: A UML-Based Modeling Language for Model–Driven Security. In *Proc. of 5th Int. Conf. on the Unified Modeling Language*, number 2460 in LNCS. Springer, 2002.
13. Interactive Objects. Arcstyler, 2005. **www.io-software.com**.

A   Operation Signatures

Operations of interface `Conference`:

```
callForPapers()
submit(a:Author,text:String):Paper
submissionDeadline()
listPapers():String
getPaper(number: int):Paper
decide()
notifyAuthors()
```

Operations of interface `Paper`:

```
readText():String
review(r: Reviewer):Review
accept()
reject()
getReviews():Review[]
getAuthor():Author
notifyAuthor()
submitFinal(text: String)
```

Operations of interface `Review`:

```
submit(text: String, rating: ABCD):Paper
modifyRating(rating: ABCD)
modifyText(text: String)
read():String
```

Possibilistic Information Flow Control in MAKS and Action Refinement*

Dieter Hutter

German Research Center for Artificial Intelligence (DFKI GmbH)
Stuhlsatzenhausweg 3, 66123 Saarbrücken, Germany
hutter@dfki.de

Abstract. Formal methods emphasizes the need for a top-down approach when developing large reliable software systems. Refinements are used to map step by step abstract algebraic specifications to executable specifications. Action refinements are used to add detailed design information to abstract actions. Information flow control is used to specify and verify the admissible flow of confidential information in a complex system. However, it is well-known that in general action refinement will not preserve information flow properties which have been proved on an abstract level. In this paper we develop criteria ensuring that these properties are inherited during action refinement. We adopt Mantel's MAKS framework on possibilistic information flow control to formulate security predicates but advance to configuration structures instead of trace event systems to cope with necessary modeling of concurrency.

1 Introduction

In order to deal with the complexity of the development of reliable software systems, formal methods propose the use of a top-down approach. Starting with an abstract specification, step by step more implementation details are added to subsequent specification layers. Various verification methods have been developed to support this stepwise refinement of specifications in order to guarantee that subsequent refined specifications satisfy the requirements of previous layers. While this approach guarantees that, for instance, an implementation level satisfies the logical requirements of the abstract level, it is well known that information flow properties are typically incompatible with refinement (e.g. [12]). Since security orderings are in general neither monotonic nor anti-monotonic with respect to safety orderings, information flow properties are in general not preserved under refinement.

Information flow control (e.g. [16, 22, 13]) relies on the idea of modeling confidentiality (and dually: privacy) of data as restrictions on the flow of information between different domains of a system. Starting with the work of Goguen and Meseguer [9, 10], the restrictions on information flow for deterministic systems

---

* This work was supported by the German Federal Ministry of Education and Research (BMBF) and the German Research Foundation (DFG).

G. Müller (Ed.): ETRICS 2006, LNCS 3995, pp. 268–281, 2006.
© Springer-Verlag Berlin Heidelberg 2006

have been formalized as independence properties between actions and observations of domains: Alice's actions are confidential wrt. Charly if his observations are independent of her actions, i.e. if Alice changes her actions this does not cause different observations for Charly. In this case Alice is said to be non-interfering with Charly. For non-deterministic systems, the intuition works backwards: Alice is possibilistically non-interfering with Charly if the observations of Charly can be explained by several, different behaviors of Alice. Thus, Charly's observation does not reveal which actions Alice has chosen.

In the area of information flow control, security predicates are typically closure properties: while an adversary may observe visible parts of a system behaviour he must not be able to predict or deduce the non-visible parts. Thus the set of system traces causing a specific visible behaviour has to contain sufficiently many traces that significantly vary in their confidential behaviour.

Technically, security predicates basically enforce that the occurrences of confidential events in a system trace are independent of the occurrences of visible events, which can be observed by an adversary. As a simple example, suppose $\langle v \rangle$ is a system trace and c a confidential event. A security predicate like the so-called *BSIA* (which we will inspect in more detail later on) demands that observing the visible part v of a system run does not imply that c has not happened at some point. That means, that besides $\langle v \rangle$ also $\langle c, v \rangle$ and $\langle v, c \rangle$ have to be possible system traces. Once we refine v to a sequence v_1, v_2, the refinement of the security property would demand $\langle c, v_1, v_2 \rangle$ and $\langle v_1, v_2, c \rangle$ to be system traces of the refined system. However, if we apply the closure property to the refined system, we additionally have to show that $\langle v_1, c, v_2 \rangle$ is a possible system trace. This phenomenon closely relates to the problem of differentiating the situations $v \| c$ (executing v and c independently) and $v; c, c; v$ (executing v and c in any sequel) which cause different perceptions of possible refinements. While $v \| c$ and $v; c, c; v$ imply the same set of traces, namely $\{\langle v, c \rangle, \langle c, v \rangle\}$ their refinements $\{\langle c, v_1, v_2 \rangle, \langle v_1, c, v_2 \rangle, \langle v_1, v_2, c \rangle\}$ and $\{\langle c, v_1, v_2 \rangle \langle v_1, v_2, c \rangle\}$, respectively, do not. In general, interleaving trace equivalence or interleaving bisimulation equivalence are not preserved under action refinement (see [4]). As a consequence, trace-based systems as they are used in MAKS are not appropriate when considering non-atomic events that can be refined later on. Given a trace based specification of an abstract system, we are not able to distinguish whether confidential and visible events run in parallel or in any arbitrary sequel. However, this difference becomes apparent if we refine the system (cf. the example above) and thus can be also observed by an adversary watching the refined system.

In this paper we transfer basic parts of MAKS to so-called configuration structures [6]. Configuration structures are known to preserve bisimulation equivalences during action refinement if some preconditions are met. We base our techniques on the notions developed for the framework MAKS [15] to specify and verify possibilistic information flow policies. We present the translation of the main basic security predicates *BSD* and *BSIA* of MAKS in terms of configuration structures and illustrate under which conditions both are preserved under action refinement.

We start with a brief introduction to the framework MAKS for possibilistic information flow in Section 2 and continue with another introduction to configuration structures in Section 3. In section 4 we introduce the basic concepts of transferring possibilistic information flow control to configuration structures and translate the most prominent security predicates of MAKS into the notion of configuration structures in 5. Finally we compare our approach with related work in 6.

2   MAKS

In this section we will shortly discuss concepts and notation and briefly present the parts of MAKS [15] that we use as a starting point of our paper. Systems are described by an *event system* $ES = (E, I, O, Tr)$, which consists of a set E of events, two sets $I, O \subseteq E$ of input and output events, respectively, and the set $Tr \subseteq 2^{E^*}$ of possible system traces. The set Tr of finite sequences of events is required to be closed under prefixes, i.e. $\alpha.\beta \in Tr$ implies $\alpha \in Tr$, where we write $\alpha.\beta$ for the sequence resulting from concatenating the sequences α and β. We write $\langle e_1, \ldots, e_n \rangle$ for the sequence consisting of the events $e_1, \ldots, e_n$.

In MAKS a security predicate Θ is defined as a conjunction of closure properties on sets of traces. The idea behind using closure properties is the following. Suppose an attacker observes the visible events of a system run (while the confidential ones are invisible). We assume that attackers know all possible system runs, thus they know the set of all possible system runs which might have caused the observed behavior. In particular, an attacker knows the confidential events occurring in these possible runs, and can try to deduce constraints on the confidential events that must have occurred in the observed run. Information flow happens if the attacker is able to deduce knowledge about the occurrence or non-occurrence of confidential events beyond the knowledge already deducible from knowing the system specification, by inspecting the set of runs that are consistent with the observed behavior. A system is secure if this set of runs contains a *sufficient* variety of different possible sequences of confidential events. Closure properties are used to describe this variety because, intuitively, they demand that if there is a possible system run τ satisfying some precondition, then there is also another possible system run τ' such that the attacker cannot distinguish both. Suppose τ' in turn satisfies the precondition. Then we can inductively deduce the existence of another trace τ'' and so on. To assess the security of a system satisfying some basic security predicates we need to understand the guaranteed variance of traces wrt. confidential events being in the transitive closure $\{\tau, \tau', \tau'', \ldots\}$ of an observed system run τ.

The closure properties of sets of possible system traces (parametrized over an arbitrary set of events E) are described by a conjunction of *basic security predicates* (BSPs) and a *view*. A view $\mathcal{V} = (V, N, C)$ for E is a disjoint, exhaustive partition of E and formalises an observer or attacker: C comprises those events whose occurrence or non-occurrence should be confidential for the observer, V represents those events that are directly visible for the observer, and N are all other events. An event system satisfies a security property if each BSP holds for the view and the set of possible system traces. BSPs that we will be using as examples in this paper are BSD and $BSIA^1$ defined as

$$BSD_{\mathcal{V}}(Tr) \iff [\forall \alpha, \beta \in E^*, c \in C. \ (\beta. \langle c \rangle .\alpha \in Tr \wedge \alpha|_C = \langle \rangle \tag{1}$$
$$\implies \exists \alpha' \in E^*, \tau' \in Tr. \ (\beta.\alpha' = \tau' \wedge \alpha'|_V = \alpha|_V \wedge \alpha'|_C = \langle \rangle))]$$

$$BSIA_{\mathcal{V}}^{\rho}(Tr) \iff [\forall \alpha, \beta \in E^*, c \in C. \ (\beta.\alpha \in Tr \wedge \alpha|_C = \langle \rangle \wedge Adm_{\mathcal{V}}^{\rho}(Tr, \beta, c)$$
$$\implies \exists \alpha' \in E^*, \tau' \in Tr. \ (\beta. \langle c \rangle .\alpha' = \tau' \wedge \alpha'|_V = \alpha|_V \wedge \alpha'|_C = \langle \rangle))] \tag{2}$$

where $\tau|_D$ is the projection of τ to the events in $D \subseteq E$. $Adm_{\mathcal{V}}^{\rho}(Tr, \beta, c)$ holds if the confidential event c is admissible after the trace β, when only events in the set $\rho(\mathcal{V})$ are considered, i.e. for all functions ρ from views over E to sets of events, we have $\forall \beta \in E^*, c \in C. \ Adm_{\mathcal{V}}^{\rho}(Tr, \beta, c) \iff \exists \gamma \in E^*. \ \gamma. \langle c \rangle \in Tr \wedge \gamma|_{\rho(\mathcal{V})} = \beta|_{\rho(\mathcal{V})}$.

3   Configuration Structures

In this section we summarize the concept of configuration structures and their essential properties. Nevertheless, the reader is referred to the literature, for instance [6, 7], for further particulars. Configuration structures provide a general model to formalize concurrent systems in a modular way while allowing for a stepwise refinement. They have been also used as semantic models for CCS-like [18] languages.

Configuration structures are based on a set of events $\mathcal{E}$ that denote *occurrences* of actions. Thus, each event e is labeled by an action $l(e)$. A concurrent system is described as a configuration structure by defining the possible states $\mathcal{S}$, so called configurations, it can reach. Each configuration is a finite set of events. The intuition behind is that this set of events represent the set of actions the system had to perform to reach this particular state. Thus, the configuration of a successor state will always contain the configuration of the original state as a subset. State transitions are implicitly defined by the subset relation of configurations. A subset $\mathcal{T}$ of the configurations is considered as terminating configurations, i.e. these configurations are maximal in the set of all configurations.

Definition 1 (Configuration Structure). *A configuration structure (over an alphabet Σ) is a triple $CS = (\mathcal{S}, \mathcal{T}, l)$ where $\mathcal{S}$ is a family of finite sets (configurations), $\mathcal{T} \subset \mathcal{S}$ a termination predicate satisfying $X \in \mathcal{T} \wedge X \subseteq Y \in \mathcal{S} \implies X = Y$ and $l : \bigcup_{X \in \mathcal{S}} X \to \Sigma$ is a labellings function. $\mathcal{ACS}$ denotes the domain of all configuration structures and $\mathcal{E}_{CS} = \bigcup_{X \in \mathcal{S}} X$ is the set of events of CS.*

Given a configuration structure $CS = (\mathcal{S}, \mathcal{T}, l)$ we use $\mathcal{S}_{CS}$, $\mathcal{T}_{CS}$, and l_{CS} to select the individual elements of the tuple CS.

---

[1] *BSD* stands for backwards-strict deletion and *BSIA* for backwards-strict insertion of admissible events.

Definition 2. *Let* $CS = (S, T, l)$ *be a configuration structure. The step transition relation* $\rightarrow$ *of* CS *is defined by* $\forall X, Y \in S : X \rightarrow Y$ *iff* $X \subset Y$, *and* $\forall Z : X \subset Z \subset Y \implies Z \in S$.

For our purposes we restrict ourselves to so-called *stable* configuration structures that are closely associated to stable event structures (see [21]). Stable configuration structures have the property that causal dependencies in configurations can faithfully be represented by partial orders.

Definition 3 (Stable Configuration Structures). *A configuration structure* $CS = (S, T, l)$ *is*

- rooted *iff* $\emptyset \in S$,
- connected *iff* $\emptyset \neq X \in S \implies \exists e \in X : X \setminus \{e\} \in S$,
- closed under bounded unions *iff* $X, Y, Z \in S, X \cup Y \subseteq Z \implies X \cup Y \in S$,
- closed under bounded intersection *iff* $X, Y, Z \in S, X \cap Y \subseteq Z \implies X \cap Y \in S$.

CS *is* stable *iff it is rooted, connected, closed under bounded union and closed under bounded intersection.*

To refine a configuration structure CS, each action $a \in \Sigma_{CS}$ is associated to an individual configuration structure CS_a that represents the refinement of this particular action. Given a configuration $X \in CS$, its refinement $\tilde{X}$ combines each event $e \in X$ with a non-empty configuration X_e in its refinement $CS_{l(e)}$. Given a configuration $\tilde{X}$ in the refinement we can compute a set $busy(\tilde{X})$ of events e for which X_e is not a terminating configuration. These events $busy(\tilde{X})$ are performed in parallel since the execution of their refinements is done more or less "interleaved". Formally we define:

Definition 4 (Refinement). *A function ref* : $\Sigma \rightarrow \mathcal{ACS} \setminus \{\epsilon\}$ *is called a refinement function. Let* $CS = (S, T, l) \in \mathcal{ACS}$ *and let ref be a refinement function. Then* $\tilde{X}$ *is a refinement of a configuration* $X \in S$ *by ref iff*

- $\tilde{X} = \bigcup_{e \in X} \{e\} \times X_e$ *where* $\forall e \in X : X_e \in S_{ref(l(e))} \setminus \{\emptyset\}$,
- $\forall Y \subseteq busy(\tilde{X}) : X - Y \in S$ *with* $busy(\tilde{X}) := \{e \in X \mid X_e \notin T_{ref(l(e))}\}$

A refinement is terminated *iff* $busy(\tilde{X}) = \emptyset$.

The refinement $ref(CS) = (S_{ref(CS)}, T_{ref(CS)}, l_{ref(CS)})$ *of a configuration structure* CS *by a refinement function ref is defined by*

- $S_{ref(CS)} = \{\tilde{X} \mid \tilde{X}$ *is a refinement of some* $X \in S$ *by ref*$\}$,
- $T_{ref(CS)} = \{\tilde{X} \mid \tilde{X}$ *is a terminated refinement for some* $X \in T$ *by ref*$\}$, *and*
- $l_{ref(CS)}(e, e') = l_{ref(l(e))}(e')$ *for all* $(e, e') \in E_{ref(CS)}$.

Refinements are well-defined operations on configurations structures, i.e. $ref(CS) \in \mathcal{ACS}$ if $CS \in \mathcal{ACS}$ and ref is a refinement function. Also $ref(CS)$ is stable if CS and all configuration structures $CS_{ref(l(e))}$ for the refinements of all actions $l(e)$ are stable.

Given a stable configuration structure $\mathcal{CS} = (\mathcal{S}, \mathcal{T}, l)$, we are able to formalize the causal dependencies in a configuration by a partial order. We define $d \leq_X e$ iff $\forall Y \in \mathcal{S} : Y \subseteq X \land e \in Y \implies d \in Y$. The *causality relation* on $X \in \mathcal{S}$ is given by $d <_X e$ iff $d \leq_X e \land d \neq e$.

As a consequence of stableness, causality relations on refined configuration structures are completely determined by the causality relations on the original configuration structure and the ones associated to the actions by the refinement function:

Lemma 1. *Let $\tilde{X}$ be a refinement of $X \in \mathcal{S}$ by a refinement function ref, i.e. $\tilde{X} = \bigcup_{e \in X}\{e\} \times X_e$. Then, $(d_1, d_1') <_{\tilde{X}} (d_2, d_2')$ iff $(d_1 <_X d_2) \lor (d_1 = d_2 \land d_1' <_{X_{d_1}} d_2')$.*

Proof. A proof of this lemma can be found in [7].

This allows us to establish a partial order on the event of a configuration. In particular, $\mathcal{X} = (X, <_X, l_X)$ represents a partial order which is labeled over Σ. Let $\mathcal{Y} = (Y, <_Y, l_Y)$ then $\mathcal{X}$ and $\mathcal{Y}$ are isomorphic iff there is a bijection between $\mathcal{X}$ and $\mathcal{Y}$ respecting ordering and labellings.

In the following we will make use of the following property.

Lemma 2. *Given two configurations $X, X' \in \mathcal{S}$ of a stable configuration structure with $X \subset X'$ there are always configurations $X_0, \ldots, X_n$ and actions $a_1, \ldots, a_n$ with $X = X_0 \rightarrow_{a_1} X_1 \rightarrow \ldots \rightarrow_{a_n} X_n = X'$.*

Proof. A proof of this lemma can be found in [7].

4   Security in Configuration Structures

In this section we will translate the ideas of MAKS to configuration structures. We introduce the notion of a view for configuration structures which classify their actions into visible, non-visible or confidential actions. Notice, that an event in a trace-based system corresponds to an action in a configuration structure. Events in a configuration structure relate to *occurrences* of events in trace-based systems. Therefore we define:

Definition 5 (View). *Let $\mathcal{CS}$ be configuration structure over an alphabet Σ. A view $\mathcal{V} = (V, N, C)$ for $\mathcal{CS}$ is a triple such that V, N, C forms a disjoint partition of Σ.*

In the following, we use the notation $U_{V|N|C} = \{e \in U \mid l(e) \in V \mid N \mid C\}$ to refer to the visible, non visible, or confidential parts of U.

The following definition formalizes possible refinements of visible, non-visible, and confidential actions. Intuitively, the refinement of non-visible actions consists again of non-visible actions only. Visible actions can be refined by using visible and non-visible actions but obviously they must not contain confidential actions. The refinement of confidential actions is more delicate. Similar to visible actions, the refinement of confidential actions can only contain confidential and non-visible actions but must not contain any visible actions. Otherwise, an adversary could easily deduce the occurrence of confidential actions by looking at its visible actions in the refinement.

However, in order to guarantee that action refinements will preserve security predicates like *BSD* or *BSIA* we have to go one step further: if an action refinement would translate a confidential action c into a sequel of confidential actions, say c_1, c_2, and suppose that both actions would occur only inside this refinement, then the refinement would introduce a dependency between confidential actions (which can be utilized by an adversary). Notice that confidential events in MAKS are closely related to high-input (rather than high-) events in other approaches. Therefore confidential events are typically used to model the *introduction* of a secret into a system rather than the *processing* of a secret, which will be modeled by non-visible events. In the following we demand that the refinement of a confidential event always results in a sequel of events in which only the first event can be confidential and all others are non-visible. Thus, roughly speaking, we assume that a secret introduced to a system is always atomic.

Definition 6 (View Refinement). *Let $CS = (S, T, l)$ be configuration structure and $V = (V, N, C)$ be a view for CS. Given a refinement function ref, a view $\tilde{V} = (\tilde{V}, \tilde{N}, \tilde{C})$ for $ref(CS)$ is called a* view refinement *of V wrt. ref iff*

- $\forall a \in N : \Sigma_{ref(a)} \subseteq \tilde{N}$
- $\forall a \in V : \Sigma_{ref(a)} \subseteq \tilde{V} \cup \tilde{N}$
- $\forall a \in C : \Sigma_{ref(a)} \subseteq \tilde{C} \cup \tilde{N}$
- $\forall a \in C : \forall \{e\}, X \in S_{ref(a)} : e \in X \implies l(X \setminus \{e\}) \subseteq \tilde{N}$

Typically basic security predicates in MAKS represent closure properties demanding that observing the visible events of a trace does not reveal any information about the confidential events of this trace. Given an admissible system trace, there must be another trace with different confidential events that cause the same visible behavior, i.e. both traces are equivalent with respect to their visible behavior. To translate this idea into configuration structures, we have to formalize the notion of visible behavior. In contrast to trace based system this includes also the branching behavior of a particular configuration. In the following we introduce the notion of V-simulation between configurations. A configuration X V-simulates another configuration Y if X behaves(with respect to successor configurations and branching behavior) as Y on the low-level. The problem of formalizing such a property that is also preserved under action refinement is closely related to the general problem of defining equivalence relations invariant under refinement. For our purposes we adopt the notion of history preserving bisimulations [5] relating two configurations with same causal history which are known to be preserved under action refinement. However, in our setting we are only interested in visible parts of the history and in simulation (instead of bisimulation):

Definition 7 (V-simulation). *Let $CS = (S, T, l)$ be configuration structure with events $\mathcal{E}$, $V = (V, N, C)$ be a view for CS, and $X, Y \in S$. Y V-simulates X iff there is relation $R \subseteq (S, S, \mathcal{P}(\mathcal{E}_V, \mathcal{E}_V))$ such that $(X, Y, id) \in R$ and whenever $(U, W, f) \in R$ then*

- f is an isomorphism between $(U_V, <_{U_V}, l\,|_{U_V})$ and $(W_V, <_{W_V}, l\,|_{W_V})$, and
- for all $U' \in \mathcal{S}$ with $U \subset U'$ and $(U' - U) \cap \mathcal{E}_C = \emptyset$
  there is $Y' \in \mathcal{S}$ and $f' \in \mathcal{P}(\mathcal{E}_V, \mathcal{E}_V)$ such that:
  $W \subseteq Y'$, $(W' - W) \cap \mathcal{E}_C = \emptyset$, $f'\,|_W = f$, and $(U', W', f') \in R$.

The following lemma guarantees that $\mathcal{V}$-simulation is preserved under action refinement if we refine $\mathcal{V}$ appropriately (cf. Def. 6).

Lemma 3. Let $\mathcal{CS} = (\mathcal{S}, \mathcal{T}, l)$ be configuration structure (with events $\mathcal{E}$) together with a view $\mathcal{V} = (V, N, C)$, ref be a refinement function for $\mathcal{CS}$, and $\tilde{\mathcal{V}}$ be a view refinement of $\mathcal{V}$ wrt. $\mathcal{CS}$.
Let $X, Y \in \mathcal{S}$ and $\tilde{X}, \tilde{Y} \in \mathcal{S}_{ref(\mathcal{CS})}$ such that $\forall e \in \mathcal{E}_V\colon X_e = Y_e$ holds. Then, $\tilde{Y}$ $\tilde{\mathcal{V}}$-simulates $\tilde{X}$ if Y $\mathcal{V}$-simulates X.

Proof. Let $\tilde{R}$ be a relation with $(\tilde{U}, \tilde{W}, \tilde{f}) \in \tilde{R}$ iff there is a $(U, W, f) \in R$ such that

$$\tilde{U} = \bigcup_{e \in U} e \times U_e \text{ with } U_e \neq \emptyset \tag{3}$$

$$\tilde{W} = \bigcup_{e \in W} e \times W_e \text{ with } W_e \neq \emptyset \tag{4}$$

$$\forall e \in \mathcal{E}_V : U_e = W_{f(e)} \tag{5}$$

$$\forall (e, e') \in \tilde{\mathcal{E}}_V : \tilde{f}(e, e') = (f(e), e') \tag{6}$$

First, we have to prove that $(\tilde{X}, \tilde{Y}, id) \in \tilde{R}$ holds. Since $R(X, Y, id)$ holds, $f = id$ obviously implies $\forall e \in V\colon X_e = Y_{f(e)}$ and $\tilde{f}(e, e') = (e, e') = (f(e), e')$.

Second, we have to prove that $\tilde{f}$ is an isomorphism between $(\tilde{U}_{\tilde{V}}, <_{\tilde{U}_{\tilde{V}}}, l\,|_{\tilde{U}_{\tilde{V}}})$ and $(\tilde{W}_{\tilde{V}}, <_{\tilde{W}_{\tilde{V}}}, l\,|_{\tilde{W}_{\tilde{V}}})$ Therefore, we have to prove that $(d, d') <_{\tilde{U}} (e, e') \leftrightarrow \tilde{f}(d, d') <_{\tilde{W}} \tilde{f}(e, e')$ and $l(\tilde{f}(e, e')) = l((e, e')$:

$$(d, d') <_{\tilde{U}} (e, e') \leftrightarrow (d <_U e) \vee ((d = e) \wedge (d' <_{ref(l(d))} e'))$$
$$\leftrightarrow (d <_U e) \vee ((d = e) \wedge (d' <_{ref(l(f(d)))} e'))$$
$$\leftrightarrow (f(d) <_W f(e)) \vee ((f(d) = f(e)) \wedge (d' <_{ref(l(f(d)))} e'))$$
$$\leftrightarrow \tilde{f}(d, d') <_{\tilde{W}} \tilde{f}(e, e')$$

$$l(\tilde{f}(e, e')) = l((f(e), e')) = l_{ref(l(f(e)))}(e') = l_{ref(l(e))}(e') = l((e, e'))$$

Third, let $(\tilde{U}, \tilde{W}, \tilde{f}) \in \tilde{R}$ then we have to prove that for all $\tilde{U}' \in \mathcal{S}_{ref(\mathcal{CS})}$ with $\tilde{U} \subset \tilde{U}'$ and $(\tilde{U}' - \tilde{U}) \cap \tilde{\mathcal{E}}_{\tilde{C}} = \emptyset$ there is $\tilde{W}' \in \mathcal{S}_{ref(\mathcal{CS})}$ and $\tilde{f}' \in \mathcal{P}(\tilde{\mathcal{E}}_{\tilde{V}}, \tilde{\mathcal{E}}_{\tilde{V}})$ such that: $\tilde{W} \subseteq \tilde{W}'$, $(\tilde{W}' - \tilde{W}) \cap \tilde{\mathcal{E}}_{\tilde{C}} = \emptyset$, $\tilde{f}'\,|_{\tilde{W}} = \tilde{f}$, and $(\tilde{U}', \tilde{W}', \tilde{f}') \in \tilde{R}$.

Let $(\tilde{U}, \tilde{W}, \tilde{f}) \in \tilde{R}$ and $\tilde{U}' \in \mathcal{S}_{ref(\mathcal{CS})}$ with $\tilde{U} \subset \tilde{U}'$ and $(\tilde{U}' - \tilde{U}) \cap \tilde{\mathcal{E}}_{\tilde{C}} = \emptyset$. Since $(\tilde{U}, \tilde{W}, \tilde{f}) \in \tilde{R}$, let (U, W, f) be the corresponding element in R as required by the construction of $\tilde{R}$. $\tilde{U}' \in \mathcal{S}_{ref(\mathcal{CS})}$ implies $U' \in \mathcal{S}_{\mathcal{CS}}$. Further, obviously $U \subseteq U'$, and $(U' - U) \cap \mathcal{E}_C = \emptyset$ because otherwise, there would be a confidential event e in $U - U'$ and thus the refinement $e \times U'_e$ would include (by the definition of 7) at least one confidential event (e, e'). Thus, there is a $(U', W', f') \in R$ with $W' \in \mathcal{S}_{\mathcal{CS}}$, $\quad W \subseteq W'$, $(W' - W) \cap \mathcal{E}_C = \emptyset$, and $f' \mid_W = f$.

Consider $\tilde{W}' = \bigcup_{e \in W'} e \times W'_e$ with $W'_e = U'_{f^{-1}(e)}$ if $e \in \mathcal{E}_V$ and $W'_e \in \mathcal{T}_{ref(l(e))}$ with $W_e \subseteq W_e$ otherwise. Obviously, $(e, e') \in \tilde{\mathcal{E}}_{\tilde{N}}$ for $e \notin \mathcal{E}_V$ and $e' \in W'_e - W_e$ because the refinement of non-visible events introduces only non-visible events while the refinement of confidential events only causes one confidential event at the start (i.e. is already included in W_e) followed by non-visible events.

We know that $busy(\tilde{W}') \subseteq \mathcal{E}_V$. Since $\tilde{U}' \in \mathcal{S}_{ref(\mathcal{CS})}$ we know also that $\forall Y \subseteq busy(\tilde{U}) : U - Y \in \mathcal{S}_{\mathcal{CS}}$ and thus $\forall Y \subseteq busy(\tilde{U}) \cap \mathcal{E}_V : U - Y \in \mathcal{S}_{\mathcal{CS}}$. Since f is an isomorphism on the pomsets, $\forall Y \subseteq f(busy(\tilde{U}) \cap \mathcal{E}_V) : W - Y \in \mathcal{S}_{\mathcal{CS}}$ holds. Thus, $\forall Y \subseteq busy(\tilde{W}') : W - Y \in \mathcal{S}_{\mathcal{CS}}$ and $\tilde{W}' \in \mathcal{S}_{\mathcal{CS}}$ $\qquad \square$

5   Basic Security Predicates

In the following subsections we will translate the two most prominent basic security predicates of MAKS, *BSD* and *BSIA*$_\rho$, into our framework based on configuration structures and prove that both notions are (under some preconditions) preserved under action refinement.

5.1   Backward Strict Deletion

Enforcing the Backward Strict Deletion property in a trace-based system guarantees that an adversary cannot deduce that a specific confidential event has happened when monitoring the visible behavior of the system. Technically, this property ensures that for each (finite) trace tr we can take the prefix of this trace up to the last confidential event and then simulate the rest of tr without confidential events (see Section 2). The translation of this property to configuration structures in straight forward. If we are in a particular configuration $X \in \mathcal{S}$ and have the possibility to perform an confidential action, i.e. $X \cup \{e\} \in \mathcal{S}$ with $e \in \mathcal{E}_C$, then X should cause the same visible behavior as $X \cup \{e\}$ would do. Formally we define:

Definition 8. *Let* $\mathcal{CS} = (\mathcal{S}, \mathcal{T}, l)$ *be a configuration structure together with a view* $\mathcal{V} = (V, N, C)$. $\mathcal{CS}$ *satisfies* Backward Strict Deletion *(or BSD for short) iff for all* $X \in \mathcal{S}$ *and* $e \in \mathcal{E}_C$: $X \cup \{e\} \in \mathcal{S}$ *implies that* X $\mathcal{V}$*-simulates* $X \cup \{e\}$.

The following theorem guarantees that the basic security predicate *BSD* is always preserved under action refinement as long as we use a view refinement as specified in Definition 6. Since secrets are considered as atomic we are able to remove the complete refinement of a confidential event since *BSD* on the abstract level guarantees that we can remove this confidential event already on the abstract level.

Theorem 1. *Let* $\mathcal{CS} = (\mathcal{S}, \mathcal{T}, l)$ *be a configuration structure together with a view* $\mathcal{V} = (V, N, C)$ *that satisfies BSD wrt.* $\mathcal{V}$. *Let* $ref(\mathcal{CS})$ *be a refinement of* $\mathcal{CS}$ *and* $\tilde{\mathcal{V}}$ *be view refinement of* $\mathcal{V}$ *wrt. ref and* $\mathcal{CS}$. *Then,* $\tilde{\mathcal{CS}}$ *satisfies BSD wrt.* $\tilde{\mathcal{V}}$.

Proof. Let $ref(CS) = (\tilde{S}, \tilde{T}, \tilde{l})$ and $\tilde{V} = (\tilde{V}, \tilde{N}, \tilde{C})$. Suppose, there is an $(e, e') \in \tilde{\mathcal{E}}_{\tilde{C}}$ and $\tilde{X} \in \tilde{S}$ such that $\tilde{X} \cup \{(e, e')\} \in \tilde{S}$. Let $\tilde{X}$ be the refinement of some $X \in CS$. Since $(e, e') \in \tilde{\mathcal{E}}_C$ we know that $e \notin X$ because confidential events (e, e') can only occur as a first step in the refinement of a confidential event e. Thus, $\tilde{X} \cup \{(e, e')\}$ is a refinement of a configuration $X' = X \cup \{e\}$. Furthermore, since CS satisfies BSD, we know that X V-simulates X'. Then, Lemma 3 ensures that $\tilde{X}$ $\tilde{V}$-simulates $\tilde{X} \cup \{(e, e')\}$, since $X_d = X'_d$ holds for all $d \in \mathcal{E}_V$ trivially. $\qquad\square$

5.2   Backward Strict Insertion

While *BSD* is concerned with the non-deducability of occurrences of actions, enforcing Backward Strict Insertion will guarantee that an adversary cannot deduce that a confidential action has *not* occurred. Technically we have to guarantee that for any possible system trace tr: if we take any prefix of tr containing in particular all its confidential events and append another confidential event to the end of prefix then we can expand this trace to a system trace that causes the same visible behavior as tr. We can easily translate this property to configuration structures as follows. If we are in a particular configuration $X \in S$ then we must be able to perform any confidential action, i.e. $X \cup \{e\} \in S$ with $e \in \mathcal{E}_C$ and $X \cup \{e\}$ must cause the same visible behavior as X would do.

It is obvious that a system satisfying *BSIA* behaves totally randomly on confidential events since they can occur in a random sequel and are also randomly interleaved with the sequel of visible events. However, any intrinsic dependencies between (confidential) events are known to an adversary since he can inspect the admissible system traces. Since there is no general solution to the problem of how much system information should be leaked to an adversary, Mantel allows one to restrict the enforcement of the *BSIA* predicate only to specific situations. He introduces an admissibility predicate ρ on traces in order to specify those situations in which we have to guarantee that *BSIA* holds (see Section 2.)

We translate this admissibility restriction into the notion of configuration structures as follows:

Definition 9. *Let $CS = (S, T, l)$ be a configuration structure with events E. A set $\rho \subseteq \mathcal{E}$ is called an* admissibility restriction. *A configuration X is ρ-admissible iff there is a configuration $X' \in S$ such that $l(X \cap \rho) = l(X' \cap \rho)$.*

Definition 10. *Let $CS = (S, T, l)$ be a configuration structure with events E and $\rho \subseteq E_S$. CS satisfies $BSIA_\rho$ iff for all $X \in S$ and all $e \in C_S$: if $X \cup \{e\}$ is ρ-admissible then $X \cup \{e\} \in CS$ and $X \cup \{e\}$ V-simulates X.*

In order to translate a security predicate $BSIA_\rho$ that is satisfied by a configuration structure CS to its refinement $ref(CS)$ we have to provide an appropriate set $\tilde{\rho}$ such that on the one hand $ref(CS)$ satisfies $BSIA_{\tilde{\rho}}$ but on the other hand $\tilde{\rho}$ lacks only that degree of information about dependencies of confidential events that we are willing to provide to the adversary. Thus, we do not provide a unique translation of ρ to some $\tilde{\rho}$ but provide sufficient conditions of $\tilde{\rho}$ to guarantee that

$BSIA_\rho$ will be preserved under refinement. In particular, a refinement has to preserve admissibility: if a configuration $\tilde{X}$ of the refined configuration structure is admissible wrt. $\tilde{\rho}$ then it abstract configuration X should be also admissible wrt. ρ. Furthermore, we have to guarantee that in all admissible situations the inserted confidential event can be executed in parallel with non-atomic previous events, the refinements of which have not been finished yet.

Definition 11. *Let $CS = (\mathcal{S}, \mathcal{T}, l)$ be a configuration structure and ref be a refinement function. An admissibility restriction $\tilde{\rho} \subseteq \tilde{\mathcal{E}}$ is a refinement of an admissibility restriction $\rho \subseteq \mathcal{E}$ wrt. ref and CS iff for all $\tilde{X} \in \tilde{\mathcal{S}}$ and all $(e, e') \in \tilde{\mathcal{E}}_{\tilde{C}}$ holds*

- *$\tilde{X} \cup \{(e, e')\}$ is $\tilde{\rho}$-admissible implies $X \cup \{e\}$ is ρ-admissible, and*
- *$\forall Y \subset busy(\tilde{X}) : X \cup \{e\} - Y \in \mathcal{S}$*

Given this definition of refining ρ-admissibility, we are now able to formulate the preconditions under which $BSIA_\rho$ is preserved under action refinement:

Theorem 2. *Let $CS = (\mathcal{S}, \mathcal{T}, l)$ be a configuration structure together with a view $\mathcal{V} = (V, N, C)$ that satisfies $BSIA_\rho$ wrt. $\mathcal{V}$. Let $ref(CS)$ be a refinement of CS, $\tilde{\mathcal{V}}$ be view refinement of $\mathcal{V}$ wrt. ref and CS, and $\tilde{\rho}$ is a refinement of ρ wrt. ref and CS. Then, $\tilde{CS}$ satisfies $BSIA_{\tilde{\rho}}$ wrt. $\tilde{\mathcal{V}}$.*

Proof. Suppose, $\tilde{X} \in \tilde{\mathcal{S}}$ and $\tilde{X} \cup \{e, e'\}$ is $\tilde{\rho}$-admissible. Therefore, $X' = X \cup \{e\}$ is ρ-admissible and $X' \in \mathcal{S}$. Since $\forall Y \subset busy(\tilde{X}) : X \cup \{e\} - Y = X' - Y \in \mathcal{S}$ and also $\forall Y \subset busy(\tilde{X}) : X - Y \in \mathcal{S}$ we know that $\forall Y \subset busy(\tilde{X} \cup \{e, e'\}) : X' - Y \in \mathcal{S}$ and thus $\tilde{X} \cup \{e, e'\} \in \tilde{\mathcal{S}}$.

Since X' is ρ-admissible, $X' \in CS$, and CS satisfies $BSIA_\rho$ we know that X' $\mathcal{V}$-simulates X. Thus, lemma 3 ensures that $\tilde{X} \cup \{(e, e')\}$ $\tilde{\mathcal{V}}$-simulates $\tilde{X}$, since $X_d = X'_d$ holds for all $d \in \mathcal{E}_V$ trivially. $\square$

6   Related Work

Action refinement has been the subject of intensive studies in between 1985 and 1995. We refer to [8] for an overview and classification of the different syntactic and semantic based interpretations of action refinement. Configuration structures are closely related to event structures which have been introduced by Winskel [21]. We refer the reader to [7] for a discussion of the various approaches, the corresponding notions of action refinements and the problems of finding appropriate bisimulation equivalences that are preserved under refinement.

Starting with the work of Goguen and Meseguer, information flow control has been subject of a large variety of different approaches introducing different formal notions of independence. Most prominent, McLean [17], Zakinthinos and Lee [22] and Mantel [13] proposed frameworks to embed these different notions in a uniform framework.

There is a large number of work that is concerned with the problem of combining information flow control and refinement. This work can be divided into different categories according to the different versions of refinements considered.

Jacob [12] as well as Mantel [14] proposed approaches for secure refinement considering refinement as a process to eliminate indeterminism. In terms of trace-based systems such a refinement reduces the set of admissible system traces while actions (or events) are considered as atomic. Mantel introduces a collection of refinement operations for specific information flow properties that ensure that these properties are preserved under refinement (i.e. reduction of the set of admissible systems traces). In contrast, Jacob allows for an uncontrolled refinement but provides measures to translate the obtained refined system into a secure one. [1] also proposes a notion of refinement of states for processes described in terms of a Security Process Algebra (SPA).

Our approach is based on action refinement in which actions are considered as non-atomic. This allows one to model procedures as actions on the abstract level and use action refinements to implementation them on an implementation level. Investigating information flow properties in the presence of action refinement has been done previously by [3]. This approach is more related to ours, since they use a CCS-like process algebra SPA as an underlying specification language. Flow event structures as a special form of event structures are particular suited for giving semantic to languages like CCS. The approach in [3] uses a bisimulation-based information flow property named P_{BNDC} and provide preconditions under which this property is preserved under refinement in SPA. Their notion of *weak bisimulation on low action* is related to our notion of $\mathcal{V}$-simulation; both are used to formalize the corresponding security predicates (see also [2]. However, both approaches strongly differ in the preconditions they impose on systems in order to guarantee that the information flow properties are preserved under refinement.

7   Conclusion

Based on Mantel's framework MAKS, we presented a framework for possibilistic information flow in configuration structures. We transfered the most prominent basic security predicates BSD and $BSIA_\rho$ in terms of configuration structures and elaborated the situations in which these properties are preserved under action refinement. The work was motivated by developing a framework to investigate the security of multi-agent systems with the help of possibilistic information flow [11]. In this work we used a scenario of comparison shopping agents as a case study. It turned out that the verification of the security properties of individual agents (and in particular the formulation of the unwinding conditions) was hindered by the large number of N-events used to formalize the internal processing of incoming messages. In the approach presented in this paper this internal processing could be easily modeled as a refinement of various N-events which allows us to abstract away from a large part of the internal computation. However, a precondition of doing such an approach is the existence of appropriate unwinding theorems to verify BSD and $BSIA_\rho$ on configuration structures.

This development is still work in progress. Future work will be concerned with weakening the restrictive definition of a view refinement which now restricts the refinement of a confidential event to a single confidential event followed by non-visible events.

References

1. A. Bossi, R. Focardi, C. Piazza, and S. Rossi. Refinement Operators and Information Flow Security In: *Proceedings of the 1st International Conference on Software Engineering and Formal Methods (SEFM'03)*, IEEE Computer Science, 2001
2. A. Bossi, R. Focardi, C. Piazza, and S. Rossi. Bisimulation and Unwinding for Verifying Possibilistic Security Properties Proceedings of the 4th International Conference on Verification, Model Checking, and Abstract Interpretation (VMCAI 2003), Springer LNCS 2575, 2003
3. A. Bossi, D. Macedono, C. Piazza, and S. Rossi. Compositional Action Refinement and Information Flow Security. Technical Report CS-2003-13. Dipartimento di Informatica, Univerista Ca Foscari di Venezia, 2003
4. L. Castellano, G. de Michelis, and L. Pomello. Concurrency vs. interleaving: an instructive example. Bulletin of the EATCS 31, pp. 12–15, 1987.
5. P. Degano, R. de Nicola, and U. Montanari. Observational equivalences for concurrency models. In: *Proceedings of the 3rd IFIP WG 2.2 working conference: Formal description of programming concepts III*, Ebberup, North-Holland, 1987
6. R.J. Van Glabbeek and G.D. Plotkin. Configuration structures. In: *Proceedings of the 10th Annual IEEE Symposium on Logic in Computer Science*, IEEE Computer Society, 1995.
7. R.J. Van Glabbeek and U. Goltz. Refinement of actions and equivalence notions for concurrent systems. Acta Informatica, Vol. 37(4-5), pp. 229–327, 2001.
8. R. Gorrieri and A. Rensink. Action Refinement. Technical report UBLCS-99-09, University of Bologna, 1999.
9. J. A. Goguen and J. Meseguer. Security policies and security models. In *Proceedings of the IEEE Symposium on Security and Privacy*. IEEE Computer Society, 1982.
10. J. A. Goguen and J. Meseguer. Inference control and unwinding. In *Proceedings of the IEEE Symposium on Security and Privacy*. IEEE Computer Society, 1984.
11. D. Hutter, H. Mantel, A.Schairer, and I. Schaefer Security in Multiagent Systems – A Case Study on Comparison Shopping. Journal of Applied Logic. Special Issue: Logic-based Verification of Multiagent Systems, Elsevier, Article in press, doi:10.1016/j.jal.2005.12.015, 2006
12. J. Jacob. On the derivation of secure components. In: *Proceedings of the 1989 IEEE Symposium on Security and Privacy*, IEEE Computer Society, 1989.
13. H. Mantel. Possibilistic definitions of security – an assembly kit. In *Proceedings of the IEEE Computer Security Foundations Workshop*. IEEE Computer Society, 2000.
14. H. Mantel. Preserving Information Flow Properties under Refinement. In: *Proceedings of the 2001 IEEE Symposium on Security and Privacy*, IEEE Computer Society, 2001.
15. H. Mantel. *A Uniform Framework for the Formal Specification and Verification of Information Flow Security*. PhD thesis, Universität des Saarlandes, 2003. Published as a manuscript.
16. J. D. McLean. Proving Noninterference and Functional Correctness using Traces. *Journal of Computer Security*, 1(1):37–57, 1992.

17. J.D. McLean. A general theory of composition for trace sets closed under selective interleaving functions. In *Proceedings of IEEE Symposium on Security and Privacy*. IEEE Computer Society, 1994.
18. R. Milner A Calculus of Communicating Systems. Springer, LNCS 92, 1980
19. J. Rushby. Noninterference, transitivity, and channel-control security policies. Technical Report CSL-92-02, SRI International, Menlo Park, CA, 1992.
20. P.Y.A. Ryan and S.A Schneider. Process algebra and non-interference. *Journal of Computer Security*, 9(1/2):75–103, 2001.
21. G. Winskel. Event structures. In: *Petri Nets: Applications and Relationships of other models of concurrency*, Advances in Petri Nets. Springer, LNCS 255, 1986
22. A. Zakinthinos and E. S. Lee. A general theory of security properties. In *Proceedings of the IEEE Symposium on Security and Privacy*. IEEE Computer Society, 1997.

Toward a Framework for Forensic Analysis of Scanning Worms

Ihab Hamadeh and George Kesidis

Pennsylvania State University, University Park, PA 16802, USA
hamadeh@cse.psu.edu, kesidis@engr.psu.edu
Department of Computer Science and Engineering
Department of Electrical Engineering

Abstract. Scanning worms have been around for a while and have had some damaging effects on the Internet. Because of their fast spread and their random selection of their target victims, building a global knowledge about which infected end-systems caused the infection of which susceptible end-systems seems fairly hard. In this paper, we propose to find the originator(s) (i.e., first infected end-system(s)) that spread the worm. The broader view is to build the complete infection tree(s) rooted at the originator(s) and which leaves consist of susceptible machines becoming infected. Besides, scanning worms could unintentionally divulge some information about the machines they infect. We will show how such information could be extracted from the scans of a victim end-system. We studied two different worms, the SQL Slammer/Sapphire worm and the Witty worm, and demonstrated the possibility of building the infection tree and gathering information about the infected end-systems.

1 Introduction

Even with the precautions taken to protect enterprise networks, the Internet has recently experienced several serious outbreaks of scanning worms that infiltrate most highly secured networks. Scanning worms have been able to spread throughout the Internet infecting computers at many sites, including universities, medical research facilities, and even military sites. Unlike e-mail worms, scanning worms exploit a software vulnerability to gain access/control of an end-system and require no human intervention to propagate. An infected end-system scans (dispatches suitably crafted packets often to randomly chosen IPv4 addresses of) potential victim end-systems. If the scanned end-system is susceptible to the exploit, it is subsequently infected and begins scanning (spreading the worm) in turn. Some of the worms were relatively benign to their hosts (e.g., SQL Slammer/Sapphire). Others were more malicious such as the CodeRed worm that caused Web pages to appear defaced and the Witty worm that overwrote random sectors of randomly chosen hard disks.

Unlike prior research that focused on detecting worms, we propose to find the originator(s) (i.e., first infected machine(s)) that spread the worm. The broader view is to build the complete infection tree(s) (i.e. causal tree) rooted at the

G. Müller (Ed.): ETRICS 2006, LNCS 3995, pp. 282–297, 2006.

originator(s) and which leaves consist of susceptible machines becoming infected. Such knowledge could be important for many reasons. In terms of Internet forensics, it could be essential in determining the stepping stone machines used in the attack and eventually the attacker himself. It also can help understand how an attack was successful in infiltrating many network security defenses. In addition, having the knowledge about the number of originators and the infection tree in general would help in recreating the attack in order to model the spread of a worm or its variants. This paper is organized as follows. In section 2, we review some of the previous research work about worms. Our assumptions and notations are introduced in section 3, followed by a discussion on how to build the framework for forensic analysis in section 4. Our case study of the SQL Slammer worm and of the Witty worm and the results are covered in section 5 followed by a concluding section.

2 Related Work

Because worms could have devastating effects and also could propagate and infect so rapidly all potential susceptibles before (human initiated) responses could be mounted, much of the existing worm research has focused on finding ways to detect and mitigate the spread of a worm. Several worm detection and containment solutions have been proposed [18, 15, 17]. Many "network telescopes" [8, 9, 7] have monitored the spread of worms and provided a base to model that spread. Some of these models have been developed in [13, 20, 16] in order to understand the worm global effect on the Internet infrastructure, and to become part in testing worm defense mechanisms.

While significant work has been done in the area of Distributed Denial of Service attack traceback [10, 12, 2], relatively little work has addressed the problem of worm traceback to determine the worm infection tree and the originator(s) of the worm. GrIDS [14] was one of the first intrusion detection systems used to aggregate data (collected from thousands of end-hosts within an enterprise network) into activity graphs to reveal the causal structure of malicious network activity. Xie et al. [19] proposed a "random moonwalk" algorithm to find the origin and the initial propagation paths of a worm attack. The algorithm is based on correlating repeatedly sampled paths from the host contact graph but requires collaboration between multiple entities in the Internet (i.e., an architecture in which network routers or end-systems record flow records and make them available for querying to obtain a global knowledge). Their algorithm along with the technique we propose in this paper aim at finding the first instance(s) of the worm and not the real attacker. Finding the real attacker would be performed the traditional way by looking at the log of the network the originator(s) reside in and checking what machine(s) contacted the originator to determine the stepping stone machines. This method can be employed recursively until the attacker is found. Kumar et al. [9] performed a forensic analysis of the Witty worm. They inferred interesting attributes of the infected end-systems in addition to tracing back the sequences of infection events. They did not,

Table 1. Summary of Notations

Notation	Description
$\mathcal{I}$	The list of infected scanning machines (i.e. infectives)
Δ	The set of 32-bit IP addresses of the network telescope
d^k	The ordered list of destination IP addresses of the scans sent by infective k to the network telescope
d_n^k	The destination IP address of the nth scan that the network telescope receives from infective k
$\mathcal{D}^k$	The ordered list of destination IP addresses of the scans sent by infective k to the Internet
$\widehat{\mathcal{D}}'^k$	The ordered list of **recreated** destination IP addresses of the scans infective k **must** have generated
$\widehat{\mathcal{D}}''^k$	The ordered list of **recreated** destination IP addresses of the scans infective k **may** have generated
$\widehat{\mathcal{D}}^k$	The total possible ordered list of **recreated** destination IP addresses of the scans sent by infective k to the Internet
$\mathcal{D}_m^k$	The destination IP address of the mth scan sent by infective k to the Internet
$T(d_n^k)$	The **measured** time the network telescope received the nth scan sent by infective k
$\widehat{T}(\mathcal{D}_m^k)$	The **estimated** time of the mth scan sent by infective k to the Internet

however, describe their traceback analysis in detail nor mention limitations of their method if there is significant packet loss (subsampling) at the telescope. In this paper, we describe a general framework to reconstruct the infection tree for both TCP and UDP scanning worms from network telescope data. Sufficient detail is given so that any researcher will be able to reproduce the results presented in this paper. We also discuss how difficult reconstruction of the infection tree becomes when the scanning worm "reseeds" while the telescope is heavily congested.

3 Assumptions and Notations

Consider a scanning worm that generates addresses for its scans (to potential victims) according to the following linear congruential pseudo-random number generator (LCPRNG) [4]

$$x_{n+1} = (ax_n + b) \bmod 2^M \tag{1}$$

where $M = 32$ for our study. Many scanning worms such as Slammer, Witty, CodeRed and MSBlaster used such pseudo random number generators. We assume that each infective (infected end-system or worm) initially (upon infection) chooses a seed x_0 at random and then thereafter uses equation (1) to generate subsequent addresses for scanning.

Network telescopes such as [9, 8, 7] can be used to observe the progress of a worm by logging all scans by a worm's infectives to the network telescope. Table 1 is a summary of the notations used throughout this paper.

For the worm under consideration, assume that the network telescope logs the header of each scan to the network telescope including the source address S^k of the infective k ($k \in \mathcal{I}$), the destination address d^k ($d^k \in \Delta$), and the local (network telescope's) time $T(d^k)$ of reception.

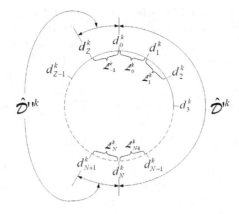

Fig. 1. Ordered sequence of IP addresses generated using equation 1

4   Steps Toward Building the Framework

Our objective is to use the network telescope's log offline to determine the infection tree of the worm (post-mortem analysis), i.e., a tree whose root is the
original infected end-system (assumed herein to be a single end-system) and
whose parent-child relationship corresponds to infector-infectee. In particular,
we wish to accurately resolve the tree structure close to the root and, of course,
the true root (original infective) itself.

To do this, we begin by considering again the LCPRNG of equation (1). The
quantities a and b are assumed known prior to our offline analysis (by reverse engineering the worm's code). Again, assuming that the iteration is seeded with x_0
initially, each infective will scan a series of addresses $x_1, x_2, x_3, \ldots$. The sequence
of addresses generated will depend on a and b and x_0.

The Witty worm used $a = 214013$ and $b = 2531011$ [6] (similar values are
used by Microsoft rand() function), while the Slammer worm used $a = 214013$
and $b = -2011082752, -2009896848, -2009990620$ or other values depending on
the sqlsort.dll version [1, 5]. Note that by choosing b even, each generated group
of addresses consisted either of all odd or all even numbers depending on x_0.

Let $\mathcal{D}^k$ be the ordered list of destination addresses generated by infective k. We
have $\mathcal{D}^k \cap \Delta = d^k$. The following analysis will be conducted for each infective $k \in \mathcal{I}$.

4.1   Building $\mathcal{D}$ for Each Infective

The challenge in building $\mathcal{D}^k$ for every infective $k \in \mathcal{I}$ resides in determining
the seed of the LCPRNG or more precisely the first scan sent by each infective.
First visualize $\mathcal{D}^k$ as a circle of numbers (2^{32} maximum) placed in clockwise
order of generation according to equation (1), see Figure 1. Let $\mathcal{L}^k$ be the list of
IP addresses infective k may have targeted (excluding the network telescope's).
$\mathcal{L}^k_{-1}$ is the sublist of possible IP addresses infective k scanned before sending

its first scan to the network telescope and $\mathcal{L}_0^k, \mathcal{L}_1^k .. \mathcal{L}_n^k$ are the set of sublists of IP addresses infective k scanned after its first scan d_0^k to the network telescope (Figure 1). Thus $\mathcal{L}_{-1}^k$ is the sublist of IP addresses between d_Z^k and d_0^k where $d_0^k, d_Z^k \notin \mathcal{L}_{-1}^k$. Similarly, $\mathcal{L}_0^k$ is the sublist of IP addresses between d_0^k and d_1^k where $d_0^k, d_1^k \notin \mathcal{L}_0^k$. Since d_0^k is the first scan sent by infective k to network telescope (i.e., the first scan the network telescope logged from k), we can deduce from Figure 1, that the destination address of the first scan $\mathcal{D}_0^k$ generated by infective k (destined to the Internet) lies between d_Z^k and d_0^k, i.e., $d_Z^k \prec \mathcal{D}_0^k \preceq d_0^k \Leftrightarrow \mathcal{D}_0^k \in (\mathcal{L}_{-1}^k \cup \{d_0^k\})$, where d_Z^k is the last possible unique scan that the network telescope could receive from infective k before the same group of scans destined to the network telescope (i.e., d_0^k, d_1^k, etc.) repeats again. Let d_N^k be the last unique scan received by the network telescope from infective k and $\mathcal{D}_M^k$ be the last scan sent by k to the Internet (e.g., the infected end-system k was powered off, crashed, inoculated, etc.).

$$d_N^k \preceq \mathcal{D}_M^k \prec d_{N+1}^k \Leftrightarrow \mathcal{D}_M^k \in (\mathcal{L}_N^k \cup \{d_N^k\}),$$

where $(M \geq N)$. Thus, we can claim that the list of IP addresses that k *must* have generated (and consequently scanned) is

$$\widehat{\mathcal{D}}'^k = \sum_{l=0}^{N-1} \mathcal{L}_n^k \cup \sum_{n=0}^{N} \{d_n^k\} \, ,$$

while it *may* have generated additional IP addresses within $\widehat{\mathcal{D}}''^k = \mathcal{L}_{-1}^k \cup \mathcal{L}_N^k$. Let $\widehat{\mathcal{D}}^k$ be the set of all IP addresses infective k may have generated, $\widehat{\mathcal{D}}^k = \widehat{\mathcal{D}}'^k \cup \widehat{\mathcal{D}}''^k$. Let $\mathcal{N}(\alpha)$ be the size of a list α. We have $\mathcal{N}(\widehat{\mathcal{D}}^k) \geq \mathcal{N}(\mathcal{D}^k)$. To determine the list of IP addresses $\widehat{\mathcal{D}}^k$ that infective k may have scanned, the LCPRNG is first seeded with d_0^k and equation 1 is repeated to generate the complete sequence of IP addresses $\mathcal{S}$ until d_0^k is revisited again. The complete list of IP addresses $\sum_{n=-1}^{N} \mathcal{L}_n^k \cup \sum_{n=0}^{N} d_n^k$ for each $k \in \mathcal{I}$ could be easily recreated from $\mathcal{S}$.

4.2   Recreating Worm Scans Timing

Recreating the time of each scan an infective k generated depends on the type of the worm. Generally, there exist two kind of worms: fast scanning worms (such as Slammer and Witty) and slow scanning worms (such as CodeRed and MS-Blaster).

Fast scanning worms usually use a single UDP packet to both scan and infect. Generally, worms that use the UDP protocol are bounded by the bandwidth capacity of its infectees link. The scanning rate of an infective could vary as neighboring susceptible end-systems (e.g., within the same subnet, within the same organization) are infected. As new infectives join the scanning operation on a shared link, congestion could occur and many scans could be dropped causing the rate of scans forwarded into the Internet per infective to drop [16].

As a result, we estimate such rates only locally in time because the effective scan-rate of an infective can substantially change because of time-varying levels of network congestion (possibly due to the worm itself). To estimate the time of each scan sent by infective k, we assume the rate of scans R^k to be constant between two consecutive scans to the network telescope, that means,

$$R_n^k = \frac{\mathcal{N}(\mathcal{L}_n^k) + 1}{T(d_{n+1}^k) - T(d_n^k)}. \tag{2}$$

Hence, the estimated time of each scan that happened between two consecutive scans d_n^k and d_{n+1}^k to network telescope is

$$\widehat{T}(\widehat{\mathcal{D}}_{m+i}^k) = T(\widehat{\mathcal{D}}_M^k) + \frac{i}{R_M^k}, \tag{3}$$

where $\widehat{\mathcal{D}}_m^k = d_n^k$, $\widehat{\mathcal{D}}_{m+i}^k \preceq d_{n+1}^k$. Thus far, we estimated the time of each scan sent by infective k after d_0^k. To estimate the time of scans that happened before d_0^k (i.e. the scans of the sublist $\mathcal{L}_{-1}^k$), we assume the rate of the scans of sublist $\mathcal{L}_{-1}^k$ to be similar to that of sublist $\mathcal{L}_0^k$.

$$R_{-1}^k = R_0^k \quad and \quad \widehat{T}(\widehat{\mathcal{D}}_{m-i}^k) = T(d_0^k) - \frac{i}{R_0^k} \tag{4}$$

Slow scanning worms require more than one packet to scan and infect a vulnerable end-system. They usually use the TCP protocol to scan and infect and thus their speed of spreading is mainly dependent on the condition of the network. A three-way handshake could take from a few milliseconds on a LAN to hundreds of milliseconds and even a few seconds on a WAN. Sometimes, a worm tries to contact IP addresses that are not populated and causes the worm to wait for about 21 seconds (Windows OS) before proceeding in scanning other IP addresses. To minimize this delay, some worms selectively reduce the timeout to few seconds (e.g., MSBlaster used 1.8 seconds, CodeRed II used 10 seconds). Moreover, some worms used non-blocking socket and multiple threads to propagate faster (e.g., CodeRed used 100 threads, CodeRed II used 300 or 600 threads). Even when equipped with these features, these kind of worms could not even closely reach the speed of single-packet-UDP worms. To estimate the time of each scan sent by infective k, we assume a burst of scans is sent (i.e. at the same time), and that the rate between consecutive burst of scans is constant. For instance, the MSBlaster worm sent 20 scans and tried to infect each responding end-system before proceeding in scanning the next 20 IP addresses. Let N_S be the number of scans sent simultaneously (this could be the number of scanning threads). Thus, the estimated rate between two consecutive burst of N_S scans is:

$$R_n^k = \frac{\left\lceil \frac{\mathcal{N}(\mathcal{L}_n^k) + 1}{N_S} \right\rceil}{T(d_{n+1}^k) - T(d_n^k)} \tag{5}$$

Hence, the estimated time of each scan that happened between two consecutive scans d_n^k and d_{n+1}^k to network telescope is

$$\widehat{T}(\widehat{\mathcal{D}}^k_{m+i}) = T(\widehat{\mathcal{D}}^k_m) + \frac{\lfloor \frac{i}{N_S} \rfloor}{R^k_m}, \tag{6}$$

where $\widehat{\mathcal{D}}^k_m = d^k_n$, $\widehat{\mathcal{D}}^k_{m+i} \preceq d^k_{n+1}$.

To estimate the time of scans that happened before d^k_0 (i.e. the scans of the sublist $\mathcal{L}^k_{-1}$), we assume the rate of the burst of scans of sublist $\mathcal{L}^k_{-1}$ to be similar to that of sublist $\mathcal{L}^k_0$.

$$R^k_{-1} = R^k_0 \quad and \quad \widehat{T}(\widehat{\mathcal{D}}^k_{m-i}) = T(d^k_0) - \frac{\lceil \frac{i}{N_S} \rceil}{R^k_0} \tag{7}$$

Estimating the time of each scan for slow scanning worms is a difficult and challenging problem. It depends on whether a scan succeeds (thus, the infection process takes few seconds before another scan is sent) or fails (and thus, another scan is sent immediately). Therefore, the time of scans is typically dependent on the status of the scans (succeeded or failed) and also, on the scanning strategy of the worm.

Algorithm 1. SQL Slammer/Sapphire Worm

---

variables: X, $b = -2011082752$, -2009896848, -2009990620 or other values depending on the sqlsort.dll version

Procedure $rand()$
  $X \Leftarrow (214013 \times X + b) \bmod 2^{32}$
  $return(X)$
end;
Procedure $Worm\_Body()$
  $X \Leftarrow GetTickCount()$
  loop
    $dest\_IP \Leftarrow rand()$
    $dest\_port \Leftarrow 1434$
    $payload\_length \Leftarrow 376$
    $Send\_Scan()$
  end loop
end;

4.3   Building the Infection Tree

Now that the list $\widehat{\mathcal{D}}_k$ (for $d^k_Z \prec \widehat{\mathcal{D}}^k_m \prec d^k_{N+1}$) and their corresponding estimated time $\widehat{T}^k_m$ have been determined, we can build the infection tree as follows. For every $k \in \mathcal{I}$, we first extract the tables Q_k with each entry containing an infectee of $k' \in \mathcal{I}$ and the estimated time of infection, i.e. $Q^k = \{(\widehat{\mathcal{D}}^k_m, \widehat{T}(\widehat{\mathcal{D}}^k_m)) \mid \widehat{\mathcal{D}}^k_m \in \mathcal{I}, \widehat{\mathcal{D}}^k_m \neq k\}$

From the collection of tables Q^k, we build an infection tree where the nodes represent the infectives. Given two infectives A and B, if A infected B (i.e., B is the child of A), then the following conditions are met.

$$\widehat{T}(\widehat{\mathcal{D}}^A_m) = max_{\widehat{\mathcal{D}}^k_m = B, \, \widehat{T}(\widehat{\mathcal{D}}^k_m) < T(d^B_0), \, A,B,k \in \mathcal{I}}(\widehat{T}(\widehat{\mathcal{D}}^k_m))$$

and

$$\widehat{T}(\widehat{\mathcal{D}}^A_m) - T(d^B_0) < \epsilon$$

The value of ϵ is expected to be less than a second for fast scanning worms (unless many scans from B to the network telescope are dropped) and tens of seconds or even minutes for slow scanning worms (since it might take a while before infective B sends a scan to the network telescope). If no infective meets the above conditions, we say that B is one of the originator of an infection (i.e., root of an infection tree). False positives may occur when two infectives A and B scan the same susceptible C at a very close time. Moreover, if A and B scan the same susceptible B, it is most likely that they will both scan the same set of addresses with different scan rates, which might create false positives in the infection tree. However, it is highly unlikely such false positives would occur at the beginning of spread of a worm (i.e. at the beginning of the infection tree), though it is possible to have two instances of the worm picking the same seed or close seeds (close in terms of distance on the ordered sequence of generated random numbers not in terms of value) and to have the rate of the earliest infected worm instance lower that the rate of the other worm instance.

5 Case Study

To assess our framework, we chose to study two different worms, the Slammer worm and the Witty worm. Both used the pseudo-random number generator of equation 1 and both provided different types of forensics about the end-systems they infected. Our ultimate goal was to test our approach with non-anonymized traces of worms. In the case of the Slammer worm, only anonymized traces (IP addresses in the scans have been modified) were available and thus could not be used to test our framework without resorting to the simulation of the spread of the SQL Slammer worm. But fortunately, in the case of the Witty Worm, non-anonymized traces were provided by CAIDA and used to validate our framework for some worm instances.

5.1 The SQL Slammer Worm

The SQL Slammer worm targeted end-systems running Microsoft SQL Server 2000, as well as Microsoft Desktop Engine (MSDE) 2000. The worm sent a single 376 bytes (payload size) UDP packet to the SQL Server Resolution Service port 1434. Once an end-system gets infected, the number of milliseconds that have elapsed since the system started is retrieved by calling the function GetTick-Count[1] and is used as the seed to the LCPRNG. Thereafter, the worm crafts a packet with a destination IP address generated according to equation 1 and dispatches it into the Internet. Algorithm 1 represents the scanning strategy of the SQL Slammer worm extracted from the worm's disassembled code [1]. Depending on the sqlsort.dll version, the value of b in equation 1 differed from one infective to another and created different groups with different sequences of IP addresses. For instance, for $b = -2011082752$, equation 1 would produce 64

---

[1] The 32-bit value will wrap around to zero if the system is run continuously for 49.7 days.

groups of random numbers (2 groups of odd numbers of size 2^{30} each and 62 different groups of even numbers of sizes ranging from 1 to 2^{29} each). Thus, for the three different values of b mentioned in Section 4, 192 different groups could be produced.

We performed a time driven simulation of the propagation of the Slammer worm. The experiment consisted of 75000 susceptibles with randomly assigned IP addresses connected to either a 10MBps (i.e., sending 2900 scans per second), 100Mbps link (29000 scans per second) or 1Gbps link (290000 scans per second). Once infected, an infective randomly chose a 32-bit seed and b from the three given values in Algorithm 1. Each scan was randomly delayed by a constant value to represent the propagation delay. We ran the experiment for 10 minutes of simulated time and saved the complete infection tree. We also logged the scans targeting a /8 network to test our framework. We extracted the log of the scans of the first 500 infectives that targeted the /8 network telescope (i.e., d^k, $1 \leq k \leq 500$). By matching, the first few consecutive scans of each infective k to one of the 192 different groups, we were able to determine the complete list of IP addresses each infective scanned and will scan. We were also able to extract $\mathcal{L}_{-1}^k$ for each infective. However, it was not possible to determine the seed[2] of each infective. The estimated time of each scan was determined using equations 3 and 4. Once the complete list of IP addresses and their corresponding estimated time was determined, the infection tree for the first 500 infective was built using the rules described in section 4.3. The infection tree we built exactly matched the one we recorded during simulation for the first 500 infectives.

Though our simulation does not take into consideration the fact that packets could be dropped due to congestion, it is easy to recover all the IP addresses each infective scanned between any two scans to the /8 network telescope. Unlike the Witty worm, building the infection tree is not affected by the loss of some scans destined to end-systems within the network telescope because it is easy to reproduce these scans. We also ran the simulation for 5 and 10 originators and we were still able to build the complete infection tree for the first 500 infectives. Looking at the SQL Slammer algorithm, two types of forensics could be deduced (if the non-anonymized traces were available): the infection tree (and IP addresses scanned) and the version of the sqlsort.dll file on each infective.

5.2 The Witty Worm

The Witty worm exploited a vulnerability in ICQ parsing by ISS products. Unlike all other worms, the Witty worm had a fixed source port number (4000) and a randomly chosen destination port number. It was also a damaging worm that overwrote random sectors of a randomly selected hard disk. Algorithm 2 represents the scanning strategy of the Witty worm extracted from the worm's disassembled code [6]. Once a susceptible is infected, it seeds its pseudo-random number generator with the value returned by GetTickCount. Then, it uses the LCPRNG to first generate the higher two bytes of the destination IP address and

---

[2] The seed falls in $(\mathcal{L}_{-1}^k \cup d_n^k)$ (refer to Figure 1).

Algorithm 2. Witty Worm

---

variables: X, $var0$, $var1$, $var2$
Procedure $rand()$
  $X \Leftarrow (214013 \times X + 2531011) \bmod 2^{32}$
  $var0 \Leftarrow (X >> 16)$
  $return(var0)$
end;
Procedure $Worm\_Body()$
  $start$:
    $X \Leftarrow GetTickCount()$
  $scan$:
  for $N = 1$ to 20000 **do**
    $var1 \Leftarrow rand()$
    $var2 \Leftarrow rand()$
    $dest\_IP \Leftarrow (var2 << 16) + var1$
    $source\_port = 4000$
    $dest\_port \Leftarrow rand()$
    $payload\_size \Leftarrow 768 + (rand() >> 7)$
    $Send\_Scan()$
  end for
  $physicalDrive \Leftarrow (rand() >> 8) \& 7$
  $status = OpenDevice(physicalDrive)$ for raw $write$ $access$
  if status = fail **then**
    goto $scan$
  else
    $write\_to\_location \Leftarrow ((rand() >> 1) << 16) + 20000$
    goto $start$
  end if

end;

---

then again to generate the lower two bytes of the destination IP address. The destination port address and the size of the scan payload are also determined using the same LCPRNG. After 20000 scans, the worm uses the LCPRNG to determine which physical drive (number 0 to 7) it will attempt to write on. If the physical drive does not exist, the worm continues scanning for another 20000 times. If the physical drive exists, the worm will write 64KB of data to a random position on the disk and reseed the LCPRNG by calling GetTickCount again. Analyzing the Witty data is much more challenging since the Witty worm kept on reseeding its LCPRNG whenever it succeeded in writing to a physical drive. Fortunately, we were able to test our framework on real non-anonymized traces of the witty worm scans provided by CAIDA[3]. Because CAIDA's /8 network telescope contains approximately 1/256th of all IPv4 addresses, the network telescope receives roughly one out of every 256 packets sent by an Internet worm with an unbiased random number generator [11].

Building $\widehat{\mathcal{D}}$ for Each Infective. To analyze the Witty worm, we first tried to understand how many groups of random numbers it generated. Since it used four consecutive generated random numbers for each crafted scan (refer to

---

[3] The CAIDA Dataset on the Witty Worm - March 19-24, 2004, Colleen Shannon and David Moore, http://www.caida.org/passive/witty/. Support for the Witty Worm Dataset and the UCSD Network Telescope are provided by Cisco Systems, Limelight Networks, the US Department of Homeland Security, the National Science Foundation, and CAIDA, DARPA, Digital Envoy, and CAIDA Members.

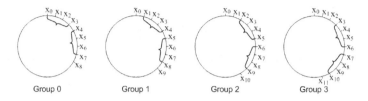

Fig. 2. The four groups of all possible 2^{32} quadruplets (2^{30} in each group) the witty worm could generate

Algorithm 2), four different groups, each consisting of 2^{30} different quadruplets, could be created as shown in Figure 2. x_0, x_1, ..., x_{11} lays consecutively on the single group of 2^{32} numbers generated using equation 1, with $a = 214013$ and $b = 2531011$ (these values of a and b generate only a single group of size 2^{32}).

By matching each content of a scan for an infective k (i.e. the upper two bytes and lower two bytes of the destination IP address, the destination port number and the payload size) to the upper two bytes of each generated number in each quadruplet in each group, it was possible to determine the group each scan belonged to and $\widehat{\mathcal{D}}'^k$ could be constructed for every 20000 scans (refer to Figure 1). $\widehat{\mathcal{D}}''^k$ was built such that:

$$\mathcal{N}(\mathcal{L}^k_{-1}) + \mathcal{N}(\widehat{\mathcal{D}}'^k) = 20000 \qquad and \qquad \mathcal{N}(\mathcal{L}^k_N) + \mathcal{N}(\widehat{\mathcal{D}}'^k) = 20000$$

Thus $\mathcal{N}(\widehat{\mathcal{D}}'^k) + \mathcal{N}(\widehat{\mathcal{D}}''^k) \geq 20000$.

Here, $\mathcal{D}^k$ and $\widehat{\mathcal{D}}^k$ consist of quadruplets (such as x_0, x_1, x_2, x_3) and not a single value (i.e. a single IP address value) like it is the case with the Slammer worm. Also, for clarity, we will denote $\widehat{\mathcal{D}}^k[i]$ here as the ith set of list of possible 20000+ consecutive quadruplets embedded in the scans of infective k. Now that i different sets are built per infective, we can deduce the seeds and consequently $\mathcal{D}^k$.

Discovering the Seeds and Other Forensics. By looking at the broader picture where each quadruplet is one entity produced by the LCPRNG, we could deduce from Algorithm 2 that the witty worm reseeded its LCPRNG in two different ways. The first way happens after each 20000 scans whenever the witty worm uses its LCPRNG to generate the number of physical drive it needs to write on but opening the target physical drive fails. For instance, assume x_0, x_1, x_2 and x_3 in Figure 2 to be the quadruplet used in the 20000th scan, x_4 will thus be used to determine the number of the physical drive to write on. If opening the physical drive for write fails, the next 20000 scans will start with the quadruplet x_5, x_6, x_7 and x_8 (i.e., the group shifted from 0 to 1 and thus seeded with x_4). The second type of reseeding happens when writing to the selected physical drive succeeds. The worm will then reuse the function GetTickCount to reseed the LCPRNG. In that case, the next 20000 scans will fall in any group 0, 1, 2 or 3 depending on the value returned by GetTickCount.

Before being able to discover the seeds, it is imperative to determine which way the worm reseeded. Given two consecutive sets $\widehat{\mathcal{D}}^k[i]$ and $\widehat{\mathcal{D}}^k[i+1]$, let $G^k[i]$

and $G^k[i+1]$ be the groups the sets fall in (or belong to) respectively. We can say that the worm tried to open a target physical drive but failed to if

$$(G^k[i] + 1) \bmod 4 = G^k[i+1] \bmod 4 \quad and \quad \mathcal{L}_N^k[i] \cap \mathcal{L}_{-1}^k[i+1] \neq \varnothing, \quad (8)$$

where $\mathcal{L}_N^k[i] \in \widehat{\mathcal{D}}''^k[i]$, $\mathcal{L}_{-1}^k[i+1] \in \widehat{\mathcal{D}}''^k[i+1]$. Otherwise, if

$$(G^k[i] + 1) \bmod 4 \neq G^k[i+1] \bmod 4 \tag{9}$$
$$or \ (G^k[i] + 1) \bmod 4 = G^k[i+1] \bmod 4 \tag{10}$$
$$and \ \mathcal{L}_N^k[i] \cap \mathcal{L}_{-1}^k[i+1] = \varnothing \tag{11}$$

then the worm wrote to the physical drive and reseeded its LCPRNG using the returned value from GetTickCount.

In the latter case, the values of the seeds returned by GetTickCount can be discovered by checking the following condition given that $\curlyvee x \in \mathcal{L}_{-1}^k[0]$ and $\curlyvee x' \in \mathcal{L}_{-1}^k[i+1]$, if

$$|(\widehat{T}(x') - \widehat{T}(x)) - (x' - x)| < \epsilon \tag{12}$$

then x is the initial seed (i.e., the first seed the worm used) and x' is another seed returned by GetTickCount when the worm succeeded to write on a physical drive. In our experience of dealing with the witty worm traces, $\epsilon = 1 \ sec$ was more than enough to capture the value of the seeds. Since this condition could yield multiple different values of x and x', it is sometimes required that the worm have reseeded (i.e. used the GetTickCount) more than once in order to accurately identify the initial seed and the remaining seeds. Once the seeds are determined, the complete list of scans can be reproduced including the destination IP addresses, destination port addresses, the size of the scan packet. We also can determine the number of physical drives that exist on each infective, the location on the physical drive the worm overwrote and the infection tree.

Results and Challenges. We concentrated our study on the first 100 infectives as they appeared on the CAIDA network telescope. The estimated time of each scan was generated using equations 3 and 4, while we recreated the complete lists of scans sent by each infective and their seeds. Surprisingly, the scanning behavior of the first infective that appeared on CAIDA's network telescope did not conform to the Witty's algorithm. The first infective scanned IP addresses of the form A.B.A.B (lower and upper two bytes are similar) and the payload size was fixed to 675 bytes. The remaining 99 infectives used Algorithm 2 to spread. By reproducing the scans of each infective, it appeared that, like CAIDA expected, most of the first 100 infectives were targeted through a hitlist. It is not possible to know if the first infective (i.e. the one that did not conform to the Witty's algorithm) was the one the attacker launched his attack from or another compromised end-system that used only a hitlist and thus never appeared on the network telescope. Table 2 shows some interesting forensics about some infected machines. As we know the witty worm reseeded its random

Table 2. Interesting forensics about some infectives

Infective's ID	Seeds Returned by GetTick-Count	Estimated Time of First Scan	Approx. Link Bandwidth	Number of physical drive	Overwriting 64KB Starting From Location		
3	2410921000, 2410945609, 2410950531, 2410957078	1079757936.71	100 Mbps	1	2089700896 (on drive 0), 2077511200 (on drive 0), 764300832 (on drive 0)		
20	2550872765, 2551156125, 2551272812, 2551572968	1079757937.04	10 Mbps	1	1291734560 (on drive 0), 579948064 (on drive 0), 534072864 (on drive 0)		
43	2168703410, 2168714927, 2168761373, 2168766301	1079757937.38	100 Mbps	1	652955168 (on drive 0), 1005145632 (on drive 0), 1263488544 (on drive 0)		
78	2169079812, 2169082515, 2169085234, 2169101937	1079757939.19	59 Mbps	3	1361202720 (on drive 2), 1175408160 (on drive 0), 413216 (on drive 1)		

number generator whenever it was able to write a portion of data onto the infected machine's physical drive. We listed the first four seeds returned by GetTickCount. The second, third and fourth seeds are generated whenever the worm succeeds to write on an existing physical drive. For instance, in the case of infective number 3, the first seed that GetTickCount returned was 2410921000. Infective 3 generated scans continuously as per Algorithm 2 until it succeeded to write 64Kbytes of data to location 2089700896 on physical drive 0. At that point, the worm reseeded its LCPRNG by calling GetTickCount again. The value returned was 2410945609. We were also able to determine how many physical drives existed on each infective and the approximate bandwidth of the network link the infectives were connected to. We also built a preliminary infection tree as depicted in Figure 3 that shows how some of the first 100 infectives infected some of the first 250 infectives. Note that we found that infective 58 infected end-system 43 even though the first scan to the network telescope from 43 appeared before the first scan from 58. This was due to the fact that the first tens of scans from 58 to the network telescope never arrived (i.e. dropped) due to congestion somewhere in the network.

During our analysis of the witty worm, we were faced with many challenges. Some scans reached the network telescope out of order but we were able to use the identification field in each scan to determine the real order they were sent in. Some infectives were attached to a 1Gbps link (i.e. spawning 120000 scans per seconds on average) and caused the Identification field to wrap around multiple times. As a result, we had to use the ordered sequence of quadruplets (Figure 2) to re-order out-of-order scans. Another problem we faced was multiple infectives behind Network Address Translations (NATs). Though it was still possible to identify each one by looking at the identification field and the group (Figure 2) the scans belonged to, recollecting the scans was a tedious matter. The most

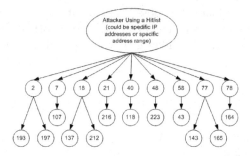

Fig. 3. An infection subtree for the first 250 infectives

serious challenge we faced while dealing with the witty traces was the loss of scans for multiple seconds and sometimes more than a minute. During that period of time, a worm may have reseeded its LCPRNG using the value returned by GetTickCount multiple times and the only way to recover those scans (that were never logged or received by the network telescope during that period of time) would be through a brute force method. However, once this interruption period stopped, we were able to continue recovering subsequent seeds and recreate the complete lists of scans. Thus unlike the analysis of slammer worm, which is much less sensitive to the loss of scans (because the Slammer worm never reseeded its LCPRNG and because we can recreate all subsequent scans using Figure 1 even if scans are lost for multiple seconds or minutes), each scan is equally important when it comes to the analysis of the witty worm.

6   Discussion and Conclusion

We introduced a framework for the forensic analysis of scanning worms. We focused on building the general infection tree and also gather information about the infected end-systems (such as the number of physical drives, the number of milliseconds since the infective was started, etc.) from scans that traverse any /8 network telescope. Actually, by simply looking at the reverse-engineered code of a worm, one could tell what information one could expect to learn about the infectives. We do not advocate that this method will work for all kinds of scanning worms but it is a very good step forward toward a framework for forensics analysis of scanning worms. For instance, the MSBlaster worm scanned linear IP addresses continuously and therefore cannot be analyzed as described in this paper unless there exists a widely spread distributed monitoring system. That justifies the need for a distributed monitoring system (for instance multiple /16 network telescopes on different /8 networks). Also, an attacker could write a worm where the value of b of the LCPRNG can be randomly modified; however, this also can be reverse-engineered since the random number generator used will always be known (either embedded in the worm payload or part of the operating system), but the analysis of such worm would be, as a result, more time consuming and difficult but possible. Thus it is good to note that the way to analyze a worm could differ from one worm to another but the general idea is to use the pseudo random number generator of scanning worms to rebuild the whole infection scenario.

References

1. Eeye Digital Security: Sapphire Worm Code Disassembled. http://www.eeye.com/html/Research/Flash/sapphire.txt (2003)
2. Hamadeh, I., Kesidis, G.: Performance of IP address fragmentation strategies for DDoS Traceback. In the Proceedings IEEE Workshop on IP Operations and Management (IPOM) (2003)
3. Kumar, A., Paxson, V., Weaver, N.: Exploiting Underlying Structure for Detailed Reconstruction of an Internet-scale Event. In the Proceedings of ACM IMC (2005)
4. Lehmer, D. H.: Mathematical methods in large-scale computing units. In the Proceedings of the 2nd Symposium on Large-Scale Digital Calculating Machinery (1951)
5. Moore, D., Paxson, V., Savage, S., Shannon, C., Staniford, S., Weaver, N.: The Spread of the Sapphire/Slammer Worm. The Cooperative Association for Internet Data Analysis. http://www.caida.org/outreach/papers/2003/sapphire/sapphire.html (2003)
6. Murphy, M.: ISS PAM/ICQ Witty Worm Analysis. http://www.netsecure.shawbiz.ca/witty-analysis.html (2004)
7. University of Michigan Internet Motion Sensor. http://ims.eecs.umich.edu/index.html
8. University of Wisconsin-Madison Advanced Internet Laboratory. http://wail.cs.wisc.edu/
9. Cooperative Association for Internet Data Analysis (CAIDA).UCSD Network Telescope. http://www.caida.org/analysis/security/telescope/
10. Savage, S., Wetherall, D., Karlin, A., Anderson, T.: Practical Network Support for IP Traceback. In the Proceedings ACM SIGCOMM (2000)
11. Shannon, C., Moore, D.: The Spread of the Witty Worm. The Cooperative Association for Internet Data Analysis. http://www.caida.org/analysis/security/witty/ (2004)
12. Snoeren, A.C., Partridge, C., Sanchez, L.A., Jones, C.E., Tchakountio, F., Kent, S.T., Strayer, W.T.: Hash-Based IP Traceback. In the Proceedings ACM SIGCOMM (2001)
13. Staniford S., Paxson, V., Weaver, N.: How to Own the Internet in Your Spare Time (2002)
14. Staniford-Chen, S., Cheung, S., Crawford, R., Dilger, M., Frank, J., Hoagland, J., Levitt, K., Wee, C., Yip, R., Zerkle, D.: GrIDS - A Graph Based Intrustion Detection System for Large Networks. In the Proceedings of the 19th National Information Systems Security Conference (1996)
15. Staniford, S.: Containment of Scanning Worms in Enterprise Networks. Journal of Computer Security (2004)
16. Weaver, N., Hamadeh, I., Kesidis, G., Paxson, V.: Preliminary results using scale-down to explore worm dynamics. In the Proceedings of the ACM CCS workshop on Rapid malcode (2004)

17. Whyte, D., Kranakis, E., Van Oorschot, P.C.: DNS-based Detection of Scanning Worms in an Enterprise Network. Network and Distributed System Security Symposium (2005)
18. Williamson, M.M.: Throttling Viruses: Restricting Propagation to Defeat Mobile Malicious Code. In the Proceedings of the 18th Annual Computer Security Applications Conference (2002)
19. Xie, Y., Sekar, V., Maltz, D., Reiter, M., Zhang, H.: Worm Origin Identification Using Random Moonwalks. In the Proceedings of the IEEE Symposium on Security and Privacy (2005)
20. Zou, C., Gong, W., Towsley, D.: Worm Propagation Modeling and Analysis under Dynamic Quarantine Defense. In the Proceedings of the ACM CCS workshop on Rapid malcode (2003)

A Comparison of Market Approaches to Software Vulnerability Disclosure

Rainer Böhme

Technische Universität Dresden
Institute for System Architecture
01062 Dresden, Germany
rainer.boehme@tu-dresden.de

Abstract. Practical computer (in)security is largely driven by the existence of and knowledge about vulnerabilities, which can be exploited to breach security mechanisms. Although the discussion on details of responsible vulnerability disclosure is controversial, there is a sort of consensus that better information sharing is socially beneficial. In the recent years we observe the emerging of "vulnerability markets" as means to stimulate exchange of information. However, this term subsumes a broad range of different concepts, which are prone to confusion. This paper provides a first attempt to structure the field by (1) proposing a terminology for distinct concepts and (2) defining criteria to allow for a better comparability between different approaches. An application of this framework on four market types shows notable differences between the approaches.

1 Introduction

Vulnerabilities are errors in computer systems which can be exploited to breach security mechanisms. They typically emerge during software development and some remain undiscovered in the final product, largely because common software testing methods are not designed to detect errors that require strategic interaction of a malicious party. However, widely deployed software is subject to public scrutiny that leads to the discovery of vulnerabilities. Information about new (i.e., recently discovered) vulnerabilities is highly valuable as it decides about the success of attack or defense in open computer networks: *malicious users* may use the information to launch attacks on vulnerable systems, whereas *honest users* have an interest to assess the security risks they are exposed to and to decide about appropriate countermeasures, such as demanding a patch from the vendor or switching to a competitor's product. Hence, as long as perfectly secure software is not available, the optimal distribution of vulnerability information is an important factor for the stability of a "network society" [1, 2, 3, 4].

The distribution of vulnerability information, however, is rarely a technical problem but rather a result of rational decision-making of the parties involved: Why should a teenage computer freak report the outcome of his leisure-time efforts to the public if he can increase his pocket money by selling crucial information on the black market? Why should a software vendor invest time and

G. Müller (Ed.): ETRICS 2006, LNCS 3995, pp. 298–311, 2006.
© Springer-Verlag Berlin Heidelberg 2006

money in secure programming, when his competitor does not, and his customers cannot measure the difference in quality? These questions motivate to regard computer security from the point of view of economics, a discipline studying rational decision-making of independent agents. A good introduction to the field of economics and information security can be found in Ross Anderson's seminal article [5].

The interest in "vulnerability markets" can be partly attributed to theoretical work in this interdisciplinary community. In addition, recent developments, such as vulnerabilities being offered on online auctions and security firms allotting rewards for vulnerability reports, contribute to the public attention. However, sometimes completely different concepts are referred to as "vulnerability markets", which is a source for confusion. Therefore, this paper aims to structure the area by presenting a typology of vulnerability markets. Moreover, a criteria-based framework for the comparison of different market types is proposed.

The remainder of this paper is structured as follows: Section 2 briefly summarises economic reasons for the deficit in nowadays computer security and explains how vulnerability markets could change this situation to the better. Section 3 presents a typology of vulnerability markets in the literature and discusses their similarities and differences. In Section 4, a set of criteria based on the anticipated positive effects (see Section 2) is defined and then applied for a systematic comparison of different market types. Section 5 concludes the paper with pointers to existing limitations and possible future research.

2   The Computer Security Market Failure

Before discussing the effects of vulnerability markets, we sketch two examples illustrating how the market currently fails in providing computer security.

The first example refers to the supply-side for security technology. Its theoretical background is George Akerlof's lemon market problem [6]. Akerlof studied the rules of a market with asymmetrical information between buyer and seller. For instance, the typical buyer of a second hand car cannot distinguish between good offers and bad ones (so-called "lemons"), because—unlike the seller—he does not know the true history of the car. So the buyer is not willing to pay more than the price of a lemon. As a result, used cars in good condition will be under-provided on the market. The same applies to computer security: security is not visible and thus becomes a trust good. Since the buyer is unable to differentiate secure from insecure products apart, the market price drops to the level for insecure products. Hence, vendors have little incentive to develop sound security technology and some might rather prefer to invest in more visible features, or to be first on the market to dominate the technological standard [7].

The second example targets to the demand-side of security. Its theoretical roots lie in the popular "tragedy of the commons", another economic theory published by Garrett Hardin [8]. Consider a computer network and the threat of botnets [9], where security is rather a property of the network than of its individual nodes: if the weakest node gets corrupted then the other nodes face a high risk of being attacked and consequently face higher expected loss. Therefore, the cost of security incidents is distributed among all nodes. On the other hand, if one node decides to invest in security, then all computers in the network benefit, because the now secure node is less likely to cause harm to others from forwarded malicious traffic. In brief, since both risk and benefits are socialised between all nodes, individuals lack the incentive to unilaterally invest in security. They prefer to remain "free riders" waiting for others to pay in their place (who'll never do so, because of the same rationale; see [10] for a rigorous analysis).

To sum it all up, the lemon market suggests that vendors under-provide security to the market, whereas the tragedy of the commons can explain why users demand less security than appropriate. A common notion for this deadlock is *market failure*.

The collection of reasons for the market failure is by far incomplete[1] but it is enough to characterise the problem and to derive objectives to mitigate it. To counter the lemmon effect, security has to become measurable [13]. The free rider problem can be solved by redistributing the costs in a way that nodes are made responsible to bear all costs and receive full utility of their own decisions. In micro-economic terms this corresponds to an "internalisation of externalities"; or, as we might frankly say, tax bad security [14].

There are two ways to fix a market failure. At first, regulation—which is least desirable as there are numerous examples where regulation renders the situation even worse. Indeed, good regulation is really difficult since it often implies a trusted third party (TTP) as "social planner", whom to make incorruptible is costly, if not impossible. There exists a large body of literature on public choice theory, which studies imperfections due to state interventions and adverse incentives in government decision-making [15, 16]. Note that we hesitate to argue that regulation of computer security is generally a bad idea or inferior to market approaches. We rather consider it as an option which needs to be studied, though it is beyond the scope of this paper.

The second possible response to a market failure is establishing new markets with mechanisms that eventually feedback and thus mitigate the problems at their source. If the markets are designed properly, then market prices serve as valid indicators for underlying security properties and thus make security measurable. Moreover, markets can well differentiate between good and bad security. For instance, cyber-insurance contracts could contain deductions for customers where good security technology and practices are in place. Conversely, users who do not invest appropriately in security pay a higher premium, which corresponds to the objective of taxing bad security.

This is the theoretical justification for vulnerability markets. In the following section we present concrete concepts for vulnerability markets before we discuss how suitable each concept is to counter the market failure.

---

[1] Another often-cited topic is the discussion on software liability [11, 12], which we omit for the sake of brevity.

Table 1. Alternative names for vulnerability markets in the literature

Proposed term	Equivalents in the literature
Bug challenges	*vulnerability markets* in [13]
	bug auctions in [17, 18]
	bug bounties on some blogs
Vulnerability brokers	*vulnerability markets* in [19]
	also *vulnerability sharing circles*
Exploit derivatives	related to *security tokens* in [20], but not the same
	prediction markets in more general contexts
Cyber-insurance	(not ambiguous)

3   Classifying Vulnerability Markets

This section contains a typology of possible market concepts for security-related information. Note that our terminology is deliberately not consistent with all prior art, because some terms have been used ambiguously in the past. Therefore, we collected alternative names for each concept together with the corresponding references in Table 1.

3.1   Bug Challenges

Bug challenges are the oldest concept to "prove" the security strength of a product, or to guarantee invisible properties of traded goods in general. In the simplest scenario, the vendor allots a monetary reward for vulnerability reports related to his product. Then the amount of the reward is a lower bound to the security strength of the product: it can be safely used to handle and secure assets totalling up to this amount because a rational adversary would prefer to report possible vulnerabilities and cash the reward over attacking the system and capitalising the information gained. Stuart Schechter coined the term *market price of vulnerability* (MPV) for a metric derived from this model [13]. Examples for simple bug challenges in the real world include the Mozilla Security Bug Bounty Program[2], the RSA factoring contests, and the Argus Security Challenges[3].

One of the main issues in bug challenges is the difficulty to find an appropriate level of reward. Therefore, several extensions to fixed-sum bug challenges have been proposed in the literature. For example, the reward could be initialised at a very low level and then gradually grow over time. The most widely known example of this type is Donald E. Knuth's reward of initially 1.28 USD for each bug in his TeX typesetting system. His reward grows exponentially with the

---

[2] http://www.mozilla.org/security/bug-bounty.html

[3] http://www.wired.com/news/technology/0,1282,43234,00.html; its aftermath demonstrates the need for a trusted third party to settle the deals: http://www.net-security.org/news.php?id=1522.

number of years the program is in use. To limit the expenses, the vulnerability buyer may decide to reset the reward after each vulnerability report [13].

This scheme allows for a certain dynamic in price-setting, which is similar to market mechanisms designed as auctions [17]. This is the reason why bug challenges are sometimes referred to as "bug auctions", which *should not be mistaken* as offering vulnerability reports on auction platforms such as eBay.[4] For a precise terminology, we propose to distinguish between *buyer-administered* bug auctions and *seller-administered* bug auctions.

Even with this extension, the price quote is not always a reliable indicator for the true security of a product. Consider the case where two vulnerabilities are discovered at the same time. A rational agent would sell the first one and then wait with the second release until the reward has climbed back to a worthwhile amount. In the meantime, the mechanism fails completely in aggregating information about the security of a product, and prudent users should stop using it until the reward signals again a desirable level of security.

As to the operational aspects, it is still questionable whether the rewards can ever be high enough to secure the accumulated assets at risk for software with large installation bases in critical environments, such as finance, health care, or governmental use. Even when taking into account that the actual amount can be smaller than the assets at stake by assuming a risk-averse adversary (the reward is certain whereas making a fortune as black-hat is risky), the so-reduced sum still requires a financial commitment of vulnerability-buyers which exceeds the tangible assets of many software vendors, let alone the case of open source software or depreciated systems, where the vendor ceased to exists.

3.2 Vulnerability Brokers

Vulnerability brokers are often referred to as "vulnerability sharing circles". These clubs are built around independent organisations, mostly private companies, who offer money for new vulnerability reports. They then circulate the acquired information within a closed group of subscribers to their security alert service. The customer bases are said to consist of both vendors, who thus learn about bugs to fix, and corporate users, who want to protect their systems even before a patch becomes available. In the standard model, only honest users are assumed to join the club, though it might be very difficult to enforce this policy in practice.[5] With annual subscription fees of more than ten times the reward for a vulnerability report, the business model seems so profitable that there are multiple players in the market: iDefense was first with its "Vulnerability Contributor Program", TippingPoint/3COM followed with a "Zero-day Initiative" and Digital Armaments also offers money or barter deals for vulnerability information. This kind of competition increased the (publicly communicated) reward sums to 4-digit dollar amounts per bug and led to sophisticated bonus schemes,

---

[4] http://it.slashdot.org/article.pl?sid=05/12/12/1215220

[5] It is remarkable that Nizovtsev and Thursby in [3] model the proportion of 'black hats' within vulnerability sharing circles equal to the proportion in the population. They justify this decision with frequent reports of insider attacks.

which resemble customer loyalty plans. This business model has been criticised as blackmail, because vendors and users are forced to subscribe to all services in order to avoid missing important information, even when the frequency of actually relevant reports is very low.

A technically similar but socially more acceptable service is offered by CERT (Computer Emergency Response Team). It also acts as a vulnerability broker, albeit on a non-profit basis. It does not pay any reward for reporting vulnerability information and disseminates that information for free. A recent paper compares the social welfare of vulnerability markets (more precisely: commercial vulnerability brokers) with the CERT approach [19]. The authors conclude that a single CERT acting as a social planner always performs better than commercial brokers.[6] Being exposed to competition with commercial brokers, however, the authors suggest for a CERT-type model to offer monetary rewards as well. This, in turn, means that it must be subsidised from public money (which reduced overall welfare) and it remains unclear how to assure that the social planner works efficiently and turns away from hidden action.

3.3 Exploit Derivatives

Exploit derivatives apply the idea of binary options, as known in the theory of financial markets, to computer security events. Instead of trading sensitive vulnerability information directly—with all its negative consequences from trading information goods—, a market is constructed for contracts with pay-out functions *derived* from security events [18].

Consider a pair of contracts $(C, \bar{C})$, where C pays a fixed amount of money, say 100 EUR, if there exists a remote root exploit against some specified server software X on platform Y at date D in the future. The inverse contract, $\bar{C}$ pays out the same face value if there is *no* remote root exploit submitted to a market authority—not a trusted third party in a strict sense—before date D. It is evident that the value of the bundle $(C, \bar{C})$ is 100 EUR at any time and that selling and buying it is risk-free.[7] Therefore, one or many market makers can issue as many bundles as demanded by the market participants. Now assume that there is an exchange platform, where the contracts C and $\bar{C}$ can be traded individually at prices determined by matching bid and ask orders. Then the ratio of the market price of C and its face value approximately indicates the probability of software X being compromised before date D.

The accuracy of the price information depends on the liquidity of the market, hence for accuracy we need a high number of participants and low transaction costs. This market type, however, has the potential to attract far more groups of participants than bug challenges or vulnerability brokers. Software users would demand contracts C in order to hedge the risks they are exposed to due to

---

[6] Note that the authors come from Carnegie Mellon University, which hosts the headquarters of CERT/CC.

[7] Ignoring interest rate yield of alternative investment, which can be easily compensated for, but is omitted here for the sake of brevity.

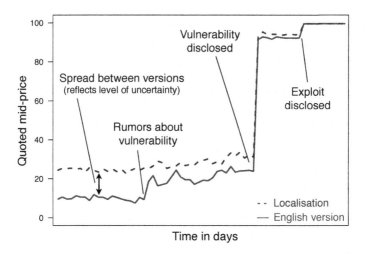

Fig. 1. Relation of events and price quotes of hypothetical exploit derivatives

their computer systems in place. The same applies for cyber-insurance companies underwriting their customers' cyber-risks. Conversely, investors would buy contracts $\bar{C}$ to diversify their portfolios. Software vendors could demand both types of contracts: contracts $\bar{C}$ that pay if their software remains secure as a means to signal to their customers that they trust their own system; or contracts C_{comp} that pay if their competitors' software gets compromised. One could even think of software vendors using exploit derivatives as part of their compensation schemes to give developers an incentive to secure programming.

Finally, security experts (a.k.a. "vulnerability hunters") could use the market to capitalise efforts in security analyses. If, after a code review, they consider a software as secure, they could buy contracts $\bar{C}$ at a higher rate than the market price. Otherwise they buy contracts C and afterwards follow their preferred vulnerability disclosure strategy. As interaction on the market influences the price, the quotes are constantly updated and can be used as reliable indicators for security strength. Note that this concept does not require the co-operation of the vendor, and the number of different contracts referring to different pieces of software, versions, localisations, etc., is solely limited by demand.

Figure 1 displays a hypothetical price development for an exploit derivative over time. The price quotes reflect changes in the expected security level of the underlying software. Combining information from more than one contract allows for even more interesting metrics. Differences between related contracts ("spreads" in financial terms) can be directly attributed to variations in security or public scrutiny between well-defined technical differences. In the figure, this is illustrated as differences in the perceived security between two localisations of the same software. In addition, joint probabilities of failure can be computed from pairs of contracts to measure the total security of cascaded protection mechanisms.

Like other market types, exploit derivatives require a trusted third party to test candidate exploits at the end of each contract and announce the result. However, if the TTP is required to publish the exploit candidates together with the announcement, it becomes verifiable and cannot cheat. The job can also be distributed to a number of TTPs. Therefore, the assumptions about the TTP are much gentler in this scenario than in other market types.

The concept of exploit derivatives is a modification of seminal work by Kanta Matsuura [20]. He studied the use of option pricing models to assess the risk of cryptographically secured digital objects being compromised. Exploit derivatives, unlike Matsuura's *security tokens*, start with modelling the risk of *components* or mechanisms being compromised rather assessing the risk of loosing the value of the *content* processed in the system. This generalisation, however, does not limit the range of applications at all, because given a set of critical components it is possible to choose a portfolio that exactly matches the risk profile of the defined system. The total value of its content can be matched in a second step by a linear adjustment of the investment volume up to the desired level. In this framework one can even think of cyber-insurance companies being merely intermediaries to whom users and firms outsource their exploit derivatives portfolio management. This guides us to the remaining type of vulnerability markets.

3.4 Cyber-Insurance

Cyber-insurance is among the oldest proposals for market mechanisms to overcome the security market failure (see [21, 22, 23, 24, 11]). The idea that cures the market failure goes as follows: end users demand insurance against financial losses from information security breaches and insurance companies sell this kind of coverage after a security audit. The premium is assumed to be adjusted by the individual risk, which depends on the IT systems in use and the security practices in place. Therefore, it would be costly to buy insurance coverage for insecure software. This gives users an incentive to invest in security technology. One would even raise the willingness to pay more for secure products if—in the long run—the total cost of ownership including insurance premiums is below the expenses for a less secure product.

In theory, on a long-term average the premiums converge to the actual security risk (plus a constant overhead) because competition sets an upper and profitability a lower bound. Premiums are never completely ill-aligned (like in bug challenges after a reset of the reward). In contrast to bug challenges and exploit derivatives, the premiums are adjusted to each individual insured's risk profile and not on the expected security strength of standard components. This tailored nature is advantageous for the application as a metric, because an organisation or a system is measured on the whole and there is no need for sophisticated and error-prone aggregation to high-level indicators.

However, despite the presence of potent insurance companies, cyber-insurance business remains on a comparatively low volume. One of the reasons could be that insurance companies hesitate in underwriting cyber-risks, because the losses from information security risks are highly correlated globally—think about viruses and worms, and the lack of diversity in installed platforms. This concentration of risk is contrary to the insurance principle of portfolio balancing and requires additional safety premiums that render cyber-insurance policies economically uninteresting [25]. Apart from the fear of "cyber-hurricanes", there are other operational obstacles, such as the difficulty to substantiate claims, the intangible nature of cyber-assets, and unclear legal grounds.

4   Comparison of Market Types

The typology presented in the previous section demonstrates that there is not one "vulnerability market" but rather a family of different concepts. It also becomes evident that the different mechanisms are hardly comparable per se. Nevertheless we try to tackle the research question which market type serves best to counter the security market failure by defining a set of criteria that allow for a more objective comparison. For an ideal vulnerability market, with respect to its ability to counter the security market failure, we have identified three functions, which are elaborated in detail below.

4.1   Information Function

The information function refers to the possibility to use market prices as forward-looking indicators for security properties. This function is important to counter the lemon effect because it makes security measurable. It can be divided in sub-dimensions, such as the accuracy of price information, its timeliness and availability to the public.

Some empirical studies show that even existing stock markets do accumulate information related to security events [26, 27, 28, 29]. However, stock markets aggregate a large set of different information so that only very extreme security events can be identified in the stochastic movements of market prices. Consequently, an ideal vulnerability market should isolate security-relevant information from other sources of noise and distortion.

4.2   Incentive Function

The incentive function addresses the monetary compensation for security research and development. It motivates firms and individuals to participate in the exchange of vulnerability information. Possible incentives from vulnerability markets include incentives for individual bug hunters as well as incentives for developers.

In the absence of operable vulnerability markets, individual bug hunters are motivated by altruism and the prospect of reputation, and—perhaps—by monetary compensation on the black market. Vulnerability markets add monetary rewards on top of the gain in reputation and, depending on the price level, may convince bug hunters to turn away from selling on the black market.

The sole motivation for software developers to invest in security is trust of satisfied customers, which can be capitalised in the long run only. Vulnerability markets add short-term profits and competitive advantage on top of the long-term benefits. With hyperbolic discounting of (uncertain) future revenues [30] and a general tendency to short-term oriented management decisions, vulnerability markets thus add a strong incentive to give security a higher priority.

4.3   Risk-Balancing Function

The risk balancing function means that the vulnerability market provides instruments to hedge against large information security risks. This is important to mitigate the financial impact of (occasional) security breaches, which may help firms to survive attacks rather than filing for bankruptcy with all its adverse social and economic consequences.

It is also the risk balancing function which contributes to the objective of taxing bad security, both directly and indirectly. The direct effect comes from the fact that instruments covering extreme events are less costly if the extreme events become less likely. The probability of failure, in turn, is related to the level of security (in terms of resistance against attacks) and exposure (in terms of likelihood of being targeted by an attack). As exposure is said to depend largely on how widely a system is deployed, diversity gets rewarded as well. Since diversity is a desirable security property on an aggregated level [31, 32, 25], the risk balancing function taxes bad security also indirectly.

4.4   Market Efficiency

Orthogonal to the functions, market efficiency is a criterion which expresses the absence of additional burden in realising the functions. Therefore, efficiency should be regarded as a property of the market, which subsumes the following aspects:

- low transaction costs (it is inexpensive to participate in the market)
- liquidity (high number of participants and possible trade counterparts)
- accountability (low counterparty risk)
- transparency (fair rules, public price quotes)

Not all of these properties are necessary to make vulnerability markets operable, but any of them increases the potential of a vulnerability market to actually counter the security market failure. There exist also a number of dependencies between these sub-dimensions. For example, low transaction costs allow more people to participate in the market and thus automatically improve the liquidity; accountability reduces the transaction costs because the average loss due to unsettled positions decreases, asf.

4.5   A Provisional Assessment of Market Types

Putting the three functions and the efficiency property together, gives us a framework for a structured comparison of the market types discussed in Section 3. A

Table 2. Comparison of Vulnerability Markets

| Market type | Criterion | | | |
	Infomation	Incentives	Risk-balancing	Efficiency
Bug challenges	−	+	− −	−
Vulnerability brokers	− −	±	− −	− −
Exploit derivatives	++	+	+	+
Cyber-insurance	+	++	++	−

Symbols ranging from − − (poor) to ++ (excellent)

summary of the correspondence of each market type to the criteria is given in Table 2. Note that the evaluation is based on a qualitative assessment and should be regarded as a starting point for exchanges of view rather than as outright evidence. Some arguments backing the relative assessment of different market types are given below.

The incentive function is fulfilled by all market types, though to varying degree. The ambivalent evaluation for vulnerability brokers is due to the questionable incentives created for adversaries to join the circle in order to obtain sensitive vulnerability information before the general public [3]. Conversely, we consider cyber-insurance as particularly good at the incentive function because the incentives to give security a higher priority are not limited to bug hunters and developers, but also affect the end user. This fosters security awareness on a large basis.

As to the information function, bug challenges fail to provide accurate indicators when vulnerabilities are reported frequently. Vulnerability brokers do not reveal timely information to the public at all. Even worse, the usual practice of requiring vulnerability discoverers to sign non-disclosure agreements hinders the vital exchange of security-relevant information. We consider exploit derivatives as superior to cyber-insurance, because insurance contracts are re-negotiated less frequently, which negatively affects the timeliness of a price indicator. And it is questionable whether price information on actual cyber-insurance contracts—not merely unspecified offers—will ever be made available to the public on a large and regular basis. This together with the presumably high transaction costs of insurance contracts justifies a slightly negative assessment of cyber-insurance with respect to efficiency.

Bug challenges and vulnerability brokers provide no risk-balancing instruments at all. Exploit derivatives are somewhat worse than cyber-insurance because it is more difficult to manage optimal portfolios for individual risk profiles when the pay-outs are defined by global events rather than by a firm's individual losses.

Overall, it appears that exploit derivatives and cyber-insurance are both acceptable concepts for vulnerability markets, and it is a matter of fact that both can complement one another.

5   Concluding Remarks

This paper contributes to the literature on vulnerability disclosure policy and economics of information security by differentiating classes for vulnerability market concepts. Moreover, criteria for a better comparability of market types with regard to their potential as tools to moderate the flow of security-relevant information have been proposed. An application of this framework to four market types resulted in a qualitative assessment, which may serve as a first guideline for practitioners in the security industry as well as for policy makers on topics related to information security. Primarily, however, it is intended to be a starting point for academic discussion on the basis of further refined analyses and more rigorous models.

As to future research, there remains to be written chapters on possible conflicts of interest, and on the consequences for disclosure policies. The entire comparison could be repeated on the basis of formal models for each of the market types. Although it might be tricky to model all properties, it will help to understand the exact conditions under which each market type performs optimal.

There is also room for more general critiques on the market approach. One might question whether vulnerability hunting actually leads to more secure products because the supply of vulnerabilities is deemed to be unlimited [4]. So why bother putting market incentives in place for something allegedly useless? (See [33] for a discussion and evidence *for* vulnerability hunting.) Moreover, it is well-known that markets tend to err in the short term—but it is still very difficult to outpace existing markets in the long run. Therefore, we need to assess the harm a "vulnerability market bubble" potentially causes, and weight it against the welfare gains from better information, more secure products, and the possibility to hedge information security risks.

Finally, it is important to ask the questions whether a closer link between information security and financial markets is desirable at all from a stability point of view. A higher interdependency between two previously separate systems implies also a larger sensitivity to mutual shocks, even if the now combined system is less likely to face extreme outcomes because of better risk sharing. Whatever mechanisms get implemented in practice, an individual virus author's potential to halt computers in offices all over the world (which already translates to enormous financial losses) must not get leveraged to cause global asset price deterioration.

Acknowledgements

The author gratefully acknowledges the valuable comments he received from Thorsten Holz, Gaurav Kataria, and Andy Ozment.

References

1. Arora, A., Telang, R., Xu, H.: Optimal policy for software vulnerability disclosure. In: *Workshop on the Economics of Information Security (WEIS)*, University of Minnesota, Minneapolis, MN (2004) http://www.dtc.umn.edu/weis2004/xu.pdf.

2. Arora, A., Krishnan, R., Telang, R., Yang, Y.: An empirical analysis of vendor response to software vulnerability disclosure. In: *Workshop on Information Systems and Economics (WISE)*, University of California, Irvine, CA (2005)

3. Nizovtsev, D., Thursby, M.: Economic incentives to disclose software vulnerabilities. In: *Workshop on the Economics of Information Security (WEIS)*, Harvard University, Cambridge, MA (2005) `http://infosecon.net/workshop/pdf/20.pdf`.

4. Rescorla, E.: Is finding security holes a good idea? In: *Workshop of Economics and Information Security (WEIS)*, University of Minnesota, Minneapolis, MN (2004) `http://www.dtc.umn.edu/weis2004/rescorla.pdf`.

5. Anderson, R.J.: Why information security is hard – An economic perspective (2001) `http://www.cl.cam.ac.uk/~rja14/econsec.html`.

6. Akerlof, G.A.: The market for 'lemons': Quality, uncertainty and the market mechanism. *Quarterly Journal of Economics* **84** (1970) 488–500

7. Shapiro, C., Varian, H.R.: *Information Rules. A Strategic Guide to the Network Economy.* Harvard Business School Press (1998)

8. Hardin, G.: The tragedy of the commons. *Science* **162** (1968) 1243–1248

9. Freiling, F., Holz, T., Wicherski, G.: Botnet tracking: Exploring a root-cause methodology to prevent distributed denial-of-service attacks. In S. de Capitani di Vimercati et al., ed.: *Proc. of ESORICS*. LNCS 3679, Berlin Heidelberg, Springer Verlag (2005) 319–335

10. Varian, H.R.: System reliability and free riding. In: *Workshop on Economics and Information Security (WEIS)*, Berkeley, CA (2002) `http://www.sims.berkeley.edu/resources/affiliates/workshops/econsecurity/`.

11. Varian, H.R.: Managing online security risks. *New York Times* (2000) `http://www.nytimes.com/library/financial/columns/060100econ-scene.html`.

12. Ryan, D.J., Heckmann, C.: Two views on security software liability. *IEEE Security & Privacy* **1** (2003) 70–75

13. Schechter, S.E.: *Computer Security Strength & Risk: A Quantitative Approach.* PhD thesis, Harvard University, Cambridge, MA (2004)

14. Camp, J.L., Wolfram, C.: Pricing security. In: *Proc. of the CERT Information Survivability Workshop*, Boston, MA (2000) 31–39 `http://www.cert.org/research/isw/isw2000/papers/54.pdf`.

15. Downs, A.: *An Economic Theory of Democracy.* Harper and Brothers, New York (1957)

16. Stigler, G.J.: *The Citizen and the State: Essays on Regulation.* University Press, Chicago (1975)

17. Ozment, A.: Bug auctions: Vulnerability markets reconsidered. In: *Workshop of Economics and Information Security (WEIS)*, University of Minnesota, Minneapolis, MN (2004) `http://www.dtc.umn.edu/weis2004/ozment.pdf`.

18. Böhme, R.: Vulnerability markets – What is the economic value of a zero-day exploit? In: *Proc. of 22C3: Private Investigations*, Berlin, Germany (2005) `https://events.ccc.de/congress/2005/fahrplan/attachments/542-Boehme2005_22C3_VulnerabilityMarkets.pdf`.

19. Kannan, K., Telang, R.: An economic analysis of markets for software vulnerabilities. In: *Workshop of Economics and Information Security (WEIS)*, University of Minnesota, Minneapolis, MN (2004) `http://www.dtc.umn.edu/weis2004/kannan-telang.pdf`.

20. Matsuura, K.: Security tokens and their derivatives. Technical report, Centre for Communications Systems Research (CCSR), University of Cambridge, UK (2001)

21. Gordon, L.A., Loeb, M.P., Sohail, T.: A framework for using insurance for cyber-risk management. *Communications of the ACM* **46** (2003) 81–85
22. Kesan, J.P., Majuca, R.P., Yurcik, W.J.: The economic case for cyberinsurance. In: *Workshop on the Economics of Information Security (WEIS)*, Harvard University, Cambridge, MA (2005) `http://infosecon.net/workshop/pdf/42.pdf`.
23. Schneier, B.: Hacking the business climate for network security. *IEEE Computer* (2004) 87–89
24. Yurcik, W., Doss, D.: Cyberinsurance: A market solution to the internet security market failure. In: *Workshop on Economics and Information Security (WEIS)*, Berkeley, CA (2002) `http://www.sims.berkeley.edu/resources/affiliates/workshops/econsecurity/`.
25. Böhme, R.: Cyber-insurance revisited. In: *Workshop on the Economics of Information Security (WEIS)*, Harvard University, Cambridge, MA (2005) `http://infosecon.net/workshop/pdf/15.pdf`.
26. Ettredge, M., Richardson, V.J.: Assessing the risk in e-commerce. In Sprague, R.H., ed.: *Proc. of the 35th Hawaii International Conference on System Sciences*, Los Alamitos, CA, IEEE Press (2002)
27. Campbell, K., Gordon, L.A., Loeb, M.P., Zhou, L.: The economic cost of publicly announced information security breaches: Empirical evidence from the stock market. *Journal of Computer Security* **11** (2003) 431–448
28. Cavusoglu, H., Mishra, B., Raghunathan, S.: The effect of internet security breach announcements on market value: Capital market reactions for breached firms and internet security developers. *International Journal of Electronic Commerce* **9** (2004) 69–104
29. Telang, R., Wattal, S.: Impact of software vulnerability announcements on the market value of software vendors – An empirical investigation. In: *Workshop on the Economics of Information Security (WEIS)*, Harvard University, Cambridge, MA (2005) `http://infosecon.net/workshop/pdf/telang_wattal.pdf`.
30. Kahneman, D., Tversky, A.: *Choices, Values, and Frames.* Cambridge University Press (2000)
31. Geer et al., D.: CyberInsecurity – The cost of monopoly (2003) `http://www.ccianet.org/papers/cyberinsecurity.pdf`.
32. Chen, P.Y., Kataria, G., Krishnan, R.: Software diversity for information security. In: *Workshop on the Economics of Information Security (WEIS)*, Harvard University, Cambridge, MA (2005) `http://infosecon.net/workshop/pdf/47.pdf`.
33. Ozment, A.: The likelihood of vulnerability rediscovery and the social utility of vulnerability hunting. In: *Workshop on the Economics of Information Security (WEIS)*, Harvard University, Cambridge, MA (2005) `http://infosecon.net/workshop/pdf/10.pdf`.

Reliable Keystroke Biometric System Based on a Small Number of Keystroke Samples

Woojin Chang

Department of Industrial Engineering, Seoul National University
San 56-1, Sillim-dong, Gwanak-gu, Seoul, 151-742, Korea
changw@snu.ac.kr

Abstract. Less than ten keystroke samples from a legitimate user can make Keystroke Biometric System (KBS) reliable. Based on user's original keystroke samples, artificial keystroke samples are produced by resampling techniques in both time and wavelets domains. KBS constructed from these original and artificial keystroke samples shows smaller error rates than KBS from original keystroke samples only. Our resampling techniques can reduce user's workload for keystroke pattern registration while maintaining practically allowable error rates of KBS.

Keywords: Keystroke Biometric System, Discrete Wavelet Transform, Training set, Resampling, Hierarchical tree-based classification.

1   Introduction

Keystroke biometric system (KBS) authenticates the legitimate user by his or her keystroke dynamics. Although KBS is cheap, accessible and unobtrusive authentication process, KBS is less reliable than other physiological biometric system (e.g. fingerprints, retinas, and iris) because KBS is the individual's behavioral biometric system using his or her keystroke patterns, which are very similar to each other in general, but not perfectly consistent. For this reason, KBS is accompanied with passwords as a secondary security system in many enhanced login processes.

KBS classifies an arbitrary password typing pattern as either the legitimate user's or imposter's and has two types of error for false acceptance and false rejection. The false acceptance rate (FAR) is the percentage that imposters' keystroke typing patterns are identified as genuine user's and the false rejection rate (FRR) is the percentage that legitimate user's keystroke typing patterns are identified as imposters'. From the nature of two errors, FAR can be reduced at the cost of FRR, and vice versa. As a combination of FAR and FRR, Peacock et al. [3] presented the average false rate (AFR): average FAR and FRR.

KBS is built using keystroke training samples . A certain size of keystroke samples, which is a double digit number in most of cases, are necessary for reliable KBS. Thus, KBS asks users (hereafter user is referred to the legitimate user) to input their keystroke typing patterns many times repeatedly, and this can be troublesome work for many users. If a KBS requires only a small size of

G. Müller (Ed.): ETRICS 2006, LNCS 3995, pp. 312–320, 2006.

keystroke samples, which is a single digit number, and is reliable as much as the KBS requiring two digit sample size, then the KBS requiring small sample size is much more attractive.

In general, a small number of user's keystroke training samples result in low FAR, but high FRR. In this case, if users having consistent keystroke patterns provide more keystroke samples, FRR tends to decrease while FAR may not change or slightly increase.

The issue here is how to reduce FRR and to keep low FAR using a small size of training samples for KBS. We focuss on expanding training sample size as a solution. To the best of our knowledge, no paper addressed the research on how to expand the training sample size without additional sample collection from user in order to enhance the performance of a given KBS. In this paper, we introduce resampling techniques to expand training sample size. Resamplings are done in both time and wavelet domains.

The remainder of this paper is organized as follows: the structure of keystroke sample is described in Section 2. How to expand the training sample size using our resampling techniques is discussed in Section 3. The evaluation of the resampling techniques, which are applied to keystroke samples collected from 12 users, is presented in Section 4. Conclusions are in Section 5.

2   Keystroke Timing Vector

A keystroke sample is expressed as a keystroke timing vector (KTV) consisting of duration and interval times measured at the accuracy of milliseconds(ms). In the timing vector, each keystroke duration time is followed by the interval time which is calculated by subtracting the key-hit time from the previous key-release time. Thus, the interval time can be a negative value when a key is stroked before a previous key is released. We include the "Enter" keystroke as the last element of KTV. In this set-up, typing a string of n characters results in a KTV of length $2n + 1$, which consists of $n + 1$ keystroke duration times including the "Enter" key and n keystroke interval times (see Figure 1).

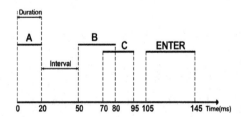

Fig. 1. "ABC" keystroke pattern is represented as keystroke timing vector, $(20, 30, 30, -10, 25, 10, 40)$

Let $\mathbf{v}_1, \ldots, \mathbf{v}_n$, where $\mathbf{v}_i = (v_{i1}, \ldots, v_{iN})$, denote n user's KTVs of length N. These n KTVs are used as the training samples for a KBS.

3   Expanding Training Sample Size for KBS

In this section, we introduce two resampling methods for expanding training sample size. We construct $p+q$ user's artificial KTVs, $\hat{\mathbf{v}}_1, \ldots, \hat{\mathbf{v}}_p$ in time domain (original domain) and $\tilde{\mathbf{v}}_1, \ldots, \tilde{\mathbf{v}}_q$ in wavelet domain, based on user's given sample KTVs, $\mathbf{v}_1, \ldots, \mathbf{v}_n$ in time domain.

3.1   Resampling in Time Domain

Using user's original KTVs, $\mathbf{v}_1, \ldots, \mathbf{v}_n$, we construct p artificial KTVs, $\hat{\mathbf{v}}_1, \ldots, \hat{\mathbf{v}}_p$, where $\hat{\mathbf{v}}_i = (\hat{v}_{i1}, \ldots, \hat{v}_{iN})$. As each element (e.g. j-th element) of user's orginal KTV has unique features of user's keystroke typing pattern, the j-th element of $\hat{\mathbf{v}}_i$, $\hat{v}_{ij}$, is randomly selected among the corresponding j-th elements of n user's KTVs, $v_{1j}, \ldots, v_{nj}$.

3.2   Resampling in Wavelet Domain

Discrete wavelet transformation (DWT) is applied to a user's KTV sample in the time domain, and then the corresponding keystroke wavelet coefficient vector (KWV) is produced in the wavelet domain. Since DWT separates a KTV into multi-resolution components, the latent features in KTV can be well observed and extracted in KWV. Since the data size that is fit for DWT should be 2 to the power of any natural number, the dummy data points need to be added to the unfit KTV.

For user's KTV sample, $\mathbf{v}_i = (v_{i1}, \ldots, v_{iN})$, the smallest 2^m larger than N ($2^{m-1} < N \le 2^m$) is the adequate vector length for DWT. We put two zero vectors of length $\lceil \frac{2^m - N}{2} \rceil$ (where $\lceil x \rceil$ is the smallest integer larger than or equal to x) and $\lfloor \frac{2^m - N}{2} \rfloor$ (where $\lfloor x \rfloor$ is the largest integer less than or equal to x) into the front and back sides of the KTV respectively, and obtained $\mathbf{u}_i = (0, \ldots, 0, v_{i1}, \ldots, v_{iN}, 0, \ldots, 0)$. When we let $\mathbf{c}_m = (c_{m0}, \ldots, c_{m2^m - 1})$ denote $\mathbf{u}_i$, and define $\mathbf{c}_j = (c_{j0}, \ldots, c_{j2^j - 1})$ and $\mathbf{d}_j = (d_{j0}, \ldots, d_{j2^j - 1})$ for $j = 1, \ldots, m - 1$, $\mathbf{c}_j$ and $\mathbf{d}_j$ are calculated as follows.

$$c_{m-1\ell} = \frac{1}{\sqrt{2}} c_{m2\ell} + \frac{1}{\sqrt{2}} c_{m2\ell+1}$$

$$d_{m-1\ell} = \frac{1}{\sqrt{2}} c_{m2\ell} - \frac{1}{\sqrt{2}} c_{m2\ell+1},$$

where $\ell = 0, \ldots, 2^{m-1} - 1$, and for each $j = 1, \ldots, m - 1$

$$c_{j-1\ell} = \frac{1}{\sqrt{2}} c_{j2\ell} + \frac{1}{\sqrt{2}} c_{j2\ell+1}$$

$$d_{j-1\ell} = \frac{1}{\sqrt{2}} d_{j2\ell} - \frac{1}{\sqrt{2}} d_{j2\ell+1},$$

where $\ell = 0, \ldots, 2^{j-1} - 1$.

Then the wavelet coefficients, $\mathbf{w}_i = (w_{i1}, \ldots, w_{i2^m}) = (\mathbf{d}_{m-1}, \mathbf{d}_{m-2}, \ldots, \mathbf{d}_1, d_{00}, c_{00})$ are obtained through cascade algorithm whose computational complexity is $O(2^m)$.

In this way, n KWVs, $\mathbf{w}_1, \ldots, \mathbf{w}_n$, which correspond to $\mathbf{v}_1, \ldots, \mathbf{v}_n$ are obtained (see [2] for full details of discrete wavelet transformation of KTVs).

From $\mathbf{w}_1, \ldots, \mathbf{w}_n$, we construct artificial q KWVs, $\tilde{\mathbf{w}}_1, \ldots, \tilde{\mathbf{w}}_q$, where $\tilde{\mathbf{w}}_i = (\tilde{w}_{i1}, \ldots, \tilde{w}_{i2^m})$. The j-th element of $\tilde{\mathbf{w}}_i$, $\tilde{w}_{ij}$, is selected using the following resampling rules.

First define

$$A = \Big\{ j : \Big| \sum_{i=1}^{n} \text{sign}(w_{ij}) \Big| \geq 0.9n, \ j = 1, 2, \ldots, 2^m \Big\}$$

$$B = \Big\{ j : \Big| \sum_{i=1}^{n} \text{sign}(w_{ij-1} - w_{ij}) \Big| \geq 0.3n, \ j = 2, \ldots, 2^m \Big\} \cup \{1\}$$

where $\text{sign}(x) = 1$ if $x > 0$, otherwise -1.

For $i = 1, 2, \ldots, q$,

- If $j \in A \cap B$, then $\tilde{w}_{ij}$ is uniformly selected between $\bar{w}_j - s_{w_j}$ and $\bar{w}_j + s_{w_j}$, where $\bar{w}_j = \frac{1}{n} \sum_{i=1}^{n} w_{ij}$ and $s_{w_j} = \sqrt{\frac{1}{n-1}(w_{ij} - \bar{w}_j)^2}$.
- If $j \in A$ and $j \notin B$, then $\tilde{w}_{ij}$ is uniformly selected between $\bar{w}_j - 2s_{w_j}$ and $\bar{w}_j + 2s_{w_j}$.
- If $j \notin A$ and $j \in B$, then $\tilde{w}_{ij}$ is uniformly selected between $\bar{w}_j - 2.3s_{w_j}$ and $\bar{w}_j + 2.3s_{w_j}$.
- If $j \notin A \cup B$, $\tilde{w}_{ij}$ is uniformly selected between $\bar{w}_j - 2.8s_{w_j}$ and $\bar{w}_j + 2.8s_{w_j}$. Note: 0.9 and 0.3 in sets A and B, and the values, $\pm 1, \pm 2, \pm 2.3, \pm 2.8$ in the above rules were empirically selected since previous experiments indicated that using those values resulted in low FAR, FRR, and AFR.

The conditions, $|\sum_{i=1}^{n} \text{sign}(w_{ij})| \geq 0.9n$ in set A and $|\sum_{i=1}^{n} \text{sign}(w_{ij-1} - w_{ij})| \geq 0.3n$ in set B are used to measure the consistency level of the wavelet coefficients at the j-th position, $w_{1j}, \ldots, w_{nj}$. The more conditions the j-th position satisfy, we assume, the narrower the range of the probable value of the coefficient at the position.

Through discrete inverse wavelet transformation (DIWT), a pattern in the time domain is recovered. As zero vectors were put into the front and back sides of the original KTVs before applying DWT, the elements whose positions correspond to these zero elements should be removed from the recovered (inverse wavelet transformed) KTVs. Then we obtain the complete artificial q KTVs, $\tilde{\mathbf{v}}_1, \ldots, \tilde{\mathbf{v}}_q$, where $\tilde{\mathbf{v}}_i = (\tilde{v}_{i1}, \ldots, \tilde{v}_{iN})$.

4   Evaluation of Resampling Techniques

After resamplings in both time and wavelet domains, we can have keystroke training sets whose sizes are up to $n + p + q$ in total: n is given, p and q are constructed in time and wavelet domains respectively.

As our keystroke training sets consist of user's original and artificial keystroke samples and exclude imposters' samples, classification methods incorporating both user's and imposter's patterns for training are inapplicable to our case.

We introduce the hierarchical tree-based keystroke classification method which needs user's pattern only and takes relatively short process time due to its simple computational algorithm.

We compare the performances of this classification method when different training sets (training set consisting of user's original keystroke samples only, training sets including user's artificial keystroke samples) are used.

4.1   Hierarchical Tree-Based Classification

Let $\mathcal{T} = \{\mathbf{x}_1, \ldots, \mathbf{x}_m\}$ denote a training set for a KBS. Define $\mathbf{X} = \mathcal{T} \cup \{\mathbf{y}\} = \{\mathbf{x}_1, \ldots, \mathbf{x}_m, \mathbf{y}\}$ as a set of KTVs consisting of user's training samples, $\mathbf{x}_1, \ldots, \mathbf{x}_m$, and the unknown KTV, $\mathbf{y}$.

The Euclidean distance between pairs of samples in $\mathbf{X}$ (e.g. $\text{dist}(\mathbf{x}_i, \mathbf{x}_j) = \sqrt{\sum_{k=1}^{n}(x_{ik} - x_{jk})^2}$) is computed, and the distances of all possible $\binom{m+1}{2}$ pairs are arranged in the order $(1,2), (1,3), \ldots, (1, m+1), (2,3), (2,4), \ldots, (m, m+1)$. Then, a hierarchical cluster tree (dendrogram) for $\mathbf{X}$ is computed using single linkage algorithm where similarity between two clusters is computed based on the minimum distance between the objects belonging to the corresponding clusters (see [1] for general review of the method). The leaf nodes in the cluster hierarchy are the samples in $\mathbf{X}$, numbered from 1 to $m+1$ ($\mathbf{y}$ is marked with $m+1$). They are the singleton clusters from which all higher clusters are built.

If the unknown KTV, $\mathbf{y}$, does not belong to any cluster comprised of elements of $\mathcal{T}$ except for the highest cluster (the cluster containing all samples of $\mathbf{X}$), then $\mathbf{y}$ is classified as imposter's rather than genuine user's. Otherwise, $\mathbf{y}$ is classified as user's. Figure 2 shows an example where $\mathbf{X} = \{\mathbf{x}_1, \ldots, \mathbf{x}_7, \mathbf{y}\}$ and $\mathbf{y}$ is classified as imposter's.

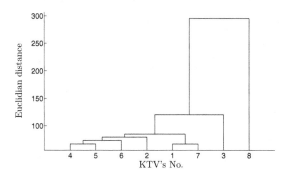

Fig. 2. Dendrogram: the user's samples are numbered from 1 to 7, and the imposter's sample is marked with 8

4.2   Classifications Using Different Training Sets

We measure FAR and FRR of three hierarchical tree-based classifications, whose training sets are $T_0 = \{\mathbf{v}_1, \ldots, \mathbf{v}_n\}$, $T_1 = \{\mathbf{v}_1, \ldots, \mathbf{v}_n, \tilde{\mathbf{v}}_1, \ldots, \tilde{\mathbf{v}}_q\}$, and $T_2 = \{\mathbf{v}_1, \ldots, \mathbf{v}_n, \hat{\mathbf{v}}_1, \ldots, \hat{\mathbf{v}}_p, \tilde{\mathbf{v}}_1, \ldots, \tilde{\mathbf{v}}_q\}$ respectively. Remind that $\hat{\mathbf{v}}_1, \ldots, \hat{\mathbf{v}}_p$ are artificial KTVs constructed in time domain, and $\tilde{\mathbf{v}}_1, \ldots, \tilde{\mathbf{v}}_q$ are those constructed in wavelet domain. The training set, $\{\mathbf{v}_1, \ldots, \mathbf{v}_n, \hat{\mathbf{v}}_1, \ldots, \hat{\mathbf{v}}_q\}$, is excluded from consideration because outcomes based on this training set are not much better than T_0.

A hierarchical cluster tree (dendrogram) is obtained using three kinds of KTV sample sets,

$$\mathbf{X}_0^i = T_0 \cup \{\mathbf{y}_i\} = \{\mathbf{v}_1, \ldots, \mathbf{v}_n, \mathbf{y}_i\}$$
$$\mathbf{X}_1^i = T_1 \cup \{\mathbf{y}_i\} = \{\mathbf{v}_1, \ldots, \mathbf{v}_n, \tilde{\mathbf{v}}_1, \ldots, \tilde{\mathbf{v}}_q, \mathbf{y}_i\}$$
$$\mathbf{X}_2^i = T_2 \cup \{\mathbf{y}_i\} = \{\mathbf{v}_1, \ldots, \mathbf{v}_n, \hat{\mathbf{v}}_1, \ldots, \hat{\mathbf{v}}_p, \tilde{\mathbf{v}}_1, \ldots, \tilde{\mathbf{v}}_q, \mathbf{y}_i\}$$

where $\mathbf{y}_i = (y_{i1}, \ldots, y_{iN})$, $i = 1, \ldots, r + s$.

FRR and FAR are computed using the test sets from user, $\mathcal{Y}_0 = \{\mathbf{y}_1, \ldots, \mathbf{y}_r\}$, and imposters, $\mathcal{Y}_1 = \{\mathbf{y}_{r+1}, \ldots, \mathbf{y}_{r+s}\}$, respectively.

4.3   Experimental Results

For the evaluation of our resampling technique, keystroke data sets from Yu and Cho [4] were used in this paper.

Keystroke patterns of 12 passwords, whose lengths range from 6 to 10, were collected from both users and imposters. Each of 12 users typed his or her password at least 150 and at most 400 times to build his or her keystroke pattern pool, and based on which three types of training sets, T_0, T_1, and T_2, are constructed. T_0 consists of 7 KTVs, $\mathbf{v}_1, \ldots, \mathbf{v}_7$, which are randomly selected from the pool. T_1 contains 13 artificial KTVs, $\tilde{\mathbf{v}}_1, \ldots, \tilde{\mathbf{v}}_{13}$, which are constructed in wavelet domain as in Section 3.2, in addition to the elements of T_0. T_2 extends T_1 by including 8 more artificial keystroke samples, $\hat{\mathbf{v}}_1, \ldots, \hat{\mathbf{v}}_8$, which are constructed in time domain as in Section 3.1.

How many artificial keystroke samples from time and wavelet domains need to be included in a training set to minimize the error rate of KBS is another research topic. The previous experiments indicate that outcomes with low error rates occurred when the size of artificial samples from time domain is similar to that of user's original samples, and the size of artificial samples from wavelet domain is almost double. For this reason, in this paper, 8 and 13 artificial keystroke samples from time and wavelet domains respectively are combined with user's 7 keystroke samples, and those 28 keystroke samples comprise a training set.

In [4], for the preparation of KBS test set, each user of 12 passwords typed his or her password 75 times, and 15 imposters also typed each of 12 passwords 5 times after some password typing practices. Thus, for each user's password, a test set from the user, $\mathcal{Y}_0 = \{\mathbf{y}_1, \ldots, \mathbf{y}_{75}\}$, and another test set from the imposters, $\mathcal{Y}_1 = \{\mathbf{y}_{76}, \ldots, \mathbf{y}_{150}\}$ are constructed.

For the comparison with performances of three hierarchical tree-based classifications whose training sets are T_0, T_1, and T_2 respectively, the classifications of $\mathbf{X}_0^i, \mathbf{X}_1^i$ and $\mathbf{X}_2^i$ for $i = 1, \ldots, 150$ are repeated 50 times using nonidentical triplet of T_0, T_1, and T_2 at each run. (Note $\mathbf{v}_1, \ldots, \mathbf{v}_7$ are randomly selected for each run.) For each of 12 users' cases, the performances of these three classifications, each of which consists of the averages of 50 FARs, 50 FRRs, and 50 AFRs respectively, are shown in Table 1.

Table 1. The test results for keystroke dynamics of 12 passwords typing: the averages of FARs, FRRs, and AFRs of the classifications using training sets T_0, T_1, and T_2

| User | User's | T_0 | | | T_1 | | | T_2 | | |
No.	Password	FAR	FRR	AFR	FAR	FRR	AFR	FAR	FRR	AFR
1	loveis.	3.79	12.85	8.32	4.83	6.80	5.82	4.80	6.75	5.78
2	i love 3	6.64	7.33	6.99	8.80	2.67	5.74	8.67	2.35	5.51
3	autumnman	0.03	10.85	5.44	0	4.13	2.07	0	3.87	1.94
4	ahrfus8	2.11	13.41	7.76	3.01	6.13	4.57	2.99	5.73	4.36
5	drizzle	7.33	9.04	8.19	7.36	3.28	5.32	7.55	3.39	5.47
6	beaupowe	2.03	11.25	6.64	3.31	4.80	4.06	3.25	4.37	3.81
7	tmdwnsll	7.65	13.97	10.81	6.13	10.83	8.48	6.11	10.69	8.40
8	yuhwa1kk	0	6.48	3.24	0	3.47	1.74	0	3.81	1.91
9	rlasus	4.53	7.63	6.08	5.23	2.40	3.82	5.31	2.67	3.99
10	dlfjs wp	0.96	14.11	7.54	2.37	5.76	4.07	2.64	5.92	4.28
11	dltjdgml	0.16	8.59	4.38	0.56	5.09	2.83	0.64	4.29	2.47
12	c.s.93/ksy 8	4.61	12.27	8.44	2.13	11.87	7.00	1.87	11.60	6.74

Note: 'c.s.93/ksy 8' contains special characters. FAR,FRR and AFR are expressed as error percentages and each error rate is the average of 50 classifications of the corresponding keystroke data set.

When T_0 is used as a training set, FAR is low, but FRR is much higher than FAR, in general. This is expected as only 7 keystroke samples are used for a training set. When T_1 or T_2 is used, FAR tends to increase a little, but FRR shows a sizeable decrease, compared with those using T_0. On the whole, for each case, AFRs based on T_0, T_1, and T_2 are arranged respectively in decreasing order, and the difference between AFRs based on T_1 and T_2 is small. This is illustrated in Figure 3. These results show that our resampling techniques for expanding the size of keystroke training samples are effective in improving the overall classification accuracy, and the resampling technique in wavelet domain plays a major role for this improvement.

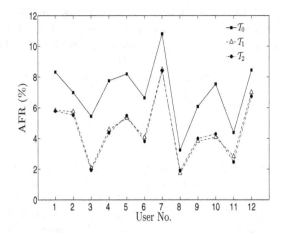

Fig. 3. AFRs of the classifications based on training sets T_0, T_1, and T_2

The results in Table 1 are inferior to those in Yu and Cho [4], in which the average FAR=0 and average FRR=3.71. This is due to the fact that the algorithm of our hierarchical tree-based keystroke classification method using 7 user's original keystroke samples for training is relatively simple and the fact that the algorithm of the method in [4], which is based on support vector machine and genetic algorithm, using 50 user's original keystroke samples for training is sophisticated. However, in terms of the time taken for classification, it takes less than three seconds for our method and more than two hours for the method in [4]. When considering the number of user's original keystroke samples used for training and the time taken for classification, our method might be more practical than Yu and Cho [4].

5   Conclusions

If a small size of training set is used for KBS, FRR tends to be high and FAR is low in general. In this case, to reduce FRR while keeping FAR below a certain allowable level, we introduce resampling techniques that expand the size of training set.

Using our resampling techniques, we constructed 21 artificial KTVs, 13 in wavelet domain and 8 in time domain, from 7 original KTVs. The KBS based on the training set consisting of both 21 artificial KTVs and 7 original KTVs showed a little increase of FAR, but a significant decrease of FRR, compared with the KBS based on the training set consisting of 7 original KTVs only. Thus, AFR, which can be regarded as an overall classification error rate, decreased when artificial KTVs constructed by our resampling techniques were included in the original training set. From this result, it can be concluded that the addition of artificial keystroke samples to a given training set consisting of a few original keystroke samples from user is effective in enhancing the performance of KBS.

In this paper, the hierarchical tree-based classification based on Euclidian distance between KTVs is used as a classification method, and the method is relatively simple. The sophisticated classification method combined with our resampling techniques may reduce FAR, FRR, and AFR much more. Finding a new classification method, which is the most harmonious with our resampling techniques, will be our future work.

Acknowledgement

We would like to thank Professor Sungzoon Cho at Seoul National University for sharing his data on keystroke dynamics. This work was supported by the Korea Research Foundation Grant (No. KRF-2005-003-D00470) funded by the Korean Government(MOEHRD) and Basic Research Program Grant (No.R01-2005-000-103900-0) funded by Korea Science and Engineering Foundation.

References

1. Duda, R.O., Stork, D.G., Hart, P.E.: Pattern Classification. Wiley (1999)
2. Chang, W.: Keystroke Biometric System using Wavelets. Lecture Notes in Computer Science, Vol. 3832 (2005) 647 - 653
3. Peacock, A., Ke, X., Wilkerson, M.: Typing Patterns: A Key to User Identification. IEEE Securiy & Privacy **2** (2004) 40–47
4. Yu, E., Cho, S.: Keystroke dynamics identy verification–its problems and practical solutions. Computers & Security **23** (2004) 428–440

Allowing State Changes in Specifications

Mike Barnett [1], David A. Naumann [2], Wolfram Schulte [1], and Qi Sun [2]

[1] Microsoft Research
Redmond, WA USA
[2] Stevens Institute of Technology
Hoboken, NJ USA

Abstract. We provide a static analysis (using both dataflow analysis and theorem proving) to allow state changes within specifications. This can be used for specification languages that share the same expression sub-language with an implementation language so that method calls can appear in preconditions, postconditions, and object invariants without violating the soundness of the system.

1 Introduction

An obvious truth is that a software specification is meant to be a description; it is clearly not the thing that it is describing. Software specifications which share the same expression language as the implementation programming language run the risk of blurring this distinction. When specifications contain expressions that change the state of the program, the meaning of the program may differ depending on whether or not the specifications are present; the two are no longer independent.

Despite this, there are many reasons for using the same expression language in both an implementation and its specification. To prevent unwanted interference, specifications are usually restricted to a side-effect free (pure) subset of the expression language. An important decision to make is whether (programmer-defined) functions belong in the subset or not: there are three main current approaches.

- The simplest approach is to forbid the use of functions in specifications altogether. While easy to implement, this solution does not scale and is overly restrictive on the practical use of specifications. ESC/Java [16] uses this solution.
- From a theoretical perspective, a pleasing solution is to allow only provably pure functions. However, an automatic static analysis must be conservative and may reject some pure functions. JML [21] uses this solution.
- An unsound solution is to request for the programmer to refrain from using functions with side-effects in specifications, but to actually allow the free use of functions. While not restrictive at all (and particularly easy to implement), this means it is not possible to guarantee that a program's meaning is unchanged when including its specification. It also is impractical for library functions that are beyond the control of the programmer. Eiffel [24] uses this solution.

We are interested in a sound, practical static analysis that goes beyond purity to allow *benevolent* side-effects [18] so programmers can use functions in specifications as freely as possible. We propose a definition of *observational purity* and a static analysis

G. Müller (Ed.): ETRICS 2006, LNCS 3995, pp. 321–336, 2006.

to determine it. The intuition behind observational purity is that a function is allowed to have side-effects only if they are not observable to callers of the function. As with programs, we restrict our attention to effects that are observable in terms of the source language (Java or C#) and ignore effects such as memory usage or power consumption. Our prototypical example of an observationally pure function is one that maintains an internal cache. Changing this internal cache is a side-effect, but it is not visible outside of the object. Other examples are methods that write to a log file that is not read by the rest of the program and methods that perform lazy initialization. Algorithms that are optimized for amortized complexity, such as a list that uses a "move to front" heuristic, also perform significant state updates that are not visible externally. Observationally pure methods often occur in library code that is highly optimized and also frequently used in specifications, e.g., the equality methods in a string library.

Our proposal uses a conservative static analysis together with a mild verification condition. It appears that for the many simple cases that occur in practice the proposal requires very little effort on the part of the programmer.

Section 2 begins by discussing the example of a function that maintains an internal cache. Then we define observational purity in semantic terms, sketching just enough formalization to make the ideas clear. The general definition entails a nontrivial proof obligation. In Section 3 we outline a static analysis that provides a conservative approximation for observational purity; for its application, the only proof obligations are ordinary assertions. In Section 4 we show the resulting annotations and apply our method to an example. Section 5 discusses related work and future directions for our work.

2   Towards Observational Purity

Figure 1 shows a class C that contains a method f which is meant to compute a function, $expensive$, of type $T \rightarrow U$. We suppose that this function is expensive to compute, so as an optimization the actual computation is done only the first time that f is called for each argument x. The class C maintains an internal cache to store already computed results. The cache is implemented as a hashtable, t, where it stores pairs $(x, expensive(x))$ so that future queries for x do a table lookup instead of recomputing $expensive(x)$. In a more complete example there would be other methods in the class. Note that class C does not include method $expensive$ in its interface. Clients use method f and need to be able to express conditions involving $c.f(\ldots)$ for some object c of type C.

We assume that $expensive$ is a (weakly) pure function and so can be used in specifications. But we address the use of f in specifications. One reason to use a function like f is that, being part of the code interface, it may be more familiar to the programmer. Another reason is that an implemented method is needed if the specification is to be executed by a runtime checker. Finally, in a case like $Object.equals$, there is no pure method analogous to $expensive$ that could be used in a specification. Each type can (and probably should) redefine equality so there is no other generally accepted method that a user could use to specify that two objects should be equal.

Assuming that no other methods in the class access t, the private field t and the hashtable it references are effectively encapsulated in f. It should be possible to allow

```
class C {
    private Hashtable  t := new Hashtable();
    invariant Forall{ T  x in t.Keys  :  t[x] = expensive(x)};
    public U  f(T  x)
        requires x ≠ null;
        ensures result = expensive(x);
    {
        if (¬t.ContainsKey(x)){
            U  y := ...; // compute expensive(x)
            t.Add(x, y); }
        return (U)t[x];
    }
}
```

Fig. 1. A class C that maintains a cache t to avoid recomputing *expensive*

f to appear in specifications since $f(x) = expensive(x)$ for any x and the side effect is not observable. The first problem is to formalize what it means to allow f in specifications. We choose the following criterion:

$$\textbf{assert } Q[f] \;\cong\; \textbf{skip} \tag{1}$$

for any formula $Q[f]$ that has invocation(s) of f but is otherwise pure. That is, we want the assertion to be equivalent to **skip** with respect to some suitable equivalence relation that is yet to be determined. It is well known how to express satisfaction of pre/post specifications in terms of assertions, so our criterion accounts for specifications as well as other annotations, provided that $\cong$ has two properties:

Preserves correctness: If $S \cong S'$ then S and S' should satisfy the same specifications.

Congruence: if $S \cong S'$ and $C[-]$ is some program context such that $C[S]$ is well formed then $C[S] \cong C[S']$.

Equation (1) formalizes both that f has no effect for runtime checking and that in terms of static verification it is sound to ignore the effect in reasoning about **assert** $Q[f]$. Preservation of correctness ensures that replacing an assertion by **skip** does not change the behavior of a program in any way that can be described (observed) by specifications. An important instance of congruence is that $S \cong S'$ implies $S; T \cong S'; T$, which allows (1) to be used to introduce or eliminate a precondition.

Preservation of correctess and congruence are properties of $\cong$ together with the programming language and specifications. It could be that a suitable $\cong$ fails to exist because programs or specifications include some unusual feature like the ability to determine the absolute number of allocated objects, reachable or not. A common feature that would be problematic is pointer arithmetic, which makes it possible to indirectly detect memory allocation. Our examples mostly follow the syntax of C#, which like Java has no pointer arithmetic, but otherwise they do not depend on the specifics of the programming language.

2.1 Semantics

Criterion (1) expresses a sense in which f has no effect, but the point is that f does have an effect. To justify our claims we need to consider a semantics for **assert** that has effects.

We write $f(x), h \rightarrow v, k$ to express that invocation of method f on arguments x in initial heap h yields value v and final heap k. We include the receiver object in the list x to simplify notation. We model the *heap* as a finite partial function that maps each object location (address) to a mutable record of the object's fields (including an immutable field that records its allocated type). So dom h is the set of locations allocated in h, $h\,o$ represents the state of object o, and $h\,o.t$ is the value of field t of object o in heap h. For brevity, we assume that local variables are somehow encoded in the heap, e.g., as a record at a distinguished location. It is not difficult to make a more precise formalization of our theory, taking proper account of local variables [28], but with these assumptions we can simply write

$$S, h \rightarrow k$$

to express that the result of executing statement S in heap h is heap k. Similarly, execution of an expression E in h, yielding heap k and value v, is written

$$E, h \rightarrow v, k$$

as in the special case of method call. Now the semantics of **assert** is defined by

$$(\textbf{assert } Q), h \rightarrow k \quad \text{iff} \quad Q, h \rightarrow true, k$$

In this paper we confine attention to partial correctness of single-threaded programs and thus it is sound to model divergence by the absence of an outcome. In our semantics, input and output can be represented by designated objects with sequence-valued fields.

2.2 Weak Purity

As a step on the way to defining $\cong$, let us consider *weak purity* as in JML. For f to be weakly pure means it has no effect on preexisting objects. But it may well allocate new ones. New objects may be allocated for a data structure used by some algorithm to compute a result; such a data structure is garbage upon termination of the algorithm. New objects may also comprise the result value, e.g., a function might return a new string. A more complicated example is a method that returns an enumeration in the form of an *Iterator* object: this new object may reference preexisting ones (a cursor reference into the underlying collection) but also new ones (e.g., an array to represent the sequence, or a *BigInteger* used for a version stamp with a long-lived collection).[1]

Definition 1. Expression E is *weakly pure* iff for any h, v, k,

$$E, h \rightarrow v, k \quad \text{implies} \quad (\text{dom } h) \triangleleft k = h$$

where $(\text{dom } h) \triangleleft k$ denotes heap k restricted to the objects allocated in h. Method f is *weakly pure* iff the call $f(E)$ is weakly pure for any weakly pure E.

---

[1] A database query could return even more elaborate structure, but might well perform internal updates and thus satisfy only the weaker observational purity.

An asserted formula Q is just a boolean expression, possibly involving quantifiers and other mathematical notations in addition to program expressions. We may as well assume that the only program expressions that have side effects are method invocations. So the only possible effects from **assert** Q are the field updates from method invocations in Q.

We expect that observational purity will subsume weak purity and thus weakly pure f should satisfy Equation (1). Let us consider what equivalence $\cong$ is suitable in the case of weak purity. Semantic equality is a correctness preserving congruence. But for weakly pure f it is not the case that the meaning of **assert** $Q[f]$ is equal to **skip**, since f may allocate new objects. So we should perhaps consider heaps equivalent if they are the same after garbage collection. But when the allocator chooses a location for a new object, the choice may be influenced by the presence of garbage, so relocation must also be considered.

Let us write $h \approx h'$ if h and h' are the same "modulo renaming of locations" and "modulo garbage collection".[2] For values we write $v \approx v'$, meaning $v = v'$ if v, v' have primitive type but equivalence modulo renaming if they are object locations.

As a candidate interpretation for $\cong$ in (1), define the relation $\approx$ on statements by lifting the state relation $\approx$ as follows: $S \approx S'$ iff for all h, h', k, k' with $h \approx h'$, if $S, h \to k$ and $S, h' \to k'$ then $k \approx k'$. In a diagram:

$$h \approx h'$$
$$S \downarrow \quad \downarrow S' \qquad\qquad (2)$$
$$k \approx k'$$

Relation $\approx$ is not correctness preserving if we admit specifications that are sensitive to garbage or to specific choices of locations, such as the postcondition "there is an even number of objects allocated and location 1024 is not allocated". But specification languages at the source code level, such as JML, do not allow such a postcondition to be expressed. For specifications that are insensitive to renaming of locations and garbage collection, $\approx$ is correctness preserving.

Relation $\approx$ is also a congruence, for the constructs of source languages like C# and Java that are designed to be insensitive to renaming of locations (which is not the case in C owing to address arithmetic). Garbage collection in these languages can be observed, via timing behavior and out-of-memory exceptions, but for reasoning about specifications an idealized model is often assumed, in which integers and memory are unbounded. Our semantics is at that level of abstraction, which justifies the assumption we shall make that $\approx$ is a correctness preserving congruence. This is certainly the case for standard OO constructs without address arithmetic or bounded memory.

Proposition 1. If Q is weakly pure then **assert** $Q \approx$ **skip**.

In the general case, Q is some formula that may include several invocations of observationally pure methods, on arguments that are pure. For simplicity we give the proof

---

[2] These notions are formalized precisely in [28], by indexing the equivalence relation with a renaming bijection. But the technical details are not necessary to follow the key points of our proposal. Note that [28] uses slightly different notations than the present paper.

only for the case where Q is $f(x)$ for some boolean valued weakly pure f. The generalization is straightforward; indeed it can encoded in this special case, at the cost of introducing a new method f.

Suppose we have

$$h \approx h'$$
$$\textbf{assert } f(x) \downarrow \quad \downarrow \textbf{ skip}$$
$$k \quad k'$$

By semantics of **skip**, $h' = k'$. By semantics of **assert**, we have $f(x), h \rightarrow true, k$. And by weak purity of f we have $(\text{dom } h) \triangleleft k = h$. We did not formalize in detail the effect of statements on local variables but it should be clear that garbage collection of k gives $(\text{dom } h) \triangleleft k$, so $k \approx (\text{dom } h) \triangleleft k$, because method call has no effect on locals at the call site and neither does **assert**. Hence $k \approx k'$ follows by transitivity of $\approx$ from

$$k \quad \approx \quad (\text{dom } h) \triangleleft k \quad = \quad h \quad \approx \quad h' \quad = \quad k'$$

This completes the diagram and the proof of **assert** $f(x) \approx$ **skip**.

If f is weakly pure, it may allocate new objects and return a reference to one of them, but it does not otherwise store references to the new objects. The preceding argument can be adapted to prove the following alternative characterization.

Lemma 1. f is *weakly pure* iff $f(x), h \rightarrow v, k$ implies $k \approx h$ for any x, h, v, k.

Having justified the use of weakly pure methods, we note that f in Fig. 1 is not weakly pure because it updates a preexisting hashtable. To allow f in specifications we need to take into account that the hashtable is encapsulated within class C.

2.3 Observational Purity

It is well known that private visibility for fields is not sufficient for encapsulation because of sharing [19, 13]. If our example included a method that returned a pointer to the hashtable, client programs could use it and thereby behave differently depending on its contents. In such a situation, **assert** $f(x)$ would not be equivalent to **skip** because the effect of f could be observed. There has been extensive work on notions of confinement or ownership to address this problem [3, 6, 13, 26]. Such a notion gives rise to an equivalence on heaps, written $h \sim^C h'$, with the meaning h *is indistinguishable from* h' *in code of any class other than* C (and, as before, modulo garbage collection and renaming).[3] The equivalence extends to statements by defining $S \sim^C S'$ iff the relation $\sim^C$ on states is preserved as in (2).

At this point one might hope to simply adapt Lemma 1, using $\sim^C$, to serve as a definition: f would be *observationally pure outside* C provided that $f(x), h \rightarrow v, k$ implies $h \sim^C k$ for any x, h, v, k. Indeed, if f satisfies this condition then we do have **assert** $f(x) \sim^C$ **skip**. But is the relation $\sim^C$ a correctness preserving congruence?

---

[3] The precise definition of $\sim^C$ exploits a renaming relation to encode which locations are confined to class C, i.e., not usable by code of other classes [28].

We claim that $\sim^C$ is correctness preserving with respect to specifications except for private specifications in class C. Public specifications would not refer to encapsulated state, but private specifications and other code annotations might well refer to it. The latter can distinguish between **assert** $f(x)$ and **skip**. Even if f has the property that $f(x), h \rightarrow v, k$ implies $h \sim^C k$, it does not make sense to use Equation (1) to replace an assert in code of C.

Unfortunately, the proposed definition is unsatisfactory because $\sim^C$ is not a congruence. As an example, suppose the following method is added to class C in Figure 1.

$$\textbf{public int } leak() \{ \quad \textbf{return } t.Count; \quad \}$$

We have **assert** $f(x) \sim^C$ **skip** because f is observationally pure outside C, but

$$\textbf{assert } f(x); y := leak() \not\sim^C \textbf{skip}; y := leak()$$

which shows that the congruence property fails for the context $-; y := leak()$.

The name "leak" hints that this is a dubious method; it clearly exposes what is intended to be encapsulated. But congruence fails even for desirable code. Consider the context $y := f(x); -$, where f is from Fig. 1. We have $y := f(x) \not\sim^C y := f(x)$ for the following reason. Consider h, h' such that $h \approx h'$ except that for some C object o, $h o.t$ and $h' o.t$ map x to different values, i.e., $o.t[x]$ in h differs from $o.t[x]$ in h'. Then $h \sim^C h'$, because $\sim^C$ ignores the t field. But $v \not\sim^C v'$ where v, v' are the corresponding results of executing $f(x)$, and so $k \not\sim^C k'$ where k, k' are the corresponding heaps after $y := f(x)$. Now clearly **skip** $\sim^C$ **skip**, but if we put **skip** into the context $y := f(x); -$ then we get

$$y := f(x); \textbf{skip} \quad = \quad y := f(x) \quad \not\sim^C \quad y := f(x) \quad = \quad y := f(x); \textbf{skip}$$

So the context $y := f(x); -$ is another counterexample to congruence.

Indeed, as soon as $S \cong S$ fails for some S then $\cong$ fails to be a congruence.

2.4 Simulation Relations

The second counterexample to congruence shows the root problem: because $\sim^C$ is defined to ignore the encapsulated fields and objects, it relates states from which methods of C may have quite different behavior. The problem can be solved by requiring that every method of C preserve $\sim^C$ but that is impractical: it would disallow any nontrivial use of the internal state of C objects.

A more practical solution is obtained by generalizing from $\sim^C$ to some relation $\asymp$ that *is* preserved by methods of C.

Example 1. Typically, $h \asymp h'$ just if the heap partitions in such a way that each C-object has an associated island of its encapsulated representation objects and with the exception of these objects everything corresponds as in the definition of $\approx$. For our running example, one possibility is the relation $\asymp$ defined by: $h \asymp h'$ iff $h \sim^C h'$ and moreover for every C-object[4] the invariant holds for both h and for h', i.e.,

---

[4] Strictly speaking we should consider pairs o, o' that correspond, i.e., $o \approx o'$.

$h\ o.t[x] = expensive(x)$ for all x in the domain of keys of $h\ o.t$, and the same for $h'\ o.t$. For this relation we have that $f \asymp f$, by contrast with the second counterexample above. The notation $f \asymp f$ is the lift of $\asymp$ from states to methods defined as follows: If $h \asymp h'$ then $f(x), h \to v, k$ and $f(x), h' \to v', k'$ imply $k \asymp k'$ and $v \approx v'$, for all x, h, k, v and their primed counterparts.

As another example, suppose class C represents a bag of objects using an array which may have null elements. Some operations may have the side effect of compacting the array (moving non-null elements into the place of nulls). Then $h \asymp h'$ just if, for corresponding pairs of arrays the only difference is possible compaction. If C has other fields, these are related by $\approx$.

Definition 2. For a given class C, a C-*simulation* is a transitive relation $\asymp$ such that the following conditions hold.

(a) $h' \approx h \asymp k \approx k'$ implies $h' \asymp k'$, i.e., the relation is insensitive to renaming and garbage collection;
(b) $h \asymp k$ implies $h \sim^C k$, i.e., related heaps cannot be distinguished in the context of code of classes other than C;
(c) $f \asymp f$ for every method f of class C, i.e., methods of C preserve $\asymp$.

Item (a) is a simple healthiness condition that is to be expected. Item (b) and transitivity are what will justify the use of $\asymp$ in the definition of observational purity; (b) says that outside C, the relation acts like the simple indistinguishability relation. Item (c) complements (b), dealing with the problem that code in C need not preserve $\sim^C$ and as a result $\sim^C$ is not a congruence.

Simulations of various kinds are of fundamental importance in the study of encapsulation [25, 14]. A standard result is that if a relation has property (c) then in fact it is preserved by every method of every class. Indeed, it is preserved by every statement and as a consequence it is a congruence: If $S \asymp S'$ then $C[S] \asymp C[S']$ for all well formed contexts $C[-]$. By well formed contexts, we mean those which respect encapsulation boundaries. Encapsulation for this purpose is studied in [3] and other disciplines for encapsulating invariants can be used as well, e.g. verification disciplines [6, 26] and type systems [17, 13]. Such disciplines typically base encapsulation boundaries on program structures such as modules and private fields and in addition some form of alias control.

For simulations used to connect different representations of an abstraction, transitivity does not make sense because the domain and range of the relation are different state spaces. For our purposes transitivity is needed; it holds for the examples we have considered, for reasons that become clear in Section 3.

2.5 Observational Purity Via Simulation

Our main definition follows the pattern of Lemma 1.

Definition 3. Expression E is *observationally pure outside* C *via* $\asymp$ if and only if $\asymp$ is a C-simulation and $E, h \to v, k$ implies $k \asymp h$ (for all h, v, k). Moreover, E is *observationally pure outside* C iff there exists $\asymp$ such that E is observationally pure outside C via $\asymp$. Finally, f is *observationally pure outside* C *(via* $\asymp$) iff the call $f(x)$ is observationally pure outside C (via $\asymp$) for variable x.

For a method f it suffices to check the method body, but we formulate it in terms of application to a variable for clarity.

If f is weakly pure then it is observationally pure, via the relation $\approx$. Taking $\asymp$ in Def. 3 to be $\approx$, the requisite condition is exactly weak purity. And $\approx$ is a simulation: (a) holds by transitivity, (b) by definition, and (c) by congruence.

If every method call in an expression E is observationally pure via $\asymp$ then it is not difficult to show that E is observationally pure via the same relation. One might want a different simulation to be used for different methods ; this generalization is discussed in [9]

Theorem 1. If Q is observationally pure outside C then for any context $C[-]$ of a class other than C we have $C[\textbf{assert } Q] \sim^C C[\textbf{skip}]$.

As with Proposition 1, we give a proof for the case that Q is a single call $f(x)$.

Suppose f is observationally pure outside C via $\asymp$. A consequence of conditions (a) and (b) of Def. 2 is that $S \asymp S'$ implies[5] $S \sim^C S'$. So to prove $C[\textbf{assert } f(x)] \sim^C C[\textbf{skip}]$ it suffices to show $C[\textbf{assert } f(x)] \asymp C[\textbf{skip}]$. Because $\asymp$ is a congruence (a consequence of condition (c)), this follows from $\textbf{assert } f(x) \asymp \textbf{skip}$. Finally, $\textbf{assert } f(x) \asymp \textbf{skip}$ can be proved by an argument similar to that for Proposition 1, using transitivity of $\asymp$ and the conditions of Def. 3 for f.

So we have justified that (1) holds, with $\sim^C$ for $\cong$, provided that there is a simulation $\asymp$ with respect to which f is observationally pure.

Relation $\sim^C$ is correctness preserving for specifications other than private ones for class C, so it is suitable for annotations and specifications of classes other than C. Thus, for $\sim^C$, Equation (1) should only be used in code outside C.

An attractive feature of our account is that simulations are intimately connected with established theories of encapsulation; our approach can be carried out given suitable forms of encapsulation such as ownership confinement [12] or the assertion based encapsulation of the Boogie methodology [6].

An unattractive feature of our account is that it appears to require the definition of a relation $\asymp$ and proof that all methods of the class C preserve it. Moreover, the program must conform to some encapsulation discipline, and possibly additional conditions be imposed on $\asymp$, to ensure that Def. 2(b) holds and that congruence follows from Def. 2(c). Such disciplines exist but impose nontrivial restrictions and/or depend on significant additional program annotations. In Section 3 we show that it is enough to have an encapsulation discipline that supports object invariants and for the programmer to reason about assertions rather than simulations.

By contrast, to check whether a method is weakly pure it suffices to check the code of the method (including overriding implementations).

3   Using Information Flow Analysis to Check Observational Purity

The requirement in Def. 3, that $f(x), h \rightarrow v, k$ implies $k \asymp h$, expresses a very strong form of encapsulation for f. Encapsulation usually means hiding of internal

---

[5] This glosses over a technicality: the relation needs to be established initially by constructors. A formalization is worked out in [28].

representations but not hiding of the represented information. By contrast, an observationally pure method reveals nothing about state, not even in terms of abstract values. This is akin to secure information flow policy, in particular confidentiality: public outputs must reveal nothing at all about secret inputs. In this section we show how static analysis for secure information flow can be used to check observational purity.

As indicated in the running example, for purposes of observational purity a simulation $\asymp$ would typically be defined so that $h \asymp h'$ if and only if

- $h \sim^C h'$ —i.e., fields of objects not of type C are related by $\approx$;
- fields of C that are not affected by the observationally pure methods are also related by $\approx$; and
- $I(h)$ and $I(h')$, where some object invariant is associated with class C and I expresses that each instance of C satisfies the invariant.

The first and second items are similar. Earlier we focused on the class as a natural encapsulation boundary, which motivated the definition of $\sim^C$, but we can combine the two items using a relation $\dot\sim$ that expresses hiding of just the fields affected by the observationally pure method. Suppose method f of class C is claimed to be observationally pure. Define $h \dot\sim h'$ iff h and h' agree, up to $\approx$, on all fields except those written by f.[6]

Anticipating the connection with secure information flow, let us assume that some methods of C are marked as *ObservationallyPure* and the fields written by those methods are marked as *Secret*.[7] Parameters and results of some private methods of C may also be marked as secret. All other fields, parameters, and results are considered *open*, the unmarked default. Now $h \dot\sim h'$ means that, up to $\approx$, heaps h and h' differ only in their secret parts.

To summarize the preceding paragraphs, we have observed that the typical $\asymp$ factors so that

$$h \asymp h' \text{ iff } h \dot\sim h' \text{ and } I(h) \text{ and } I(h') \tag{3}$$

The next observation is that if we instantiate Def. 2 with $\dot\sim$ for $\asymp$ then condition (c) is exactly the *termination-insensitive noninterference* property checked by dependency or information flow analysis [1, 31]. Condition (a) of Def. 2 holds by definition of $\dot\sim$. If all secret fields are in class C then (b) also holds by definition of $\dot\sim$.

For OO programs there are modular, type based information flow analyses that check each method implementation separately, relative to a fixed security labelling of method parameters and returns that is invariant under subclassing [27, 4, 33]. Restrictions are imposed only on methods that read or write secret fields or have secret parameters or results. Thus, in our application where only the putatively pure methods involve secrets, only their implementations need to be checked by the analysis.

Our proposal is therefore to use $\dot\sim$ as the standard simulation to witness observational purity. Two issues remain to be addressed:

---

[6] This glosses over the considerations mentioned in Footnote 3.

[7] We use the term "open" instead of "public" to avoid confusion with the visibility modifiers (private, protected, public) that are common in object-oriented programming. The security literature often uses "high" for secret and "low" for open.

- how can we check whether a method marked observationally pure does have the property in Def. 3 (that $f(x), h \rightarrow v, k$ implies $k \overset{.}{\sim} h$) with respect to $\overset{.}{\sim}$?
- do the examples of interest satisfy the restrictions of standard information flow analysis?

The first item is easy. The property is familiar in information flow analysis: The rule for checking a conditional "**if** E **then** S **else** S'" requires that, if E reads secrets then S and S' do not write open fields [15]. Not writing open fields is expressed by the property that $S, h \rightarrow k$ implies $k \overset{.}{\sim} h$. The ability to check this property is included in any information flow analysis.

The second item is problematic. Of course any fully automatic analysis is conservative and will reject some programs that are acceptable semantically. What we hope is that a large class of typical examples will be accepted. Unfortunately, all of our examples will be rejected by the standard rules, because of manifest dependence of (open) results on secret state. For example, the return expression of method f in Fig. 1 is $(U)t[x]$, which is considered secret because t is. The standard rule [15] for assignment is that

> If y is secret or E is open then "$y := E$" has secure flow.

We model the statement **return** E as assignment $result := E$ to a special variable. The example is rejected because a secret expression is assigned to the open result.

It would seem that, for f in our running example, (c) with $\overset{.}{\sim}$ for $\asymp$ fails, for the same reason (c) with $\sim^C$ for $\asymp$ fails, i.e., these relations allow the secret state to differ arbitrarily. But recall the factorization (3); what is preserved by code of C is the conjunction of $\overset{.}{\sim}$ with the object invariant. Hence, if we restrict attention to heaps satisfying the invariant then $\overset{.}{\sim}$ is preserved, because, in such heaps, $f(x)$ returns $expensive(x)$ regardless of whether x is in the cache or not.

One could devise information flow rules that directly take an invariant into account. Instead, we propose the following rule for assignments, which is of interest in the case that y is open and E secret.

> If E' is open then "**assert** $E = E'; y := E$" has secure flow.   (4)

It is not difficult to show that this is sound with respect to the noninterference property, i.e., condition (c). For our running example, the code would be annotated like this:

$$\textbf{assert } (U)t[x] = expensive(x); \ result := (U)t[x]$$

If $h \overset{.}{\sim} h'$ initially but $I(h)$ or $I(h')$ fails then one of the assertions fails and there is no pair k, k' of result heaps —and thus no counterexample to the noninterference property. On the other hand, if the invariant holds in both initial heaps then the corresponding results are equivalent (modulo $\approx$) as required. The role of the invariant is now to prove that the assertion is valid.

4   The Running Example

To support flow analysis, class C is annotated as shown in Figure 2. Note that the required assertion preceding the **return** is an immediate consequence of the class

```
class C {
    [Secret]
    private Hashtable  t := new Hashtable();
    invariant Forall{ T  x in t.Keys  :  t[x] = expensive(x)};
    [ObservationallyPure]
    public U  f( T  x)
        requires x ≠ null;
        ensures result = expensive(x);
    {
        if (¬t.ContainsKey(x)){
            U  y :=  ...; // compute expensive(x)
            t.Add(x, y); }
        assert (U)t[x] = expensive(x);
        return (U)t[x];
    }
}
```

Fig. 2. The annotated class C . The "leak" of secret information has been guarded by an assertion.

invariant that has been introduced as part of specifying the correctness of f regardless of the issue of purity.

Our approach would prevent the method *leak* (from Section 2.3) from being added to class C . Because t is secret, expression $t.Count$ is secret but the result is open. To include such a method, the programmer would have to validate an assertion relating $t.Count$, the number of items in the hashtable, to some open data, which is unlikely to be possible.

It is important to also consider how information can be revealed via control flow. Suppose the programmer added the following method to the example class C .

```
[ObservationallyPure]
public U  problem( T  x)
    requires x ≠ null;
    ensures result = expensive(x);
{  if (t.ContainsKey(x))  throw new Exception(...);  else return f(x);   }
```

If x had been an argument to f in a previous state, then $problem(x)$ throws an exception, otherwise it returns $expensive(x)$. As mentioned earlier, information flow analyses check that in the branches of a conditional with secret guard, there are no flows on open channels (e.g., assignments to an open variable, normal or exceptional return) [31]. For exceptional flows and unstructured code, control dependencies are tracked [11]; an open flow is not allowed if the program counter is influenced by secrets. Method *problem* is thus rejected as insecure.

Following the pattern of our new rule (4) one can introduce the following assertion/conditional rule:

If E' is open and S_0 and S_1 have secure flow then so does
" **assert** $E = E'$; **if** (E) **then** S_0 **else** S_1 ".

In fact this is a direct consequence of (4) as the code can be rewritten using a fresh, open variable y as follows: **assert** $E = E'$; $y := E$; **if** (y) **then** S_0 **else** S_1. For field update $x.f := E$ the rule is similar to the rule for assignment in that if E is secret then f must also be marked as secret.[8]

The assertion/conditional rule would not apply to method *problem* unless the programmer could find an open expression equal to $t.ContainsKey(x)$ which is unlikely. The method is rejected as it should be.

5 Conclusions

When specifications do not modify the observable state of a program, specifications can be combined with programs without changing their meaning. This makes it much easier to implement both static and dynamic analysis tools. The distinction can be made by completely separating the functions used in specifications from those in the program, which is attractive in theory. But OO code includes many purely functional methods, indeed many that only read state, and terminate for obvious reasons, often under no preconditions. For runtime checking it is surely better to use such a method in specifications rather than re-implementing it merely for theoretical elegance. Moreover, requiring the use of a special specification library for functions that are manifestly present in the code creates an unnecessary impediment to programmers' writing and using specifications.

Specifications are usually at a high level of abstraction that ignores phenomena such as real time, power consumption, and even memory size. Once the door is opened to using program functions in specifications, it is natural to allow those that have an effect such as memory allocation that is not observable at the level of reasoning. We push this idea further, arguing that effects can be ignored in the context of a specification if encapsulation prevents the effects from being observable in that context.

Many library methods are weakly pure. But there are also many accessor methods that are intended to be pure, as indicated by the names and by documentation, but which are not weakly pure. It would be convenient to have them available for use in contracts.

5.1 Related Work

Runtime verification using AsmL [10] does not restrict the use of functions in specifications. It provides an alternative data space from the implementation so that side-effects in this space are insulated from the data space of the implementation. But AsmL is unsound since it allows full interoperability with arbitrary components.

JML has decided on the conservative approach of outlawing all side-effects [20] except construction of new objects. Library methods that cause side-effects cannot be used in specifications; instead, pure replacements must be used. This complicates life for specifiers: one must always be aware of which methods one can use and which are outlawed. Also, not all of the current JML tools are capable of using the replacement methods.

---

[8] There is an additional restriction that if x is secret then f must be so too; open fields could be updated through an open alias of x. See [4] for an explanation.

These issues have long been known in the Eiffel community; Meyer [24] discusses at length the desire to allow benevolent side-effects. However, Eiffel does not enforce any policy, but leaves it as a design principle.

Leino [22] explores benevolent side effects with respect to modifies specifications.

Sălcianu and Rinard [32] have designed a purity analysis that is able to distinguish updates to pre-existing objects and newly allocated objects. The mutation of the latter is allowed in a pure method. They also are able to extract regular-expression descriptions of updates that violate purity. This analysis supports the intended notion of purity of JML but is less conservative than the analysis used in the JML tools.

A preliminary version of this paper appeared as [8]. Naumann [28] subsequently formalized the general theory in terms of simulations (justifying our Section 2) but did not develop the connection with information flow or consider extensive examples.

Banerjee and Naumann [3] give a general theory of simulations for encapsulated data representations, using an instance-based notion of heap encapsulation closely related to ownership types [12, 13]. In recent work [5] they give an instance-based theory of simulations using an adaptation of the Boogie methodology [6, 23] which uses mutable notion of ownership for modular reasoning about object invariants. It seems likely that a notion of simulation suitable for observational purity could be based on other units of modularity such as the package [17]; in some sense that's closer to what an information flow analysis does.

A prototype checker for secure information flow in single-threaded Java programs, based on proven sound rules [4], is being developed as part of the dissertation research of Qi Sun [33]. The Jif prototype[9] checks information flow for Java; based on work of Andrew Myers [27], it deals with more sophisticated flow policies. The FlowCaml system[10] is based on provably sound rules [29, 30] and handles a substantial fragment of Objective Caml, though omitting object-oriented features. Amtoft et al. [2] have developed a logic for checking information flow and shown how it applies to our leading example.

The security literature has extensive work on declassification, i.e., intentional flows from secret to open. Our rule (4) may appear to be a form of declassification, but it does not allow any leakage of information which is the point of declassification [31].

5.2 Future Work

We plan to perform an analysis of the .NET base class library to see how many functions that would informally be considered as pure are actually observationally pure, but not weakly pure. We are also implementing our observational purity system in the context of the Spec# project [7] within Microsoft Research. This context provides automated theorem-proving support to check assertions. For simple examples involving lazy initialization and caches, superficial syntactic heuristics might be adequate for checking the relevant assertions.

Acknowledgements. We thank the participants at the Formal Techniques for Java-like Programs workshop (FTfJP 2004) for comments and discussion. Thanks also to Gary

---

[9] On the web at http://www.cs.cornell.edu/jif/

[10] On the web at http://cristal.inria.fr/~simonet/soft/flowcaml/

Leavens, Rustan Leino, and Alexandru Sălcianu. Dave Naumann and Qi Sun grate-fully acknowledge support from Microsoft Research as well as the US National Science Foundation (awards CCR-0208984 and CCF-0429894).

References

1. Martín Abadi, Anindya Banerjee, Nevin Heintze, and Jon G. Riecke. A core calculus of dependency. In *ACM Symp. on Princ. of Program. Lang. (POPL)*, 1999.
2. T. Amtoft, S. Bandhakavi, and A. Banerjee. A logic for information flow in object-oriented programs. In *POPL*, 2006. Extended version available as KSU CIS-TR-2005-1.
3. Anindya Banerjee and David A. Naumann. Ownership confinement ensures representation independence for object-oriented programs. *Journal of the ACM*, 52(6):894–960, November 2005.
4. Anindya Banerjee and David A. Naumann. Stack-based access control for secure information flow. *Journal of Functional Programming*, 15(2):131–177, 2005. Special issue on Language Based Security.
5. Anindya Banerjee and David A. Naumann. State based ownership, reentrance, and encapsulation. In *European Conference on Object-Oriented Programming (ECOOP)*, pages 387–411, 2005.
6. Mike Barnett, Robert DeLine, Manuel Fähndrich, K. Rustan M. Leino, and Wolfram Schulte. Verification of object-oriented programs with invariants. *Journal of Object Technology*, 3(6):27–56, 2004. Special issue: ECOOP 2003 workshop on Formal Techniques for Java-like Programs.
7. Mike Barnett, K. Rustan M. Leino, and Wolfram Schulte. The Spec# programming system: An overview. In *CASSIS post-proceedings*, 2004.
8. Mike Barnett, David A. Naumann, Wolfram Schulte, and Qi Sun. 99.44% pure: Useful abstractions in specifications. In *ECOOP workshop on Formal Techniques for Java-like Programs (FTfJP)*, 2004. Technical Report NIII-R0426, University of Nijmegen.
9. Mike Barnett, David A. Naumann, Wolfram Schulte, and Qi Sun. Allowing state changes in specifications. Technical Report MSR-TR-2006-22, Microsoft Research, 2006.
10. Mike Barnett and Wolfram Schulte. Runtime verification of .NET contracts. *The Journal of Systems and Software*, 65(3):199–208, 2003.
11. Gilles Barthe, David A. Naumann, and Tamara Rezk. Deriving an information flow checker and certifying compiler for java. In *27th IEEE Symposium on Security and Privacy*, May 2006. To appear.
12. David Clarke. Object ownership and containment. Dissertation, Computer Science and Engineering, University of New South Wales, Australia, 2001.
13. David Clarke and Sophia Drossopoulou. Ownership, encapsulation and the disjointness of type and effect. In *OOPSLA*, pages 292–310, November 2002.
14. Willem-Paul de Roever and Kai Engelhardt. *Data Refinement: Model-Oriented Proof Methods and their Comparison*. Cambridge University Press, 1998.
15. D. Denning and P. Denning. Certification of programs for secure information flow. *Communications of the ACM*, 20(7):504–513, 1977.
16. Cormac Flanagan, K. Rustan M. Leino, Mark Lillibridge, Greg Nelson, James B. Saxe, and Raymie Stata. Extended static checking for Java. In *ACM Conf. on Program. Lang. Design and Implementation (PLDI)*, pages 234–245, 2002.
17. Christian Grothoff, Jens Palsberg, and Jan Vitek. Encapsulating objects with confined types. In *OOPSLA*, 2001.

18. C. A. R. Hoare. Proofs of correctness of data representations. *Acta Informatica*, 1:271–281, 1972.

19. John Hogg, Doug Lea, Alan Wills, Dennis deChampeaux, and Richard Holt. The Geneva Convention on the treatment of object aliasing. *OOPS Messenger*, 3(2):11–16, 1992.

20. Gary Leavens, Yoonsik Cheon, Curtis Clifton, Clyde Ruby, and David R. Cok. How the design of JML accomodates both runtime assertion checking and formal verification. Technical Report 03-04, Department of Computer Science, Iowa State University, March 2003.

21. Gary T. Leavens, Yoonsik Cheon, Curtis Clifton, Clyde Ruby, and David R. Cok. How the design of JML accommodates both runtime assertion checking and formal verification. In Frank S. de Boer, Marcello M. Bonsangue, Susanne Graf, and Willem-Paul de Roever, editors, *Formal Methods for Components and Objects (FMCO 2002)*, volume 2852 of *LNCS*, pages 262–284. Springer, 2003.

22. K. Rustan M. Leino. A myth in the specification of programs. Manuscript KRML62, available from the author.

23. K. Rustan M. Leino and Peter Müller. Object invariants in dynamic contexts. In *European Conference on Object-Oriented Programming (ECOOP)*, pages 491–516, 2004.

24. Bertrand Meyer. *Object-oriented Software Construction*. Prentice Hall, New York, second edition, 1997.

25. John C. Mitchell. *Foundations for Programming Languages*. MIT Press, 1996.

26. P. Müller, A. Poetzsch-Heffter, and G.T. Leavens. Modular invariants for object structures. *Science of Computer Programming*, 2006. To appear.

27. Andrew C. Myers. JFlow: Practical mostly-static information flow control. In *ACM Symp. on Princ. of Program. Lang. (POPL)*, pages 228–241, 1999.

28. David A. Naumann. Observational purity and encapsulation. In *Fundamental Aspects of Software Engineering (FASE)*, pages 190–204, 2005.

29. F. Pottier and S. Conchon. Information flow inference for free. In *Proceedings of the fifth ACM International Conference on Functional Programming*, pages 46–57, 2000.

30. François Pottier and Vincent Simonet. Information flow inference for ML. *ACM Transactions on Programming Languages and Systems*, 25(1):117–158, January 2003.

31. Andrei Sabelfeld and Andrew C. Myers. Language-based information-flow security. *IEEE J. Selected Areas in Communications*, 21(1):5–19, January 2003.

32. Alexandru Sălcianu and Martin Rinard. A combined pointer and purity analysis for Java programs. Technical Report MIT-CSAIL-TR-949, Department of Computer Science, Massachusetts Institute of Technology, May 2004.

33. Qi Sun, Anindya Banerjee, and David A. Naumann. Modular and constraint-based information flow inference for an object-oriented language. In Roberto Giacobazzi, editor, *Static Analysis Symposium (SAS)*, volume 3148 of *LNCS*, pages 84–99. Springer-Verlag, 2004.

Field Access Analysis for Enforcing Access Control Policies

Kathrin Lehmann[1] and Peter Thiemann[2]

[1] TU München
[2] Universität Freiburg
http://www.informatik.uni-freiburg.de/~thiemann

Abstract. A field access analysis computes for each object the set of places where its fields are accessed and modified. Such an analysis is the formal basis for a code instrumentation algorithm that inserts access control checks in a program to enforce an access control policy.

The present work formalizes field access analysis in terms of a type-based program analysis for Java, proves type preservation for the underlying annotated type system, and demonstrates its use with an example specification and instrumentation. A variant of the analysis has been implemented.

1 Introduction

Security considerations are an important part of contemporary system development efforts. Although programming languages enter at a late stage in the development process, they do provide the ultimate building blocks for the system. Thus, to obtain high confidence in the security properties of a system, the programming language must be aware of these properties at best or it must facilitate static analysis of these properties. These issues are the driving forces of research on language-based security [19].

Security has three main facets, integrity, confidentiality, and availability, all of which have been formalized to various degrees and incorporated in type systems and other kinds of static analyses. The present work deals with one particular mechanism to help enforce confidentiality, namely access control.

There are a variety of access control models ranging from mandatory access control (MAC) in military systems to discretionary access control (DAC) as used in the UNIX file system to more recent models, like role-based access control (RBAC) [7], which is now widely accepted for describing roles and permissions in business applications.

The ISO-Standard 10181-3 [1] defines a general access control framework, which is independent of RBAC, DAC, or other access control strategies. An initiator, the "subject", poses a request to be executed on a defined object, the "target". This request is forwarded to an "access enforcement function" (AEF), which is responsible for enforcing the access control policies. The AEF in turn asks the "access decision function" (ADF) responsible for answering the access control request for an access control decision. Access is granted

G. Müller (Ed.): ETRICS 2006, LNCS 3995, pp. 337–351, 2006.
© Springer-Verlag Berlin Heidelberg 2006

according to the ADF's decision. Similar ideas, *i.e.*, separation of AEF and ADF components, are also presented in the XACML Standard 2.0 [10], which is an XML-based language for the description of an access control policy based on rules.

In the last years mechanisms and standards have been developed that provide a unified framework and APIs for expressing access control needs. These mechanisms mainly focus on ADF functionality. For example, Sun developed JAAS, the Java Authentication and Authorization Service [21], which builds on the SecurityManager already present in Java. JAAS and the Java Security Architecture [22] enable the definition of access control policies (*i.e.*, ADF), but their enforcement (*i.e.*, AEF) requires manual coding. A systematic approach for constructing AEF-components is still missing.

The present work explores the question of how to identify earliest places in source code where enforcement of an access control policy should take place and which parts of the access control policy must be enforced at this point of program flow. This instrumentation should be efficient in the sense that it does not perform redundant checks. There are two steps toward this goal. The first analysis step yields a field-access model that exhibits all field accesses and updates relevant for access control that may be performed by a piece of code. The second step performs the actual instrumentation of the code by checking which permissions are required to run the subsequent code.

The primary concern of this paper is the analysis step. We define a type-based analysis for Java programs that constructs essentially an annotation scheme on top of an underlying Java type derivation. The resulting, annotated type derivation contains sufficient information to construct a suitable access-path model. We prove that the access-path model is a sound approximation of the actual access paths. There is an implementation of a variant of the analysis on top of the SOOT framework [24].

Outline

Section 2 contains a worked out example. It presents a walk-through of the analysis and sketches the insertion of AEF-code. Section 3 introduces the theoretical framework in terms of AccessJava, a typed Java core calculus. Section 4 contains the technical results, in particular, the annotations inferred by the analysis support a non-interference property that rules out violations of the access-control policy. Section 5 reviews related work and Sec.6 concludes.

2   Motivation

This section introduces our method informally with an example.

2.1   An Example

Figure 1 contains an excerpt from the UML data model of a web log community. Each web log is owned by a person and consists of web log entries that are ordered

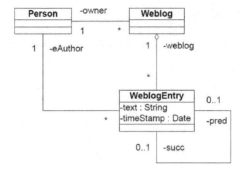

Fig. 1. Example class diagram of web log community

Table 1. Example permissions. (W = Weblog, WE = WeblogEntry)

permission	subject	object	action
UpdatePropWE	eAuthor of weblog entry OR owner of weblog	properties of WE	write prop.
CreateAssocWE_W	eAuthor of weblog entry OR owner of weblog	assoc. instance from WE to its W	create assoc.

in reverse chronological order. The role name **eAuthor** denotes the author of the web log entry.

Table 1 shows some example permissions for administrating web log entries. This list is by no means complete. It only shows permissions relevant to the running example. Protected resources, the *objects*, are the properties and association instances of the application objects. In ACCESSJAVA both kinds of *objects* are modelled as fields. A *subject* is a principal, given by objects of the type Person. *Actions* can be read and write actions to properties of primitive data type or read, create, and remove actions of associations between application objects. To keep the example short, only properties of **WeblogEntry** and instances of the **weblog** association are protected.

Listing 1.1 contains example code from a web log implementation. The method **serve()** in **EmailEntryService** receives a user id and password, a weblog, and text for a new weblog entry to create. The new entry's attributes are set and the entry is inserted at the first position in the web log. The code does not set an explicit first pointer because the **Weblog** class does not maintain one. Instead, a database table maintains the association between **Weblog** and **WeblogEntry** objects with the sequence defined by the time stamps. Given the permissions above, the task is to find out which permissions are required to execute this service. From this information, we generate an access enforcement function that checks if the current principal has permission to execute the service.

```
1  public class EmailEntryService {
       public void serve(/* request data */){
3          String uid = /* get user id from request*/;
           String pwd = /* get password from request*/;
5          Weblog weblog = /* get weblog from request */;
           String text = /* get entry text from request */;
7
           Person user = AuthenticationService.authenticate(uid, pwd);
9          WeblogEntry entry = WeblogCommunity.createWeblogEntry(user);

11         /** set attributes **/
           entry.setText(text);
13         entry.setPublished(new Date());
           entry.setWeblog(weblog);
15
           /** insert new entry at the beginning **/
17         WeblogEntry first = weblog.getFirstEntry();
           entry.setSuccessor(first);
19         first.setPredecessor(entry );
           }
21 }

23 public class WeblogCommunity {
       public static WeblogEntry createWeblogEntry(Person p){
25         WeblogEntry newEntry = new WeblogEntry();
           newEntry.setAuthor(p);
27         return newEntry;
       }
29 }

31 public class WeblogEntry {
       private Weblog weblog;
33     private String text;
       private Date timeStamp;
35     private Person author;
       private WeblogEntry succ;
37     private WeblogEntry pred;

39     public void setWeblog(Weblog w){
           this.weblog = w;
41     }
       public void setText(String text){
43         this.text = text;
       }
45     public void setPublished(Date time){
           this.timeStamp = time;
47     }
       public void setAuthor(Person p){
49         this.author = p;
       }
51     public void setPredecessor(WeblogEntry p){
           this.pred = p;
53     }
       public void setSuccessor(WeblogEntry s){
55         this.succ = s;
       }
57 }
```

Listing 1.1. Example source code of a web log community

To compute the required permissions, our static analysis builds type graphs for each variable and for each program point in the source code. This type graph holds information about all field accesses and updates that may be executed along any execution path starting from the program point.

```
class WeblogEntry {
  ...
    //entry = WeblogEntry {t1  weblog  [W, {S40}] }
    public void setWeblog(Weblog w) {
      this.weblog = w;  //@set  weblog;  line 40
    }
  ...
}
```

Listing 1.2. Get- and set-methods of `WeblogEntry` after second iteration

2.2   Analysis of the Example

The first step in building such a type graph is to map all defined actions to concrete source code artefacts. The "write" action of a web log entry described in the table above takes place when a property of a web log entry is set. In our example code, expressions of the form "obj.property = var;" serve as anchors for the write access.

The algorithm for building the type graph starts with annotating every statement corresponding to one of the anchor forms just defined. The source code is then analyzed iteratively by adding new annotations in each iteration in order to further propagate the anchors and construct a type graph.

The annotations of the statements within a method give rise to annotations describing all read and write accesses to all properties of the base object itself (`this`), all objects defined within the method and subsequent methods called from within the method's body, and all parameter objects to this method. This type graph fragment is then transferred to all statements that call this method.

Listing 1.2 shows the status of our example code after the second iteration. The set-method shown consist of only one anchor statement. This completes the analysis of the method body and annotations may be added to the method's definition. The annotation for the method `setWeblog(Weblog w)` sets (S) the field `weblog` in line 40. In the algorithm, each field collects a set of these annotations, fields with empty annotation set are omitted from the listing. For that reason the listing does not contain an annotation for the argument `Weblog w` of method `setWeblog()`.

After several iterations the method `serve()` in `EmailEntryService`, which represents the entry point of our example code, can be annotated with the complete type graph. Listing 1.3 contains the result. The final annotation shows that `serve()` sets all properties and associations of the newly created weblog entry.

Not all statements are interesting with respect to access control. These statements can be annotated with an *out-of-scope* note. Examples for such statements are method calls whose call graph will not reach any of the defined anchor statements. Our example tracks operations on properties and associations of application objects. All method calls of objects of the Java Runtime can be skipped. Also return statements that are no anchors, if-statements, and other control flow directives may be skipped. However, the example source code is stripped of all these kinds of processing statements.

```
user      : p1 = Person {}

weblog    : w1 = Weblog {}

entry     : WeblogEntry {
                w1        weblog      [W, {S40}  ]
                String    text        [W, {S43}  ]
                Date      timeStamp   [W, {S46}  ]
                p1        author      [W, {S49}  ]
                e1        succ        [W, {S55}  ]
          }

first     : e1 = WeblogEntry {
                e         pred        [W, {S52}  ]
          }
```

Listing 1.3. Final type graph at invocation of **serve**

```
public class EmailEntryService {
    public void serve(/* request data */){
        String uid = /* get user ID from request*/;
        String pwd = /* get password from request*/;
        Weblog weblog = /* get weblog from request */;
        String text = /* get entry text from request */;

        Person user = AuthenticationService.authenticate(uid, pwd);
        WeblogEntry entry = WeblogCommunity.createWeblogEntry(user);

        if (!(((weblog.getOwner().equals(user)) ||        // CreateAssocWE_W
                entry.getAuthor().equals(user)))           // UpdatePropWE
        throw new AccessControlException();
        ...
    }
}
```

Listing 1.4. Instrumented example access control source code

As any program analysis, this analysis is approximative to retain computability when analyzing programs with recursive data or control flow. Hence, type graphs do not record dependencies from conditionals (although that might yield more accurate information) and they are restricted to regular trees. To enforce the restriction to regular trees, type graphs must not contain more than one node for each combination of the program point of the creating **new** expression and node annotation. For readability, Listing 1.3 elides program points although the formal framework in Sec.3 includes them.

2.3   Code Instrumentation

The type graph yields for each object a description about the locations where the object's properties and associations are accessed. When inserting code with access control functionality, this type graph is analyzed. In a conservative approach (neglecting control flow) access control statements are inserted just before the first usage of the object, checking all property accesses.

In our example, the type graph shows that all properties and associations of the weblog entry **entry** are set. Therefore, the corresponding policies

$$
\begin{array}{lll}
P & ::= defn^*\ e \\
defn & ::= \textbf{class}\ cl\ \textbf{extends}\ c\ \{\ field^*\ meth^*\ \} \\
field & ::= t\ fd \\
c & ::= cl\ |\ \textbf{object} \\
t & ::= rt\ |\ \underline{\tau}\ |\ \mu\tau.t \\
rt & ::= (c,\underline{tg})\ |\ \overline{\textbf{int}}\ |\ \textbf{boolean}\ |\ \ldots \\
tg & \in\ ClassName \rightarrow \{field[F,fa]^*\} & \text{type graph} \\
F & ::= \mathsf{F}\ |\ \mathsf{R}\ |\ \mathsf{W} & \text{polarity annotation} \\
fa & ::= \psi\ |\ \emptyset\ |\ G\ell\ |\ S\ell\ |\ fa \cup fa & \text{field annotation} \\
meth & ::= \underline{\underline{\forall\psi^*}}.C \Rightarrow t\ \underline{[t]}\ md\ (arg^*)\ \{\ e\ \} \\
arg & ::= t\ var \\
\underline{\underline{C}} & ::= fa \leq^{fa} fa\ |\ G\ell \in fa\ |\ S\ell \in fa\ |\ C \wedge C\ |\ \textsc{True}\ |\ \textsc{False} \\
e & ::= [\textbf{new}\ c]^\ell\ |\ [var]^\ell\ |\ [\textbf{null}]^\ell\ |\ [e\underline{:\ cl}.fd]^\ell\ |\ [e\underline{:\ cl}.fd = e]^\ell \\
& \quad |\ [e.md(e^*)]^\ell\ |\ [\textbf{let}\ var = e\ \textbf{in}\ e]^\ell\ |\ [\textbf{cast}\ c\ e]^\ell \\
cl & \in\ ClassName, fd \in FieldName, md \in MethodName
\end{array}
$$

Fig. 2. Syntax of AccessJava

defined in table 1 have to be checked. Writing properties and creating an association between a weblog entry instance and a weblog instance depend on the relationship eAuthor and owner between the subject, the entry and web log objects respectively. So, code that checks these permissions must be added after the objects in question are defined and before they are first used. In our example we may generate the code depicted in listing 1.4 for the service EmailEntryService. The permissions for updating a propery of a weblog entry and for creating a new weblog entry, which adds a new association from a weblog instance to a weblog entry instance, both depend on the weblog, the weblog entry, and the principal in question. Hence, the access control check is inserted at line 10 in the original source code just after these three objects have been defined.

3   Analysis

The theoretical framework of the access path analysis is based on AccessJava, a subset of ClassicJava[8], which models the core expression language of Java with imperative field update. The formalization omits interfaces and **super** method calls, which would be straightforward to add.

Figure 2 defines the syntax of AccessJava. Analogously to ClassicJava, the AccessJava grammar contains underlined parts which are not written by the programmer, but rather filled in by type elaboration (singly underlined) and the analysis algorithm (doubly underlined). The former are inherited from ClassicJava and simplify the definition of the dynamic semantics. The latter concern polarity and field annotations, fa, and the corresponding universal quantification over field annotations.

$$R \leq^p F \qquad W \leq^p F \qquad F \leq^p F$$

$$\frac{L \subseteq L'}{C \vdash L \leq^{fa} L'} \qquad C \vdash fa \leq^{fa} fa \qquad C \wedge fa \leq^{fa} fa' \vdash fa \leq^{fa} fa'$$

$$C \vdash fa \leq^{fa,F} fa \qquad \frac{C \vdash fa \leq^{fa} fa'}{C \vdash fa \leq^{fa,R} fa'} \qquad \frac{C \vdash fa' \leq^{fa} fa}{C \vdash fa \leq^{fa,W} fa'}$$

$$C \vdash t \leq^{t,F} t \qquad \frac{C \vdash t \leq^t t'}{C \vdash t \leq^{t,R} t'} \qquad \frac{C \vdash t' \leq^t t}{C \vdash t \leq^{t,W} t'}$$

$$\frac{P, C \vdash t \leq^{t,F'} t' \quad F \leq^p F' \quad C \vdash fa \leq^{fa,F'} fa'}{P, C \vdash t \, fd[F, fa] \leq^f t' \, fd[F', fa']}$$

$$\frac{(\forall j) \, P, C \vdash field_j \leq^f field'_j}{P, C \vdash field_1 \ldots field_n \leq^{f*} field'_1 \ldots field'_n}$$

$$\frac{dom(tg) = dom(tg')}{(\forall cl \in dom(tg)) \, P, C \vdash tg(cl) \leq^{f*} tg'(cl)}{P, C \vdash tg \leq^{tg} tg'} \qquad \frac{cl \preceq^c_P cl' \quad P, C \vdash tg \leq^{tg} tg'}{P, C \vdash (cl, tg) \leq^t (cl', tg')}$$

Fig. 3. Subtyping

The doubly underlined parts extend Java's type language in two ways.

1. Each class type comes with a type graph tg that associates every class name with all its fields and their annotated types. The type graph for a class cl records analysis information about the field accesses through the objects of class cl. Without the type graph, analysis information would vanish through subsumption (which hides some fields) whereas downcasts (which expose some fields) would have to invent analysis information.

2. A class type may be recursive through its type graph. The presence of explicit information on fields and their types requires a recursive record type for objects [4, 5]. The operator $\mu\tau.t$ introduces a recursive type using τ as a type variable. The reading of the μ operator is equi-recursive: no extra typing rules are needed, but the existing ones have a coinductive interpretation.

The main technical novelty of ACCESSJAVA is the presence of field annotations, fa. This notion is in contrast to the more usual placement of annotations on types or type constructors [20].

The field annotations arise in the class graph together with the polarity annotations, F. The polarity annotation indicates the further use of the field (reading or writing) and directs the allowed subsumptions as explained in Sec.3.1. Field annotations themselves may be variables, empty, $G\ell$ (the field may be read at location ℓ), $S\ell$ (the field may be written to at location ℓ), or a union of field annotations. The union operator is associative, commutative, and idempotent.

3.1   Static Semantics

Figure 3 defines the subtyping relation through a set of coinductive inference rules. Starting with the rule at the bottom, subtyping $\leq^t$ on types arises from

$$\frac{c \precsim_P t}{P,C,A \vdash_e [\mathbf{new}\ c]^\ell : t} \qquad \frac{A(var) = t}{P,C,A \vdash_e [var]^\ell : t} \qquad \overline{P,C,A \vdash_e [\mathbf{null}]^\ell : (c, tg)}$$

$$\frac{\langle cl, fd, t', \mathsf{R}, fa \rangle \in_P t}{P,C,A \vdash_e e : t \quad C \Vdash G\ell \in fa}{P,C,A \vdash_e [e:\underline{cl}.fd]^\ell : t'} \qquad \frac{\langle cl, fd, t', \mathsf{W}, fa \rangle \in_P t}{P,C,A_1 \vdash_e e : t \quad P,C,A_2 \vdash_e e' : t' \quad C \Vdash S\ell \in fa}{P,C,A \vdash_e [e:\underline{cl}.fd = e']^\ell : t'}$$

$$\frac{P,C,A \vdash_e e_0 : t'_0 \quad (\forall j)\ P,C,A \vdash_e e_j : t'_j}{t'_0, md \leadsto_P \forall \psi^*.C' \Rightarrow t\ [t_0]\ md\ (t_1\ var_1 \ldots t_n\ var_n)}{C \Vdash S(C') \quad t'_j = S(t_j) \quad t'_0 = S(t_0)}{P,C,A \vdash_e [e_0.md(e_1, \ldots, e_p)]^\ell : S(t)}$$

$$\frac{P,C,A \vdash_e e : t}{t = (c, tg)}{P,C,A \vdash_e [\mathbf{cast}\ c\ e]^\ell : t} \qquad \frac{P,C,A \vdash_e e : t_1}{C \vdash t_2 \leq^t t_1 \quad t_2 = (c, tg)}{P,C,A \vdash_e [\mathbf{cast}\ c\ e]^\ell : t_2} \qquad \frac{P,C,A \vdash_e e : (cl', tg)}{cl \not\preceq^c_P cl' \quad cl' \not\preceq^c_P cl}{P,C,A \vdash_e [\mathbf{cast}\ cl\ e]^\ell : (cl, tg)}$$

$$\frac{P,C,A \vdash_e e_1 : t_1}{P,C,A, var : t_1 \vdash_e e_2 : t_2}{P,C,A \vdash_e [\mathbf{let}\ var = e_1\ \mathbf{in}\ e_2]^\ell : t_2} \qquad \frac{P,C,A \vdash_e e : t_1 \quad C \vdash t_1 \leq^t t_2}{P,C,A \vdash_e e : t_2}$$

Fig. 4. Typing rules for expressions

the declared subtyping relation among classes, $\preceq^c_P$, and from the annotations present in the type graph, tg. The relation $\preceq^c_P$ is the reflexive transitive closure of the single-step inheritance relation $\prec^c_P$ defined by

$$cl \prec^c_P c \quad \text{iff} \quad \mathbf{class}\ cl\ \mathbf{extends}\ c\ \{\ field^*\ meth^*\ \} \in P.$$

The type graph is essentially a class-indexed product of field descriptions where a field description is also a product of descriptions of single fields so that subtyping propagates covariantly in both cases, for $\leq^{tg}$ and for $\leq^{f*}$. The most complicated case is the one for single fields, $\leq^f$. The polarity annotation F indicates if the field will be used for reading $F = \mathsf{R}$, for writing $F = \mathsf{W}$, or for both $F = \mathsf{F}$ (see [17, Chapter 15.5]). The rule first allows the F annotation to change to F' according to the top three axioms. Then, F' determines whether the field type t and the field annotation fa are handled in a covariant ($F = \mathsf{R}$), contravariant ($F = \mathsf{W}$), or invariant ($F = \mathsf{F}$) manner. It remains to explain the subtyping of field annotations $\leq^{fa}$. A field annotation is either a variable or a set of labels indexed with G or S. The field annotation represents the set of locations of potential getters or setters so it is propagated by subsetting. The other two axioms treat the case where one or both annotations are variables.

Figure 4 defines the typing rules for expressions. The rule for **new** relies on the auxiliary relation $c \precsim_P t$ (see definition in Fig.5) that relates a class c to a type of the form $t = (c, tg)$ where tg is a type graph with slots for the fields of c and its subclasses.

The rules for variables and **null** are unsurprising. The rules for getting and setting the field of an object both rely on a relation $\langle cl, fd, t, fa \rangle \in_P t'$ which associates a field (identified by cl and fd), its type, and its field annotation with an object type t'. Each rule registers the location and the kind of access ($G\ell$

$$\frac{tg(\textbf{object}) = \{\}}{\textbf{object} \precsim_P (\textbf{object}, tg)}$$

$$\frac{\textbf{class } cl \textbf{ extends } c \ \{ \ \textit{field}^* \ \textit{meth}^* \ \} \in P \qquad tg(cl) = \textit{field}[F, fa]^* \qquad c \precsim_P (c, tg)}{cl \precsim_P (cl, tg)}$$

$$\frac{t \ fd[F, fa] \in tg(cl)}{\langle cl, fd, t, F, fa \rangle \in_P (cl, tg)}$$

$$\frac{fd \notin tg(cl) \qquad cl \prec_P^c cl' \qquad \langle cl'', fd, t, F, fa \rangle \in_P (cl', tg)}{\langle cl'', fd, t, F, fa \rangle \in_P (cl, tg)}$$

$$\frac{cl \precsim_P (cl, tg) \qquad \langle cl', fd', t', F', fa' \rangle \in_P (cl, tg)}{\langle cl', fd', t' \rangle \in'_P}$$

$$\frac{\textbf{class } cl \textbf{ extends } cl' \ \{ \ \textit{field}^* \ \textit{meth}^* \ \} \in P \qquad \forall \psi^*.C \Rightarrow t \ [t_0] \ md \ (arg^*) \ \{ \ body \ \} \in \textit{meth}^*}{(cl, tg), md \rightsquigarrow_P \forall \psi^*.C \Rightarrow t \ [t_0] \ md \ (arg^*)}$$

$$\frac{\textbf{class } cl \textbf{ extends } cl' \ \{ \ \textit{field}^* \ \textit{meth}^* \ \} \in P \qquad md \notin \textit{meth}^* \qquad (cl', tg), md \rightsquigarrow_P \forall \psi^*.C \Rightarrow t \ [t_0] \ md \ (arg^*)}{(cl, tg), md \rightsquigarrow_P \forall \psi^*.C \Rightarrow t \ [t_0] \ md \ (arg^*)}$$

Fig. 5. Auxiliary relations

$$\frac{cl \precsim_P t_0 \qquad \psi^* = fv(C, t, t_0, t_1, \ldots, t_n) \qquad P, C, [\textbf{this} : t_0, var_1 : t_1, \ldots, var_n : t_n] \vdash_e e : t}{P, cl \vdash_m \forall \psi^*.C \Rightarrow t \ [t_0] \ md \ (t_1 \ var_1 \ldots t_n \ var_n) \ \{ \ e \ \}}$$

$$\frac{(\forall j) \ P, cl \vdash_m \textit{meth}_j}{P \vdash_d \textbf{class } cl \textbf{ extends } c \ \{ \ \textit{field}^* \ \textit{meth}_1 \ldots \textit{meth}_m \ \}}$$

$$\frac{\textsc{ClassesOnce}(P) \quad \textsc{MethodsOncePerClass}(P) \quad \textsc{FieldOncePerClass}(P) \quad \textsc{CompleteClasses}(P) \quad \textsc{WellFoundedClasses}(P) \quad \textsc{ClassFieldsOK}(P) \quad \textsc{ClassMethodsOK}(P) \quad P = \textit{defn}_1 \ldots \textit{defn}_m \ e \quad (\forall j) \ P \vdash_d \textit{defn}_j \quad P, C, \emptyset \vdash_e e : t}{C \vdash_p P : t}$$

Fig. 6. Typing rules for method definitions and programs

or $S\ell$) in the corresponding field annotation. Both make use of the judgment $C \Vdash G\ell \in fa$ defined by

$$C \Vdash G\ell \in G\ell \qquad C \wedge G\ell \in \psi \Vdash G\ell \in \psi \qquad \frac{C \Vdash G\ell \in fa}{C \Vdash G\ell \in fa \cup fa'}$$

Analogous definitions hold for $C \Vdash S\ell \in fa$.

The rule for method call retrieves the method definition of the called method md for static receiver type t_0 using the auxiliary relation $t_0, md \rightsquigarrow_P \ldots$. It also provides the full method signature (which is to be inferred). The type at which the method is used in the program must be a substitution instance of the signature as indicated in the rule by the substitution S.

The rule for **let** models the definition of a local variable with inferred type. **cast** expressions have three rules, one for upcasts that never fail, one for downcasts, and one for stupid casts [12]. The final subsumption rule is standard.

Figure 6 contains the rules for definitions and programs. Starting from the bottom, the judgment for programs ($C \vdash_p P : t$) enforces some global well-formedness conditions through predicates with telling names. Definitions for these predicates may be found in the work on CLASSICJAVA[8].

In a valid program, each class definition must be valid (judgment $P \vdash_d \textit{defn}$) which in turn requires that each method definition of a class cl must be valid (judgment $P, cl \vdash_m \textit{meth}$). The rule for the latter judgment constructs the type of **this** using $\precsim_P$, type checks the method body with the variable assumptions resulting from the **this** type and the method signature, and yields the constraint required for the method from the expression judgment. It also abstracts over all annotation variables which occur free in the constraint or in any of the types. This abstraction corresponds to the standard introduction rule for universal quantification for the special case when the context is empty.

3.2 Dynamic Semantics

Figure 7 defines the dynamic semantics of ACCESSJAVA. The auxiliary definitions extend expressions, e, by locations l, drawn from an infinite set $\textit{Loc}$. A value is either a location, l, or a null pointer, **null**. The language of evaluation contexts, E, defines the standard left-to-right call-by-value evaluation order. $\mathcal{F}$ is a field map that maps a pair of a class name and a field name to a value. The underlined portions indicate information inferred during type checking: for field access and update the effective class.

$$
\begin{aligned}
e &::= l \mid \ldots & E &::= [\,] \mid [E.fd]^\ell \mid [E.fd = e]^\ell \mid [v.fd = E]^\ell \mid [E.md(e^*)]^\ell \\
v &::= l \mid \textbf{null} & &\quad \mid [v.md(v^*\, E\, e^*)]^\ell \mid [\textbf{let } var = E \textbf{ in } e]^\ell \mid [\textbf{cast } ci\, E]^\ell \\
l &\in \textit{Loc} & \mathcal{F} &::= \{\,\} \mid \mathcal{F}\{cl.fd \mapsto v\}
\end{aligned}
$$

$P \vdash \langle E[[\textbf{new } cl]^\ell], \mathcal{S} \rangle \overset{\ell}{\hookrightarrow} \langle E[l], \mathcal{S}' \rangle$
   if $l \notin dom(\mathcal{S})$ **and** $\mathcal{S}' = \mathcal{S}[l \mapsto \langle cl, \{cl'.fd \mapsto \textbf{null} \mid \langle cl', fd, t' \rangle \in'_P cl\} \rangle]$

$P \vdash \langle E[[l: \underline{cl}.fd]^\ell], \mathcal{S} \rangle \overset{\ell}{\hookrightarrow} \langle E[v], \mathcal{S} \rangle$
   if $\mathcal{S}(l) = \langle cl', \mathcal{F} \rangle$ **and** $\mathcal{F}(cl.fd) = v$

$P \vdash \langle E[[l: \underline{cl}.fd = v]^\ell], \mathcal{S} \rangle \overset{\ell}{\hookrightarrow} \langle E[v], \mathcal{S}[l \mapsto \langle cl', \mathcal{F}[cl.fd \mapsto v] \rangle] \rangle$
   if $\mathcal{S}(l) = \langle cl', \mathcal{F} \rangle$

$P \vdash \langle E[[l.md(v^*)]^\ell], \mathcal{S} \rangle \overset{\ell}{\hookrightarrow} \langle E[e[var^* \mapsto v^*, \textbf{this} \mapsto l]], \mathcal{S} \rangle$
   if $\mathcal{S}(l) = \langle cl, \mathcal{F} \rangle$ **and** $\langle md, var^*, e \rangle \in^c_P cl$

$P \vdash \langle E[[\textbf{let } var = v \textbf{ in } e]^\ell], \mathcal{S} \rangle \overset{\ell}{\hookrightarrow} \langle E[e[var \mapsto v]], \mathcal{S} \rangle$

$P \vdash \langle E[[\textbf{cast } cl\, v]^\ell], \mathcal{S} \rangle \overset{\ell}{\hookrightarrow} \langle E[v], \mathcal{S} \rangle$
   if $(v = l \in \textit{Loc}$ **and** $\mathcal{S}(l) = \langle cl', \mathcal{F} \rangle$ **implies** $(cl' \preceq^c_P cl))$

$P \vdash \langle E[[\textbf{cast } cl\, l]^\ell], \mathcal{S} \rangle \overset{\ell}{\hookrightarrow} \langle \text{error: bad cast}, \mathcal{S} \rangle$
   if $\mathcal{S}(l) = \langle cl', \mathcal{F} \rangle$ **and not** $(cl' \preceq^c_P cl)$

$P \vdash \langle E[[\textbf{null}.fd]^\ell], \mathcal{S} \rangle \overset{\ell}{\hookrightarrow} \langle \text{error: dereferenced null}, \mathcal{S} \rangle$

$P \vdash \langle E[[\textbf{null}.fd = v]^\ell], \mathcal{S} \rangle \overset{\ell}{\hookrightarrow} \langle \text{error: dereferenced null}, \mathcal{S} \rangle$

$P \vdash \langle E[[\textbf{null}.md(v^*)]^\ell], \mathcal{S} \rangle \overset{\ell}{\hookrightarrow} \langle \text{error: dereferenced null}, \mathcal{S} \rangle$

Fig. 7. Dynamic semantics of ACCESSJAVA

The semantics is formalized by a transition system on configurations $\langle e, \mathcal{S} \rangle$, where e is an expression and $\mathcal{S}$ is a store that maps locations to values. It is essentially CLASSICJAVA's semantics [8] with the transition for $[\mathbf{cast}\ cl\ v]^\ell$ extended to the case $v = \mathbf{null}$, the expressions modified to carry program points, ℓ, and with each transition labeled with the program point of the redex.

4   Technical Results

The type system presented in Sec.3 enjoys a type preservation property. To state that property requires to extend typing to configurations using the rules in Fig.8. The typing judgment for configurations treats locations like variables, that is, the environment A contains assumptions about locations, too. The judgment $\vdash_s$, which states the consistency of the assumptions about the store, has a standard inductive reading because all cyclic references are broken by the explicit use of the type environment A.

$$\frac{P, C \vdash_S \mathcal{S} : A \quad P, C, A \vdash_e e : t}{P, C, A \vdash_c \langle e, \mathcal{S} \rangle : t}$$

$$\frac{dom(A) = dom(\mathcal{S}) \quad (\forall l \in dom(\mathcal{S}))\ P, C, \mathcal{S}, A \vdash_s l}{P, C \vdash_S \mathcal{S} : A}$$

$$\frac{(cl, tg) = A(l) \quad \mathcal{S}(l) = \langle cl, \mathcal{F} \rangle \quad ran(\mathcal{F}) \subseteq dom(\mathcal{S}) \cup \{\mathbf{null}\}}{(\forall cl'.fd' \in dom(\mathcal{F}))\ t'\ fd'[F', fa'] \in tg(cl') \Rightarrow C \vdash A(\mathcal{F}(cl'.fd')) \leq^t t'}{P, C, \mathcal{S}, A \vdash_s l}$$

Fig. 8. Typing rules for configurations

Theorem 1. *If $P, \text{TRUE}, A \vdash_c \langle e, \mathcal{S} \rangle : t$ and $\langle e, \mathcal{S} \rangle \hookrightarrow \langle e', \mathcal{S}' \rangle$ then there exists A' with $(\forall l \in dom(A))\ A'(l) = A(l)$ such that $P, \text{TRUE}, A' \vdash_c \langle e', \mathcal{S}' \rangle : t$ or $e' = \mathsf{error} : ....$*

The more interesting result is a non-interference style result which demonstrates that the field annotations of the object types in a method signature reflect the access pattern of the objects in the method. That is, whenever the field annotations indicate that a field is not read, then the result of the method invocation is independent of the value of that field. Also, whenever the field annotations indicate that a field is not written, then its content will not change for the time of the method invocation.

To prove such a statement it has to be generalized to cover the execution of expressions and to consider the effect exerted on the store through the free locations in the expression.

Theorem 2. *Suppose that $P, \text{TRUE}, A \vdash_c \langle e_1, \mathcal{S}_1 \rangle : t_1$ and $P \vdash \langle e_1, \mathcal{S}_1 \rangle \overset{\ell}{\hookrightarrow} \langle e_2, \mathcal{S}_2 \rangle$. Let further $l \in dom(\mathcal{S}_1)$, $A(l) = (cl, tg)$, $\mathcal{S}_1(l) = (cl, \mathcal{F}_1)$, $\mathcal{S}_2(l) = (cl, \mathcal{F}_2)$, $cl'.fd \in dom(\mathcal{F}_1)$, and $t\ fd[F, fa] \in tg(cl')$.*

1. *If $fa \cap \{S\ell\} = \emptyset$ then $\mathcal{F}_1[cl'.fd] = \mathcal{F}_2[cl'.fd]$.*
2. *If $fa \cap \{G\ell\} = \emptyset$ and $\mathcal{S}_1' = \mathcal{S}_1[l \mapsto (cl, \mathcal{F}_1[cl'.fd \mapsto v])]$, for some arbitrary v, then $P \vdash \langle e_1, \mathcal{S}_1' \rangle \overset{\ell}{\hookrightarrow} \langle e_2, \mathcal{S}_2' \rangle$ such that $\mathcal{S}_2' = \mathcal{S}_2[l \mapsto (cl, \mathcal{F}_2[cl'.fd \mapsto v])]$.*

5   Related Work

In previous work [23], the last author proposes an analysis to track invariants of the DOM API. The DOM work relies on an annotated type system with polymorphism like the present work. However, the nature and the semantics of the annotations is quite different. The DOM analysis annotates **types** to model affine properties, *i.e.*, properties of values that change over time. In contrast, the present work yields summaries of access patterns collected by annotating **fields**. In the DOM work, type soundness is the key property, whereas the present work requires non-interference. Furthermore, the DOM work considers a language without inheritance, whereas the present work covers inheritance, too. The technical way that polymorphism is added to Java's type system and the particular style of expressing method signatures is common to both works. It is inspired by the work on HM(X) [16].

The present work is very related to effect systems [14], in particular to recent variants for Java core languages [3]. However, in these languages effects have the form **reads** *regions* **writes** *regions*, where a region is an abstraction for a set of fields of an object. In contrast, ACCESSJAVA has effects of finer granularity that include the description of the access path.

Our work falls into the realm of language-based security [19, 18]. One strand of work here deals with enforcing secure information flow. A typical approach is to extend a type system by labeling each type with values from a secrecy lattice ranging between *high* or *low* [6]. The goal of the security typed languages is to prevent information release from information qualified as *high* into variables classified as *low*. An example of a security typed programming language is JiF (Java + information flow) [15], an extension of Java, which adds a security label to each Java type.

In the area of access control models, Guelev et al. [11] present an agent based access control model that is able to express delegation of permissions and find indirect access paths. Abadi et al. [2] enhance the mechanism of stack inspection to associate rights with code by a history component. An access control decision is based not only on the state of the stack but also on code that has run before. Fournet and Gordon [9] define a formal semantics for stack inspection. In contrast, our model does not rely on stack inspection but computes access rights from access paths in the data model.

Further research concerns automatic code instrumentation for inserting access control checks into source code. Basin et al. [13] enrich a UML diagram by annotations expressing the (role-based) access control policy of the system (SecureUML). This diagram is the basis for generating Java code which includes the required security checks in each method body.

6 Conclusion

The present work defines a field access analysis for Java that provides sufficient information to guide the instrumentation of code with AEFs so that access control policies based on paths in the data model can be enforced. We prove a non-interference property required to guarantee correct enforcement and sketch an instrumentation algorithm. A simplified variant of the analysis is implemented on top of SOOT [24].

Further work includes the refinement of the implementation to the point that it can analyze existing business application code. In addition, ACCESSJAVA must be extended to track create and delete operations in addition to the read and write actions that it currently models. Create and delete are important because they also create and delete associations between objects.

References

1. I. 10181-3. Security frameworks for open systems: Access control framework, 1996.
2. M. Abadi and C. Fournet. Access control based on execution history. In *Network and Distributed System Security Symposium (NDSS'03)*, pages 107–121, San Diego, Feb. 2003. Internet Society.
3. G. M. Bierman, M. J. Parkinson, and A. M. Pitts. An imperative core calculus for Java and Java with effects. Technical Report 563, University of Cambridge Computer Laboratory, Apr. 2003.
4. L. Cardelli. A semantics of multiple inheritance. *Information and Computation*, 76(2/3):138–164, 1988.
5. W. Cook and J. Palsberg. A denotational semantics of inheritance and its correctness. *Information and Computation*, 114(2):329–350, 1995.
6. D. Denning. A lattice model of secure information flow. *Communications of the ACM*, 19(5):236–242, 1976.
7. D. Ferraiolo, R. Sandhu, S. Gavrila, R. Kuhn, and R. Chandramouli. Proposed nist standard for role-based access control. *ACM Trans. on Information and Systems Security*, 4(3):224–274, 2001.
8. M. Flatt, S. Krishnamurthi, and M. Felleisen. A programmer's reduction semantics for classes and mixins. In *Formal Syntax and Semantics of Java*, number 1523 in LNCS, pages 241–269. Springer, 1999.
9. C. Fournet and A. D. Gordon. Stack inspection: Theory and variants. In J. Mitchell, editor, *Proc. 29th ACM Symp. on Principles of Programming Languages*, pages 307–318, Portland, OR, USA, Jan. 2002. ACM Press.
10. S. Godik, T. Moses, et al. eXtensible Access Control Markup Language (XACML), 2003.
11. D. P. Guelev, M. D. Ryan, and P.-Y. Schobbens. Model-checking access control policies. In Y. Z. Kan Zhang, editor, *Seventh Information Security Conference (ISC'04)*, number 3225 in LNCS, pages 219–230. Springer, Sept. 2004.
12. A. Igarashi, B. C. Pierce, and P. Wadler. Featherweight Java: a minimal core calculus for Java and GJ. *ACM Trans. on Programming Languages and Systems*, 23(3):396–450, May 2001.

13. T. Lodderstedt, D. A. Basin, and J. Doser. SecureUML: A UML-based modeling language for model-driven security. In J.-M. Jézéquel, H. Hussmann, and S. Cook, editors, *UML 2002 - The Unified Modeling Language. Model Engineering, Languages, Concepts, and Tools. 5th International Conference, Dresden, Germany, September/October 2002, Proceedings*, number 2460 in LNCS, pages 426–441. Springer, 2002.

14. J. M. Lucassen and D. K. Gifford. Polymorphic effect systems. In *Proc. 15th ACM Symp. on Principles of Programming Languages*, pages 47–57, San Diego, California, Jan. 1988. ACM Press.

15. A. C. Myers. JFlow: practical mostly-static information flow control. In A. Aiken, editor, *Proc. 1999 ACM SIGPLAN Symp. on Principles of Programming Languages*, pages 228–241, San Antonio, Texas, USA, Jan. 1999. ACM Press.

16. M. Odersky, M. Sulzmann, and M. Wehr. Type inference with constrained types. *Theory and Practice of Object Systems*, 5(1):35–55, 1999.

17. B. C. Pierce. *Types and Programming Languages*. MIT Press, 2002.

18. A. Sabelfeld and A. C. Myers. Language-based information-flow security. *IEEE J. Selected Areas in Communications*, 21(1):5–19, Jan. 2003.

19. F. B. Schneider, J. G. Morrisett, and R. Harper. A language-based approach to security. In R. Wilhelm, editor, *Informatics - 10 Years Back. 10 Years Ahead*, number 2000 in LNCS, pages 86–101. Springer, 2001.

20. K. L. Solberg. *Annotated Type Systems for Program Analysis*. PhD thesis, Odense University, Denmark, July 1995. Also technical report DAIMI PB-498, Comp. Sci. Dept. Aarhus University.

21. Sun. Java authentication and authorization service (JAAS), reference guide. http://java.sun.com/j2se/1.4.2/docs/guide/security/jaas/JAASRefGuide.html[17.5.2004], 2001.

22. Sun. Java security architecture. http://java.sun.com/j2se/1.5.0/docs/api [10.2.2005], 2005.

23. P. Thiemann. A type safe DOM API. In G. Bierman and C. Koch, editors, *Tenth International Symposium on Database Programming Languages (DBPL'05)*, number 3774 in LNCS, Trondheim, Norway, Aug. 2005. Springer.

24. R. Vallée-Rai, L. Hendren, V. Sundaresan, P. Lam, E. Gagnon, and P. Co. Soot - a Java optimization framework. In *Proc. CASCON 1999*, pages 125–135, 1999.

Controlling Access to Documents: A Formal Access Control Model[*]

Paul E. Sevinç[1], David Basin[1], and Ernst-Rüdiger Olderog[2]

[1] Department of Computer Science, ETH Zurich, 8092 Zurich, Switzerland
{paul.sevinc, basin}@inf.ethz.ch
[2] Dept. of Computing Science, University of Oldenburg, 26111 Oldenburg, Germany
olderog@informatik.uni-oldenburg.de

Abstract. Current access-control systems for documents suffer from one or more of the following limitations: they are coarse-grained, limited to XML documents, or unable to maintain control over copies of documents once they are released by the system. We present a formal model of a system that overcomes all of these restrictions. It is very fine-grained, supports a general class of documents, and provides a foundation for usage control.

1 Introduction

Sensitive data is often protected by controlling access to its container. Two examples of containers are databases and file systems. Typically, databases are based on the relational model, whereas file systems are modeled as trees whose inner nodes are directories and whose leaves are files. For both examples, there are access-control models and systems (e.g., [1, 2, 3]) that take the inner structure of the respective container into account and thus allow for fine-grained access control. This means that access is not granted or denied to a database or a file system as a whole, but rather to individual tables or rows of the database and to individual directories or files of the file system.

A third example of a data container is a document. When documents are protected by controlling access to the file system where they reside, users either have full access to a document or no access at all. However, in some contexts (cf. §2), fine-grained access control is also required for documents. There exist access-control models for a specific class of documents, namely Extensible Markup Language (XML) [4] documents (cf. §5). However, most of these models are limited to XML-encoded databases. Furthermore, the systems based on these models cannot protect data once it has been released to users.

What has been missing until now is an access-control system that is based on a fine-grained access-control model for documents, such as texts, spreadsheets, and presentations, and whose mechanisms not only enforce policies on a server but also on clients, both while data is within documents and in transit between documents. In this paper, we present a formal model of such a system.

---

[*] This work was partially supported by the Zurich Information Security Center. It represents the views of the authors.

G. Müller (Ed.): ETRICS 2006, LNCS 3995, pp. 352–367, 2006.

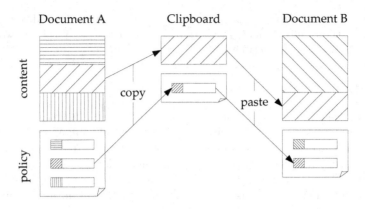

Fig. 1. Sticky Policies

1.1   Contributions

We have defined a fine-grained model of a system for processing documents. As natural languages and semi-formal modeling languages like UML are not sufficiently precise, we have used the specification language Z [5] to define the states and operations of the system. Hence our first contribution is a formal model of an unprotected document-processing system.

Our second contribution is a policy language that allows users to formalize protection requirements that we have gathered for banking environments. Again we have taken a formal approach here and defined the policy language's abstract syntax in Z and its semantics (how access requests are evaluated) in a combination of (Object-)Z and the specification language Communicating Sequential Processes (CSP) [6] called CSP-OZ [7].

Our third contribution is to provide a foundation for controlling usage of documents. *Usage control* [8] is a notion that subsumes both server-side and client-side access control.[1] It is important in the document context as owners need assurance that the policies governing access to their documents are respected, even when other users incorporate parts of these documents in their own documents. To achieve this, we associate parts of each document with the respective parts of its policy and maintain this association over the document life-cycle. This amounts to a fine-grained variant of the sticky-policies paradigm [9, 10]: when content is copied (or cut) from a document to the clipboard and pasted into a document, then so is the respective part of the policy (cf. Figure 1).

1.2   Organization

In Section 2, we explain the context of this work and we derive high-level requirements from representative use cases. In Section 3, we introduce our document

---

[1] Client-side access control is also called *rights management*. Note that enforcement requires the combination of classical access-control mechanisms with hardware-based or software-based rights-management mechanisms.

model and we formalize document content. In Section 4, we formalize document policies and their enforcement. In Section 5, we compare with related work, and we draw conclusions in Section 6.

2   Requirements

Documents take many forms and serve many purposes. In this paper, we will restrict our focus to a setting common in the context of companies and other organizations. Stakeholders in these companies (i.e., users) create, exchange, read, and edit documents that contain security-sensitive data. In general, users cannot be trusted by the company because they may not understand the company's security requirements, they may be careless in their use of data, they may have an untrustworthy platform (e.g., compromised by a Trojan horse), or they may simply be untrustworthy themselves.

In what follows, we will assume that systems are trustworthy but users are not. That is, we focus on the functional security requirements for document processing necessary to handle careless or dishonest users. Due to space limitations, we will restrict our attention to the following representative use cases:

Annual Report: To mitigate the risk of insider trading, public access to the company's annual report must not be granted until a given date.

Company Guidelines: Before employees are granted access to data, they must first acknowledge the company guidelines governing the handling of that data.

Presentation Slides: Presenters must be able to define different rules (policy) for different parts (content) within one and the same presentation document so that they need not create multiple differently censored versions.

From the first use case, we derive the requirement for *conditional access control*, i.e., for access-control decisions that depend on request parameters other than the subject, the object, and the action. From the second use case, we derive the requirement for *provisional access control*, i.e., for access-control decisions that depend on whether provisions have been made. From the third use case, we derive the requirement for *fine-grained access control*, i.e., for access-control models and systems where the objects protected are not the data containers (in our case documents) as a whole, but rather their constituent parts. We can derive the same requirements in other document-processing contexts. Examples include the review process of papers, the distribution of sample chapters of books, and the acceptance (or not) of end-user license agreements.

A notion related to *provisions* is *obligations*. Roughly speaking, provisions must hold when access is granted, while obligations must hold after access has been granted [11, 12, 13]. For example, a subject may be obliged not to disclose any information learned as a result of being granted access to some data. Since, by definition, this obligation cannot be enforced technically at the time of access, it is mapped to a provision which can be, namely the subject must have signed a non-disclosure agreement. Our model will not directly support obligations, but will support both conditions and provisions.

3   Document Content Model

In our model, documents are pairs consisting of a *content* component and a *policy* component. The content is where the data is stored and the policy describes what operations are allowed on both the content and the policy itself. Further components—which we do not model in this paper—are either application-specific (e.g., a style sheet) or related to the security mechanisms (e.g., encrypted component-decryption keys). We model the content component in this section and the policy component in the next. Due to space limitations, we omit formal definitions of most operations and auxiliary functions and instead provide three illustrative examples: operations for adding an attribute, copying a node, and adding a role-permission mapping. The full specification can be found in our technical report [14].

We have formalized our model in Z, which is a popular formal language based on typed set theory and first-order logic with equality. We have chosen Z as document processing is heavily data-oriented and Z is well-suited for data modeling. In particular, Z provides constructs for structuring and compositionally building data-oriented specifications: schemas are used to model the states of the system (*state schemas*) and operations on the state (*operation schemas*), and a *schema calculus* is provided to compose these subspecifications. We explain Z notation as it is encountered.

3.1   Content Model

Many kinds of content are structured hierarchically. For example, a book consists of chapters, sections, and paragraphs. To reflect this, we model content as a rooted tree whose nodes have attributes (i.e., name-value pairs). This model is quite general and we can easily specialize it not only to different document formats, like XML, but also to directory information bases and to file systems [14].

Data Types. We introduce four data types: *Name* and *Value* are basic types (declared in Z by placing them in square brackets). *Name* represents the set of attribute names and *Value* the set of attribute values. As we shall see, security-sensitive data is stored as attribute values. *Attributes* is the set of finite sets of name-value pairs in which a name maps to at most one value, i.e., members of this type are functions mapping finitely many names to values. Finally, *Tree* is a recursive type where each node has attributes and a sequence of subtrees. In Z, we express all this as follows:

$$[Name, Value]$$
$$Attributes == Name \nrightarrow Value$$
$$Tree ::= Node \langle\!\langle Attributes \times \text{seq } Tree \rangle\!\rangle$$

We have specified three auxiliary functions on these data types, which we will use below: *TreeDomainF*, which given a tree returns the set of all valid paths in the tree, *ReadNodeF*, which given a tree and a valid path returns the subtree at (the end of) the path, and *ReadAttributesF*, which given a tree and a valid path returns the attributes of the root node of the subtree at the path [14].

Containers (State). The state of documents and the clipboard are represented as schemas. A schema in Z has a name, a declaration part, and optionally a predicate part that expresses properties (i.e., invariants, preconditions, relationships between states) that (instances of) the variables must satisfy.[2] As mentioned in Section 1.1, making the clipboard and the clipboard-related operations part of the model is a prerequisite for fine-grained *sticky policies*. The first schema below represents the content component of documents. The second schema represents the content component of the clipboard. Both consist of a single binding stating that the document content is a tree called *root* and the clipboard content is a tree called *cCache*.

$$\begin{array}{|l}\hline \text{--- } DocumentContent \text{ ---------}\\ root : Tree \\ \hline \end{array} \qquad \begin{array}{|l}\hline \text{--- } ClipboardContent \text{ ---------}\\ cCache : Tree \\ \hline \end{array}$$

In general, each state schema comes with an initialization schema (not given here) that specifies the initial state and establishes the state invariants. In the case of document content, for example, the empty node is assigned to the root.

Operations. We have defined more than a dozen operations[3], most of which change the state of the document, or the clipboard, or both. Here we consider two representative examples.

The *AddAttributeC* schema specifies that adding an attribute changes the document content (Δ specifies a relation between a pre-state and a post-state). The operation expects input, namely the path to the parent node (*path?*), as well as the name and the value of the attribute to add (*name?* and *value?*), and has no output. Paths are sequences (seq) of non-negative integers ($\mathbb{N}_1$). The preconditions are that the given path is in the document content's domain and that the parent node does not already have an attribute with the given name. The post-state of the document content (*root'*) is the pre-state (*root*) with the sole exception that the parent node additionally has the given name-value pair as attribute. By convention, variables whose names end in a question mark or a prime denote input variables and post-state variables, respectively. Our own convention is that schemas whose names end in C or P specify a content-related operation and a policy-related operation, respectively.

---

[2] Graphically, a schema is written as a three-sided box with the name on the top edge, followed by declarations, and optionally followed by a line and predicates.

[3] They are reading, adding, deleting, copying, cutting, and pasting a node as well as reading, adding, deleting, changing, copying, cutting, and pasting an attribute. Reading a node is special in that it returns the names of its attributes and the number of its children, but not any value. There is no change-node operation. [14]

AddAttributeC

$\Delta DocumentContent$
$path? : \text{seq } \mathbb{N}_1$
$name? : Name$
$value? : Value$

$path? \in TreeDomainF(root)$
$name? \notin \text{dom } ReadAttributesF(root, path?)$
$TreeDomainF(root') = TreeDomainF(root)$
$\forall\, p : \text{seq } \mathbb{N}_1 \mid p \in TreeDomainF(root) \land p \neq path? \bullet$
    $ReadAttributesF(root', p) = ReadAtrributesF(root, p)$
$ReadAttributesF(root', path?) =$
    $ReadAttributesF(root, path?) \cup (name? \mapsto value?)$

The *CopyNodeC* schema specifies that copying a node does not change the document content (Ξ specifies that the pre-state and post-state are identical), but changes the clipboard content. The operation expects input, namely the path to the node to copy (*path?*), and has no output. The precondition is that the given path is in the document content's domain. The post-state of the clipboard content (*cCache'*) is a copy of the node.

CopyNodeC

$\Xi DocumentContent$
$\Delta ClipboardContent$
$path? : \text{seq } \mathbb{N}_1$

$path? \in TreeDomainF(root)$
$cCache' = ReadNodeF(root, path?)$

---

4 Document Policy Model

In this section we present our policy language and access-control architecture. We have designed the language to meet our domain-specific requirements for controlling access to document content (as just modeled). Our architecture is an adaptation of the XACML data-flow model [15]. We first present these ideas informally and afterwards present excerpts from the formal specification.

4.1 Informal Description

Policy Language. Our access-control model is role-based, where policies express relations between roles and permissions and where subjects are *users* acting in a *role*. Additionally, policies incorporate a concept of ownership adapted from discretionary access control (DAC), where every object has an owner, namely the user that created it. Users are allowed all forms of access to objects they own and can arbitrarily add and delete role-permission assignments for these objects as well. However, unlike DAC models, our model does not leave to a subject's discretion any data the subject has (read) access to.

Permissions relate *objects* with *actions* (not to be confused with operations) that are further constrained by *conditions* and *provisions*. That is, permissions only apply when the condition evaluates to *true* in the current *environment*. As their name implies, permissions always *grant* access. Nevertheless, grants are tentative until the provisions have been made. By design, conflicts (i.e., different sets of provisions) cannot arise from more than one permission applying to a request and as a result there is no need for conflict-resolution strategies. Subjects can be permitted to delegate their reading and editing permissions to other subjects.

We limit ourselves to a single editing action, which we call *change*. This is in contrast to other models (cf. §5), which typically have the actions add, delete, and update (when integrity is a concern). In our model, to add or delete a child node or an attribute, a subject must be allowed to change the parent.

Let us discuss the change action in more detail. Table 1 lists the operations permitted by our change action and by the usual add, delete, and update actions. We claim that giving add, delete, and update permissions individually is unsatisfactory, in particular in the context of document editing which requires the ability to undo operations. Suppose, for example, that a subject has the permission to add an object to a node. Undoing adding an attribute or a node could be supported by giving the subject the permission to delete the attribute or the node. However, the permissions required to undo pasting an attribute or a node (i.e., a subtree) are less clear. Similarly, does deleting a node require the permission to delete all descendants of the node? And does deleting an object require the permission to read the object? Now suppose that a subject has the permission to delete an object but not the permission to add an object to the object's parent node. Can deleting the object be undone without giving the subject "new" (add) permissions on "old" nodes? We avoid these questions with our approach and instead provide users with a simple semantics of an editing action whose consequences are easy to understand: a subtree can either be changed in arbitrary ways or not at all. Note that this simplification has no negative effects when confidentiality is the main security goal, as it is in the use cases in Section 2.

Table 1. Operations permitted by Actions

Object Action	attribute	node
change	*not applicable*	add attribute to node add child node to node delete an attribute from node delete subtree rooted at a child node change an attribute's value
add	*not applicable*	add attribute to node add child node to node
delete	delete attribute	delete subtree rooted at node
update	change attribute value	*not applicable*

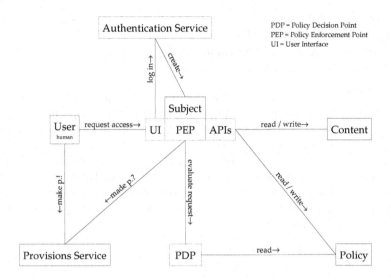

Fig. 2. Access-Control Actors

Access-Control Architecture. The architecture of our system is an adaptation of the XACML data-flow model [15] and is shown in Figure 2. The system runs on a User's client. Content and Policy are components of a document that the user has opened with the system. When several documents are open, only one is currently active. After successful login, the user is represented by a Subject and accesses documents through the user interface (UI). If security were not a concern, there would be no policy and the UI would directly access the document application programming interfaces (APIs)[4] when reading and writing content. However, since security is indeed a concern, the UI accesses the document APIs via the policy execution point (PEP). The PEP grants or denies access (i.e., blocks operations) based on access decisions made by the Policy Decision Point (PDP) and based on whether certain provisions have been made, for which the PEP consults the Provisions Service. That is, the PEP mediates access while the PDP makes (tentative) access decisions.

4.2   Formal Specification

Data Types The most elementary concepts of any access-control model are subjects, objects, and actions. In our model, subjects are pairs consisting of a role ID and a user ID. The set of all role IDs and the set of all user IDs are basic types of the specification. Objects are nodes or attributes at a given path. The ability to speak about nodes and attributes at arbitrary positions in the document content is straightforward, given our content model, and allows for very fine-grained access control. In this paper, we discuss in detail only one of the four actions we have defined, namely the *change* action.

---

[4] In the context of XML documents, the Document Object Model (DOM) [16] is a well-known example for such an API.

$[RoleID,\ UserID]$
$Subject == RoleID \times UserID$
$Object ::= Node\langle\!\langle\mathrm{seq}\,\mathbb{N}_1\rangle\!\rangle \mid Attribute\langle\!\langle\mathrm{seq}\,\mathbb{N}_1 \times Name\rangle\!\rangle$
$Action ::= read \mid change \mid print \mid delegate$

The applicability of permissions can be limited by conditions on the environment and user. For now, *time* is the only environmental property modeled. To satisfy a condition, the request environment must be in the condition's set of environments and the requesting user must be in the condition's set of users. Time-dependent permissions are motivated by the use cases given in Section 2. User-dependent permissions are necessary for delegation. For example, if a manager wants to delegate some of her permissions to her secretary (but not to all employees whose role is secretary) she can make the delegated permissions depend on the secretary's user ID.

$Environment ::= Timestamp\langle\!\langle\mathbb{Z}\rangle\!\rangle$
$Condition == \mathbb{P}\,Environment \times \mathbb{P}\,UserID$

We support two kinds of provisions: *log* and *sign*.[5] When a permission depends on a log provision, the system providing access must log the message specified in the provision before access can be granted. When a permission depends on a sign provision, the user requesting access must have signed the agreement specified in the provision before access can be granted. Examples for agreements are end-user license agreements and non-disclosure agreements as well as company guidelines. The set of all messages and the set of all agreement IDs are basic types of the specification.

$[Message,\ AgreementID]$
$Provision ::= Log\langle\!\langle Message\rangle\!\rangle \mid Sign\langle\!\langle AgreementID\rangle\!\rangle$

Now we have specified all components of permission tuples. Given the request parameters, the PDP checks whether a permission matches the request. If so, the PDP responds with *Grant* parameterized with the permission's set of provisions and if not, the PDP responds with *Deny*.

$Permission == Object \times Action \times Condition \times \mathbb{P}\,Provision$
$Response ::= Grant\langle\!\langle\mathbb{P}\,Provision\rangle\!\rangle \mid Deny$

Containers (State). The first schema shown below specifies what constitutes the policy component for documents. Its predicate states that permissions with the action *change* must have a node as object and that at most one permission can match a given request. The second schema specifies what constitutes the policy component for the clipboard. Both schemas declare variables of the same type, a partial, finite function that maps objects to their owner and the role-permission relation for role-based access control.

---

[5] These two provisions are essential given our requirements, but others could be added simply by extending the *Provision* data type.

```
┌─ DocumentPolicy ─────────────────────────────────────────
│ ObjectOwner : Object ⇸ UserID
│ RolePermission : RoleID ↔ Permission
├──────────────────────────────────────────────────────────
│ ∀ r : RoleID; p : Permission | r ↦ p ∈ RolePermission •
│     p.2 ≠ change ∨ (∃ path : seq ℕ₁ • p.1 = Node(path))
│ ∀ r₁, r₂ : RoleID; p₁, p₂ : Permission | r₁ ↦ p₁ ∈ RolePermission ∧
│     r₂ ↦ p₂ ∈ RolePermission • r₁ ≠ r₂ ∨ p₁ = p₂ ∨
│     p₁.1 ≠ p₂.1 ∨ p₁.2 ≠ p₂.2 ∨
│     first(p₁.3) ∩ first(p₂.3) = ∅ ∨ second(p₁.3) ∩ second(p₂.3) = ∅
└──────────────────────────────────────────────────────────
```

```
┌─ ClipboardPolicy ────────────────────────────────────────
│ ooCache : Object ⇸ UserID
│ rpCache : RoleID ↔ Permission
└──────────────────────────────────────────────────────────
```

Using Z's schema calculus, here schema conjunction, we can now formally express that both documents and the clipboard are pairs consisting of a content component and a policy component (cf. the pairs depicted in Figure 1).

$$Document \;\widehat{=}\; DocumentContent \wedge DocumentPolicy$$
$$Clipboard \;\widehat{=}\; ClipboardContent \wedge ClipboardPolicy$$

Operations. The *AddAttributeP* schema below specifies that adding an attribute changes the document policy. The operation expects the subject who is adding an attribute (*subject?*), the path to the parent node (*path?*), and the name of the attribute (*name?*) as input and has no output. The post-state of the document policy (*ObjectOwner'* and *RolePermission'*) is the pre-state (*ObjectOwner* and *RolePermission*) with the sole exception that the set of object owners has an additional entry (*Attribute(path?, name?)* ↦ *second(subject?)*).

```
┌─ AddAttributeP ──────────────────────────────────────────
│ ΔDocumentPolicy
│ sub? : Subject
│ path? : seq ℕ₁
│ name? : Name
├──────────────────────────────────────────────────────────
│ ObjectOwner' = ObjectOwner ∪ {Attribute(path?, name?) ↦ second(sub?)}
│ RolePermission' = RolePermission
└──────────────────────────────────────────────────────────
```

The *CopyNodeP* schema specifies that copying a node changes the clipboard policy but not the document policy. The operation expects the path to the node to copy (*path?*) as input and has no output. As specified in *CopyNodeC* above, the subtree being copied becomes the tree in the clipboard content. Therefore, by using a number of standard functions to manipulate sequences, the common path prefix (*path?*) is removed in the course of copying those parts of the document policy related to the subtree being copied.

$\quad$ *CopyNodeP* $\rule{6cm}{0.4pt}$
$\Xi\, DocumentPolicy$
$\Delta\, ClipboardPolicy$
$path?\,:\,\text{seq}\,\mathbb{N}_1$

$ooCache' = \{p : \text{seq}\,\mathbb{N}_1;\ u : UserID\ |$
$\quad path?\,\text{prefix}\,p \wedge Node(p) \mapsto u \in ObjectOwner \bullet$
$\quad Node((\#path? + 1 \mathbin{..} \#p)\upharpoonright p) \mapsto u\} \cup \{p : \text{seq}\,\mathbb{N}_1;\ n : Name;$
$\quad u : UserID\ |\ path?\,\text{prefix}\,p \wedge Attribute(p, n) \mapsto u \in ObjectOwner \bullet$
$\quad Attribute((\#path? + 1 \mathbin{..} \#p)\upharpoonright p, n) \mapsto u\}$
$rpCache' = \{r : RoleID;\ p : \text{seq}\,\mathbb{N}_1;\ a : Action;\ c : Condition;$
$\quad ps : \mathbb{P}\,Provision\ |\ path?\,\text{prefix}\,p \wedge$
$\quad r \mapsto (Node(p), a, c, ps) \in RolePermission \bullet$
$\quad r \mapsto (Node((\#path? + 1 \mathbin{..} \#p)\upharpoonright p), a, c, ps)\} \cup \{r : RoleID;\ p : \text{seq}\,\mathbb{N}_1;$
$\quad n : Name;\ a : Action;\ c : Condition;\ ps : \mathbb{P}\,Provision\ |$
$\quad path?\,\text{prefix}\,p \wedge r \mapsto (Attribute(p, n), a, c, ps) \in RolePermission \bullet$
$\quad r \mapsto (Attribute((\#path? + 1 \mathbin{..} \#p)\upharpoonright p, n), a, c, ps)\}$

Now we can formally express that adding an attribute and copying a node are transactions operating simultaneously on both the content and policy components.

$$AddAttribute \mathrel{\widehat{=}} AddAttributeC \wedge AddAttributeP$$
$$CopyNode \mathrel{\widehat{=}} CopyNodeC \wedge CopyNodeP$$

Three more operations are policy-related only: adding a role-permission mapping, deleting a role-permission mapping, and delegating a permission to another subject. Here we consider the first of these. The *AddRolePermission* schema specifies that adding a role-permission mapping changes the document policy, in particular the role-permission relation (*RolePermission'*). The operation expects input, namely the role (*role?*) and the permission (*permission?*), and has no output. The precondition is that the invariant specified in the *DocumentPolicy* schema above will still hold after the role-permission mapping has been added.

$\quad$ *AddRolePermission* $\rule{6cm}{0.4pt}$
$\Delta\, DocumentPolicy$
$role?\,:\,RoleID$
$permission?\,:\,Permission$

$permission?.2 \neq change \vee (\exists\, path : \text{seq}\,\mathbb{N}_1 \bullet permission?.1 = Node(path))$
$\forall\, r : RoleID;\ p : Permission\ |\ r \mapsto p \in RolePermission \bullet r \neq role? \vee$
$\quad p.1 \neq permission?.1 \vee p.2 \neq permission?.2 \vee$
$\quad first(p.3) \cap first(permission?.3) = \varnothing \vee$
$\quad second(p.3) \cap second(permission?.3) = \varnothing$
$ObjectOwner' = ObjectOwner$
$RolePermission' = RolePermission \cup \{role? \mapsto permission?\}$

4.3   Policy Interpretation

In classical access-control architectures, the PDP interprets the policy to decide whether access is granted and the PEP enforces this decision. As explained in Section 4.1, in architectures with support for provisions, the control flow is more complex and additionally involves interaction with a provisions service. We have specified the PDP and provisions service in Z: the PDP takes a request and a policy and responds with grant or deny, and the provisions service takes a set of provisions and responds with an empty set (denoting that all provisions have been satisfied) or with the set of provisions not yet satisfied. In what follows, we provide excerpts from the PEP specification.

The modeling requirements for the PEP are different than for the other subsystems. The UI is event-driven and the PEP must synchronize (interact) with the UI as well as the other architectural components and its control flow is data-dependent. While Z is well-suited for data modeling, it cannot easily describe such process interaction. Therefore we employed CSP-OZ, which combines Z with the process calculus CSP as mentioned in the introduction.

A CSP-OZ class describes both operations (in Z) and their synchronization (in CSP). The excerpt in Figure 3 formalizes the generic description given in Section 4.1 for the operation of adding an attribute. It leaves open the application-specific mechanisms of receiving events (e.g., *AddAttribute_event*) and of updating the UI (e.g., *AddAttribute_ret*). The other operations (copying a node, reading an attribute, etc.) are declared analogously. The formalization of the UI (not shown) is similar but simpler than that of the PEP. CSP processes synchronize

```
┌─PEP────────────────────────────────────────────────────
│
│ chan login : [ u? : UserID; ok! : B ]
│ chan logout
│ chan abort
│
│ main = login?u?ok →
│           (ok & getSubject?subject → PEPL(subject)
│           □ ¬ok & main)
│ PEPL(subject) =
│     logout → main
│     □ AddAttribute_event?path?name → GetEnv?environment →
│        AddAttributeRequest!subject!path!environment?response →
│        (response = Deny & abort → PEPL(subject)
│        □ response = Grant(ps) &
│           MadeProvisions!subject!ps?rem_ps →
│           (rem_ps = ∅ & AddAttribute!subject!path!name →
│              AddAttribute_ret → PEPL(subject)
│           □ rem_ps ≠ ∅ & abort → PEPL(subject)))
│     □ ...
│
└────────────────────────────────────────────────────────
```

Fig. 3. Policy Execution Point

along so-called channels. Explicitly declared (**chan**) are the channels *login*, *logout*, and *abort*. Operations specified in Z are also channels. The UI and the PEP execute in parallel. At first, both processes are in the main loop (**main**) until a user successfully logs in, at which point they enter their event-processing loops (*PEPL* in the case of the PEP). When a user logs out via the UI, the PEP follows suit and returns to its main loop. Unlike the UI, the PEP must take additional steps between receiving an event and handling it or aborting, in order to make an access decision. First, it determines the current environment (*GetEnv*) and then it communicates with the PDP (via *AddAttributeRequest*) and, provided the PDP has not denied the request, with the provisions service (via *MadeProvisions*). The PEP signals access denied on the *abort* channel, which forces the UI to abort without having handled the event.

Hence the PEP class brings together the various Z specifications from before and formalizes how policies are interpreted and enforced. Overall, our model provides a precise description, with a formal mathematical semantics, of secure document processing, i.e., documents, operations on them, and access control.

5 Related Work

A number of commercial document-processing systems offer security functionality, for example those of Adobe[6] and Microsoft[7]. In contrast to our work, these systems offer only coarse-grained protection. Moreover, once data is copied, it is at the user's discretion.

The work closest to ours is in *XML access control*, which is an active research area concerned with controlling access to constituent parts of XML documents (e.g., [17, 18, 19, 20, 21, 22, 23]). We shall first discuss the primary characteristics of this work, and then examine several prominent proposals.

XML access control models are fine-grained, although the different proposals differ in their granularity and the types of their constituent parts. Moreover, they differ in the operations offered and their semantics. Some XML access control systems only provide a read operation with no arguments and thus expect their users to request entire XML documents (typically, there is only one instance, namely the XML-encoded database), in which case they respond with a censored copy called the *view* (Gabillon [23] compares several view-generation strategies). The current proposals differ considerably in the policy languages they offer, e.g., their features and syntactic sugar. Although these additions are intended to ease a policy writer's life, they are also a double-edged sword: they not only make the policy language more complex, they also necessitate conflict-resolution strategies [17, 18, 19]. In contrast, we have focused on a simple, yet expressive, core language with a clean, formal semantics. All current proposals for XML access control are limited in that they leave data at the user's discretion once it is copied. In contrast, we have solved this problem by adapting the idea of sticky policies to our model.

---

[6] http://www.adobe.com/security/
[7] http://www.microsoft.com/windowsserver2003/technologies/rightsmgmt/

The XML Access Control Language (XACL) [18, 19] has up to now been the only proposal for XML access control with concrete support for provisions. Our model differs from that of the XACL, in this respect, in that provisions never have to be made (not even by the system) when access is denied. More importantly, XACL policies may be ambiguous in terms of which provisions must hold for a given request. In our model, at most one permission matches a request, so there is no such ambiguity.

Bertino *et al.* [20, 21] have proposed an approach to XML access control consisting of two parts: an access-control system *Author-χ*, and a credentials and policy language *χ-Sec*. Their proposal goes beyond XML access control in that they actually consider semi-structured data encoded in XML documents. They allow arcs (i.e., references or hyperlinks) to be secured with what they call the *navigate* privilege (privileges are what we call actions). Our model does not encompass semi-structured data. However, arcs can be encoded as attributes (as is done in the XML), whereby read access can be interpreted as navigate access. This proposal has a rich language for expressing temporal conditions, based on periodic time expressions [24]; from our requirements analysis, these are not necessary in our context.

Gabillon *et al.* [22, 23] go beyond XML access control and consider tree-structured data. However, nodes in their trees have no properties other than child nodes. This has the unfortunate consequence that the policy language must be adapted to every specialization. In contrast, we can refine our document-content model without changing our policy language. The work by Gabillon *et al.* [22, 23] is the only closely related work in which object ownership and policy editing are not foreign concepts, and permission delegation is supported as well. All other approaches assume that policies are schema-based, static, and provided by (not further specified) administrators.

6   Conclusion

We have presented a formal model of an access-control system for document security. This model reflects real-world requirements and provides a precise design for solving this problem in a general way. Hence it represents a large step towards a general-purpose document-security system.

As future work, we will take the remaining steps in building a prototype implementation. First, we shall define a concrete syntax for our policy language and implement a PDP that interprets this syntax and can evaluate requests. A likely candidate for the concrete syntax is an eXtensible Access Control Markup Language (XACML) [15] profile in which case our PDP could be based on an existing XACML PDP, such as the one from Sun Microsystems Laboratories[8]. Because the XACML lacks a formal semantics, an alternative is to directly implement the PDP as a refinement of our formal model. Second, we will employ cryptographic mechanisms to secure documents during storage and while in transit so that only trusted systems can access them. Third, as a proof of concept, we will implement an XML

---

[8] http://sunxacml.sourceforge.net/

editor along the lines of the architecture in Section 4.1 on page 357. Finally, we plan to embed the XML editor in a trustworthy client environment, where master keys are secured in Trusted Platform Modules (TPMs) [25]. All of these steps are realistic and should contribute to a practical solution that represents a large advance in the way that documents, and more generally hierarchically structured content, are secured.

Acknowledgments

We would like to thank Achim Brucker, Manuel Hilty, Günter Karjoth, Michael Näf, Beat Perjés, Alexander Pretschner, Gritta Wolf, and Burkhart Wolff for their assistance on this topic and their feedback on this paper.

References

1. Bertino, E., Sandhu, R.: Database security—concepts, approaches, and challenges. IEEE Transactions on Dependable and Secure Computing **2** (2005) 2–19
2. Castano, S., Fugini, M., Martella, G., Samarati, P.: Database Security. ACM Press (1995)
3. Smith, B., Komar, B.: Microsoft Windows Security Resource Kit. Second edn. Microsoft Press (2005)
4. W3C (World Wide Web Consortium): Extensible Markup Language (XML). (W3C Recommendation)
5. International Organization for Standardization: Information technology – Z formal specification notation – Syntax, type system and semantics. First edn. (2002)
6. Hoare, C.: Communicating Sequential Processes. Prentice Hall (1985)
7. Fischer, C.: CSP-OZ: a combination of Object-Z and CSP. In: Proc. 2nd IFIP Workshop on Formal Methods for Open Object-Based Distributed Systems (FMOODS). (1997) 423–438
8. Park, J., Sandhu, R.: The $UCON_{ABC}$ usage control model. ACM Transactions on Information and System Security **7** (2004) 128–174
9. Karjoth, G., Schunter, M., Waidner, M.: Platform for enterprise privacy practices: Privacy-enabled management of customer data. In Dingledine, R., Syverson, P., eds.: Privacy Enhancing Technologies. Volume 2482 of Lecture Notes in Computer Science., Springer-Verlag (2003) 69–84
10. IBM Zurich Research Laboratory: Enterprise privacy technologies. (WWW)
11. Bettini, C., Jajodia, S., Wang, X.S., Wijesekera, D.: Provisions and obligations in policy rule management. Journal of Network and Systems Management **11** (2003) 351–372
12. Bettini, C., Jajodia, S., Wang, X.S., Wijesekera, D.: Reasoning with advanced policy rules and its application to access control. International Journal on Digital Libraries **4** (2004) 156–170
13. Hilty, M., Basin, D., Pretschner, A.: On obligations. In de Capitani di Vimercati, S., Syverson, P., Gollmann, D., eds.: Proceedings of the 10th European Symposium on Research in Computer Security (ESORICS 2005). Volume 3679 of Lecture Notes in Computer Science., Springer-Verlag (2005) 98–117
14. Sevinç, P.E., Basin, D.: Controlling access to documents: A formal access control model. Technical report, Swiss Federal Institute of Technology Zurich (2006)

15. OASIS: eXtensible Access Control Markup Language (XACML). (Specification)
16. W3C (World Wide Web Consortium): Document Object Model (DOM) Level 3 Core Specification. (W3C Recommendation)
17. Damiani, E., De Capitani di Vimercati, S., Paraboschi, S., Samarati, P.: A fine-grained access control system for XML documents. ACM Transactions on Information and System Security **5** (2002) 169–202
18. IBM Tokyo Research Laboratory: XML Access Control Language (XACL). (WWW)
19. Kudo, M., Hada, S.: XML document security based on provisional authorization. In: Proceedings of the 7th ACM conference on Computer and communications security, Athens (2000) 87–96
20. Bertino, E., Castano, S., Ferrari, E.: Securing XML documents with Author-X. IEEE Internet Computing **5** (2001) 21–31
21. Bertino, E., Carminati, B., Ferrari, E.: Access control for XML documents and data. Information Security Technical Report **9** (2004) 19–34
22. Gabillon, A., Munier, M., Bascou, J.J., Gallon, L., Bruno, E.: An access control model for tree data structures. In: Proceedings of the 5th International Conference on Information Security. (2002) 117–135
23. Gabillon, A.: An authorization model for XML databases. In: Proceedings of the 11th ACM conference on Computer and communications security. (2004)
24. Niézette, M., Stévenne, J.M.: An efficient symbolic representation of periodic time. In: Proceedings of the ISMM International Conference on Information and Knowledge Management (CIKM-92). (1992) 161–168
25. Trusted Computing Group: TCG TPM Specification Version 1.2. (TCG Specification)

How to Increase the Security of Digital Rights Management Systems Without Affecting Consumer's Security

Jürgen Nützel and Anja Beyer

Technische Universität Ilmenau, Institut für Medien und Kommunikationswissenschaft
D-98693 Ilmenau, Germany
{Juergen.Nuetzel, Anja.Beyer}@tu-ilmenau.de

Abstract. The paper starts with a description of the fundamental principles of modern Digital Rights Management Systems. This is the basis for the discussion of their most important security aspects from the provider's view on the one hand and the customer's view on the other hand. The second half of the paper focuses the new DRM standard from the Open Mobile Alliance (OMA) and its implementation on "open" systems like Windows. The security anchor of the OMA DRM is the device private key. As long as no trusted storage facilities for open systems work effectively, techniques for software obfuscation could be a solution. Therefore the obfuscation of the device private key and its secure download is described. Currently on Windows PCs there is no chance for a full tamper-proof solution, but the authors try to make the job of an attacker as hard as possible, without affecting the consumer's security.

1 Motivation and Introduction

After the appearance of illegal services like Napster the music industry needed a few years and technology partners like Apple and Microsoft to setup legal download services which brought digital rights management (DRM) onto end users' devices. DRM systems (DRMS) now allow the rights owners to restrict and control the usage of the music a consumer has downloaded. Content will only be delivered encrypted. In order to render the content an appropriate license is needed. A license includes the content encryption key and some usage rights. The license has to be delivered and stored on the consumer's device in a secure manner. Only the DRM controller which resides on the consumer's device is able to apply the key if the according usage rights allow this.

The DRM technology was developed to increase the security of the business models of the content industry. This security is based on the proper function of the DRM controller. But it is very hard to secure a DRM controller, because it resides on the device of the user which cannot be trusted by the DRMS provider. In spite of the conflict between DRMS providers and device owner, the providers must not affect the security needs of ordinary PCs or mobile phone users. The implementation of a DRMS must not weak the security of the device against attacks and intrusion from external.

Although the DRM standard of the Open Mobile Alliance (OMA) [1] was originally designed for mobile phones the version 2 became now attractive to adopt it

G. Müller (Ed.): ETRICS 2006, LNCS 3995, pp. 368–380, 2006.

for environments like Windows XP. The description of the implementation of such an adoption shows several security problems to solve. Some are critical for the device owner and some are critical for the content owner.

2   Digital Rights Management

In times when virtual goods, such as novels, music and movies where bound to a physical medium (e.g. books, CDs, cassettes) the publishers did not have to worry about people misusing their intellectual property [2, p. viii]. By purchasing a book or a CD the complete usage rights (e.g. reading, copying, giving away and retailing) devolved to the customer. It took some time and effort to take a copy of a book or a CD. Nowadays, in times of digitization, it needs nearly no time duplicating virtual goods (digitized goods) and is low in costs. In order to cut down the illegal transmission the vendors established the so called Digital Rights Management systems (DRMS).

With DRMS they try to pass the usage rights granularly to the customer. With DRMS the content provider is able to allow its customers only certain operations which are defined in a license file (e.g. take five copies, print two times, etc.) [3, p. 59]. The rights are expressed machine readable using a rights expression language (REL). Several REL exist in parallel. Their common basis is XML (Extensible Markup Language). In [4] a family tree of most popular REL is given. ODRL (Open Digital Rights Language) [5] for instance is the REL of the new DRM standard developed by OMA [3, p. 63].

2.1   Some Definitions for DRM

There is still no standardized definition for the term Digital Rights Management. Iannella differentiates between DRM of the first and second generation. While for him the first generation only applies to copy protection, „[t]he second-generation of DRM covers the description, identification, trading, protection, monitoring and tracking of all forms of rights usages over both tangible and intangible assets including management of rights holders relationships. Additionally, it is important to note that DRM is the "digital management of rights" and not the "management of digital rights". That is, DRM manages all rights, not only the rights applicable to permissions over digital content" [6].

With his three-legged stool with the legs law, business and technology Nils Rump [7] shows that the domain is complex and not only narrowed on technical issues [3, p.60].

Rüdiger Grimm apprehends DRM as procedures that help to protect the rights of the virtual goods in a way that we are accustomed from the intellectual products bound to physical media. Copy and transfer shall be linked to the rules of the rights holder, thus the content provider [8].

2.2   The DRM Reference Model

In [2] a DRM reference model was introduced which well describes the fundamental structure and functions of most of the existing DRMS [3, p. 60].

The reference model contains three major components: the content server, the license server and the DRM client (see figure 1).

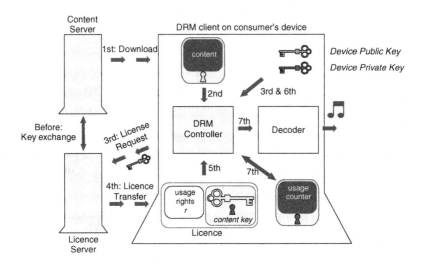

Fig. 1. The DRM reference model with usage counter and device key pair (Public and Private Key) for device identification

Figure 1 describes the DRM reference model. Prior to a download the content server has to prepare the encrypted content for distribution. Therefore, the DRM packager located in the content server encrypts the content and puts some additional metadata (like a unique content ID and the address of the license server) to the content package and hands the applied content encryption keys (or a seed information to retrieve the keys from) over to the license server (OMA calls this the rights issuer). The license server stores the encryption keys and provides them on request (3rd step in figure 1) together with the appropriate usage rights. This will be done in the DRM license generator which creates the licenses (OMA calls this rights objects) containing identity, rights specifications and encryption keys. The client of the DRM system is located at the user's side. It contains the DRM controller, the decoder to render the content and the user's or device's identification mechanism. In the OMA DRM standard (version 2) a RSA key pair identifies the device. In [2, p. 82] the DRM controller is described as "…the real nerve center of the DRM system." It enables the user to exercise his rights, to render the content and it organizes the communication with the content and the license server [2, p. 79ff].

The following section outlines a typical sequence for a DRM system: In the first, step (in figure 1) the user must receive the content package either by downloading it from a content server or from another user, which is part of superdistribution. In order to render it, the customer's device has to make a request (in the 3rd step) for an appropriate license. This action follows after the DRM controller has opened the content (the second step) and has retrieved the content ID and license server address. If no local stored license was found the DRM controller sends a license request to the license server. The request includes the identity of the user, information about the client device (e.g. by sending a certificate which includes the device public key) and the content ID from the content package. The license generator verifies the request parameters and looks up the rights information for the content in the rights database. Before the following step might happen a financial transaction is initiated. Afterwards, the license generator creates the license containing rights and the content encryption key. The content key in the license is encrypted with device public key. Then (in step four), the license is sent to the client. After that the DRM controller is able (in step 5 und 6) to access the content encryption key using the device private key. Depending on the usage counters and the usage rights ("play three times") the content will be decrypted and rendered in the decoder. The device private key is the security anchor of the DRM client. If that private key becomes visible for the user, the user will be able to decrypt every content package without a proper license. In chapter 5 we will show how to obfuscate this key on a Windows PC.

3   Security Aspects for DRM Systems

In the second chapter we have described the functional model of modern DRMS with a focus on the client side. This description gave us a general view over the involved components and the potential security problems that might arise. The following chapter goes more into the details of the security aspects for DRMS. We start the chapter with the general security goals which we map onto DRM.

3.1   General Goals and the Realization of DRM Security

The three protection goals confidentiality, integrity and availability are considered to be the basic requirements for IT security. In the area of e-commerce (we see DRMS belonging to e-commerce) the additional goals privacy and accountability are important as well.

- **Confidentiality** means the protection against unauthorized access to data and information. The communication between two partners is thought to take place secretly. That means that no third party is allowed to acquire knowledge about the communication. In case of music download shops (which often apply DRM systems) this means no information about the chosen music or the transmitted payment data (e.g. credit card numbers) may become visible for a third person.
- **Integrity** refers to protection against unauthorized modification of data or information: the user of a music download portal must be sure that the shown prices are correct and are presented unmodified.
- **Availability** indicates the protection against unauthorized interference of functionality. The music enthusiast expects a stable usage of the content or license server and does not want to wait for the server being available until he can use it.
- **Privacy**, also regulated by the EU Directive 95/46/EC on the protection of personal data [9], is the right of an individual person on informational self-determination. It allows an individual person to decide about the usage of their personal data.

- **Accountability** expresses the unauthorized non-commitment, meaning the loss of bindingness. The content provider has to be sure that the customer cannot withdraw his desire to buy after the ordering [10].

These general security objectives apply to all business to consumer e-commerce systems and so for DRM systems. On the customers side mainly the confidentiality of the personal data (privacy) and accountability. On the merchants side particularly the integrity of the product data, the availability of the service and a mandatory warranty about the payment of the goods. A secure transmission of data and information about an insecure communication channel like the Internet is compulsory [cp. 11].

3.2   The Competition of Provider's and Consumer's Security

The closer examination of the security of a DRM system necessitates a view on the requirements of more than one side (multilateral security). The following description reveals that the content provider's goals compete with the goals of the customer.

- **Confidentiality/privacy**: it is not obviously how the merchants are dealing with the private data of their customers. In the general terms and conditions they often claim that they do not refer personal data to third parties and that they handle discreet with it. But the customer has no possibility to examine that. Through evaluation of its system it might be possible that a merchant gains the trust of the user.

The objective of available services is already implemented in a good manner by applying back-up systems. With the implementation of Intrusion Detection Systems and appropriate escalation routines it is possible to meet the threat of denial-of-service attacks.

- **Accountability** is important on both sides: merchant's and customer's side. The provider forces the customer to pay for the content before he can download it. With this constellation the clients do not have the possibility to withdraw from the contract. Above this, the user has to trust the provider receiving the paid goods. It is not expected to happen that the provider does not deliver because the provider's success depends on satisfied customers.

3.3   The Content Is the Most Valuable Asset of the Provider

The content provider's revenue depends on the sale of digital goods, like music files, videos or e-books which are generally called "content". Therefore it is the most valuable asset for it and the objective is the protection against unauthorized usage of the content (see table 1).

To prevent abusiveness certain security mechanisms are installed: the content is transferred only encrypted to the client's system. In order to use it, the customer needs a license which contains the decryption key (see chapter 2).

Obfuscation techniques are used in order to hide the device private key, the usage counter and content encryption keys somewhere on the end user's device, so that the user cannot extract it and hand it over. Nevertheless, there is the risk especially on ordinary Windows PCs that a potential attacker may try to spy out the private device key. If this happens, the whole system is compromised and the total DRM mechanisms become ineffective. In chapter 5 we describe methods how the device private key, the content key and the usage counter can be secured on insecure PCs.

Table 1. The valuable assets of the content provider and the user

	Content provider	User
Asset	Content - virtual goods, e.g. music, video, e-books (copyright)	System
Objectives	Confidentiality (protection against unauthorised usage of licenses)	Integrity of the system (hardware and software)
Threat	Extraction of the private decryption/license key	Loss of integrity of the system

3.4 A Stable System Is the Most Valuable Asset of the User

The objective of the customer is to protect the stability and integrity of the system, mainly a personal computer. The outcome of this is a direct competition to the content provider's objective: the protection against unauthorized usage of the license. But in order to accomplish a proper usage it is necessary to install software on the end users system and this in turn may have effects on the integrity of different already installed software. It is a severe intervention in the users system what can have fatal consequences, e.g. it is possible that with this interface the program opens the door to potential attackers and malware. Practically it lately happened with the Sony DRM XCP (Extended Copy Protection): once installed on the computer as a rootkit, World of Warcraft hackers used it to hide cheat-software [12], [13].

In order to supply evidence that there is no program code that allows the execution of additional malicious functions an extra procedure is needed. A possibility to proof this is the evaluation of the software. The Common Criteria for Information Technology Security Evaluation (in short Common Criteria) are an international standard for determining if products actually meet their claims [14].

4 Open Mobile Alliance (OMA) DRM

The Open Mobile Alliance (OMA) [1] is an organization which develops open standards to increase the interoperability of mobile services. Almost every mobile operator and device manufacturer is member of OMA. One of OMA's standardization activities focuses DRM.

4.1 OMA DRM Version 1

The first release of the DRM specification [15] is in practice since 2004. Many mobile devices e.g. from Nokia [16] have implemented this first version. It was only developed to protect content with a short lifetime like logos or simple Java games. OMA DRM Version 1 uses the open standard ODRL 1.1 (Open Digital Rights

Language) as its rights expression language (REL) to express granted usage rights. Version 1 only provides three simple protection schemes:

- **Forward-lock:** The content is prevented from forwarding by the user. In this case no rights object (license file) is needed. The forward-lock is signaled by a specific mime-type or file extension. This scheme relies on the fact that the user has no direct access to the file system of the mobile phone. For many business models (e.g. the download of simple Java games or ring tones) this easy protection is sufficient.
- **Combined delivery:** In contrast to forward-lock a specific rights object with individual usage rights (specified using ODRL) is available. Unlike modern DRMS content and rights object will be delivered together. Usage rights like "play only three times" enable new business models.
- **Separate delivery:** This comes very close to the DRM reference model. The content is encrypted using AES (Advanced Encryption Standard). For the encrypted content OMA defines its own file format with the file extension DCF (DRM Content Format). The rights object with the content encryption key comes along a separate channel (WAP push or SMS).

These simple protection schemes do not fulfill the requirements of a second generation DRMS (see chapter 2.1). Therefore OMA developed a second release.

4.2   Trust and Security Model of OMA DRM Version 2

The first release of the DRM specification lacks the complete security necessary for a robust, end-to-end DRMS that enables a secure distribution, the authentication of devices, revocation and other aspects like a domain concept [17]. The second version which is the focus of this paper addresses these missing aspects of the OMA DRM.

The second release was published in 2004. While the first release strongly focused the limited capabilities of mobile devices the second version is now not limited to certain devices or platforms. OMA DRM V2 is the only widespread DRMS which is independent from media object format, operating system and runtime environment. The authors of this article are of the opinion that OMA DRM will become the only successful competitor of Microsoft's Windows Media Rights Manager and Apple's FairPlay.

The main goal of any DRM solution is the enforcement of permissions and constraints associated with the content. The main threat comes from unauthorized access to protected content beyond the grants of the associated rights objects (RO, the license in the OMA DRM specification).

RO (rights objects) and their protection are enforced at the point of content consumption on the client's device. This is modeled in the OMA DRM specifications by the introduction of a so called DRM agent. The DRM agent (the DRM client in figure 1) embodies a trusted environment within protected content can securely be consumed. Its role is to enforce permissions and constraints (found in the RO) and to control access to the content [18].

- **Symmetric encrypted content:** In the same manner as every modern DRMS, the content is packaged in a secure container (DCF, DRM Content Format). The content is encrypted with a symmetric content encryption key (CEK). Although it is required in the OMA specification, it is recommended not to use the same CEK for all instances of a media object. Using the same CEK would pose a greater risk if a device becomes compromised and a CEK becomes public.

- **Device authentication:** All DRM agents (the client devices) have a unique private/public key pair (the device key pair) and a certificate. The certificate includes additional information such as issuer, device type, software version, serial numbers, etc. This allows the rights issuers to securely authenticate a user's device (the DRM agent). The certificate and the device public key are transferred during the rights object acquisition protocol (ROAP) from the DRM agent to the rights issuer (RI). Like the CEK the device private key may not leave the trusted environment of the DRM agent.
- **Rights object (RO):** A RO is an XML document, expressing the permissions and constraints (using ODRL 2.1) associated with the content. The RO also contains the CEK. Therefore the content cannot be used without the appropriate RO. Before delivering the RO (from RI to the client device), sensitive parts like the CEK are additionally encrypted using the symmetric REK (right object encryption key). The RO is cryptographically bound to the target DRM agent. This is done by using device public key which encrypts the REK. This ensures that only the target DRM agent with corresponding device private key can access the RO and thus the content. In addition, the RI digitally signs the RO.
- **Delivery:** Since both RO and DCF are inherently secure, they can now be delivered to the target DRM agent using any transport mechanism (e.g. HTTP/WSP, WAP Push, MMS). They can be delivered either together or separately.

These are the most important aspects of the OMA DRM security model. Further aspects refer to state of the RO (e.g. remaining number of play-back or usage time) and the time on the user's device which may not be modified by the user. An unauthorized modification of the play-back counters or the device time has to be prevented as well.

5 Obfuscation of OMA DRM Agents

The device private key is the most critical information which has to be kept secret in the trusted environment of the DRM agent. The REK in all locally stored RO could be deciphered with the private key. With the REK an attacker could retrieve the CEK from the RO.

A second possible threat is the loss of the device authentication. The complete security of the communication between the RI and the DRM agent relies on the device key pair. If a private key gets "lost" an attacker could implement (according to the open OMA protocols) a corrupt DRM agent which simply decrypts the DCF instead of rendering it. The RI can react (if it is detected) on this threat only with the revocation of this corrupted device (identified by the device certificate) or even with the revocation of all devices of this device type. After the revocation the revoked device is no longer able to receive valid ROs. The developer of the agent's software gets seriously into trouble with the revocation of DRM agents.

5.1 Obfuscation of the Key Store

Mobile devices are the main focus of OMA DRM. Nevertheless there is a great interest in the industry to port the OMA DRM agent also to other platforms, especially to ordinary Windows XP PCs. The problem is that the Windows XP operating system supports no trusted storage facilities to hide the device private key on the hard disk even against the access of the system administrator.

The TCG (Trusted Computing Group) [19] is an industrial organization which develops and promotes open, vendor-neutral industry standard specifications for trusted computing building blocks and software interfaces. The TPM (Trusted Platform Module), which comes (only optional for the system partition) into play in the new Windows Vista [20] operating system, is one of the developments of the TCG. The TPM is a cryptographic co-processor on the PC's main board which provides cryptographic operations (like RSA, AES, SHA-1) and stores individual private keys generated by the TPM. It is able to provide a root of trust. The current TPM specification (version 1.2), which is used by Windows Vista was published in 2005.

We have to recognize that secure computing even with Windows Vista comes very slowly onto Windows platforms. Therefore we have to think about less secure software solutions based upon obfuscation techniques. Such obfuscated software solutions have to solve two goals:

- **Hiding and device binding:** The device private key must not become visible and must not be transferred to any other device (PC). Our solution is to store the private key encrypted in a key store file (see figure 2). The encryption is done by a randomly generated symmetric key (RK). RK will be stored also in the key store. The RK will be encrypted by symmetric keys (the hardware keys, HWK), which will be derived directly from several hardware (or system) parameters like MAC address, hard disc and graphic card IDs and others. To avoid the loss of the key store after the replacement of the hard disk RK has to be encrypted several times with different subsets of the system parameters (three from four parameters in figure 2). The state of the rights objects (RO) is stored using the same method. In the final implementation we have 8 different hardware parameters and we allow the loss of two of them. In this case RK has to be encrypted more than 50 times with different subsets of the 8 parameters.

- **Obfuscation of the software:** A way to retrieve the private key even if it is protected as shown in figure 2 is to reverse engineer the software. In [21] and [22] the reader may learn a lot about such reversing techniques and about techniques to prevent reverse engineering of program code. If an attacker is able to trace the software using a debugger after a while he will find the location where the private key will be applied. This allows him to locate the key in the memory. To avoid this attack several obfuscation techniques should be applied. We mention only a few of them here. Many obfuscation tools encrypt or pack the code to avoid the simple disassembly. The decryption and unpacking will be done shortly before the code execution. Before the encryption additional injected code checks for installed and running debuggers. If such tools are found, the execution aborts. Further techniques complicate the machine code by the insertion of useless jumps and sub routine calls. Another (very difficult) method is to modify parts of the operating system. This was done by Sony (see chapter 3.4) with big drawbacks for the user's security. Beside the low-level methods some high-level techniques should also be applied. A secret operation like the loading of secret keys should be split into many smaller portions. A series of such modifications extensively complicate the effort for a potential attacker to compromise the system.

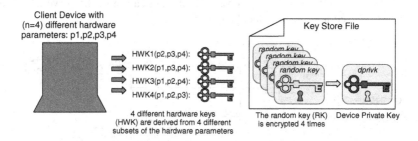

Fig. 2. The hiding and device binding of the device private key using (in this example four) different hardware parameters

5.2   Different Options to Install the Device Private Key

In the case of a Windows XP PC the user has to install additional software to receive rights objects from an OMA compatible rights issuer. The option to install an additional device which hides the private key like a smartcard or a dongle is not practical, because these additional devices are too expensive.

- **Embedded in installation package:** One option would be to embed (in an obfuscated way) the private key in an individualized installation package. This solution is insufficient because the individual installation package could be installed on several PCs.
- **Created in the DRM agent:** Another option is to create the device key pair within the DRM agent. This option has many drawbacks and security risks. The DRM agent has to send the device public key to a certification authority (CA) to receive a signed certificate (for the authentication against the RI). This communication has to be secured to make the CA believe the public key comes from a valid DRM agent.
- **Hidden download:** The authors of this paper are of the opinion that the hidden download of a unique device private key is the most practicable software based solution. We discuss our decision in chapter 5.3. The security anchors for this download are two shared master keys ($mk1$, $mk2$). The keys are embedded in the installation package (which is the same for all users) for the DRM agent. To obfuscate the two 128 bit AES keys they will be split into small parts (e.g. of 8 bits) and will be spread over many kilobytes of random data.

Figure 3 shows the proposed communication between the client PC and the specialized CA (the "Device CA") during a successful download. At the beginning the installation package with a specified software ID (sw_id) will be downloaded and installed. After the DRM agent is started for the first time it contacts the Device CA. It sends the software ID, a random session ID (*session1*), the local time and a first message authentication code (*mac1*). The server uses *mac1* to proof that the transferred parameters are unmodified and that the sender is a valid DRM agent. The correct local time has to be sent to prevent reply attacks. If the local time is within a defined tolerance the server answers with the server time (*time2*) and a second MAC (*mac2*), which enables the client to proof the authentication of the server. The server time could be used to adjust the local clock.

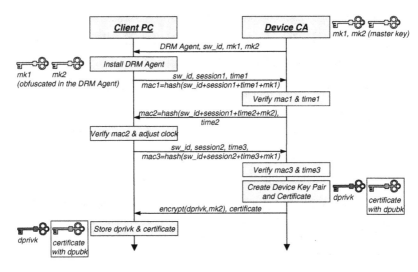

Fig. 3. Sequence diagram for the proprietary communication between client PC and the device certification authority (CA)

After this mutual authentication the client requests the device certificate and the device private key. This second request uses a new session ID (*session2*). If the sent parameters could be verified the server creates a new key pair. Every request produces a new key pair. Finally the certificate and the encrypted device private key are transferred. The client PC receives the encrypted device private key. It decrypts the key and re-encrypts it using the RK (see figure 2). After this step the key store is initialized and the DRM agent is ready to request RO.

5.3 Hidden Key Download in Practice

The proposed hidden key download protocol was designed for media player software with integrated shop functionality. We know that software obfuscation solutions provide only limited security (see chapter 6). Therefore we recommend this solution mainly for pay-per-track business models. In subscription models the financial risk for the provider would be much higher. In such risky business models the users pay only a monthly fee to gain access to huge media database. If the DRM solution will be circumvented the user will receive free access to this media catalog.

The alternative approach to create the device key within the DRM agent software does not increase the security level. Because there is no chance for the CA to be sure that the private key is not visible to the user. To achieve that way the higher security level, which is needed for subscription, a hardware solutions like a TPM (trusted platform module) [19] is needed. We already started working on such solutions using a TPM.

6 Conclusions and Further Work

To generate a balance between raising the security for DRM systems without affecting the consumers' security is a great challenge we faced up to in this paper. The OMA DRM standard implies methodologies to control access to copyright protected content in trusted environments, especially mobile devices. Our solution adopts this standard to untrustworthy platforms like Windows. The OMA approach has been expanded to procedures for a secure distribution of the device private key which is the security anchor of the DRMS and the authentication of devices. "Given enough time, effort and determination a competent programmer will always be able to reverse engineer an application" [23] or to annul a security mechanism. Obfuscation is a technique that "renders software unintelligible but still functional" [25]. Its aim is to reduce the program's vulnerability to any kind of static analysis [21]. In our case it allows to protect the reverse engineering of the device private key is and is currently the most viable method for that. In the end, the authors are conscious that the obfuscation is not a panacea and Barak et al [24] even argue that obfuscation is impossible [24]. Nevertheless, at least it raises the security level, so that it is much more difficult to deobfuscate the software than to reverse engineer it. Deobfuscating is more time-consuming that reverse engineering and technically more difficult or at least economically unviable. As a conclusion, one could say that a successful fighting against hackers must combine several approaches of anti-reversing such as Trusted Computing, code encryption and obfuscation [21]. We have shown that the providers' security could be established sufficiently without risky modifications of the user-system.

Further work will focus a proof of concept to show that the suggested design is feasible and raises the security level of DRMS. We also work on hardware based solutions which are closely related to Trusted Computing [19]. Beyond, future research will concentrate on the integration of evaluation in the DRMS developing process to provide guaranty to customers that the software is not able to "open" back doors for hackers.

References

1. Website of the Open Mobile Alliance, www.openmobilealliance.org
2. Rosenblatt, B.; Trippe, B.; Mooney, S.: Digital Rights Management, Business and Technology, M&T Books, New York, 2002
3. Nützel, Jürgen: Die informatorischen Aspekte virtueller Güter und Waren, Habilitationsschrift (venia legendi), Technische Universität Ilmenau, 2006, www.juergen-nuetzel.de/habilitation.html

4. Schmidt, A. U.; Tafreschi, O.; Wolf, R.: Interoperability Challenges for DRM Systems., 2nd Virtual Goods Workshop, Ilmenau, May, 2004, http://virtualgoods.tu-ilmenau.de/2004/Interoperability_Challenges_for_DRM_Systems.pdf
5. Website of the ODRL initiative, www.odrl.org
6. Iannella, Renato: Digital Rights Management (DRM) Architectures. D-Lib Magazine, Volume 7 Number 6, June, 2001, www.dlib.org/dlib/june01/iannella/06iannella.html
7. Rump, Niels: Managing Meaning - How can standards help? 2nd Virtual Goods Workshop, Ilmenau, May, 2004, http://virtualgoods.tu-ilmenau.de/2004/VirtualGoodsRump.pdf
8. Grimm, Rüdiger: Digital Rights Management: technisch-organisatorische Lösungsansätze. pp. 93-106 in Digital Rights Management, Münchner Kreis, Eds.: Picot, Arnold, Springer-Verlag, Berlin, Heidelberg, New York, 2004
9. Directive 95/46/EC of the European Parliament and of the Council of 24 October 1995 on the protection of individuals with regard to the processing of personal data and on the free movement of such data
10. Müller, Günter; Pfitzmann, Andreas: Sicherheit, insbesondere mehrseitige IT-Sicherheit in: Mehrseitige Sicherheit in der Kommunikationstechnik – Verfahren, Komponenten, Integration; Addison-Wesley-Longman, Bonn u.a. 1997, p. 21-29
11. Röhrig, Susanne; Knorr, Konstantin; Noser, Hansrudi: Sicherheit von E-Business-Anwendungen - Struktur und Quantifizierung, WIRTSCHAFTSINFORMATIK 42 (2000) 6, p. 499-507
12. Russinovich, Mark: www.sysinternals.com/blog/2005/10/sony-rootkits-and-digital-rights.html, published 31.10.2005
13. World of warcraft hackers using Sony BMG rootkit, www.securityfocus.com/brief/34
14. Website of Common Criteria, www.commoncriteriaportal.org
15. OMA Digital Rights Management V1.0, DRM Specification, Approved Enabler, www.openmobilealliance.org/release_program/drm_v1_0.html, Release Date: 2004/06/25
16. Nokia: DRM Developer's Guide for Nokia Devices v2.1., 2004, http://sw.nokia.com/id/418a9cf9-9d49-44b7-911d-f6c24f9d77d2/DRM_Developers_Guide_For_Nokia_Devices_v2_1_en.pdf
17. OMA Digital Rights Management V2.0, DRM Specification, Candidate Enabler, www.openmobilealliance.org/release_program/drm_v2_0.html, Release Date: 2005/09/15
18. OMA Digital Rights Management V2.0, DRM Architecture, Candidate Enabler, www.openmobilealliance.org/release_program/drm_v2_0.html, Release Date: 2005/09/15
19. The website of the Trusted Computing Group, www.trustedcomputinggroup.org
20. Website of Microsoft's Windows Vista, www.microsoft.com/windowsvista/
21. Eilam, Eldad: Reversing: Secrets of Reverse Engineering, Wiley Publishing, Inc., Indianapolis, USA, 2005
22. Cerven, Pavol: Crackproof Your Software, No Starch Press, San Francisco, 2002
23. Collberg Christian, Thomborson Clark, Low Douglas: A taxonomy of obfuscating transformation, Technical report #148, Department of Computer Science, University of Auckland, New Zealand, 1997
24. Barak, B., O. Goldreich, R. Impagliazzo, S. Rudich, A. Sahai, S. Vadhan and K. Yang, "On the (im)possibility of obfuscating programs (extended abstract)," in J. Kilian, editor, *Advances in Cryptology - CRYPTO 2001*, Lecture Notes in Computer Science 2139, www.eecs.harvard.edu/~salil/papers/obfuscate-abs.html
25. Collberg Christian, Thomborson Clark: Watermarking, Tamper-Proofing and Obfuscation – Tools for Software Protection, Department of Computer Science, University of Auckland, New Zealand, 2000

Secure End-to-End Transport over SCTP

Carsten Hohendorf[1], Erwin P. Rathgeb[1],
Esbold Unurkhaan[2], and Michael Tüxen[3]

[1] University of Duisburg-Essen
Institute for Experimental Mathematics
Computer Networking Technology Group
45326 Essen, Germany
Tel.: +49-201-183-7637
hohend@iem.uni-due.de
erwin.rathgeb@iem.uni-due.de
[2] Mongolian Science and Technological University
Computer Science and Management School
P.Box 313/49 Ulaanbaatar, Mongolia
esbold@csms.edu.mn
[3] Münster University of Applied Sciences
Stegerwaldstr. 39
48565 Steinfurt, Germany
Tel.: +49-2551-962-550
tuexen@fh-muenster.de

Abstract. The Stream Control Transmission Protocol is a new transport protocol initially developed to transport signaling messages over IP networks. The new features of SCTP make it also a suitable candidate for applications which nowadays use the standard transport protocols TCP and UDP. Many of these applications have strict requirements regarding the end-to-end security. Providing end-to-end security by using IPsec or the Transport Layer Security (TLS) protocol in combination with SCTP is subject to functional and performance related limitations. These can be avoided by integrating security functions directly into SCTP (S-SCTP). Although S-SCTP in principle solves all limitations, some issues remain hindering broad deployment of this solution. Therefore, we propose an alternative solution which preserves the advantages of S-SCTP while avoiding major modifications to existing standards and operating systems.

1 Introduction

The Stream Control Transmission Protocol (SCTP) is a new transport protocol, which has been approved by the IETF as a proposed Standard [4] in 2000. Originally SCTP was developed to transport telephone signaling messages over an IP network. The goal was to provide a similar reliability and quality of service like a SS7 signaling network. The original framework for the SCTP definition is described in [3].

G. Müller (Ed.): ETRICS 2006, LNCS 3995, pp. 381–395, 2006.
© Springer-Verlag Berlin Heidelberg 2006

Although SCTP has been developed to transport signaling messages, it is a general purpose transport protocol with distinctive features which make it suitable for many applications currently using the classical transport protocols TCP and UDP. The first protocol - apart from signaling transport (SIGTRAN) - to standardize the use of SCTP was Reliable Server Pooling (RSerPool, [6]). The use of SCTP is also defined for the Authentication, Authorization and Accounting (AAA) protocol [5] and the IP Flow Information Export (IPFIX) protocol [12]. Due to the fact that SCTP is already available in most of the major operating systems (Linux, FreeBSD, Solaris, Cisco IOS), it can be anticipated that other applications for SCTP will follow soon. Most of these applications have strict security requirements which are, e.g. for SIGTRAN [11] and RSerPool [20], already specified in standards documents. Therefore it is crucial for the success of SCTP to have an efficient and flexible security solution which supports all features of SCTP.

This paper shortly describes the already standardized SCTP security solutions, namely SCTP over IPsec and TLS over SCTP and identifies their limitations. It will be shown that these functional and performance related limitations can be overcome by integrating security functions directly into SCTP as proposed by us in earlier publications under the name S-SCTP ([21], [22], [23]). One problem remaining with S-SCTP is that a full scale introduction would require these extensions of SCTP to be included in future operating system kernels. Therefore, and based on the discussion in the IETF [21], we propose an alternative security solution for SCTP which is based on the use of the newly defined Datagram TLS protocol ([27] and [28]) in combination with the chunk authentication extension of SCTP [19] currently under standardization in the IETF. We will describe the concept of this "SCTP aware DTLS" solution in detail to substantiate its feasibility. In addition, we will discuss some aspects of a planned prototype implementation based on OpenSSL.

2   Introduction to SCTP

In this section we shortly review some new features of SCTP which are crucial for end-to-end security. A more detailed SCTP description can be found e.g. in [7], [24] and [25].

An SCTP connection called "association" is established with a 4-way handshake protected by a cookie mechanism which makes it less susceptible to blind denial-of-service attacks. SCTP packets consist of a common header followed by a sequence of data units called "chunks". The association is managed by using specific control chunks, user messages are transported in data chunks. Multiple chunks can be bundled into one SCTP packet, so that the resulting SCTP packet best uses the Path Maximum Transmission Unit (PMTU). SCTP is message oriented and provides a more flexible data delivery than current transport protocols. An important feature to achieve this flexible data delivery is the streaming function of SCTP. With this function several message streams can be multiplexed into one association. Only the messages within one stream are delivered in sequence, so a message lost in one stream will not affect the delivery of messages in another stream. This eliminates the head-of-line blocking known from TCP. It is optionally also possible to deliver data out of order within a stream. Data chunks can be delivered in reliable or unreliable mode, so SCTP can provide a TCP or UDP like service to an application.

Another distinctive core feature of SCTP is multi-homing, i.e. the ability for a single SCTP endpoint to support multiple IP addresses. So a SCTP endpoint can have several paths to its peer. Only one path, the primary path, is used for normal data transmission. The other paths are only used in the case of transmission failures. The benefit of multi-homing is a better protection of the association against network failures.

In addition to these standard features of SCTP, two extensions have been proposed which also have to be dealt with when providing end-to-end security for SCTP. These extensions are the Partial Reliability SCTP [10] and the Add IP extension [17]. The Partial Reliability extension describes a mechanism how a SCTP endpoint can specify a time-to-live for a data chunk. This means that a data chunk is not retransmitted once its time-to-live has expired. A control chunk, called FORWARD-TSN (Transmission Sequence Number), is sent to the receiving side signaling that all chunks with a lower sequence number will not be retransmitted, so that the receiver does not wait any more. This extension is useful to transport real time traffic, where out of date data is useless anyway. The Add IP extension allows to dynamically reconfigure IP addresses of an existing SCTP association. So it is possible that the available paths between the endpoints change during an association lifetime. It is also possible to change the primary path with this extension. This extension was proposed to support long lived associations, where it is sometimes necessary to change some network connections. A new application for SCTP was presented on the basis of this extension, called Mobile SCTP [18].

3   Existing Security Solutions

In this section we will present the three security solutions already proposed, namely SCTP over IPsec, TLS over SCTP and S-SCTP. All of these solutions can use the same cipher suites and Hash MAC (HMAC) algorithms, so there is no difference in the provided security, as far as the algorithms are concerned. All of them provide similar mechanisms for key exchange and security session management. Therefore, the major difference with respect to security is that TLS over SCTP – residing on top of SCTP – cannot protect SCTP control information. However, there exist several functional and performance related differences and issues which will be discussed in the remainder of this section.

3.1   SCTP over IPsec

SCTP is typically used in IP based networks. If secure transfer is required SCTP can utilize the IP security protocol suite [13], [14], [15] for integrity, authentication and confidentiality. To establish IPsec Security Associations (SAs), a key negotiation such as IKE [16] may be used. The management and handling of IPsec security associations is complex even when TCP is used. Since SCTP has some features, like multihoming, which are not well supported by IPsec, the management and handling of the SAs is even more complicated. The use of SCTP with IPsec is defined in [9]. This RFC identifies the problems of SCTP over IPsec, i.e. the management of IPsec SAs in the case of multihoming and the support of the Dynamic Address Reconfiguration extension of SCTP. The proposed solution to these problems is to use a list of IP addresses in the security policy database instead of single IP addresses. However, there are no implementations available to date which fully support this RFC.

If the Authentication Header (AH) or the Encapsulation Security Payload (ESP) is used to provide security services for SCTP frames, SCTP is treated as just another transport layer protocol on top of IP (such as TCP, UDP, etc.). Without the proposed modifications to IPsec introduced in [9], this solution requires the configuration of multiple IPsec Security Associations (SA) to support a multi-homed SCTP association. In the OSI model IPsec is one layer beneath SCTP, so it is not capable of differentiating between application data that must be secured and data that does not need to be secured. As a result, IPsec secures all data traffic resulting in an increased computational effort. Another disadvantage of this is that each SCTP packet is secured separately by IPsec. So in the case of long messages which must be fragmented by SCTP the overhead increases since two or more SCTP packets have to be secured.

3.2   TLS over SCTP

RFC3436 [8] describes the usage of the Transport Layer Security (TLS, [2]) protocol over SCTP. TLS is designed to operate on top of a byte-stream oriented transport protocol providing a reliable, in-sequence delivery. Thus, TLS is currently mainly used on top of the Transmission Control Protocol [1].

TLS over SCTP uses one TLS session per stream. This potentially leads to performance problems when the association needs many secured streams. Every message is secured by TLS before it is sent over SCTP. If the application sends many small messages, each message is secured separately, which results in an increased overhead. Since each TLS record depends on the state of the previous record, the unordered delivery service of SCTP is not supported. For the same reason, the Partial Reliable Transport extension cannot be used. In the OSI model, TLS is located above the transport layer, so it cannot protect SCTP control chunks or the SCTP common header, as they are added after TLS passes the data to SCTP.

An advantage of TLS over SCTP compared to SCTP over IPsec is that this solution can mix secured and unsecured traffic within one SCTP association efficiently. The TLS user can also take full advantage of the multi-homing feature and the proposed Add IP extension of SCTP without modification of TLS.

3.3 Secure SCTP (S-SCTP)

The usage of SCTP together with standard security protocols (TLS or IPsec) leads to significant limitations and potential inefficiencies as discussed above. Neither TLS nor IPsec support all SCTP features and due to multi-streaming at the upper service access point and multihoming at the lower service access point, non-integrated solutions are always potentially inefficient in some scenarios. Therefore, the security extension S-SCTP was proposed by us in some earlier work [21], [22], [23]. S-SCTP integrates crypto functions into SCTP itself in an efficient and user-friendly way. This extension is designed to avoid the drawbacks of the non-integrated solutions, whilst still providing full compatibility with the original SCTP protocol when no protection is being used.

S-SCTP is an extension to standard SCTP, designed to be fully compatible to SCTP. The secure session is initialized after the normal SCTP association is established. If one endpoint does not support the S-SCTP extension or the setup of the secure session fails, e.g. due to wrong certificates, the application can decide if it wants to use the unsecured association or if it shuts down the association.

The basic concept of the S-SCTP solution is that an association has only one secure session for all data streams in a multi-streaming case and for all addresses in a multihoming scenario. In order to achieve this, the security mechanism is integrated between the upper functional block of SCTP which performs grouping of SCTP chunks to SCTP packets (bundling) and the lower functional block which performs the selection of network paths by choosing a destination address to send the SCTP packet as shown in Fig. 1.

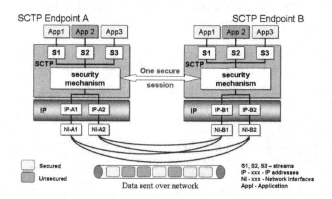

Fig. 1. S-SCTP concept

S-SCTP provides the same security features as the two standardized security solutions, namely authentication, integrity and confidentiality. For that, S-SCTP uses the same standard cipher and HMAC algorithms like IPsec and TLS. To keep the protocol overhead of S-SCTP as small as possible it supports a flexible mix of secured and unsecured data, not only on a per-stream basis as TLS over SCTP, but even on a per chunk basis. To further reduce the overhead, chunks marked for encryption are grouped together and encrypted into one ciphertext block. The HMAC is calculated per packet and not per chunk for the same reason.

To avoid the complexity of secure session management known from IPsec S-SCTP provides the user a simple API for configuration:

- simple initialisation, re-keying and termination of secure sessions,
- flexible choice of standard cipher suites,
- easy integration of newly defined cipher suites if required and
- simple selection and modification of security levels.

S-SCTP also offers a set of predefined security levels, which are easy to select and, furthermore, can be changed during a secure session lifetime.

S-SCTP's only performance disadvantage compared to TLS over SCTP occurs when long messages have to be fragmented at the SCTP layer. In that case S-SCTP has to secure two or more packets separately, so the overhead is bigger compared to TLS where the message is first secured and then fragmented. With respect to all other criteria S-SCTP performs as good as or better than any of the other two security solutions.

The following table provides a summary of the qualitative comparison of the security solutions with respect to usability, overhead, management cost and performance. In the table a "+" indicates that the feature is well supported by the solution, a "-" denotes disadvantages of the solution with the feature and a "no" shows that this feature is not supported at all. The "(-)" for the multihoming support of IPsec indicates that this problem is theoretically solved, however there are no implementations of this solution to date.

Table 1. Comparison of security solutions

Criteria	TLS	IPsec	S-SCTP
Scalability for multiple streams	-	+	+
Support for SCTP multihoming	+	(-)	+
Overhead for small messages (bundling)	-	+	+
Overhead for long messages (fragmentation)	+	-	-
Protection for unordered delivery service	no	+	+
Protection for SCTP control chunks	no	+	+
Flexible multiplexing of secure/insecure streams	+	no	+
Management of security sessions (handling, automation)	+	-	+
Partial Reliable Transport (SCTP extension)	no	+	+
Dynamic Address Reconfiguration (SCTP extension)	+	-	+

4   Quantitative Comparison of the Existing Security Solutions

In order to quantify the effect of the issues identified in Sect. 3, a testbed has been set up and configured with the three security solutions. All three security solutions used the same crypto algorithm, namely the 3DES-SHA cipher. The testbed consisted of 2 Linux PCs (multi-homed) and a FreeBSD PC used as a router. The endpoint PCs had an Athlon AMD 2000 MHz processor and 512 MB of RAM, the router had a 64-bit AMD 3,0 GHz processor and 1 GB of RAM. All PCs were equipped with 1 GBps Ethernet cards.

The tests were performed using a traffic generator sending random data to a traffic analyzer which calculated the throughput in 1 second intervals. Each point in the result figures represents the average of a 5 minute measurement period which was repeated five times. The different link speeds used in the measurements were simulated by Dummynet [26] which was installed on the router. The measurements in Fig. 2 represent scenarios where the link is the bottleneck

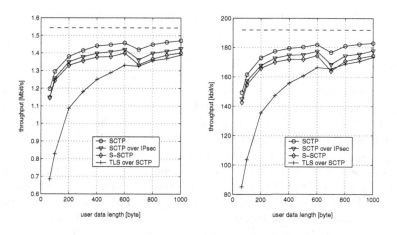

Fig. 2. Throughput of security solutions over different links

of the transmission which is typically the case for WAN connections. The left figure shows the throughput of the three security solutions over a T1-link with 1,544 Mbps and the right one over a DSL-uplink with 192 kbps (note the different scale on the y-axis). In such a scenario the throughput penalty for the three security solutions depends only on the overhead added to secure the data. As TLS secures each user message separately, the overhead added for small messages is higher as for the other two security solutions where small messages are first bundled and then secured as a whole. This is the reason why the throughput of the TLS solution is significantly lower in this case compared to the other solutions allowing bundling. Considering the typically small size of signalling messages, this result is of particular interest if a security solution for signalling transport – the genuine SCTP application – has to be selected.

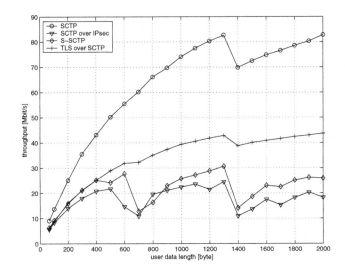

Fig. 3. Throughput of security solutions in a 1GBps Ethernet

Figure 3 shows a scenario where the link is not the bottleneck of the transmission, so the throughput of the security solutions depends on the protocol, its implementation and the performance of the CPU. Such a scenario can be found in LANs, especially in todays 1 Gbps ethernets. In this scenario where the host performance is the bottleneck, the cryptographic functions, in particular encryption, introduce a significant throughput penalty. This can be clearly seen by comparing the solutions to plain standard SCTP. Therefore, the ability to mix secured and unsecured data in one association is highly beneficial – favouring TLS over SCTP and S-SCTP. The measurement results show that the TLS solution achieves the highest throughput of all three security solutions for most packet sizes. The throughput of IPsec and S-SCTP is lower because the encryption of the data and the transmission occur in the same process. If the send queue of this process is full, the send call blocks and waits until new packets can be transmitted. During this time the process runs idle. In the case that bundling cannot be used any more (around 700 bytes of user data length) or when long messages have to be fragmented (1400 bytes of user data length) the throughput drops because there is more overhead contained in packets and the process cannot send more packets due to the blocking send call. When using TLS, encryption and transmission are handled by different processes. In this case, even if the send call blocks and waits until new packets can be transmitted, TLS can still encrypt data for future transmission.

The last figure (Fig. 4) shows the time needed to establish TLS sessions over the given number of streams. As mentioned before, TLS has to establish a new secure session for each stream and as the measurements show, this can be very time consuming if many streams have to be secured or the link bandwidth is limited. Similar problems arise when TLS regularly performs a re-keying using

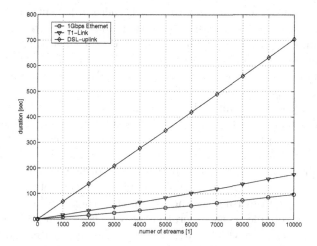

Fig. 4. Duration to complete TLS hanshakes

an abbreviated handshake. This abbreviated handshake does not take as long as the inital handshake because there is no need to exchange certificates, but for a high number of streams this can also take several seconds to minutes, depending on the link.

From the measurements presented in this section and previous measurements [23] we can identify some limitations for the three security solutions. Over high bandwidth links, the throughput of IPsec is lower compared to the other solutions. If only a small portion of the transmitted data has to be secured, the disadvantage of IPsec is more severe because it can not differentiate between data that has to be secured and data that can be send unsecured. TLS over SCTP's major performance limitation is linked to the number of streams which have to be secured. With an increasing number of streams the memory usage and the time to establish the secure sessions for all streams also increase. A throughput degradation occurs when TLS has to secure small messages which can be bundled in the other solutions. S-SCTP was designed to overcome the performance limitations of SCTP over IPsec and TLS over IPsec, so we only identified some performance limitations using high bandwidth links. The main reason for this is the use of a prototype S-SCTP implementation developed to validate the design decisions which was not yet optimized for performance.

5   An Alternative Approach to SCTP End-to-End Security

With S-SCTP, the major functional and performance issues associated with end-to-end security solutions for SCTP are – in principle – solved. However, broad acceptance and deployment would require full standardization in the IETF followed by providing S-SCTP kernel implementations for the major operating systems. One concern with respect to such kernel implementations is, that the kernel would have to perform some operations, like certificate verification and key establishment procedures, which could block the operating system for significant and unpredictable periods of time. Such a behaviour could compromise the responsiveness of the operating system and decrease its ability to handle real-time critical applications.

To strictly avoid this while still preserving the advantages of S-SCTP – in particular the capabilities to protect SCTP control traffic and to efficiently mix secured and unprotected traffic – we propose an alternative solution where the security functionality is split up. Encryption of data, data integrity and authentication are predictable and hence they can – in principle – be integrated into SCTP and implemented in the kernel. Session management, key management and user authentication using certificates on the other hand depend on factors that are not controllable by the operating system. For example user authentication depends on the user who has to present a valid certificate, additionally this certificate has to be checked. As a consequence, these functions have to be implemented in the user space and consequently above SCTP. Taking advantage of two IETF standardization efforts already in progress, namely DTLS ([27], [28]) and SCTP-AUTH [19] such a hybrid solution can be designed with minimal additional standardization impact as described below.

The new Datagram TLS is a modification of TLS allowing to support unreliable transport. The main difference to TLS is that the interdependence of successive TLS records is removed such that each received DTLS segment can be decrypted independently. This feature of DTLS can be used to support both the unordered delivery mode of SCTP as well as the SCTP extension for partial reliability. In addition, it also allows to use one common DTLS session for multiple SCTP streams avoiding the scalability problems with respect to the number of concurrent streams. The other weakness of TLS over SCTP, namely the inability to protect SCTP control traffic, has to be avoided by combining DTLS with the authentication chunk (SCTP-AUTH) extension currently under standardization for SCTP. This SCTP extension allows to protect selected SCTP chunks by means of an HMAC in order to avoid attacks on SCTP association management. SCTP-AUTH defines a new control chunk, called the AUTH chunk, which is used to compute a HMAC of all chunks after the AUTH chunk contained in that packet. The key used for the HMAC computation is called the endpoint pair key. It is based on two random numbers exchanged during the association setup and some endpoint based secrets which will in our case be established by using DTLS. Multiple endpoint based secrets and therefore endpoint based keys are supported and identified by a key identifier. During the association setup both endpoints negotiate which chunks are accepted in an authenticated way only.

The only limitation of such a hybrid approach compared to S-SCTP is that it cannot provide confidentiality (encryption) for SCTP control chunks. However, this is outweighed by the fact that neither additional changes to SCTP (which would be difficult to standardize) nor operating system kernel modifications are required.

With this combination of SCTP, DTLS and SCTP-AUTH, some modifications to DTLS are necessary. In addition, some functionality, e.g. replay protection and reliable transport for secure session management information, can be provided at different levels. Therefore, the following section will describe the resulting solution called "SCTP aware DTLS" proposed by us in some more detail.

6   Concept of SCTP Aware DTLS

The functional block diagram of SCTP aware DTLS is shown in Fig. 5.

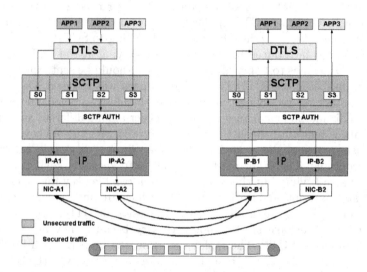

Fig. 5. Concept of SCTP aware DTLS

If an application requires a secure end-to-end session, it first establishes a SCTP association. During the handshake both peers have to exchange some parameters regarding the SCTP-AUTH extension, including a list of chunks that are only accepted in an authenticated way. SCTP aware DTLS requires at least the authentication of all DATA, SACK (Selective Acknowledgement) and FORWARD-TSN chunks, the other chunk types (e.g. HEARTBEAT) can also be authenticated if required by the application using SCTP-AUTH. Initially an empty endpoint pair secret is used with the key identifier 0, later on the endpoint pair secret is derived from the master secret of the DTLS session. Whenever DTLS changes the cipher spec a new endpoint pair secret is derived from the master secret and the key identifier is incremented.

When the application requests secure transport and triggers the handshake of the SCTP aware DTLS session it passes down the relevant details of the association which has to be protected. The handshake messages for session establishment and management are sent over stream 0, which is reserved for management traffic and provides reliable and ordered transport. Once a DTLS session is established, application data is protected by the DTLS security mechanisms and forwarded to the SCTP layer together with the SCTP specific control information (e.g. stream number).

If multiple applications (streams) require protection, they use the same DTLS session. Thus the scaling problem of TLS over SCTP is avoided. In the case an application does not need security, it can directly pass its data to SCTP. Even if no security is required, some chunks of this application will be authenticated by SCTP-AUTH, but this does not introduce any problems.

The usage of DTLS has one restriction regarding the message size an application can send over SCTP aware DTLS. A DTLS record only supports a maximum length of 2^{14} bytes of user data, all longer messages are rejected. At the moment there are no SCTP applications known which send longer messages, as long messages also introduce head-of-line blocking to SCTP.

A new issue is introduced in the case of a re-keying at the DTLS layer. The sender side DTLS has to buffer all new data that should be sent, until it receives a notification, based on SCTP TSNs, that all data was received. Only then the sender can start the re-keying process and both sides can delete the old keying material. This method can cause a blocking effect among different streams since no new data is sent until the last message encrypted with the old keys is successfully transported and the re-keying was done. Since re-keying is not frequent, this is acceptable. The other method would be to keep old keying material in the case of a re-keying, but this would require a complex key management.

There are some optional features of DTLS which are unnecessary when DTLS is used over SCTP. First of all, the retransmission of DTLS control messages in the DTLS handshake layer is not necessary because they are transported in reliable mode by SCTP. The replay detection can be performed by SCTP in combination with SCTP-AUTH and is therefore not necessary at the DTLS layer. Since the replay detection at the DTLS layer might even result in dropping user messages it must not be used. The optional cookie exchange during DTLS session setup within the DTLS layer is not necessary because the SCTP association establishment procedure provides a similar service and is performed first.

6.1   Implementation Considerations for SCTP Aware DTLS

The concept of SCTP aware DTLS tries to keep the differences to standard DTLS as small as possible, in order to reuse the existing protocol infrastructure and implementation. This is benefial when creating a secure and stable (prototype) implementation. Additionally, acceptance in the standardization process is easier if only small changes have to be made.

The current reference implementation of DTLS is based on the OpenSSL library. OpenSSL is an open source implementation of TLS which runs on all major operating systems. Since our previous TLS over SCTP and S-SCTP implementations are also based on OpenSSL, we can benefit from this experience when developing a prototype implementation. Figure 6 shows the structure of the modules in the DTLS implementation including the proposed modifications, the planned modifications are marked dark.

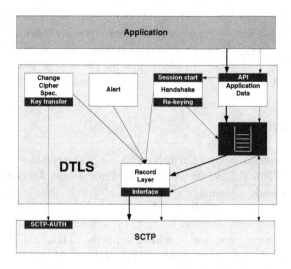

Fig. 6. Structure of SCTP aware DTLS

SCTP aware DTLS requires modifications to DTLS. First of all, the interface of DTLS to the upper layer must be modified and extended. The API of DTLS has to support an SCTP API enhanced by methods to specify the parameters of DTLS, in order to avoid major changes in applications using SCTP aware DTLS.

If an application needs security, it starts a DTLS session and specifies the SCTP association which should be used to transport the data. When the first DTLS session is requested, the Handshake Layer starts the establishment of the secure session. During the handshake, the Record Layer binds the new session to the SCTP association specified by the application. For subsequent requests of other applications to open a secure session, DTLS can skip the handshake and signal the application that the session is ready for data transmission.

The Record Layer of DTLS is responsible for the transmission of Application Data, Alert, Handshake and Change Cipher Spec messages. If the Record Layer has to send Application Data it encrypts the data and uses the SCTP information provided by the application (e.g. stream number) to send it. All other messages are control messages and must be sent over stream 0 on the bound association.

The handshake layer is responsible for re-keying. However, before a re-keying can take place all outstanding data must be acknowledged. This can be checked by using a specific socket option of SCTP. Newly arriving messages from the application have to be buffered at the DTLS layer during this period. The additional buffering mechanism and its communication with both SCTP and the handshake module are some of the major adaption efforts for the scheme.

Also all optional features of DTLS which are unnecessary when used over SCTP, are located in the handshake layer. Further analysis will show if it is beneficial to remove them or not.

In the Change Cipher Spec module only one modification must be made, when SCTP aware DTLS sends an Change Cipher Spec message, the new Master Secret must be passed down to the AUTH extension of SCTP and the key identifier must be incremented. There are no changes expexted in the Alert protocol of DTLS.

7   Conclusion

Based on a comprehensive set of criteria we have evaluated the standard security solutions for SCTP and have identified their limitations. An optimized solution solving these issues has been presented and lab tests based on a prototype implementation have confirmed the validity of the design choices. Acknowledging issues for the broad introduction of S-SCTP - which are mainly standardization related - we have proposed a new alternative. This "SCTP aware DTLS" solution preserves the advantages of S-SCTP while using emerging standard protocol components which hopefully increase the acceptance in the standardization groups. In addition to describing the overall concept of SCTP aware DTLS and its features in detail, we have also discussed the major aspects to be taken into account for our planned prototype implementation.

Both standard components which we used in our solution, DTLS [28] and SCTP-AUTH [19], are expected to reach official RFC status soon. An Internet Draft describing our proposed SCTP aware DTLS solution in detail is currently in preparation and will be submitted to the IETF for one of the next meetings.

References

1. J. Postel "Transmission Control Protocol", STD7, RFC793, September 1981.
2. T. Dierks and C. Allen "The TLS Protocol", RFC2246, January 1999.
3. L. Ong, I. Rytina, M. Garcia, H. Schwarzbauer, L. Coene, H. Lin, I. Juhasz, M. Holdrege and C. Sharp, "Framework Architecture for Signaling Transport", RFC2719, October 1999.
4. R. Stewart, Q. Xie, K. Morneault, C. Sharp, H. Schwarzbauer, T. Taylor, I. Rytina, M. Kalla, L. Zhang and V. Paxson, "Stream Control Transmission Protocol", RFC2960, October 2000.
5. D. Mitton, M. St.Johns, S. Barkley, D. Nelson, B. Patil, M. Stevens and B. Wolff, "Authentication, Authorization, and Accounting: Protocol Evaluation", RFC3127, June 2001.
6. M. Tuexen, Q. Xie, R. Stewart, M. Shore, L. Ong, J. Loughney and M. Stillman, "Requirements for Reliable Server Pooling", RFC3237, January 2002.
7. L. Ong and J. Yoakum, "An Introduction to the Stream Control Transmission Protocol (SCTP)", RFC3286, May 2002.
8. A. Jungmaier, E. Rescorla and M. Tuexen "Transport Layer Security over Stream Control Transmission Protocol", RFC3436, December 2002.
9. S. Bellovin, J. Ioannidis, A. Keromytis and R. Stewart "On the use of Stream Control Transmission Protocol (SCTP) with IPsec", RFC3554, July 2003.

10. R. Stewart, M. Ramalho, Q. Xie, M. Tuexen and P. Conrad, *"Stream Control Transmission Protocol (SCTP) Partial Reliability Extension"*, RFC3758, May 2004.
11. J. Loughney, M. Tuexen and J. Pastor-Balbas, *"Security considerations for signaling Transport (SIGTRAN) Protocols"*, RFC3788, June 2004.
12. S. Leinen, *"Evaluation of Candidate Protocols for IP Flow Information Export (IPFIX)"*, RFC3955, October 2004.
13. S. Kent and K. Seo *"Security Architecture for the Internet Protocol"*, RFC4301, December 2005.
14. S. Kent *"IP Authentication Header"*, RFC4302, December 2005.
15. S. Kent *"IP Encapsulation Security Payload (ESP)"*, RFC4303, December 2005.
16. C. Kaufman *"Internet Key Exchange (IKEv2) Protocol"*, RFC4306, December 2005.
17. R. Stewart, M. Ramalho, Q. Xie, M. Tuexen and P. Conrad, *"Stream Control Transmission Protocol (SCTP) Dynamic Address Reconfiguration"*, draft-ietf-tsvwg-addip-sctp-14 (work in progress), March 2006.
18. M. Riegel and M. Tuexen *"Mobile SCTP"*, draft-riegel-tuexen-mobile-sctp-05 (work in progress), July 2005.
19. M. Tuexen, R. Stewart, P. Lei and E. Rescorla, *"Authenticated Chunks for Stream Control Transmission Protocol (SCTP)"*, draft-ietf-tsvwg-sctp-auth-01 (work in progress), October 2005.
20. M. Stillman, R. Gopal, S. Sengodan E. Guttman and M. Holdrege, *"Threats Introduced by Rserpool and Requirements for Security in response to Threats"*, draft-ietf-rserpool-threats-05 (work in progress), July 2005.
21. C. Hohendorf, E. Unurkhaan and T. Dreibholz, *"Secure SCTP"*, draft-hohendorf-secure-sctp-00 (work in progress), July 2005.
22. E. Unurkhaan, *"Secure End-to-End Transport - A new security extension for SCTP"*, Dissertation, University of Duisburg-Essen, June 2005.
23. U. Esbold, E.P. Rathgeb and A. Jungmaier, *"Secure SCTP - A Versatile Secure Transport Protocol"*, Telecommunications 27:2-4, p.273ff, 2004.
24. R. Stewart and Q. Xie, *"Stream Control Transmission Protocol - A Reference Guide"*, Addison-Wesley, 2002.
25. A. Jungmaier, *"SCTP for beginners"*, http://tdrwww.exp-math.uni-essen.de/inhalt/forschung/sctp_fb/, 2003.
26. L. Rizzo, *"Dummynet"*, http://info.iet.unipi.it/~luigi/ip_dummynet/
27. N. Modadugu and E. Resorla *"The Design and Implementation of Datagram TLS"*, Network and Distributed System Security Symposium, February 2004.
28. E. Resorla and N. Modadugu *"Datagram Transport Layer Security"*, draft-rescorla-dtls-05.txt, June 2004.

An Extended Model of Rational Exchange Based on Dynamic Games of Imperfect Information

Almudena Alcaide, Juan M. Estevez-Tapiador,
Julio C. Hernandez-Castro, and Arturo Ribagorda

Computer Science Department – Carlos III University
Avda. Universidad 30, 28911, Leganes, Madrid
{aalcaide, jestevez, jcesar, arturo}@inf.uc3m.es

Abstract. The notion of rational exchange introduced by Syverson in 1998 is a particularly interesting alternative when an efficient scheme for fair exchange is required but the use of a trusted third party is not allowed. A rational exchange protocol cannot provide fairness, but it ensures that rational (i.e. self-interested) parties would have no reason to deviate from the protocol. Buttyán et al (2003) have recently pointed out how rationality in exchange protocols can be formalized and studied within the framework provided by Game Theory. In this paper, we identify some vulnerabilities in Syverson's protocol which were not detected by Buttyán et al's analysis. These motivate us to extend the model to consider new aspects, never formalized before when analyzing security protocols. These aspects are related to participants' reputation, protocol's robustness, and the impact that scenarios where the protocol is executed repeatedly have on the outcome of the protocol execution.

1 Introduction

It is not only the design and definition of security protocols that has been the focus of researchers in recent years. The definition of formal models to validate and verify such protocols has also been an area of intense research and development. Since the definition of the Dolev-Yao adversary model [4], many tools and techniques have been developed to prove the correctness of a protocol. Informally, a protocol is assumed to be correct when it satisfies all its goals, requirements, and properties. However, correctness does not mean that the protocol offers protection against every type of attack. Most of those validation methods and tools have been very successful at finding security flaws and providing counterexamples in many protocols. At the same time, each one of those tools has also got very significant limitations based on one single factor: the way to model unpredictable behavior; that is, how to predict the way in which a set of events, outside the protocol specifications, can subvert a protocol execution, and what the outcome would be. To attack a security protocol we only need to step out of the set of restrictions imposed by the model used to verify its properties [5]. On the other hand, without limiting the actions of each of the entities involved in a protocol the resulting model would be too wide, too difficult –if not impossible

G. Müller (Ed.): ETRICS 2006, LNCS 3995, pp. 396–408, 2006.

to manage– and, ultimately, an *undecidable* problem. There are also other types of limitations regarding existing tools and models to validate protocols, such as the constantly new pointed out properties of security services and definitions of new cryptographic primitives. Models and validation tools have to be enhanced or modified to verify compliance with the new service properties. Consider, for instance, *timeliness* and *composability*. The first one states that a security property has to be achieved in a finite amount of time, either by successful completion of the protocol or by forcing protocol termination. On the other hand, composability establishes that, given a collection of protocols executed simultaneously, it is necessary to demonstrate that no protocol in the collection will accept a message sent by another protocol in the same collection. Usually new properties such as the previous arise from new attacks and threats on breaking security services, and it is not always easy to formally define and validate them. In this context, the notion of *rational exchange* constitutes a relatively recent proposal that still poses new challenges despite its similarities with fair exchange. Before presenting our contribution, we further elaborate on this topic in the following.

1.1   Fairness and Rationality in Exchange Protocols

The problem of how to design a general procedure according to which two parties can exchange items in a *fair* manner has attracted much attention lately. Interest in this class of protocols stems from its importance in many applications where disputes among parties can occur, such as digital contract signing, certified e-mail, exchange of digital goods and payments, etc. In particular, assurance of fairness is fundamental when the exchanged items include any kind of evidences of non-repudiation, for this constitutes a key service in most of the previously mentioned applications. As a result, fair non-repudiation has experienced an explosion of proposals in recent years (see [10]) for an excellent survey).

Roughly, the property of fairness means that no party should reach the end of the protocol in a disadvantageous position, e.g. having sent her item without having received anything valuable in return. Formally, there exists no protocol according to which a number of parties can exchange items in a fair manner exclusively by themselves, and assuming that misbehaving parties can take part in the protocol. Pagnia and Gärtner provide a formal treatment of this problem in [14].As a result, the simplest protocol than can provide true fairness requires a trusted third party (TTP) in order to preserve the property during the exchange.

Recent computing paradigms, such as ad hoc and peer-to-peer networks, pose a challenge from the point of view of the security mechanisms that should be applied. In many cases, the operation of these systems is based on a complete absence of fixed infrastructures. Generally, it is not realistic to assume that services such as those provided by a TTP will be available in those environments. It is precisely in this context where notions such as *rationality* become particularly interesting. This concept, widely known to game theorists, was applied to security protocols by Syverson in 1998 [15]. Informally, a rational exchange protocol cannot provide fairness, but it ensures that rational (i.e. self-interested) parties would have no reason to deviate from the protocol as misbehaving does not result in any benefit. Since rational exchange protocols provide fewer guarantees, one would expect that they also demand fewer requirements, so they can be viewed as a trade-off between complexity and true fairness. In particular, rational exchange protocols do have the enormous advantage of not needing a trusted third party.

1.2   Overview

Syverson's rational exchange protocol was formally analyzed by Buttyán et al in [3], using their definition of rationality within a game-theoretical model proposed in the same work. However, we will see that the protocol presents significant weaknesses which were not detected by previous analysis, so a series of attacks can be successfully carried out. Our intention has been to highlight the protocol's vulnerabilities and also to extend the model in order to capture other relevant aspects involved in the protocol execution. Our proposal relies on modeling the protocol as a game of imperfect information, in which protocol participants have to establish levels of confidence based on bayesian considerations.

The rest of the paper is organized as follows. Section 2 presents the Syverson's protocol, its vulnerabilities and possible attacks, and the appropriate modifications needed to prevent them. In Section 3, we give a brief description of Buttyán et al's model and describe some enhancements. Finally, in Sections 5 and 6 we present our extended model and describe the main conclusions reached.

2   Analysis of Syverson's Rational Exchange Protocol

The scheme is illustrated in Fig. 1. A and B denote the two protocol parties, with private keys k_A^{-1} and k_B^{-1}, respectively. We assume that $item_A$ and $item_B$ are the items they would like to exchange, being $desc_{item_A}$ a description of $item_A$. (There is no equivalent description for $item_B$ because the scheme was introduced to serve as a payment protocol, in such a way that $item_B$ has the role of the payment for buying $item_A$). Moreover, $enc(k,m)$ is a symmetric encryption algorithm that encrypts message m with key k_i. Likewise, $sig(k_i^{-1},m)$ provides a digital signature on m by using secret key k_i^{-1}. Finally, $w(\cdot)$ is a WSBC (Weakly Secret Bit Commitment) function [15]. For our analysis, it suffices to know that $w(x)$ keeps x secret, but it can be broken in acceptable bounds on time.

In step one, A sends B her item $item_A$ in a weakly encrypted form. Next, B sends A her item $item_B$ in return, along with acknowledgment of the first message. Finally, A sends the appropriate key k and acknowledgment of the second message.

There are two potentially critical situations which can take place: A might fail to send message m_3 or it might not send it for a long time and, as B can only disclose the encrypted $item_A$ when the payment has already taken place, A could send a forged $item_A$ and still receive payment in return. The first deterrent against A delaying sending message m_3 is that A gains nothing by doing so, except a bad reputation that could ruin its business. In the case of A sending B

$$A \rightarrow B : m_1 = (desc_{item_A}, enc(k, item_A), w(k), \sigma_1)$$
$$B \rightarrow A : m_2 = (item_B, m_1, \sigma_2)$$
$$A \rightarrow B : m_3 = (k, m_2, \sigma_3)$$

where:

$$\sigma_1 = sig(k_A^{-1}, (desc_{item_A}, enc(k, item_A), w(k)))$$
$$\sigma_2 = sig(k_B^{-1}, (item_B, m_1))$$
$$\sigma_3 = sig(k_A^{-1}, (k, m_2))$$

Fig. 1. Syverson's rational exchange protocol

the wrong $item_A$, B holds message m_3 as a proof of such misbehavior. However, an important issue arises from both of the previous statements: both participants must exchange during the protocol execution irrevocable evidences to prove the other participant's misbehavior. For example, a scheme on entity A's reputation can only be implemented when it is not possible for B to accuse A of misbehaving if A was honest, and vice versa. A fourth message could be added in which customer B acknowledges timely receipt for message m_3. Likewise, for B to be able to prove in front of an external judging entity that A sent an invalid $item_A$, B must hold irrevocable proof of such a message. The context in which this protocol might be executed has to be carefully checked, as Syverson's protocol is not always appropriate. The author identifies scenarios where the scheme could be used for: (1) If the vendor A is selling relatively low value items, so it is not worth for the customer (in terms of computational cost or the inconvenience of delay) to break the encryption to recover the item; (2) the vendor A might be selling something that might be of timely and diminishing value, such as short term investment advice or regularly changing lists of bargain items for sale; or (3) the protocol might begin one step earlier with a signed customer request for $item_A$. The vendor A can then take the chance of trading with unknown customers and refuse to service customers who repeatedly fail to pay.

2.1   Vulnerabilities

Syverson protocol, as defined by its author, presents some vulnerabilities that allow a series of attacks to be successfully carried out.

Attack I. Consider the following scenario, where $P(Q)$ means that party P acts impersonating the role of party Q:

$$A \rightarrow B \quad : m_1 = (desc_{item_A}, enc(k, item_A), w(k), \sigma_1)$$
$$B(A) \rightarrow C \quad : m_1 = (desc_{item_A}, enc(k, item_A), w(k), \sigma_1)$$
$$C \rightarrow B(A) : m_2 = (item_C, m_1, \sigma_2)$$

This attack is based on B impersonating A, sending the same message m_1 to C and receiving $item_C$ in return. B would have to quit the protocol after receiving the payment, as she has no key to send to C. Although C has paid a full price for

$item_A$, by the time that k is disclosed to C, $item_A$ would be of very little value to C. The customer C could only present message m_1 to prove A misbehaved. However, A will claim that m_1 was never intended for C and that she was not part of such a communication. Indeed, there is nothing in m_1 linking A and C as participants on the same protocol run. To overcome this attack, some amendments should be made to the structure of m_1.

Attack II. Let us suppose the following simplistic scenario: A is selling an access code to enable the viewing of a football match on a private television network. Let us suppose that A and B carried out a successful Syverson's protocol execution and that they properly exchanged the encrypted access code, $item_B$ and the corresponding key k in messages m_{11}, m_{12}, and m_{13}, respectively. The access code that B has bought from A is obviously of timely diminishing value, but B could still have time to impersonate A and sale the access code to other customers, receiving payment in return:

$$B(A) \rightarrow C \quad : m_{21} = m_{11} = (desc_{item_A}, enc(k, item_A), w(k), \sigma_A)$$
$$C \rightarrow B(A) : m_{22} = (payment_C, m_{21}, \sigma_C)$$
$$B(A) \rightarrow C \quad : m_{23} = m_{13} = (k, m_{12}, \sigma_A)$$

In this scenario, by the time C receives message three and realizes that there is a fraud going on, C has no evidence of such a fraud to present in front of a judge, and has got the key k to decrypt the football match access code and watch the match. However, A could claim that C is watching a program without a license and take action against her. If the number of reselling codes is large, the scale of the fraud would make it impractical to pursue each one of the individuals watching the match with no license. Furthermore, trying to trace back the origin of such messages would be practically impossible. Again, to address this problem the content of message one should be amended.

Attack III. If a vendor sends the customer a message m_1 containing garbage (i.e, a ciphertext which does not correspond with the actual $item_A$), the vendor is indeed providing the customer with evidence of such a form of cheating. Message m_1 could be presented to a judge and the vendor would be charged with the appropriate penalty. Such a penalty could greatly exceed the value of the goods, so the vendor is completely discouraged from performing such a scheme. However, the vendor could not be sued and penalized twice for the same offense and, on these terms, a vendor A could carry on sending the forged message m_1 to many others customers, receiving payments in return. These new angry customers would only have message m_1 to inculpate vendor A. Vendor A would claim that she never sent m_1 to them and that they must have got it from the first resentful customer. As a matter of fact, there will be nothing in m_1 to prove that A is reselling the same forged message all over again.

2.2 Fixing the Protocol

Even though the attacks described above correspond to simple deviations from the protocol description, they represent real threats to parties using the scheme to exchange their items. In e-commerce transactions, neither vendor A nor customer B would want to take the risk of being cheated on. However, the previous attacks can be avoided if a better cryptographic evidence is constructed. This can be done in many ways. Probably the easiest one is just by including the identity of B in m_1, thus linking the message with its intended receiver[1]:

$$A \rightarrow B : m_1 = (\mathbf{B}, desc_{item_A}, enc(k, item_A), w(k), \sigma_1)$$

where:

$$\sigma_1 = sig(k_A^{-1}, (\mathbf{B}, desc_{item_A}, enc(k, item_A), w(k)))$$

This modification suffices to prevent attacks one to three.

3   Buttyán et al's Model: Game Theory and Protocol Games

Syverson's protocol was analyzed by Buttyán et al in [3]. For readability and completeness, we first provide a brief introduction to the game-theoretical model of rational exchange introduced by Buttyán et al. Please refer to [3] for further details. Where possible, we have adopted the same notation as used in [3].

3.1   Protocol Games

The protocol game of an exchange protocol is intended to model all possible interactions of the protocol participants, even the potentially misbehaving actions (i.e., those different from the prescribed by the protocol). A protocol game is constructed from the protocol description. Each of the parties involved in the protocol becomes a player of the protocol game, including the network. Every participant, apart from the network, has strategies to quit, to do nothing, to send a message following the protocol steps, or to send a message deviating from the steps of the original protocol. Each player can send messages which have been defined as *compatible* with the protocol, i.e., messages which are within the context of the protocol. The set of messages compatible with a protocol is formally defined within Buttyán et al's model. Participants can alter the order in which those messages are sent. When the protocol game is over, every participant can assess the profit or the loss they have incurred in, by using a payoff function. Informally, a two-party rational exchange protocol is an exchange protocol in which both main parties are motivated to behave correctly and to follow the protocol faithfully. If one of the parties deviates from the protocol, then she may bring the other, correctly behaving party in a disadvantageous situation, but she cannot gain any advantages by her misbehavior. Buttyán et al define the concept of rationality in terms of a Nash equilibrium in the protocol game.

---

[1] As usual, we assume that A's identity is implicit in m_1, since the message contains A's signature. If this was not the case, then we must include it explicitly to avoid a different class of attacks.

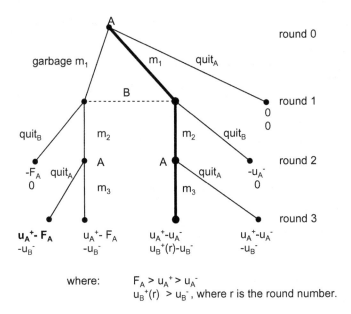

Fig. 2. Partial representation of Syverson's protocol game in extensive form

It is required that the strategies that correspond to the behavior described by
the protocol form a Nash equilibrium in the protocol game and that no other
Nash equilibrium is strongly preferable for any of the participants.

In Fig. 2, we have represented Syverson's protocol game in an extensive form.
The tree represents the different moves each participant can make and all the
different possible outcomes. The vectors assigned to each terminal node represent
the outcome for A (first value) and B (second value) when A and B follow the
path of strategies to finish the protocol at that end. These values are given by
Buttyán et al in their model.

The values u_A^+ and u_B^+ denote the values that $item_B$ and $item_A$ are worth to
parties A and B respectively. In a similar way, the values u_A^- and u_B^- denote the
values that $item_A$ and $item_B$ are worth to A and B, respectively. The value of
F_A represents the penalty A has to pay when proved to be the author and sender
of a forged message m_1. Note that this is possible only when the enhancement
described in section 2.2 is added to the protocol description. The model designed
by Buttyán et al assume that evidences are well constructed and fails to reflect
the actual content of message m_1, as it is described in the protocol.

We have highlighted in the tree the *strategy profile* for A and B which would
result in a rational exchange of items $item_A$ and $item_B$. As noted by Buttyán et
al's model this profile constitutes a Nash Equilibrium so, by definition, neither
of the players would want to deviate from it. Therefore Buttyán's model serves
to formally define rationality and to prove that Syverson's enhanced protocol is
a rational exchange protocol. However, as we can see in the diagram, A is not
motivated to be fair to B in the last round of the protocol. A could threat B to

execute $quit_A$ or to get delayed in sending m_3 to B. This is a feasible threat. In the following section we will see the consequences this threat has on B's behavior and on the equilibrium previously found.

4 Discussion

In this section we intend to analyze new aspects of the protocol, extending the model described above and introducing new parameters into the extensive form of the protocol game.

4.1 Other Nash Equilibriums in Repeated Executions

As we mentioned before, A is not motivated to be fair to B in the last round of the protocol. Therefore, A could threaten B to quit or to delay sending m_3 to B. B would then be safer quitting the protocol before round 2 and aborting the exchange. The best response that A can give to B's quit strategy is to quit as well. Therefore strategies $(alwaysquit_A, alwaysquit_B)$ also form a Nash Equilibrium for the protocol game described in Fig. 2. In order to solve this issue, A should be given some kind of incentive to be fair to B in the last round of the protocol. This incentive may have the form of a "reputation factor", surely managed by external parties, which will be made public. This reputation factor will give entity B the means to place an appropriate level of confidence in entity A. In the extended model which we propose, participant B will be forced to form a conjecture or set of beliefs over A's behavior based on its reputation factor (this implies repeated scenarios) or similar (other criteria for first time executions). This way, our model will capture the uncertainty B has over A's behavior at the last step in the protocol. A certain value δ will define the probability that entity B assigns to the event of A sending m3 at round three according to the protocol description. Consequentially, the value $(1-\delta)$ will determine the probability of A getting delayed in sending m_3 or not sending it at all. The fact that, most likely, entity A will be using Syverson's protocol to interact with a variety of entities B, in various occasions (repeated executions) can also help B in adjusting the value for δ.

4.2 Reputation Factors

Any given entity wishing to participate in a security protocol must place a degree of confidence in the protocol design as it is not possible to model and anticipate all malicious protocol attacks. Although a well verified and validated protocol will offer the participants enough guarantees to preserve security, nevertheless any given protocol carries a reputation factor. In the case of Syverson protocol, B is the entity taking a greater risk so B must be sure that A will behave according to the protocol description and B must also be confident that the protocol is well designed so A cannot deviate without being noticed. Our extended model will capture the level of uncertainty that participant B holds over the robustness of the Syverson protocol. A certain probability α can be considered as the level of confidence a customer B has in the protocol's design. It represents the possibility that a forged message sent by A could actually be part of the protocol execution, breaking the rationality property and enabling A to finish the protocol in a advantageous position. It establishes the fact that the protocol could present unknown vulnerabilities identified only by A. It is assumed that the kind of forged message A could send is different from gm_1 (garbage m_1) in Fig. 2, because gm_1 will always be detected and penalized. This fact would be represented as a new branch in the tree, labelled as *unpredictable gm_1*.

4.3 Extended Local History Records

It is specified in Buttyán et al's model that each player creates a history record of all the events that were generated by her and the round number of their generation. Possible entries in the history record file of protocol participant A would be $\mathsf{send}(m_1, party_B)$ or $\mathsf{rcv}(m_2)$, in round r. Based on the entries stored in this record each player is allowed, or not allowed, to send a particular message. For instance, a valid digital signature s_A, can only be generated by A, therefore, B can send a message containing s_A iff B received a message containing s_A *earlier and during the current protocol execution*. Indeed, as the model was defined, this history record is newly created for each protocol run so information received in previous protocol runs is discarded at the end of the execution. It is precisely this aspect of the model that hides the protocol vulnerabilities described in section 2.1. Any participant of the protocol could have compatible messages from previous runs and will be able to use them. Buttyán et al's model, by discharging old messages, fails to detect attacks as those described in section 2.1.

Furthermore, the protocol participants will have to be trained to identify such fraud messages and discharge them. Within Buttyáns model, each participant is given a program π_i to execute at each step in the protocol execution. The logic of these programs must be extended to include various tests to verify whether evidences are properly constructed [7] and the appropriate mechanisms designed to be able to reject old or/and forged messages. The protocol design and verification processes have to guarantee the participants some essential required security properties.

4.4 Entity A's Conjecture

In a similar way, A will be asked to conjecture about B's behavior at round two of the protocol. B could, at step two, continue or quit. A will assign a certain probability β to the event of B sending m_2 at round two of the protocol. Therefore $(1-\beta)$ will be the probability of B misbehaving at round two by quitting the execution. Note that A can always verify the freshness of m_2 as it is an irrevocable receipt and an irrefutable proof of origin of m_1. B cannot cheat sending the wrong m_2 as this will always be detected and punished. For simplification, we have omitted this path in the tree.

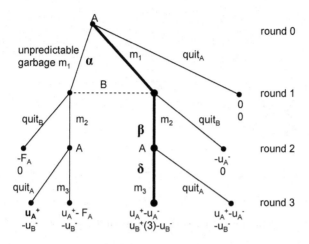

Where B's conjectures are:
α = prob{A is able to misbehave at round one}
δ = prob{A sends m3 at round three of the protocol}
and A's conjectures are:
β =prob{B sends m2 at round two of the protocol}

Fig. 3. Partial representation of Syverson's protocol game in extensive form

5   Extended Model Based on Dynamic Games of Imperfect Information

By considering the protocol as a game of imperfect information, we are forcing both entities, A and B, to form conjectures about each other, and also about the correctness and *robustness* of the protocol. Those conjectures will be represented by probabilities α, β, and δ introduced before. See Fig. 3 for a partial extensive-form representation, of the Imperfect Information Protocol Game. Fig. 3 extends Fig. 2 showing a completely new scenario. In 3 there exists the possibility that A could send B a forged message, for which A would obtain message m_2 in return and for which entity A will not be fined or penalized. This would only be possible by stepping outside the previous model and assuming that there still are vulnerabilities in the protocol design. A could well identify such flaws and try to take advantage of them. However, it is not always clear that there still exist vulnerabilities and that entity A could recognize them. So the uncertainty B holds over the protocol correctness can be captured and modelled by this new branch in the tree. We have omitted the other gm_1 path to simplify the analysis of this new aspect. The following calculations will establish the criteria for A and B to be participants of the protocol, and they will also help to define different equilibria for the different values of α, β and δ, from which neither of the two entities will want to deviate.

Entity B can formulate the following considerations for each one of the possible strategies:

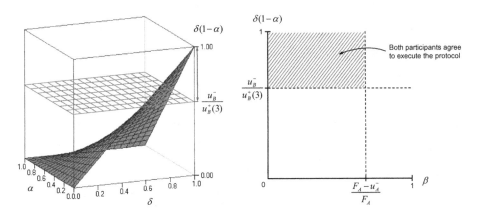

Fig. 4. Graphic representation of Nash equilibrium space

$$EG(quit_B) = 0$$
$$EG(m_2) = \alpha * [(1 - \delta) * (-u_B^-) + \delta * (-u_B^-)] +$$
$$(1 - \alpha) * [\delta * (u_B^+(3) - u_B^-) + (1 - \delta) * (-u_B^-)] = \qquad (1)$$
$$u_B^+(3) * \delta * (1 - \alpha) - u_B^-$$

Where $EG(m)$ represents the expected gain after message m. Note that:

$$EG(m_2) \geq EG(quit_B) \Leftrightarrow u_B^+(3) * \delta * (1 - \alpha) - u_B^- \geq 0$$

Therefore:

$$EG(m_2) \geq EG(quit_B) \Leftrightarrow \delta * (1 - \alpha) \geq u_B^-/u_B^+(3) \qquad (2)$$

The graph shown in Fig. 4 (left) represents the function $\delta*(1-\alpha)$. For all those values α and δ for which the graph is over the value $u_B^-/u_B^+(3)$, the best strategy for B would be to carry out the exchange and follow the protocol description. Below that line, B's best strategy is to quit, as the expected gain value would be less than zero. In a similar way, A can formulate the following considerations: For each one of the possible strategies that A can follow, the expected gains would be (ugm_1 stands for unpredictable garbage m_1):

$$EG(m_1, quit_A) = \beta * (u_A^+ - u_A^-) + (1 - \beta) * (-u_A^-) = \beta * u_A^+ - u_A^-$$
$$EG(m_1, m_3) = \beta * (u_A^+ - u_A^-) + (1 - \beta) * (-u_A^-) = \beta * u_A^+ - u_A^-$$
$$EG(ugm_1, quit_A) = \beta * (u_A^+) + (1 - \beta) * (-F_A) = \beta * (F_A + u_A^+) - F_A$$
$$EG(ugm_1, m3) = \beta * (u_A^+ - F_A) + (1 - \beta) * (-F_A) = \beta * u_A^+ - F_A$$

Note that the omitted strategies (ugm_1, m_3) and $(ugm_1, quit_A)$ do not affect the following rationale, as they are strictly dominated strategies where the pay-off function $(\beta * u_A^+ - F_A)$ is always less than zero. Furthermore, the strategy (ugm_1, m_3) is also a strictly dominated strategy with a payoff value below zero. The strategy $(ugm_1, quit_A)$ plays an important role, as there will be a threshold value for β to establish whether A, having the opportunity to attack the protocol, would take the risk to be detected at the first step of the protocol.

From previous expressions, we obtain that:

$$EG(ugm_1, quit_A) \geq EG(m_1, m_3) \Leftrightarrow \beta \leq (F_A - u_A^-)/F_A \qquad (3)$$

Fig. 4 (right) shows the intersection between the space of values for α and δ from Fig. 4 (left) and the new threshold for A's conjecture β. The shadowed area represents the equilibrium space. There are infinite Nash equilibriums depending on the different conjectures, all of them formed by mixed strategies. The values of α, β and δ will be regulated by the public reputation factor, so they will be in favor of the exchange or not *at the same time*. This is: if A's reputation is not too good or if it is the first time A participates in an exchange, B will show a high level of distrust, but A will be aware of this and will adjust the value of β accordingly. When considering a repeated scenario, the total profit for participants A and B is calculated adding all the profits obtained at each one of the protocol executions. Misbehaving will then have a global impact on the total expected gains. The values for α, β, and δ serve to formally model such an effect.

6   Conclusions

In this paper, we have studied new aspects of Syverson's protocol. First, we analyzed the evidence tokens constructed during the protocol execution, which were meant to preserve rationality in case of misbehavior. We found some vulnerabilities related to those, and provided an enhancement which overcame the problems. Secondly, we formally considered the most common context for Syverson's protocol, which is based on repeated scenarios. These were formally taken into account when studying the participants' behavior. In repeated scenarios, participants care about their reputation, so it is possible to analyze part of their future conduct based on such a factor. Finally, we studied a new aspect never modelled before: The uncertainty over the protocol's robustness and the impact this has on the participants behavior.

Our model brings into consideration Syverson's protocol reputation when assessing the risk undertaken when it is executed. We have taken Buttyán et al's model, based on game theory, and extended it to add three new parameters which serve to analyze the new aforementioned aspects. A completely new space of Nash equilibrium has emerged as a result.

References

1. L. Buttyán, J.P. Hubaux. "Rational exchange– a formal model based on game theory". In *Proceedings of the 2nd International Workshop on Electronic Commerce*, LNCS Vol. 2232, p. 114. November 2001. Springer-Verlag.
2. L. Buttyán, J.P. Hubaux. "A formal Analysis of Syverson's Rational Exchange protocol". In *Proceedings of the 15th IEEE Computer Security Foundations Workshop*, pp. 181–193, June 2002.

3. L. Buttyán, J.P. Hubaux, S. Čapkun. "A Formal Model of Rational Exchange and Its Application to the Analysis of Syverson's Protocol". *Journal of Computer Security*, Vol. 12, Issue 3/4, 2004, pp. 551–588. IOS Press, 2004.

4. D. Dolev and A. Yao. "On the security of public-key protocols". *IEEE Transactions on Information Theory*, Vol. 29, pp. 198–208, 1983.

5. D.E. Denning. "The limits of Formal Security Models". National Computer System Security Award Acceptance Speech, 1999.

6. R. Gibbons. *Game Theory for Applied Economists*. Princeton University Press, 1992.

7. [ISO/IEC 13888-3] Information Security. Security Techniques. Non Repudiation. 1997.

8. M. Jakobson. "Ripping coins for a fair exchange". In *EUROCRYPT'95*, LNCS Vol. 921, p. 220. May 1995. Springer-Verlag.

9. S. Kremer and J.F. Raskin. "A game Approach to the Verification of Exchange Protocols". In *Proceedings of the 1st Workshop on Issues in the Theory of Security*, July 2000.

10. S. Kremer, O. Markowitch, and J. Zhou. "An intensive survey of fair non-repudiation protocols". *Computer Communications*, 25(17):1606–1621. Elsevier, 2002.

11. S. Kremer. "Formal Analysis of Optimistic Fair Exchange Protocol. PhD Thesis. UniversitLibre de Bruxelles. Facultde Sciences. 2003-04.

12. R.M. Needham. "The changing environment for security protocols". *IEEE Network*, Vol. 11, No. 3, pp. 12–15, May-June 1997.

13. Petteri Nurmi. "A framework for online reputation systems". Department of Computer Science, University of Helsinki. March 2005.

14. H. Pagnia and F.C. Gärtner. "On the impossibility of fair exchange without a trusted third party". Darmstadt University of Technology, Department of Computer Science. Technical Report TUD-BS-1999-02. March 1999.

15. P. Syverson. "Weakly secret bit commitment: Applications to lotteries and fair exchange". In *Proceedings of the 11th IEEE Computer Security Foundations Workshop*, pp. 2–13, 1998.

Filtering for Private Collaborative Benchmarking

Florian Kerschbaum and Orestis Terzidis

SAP Research, Karlsruhe, Germany
Florian.Kerschbaum@sap.com
Orestis.Terzidis@sap.com

Abstract. Collaborative Benchmarking is an important issue for modern enterprises, but the business performance quantities used as input are often highly confidential. Secure Multi-Party Computation can offer protocols that can compute benchmarks without leaking the input variables. Benchmarking is a process of comparing to the "best", so often it is necessary to only include the k-best enterprises for computing a benchmark to not distort the result with some outlying performances. We present a protocol that can be used as a filter, before running any collaborative benchmarking protocol that restricts the participants to the k best values. Our protocol doesn't use the general circuit construction technique for SMC aiming to optimize performance. As building blocks we present the fastest implementation of Yao's millionaires' protocol and a protocol that achieves a fair shuffle in $O(\log n)$ rounds.

1 Introduction

Benchmarking is a management process where multiple companies evaluate their processes in comparison to each other, usually their competitors in their industry segment. Collaborative benchmarking is when multiple companies engage in this process together. Common statistical quantities, such as the average or variance, of business process performance quantities, e.g. time to ship, cash flow or return on investment, are used to compare performance. But many of the input variables to this stochastic calculation are very sensitive and highly confidential, even within one company. Gathering statistics over these variables is therefore a privacy-critical task. Current solutions solve this problem by anonymizing the data and use a trusted third party. Protocols that don't require a trusted third party are expected to increase customer acceptance.

Secure Multi-Party Computation (SMC) allows to compute such statistics without revealing anything about the input variables that cannot be inferred by the result. This paper focuses on enabling an important calculation for benchmarking. Often there is a small fraction of the participating companies whose performance is so outrageously bad that their inclusion in the benchmark, e.g. average, would distort the result and hamper the benchmarking process. Since benchmarking aims at process performance improvement, one could get a falsified picture of his standing compared to the competition.

G. Müller (Ed.): ETRICS 2006, LNCS 3995, pp. 409–422, 2006.

We present a filter protocol that runs before the protocol that computes the statistical quantity and restricts the computation to the k best values. Restricting to the k best values is equivalent to excluding the $n - k$ worst values when n is publicly known. It is general, because it can be applied before most other protocols that collaboratively compute benchmarks, e.g.[12], and that wants to exclude outlying values. The protocol is multi-party and each party holds one input value to the computation. The privacy requirements are that no one learns anything about anybody else's value, i.e. each value is kept private to its party. Also no one should learn anything about the k-partitioning of the values, i.e. no one should know whether anybody's - including his own - value is in the set of the k included values or not.

The protocol sorts privately the input values: Each participant is assigned a rank $(1...n)$ and the idea is that at the end of the protocol, the values are sorted, such that the ith-ranked element is at the ith participant. The protocol emulates a sorting network [10] where each participant is connected to one input wire. The only operation in a sorting network is the comparison of two values at two participants, and eventually exchanging them. In a sorting network there are many comparison gates that are arranged in layers. Executing all comparison gates will sort the values. Each comparison gate performs the comparison between two parties' values and exchanges them if necessary. We are using an implementation of Yao's millionaire's protocol to protect the values during the comparison. Yao's millionaires' protocols make the result of the comparison public and in order to avoid leaking information in the sorting network we shuffle the input values with a random permutation unknown to all participants. Then the result of the comparison is a random variable and no one can track his own value through the sorting network. The only cryptographic tools our protocol uses are mix networks [9] and homomorphic encryption [21, 22].

The remainder of this paper is organized as follows: The next section reviews related work, section 3 presents one comparison step in the sorting network, section 4 shows how to start the protocol using mix networks and section 5 concludes the paper.

2   Related Work

There are few business-oriented applications of SMC related to our application of SMC to benchmarking in the literature. Specifically for benchmarking there is only one [7]. It presents a protocol to compute division with a secret divisor. It is extended to a number of useful protocols for benchmarking and forecasting and is an ideal candidate to be applied after our filter protocol. Another business application of SMC has been presented in [2]. Protocols for secure supply chain management are defined that protect a retailer such that its profit is not consumed by the supplier. Most protocols are simple, yet well motivated for this business application.

There are several protocols that solve algorithms privately that are related to our sorting problem. There is a protocol in [3] that finds the maximum of two additively split vectors. It uses homomorphic encryption and a protocol for Yao's millionaire's problem. In [1] the kth ranked element is computed. The solution for the two-party case is very clever, if k is close to the median. It uses a solution to Yao's millionaire's problem. Its multiparty solution guesses the element by searching over its domain. Frikken et al. present solutions to private binary sort [12]. In several of their protocols they use solutions to Yao's millionaire's protocol.

Our protocol is also not the first to use mix networks for SMC. There is a class of protocols for private distributed constraint solving that use mix networks [25, 26]. For general SMC circuit constructions Jakobsson and Juels present a solution using homomorphic encryption and mix networks [19]. In addition to the examples above there are many SMC protocols not listed here that use homomorphic encryption.

Mix networks were invented in [9]. Many different cryptographic protocols have been derived from it. The idea of [9] has been put to practice for anonymous communication in [28]. The research in this area is very active and there are many more excellent results also not listed here.

Homomorphic encryption is available for many homomorphisms. We need a homomorphism over the addition group and two encryption schemes that can achieve that in practice are [21, 22].

We have avoided general SMC constructions, even though there are clever results on special protocols such as Yao's millionaire's problem. In [8] a protocol using a third party and a clever number theoretic construction is presented. Homomorphic encryption solves the problem in [11]. Although [11] is the best two-party solution known, it is still linear in the number of bits. Another cryptographic tool we have avoided for performance reasons in our protocol is Oblivious Transfer [23] which can be used to solve any SMC problem.

SMC was introduced in [30]. [30] also presents a general solution and Yao's millionaire's problem in which two millionaires want to compare their wealth, but do not want to reveal the exact number. Clever general constructions for SMC have been found in [6, 14]. Goldreich extends their presentation into an excellent expose [13]. The general idea is to construct a binary circuit of the function and evaluate it obviously. This can be done in one round, but the constructed circuit can be quite large. There exists a practical implementation of this general solution for two-party problems [20]. Nevertheless it is argued that for practical problems, faster solution are sought [15].

3   A Comparison Gate in the Sorting Network

Our protocol emulates a sorting network where each participant is connected to one input wire. The sorting then proceeds by executing the "compare and exchange" gates for all pairs of input wires. The gates in one layer of the network can be executed in parallel. Most practically efficient sorting networks have a depth of $O(\log^2 n)$ and a communication complexity of $O(n \log^2 n)$ and, since our comparison gates operate in $O(1)$ rounds, this step of the protocol can be completed in $O(\log^2 n)$ rounds with a communication complexity of $O(n \cdot \log^2 n)$. The comparison gates are preceded by a secret, random permutation protocol that can be of independent interest. Our protocol uses a solution to Yao's millionaires' problem that outperforms the best-known solution which can also be used in other contexts. The complexity of $O(\log^2 n)$ rounds and communication complexity of $O(n \log^2 n)$ of the overall protocol is therefore as efficient as the non-secure version.

3.1   Preliminaries

Security Model. Our protocol works in the semi-honest or honest-but-curious model [13]. Each party follows the protocol as specified, but keeps a record of the messages and tries to gain as much information as possible from them.

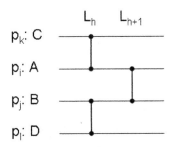

Fig. 1. A section of the sorting network

Definitions. Let $p_1, \ldots, p_n$ be the participants of the protocol and $\boldsymbol{x} = (x_1, \ldots, x_n)$ be their input values, i.e. p_i has input value x_i for $i = 1, \ldots, n$.

Figure 1 shows a section of a sorting network. We compare the input values of the participants $p_i : A$ (Alice) and $p_j : B$ (Bob). Without loss of generality we will assume that $i < j$. We also assume that $k \neq j$ and $i \neq l$, since duplicate gates in subsequent layers are superfluous and can safely be removed. Furthermore, we assume, also without loss of generality, that $k < i$ and $j < l$, as depicted in figure 1.

We use public-key, semantically secure, homomorphic encryption that is homomorphic in the addition group (modulo some m). We denote such encryption with the public key of Alice as $E_A(\cdot)$ and decryption as $D_A(\cdot)$. The homomorphic property then states that there is an operation $\times$, such that $E_A(x) \times E_A(y) = E_A(x + y)$, and an operation $\star$, such that $E_A(x) \star y = E_A(x \cdot y)$. We used Paillier's encryption scheme [22] for implementation where $\times$ is (modular) multiplication and $\star$ is (modular) exponentiation. We assume that the public key of each participant in the homomorphic encryption scheme is known to all participants.

The comparison gate protocol interlocks the variables from several gates and we use this notation to differentiate variables from previous gates to newly introduced ones. We use subscript $[CA]$ to denote variables from the comparison

Participants	Message / Operation
$C \longrightarrow B$	$a_B = a_{C[CA]}$
$D \longrightarrow A$	$b_A = b_{D[BD]}$
$A \longleftrightarrow B$	$\rho = \mathsf{Yao}(a_A - b_A, b_B - a_B)$
A	if $\neg\rho$ then $\mathsf{swap}(a_A, b_A)$
B	if $\neg\rho$ then $\mathsf{swap}(a_B, b_B)$

Fig. 2. The protocol for one comparison gate

gate between Charlie (C) and Alice (A), e.g. $r_{[CA]}$ is the variable r from that gate. We do not write the subscript $[AB]$ for variables introduced for the current comparison between Alice and Bob. Furthermore each participant has one input value, i.e. Alice has a, Bob has b, Charlie has c and so on. The comparison at each gate is between those input values, e.g. in the comparison gate between Charlie and Alice compares c and a.

3.2 Protocol

Let, Alice (A) and Bob (B) be the two participants of the comparison gate protocol. Then Alice has value a, and Bob has value b. The goal of the comparison gate is to compute $a < b$ and eventually exchange them.

The privacy requirement is that neither Alice nor Bob may learn their value, since they flow through the sorting network. Therefore each input value a, b is split between the two participants using addition, such that no party can infer a value by its local view of its share. This means, that Alice has the shares a_A and b_A and Bob has the shares a_B and b_B and that $a = a_A + a_B$ and $b = b_A + b_B$.

Alice and Bob can still compare the values.

$$a < b \Leftrightarrow a_A - b_A < b_B - a_B$$

The communication consequence of this splitting is that the predecessors need to transmit shares to the participants. Consider, the scenario in figure 1. Alice and Bob are engaging in the comparison gate protocol and have done so previously with Charlie (C) and Donna (D) (Alice with Charlie and Bob with Donna). From the previous comparison gate protocols Charlie and Donna, have shares of Alice's and Bob's values left. So, Charlie must send his share $a_{C[CA]}$ of Alice's input value to Bob and Donna her share $b_{D[BD]}$ of Bob's value to Alice. They become a_B and b_A, respectively. We will present in the next section how Alice and Bob can do the comparison using a Yao's millionaires' protocol. After the comparison Alice and Bob need to eventually exchange the values depending on the result. They can do so by exchanging their local share, i.e. no interaction is necessary. The entire protocol is summarized in figure 2.

3.3 Yao's Millionaires' Protocol

The basic idea of our approach is to hide the difference by a hiding factor. To efficiently hide a number of size $O(m)$ by multiplication the random hiding factor has to be of size at least $O(m^2)$. We want to preserve the greater-than relation, so we have to prevent "wrap-around" modulo n. Negative values are not represented in modular arithmetic, we therefore define the upper half of the range $[0, n - 1]$ to be negative numbers:

$$[\lceil \frac{n}{2} \rceil, n - 1] \equiv [-\lfloor \frac{n}{2} \rfloor, -1]$$

The multiplicative hiding has a draw-back, if the difference of a and b is 0, i.e. they are equal. Then the result of the hiding will be 0 regardless of the chosen hiding factor. This can be avoided by subtracting another (positive) random number that does not change the result, i.e. that is strictly smaller than the multiplicative hiding factor. The entire protocol is listed in figure 3.

---

1. Alice sends $E_A(a)$ to Bob.
2. Bob chooses random numbers r and r' with $0 \leq r' < r$.
3. Bob computes $E_A(c) = E_A(a)^r \cdot E_A(-r \cdot b + r') = E_A(r \cdot a - r \cdot b + r')$.
4. Bob sends $E_A(c)$ to Alice.
5. Alice decrypts $c = D_A(E_A(c))$ and decides $a < b$ if and only if $c \geq \frac{n}{2}$. The following derivation shows this equivalence:

$$c \bmod n \geq \frac{n}{2}$$

$$c < 0$$

$$r \cdot (a - b) + r' < 0$$

$$a - b \leq -1 < -\frac{r'}{r} < 0$$

6. Alice sends the bit $a < b$ to Bob.

Fig. 3. Yao's millionaires' protocol

If the numbers a and b to be compared are drawn from the domain $\mathcal{D}_a = [l_a, h_a]$, then the difference is in the domain $\mathcal{D}_- = [l_a - h_a, h_a - l_a]$. We can then choose the random numbers r from the domain $\mathcal{D}_r = [l_r, h_r] = [1, (h_a - l_a)^2]$ and the random numbers r' from the domain $\mathcal{D}_{r'} = [0, r]$. One can randomly choose one of many possible distributions for choosing the numbers to increase the Alice's difficulty of guessing b. To run the protocol correctly the modulus n of Paillier's encryption scheme needs to be larger than $2 \cdot ((h_a - l_a)^3 + (h_a - l_a)^2)$ to prevent "wrap-around".

There is a small leak in the protocol that occurs with very minor probability. If c is lower than l_r, the lower bound of domain $\mathcal{D}_r$ (, i.e. $c = 0$), Alice knows that $a = b$. If r and r' are chosen uniformly from $\mathcal{D}_r$ and $\mathcal{D}_{r'}$, respectively, then probability p of accidentally revealing $a = b$ (if a is indeed equal to b) is:

$$p = \sum_{i=1}^{h_r} \frac{1}{h_r} \cdot \frac{1}{i} \approx \frac{\ln h_r}{h_r}$$

For large numbers h_r this probability is negligible. E.g. when comparing 160-bit numbers, $p < 2^{-314}$.

Performance. We have implemented the best-known Yao's millionaires protocol by Fischlin [11] to compare the performance to ours. The implementation was done in Java [17] and evaluated on a computer with a 1.6 GHz Pentium Mobile processor and 1 GB of RAM running Windows XP using version 1.4.2 of Sun's Java SDK [27].

The implementation of Fischlin's scheme is based on his optimized version which already provided a significant speed-up compared to an earlier version using more re-randomization steps. The algorithm for computing the Jacobi symbol for decrypting is from [4]. No sanity checks were performed, e.g., on the messages allowing the decryption algorithm to be supplied with a message with Jacobi symbol $J(m|n) = -1$. Instead the performance of each implementation was optimized, as long as the security of the protocol was not violated. This reduced the decryption of the Goldwasser-Micali (GM) encryptions [16] to one Jacobi computation modulo an RSA prime factor per cipher-text.

We used a 512-bit RSA modulus for the GM encryption. For our scheme we used the following formula to compute the key length of Paillier's encryption scheme from the bit length $bits_m$ of the numbers to be compared: $bits_n = \max(512, (\lfloor \frac{bits_m}{32} \rfloor + 2) \cdot 32)$ which satisfies our requirement for the modulus above. The choice of a minimum key-length of 512-bit seems to be acceptable only for low security requirements, since RSA keys with more than 640 bits have been successfully factored [5], but we expect similar advantages for larger key sizes.

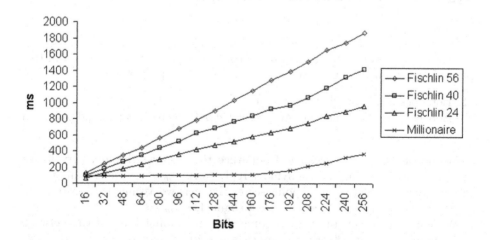

Fig. 4. Performance results

The term "low security requirement" refers to the time it takes to break the encryption and not the amount of information revealed in an information-theoretic sense.

We optimized the implementation of our scheme in two ways. First, we used the pre-computation of the dividend for decryption as suggestion in [22]. Second, we saved one more modular exponentiation by not randomizing the encryption of b. Instead, we just multiply with g^b and rely on the randomization done by the multiplication with r. This leaves the 5 modular exponentiations: two for encryption of a, one for multiplying with r, one for subtracting b and finally one for decrypting c. All modular exponentiations done modulo n^2.

Our performance results for the comparison of the two protocols are depicted in figure 4. We have run Fischlin's scheme with three different parameters for the error of probability: 2^{-24}, 2^{-40} and 2^{-56}. They are denoted as Fischlin 24, Fischlin 40 and Fischlin 56 in the figure. Our scheme is denoted as Millionaire.

4   Bootstrapping the Protocol

In the protocol above Alice and Bob learn the result of the comparison, i.e. they can track a value's partial flow through the sorting network. In the worst case Alice or Bob learns the rank of her or his value. Note, that if neither Alice nor Bob know where their input values come from, they cannot deduce anything about the input vector x. We can achieve this with an initial permutation of all input values that is known to no participating party. Such permutations have been used in other SMC protocols [25, 26], but we need our own method to prepare the values for the comparison gate protocol. Also our randomized construction achieves such a permutation in $O(\log n)$ expected steps compared to their $O(n)$ protocol and thereby keeps the $O(\log^2 n)$ complexity of the overall protocol. The overall communication complexity of this protocol is $O(n)$.

4.1   Setup

We use a mix network [9] as a sub-protocol. The construction presented in this paper fits our purposes very well. It has the following properties:

1. Bob does not know that a message came from Alice.
2. Bob has an anonymous reply channel $c_{[BA]}$ where he can send Alice an answer.

We denote sending a message from Alice to Bob over the mix network as $A \rightarrow_{mix} B$ and sending the anonymous reply as $A \leftarrow_{mix} B$. Additionally to the mix network and the point-to-point secret channels we assume the existence of a synchronous, authenticated broadcast channel $c_{broadcast}$.

Without loss of generality we assume that in the first layer of the network the comparisons are between the participants p_{2i-1} and p_{2i} for $i = 1, \ldots, \frac{n}{2}$. We denote the sets of odd and even numbered participants as P_{odd} and P_{even}, respectively.

4.2 Permutation Protocol

We will first show how to achieve a random permutation of the participants where part of the permutation is still known to the participants. Then we will modify the protocol slightly, such that it computes a derangement with the same properties. A derangement is a permutation with no fixed points, i.e. no participant remains at its position. Then we will use that protocol to achieve a permutation of the input variables, such that no participant knows anything about the permutation and no input variable is traceable, i.e. they are re-randomized.

First we will show how to compute a random permutation Π, such that each participant p_i only knows $\Pi(p_i)$, i.e. he knows his position in the permuted vector. The protocol $\mathcal{P}_{permutation}$ proceeds as follows:

1. Each participant p_i who has no incoming partner announces itself as p_i over the broadcast channel $c_{broadcast}$. Let s_{free} be the set of those participants. Initially this set contains all participants. If it is empty the protocol halts.

$$p_i \rightarrow c_{broadcast} : p_i \qquad \text{if } \nexists x \Pi(x) = i$$

2. Each participant p_{in} who has no outgoing partner chooses randomly a participant p_{out} from s_{free}. He sends to p_{out} a message m over the mix network.

$$p_{in} \rightarrow_{mix} p_{out} : m \qquad \text{if } \nexists \Pi(in)$$

3. Let s_i be the set of incoming message over the mix network at participant p_i. Each participant p_i then chooses randomly one participant p_j from s_i (if s_i is not empty). p_i sends over the anonymous reply channel to p_j the message *accept* and to all other members p_k of s_i the message *reject* (if there are any).

$$p_j \leftarrow_{mix} p_i : accept \qquad p_j \in s_i$$

$$p_k \leftarrow_{mix} p_i : reject \qquad \forall p_k \in s_i \wedge k \neq j$$

4. On the receipt of the message *accept* participant p_{in} adds $\Pi(in) = out$ to the permutation.

$$accept \Rightarrow \Pi(in) = out$$

5. The protocol continues at step 1.

This protocol can take $O(n)$ rounds in the worst case, if every participant chooses the same partner p_{out} every time. But, since this is a randomized algorithm, its expected running time is much more interesting.

Assume that each participant chooses its outgoing partner p_{out} in succession, i.e. first p_1, then p_2, and so on until p_n. If each participant chooses a different partner the protocol finishes in this round. Let E_i be the expected number of participants that have an ingoing partner when it has been participant p_i's turn. We can compute E_n as follows:

$$E_i = E_{i-1} + \frac{n - E_{i-1}}{n} = 1 + \frac{n-1}{n} E_{i-1} = \sum_{j=0}^{i-1} \left(\frac{n-1}{n}\right)^j$$

$$E_n = \lim_{i \to \infty} E_i \approx 0.6321 \cdot n$$

This means a constant fraction of the participants are expected to find their partners in each round. From the resulting recurrence $T(n) = 1 + T(n - E_n)$ we can conclude that the expected number of rounds is $O(\log n)$ and the overall communication complexity $O(n)$.

4.3   Derangement Protocol

The protocol $\mathcal{P}_{derangement}$ modifies $\mathcal{P}_{permutation}$ slightly, such that it computes a derangement. Recall, that a derangement is a permutation where no element remains at its place. The only modification is to step 2 of the protocol:

2. Each participant p_{in} who has no outgoing partner chooses randomly a participant p_{out} from s_{free} that is not himself. If he finds such a partner, he sends to p_{out} a message m over the mix network. If there is only him who has no ingoing partner, he announces $fail$ over the broadcast channel and the protocol will restart with an empty permutation Π.

$$p_{in} \to_{mix} p_{out} : m \qquad \text{if } \nexists \Pi(in) \wedge out \neq in$$

$$p_{in} \to c_{broadcast} : fail \qquad \text{if } s_{free} = \{in\}$$

Protocol $\mathcal{P}_{derangement}$ can theoretically never terminate, since it is not guaranteed that a derangement is found. The probability p that a random permutation is a derangement is $p = \frac{1}{e}$ [29]. We are not choosing a random permutation in $\mathcal{P}_{derangement}$, but are already tilting the odds towards a derangement by not picking oneself as a partner in step 2. Nevertheless we are upper bounded by the random permutation and the expected number of restarts is $O(1)$ and we can find a derangement in $O(\log n)$ expected rounds.

4.4   Final Protocol

We will now put the pieces together and construct a protocol $\mathcal{P}_{final}$ that can be run as the initiation protocol for the sorting network. First the participants choose a random derangement. The values are sent along that derangement twice. In the first step the source of the value is already hidden and the second step hides the target from the source. This results in a permutation (and not a derangement any longer) that is unknown to all participants, since it is based on a derangement and no party is source and target of a single message.

We need to take some steps in order to prepare for the comparison gate protocol. The input values (e.g. a and b) need to be split between Alice and Bob. Recall, that the initial comparisons are between p_{2i-1} and p_{2i} for $i = 1, \ldots, \frac{n}{2}$. We apply the random permutation only between those fixed pairs, i.e. each "odd" participant sends his value to his "even" partner. He does so in a split fashion and encrypts the shares with the public key from another random party in P_{odd}, such that no intermediate (even) party may learn the entire share.

Since in the resulting permutation a party may receive its own value, we must prevent it from learning that fact by viewing its local shares. This is done by re-randomizing the shares with two random variables r_a and r_b at the intermediate party, which makes the resulting shares independent again. This party also has to re-encrypt the value, since the choice of encryption key may reveal the value as well. He does so by forwarding the encrypted value to the key owner (an "odd" participant) who responds with the re-encrypted value. The key owner only learns the split values, neither source nor target, (as any participant in the comparison gate protocol could), and therefore cannot infer anything about an input value.

The entire protocol $\mathcal{P}_{final}$ is as follows:

1. Each "odd" participant p_{2i-1} chooses randomly a public-key from another participant p_j in P_{odd}. He sends:

$$p_{2i-1} \longrightarrow p_{2i} : j, r_{2i-1}, E_{p_j}(x_{2i-1} - r_{2i-1}) \qquad j \neq 2i - 1$$

2. Each "even" participant p_{2i} engages in the $\mathcal{P}_{derangement}$ protocol. They obtain the derangement Π of the even participants.

3. Each "even" participant p_{2i} sends over the mix network to his partner $p_{intermediate} = p_{\Pi(2i)}$:

$$p_{2i} \rightarrow_{mix} p_{intermediate} : j, r_{2i-1}, E_{p_j}(x_{2i-1} - r_{2i-1}), r_{2i}, E_{p_j}(x_{2i} - r_{2i})$$

$$intermediate = \Pi(2i)$$

4. Each intermediate participant $p_{intermediate}$ (which is every "even" participant) sends to p_j:

$$p_{intermediate} \longrightarrow p_j : E_{p_j}(x_{2i-1} - r_{2i-1}), E_{p_j}(x_{2i} - r_{2i})$$

5. Each contacted p_j chooses randomly a public-key from participant p_k in P_{odd} (including himself) for each message. He returns to $p_{intermediate}$:

$$p_j \longrightarrow p_{intermediate} : k, E_{p_k}(x_{2i-1} - r_{2i-1}), E_{p_k}(x_{2i} - r_{2i})$$

6. Each intermediate participant $p_{intermediate}$ chooses the random values r_a, r_b. He computes:

$$E_{p_k}(a_A) = E_{p_k}(x_{2i-1} - r_{2i-1}) \times r_a = E_{p_k}(x_{2i-1} - r_{2i-1} + r_a)$$

$$a_B = r_{2i-1} - r_a$$

$$E_{p_k}(b_A) = E_{p_k}(x_{2i} - r_{2i}) \times r_b = E_{p_k}(x_{2i} - r_{2i} + r_b)$$

$$b_B = r_{2i} - r_b$$

7. Each intermediate participant $p_{intermediate}$ sends over the mix network to his partner $p_{last} = p_{\Pi(P_{intermediate})}$:

$$p_{intermediate} \rightarrow_{mix} p_{last} : k, a_B, E_{p_k}(a_A), b_B, E_{p_k}(b_A)$$

$$last = \Pi(intermediate)$$

8. Each last participant p_{last} (which is again every "even" participant) sends to his partner in the sorting network p_{last-1}:

$$p_{last} \longrightarrow p_{last-1} : k, E_{p_k}(a_A), E_{p_k}(b_A)$$

9. Each participant p_{last-1} chooses random values r'_a and r'_b to blind his shares and sends the result to participant p_k (if necessary):

$$p_{last-1} \longrightarrow p_k : E_{p_k}(a_A) \times E_{p_k}(r'_a), E_{p_k}(b_A) \times E_{p_k}(r'_b)$$

10. Each contacted participant p_k replies with the decrypted content to each message and p_{last-1} de-blinds:

$$p_k \longrightarrow p_{last-1} : a_A + r'_a, b_A + r'_b$$

We have now achieved a random permutation between all (pairs of) participants and the sharing of input values is such that the processing of the sorting network can start. The content of each message is untraceable due to the intermediate node switching the keys, such that the encryption key does not give a hint, about the origin and re-randomizing the contents itself. Nodes contacted for decrypting the contents cannot make any deductions based on the contents, since they are blinded to the contents by random variables, and even if they interact with the contacting party in the next layer, they cannot infer possible values in x.

5   Conclusion

We have shown how to sort the input variables of n nodes using a protocol based on a sorting network. First, the values are permuted, such that no participant knows where its input value came from. Then each comparison gate is processed, such that no information is leaked due to the interlocking mechanism used by the protocol, although no protocol for Yao's millionaire's problem is being used.

After processing the sorting network, we can run any benchmarking algorithm and easily restrict to the k best values by excluding the shares of the $n-k$ highest or lowest ranked participants. Just the input variables of the nodes containing the k maximum (or minimum depending of the definition of "best") need not be included in the computation. No participants gains additional information about the input vector or the sorting.

We can compute the average of the k best input variables in the following way (see [24]): First, run the sort protocol defined above. Then, the first participant chooses a random variable r and sends $sum = r + a_A + b_A$ to the second participant. Each participant then adds his shares $sum = sum + a_B + b_B$, if they are still in the range of the k best values, and forwards it to the next participant. The last participant forwards the result sum to the first participant who broadcasts $sum - r$ to all participants. The average is $\frac{sum}{k}$. To compute the variance each participant subtracts the average from his input value and squares it. They run the protocol outlined above on the result to obtain the variance.

References

1. G. Aggarwal, N. Mishra, and B. Pinkas. Secure Computation of the kth-Ranked Element. *Proceedings of EUROCRYPT*, 2004.
2. M. Atallah, H. Elmongui, V. Deshpande, and L. Schwarz. Secure supply-chain protocols. *Proceedings of the 5th IEEE International Conference on Electronic Commerce*, 2003.
3. M. Atallah, F. Kerschbaum, and W. Du. Secure and Private Sequence Comparisons. *Proceedings of the 2nd annual Workshop on Privacy in the Electronic Society*, 2003.
4. E. Bach, and J. Shallit. Algorithmic Number Theory. *MIT Press*, 1996.
5. F. Bahr, M. Boehm, J. Franke, and T. Kleinjung. RSA200. Available at *http://www.crypto-world.com/announcements/rsa200.txt*, 2005.
6. M. Ben-Or, and A. Wigderson. Completeness theorems for non-cryptographic fault-tolerant distributed computation. *Proceedings of the 20th annual ACM symposium on Theory of computing*, 1988.
7. M. Bykova, M. Atallah, J. Li, K. Frikken, and M. Topkara. Private Collaborative Forecasting and Benchmarking. *Proceedings of the 3rd annual Workshop on Privacy in the Electronic Society*, 2004.
8. C. Cachin. Efficient private bidding and auctions with an oblivious third party. *Proceedings of the 6th ACM Conference on Computer and Communications Security*, 1999.
9. D. Chaum. Untraceable electronic mail, return addresses, and digital pseudonyms. *Communications of the ACM*, Vol. 24(2), 1981.
10. T. Cormen, C. Leiserson, R. Rivest, and C. Stein. Introduction to Algorithms, 2nd Edition. *MIT Press*, 2001.
11. Marc Fischlin. A Cost-Effective Pay-Per-Multiplication Comparison Method for Millionaires. *RSA Security Cryptographer's Track*, 2001.
12. K. Frikken, and M. Atallah. Privacy Preserving Electronic Surveillance. *Proceedings of the 2nd annual Workshop on Privacy in the Electronic Society*, 2003.
13. O. Goldreich. Secure Multi-party Computation. Available at *http://www.wisdom.weizmann.ac.il/~oded/pp.html*, 2002.
14. O. Goldreich, S. Micali, and A. Wigderson. How to play any mental game. *Proceedings of the 19th annual ACM conference on Theory of computing*, 1987.
15. S. Goldwasser. Multi party computations: past and present. *Proceedings of the 16th annual ACM symposium on Principles of distributed computing*, 1997.
16. S. Goldwasser, and S. Micali. Probabilistic Encryption. *Journal of Computer and Systems Science 28(2)*, 1984.
17. J. Gosling, B. Joy, G. Steele, and Gilad Bracha. Java Language Specification, 2nd Edition. *Addison-Wesley*, 2000.
18. J. Groth. A Verifiable Secret Shuffle of Homomorphic Encryptions. *Proceedings of Practice and Theory in Public Key Cryptography*, 2003
19. M. Jakobsson, and A. Juels. Mix and Match: Secure Function Evaluation via Ciphertexts. *Proceedings of ASIACRYPT*, 2000.
20. D. Malkhi, N. Nisan, B. Pinkas, and Y. Sella. Fairplay - A Secure Two-party Computation System *Proceedings of the 13th USENIX Security Symposium*, 2004.
21. D. Naccache, and J. Stern. A New Public-Key Cryptosystem Based on Higher Residues . *Proceedings of the 5th ACM Conference on Computer and Communications Security*, 1998.
22. P. Paillier. Public-Key Cryptosystems Based on Composite Degree Residuosity Classes. *Proceedings of EUROCRYPT*, 1999.

23. O. Rabin. How to exchange secrets by oblivious transfer. *Technical Memo TR–81, Aiken Computation Laboratory*, 1981.

24. B. Schneier. Applied Cryptography, 2nd Edition. *John Wiley & Sons*, 1996.

25. M. Silaghi. Solving a distributed CSP with cryptographic multi-party computations, without revealing constraints and without involving trusted servers. *Proceedings of the 4th International Workshop on Distributed Constraint Reasoning*, 2003.

26. M. Silaghi. Meeting scheduling system guaranteeing n/2-privacy and resistant to statistical analysis (applicable to any DisCSP). *Proceedings of the IEEE/WIC/ACM International Conference on Web Intelligence*, 2004.

27. Sun Microsystems. J2SE 1.4.2 SDK. Available at *http://java.sun.com/j2se/1.4.2/*, 2005.

28. R. Dingledine, N. Mathewson, P. Syverson. Tor: The Second Generation Onion Router. *Proceedings of USENIX Security Symposium*, 2004.

29. N. Sloane. The On-Line Encyclopedia of Integer Sequences. Available at *http://www.research.att.com/˜njas/sequences/*, 2005.

30. A. Yao. Protocols for Secure Computations. *Proceedings of the annual IEEE Symposium on Foundations of Computer Science* 23, 1982.

On the Use of Word Networks to Mimicry Attack Detection*

Fernando Godínez[1], Dieter Hutter[2], and Raúl Monroy[1]

[1] Department of Computer Science, ITESM–Estado de México
Carr. Lago de Guadalupe, Km. 3.5, Estado de México, 52926, Mexico
{fgodinez, raulm}@itesm.mx
[2] DFKI, Saarbrücken University
Stuhlsatzenhausweg 3, D-66123 Saarbrücken, Germany
hutter@dfki.de

Abstract. Intrusion detection aims at raising an alarm any time the security of an IT system gets compromised. Though highly successful, Intrusion Detection Systems are all susceptible of mimicry attacks [1]. A *mimicry attack* is a variation of an attack that attempts to pass by as normal behaviour. In this paper, we introduce a method which is capable of successfuly detecting a significant and interesting sub-class of mimicry attacks. Our method makes use of a word network [2, 3]. A *word network* conveniently decomposes a pattern matching problem into a chain of smaller, noise-tolerant pattern matchers, thereby making it more tractable. A word network is realised as a finite state machine, where every state is a hidden Markov model. Our mechanism has shown a 93% of effectivity, with a false positive rate of 3%.

1 Introduction

Intrusion detection is concerned with the timely discovery of any activity that jeopardises the integrity, availability or the confidentiality of an IT system. It often amounts to detecting a known pattern of computer misuse, a deviation to ordinary, expected system behaviour, or a combination thereof. Regardless of which of these approaches is adopted, current Intrusion Detection Systems (IDSs) are easy to bypass with a mimicry attack.

A *mimicry attack* is a variant of an attack which aims to masquerade as normal behaviour [1]. A mimicry attack is built out of the original one using any conceivable transformation, provided that harmfulness is not lost. For example, at a host level, where an attack takes the form of a sequence of system calls, a mimicry attack is built using at least 3 transformations: i) replace a subsequence of system calls for other one, functionally equivalent; ii) swap two or more (subsequences of) independent system calls; and iii) randomly insert system calls that do not change the harmful intent of the attack.

---

* This research was partially supported by three grants: FRIDA, CONACYT 47557 and ITESM CCEM-0302-05.

G. Müller (Ed.): ETRICS 2006, LNCS 3995, pp. 423–435, 2006.

In this paper, we introduce a host-based Misuse IDS (MIDS), capable of successfully detecting a great variety of mimicry attacks. The method makes use of a word network [2, 3]. A *word network* is a technique that aims to conveniently decompose a pattern matching problem into a chain of smaller, noise-tolerant pattern matchers, thereby making it more tractable. A word network is realised as a finite state machine, where every state is a hidden Markov model. A *Hidden Markov Model* (HMM) is a doubly stochastic process, characterised by internal events that drive the model external behaviour in a random manner [4].

To approach mimicry attack detection, we divided each of the attacks under consideration into n segments, each of which is the same size. We then built n HMM's, tailored to recognise the appearance of one of these segments, as well as of some of its variants. We built an HMM to recognise the appearance of spurious system calls that do not affect the harmfulness of the attack. We then linked all these HMM's properly, forming a word network capable of recognising mimicry attacks, while filtering spurious system calls. For all our experiments we used the "Hidden Markov Model Toolkit (HTK)". This software allows for large HMMs to be used and it also has the ability to use word networks.

1.1   Paper Overview

In what follows, we discuss the rationale behind using a word network for discriminating an ordinary sequence of system calls from an intrusion one (§2). Then we describe the attacks targeted throughout our investigations (§3) and show how to obtain their mimicries (§4). Then we describe our methodology both for building (§5) and for testing (§6,§7) a word-network-based MIDS capable of detecting and attack and a number of their mimicries. Finally, we compare our results against rival techniques (§8) and discuss the conclusions drawn from our experiments (§9).

2   Sequence Analysis

2.1   Hidden Markov Models

A Hidden Markov Model (HMM) captures hidden, internal events that generate an observable, external behaviour in a probabilistic manner. An HMM is a probabilistic generative model [4, 5]. It outputs a string moving through a discrete state space using Markov decisions indexed by time. At any time, the current state generates a symbol according to a probabilistic rule. An HMM takes two parameters: i) the transition probabilities and ii) the emission probabilities. At each state, the transition probabilities determine which state the HMM should move to, while the emission probabilities which symbol should be output.

An HMM has one or more starting and final states. Possible transitions are successively carried out from a starting state to a final one. Given an input sequence, the HMM computes all the HMM transition paths that could have yielded it, associating with each of them a path probability. This path probability is calculated multiplying the path transition probabilities and the emmision probabilities. The transition and emmision probabilities are calculated using the Baum-Welch Algorithm. The sum of all the path likelihoods is regarded as the overall likelihood that the sequence was generated by the HMM and is called the *evaluation of the sequence*. To perform such evaluation Viterbi algorithm is used. A detailed description of HMMs is out of the scope of this paper but the reader is refered to [6, 4, 5] for a complete description of the algorithms involved in training and decoding HMMs.

HMMs have been widely used in anomaly detection, e.g. [7, 8, 9, 10]. Roughly, an HMM is built for modelling sequences of system calls output by an ordinary system user. Then the HMM is made evaluate unseen system call sequences. Using the output probability, one may determine whether the sequence should be considered normal (if likely) or an anomaly (otherwise).

2.2   Word Networks

A word network is a pattern matching technique specially designed to recognise speech. It is realised by means of a directed graph. Each node is an HMM, aimed at detecting a word or a phoneme; node transitions capture word dependency [2, 3]. Using word networks, the analysis of a grammatical structure is made independent of the word detection process. Each HMM is built towards the detection of a single object regardless of the object position within the input sequence of symbols. Word networks are highly robust: noise or long silences may occur in between the phonemes an the word can still be recognised. Probabilities are usually attached to the arcs making the pattern recogniser more flexible.

A word network may have one or more *silent states*. A silent state, as the name suggests, yields no productions; it is virtual in that it is given a label but does not come with an HMM. A word network gracefully degrades into an HMM. Then, the word network consists of only three states, two of them being silent: the entry and the exit states. More complex word networks will have many arcs departing from any given node and thus different paths can be tested.

To calculate the probability of a sequence over a word network, a weight is assigned to each possible transition. The weight would be positive if it is to denote a partial pattern matching success, and negative otherwise.

To approach mimicry attack detection, we have divided each attack under consideration into n segments of fixed size. For every attack segment, we have built an HMM, tailored to recognise the appearance of it, as well as of some of its variants. We have also built an HMM to recognise the appearance of spurious system calls that do not affect the harmfulness of the attack. Properly linking all the HMM's associated with an attack, we have formed a word network capable of recognising a number of variants of an attacks, filtering out redundant system calls.

We have split each attack under consideration in segments of size 6. Tan and Maxion have found that 6 is the size of the smallest unique subsequence for the log files used by Forrest [8]. Thus, for any intrusion detection method to be effective, it must consider sequences of size 6 or larger; in symbols: $\Sigma^2 \subset \Sigma^3 \subset \Sigma^4 \subset \Sigma^5 \subset \Sigma^6$ and $6-gram \not\subset 7-gram$. While Forrest's log files and DARPA's are different, it is reasonable not to use an sliding window of size lesser than 6.

3   The Attack Database

In our experiments, we have used the attacks described in Kendall's thesis [11], shown in table 1.[1] As working examples, we will use two known attacks to the Solaris operating system, *Eject* and *FFB*, reported in the DARPA repository [12].

Table 1. Selected Attacks From the 1998 DARPA Repository

Attack Name	Attack Type	Variation	Service
Eject 1	Buffer Overflow(U2R)	*	telnet
Eject 2	Buffer Overflow(U2R)	No Sniffing, Stealthy	telnet
FFB 1	Buffer Overflow(U2R)	*	telnet
FFB 2	Buffer Overflow(U2R)	No Sniffing, Stealthy	telnet
Loadmodule	Shell as Root(U2R)	*	telnet
Format 1	Buffer Overflow(U2R)	*	telnet
Format 2	Buffer Overflow(U2R)	chmod exploit files	telnet
Ftp-Write	R2U	*	ftp
warezclient	Unauthorised Software	*	ftp
Satan	Probe	*	All Services
ipsweep	Probe	*	*

3.1   The Eject Attack

The Eject attack exploits a buffer overflow in the `eject` utility, distributed within Sun Solaris 2.5. Removable media devices that do not have an eject button or that are managed by the Volume Management use the `eject` utility. Due to an insufficient bound checking of the arguments in the volume management library, `libvolmgt.so.1`, it is possible to overwrite the internal stack space of `eject`. If exploited, this vulnerability can be used to gain root access.

The Eject attack consists of 4 steps: i) inject the exploit script to the victim's host computer; ii) compile the exploit script; iii) execute the compiled exploit script; and iv) use the root console. If the exploit script is already in the victim's host and if it has been compiled, then the first two steps become unnecessary. We will refer to the long version and to the short version of Eject as *Eject 1* and as *Eject 2* respectively.

3.2   The FFB Attack

The FFB attack exploits a buffer overflow in the `ffbconfig` utility, also distributed within Sun Solaris 2.5. `ffbconfig` configures the Creator Fast Frame Buffer (FFB) Graphics Accelerator, which is part of the FFB Configuration Software Package, SUNWffbcf. This software is used when the FFB Graphics accelerator

---

[1] U2R and R2U respectively stand for user to root and remote to user. In a U2R attack, the attacker gains the privileges of `root`, whereas in an R2U one, he gains the privileges of a valid user.

card is installed. Due to an insufficient bound checking on the arguments, it is possible to overwrite the internal stack space of ffbconfig.

The attack follows an execution path similar to Eject. We also consider two versions of FFB. One, called *Ffb 1*, injects, compiles and then executes the exploit script; and the other, called *Ffb 2*, only executes the compiled exploit script.

4   On the Generation of Mimicry Attacks

We have generated a collection of mimicry attacks using the following 3 transformation methodology [1]:

S: System Call Substitution: Replace a sequence of system calls with other one, functionally equivalent. Often, newer versions of an operating system come with system calls that replace, or at least provide the same functionality of, one or more system calls from a previous version. Example system calls that can be replaced one another for the Sun Solaris operating system are the following:

1. read applied to a file, provided that the file is open, and mmap, followed by a memory access; and
2. sysinfo, with appropiate parameters, and getdomainname (sysinfo can also accomodate both gethostid and gethostname).

I: System Call Interchange: Replace a sequence of system calls with any valid permutation of it. Two system calls are interchangeable, if neither their effect nor their execution depend one another.

N: No-op Insertion: Insert a system call within the input sequence, provided that the inserted system call does not change the harmfulness of the attack. This kind of a redundant system call is sometimes called a *no-op*.

To uderstand how a mimicry attack is generated and how our methodology is applied we need to define how an attack is composed. When we refer to an *attack* it is the sequence of events that tka a system from a secure to an insecure state. Since we are working at host level the building blocks of an aattack or any program are system calls. Every attack is composed of a number of system calls which can be grouped in segments. Each segment is a small sequence of system calls, in our case each segment is composed of 6 systems calls which is the size of the window used to train our HMMs and to detect the attack. This window also defines the insertion points for *no-ops*.

4.1   Generating Base Mimicry Attack

Given the difficulty of detecting mimicry attacks, we first identified a subproblem, we call *base*, that is still of interest but that is more manageable. The base problem consists of detecting all the variants that can be generated from an attack using only transformations **S** and **I**. More formally, let Σ denote the set of system calls and $\Sigma^{\star}$ the set of sequences over Σ. Then, given an attack, $A \in \Sigma^{\star}$, we aim to build an IDS capable of detecting a member of $\mathcal{V}_{\mathbf{SI}}(A) \stackrel{\text{def}}{=} \{A'|A' = \mathbf{S}(A) \vee A' = \mathbf{I}(A)\}$.

Table 2. Some system calls and their equivalents

Original System-Call	Equivalent System-Call Sequence
memcntl	mctl
read	pread, readv, mmap
write	pwrite, writev
open_read	read
open_write	write
execv	execve, execvp, execl, execle, execlp
exit	_exit
acl	facl
chdir	fchdir
chmod	fchmod
chown	fchown, lchown
stat	fstat
brk	sbrk

While finite, $\mathcal{V}_{\mathbf{SI}}(A)$ is huge! Take, for example, a short attack like FFB, which is 192 system call long, and uniformly divide it into segments of size 8. We have found that on average each segment accepts 3 transformations, yielding 3^{24} attack variations! To generate base mimicry attacks, we identified system calls that can be emulated by means of a sequence of other system calls. Some of these system calls, and their associated equivalent sequence, are shown in table 2.

The number of variations that can be generated for the Eject and FFB attacks, using the $\mathbf{S}$ and $\mathbf{I}$ transformations, together with the system call equivalences given in table 2, is shown in table 3. This figure is obtained as follows: the number of segments subject to modification is equal to the number of attack segments that include a replaceable system call. The maximum number of attacks is then the number of possible values for a system call multiplied by the number of replaceable system calls. The numbers in the last column are calculated assuming an average of 3 possible values for each replaceable system call.

Clearly, if we were to detect mimicry attacks using a simple matching mechanism, the time to search the entire database would be prohibitively large, let alone storage space.

Table 3. Number of variants obtained from each attack

Attack	# of segments	# of segments subject to modification	# of replaceable system calls	# of attacks that can be generated
Eject 1	106	72	175	3^{175}
Eject 2	38	22	26	3^{26}
FFB 1	32	17	24	3^{24}
FFB 2	44	15	43	3^{43}

4.2   Generating Full Mimicry Attacks

The full problem of detecting mimicry attacks is much more complicated, since what counts as a no-op depends on the attack. As Wagner and Soto have pointed out, almost any system call can be turned into a no-op. For instance, passing it an spurious value, any parameterised system call may become a no-op. In the Sun Solaris system, for example, many system calls take parameters that we can exploit, including pointers, memory addresses, file descriptors, uid's, pid's and gid's. System calls that cannot be turned into a no-op include exit, pause, vhangup, fork, alarm, and setsid, as they abandon the current session.

Yet, not every unsuccessfully executed system call counts as a no-op. Consider the portion of the eject attack shown in figure 1. The first occurrence of stat is part of the attack signature and specifically provides an address jump to the buffer overflow. The second occurrence of stat is however a no-op: it does not affect the effect of the attack. Note that, in particular, the value returned in both cases is failure. Thus, simply filtering out unsuccessfully executed system calls will not work as it modifies the attack signature. To get around this problem, we may consider other system call audit information but at the expense of computer resources.

```
n.    open(2)_-_read|/etc/openwin|failure:_No_such_file_or_directory
n+1. stat(2)|/export/home/alie/ÁÁÁÁÁ-n|failure:_No_such_file_or_directory
n+2. execve(2)|ksh|success
n+3. stat(2)|/tmp/115553|failure:_No_such_file_or_directory
```

Fig. 1. Part of the FFB attack

Conversely, not every successfully executed system call is not a no-op. For example, chdir with argument "." will always be successful but will not affect the effect of an attack.

We have identified a moderate collection of 210 no-op. With them, we have generated an attack data base. One third of it was used for building the word networks modelling each attack. The remaining, larger portion was used only for validation purposes. The modelling methodology is described in the following section.

5   Modelling Attacks Using Word Networks

Having built the attack database, we use a third part of it to build all the HMM's involved in the detection of each attack. Each group of HMM's was then linked properly forming the associated word network. Built this way, these word networks cannot deal with no-ops. Yet, they are an effective means for detecting base mimicry attacks.

To approach the general problem, we have built an automaton aimed at detecting the appearance of one or more occurrences of no-ops. Linking this automaton to an attack word network enables the network to recognise a mimicry attack, even if it comes along with an arbitrary number of no-ops inserted at the end of every attack segment (but not in between). The automaton ignores all the sequences of no-ops that are also part of the attack. This is to avoid confusion when parsing in parallel an attack segment node and a no-op node.

Figure 2 portrays the architecture of the word network for the eject attack. Nodes labelled S1,..., SN represent the HMM's aimed at detecting the corresponding attack segments. Nodes labelled No-Op(1),..., No-Op(M) are part of the automaton, built to filter out no-ops. All the no-ops can be combined in a single HMM for optimization.

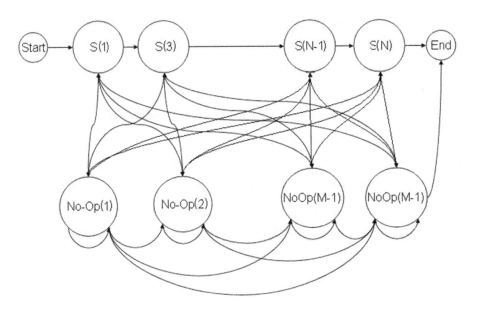

Fig. 2. Word network for a general case mimicry attack

Table 4 contains a piece of the grammar that generates the word network for Eject. There, we use strings starting with $ to denote variables, brackets, { }, to denote the reflexive-transitive closure of sequence construction, and use square brackets, [ ], to denote the optional appearance of the enclosed symbol.

We use the same word network to evaluate Eject 1 and Eject 2, only that the entry point is different. Upon evaluation, results yielded by any HMM node will contribute positively to the total outcome of the word network. Conversely,

Table 4. A grammar corresponding to the eject attack word network

$no-op $\qquad= no\text{-}op_1 \vert no\text{-}op_2 \vert \ldots \vert no\text{-}op_m;$
$code_insertion $= eject\text{-}s_1 \{\$no\text{-}op\}\ eject\text{-}s_2 \{\$no\text{-}op\} \ldots eject\text{-}s_i;$
$code_execution $= eject\text{-}s_j \{\$no\text{-}op\}\ eject\text{-}s_{j+1} \{\$no\text{-}op\} \ldots eject\text{-}s_n;$
([$code_insertion] \{$no-op\} $code_execution)

results yielded by the no-op automaton will contribute negatively, represented as a small penalisation.

The same HMMs can be used for other attacks, they serve as building blocks since the variations for the same segment, will be the same, regardless the attack it belongs to. Word networks can also be used to organise all our misuse database in the same place and only calculate the most likely path of an attack.

Since training data is sparse, training time is reasonably short. For a word network with 110 HMMs with up to 3^6 training sequences of 6 system calls for each HMM, and each HMM with 115 states, training time was about 120 minutes. We also trained each HMM with 250 states and the training time was about 300 minutes. All the tests were made on a PIV HT @ 2.6 GHz with 1 GB of dual channel RAM @ 400MHz running Linux Mandrake 9.0.

6   Base Validation Experiments

This section summarises the results output by two tests run on our IDS. One test, the false positive test, involves non-attack sessions, gathered from the DARPA repository and the other, the false negative test, involves the mimicry attacks that we generated using Wagner and Soto's methodology. For the false positive test, we randomly picked 2000 non-attack sessions coming from 4 different services: telnet (800), smtp (1000), ftp (50) and finger (150). For the false negative test, we picked 2500 unseen variants of each attack. With this size, the sample is representative with a 97.5% confidence.

On average, the IDS true positive rate is 98% while the false positive one is about 10%. These results were obtained using a 90% similarity threshold. Setting this threshold up to 95% causes a reduction in the false positive rate, from 10% to 3% on the average. Yet, the true positive rate is also reduced, from 98% to 93%. Table 5 summarises the results we obtained for each attack.

Table 5. Detection and false positive rates with different similarity thresholds. S and FP respectively stand for similarity and false positive rate.

Attack Name	Detection % $S=90\%$	FP % $S=90\%$	Detection % $S=95\%$	FP % $S=95\%$
Eject 1	97%	9%	92%	2%
Eject 2	96%	8%	90%	3%
FFB 1	98%	10%	93%	4%
FFB 2	99%	8%	95%	1%
Loadmodule	97%	7%	91%	1%
Format 1	98%	9%	92%	4%
Format 2	96%	7%	89%	3%
Ftp-Write	99%	11%	96%	5%
warezclient	99%	12%	95%	5%
Satan	98%	9%	90%	2%
ipsweep	97%	10%	91%	3%

It is worth mentioning that false positive detections arose out of sessions belonging to the same service. If an HMM is trained to detect a `telnet` attack then only `telnet` sessions yield a false positive. The high false positive rate is because an attack is usually present in a small fragment of a session; therefore the rest of the session used to train the HMM might contain normal segments. This will cause the HMM to detect a normal session as an attack.

7   General Validation Experiments

For the general problem, we also run two tests on our IDS; one is the false positive test and the other the false negative one. The false positive test set was built the same way as for the base case. The false negative test set, however, was built slightly different.

Since the number of distinct attack variants that can be possibly built inserting no-ops is infinite, we limit ourselves to a subclass that considers the insertion of 10 different randomly generated sequences of no-ops between each attack segment. This subclass is still important because it includes some context-dependant no-ops, and no-ops derived from system calls returning failure. In both cases a normalisation is not possible. With a data base of 2,500 variations for each attack, we may produce 25,000 different attacks for the general case of mimicry attacks. With this sample size, the sample is representative with a 99.2% of confidence.

In our experiments, our IDS showed capable of detecting a significant subclass of the mimicry attacks with 92% of accuracy. The false positive detection rate is high: about 4% of the sequences were wrongfully labelled as an attack. The increment on the false positive rate over modified attacks without inserted no-ops was to be expected. The noise that the no-ops insert to the model gets in the way of a correct discrimination. Table 6 summarise our results.

Table 6. Detection and false positive rate for general case mimicry attacks

Attack Name	Detection Rate	False Positive Rate
Eject 1	93%	4%
Eject 2	91%	2%
FFB 1	93%	2.8%
FFB 2	94%	3.2%
Loadmodule	91%	3%
Format 1	92%	2.5%
Format 2	89%	2%
Ftp-Write	93%	4%
warezclient	92%	3%
Satan	90%	4%
ipsweep	91%	5%

For all our experiments we used the "Hidden Markov Model Toolkit (HTK)". This software allows for large HMMs to be used and it also has the ability to use word networks. HTK can be found at `http://htk.eng.cam.ac.uk/`, whereas the HTK file format and word network definitions we used in our HMMs are described in [2].

8   Related Work

Warrender, Forrest and Pearlmutter have built an AIDS using an HMM [7]. Their method uses a sliding window of size 6, with which they take an observation of current user behaviour and then compare it against the profile of that user's ordinary behaviour. If the input observation and the profile do not match, an alarm is triggered. Warrender et al report a true positive rate of 96.6%. Other researchers, e.g. [9, 10, 8], have also explored the use of HMMs to intrusion detection, improving only slightly Warrender et al's results.

Tan and Maxion have shown that the size of the window, meaning the depth of the grammar, that Warrender et al is actually the minimal for an anomaly to be detected [8]. However, Wagner and Soto have disagreed with this result, demonstrating that a sliding window of size 6 is insufficient to detect a lot of mimicry attacks [1].

Giffin, Jha and Miller approach mimicry attack detection using a static analysis of the application(s) to be protected [13]. The model is extremely precise, it yields a high true positive and a low false positive one, but at the expense of modifying every application and having a monitor to watch over the appearance of a (sequence of) system call(s) which is not accounted for the model.

Slightly related to detecting mimicry attacks, detecting masqueraders has captured increasing interest within the community. On their seminal work, Schonlau et al [14] analyse the performance of various masquerader detection methods. They analyse six distinct detection methods: *Uniqueness, Bayes 1-Step Markov, Hybrid Multi-Step Markov, Compression, IPAM* and *Sequence-Match*. These methods are all anomaly detection methods and use sets of user commands to build profiles of normal user behaviour. Uniqueness is the most informed method, as not only does it use the profile of a given user but it also uses the profile of the others.

An alternative method, proposed by [15], uses naïve Bayes to estimate the probability that a command c can be issued by user u. This method builds a profile for a user, so-called self, from a set of training data. The self of other users is then taken as the user's non-self. This method shows a detection rate of 61.5% and a false positive rate of 1.5%.

An alternative way of approaching mimicry detection is proposed by [16]. The method is based on a widely used technique for the comparison of genetic material, e.g. DNA or RNA. The method aims at detecting how well two sequences align one another and thus how similar they are. However, if enough no-ops are inserted within an attack, this alignment test is more likely to return true. The technique assigns a small penalty for gaps occurring between normal user commands. The gaps are non-matching objects in the sequence. This allows to deal with no-ops, but the larger number of no-ops, the lower the alignment score. The authors reported a detection ratio of 75.8%, and false positive rate is 7.7%.

A recursive data mining approach is proposed by [17]. It recursively extracts repetitive sequences, and replaces them by a new symbol until no repetitive patterns are left. After the substitution, different features are extracted, such as the number of distinct patterns, the number of repetitive patterns, the frequency of repetition of each distinct pattern, the reduction factor, etc. Then, a support vector machine is trained using user patterns as negative examples and other patterns as positive ones. The authors report a detection rate of 68% and a false positive rate of 9%.

These approaches all have the same limitation: they are all susceptible to overlook mimicry attacks. By contrast, our approach is able to detect a wider class of mimicry attacks thanks to the use of word networks, which provide a way to sequence matching decomposition.

9   Conclusions

In this paper, we introduced a method which is capable of successfuly detecting a significant and interesting sub-class of mimicry attacks. Our method makes use of a word network [2, 3]. A *word network* conveniently decomposes a pattern matching problem into a chain of smaller pattern matchers, thereby making it more tractable. A word network is realised as a finite state machine, where every state is a hidden Markov model. The use of word networks to mimicry attack detection is promising and more research should be conducted.

References

1. Wagner, D., Soto, P.: Mimicry Attacks on Host Based Intrusion Detection Systems. In: Proceedings of the Ninth ACM Conference on Computer and Communications Security, Washington, DC, USA, ACM (2002) 255–265
2. Young, S., Evermann, G., Kershaw, D., Moore, G., Odell, J., Ollason, D., Povey, D., Valtchev, V., Woodland, P.: The HTK Book for HTK Version 3.2. Cambridge University Engineering Department (2002)
3. Pereira, F., Riley, M.: Speech Recognition by Composition of Weighted Finite Automata. In Roche, E., Schabes, Y., eds.: Finite-State Language Processing. MIT press, Cambridge, MA (1997) 431–453
4. Brown, M.: RNA Modeling Using Stochastic Context-Free Grammars. PhD thesis, University of California, Santa Cruz (1999)
5. Manning, C.D., Schütze, H.: Foundations of Statistical Natural Language Processing. MIT Press, Massachusets Institute of Technology, Cambridge, Massachusets 02142 (1999)
6. Rabiner, L.R.: A Tutorial on Hidden Markov Models and Selected Applications in Speech Recognition. Proceedings of the IEEE **77** (1989) 257–286
7. Warrender, C., Forrest, S., Pearlmutter, B.: Detecting Intrusions Using System Calls: Alternative Data Models. In: Proceedings of the 1999 IEEE Symposium on Security and Privacy, IEEE Computer Society Press (1999) 133–145

8. Tan, K.M.C., Maxion, R.A.: Why 6?" Defining the Operational Limits of STIDE, an Anomaly-Based Intrusion Detector. In: Proceedings of IEEE Symposium on Security & Privacy. (2002) 188–201
9. Qiao, Y., Xin, X., Bin, Y., Ge, S.: Anomaly Intrusion Detection Method Based on HMM. Electronic Letters **38** (2002) 663–664
10. Yeung, D., Ding, Y.: Host-Based Intrusion Detection Using Dynamic and Static Behavioral Models. Pattern Recognition **Vol. 36** (2003) pp. 229–243
11. Kendall, K.: A Database of Computer Attacks for the Evaluation of Intrusion Detection Systems. Master's thesis, Massachusetts Institute of Technology (1998)
12. Lippman, R.P., Cunningham, R.K., Fried, D.J., Graf, I., Kendall, K.R., Webster, S.E., Zissman, M.A.: Results of the DARPA 1998 Offline Intrusion Detection Evaluation. Slides Presented at RAID 1999 Conference (1999)
13. Giffin, J., Jha, S., Miller, B.: Efficient Context-Sensitive Intrusion Detection. In: Proceedings of the 11th Annual Network and Distributed Systems Security Symposium (NDSS), San Diego, California, The Internet Society (2004)
14. Schonlau, M., DuMouchel, W., Ju, W., Karr, A., Theus, M., Vardi, Y.: Computer Intrusion: Detecting Masquerades. Statistical Science **16** (2001) 1–17 To appear.
15. Maxion, R., Townsend, T.: Masquerade Detection Using Truncated Command Lines. In: Proceedings of the International Conference on Dependable Systems & Networks, Washington, DC, IEEE (2002) 219–228
16. Scott, C., Joel, B., Boleslaw, S., Eric, B.: Intrusion Detection: A Bioinformatics Approach. In: Proceeding of the 19th Annual Computer Security Applications Conference, Las Vegas, Nevada (2003) 24–33
17. Boleslaw, S., Yongqiang, Z.: Recursive Data Mining for Masquerade Detection and Author Identification. In: Proceedings of the 5th IEEE System, Man and Cybernetics Information Assurance Workshop, West Point, NY, IEEE (2004) 424–431

Simplifying Signature Engineering by Reuse

Sebastian Schmerl[1], Hartmut Koenig[1], Ulrich Flegel[2], and Michael Meier[2]

[1] Brandenburg University of Technology Cottbus
03013 Cottbus, Germany
sbs@informatik.tu-cottbus.de
koenig@informatik.tu-cottbus.de
[2] University of Dortmund
44221 Dortmund, Germany
ulrich.flegel@udo.edu
michael.meier@udo.edu

Abstract. Most intrusion detection systems deployed today apply misuse detection as detection procedure. Misuse detection compares the recorded audit data with predefined patterns, i.e. signatures. A signature is usually empirically developed based on experience and expert knowledge. Methods for a systematic development are scarcely reported yet. Automated approaches to reusing design and modeling decisions of available signatures also do not exist. This induces relatively long development times for signatures causing inappropriate vulnerability windows. In this paper we present an approach for systematic signature derivation. It is based on the reuse of existing signatures to exploit similarities with existing attacks for deriving a new signature. The approach is based on an iterative abstraction of signatures. Based on a weighted abstraction tree it selects those signatures or signature fragments, which are similar to the novel attack. Finally, we present a practical application of the approach using the signature description language EDL.

Keywords: Computer Security, Intrusion Detection, Misuse Detection, Attack Signatures.

1 Motivation

The growing dependencies of social processes on IT infrastructures as well as their increasing complexity provide a large potential of threats that jeopardizes these processes. To counter these threats intrusion detection systems (IDS) possess a prime importance as reactive measures. They provide means to automatically detect occurred security violations and to trigger appropriate countermeasures. IDSs apply two complementary approaches: anomaly and misuse detection. Anomaly detection aims at the exposure of abnormal user behavior. It requires a comprehensive set of data describing the normal user behavior. This is often difficult to provide so that anomaly detection has currently only a limited practical importance. Misuse detection focuses on the detection of attacks in audit trails described by patterns of known security violations, i.e. so-called signatures. The effectiveness of misuse detection strongly depends on the conciseness and the timeliness of the applied signatures. Imprecise signatures

G. Müller (Ed.): ETRICS 2006, LNCS 3995, pp. 436–450, 2006.

heavily confine the detection capability of the intrusion detection systems and lead to false positives. The reasons of this detection inaccuracy can only be in part imputed to qualitative restrictions of the audit functions. Rather they must be sought in the signature derivation process itself. In particular, the derivation of signatures starting from given exploits often appears as weak point. An attack represents a sequence of actions that exploits a vulnerability in a program, operating system, or network. The derivation of a signature to detect the attack is mostly based on experience and expert knowledge. Methods for a systematic derivation have scarcely been reported yet. Automated approaches to reusing design and modeling decisions of available signatures also do not exist. This results in relatively long development times for signatures, causing an inappropriate window of vulnerability [7].

The development time of signatures could be shortened and their conciseness improved, if - analogously to software technology - methods for the reuse of design and implementation decisions of available signatures are applied. Only a few approaches have been published which deal with this subject. Cheung et al. propose to simplify the signature design by applying attack models [1]. This approach corresponds to the design patterns of software engineering [2]. It allows the reuse of architectural design decisions. The reuse of specified signatures or signature fragments is not supported. Rubin et al. describe how mutants can be generated for a given attack [3]. Mutants exploit the same vulnerabilities as the basic attack without, however, performing the same security relevant actions. If a signature for an attack mutant is supposed to be developed, the signature of the basic attack could be reused, if available. The approach of Rubin et al. could be reused for this purpose by deriving an abstracted attack. The required transformations though (except simple transformations like IP fragmentations) strongly depend on the specific attack. A universally valid procedure for all kinds of attacks is not implementable with this approach. Rubin et al. further describe a refinement of signatures based on formal languages [4]. This approach may help the signature developer to remove triggers for false positives caused by imprecise signatures. The procedure, however, assumes an almost error-free reference signature. Larson et al. present a tool for extracting the significant events of an attack from the audit trail [8]. It executes the attack and records the respective audit data. Then the differences between this audit data and attack free audit data are determined. The problem of deriving a signature from the differences, however, remains unsolved.

In this paper we present an approach for systematic derivation of signatures from given exploits and signatures. It is based on the reuse of existing signatures or signature fragments. The approach can be automated. It selects signatures from a set of existing signatures that are similar to the new attack. These signatures help the signature developer to orient itself and, if possible, to reuse former design decisions. The paper is organized as follows. In Section 2 we describe the general principle of the approach. Next in Section 3 we adapt the procedure to a concrete signature description language. Section 4 describes the practical application of the approach. The final remarks contain some conclusions and give an outlook on future research.

2 Principle of the Approach

The development of a signature for a novel attack can be divided in the following steps: (1) execution of the attack on a dedicated system to record its traces in an audit trail. The traces are security relevant events (basic events) which are observed by sensors. (2) The signature developer investigates the basic events, identifies the relevant ones, and (3) step-by-step derives the new signature w.r.t. the approach of the attack to exploit the vulnerability of the attacked system. An important aspect in this context is the detection of patterns allowing the intrusion detection system to find attack traces. (4) After specifying the signature it must be validated to prove its correctness and conciseness. If needed, corrections or changes have to be introduced. The signature development process is time-consuming, in particular for phases (3) and (4). If knowledge of former signature designs may be reused, the time exposure for the signature development could be significantly reduced and their quality could be improved. Therefore the reuse of signatures is of great importance. Beside savings during design, the reuse of approved, i.e. validated, signature fragments may also considerably shorten the expensive validation phase.

In the following, we show how signatures can be automatically selected from a set of existing signatures which are qualified to be reused for a novel attack. This is based on the assumption that the signatures of related attacks are alike. After selecting the relevant signatures w.r.t. the new attack the signature developer can look for similarities and adapt the selected signatures. The identification of relevant signatures can be accomplished by an iterative abstraction of existing signatures until traces of the novel attack are covered. Abstraction means a generalization of signatures. Whether an abstracted signature detects the traces of the new attack can be easily decided by matching the signature to the traces. Abstractions are accomplished by iteratively applying transformations to the basic signatures. The abstraction procedure results in an abstraction tree. Each kind of transformation is weighted by a metric which defines a similarity measure related to the original signature. In order to identify reusable signature fragments the signature developer should focus on the least abstracted signatures. In the following sections we discuss transformations, abstraction trees and similarity measures.

2.1 Signature Transformations

A signature defines the set of identifiable manifestations of an attack. An attack manifestation is characterized by the events occurring during attack execution. The events form traces of the attack in the audit trail. In order to develop new signatures based on the reuse of existing ones, signatures that detect similar attack manifestations need to be identified. Although signatures may be similar, each signature is specialized to detect a specific attack. Signature transformations strongly depend on the signature model used in the applied signature description language. To identify reusable signatures it is necessary to abstract from the attack-specific elements. This is done by iteratively removing the semantic features w.r.t. the applied signature description language. The semantic features determine the set of attack manifestations a signature can detect. New signature abstractions can be obtained by removing restricting features from a signature or by weakening them. Transformations enlarge the set of attack manifestations M_{AS} that can be detected by an abstracted signature AS. A transformation T only abstracts a signature S to AS if $M_S \subseteq M_{AS}$ holds for the related sets of manifestation M_A and M_{AS}.

We apply the following rules for selecting appropriate transformations: (a) No transformations should be defined which produce the same abstraction. This rule prevents redundant transformations. (b) Transformations should always be selected such that they semantically weaken the signature only slightly. Such transformations lead to fine-granular abstractions of signatures. (c) A transformation generating an abstraction AS from a signature S should preferably meet the condition that the respective manifestation sets M_S and M_{AS} are disjoint.

2.2 Signature Abstraction Tree

There exists a relation between the derived signatures concerning their abstraction. Two signatures A and B are related, if B is abstracted from signature A. The relations between a basic signature S and all its abstractions can be represented by a signature abstraction tree in which S represents the root node. Direct children of S are those abstractions that can be generated by applying a single transformation to S. The signature abstraction tree and the related abstracted signatures can be generated successively. The tree structure determines the abstraction degree of S.

An abstracted signature associated to a node of the abstraction tree may detect all signature manifestations of the signature of the parent node, i.e. an abstraction tree defines a *contained in* relation over all sets of attack manifestations. Figure 1 depicts an example abstraction tree of S. Abstraction AS_1 is, for instance, directly generated from S by transformation 1, whilst signature AS_7 is derived from AS_1 using transformation 2. Their manifestation sets M_S, M_{AS1}, M_{AS7} must fulfill the condition $M_S \subseteq M_{AS1} \subseteq M_{AS7}$.

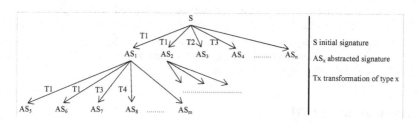

Fig. 1. Example of a signature abstraction tree

The signature abstraction tree may contain identical nodes. Two nodes are identical if the associated signatures are identical. The sub trees of these nodes are equal. Therefore one of the identical nodes and its sub tree can be removed.

After deriving the abstraction tree the abstracted signatures have to be tested to prove to what extend they identify the traces T of the new attack. These tests can be supported by the use of an intrusion detection system. The test applies a breadth-first search. It stops, when an abstracted signature is found which detects the traces T and if there is no other untested signature which has a larger similarity to the root signature. In practice, the generation and evaluation of abstracted signatures should be performed in an interleaved manner. This ensures that only the signatures required for the test are generated and that in case of identical nodes the test is limited to the respective tree fragment.

2.3 Similarity Measures of Signatures

The similarity of an abstracted signature compared to the basic signature decreases with each applied transformation. In order to estimate the similarities of different abstracted signatures the edges of the abstraction tree are weighted with a metric δ. This metric maps the type of the transformation onto real numbers. If a signature AS is generated from signature S by transformation X then the related edge between nodes P and P' is weighted with the metric value of the transformation X. The metric rates the degree of the semantic abstraction of the transformation. After weighting the edges of the tree the similarities of different abstracted signatures related to the basic signature S can be assessed. This is done by cumulating the edge weights on the path from the abstracted signature to the root node, i.e. the abstraction degree of a signature is determined by the sum of the edge weights.

2.4 Selection Procedure

Now we describe how signatures are selected from a set K of known signatures for a new attack. First the traces T of the new attack, which are received by executing the exploit on a system, are logged. Next the abstraction degree of each signature S in K is determined. It summarizes the abstractions which have to be applied to S to recognize the traces T. The procedure comprises five steps: (1) Successive application of transformations to S to derive all possible signature abstractions. (2) Generation of the abstraction tree. (3) Weighting the edges in the tree using a metric δ. (4) Applying all abstracted signatures of S to the traces T by using an IDS and indicating all signatures which identify T. (5) Selecting the abstracted signature with the smallest edge weight to root S from this subset. This abstraction degree is assigned to the signature S. After accomplishing this procedure for all signatures S in K, the abstraction degree of each signature is given. The signatures in K with the lowest abstraction degrees are suggested to the signature developer for reuse. The selection steps may be optimized and executed in parallel as indicated in Section 2.2.

3 Application to EDL

Signatures are specified using various languages. Therefore the selection procedure has to be adapted to the given signature description language or semantic model. We now demonstrate this for EDL (*Event Description Language*) [5], [6]. EDL is a signature description language which is based on a Petri-net like modeling approach. It supports the specification of complex multi-step attacks and possesses a high expressiveness and nevertheless allows for efficient analysis (cf. [6]). Before we describe the possible transformations we outline the essential features of EDL. A detailed description of EDL can be found in [5].

3.1 Modeling Signatures with EDL

The descriptions of signatures in EDL consist of places and transitions which are connected by directed edges. *Places* represent states of the system which are traversed by the related attack. *Transitions* represent the state changes. They describe the specific events which cause the state change, e.g. security relevant actions. These events are contained in the audit data stream recorded during the attack. The signature execution is represented by tokens which flow from state to state. *Tokens* represent concrete signature instances. They can be labeled with values as in colored Petri-nets.

Places describe the relevant system states of an attack. They are characterized by a set of features and a place type. Features specify the properties of the tokens which are located in a place. The information contained in a token can change from place to place. EDL distinguishes four place types: *initial, interior, escape*, and *exit places*. *Initial places* are the starting places of a signature. They are marked with an initial token at the start of analysis. Each signature has exactly one *exit place* which describes the final place of signature. If a token reaches this place, then the signature has identified a manifestation of an attack in the audit data stream. *Escape places* indicate an analysis stop of an attack instance. They are reached if events occur which make the completion of the attack instance impossible. Tokens which reach these places are discarded. All other places are *interior places*. Figure 2 shows a simple signature with places P_1 to P_4 for illustration.

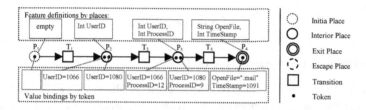

Fig. 2. Features and places

Transitions represent events which trigger state changes of signature instances. A transition is characterized by input places, output places, event type, conditions, feature mappings, consumption mode, and actions. *Input places* of transition t are places with an edge leading to the transition t. They describe the required state of the system before the transition can fire. *Output places* of transition t are places with an incoming edge from the transition t. They characterize the system state after the transition has fired. A change between system states requires a security relevant event. Therefore each transition is associated with an event type. Further, a system change can require additional conditions which specify that certain features of the event (e.g. user name) are assigned with particular values (e.g. root). Conditions can require distinct relationships between event and token features on input places (e.g. same values).

If a transition fires, tokens are created on the transition's output places. These tokens describe the new system state. To bind values to the features of the new tokens the transitions contain *feature mappings*. These are bindings which can be parameterized with constants, references to event features, or references to input place features. The *consumption mode* (cf. [5]) of a transition controls whether tokens that activate the transition remain on the input places after the transition fired. This mode can be individually defined for each input place. The consumption mode can be considered as a property of a connecting edge between input place and transition. Only in the consuming case the tokens which activate the transition are deleted on the input places.

Figure 3 illustrates the properties of a transition. The transition T_1 contains two conditions. The first condition requires that feature *Type* of event *E* contains the value *FileCreate*. The second condition compares feature *UserID* of input place P_1, referenced by *"P1.UserID"*, and feature *EUserID* of event type *E*, referenced by *"EUserID"*. This condition demands that the value of feature *UserID* of tokens on input place P_1 is equal to the value of event feature *EUserID*. Transition T_1 contains two feature mappings. The first one binds the feature *UserID* of the new token on the output place P_2 with the value of the homonymous feature of the transition activating token on place P_1. The second one maps the feature *Name* from the new token on place P_2 to event feature *EName* of the transition triggering event of type *E*.

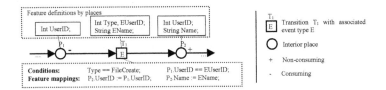

Fig. 3. Transition properties

3.2   Signature Transformations for EDL

In the following we present seven transformations for abstracting EDL signatures. We distinguish between transformations that retain the structure of the input signature (transformations 1 to 3), i.e. which modify only the properties of the transitions, and transformations that change the signature structure (transformations 4 to 7), i.e. which modify the topology of the places, transitions and their connecting edges. For each transformation, we describe the objective, the procedure, and the pre-conditions. The transformations abstract a given signature S with a given set of manifestations M_S, if and only if for the resulting signature AS and the corresponding set of manifestations M_{AS} holds $M_S \subseteq M_{AS}$. Note that this is not necessarily the case for arbitrary transformations. We provide appropriate pre-conditions for transformations that ensure that the transformations indeed abstract the signatures and the resulting abstract signatures are syntactically correct w.r.t. the modeling framework. If a transformation Tx may violate its pre-condition but not when applying another transformation Ty, $y!=x$, then Tx may only be used after Ty. Such dependencies are indicated where appropriate.

Transformation 1 (*broadening event correlation*): The consumption property of a given transition determines which events in a given trace should be correlated. The consuming mode restricts the set of events that are considered for correlation (see T_1 in Figure 3). The consumption of a token removes collected information about observed attack steps. Therefore, by transforming a consuming edge into a non-consuming one we broaden the set of events considered for correlation. As result, the number of manifestations detected by the signature may increase.

Procedure: If there is a consuming edge from an input place to a transition, the edge is transformed into a non-consuming edge.

Pre-conditions: The transition connected to the edge must not have an escape output place. Otherwise the effect of the transformation equals the effect of transformation 7.

Remarks: Transforming a consuming edge into a non-consuming one may significantly increase the number of tokens to be considered simultaneously. This negatively affects the performance of the IDS.

Transformation 2 *(relaxing static conditions)*: A given transition can restrict the events that may activate the transition by constraining the event features to constant values (*static conditions*), e.g. the first condition of T_1 in Figure 3 (*Type==FileCreate*) restricts the set of events that may activate T_1 to events where the feature *Type* is valued *FileCreate*.

Procedure: If there is a transition with a static condition, remove the static condition of the transition.

Pre-condition: The modified transition must not have consuming incoming edges. Otherwise tokens may be consumed and evolved, which may never reach an exit place, due to conditions of subsequent transitions. Consequently the number of detected manifestations is effectively reduced. Transformation 1 may be used to ensure the pre-condition.

Remarks: Instead of completely removing a condition, we could (a) remove only subterms of the condition or (b) relax restrictive test operations. We believe that such a refinement does not result in a relevant degree of abstraction.

Transformation 3 *(relaxing dynamic conditions)*: A given transition can restrict the events that may activate the transition by constraining the event features to values binded to input tokens (*dynamic conditions*), e.g. the second condition of T_1 in Figure 3 (*$P_1.UserID==EUserID$*). Evaluating dynamic conditions means correlating token features and event features, i.e. restricting the set of events that may activate the transition by enforcing relations between these events and events that have previously fired some transition(s). Such restrictions can be revoked by removing dynamic conditions, resulting in an increased number of events that may activate the corresponding transition.

Procedure: If there is a transition with a dynamic condition, remove the dynamic condition of the transition.

Pre-condition: See the pre-condition of transformation 2.

Remarks: By removing dynamic conditions the corresponding feature definitions of the input places and the token bindings of preceding transitions may become obsolete and should be removed. Moreover, we could relax dynamic conditions in a finer-grained way, as described for static conditions for transformation 2.

Transformation 4 *(removing pre-conditions)*: The topology of places and transitions implies a temporal constraint on events for transition activation. If we intend to modify temporal pre-conditions, we can modify signature elements that are connected to initial places, ignoring the event expected first in the temporal order. More specifically, if we intend to ignore temporal pre-conditions of the signature, we can remove transitions connected to initial places.

Procedure: If there exists a transition *T*, where all connected input places are initial places, remove *T* as well as all of its input places that are not connected to other transitions. The output places of *T* are transformed into initial places of the resulting signature, if not already removed due to a loop (input place == output place). Applying transformation 4 to transition T_1 of the example signature in Figure 4 results in the signature depicted in Figure 5.

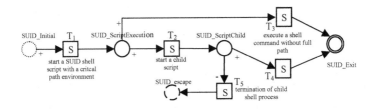

Fig. 4. Input signature to be transformed

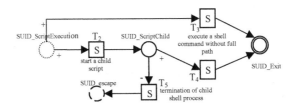

Fig. 5. Abstracted signature by means of transformation 4

Pre-condition: Transformation 4 may only be applied, if the following conditions are met. (1) The resulting signature would contain at least one path from some initial place to some exit place. Note that applying transformation 4 may imply to transform interior places with feature bindings into initial places without feature bindings. Thus, (2) we may only remove transitions, where the output places do not bind features to tokens that are referenced by subsequent transitions. Note that removing feature bindings affects the transitive closure of feature bindings. Moreover, (3) the newly transformed initial places must not be connected to consuming edges. Transformations 1 and 3 may be applied to ensure the aforementioned conditions.

Transformation 5 (*removing post-conditions*): If we intend to ignore temporal post-conditions of a signature, we can remove transitions connected to exit places, ignoring the event expected last in the temporal order.

Procedure: If there exists a transition *T*, where all connected output places are exit places, remove *T*, as well as all of its output places that are not connected to other transitions. The input places of *T* are transformed into exit places of the resulting signature. Applying transformation 5 to transition T_4 of the example signature in Figure 4 results in the signature depicted in Figure 6.

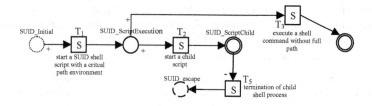

Fig. 6. Abstracted signature by means of transformation 5

Pre-condition: As for transformation 4, the resulting signature would have to contain at least one path from some initial place to some exit place.

Remarks: As a result of transformation 5 there may be more than one exit place. This is okay as long as none of the hierarchical concepts of EDL are used. The abstracted signature may contain transitions that have exit places as input places, e.g. T_5 in Figure 6. Since these transitions will never be activated, this is semantically correct. However, in order to avoid confusion of the signature engineer, such transitions should be pruned. When removing a transition, the feature definitions of preceding places and token bindings of preceding transitions may become obsolete and should be removed.

Transformation 6 (*removing intermediary conditions*): If we intend to ignore the intermediary temporal conditions of a signature, we can remove transitions not connected to initial and exit places, ignoring an event expected to occur after the first and before the last event in the temporal order.

Procedure: If there is a transition T that is connected to interior places only, then remove T as well as all of its output places. The former input places of T are transformed into input places of the transitions connected to the former output places of T. Applying transformation 6 to transition T_2 of the example signature in Figure 4 results in the signature depicted in Figure 7.

Pre-conditions: The transition selected for removal must not bind features to tokens that are referenced by subsequent transition conditions. As for transformation 4 the transitive closure of feature bindings needs to be considered for this criterion. Transformation 3 may be used to ensure the pre-condition.

Remarks: As for transformation 5, spurious feature definitions of places and feature bindings of transitions should be removed.

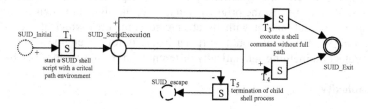

Fig. 7. Abstracted signature by means of transformation 6

Transformation 7 (*removing escape conditions*): Ignoring escape conditions may abstract a signature, because the removal of such a condition may result in further consideration of tokens that otherwise would have been removed. Escape conditions are modeled by transitions where the output place is an escape place.

Procedure: If there is a transition T that is connected to an escape place, then remove T as well as its output place, unless it is not connected to further transitions. Applying transformation 7 to transition T_5 of the example signature in Figure 4 results in the signature depicted in Figure 8.

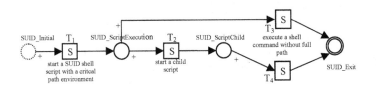

Fig. 8. Abstracted signature by means of transformation 7

Pre-conditions: None.

Remarks: As with transformation 1, the number of tokens to be considered for the abstract signature may significantly increase, thereby impairing the performance of the IDS. Moreover, as for transformation 5, spurious feature definitions of places and feature bindings of transitions should be removed.

The given transformations meet the rules (a) and (b) from Section 2.1. For transformations 1, 2, 3 and 7, rule (c) ($M_S \subset M_{AS}$) is only met, if additional signature instances in existence due to the transformation can be correlated such that the corresponding tokens reach an exit place. If this is impossible due to certain transition constraints, the transformations result in an increased number of tokens, but the number of detected manifestations is not increased.

The proposed transformations cover the whole range of syntactical elements of the signature language EDL. The transformations allow removing or relaxing arbitrary elements provided by EDL for restricting the flow of tokens from an initial to an exit place, effectively restricting the number of signature instances. Transformations are restricted to removing or relaxing constraining elements, thereby generalizing the original signature. We ignore the possibility of aggregating and (de-)composing signatures here, because - in contrast to more general signatures - we consider the resulting signature as semantically different from the original signature. Our approach is based on the idea to suggest the original signature to the signature engineer for further consideration in combination with its abstracted signatures which detect the given manifestation. We believe it would be rather irritating for the engineer, if the original signature detects something semantically different than the abstracted signature.

3.3 Complexity

We demonstrate that our approach can be used under real-world resource limitations by determining the space requirements for the abstraction tree (see Section 2.2) w.r.t.

the EDL signature transformations given in Section 3.2. Since the abstraction tree is constructed during run-time, its size also provides an intuitive measure for the computational complexity of our approach.

Suppose that for a given signature S the pre-conditions for all transformations are met. The number of nodes in the abstraction tree for a given signature S is the number of signatures that can be abstracted from S. The number of abstract signatures for S depends on the following parameters: N the set of transitions with no escape output places, E the set of transitions with escape output places, where $N \cap E = \emptyset$, b the number of conditions used by the transitions in N, and c the number of transitions in N that are connected to consuming edges.

Given the transformations from Section 3.2 $m = c + b + |E| + |N|$ elements of S can be transformed. Along a path from the root node of the abstraction tree of S, in each level a transformable element is removed. Hence, the tree depth is at most m. Moreover, in level k of the abstraction tree we have chosen to transform k from m transformable elements of S. Thus, there are $h_k = \binom{m}{k} = \frac{m!}{(m-k)! * k!}$ nodes in level k, representing all distinct abstract signatures that can be derived from S by k transformations. Consequently, the number of nodes from the root node to level k is $g_k = \sum_{i=0}^{k} \binom{m}{i}$. Further, there are at most $g = 2^m$ combinations how the transformations can be applied to S. Thus, g is the lowest upper bound of the total number of nodes of the abstraction tree.

The further investigations consider the set of signatures that was described in more detail in [6]. Table 1 gives the parameters for the signatures with the smallest, the largest, and an average number m of transformable elements. The average signature is a virtual signature, where the average parameter values of all signatures are assumed. For these signatures Table 1 also gives the depth m of the abstraction tree and the number g_m of abstracted signatures. The signature with the largest m describes a pretty complex shell link attack which can be considered as a special case. Note that while g_m considers identical nodes, all pre-conditions of transformations were ignored. However, Table 1 demonstrates that deriving all abstract signatures is feasible for average signatures, but infeasible for complex signatures. This result is further illustrated in Table 2. Execution times s_k were measured for the IDS SAM [7] on a Pentium III 800 MHz w.r.t. an attack manifestation with 10 events. s_k is the aggregate execution time of SAM in seconds (if not noted otherwise) for matching g_k signatures against the given attack manifestation.

Table 1. Signature parameters and size of corresponding abstraction trees

Parameter		min	max	average
number of non-escape transitions	$|N|$	3	7	4,25
number of conditions	b	7	18	8
number of consuming edges	c	0	4	1,25
number of escape transitions	$|E|$	2	2	2,5
max. depth of tree	m	12	31	16
number of abstracted signatures	g_m	4.096	2.147.483.648	65.536

The results suggest that we can generate and test all abstract signatures for average signatures in a reasonable time. Complex signatures obviously pose a problem. We propose to reduce their complexity by testing their static conditions before applying transformations. Abstracted signatures can be excluded from generation and the test, if each path from an initial place to an exit place contains some static condition that cannot be met by any event in the given attack manifestation. Additionally, it is not necessary to generate and test all abstract signatures of a given set K of signatures. It is sufficient to select t signatures that had to be abstracted the least. Suppose we found abstract signatures for the first t signatures S_i, $i=1..t$ in K with minimum similarity measures of a_i. Then it is sufficient for signature S_{t+1} to generate and test abstract signatures only as long as their similarity measure is lower or equal $max(a_i)$.

Table 2. Execution time for abstraction tree testing

signature		h_k, g_k and s_k for testing k tree levels						
	k=	2	4	6	8	10	12	m
min	h_k	66	495	924	495	66	1	1
	g_k	79	794	2.510	3.797	4.083	4.096	4.096
	s_k	0.1	1.2	3.8	5.7	6.1	6.2	6.2
max	h_k	465	31.465	736.281	7.888.725	44.352.165	141.120.525	1
	g_k	497	36.457	942.649	11.460.949	75.973.189	301.766.029	2.147.483.649
	s_k	0.7	55.2	23.8m	4.8h	31.9h	5.2d	37.6d
average	h_k	120	1.820	8.008	12.870	8.008	1.820	1
	g_k	137	2.517	14.893	39.203	58.651	64.839	65.536
	s_k	0.2	3.8	22.5	59.3	88.8	98.2	99.2

4   Example

In order to prove the suitability of the approach, an analysis of different signature engineering cycles of several signature developments has to be performed. Thereby traditional development processes as well as processes incorporating the proposed procedure have to be considered. By comparing the relevant parameters of the processes, e.g. the development times and the quality of the developed signatures, the suitability of the approach can be evaluated. Such an evaluation requires large financial efforts as well as a lot of human resources. To get an impression of the suitability of the proposed procedure we applied the procedure several times exemplarily. Thereby we made consistently positive experiences. In the following we describe an application example. The modus operandi, the results as well as possible improvements are explained.

The set of known signatures contains (amongst others) the signatures of a *Suid-Script-*, a *Link-* and a *Failed-Login-*Attack which are described in [7]. As new attack we used a candidate that has substantial similarity to the *Suid-Script-*Attack. Both attacks exploit the environment variable path and the suid mechanism. By using the variable path, a user specifies a list of directories to be searched for executable files. As a precondition of the *Suid-Script-*Attack a directory (*Dir*) must exist, that can be written by the attacker. Further a *Suid-Root-*Script must exist that calls a command (*Cmd*) without using its complete path. In this case an attacker can place a script in directory *Dir* that is equally named with *Cmd*. When the *Suid-Root-*Script is executed, the attacker script is called and executed with the privileges of the root user. Figure 4 sketches the corresponding EDL signature. The mechanisms used by the new attack and the traces generated by its execution are much the same. But, instead of using a suid script a binary suid application is used. The execution of applications is logged by different events and values than the execution of scripts.

Using the audit trail documenting the new attack and the set of known signatures the proposed procedure is applied. We use a metric δ that associates each transformation with value 1. Table 3 summarizes the results. It shows the applied transformations, their frequency, the level of abstraction, as well as the number of places and transitions of the four least abstracted known signatures.

Table 3. Signature ranking

Signature name	Level of abstraction (concerning $\Delta(x)=1$)	Applied transformations	$M = c+b+|E|+|N|$
Suid-Script	1	1*Transform. 2	12
JoinMailFile	3	3*Transform. 2	12
Link-Shell	4	3*Transform. 2 + 1*Transform. 3	31
Failed-Login	6	6*Transform. 2	13

The *Suid-Script*-Signature is suggested as signature for the new attack. Merely one condition of transition T_1 needs to be adapted. Even if the attack is modified in a way such that instead of a script an application that is equally named to *Cmd* is placed in *Dir*, the *Suid-Script*-Signature is selected from the set of known signatures and suggested as most suitable for reuse. In order to detect the modified attack, the conditions of the transitions T_2, T_3 and T_4 need to be adapted additionally. But the intrinsic signature characteristic, which realizes the tracking of child processes, persists.

5 Final Remarks

In this paper we have presented an approach to reusing patterns of existing signatures for the development of new signatures. The approach is geared to systematic development of signatures and exploits the fact that similar attacks produce similar traces, such that existing signatures may provide a substantial basis for developing new signatures. The reuse of approved structures may not only reduce the effort of the signature engineering process, but can also considerably shorten the costly test and correction phase. Moreover, the proposed procedure allows the signature engineer to revert to experience with existing signatures.

A signature base K typically contains a number of signatures that are specialized to a certain attack. The proposed approach selects the signatures of K that are most similar to the new attack by systematically relaxing the specializations of signatures in K. The procedure can be automated. For the selection process, the following preconditions have to be fulfilled: (1) The quality of the signatures in the set K is good. (2) The transformations must be chosen carefully and follow the rules mentioned in Section 2.1. (3) The metric used to measure signature similarities rates the semantic abstractions of the transformations appropriately.

There are several future research directions. In this paper we focus on suggesting reusable signatures for a new attack. An alternative way to support the signature engineer is a catalogue of design patterns for signatures. So we intend to examine larger sets of signatures for recurring patterns to derive and generalize these to design patterns. We envision that signature design patterns provide the same advantages like design patterns in object oriented software (cf. [2]). Another direction is the automatic derivation of test scenarios from a signature, in order to improve the testing of signature correctness and conciseness.

References

[1] Cheung S.; Lindqvist U.; Fong M.: Modeling Multistep Cyber Attacks for Scenario Recognition. In Proceedings of the 3rd DARPA Information Survivability Conference and Exposition, Washington, USA, IEEE Computer Society Press, pp. 284-292, 2003.

[2] Gamma E., Helm R., Johnson E. R., "Design Patterns – Elements of Reusable Object-Oriented Software", Addison-Wesley Professional, 1997, ISBN: 0201633612.

[3] Rubin S., Jha S., Miller B.: Automatic Generation and Analysis of NIDS Attacks. In Proceedings of the 20th Annual Computer Security Applications Conference, Tucson, AZ, USA, IEEE Computer Society Press, pp. 28-38, 2004.

[4] Rubin S.; Jha S.; Miller P. B.: Language-based generation and evaluation of NIDS signatures. In Proceedings of the IEEE Symposium on Security and Privacy, Oakland, CA, USA, IEEE Computer Society Press, pp. 3-17, 2005.

[5] Schmerl S.: Entwurf und Entwicklung einer effizienten Analyseeinheit für Intrusion-Detection-Systeme (in German). Master Thesis, Group Communication Systems, Brandenburg University of Technology Cottbus, 2004.

[6] Meier M.; Schmerl S.: Improving the Efficiency of Misuse Detection. In Proc. of the 2nd Conf. on Detection of Intrusions and Malware, and Vulnerability Assessment, Vienna, Austria, Lecture Notes in Computer Science, Vol. 3548, pp. 188-205, 2005.

[7] Lippmann, R.; Webster, S.; Stetson, D.: The Effect of Identifying Vulnerabilities and Patching Software on the Utility of Network Intrusion Detection. In Proceedings of the Symposium on Recent Advances in Intrusion Detection, Zurich, Switzerland, Lecture Notes in Computer Science, Vol. 2516, pp. 307-326, 2002.

[8] Larson U., Lundin Barse E., Jonsson E.: METAL - A Tool for Extracting Attack Manifestations. In Proceedings of the 2nd Conference on Detection of Intrusions and Malware, and Vulnerability Assessment, Vienna, Austria, Lecture Notes in Computer Science, Vol. 3548, pp. 85-102, 2005.

Redesign and Implementation of Evaluation Dataset for Intrusion Detection System

Jun Qian, Chao Xu, and Meilin Shi

Tsinghua University, Department of Computer Science,
Beijing 100084, P.R. China
{qjun, xchao, shi}@csnet4.cs.tsinghua.edu.cn

Abstract. Although the intrusion detection system industry is rapidly maturing, the state of intrusion detection system evaluation is not. The off-line dataset evaluation proposed by MIT Lincoln Lab is a practical solution in terms of evaluating the performance of IDS. While the evaluation dataset represents a significant and monumental undertaking, there remain several issues unsolved in the design and modeling of the resulting dataset which may make the evaluation results biased. Some researchers have noticed such problems and criticized the design and execution of the dataset, but there is no technical contribution for new efforts proposed *per se*. In this paper we present our efforts to redesign and generate new dataset. We first study how network applications and user behaviors characterize the network traffic. Second, we apply ourselves to improve on the background traffic simulation (including HTTP, SMTP, POP, P2P, FTP and other types of traffic). Unlike the existing model, our model simulates traffic from user level rather than from packet level, which is more reasonable for background traffic modeling and simulation. Our model takes advantage of user-level web mining, automatic user profiling and Enron email dataset etc. The high fidelity of simulated background traffic is shown in experiment. Moreover, different kinds of attacker personalities are profiled and more than 300 instances of 62 different automated attacks are launched against victim hosts and servers. All our efforts try to make the dataset more "real" and therefore be fairer for IDS evaluation.

1 Introduction

For more than a twenty-year's evolution, intrusion detection system (IDS) now has become an essential part of network security metrics. While the IDS industry is rapidly maturing, the state of IDS evaluation is not. Evaluations that focus on intrusion detection algorithm and system performance are essential for ongoing research because they can contribute to rapid research progress by revealing the weak points of current algorithms and systems. For example, the yearly evaluations sponsored by DARPA in speech recognition area have contributed substantially to rapid technical progress[1].

Although the best way to evaluate IDS is to test it in a live circumstance with real network traffic, the repeatability of experiment and concerned privacy of real network traffic deny it as a general solution. While there is no substitute for live network traffic, there are ways of designing tests around real-world environments, so synthetic traffic comes close to that of real-world conditions.

G. Müller (Ed.): ETRICS 2006, LNCS 3995, pp. 451–465, 2006.
© Springer-Verlag Berlin Heidelberg 2006

In 1998 (again in 1999), MIT Lincoln Lab (MIT LL) conducted a comparative off-line evaluation of intrusion detection systems[2,3]. It is the most comprehensive evaluation of research intrusion detection systems that has been performed to date and provides a basis for pointing out the flaws and weakness of existing intrusion detection systems. Many researchers used the resulting dataset in their researches and experiments, such as [4-8]. The open evaluation and shared dataset have focused research on difficult technical problems, motivated researchers to build advanced systems, facilitated information sharing and contributed to other researchers. For example, KDDCup'1999 (Knowledge Discovery in Databases) is a derivative of MIT LL evaluation dataset, which is specially formatted for intrusion detection data mining.

Although the dataset evaluation represents a significant and monumental undertaking, a number of issues associated with its design and execution were questionable. Some researchers have noticed such problems and criticized the design and execution of the dataset[9,10], but it is a pity that there is no technical contribution for new efforts proposed *per se*. Thus, the unsolved problems clearly remain. Besides the shortcomings of the dataset itself, the network has changed much during the last five years. New applications and attacks are booming. Such factors reshape the network streams which also have effect on performance of IDS. The applications and attacks of existing dataset are old for today's evaluation. Thus an improved and updated dataset is required.

The remainder of this paper presents our efforts to redesign and generate a more reasonable and "real" dataset for intrusion detection evaluation. We discuss the previous and ongoing efforts made by research community in section 2. In section 3, we give a brief summary of our test bed and reference network. Details concerning the background traffic generation and attack scenarios design are discussed in section 4 and 5. We make our resulting dataset a brief comparison with that of MIT LL in section 6. Finally a conclusion is given in section 7.

2   Related Works

Besides the research of MIT LL, the previous academic efforts include UC Davis (University of California, Davis) and IBM Zurich Research Lab. UC Davis aimed at a software platform that supports a methodology for testing various aspects of an IDS[11]. The emphasis of the software platform is to simulate real user's activities, especially the concurrent intrusions. The software platform allows users to create scripts simulating both intruders and normal users in UNIX environment simultaneously. The primary limitation of the software platform is that it only tests the IDS capability against known attacks.

IBM Zurich Research Lab have designed and implemented an experimentation workbench to support a comparative evaluation of several techniques they developed [12]. The workbench is able to compare the respective efficiency of IDS prototypes in terms of false alarm rates. But the implementation of the benchwork is limited to creating normal activities on an ftp server and attacks against it.

The commercial efforts include NIDSbench, Neohapsis and NSS Group. NIDSbench is a lightweight toolkit allows for the replay of various attacks or dumped network traffic for comparative testing of NIDS[13]. It consists of three components: fragrouter, tcpreplay and idstest. However, the key component idstest is never publicly released.

Neohapsis is an industrial research lab that proposes a framework called Open Security Evaluation Criteria (OSEC) for the evaluation of security products[14]. While OSEC is a trademark of Neohapsis, its criteria are open to view and critique, and were formulated with input from vendors, end-users and many from the security community actively working in the product spaces. The test suite is based around a common core (can be applied to any networked device), plus a suite of tests specific to each product category. However, the background traffic simulation and attack design are not receiving deserved consideration. Thus, OSEC still has a long way to go to reach its goal.

As a professional independent security testing facility, NSS Network Testing Lab provides evaluation and certification of a wide range of security products, including IDS/IPS appliances, firewalls, etc[15]. The persistent effort keeps NSS in a leading edge position and accumulates a wealth of experience in benchmarking and evaluations. The NSS Group has developed a specialized lab environment for IDS testing and evaluation. The test suite contains over 500 individual tests that evaluate IDS products in three main areas: performance and reliability, security accuracy, and usability. However, the test suite is not portable, neither suitable for research prototypes. And most importantly, the details of implementation are proprietary and not open to view for researchers.

The IDS evaluation methodology seems to be developing in a two-parallel way. Render unto vendors the things that are commercial, and unto researchers the things that are open.

3 Overview of Testbed and Reference Network

A reference network is required for comparative analysis in dataset evaluation methodology. We choose a university laboratory LAN as our reference network. Figure 1 shows the isolated testbed network of our experiment to generate background traffic and attacks. The left side by CISCO ROUTER of Figure 1 represents the inside of the emulated reference network and the right side represents the outside Internet. Both automated and manual attacks were launched outside against the inside victim servers (Linux 2.4.20-8, Windows 2000 Server SP2, etc) and a Cisco 2621 router. The generated live background traffic (includes HTTP, SMTP, TELNET, POP, P2P and other types of normal traffic) is similar to reference network. Inside and outside machines labeled TCPDUMP capture all packets transmitted over the attached network. The data used for evaluation also include the audit data collected from the victim servers, such as Internet Information Services logs, Windows NT event logs, file integrality check listings and etc.

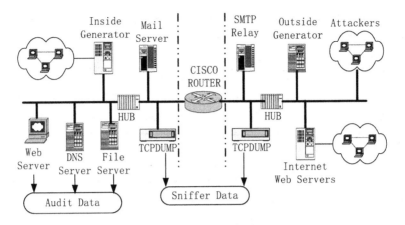

Fig. 1. Test bed of background traffic and attacks generation

Figure 2 shows the average number of connections per day for the dominant TCP services on our reference network. A three-month of continuous sniffing data was collected on reference network and used to create statistics.

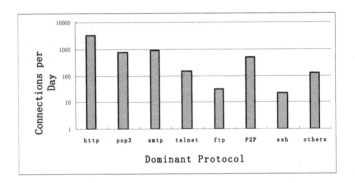

Fig. 2. Average connections per day for dominant TCP services

4   Background Traffic Simulation

The contents of the dataset consist of a large amount of normal traffic (also called background traffic) and a small amount of elaborate attacks (also called attack traffic). The background traffic is crucial for evaluation because the background traffic represents the network traffic characteristics, including details that affect false alarm rates. Thus, a well designed dataset can make it possible to measure baseline false alarm rates of evaluated intrusion detection systems while a poorly designed dataset may predicatively bias the evaluation results.

4.1   HTTP Traffic Simulation

As show in Figure 2, HTTP connections account for a dominant proportion of background traffic. The problem with the model of HTTP traffic simulation of MIT LL is that the traffic is simply simulated in terms of broken sessions rather than individual personalities. Only a list of web sites visited by folks is gathered and shared by all users in simulation. The user for each session is randomly chosen, as well as the number of pages accessed per session (randomly chosen between 1 and 15). While it is easy for execution, user personalities are melting. Although the dataset claimed a wide feasibility for the evaluation of both anomaly-based systems and signature-based systems, the simplicity of web traffic design and simulation may affect the effectiveness of some anomaly-based systems because they are studying the network traffic and user behaviors. Such systems are sensitive to the background traffic and client behaviors.

User behaviors are very likely to be concurrent and interlaced since windows are ubiquitous nowadays, it also offers the challenge to simulate user behaviors. The method used by MIT LL is limited to provide user personalization and simulate concurrent user behaviors. We are interested in how to profile personal patterns, and more importantly, how to simulate a group of web users browsing Internet simultaneously.

4.1.1   User Level Web Mining and Personalization

The web browser can be a key element in studying personal behaviors because it is the gateway to Internet. Therefore we develop a plug-in program monitoring at user level to audit individual web behaviors. It enables richer data collection and better personalization. The program is provided as a dynamic library link (DLL) so that the data collection process is transparent to user and won't interfere with user activities. Table 1 shows some of the events we used for audit.

Table 1. Internet explorer events

Event Name	Event fire condition
BeforeNavigate2	Fires before a navigation occurs in the given object (on either a window or frameset element).
DocumentComplete	Fires when a document has been completely loaded and initialized.
TitleChange	Fires before the Internet Explorer application quits.
OnQuit	Fires when the title of a document in the object becomes available or changes.

Every user's audit log is preprocessed for data reduction and converted into a program readable format for personalization. We use probability transition diagram as part of our personalization model. Several definitions are necessarily declared before taking further steps.

Definition 1 (Navigation Request). A navigation request is notated as a four-tuple R=(URL, sT, dT, wID). URL is the requested web page. sT is the start time of the navigation request, dT is the duration of the navigation request, wID is the handle of browser window (a long integer) where the navigation behavior happens.

Definition 2 (Class). If there exists a set of URLs which have the same *domain name*, then we define them as a Class $C=\{url_1,url_2,...,url_n\}$, with *domain name* defined as the class name of C. The number of the elements that belong to a class C is defined as the degree of the class, notated as $|C|$.

Definition 3 (Subsession). A subsession is a set of navigation requests launched in time sequence, notated as $U=(r_1,r_2,...,r_n)$. $\forall i, j, 1 \leq i < j \leq n$, $sT(r_i)<sT(r_j)$, $wID(r_i)=wID(r_j)$, and all the navigation requests of U belong to the same class. The start time of subsession is identical with that of the first navigation request. The length of a subsession is defined as the number of its members.

Definition 4 (Trigger Relationship). If the first navigation request of subsession u_2 is triggered by the last navigation request of subsession u_1, then we define a trigger relationship t between u_1 and u_2, t is a pair of class names. If $u_1 \in C_{name1}, u_2 \in C_{name2}$, then $t=(C_{name1}, C_{name2})$.

Definition 5 (Session). Session is defined as $S=(\varSigma U, T)$, $\varSigma U=\{u_1,u_2,...,u_n\}$, $T=\{t_1,t_2,...,t_{n-1}\}$, $n \geq 1$. $\forall i, 1 \leq i \leq n, \exists j, 1 \leq j \leq n, j \neq i$. Where either subsession u_i triggers subsession u_j or is triggered by subsession u_j, i.e. $t_i=(C_{namei}, C_{namej})$ or (C_{namej}, C_{namei}). The session length equals to the number of members of $\varSigma U$.

The context mining is to label the trigger relationships between subsessions. Two kinds of trigger relationships are labeled. One is between the subsessions launched in the same window. The other is between the subsessions in different windows that one clicks a link and pop up a new window. For example, figure 3(a) shows four browser windows launched by a user. Windows are listed in time sequence. Window #1 contains six navigation requests belong to two different subsessions, u_{11} and u_{12}. Window #2 is triggered by r_{12}, containing a single subsession u_{21}. And so do with Window #3 and Window #4. Suppose u_{11}, u_{12}, u_{21}, u_{31}, u_{41} and u_{42} belong to class C_1, C_2, C_3, C_4, C_5 and C_6 respectively, then we can deduce the trigger relationships between the subsessions. The corresponding probability transition diagram is shown as figure 3(b).

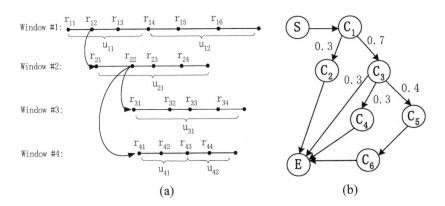

Fig. 3. Illustration of (a)trigger relationship, (b)session probability transition diagram

The *S* and *E* in figure 3(b) indicate the start and end state. Each edge of the diagram is labeled with the probability that the corresponding trigger relationship occurs in the sessions (some of the edges are not labeled explicitly if the probability is 1). Each path from the start to end corresponds to one of the sessions. Each node the path passes by is a class that consists of a set of subsessions with statistical information. The session probability transition diagram of a real user's web browser log is much more complicated than the given example.

4.1.2 User Profile and Virtual User Profile

Besides the session probability transition diagram, a user profile also includes daily connection distribution, daily connection cumulative density function and session length distribution. Figure 4 shows a user's daily connection distribution and daily connection cumulative density function respectively. We analyzed the connections in five-minute intervals over three-month continuous logs to discovery user patterns.

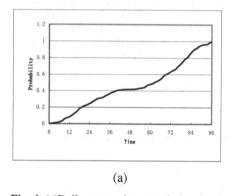
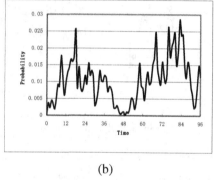

(a)   (b)

Fig. 4. (a)Daily connection cumulative density function and (b)Daily connection distribution

After user personalization, a corresponding user profile is created and stored as a knowledge base for simulation. The user profiles can't be used for traffic simulation directly without a configuration file. The configuration file includes the global information that is essential to simulation, such as the total connections during a day, IP address of every simulated user, the amplification factor (notated as *AF*) and the algorithm of generating virtual user profiles (if *AF* is set greater than 1). Each virtual user profile is synthesized by existing user profiles. The virtual user profile is useful because we don't have to gather the equivalent number of profiles if we want to simulate a large group of web users. We can achieve the goal by adjusting the value of *AF*. For example, we can achieve 20 different browsing plans by setting the value of *AF* as 2 if only 10 user profiles are available.

4.2 POP and SMTP Traffic Simulation

4.2.1 POP Traffic Modeling and Simulation

POP traffic simulates inside users connect to the inside mail server and download mail messages from the server. The problem with POP traffic simulation of MIT LL is that it models the traffic in terms of sessions rather than user personalities. The POP session start times are supposed to be Poisson distributed with a time-varying rate given in a timetable. The user with connected mail server is randomly chosen from a list of possible candidates, which eliminates the characters of real user.

We analyze four-month of continuous sendmail[16] and POP logs, and totally 21,142 emails to find out the traffic and user characteristics. Figure 5 shows the daily POP connection statistics. As can be seen, the curve regularly repeats in a period of seven days. We classify POP users into two types. One is with regular connection intervals; the other is with irregular connection intervals. An example of each type is shown in Figure 6. The statistics are based on weekday's data of one week.

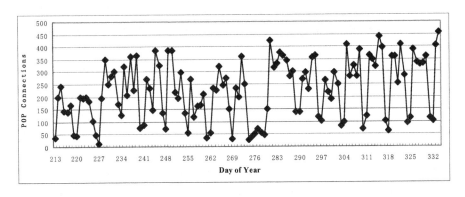

Fig. 5. POP connections of four-month statistics on reference network

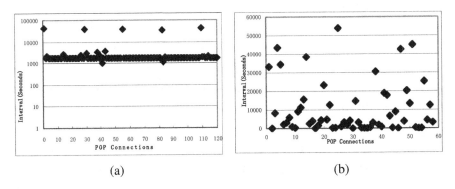

(a)   (b)

Fig. 6. (a)User with regular connection intervals (b)User with irregular connection intervals

4.2.2 SMTP Traffic Modeling and Simulation
SMTP traffic simulates emails being sent to and from users on the LAN and Internet. Figure 7 shows the SMTP connections of four-month statistics on reference network. As can be seen, the curve is self-similar in a regular period of seven days (a week). From which we argue that the reasonable duration of dataset is one week. Each dataset provided by MIT LL contains synthetic traffic of five days (from Monday to Friday), but it didn't explain why. We find a strong argument to support this conclusion.

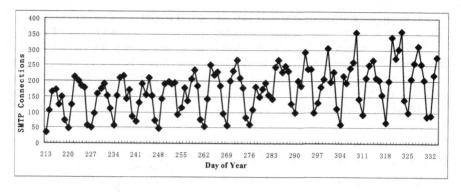

Fig. 7. SMTP connections of four-month statistics on reference network

The difficulties of SMTP traffic simulation mainly focus on message classification, contents generation and thread maintenance. MIT LL manually classifies the mail messages into seven different types. Each type accounts for a specified percentage of total messages. Unlike MIT LL, we use a clustering method to automatically classify the mail messages.

Definition 6 (Message). A message is defined as a nine-tuple, notated as emsg=(FROMADDR, RCPT, TOADDR, TITLE, TIMESTAMP, SIZE, STAT, ERRMSG, CONTENT). FROMADDR and TOADDR denote the sender and receiver respectively. RCPT is the receiver quantity of this message. TITLE, SIZE and CONTENT denotes the title, size and content of the message respectively. TIMESTAMP is the sent time of the message. STAT denotes the status of the message, successfully sent or failed. The error information is stored in ERRMSG.

Definition 7 (Message Class and Degree of Message Class). A message class C contains messages that have identical (FROMADDR, TOADDR) pairs. The quantity of messages contained by a class is defined as the degree of the class, notated as $|C|$.

Definition 8 (Supporting Rate and Frequency). For each class C, defines the supporting rate $s_c \Box |D_c|$, where D_c is a set of integers. Every member of D_c is between [0,365], which denotes the day of year of message TIMESTAMP. The frequency of class C is defined as $f_c = |C|/s_c$.

Figure 8 shows the clustering results. The classes can be mainly classified into four groups. Each group is briefly described in table 2.

Message contents generation and thread maintenance are of implicit relationship. MIT LL generates messages in two ways. Some messages are actual messages downloaded from a variety of public-domain mail list servers. The others are created by using statistical bi-grams frequencies to preserve word and two-word sequence statistics from a sampling of roughly 10,000 actual messages. To avoid concerned privacy, all the email messages are filtered by a 40,000 words dictionary to remove names and other private information. The model adopted by MIT LL is questionable because it has several shortcomings. Using filtered actual messages as SMTP traffic is the same as using filtered real network traffic as background traffic in essence. Since

MIT LL thought that filtered real network traffic is a negative solution to background traffic simulation, it is not reasonable to using filtered actual messages as SMTP traffic. In addition, neither a 40,000 words dictionary is big enough for privacy filtering nor it is practical for administrators to check through all the created messages to avoid concerned privacy. And more importantly, after filtering by such a huge words dictionary, most of the filtered emails are predictably unreadable or hardly understandable for human, not mention to IDS.

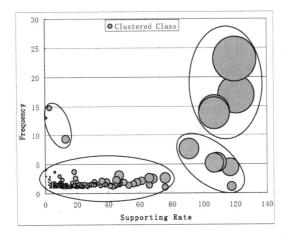

Fig. 8. Distribution of clustered classes

Table 2. Class groups and brief description

Type	Supporting Rate	Frequency	Quantity	Description
I	<80	<9	Large	Most are normal messages
II	<80	>9	Small	Spams, viruses or worms
III	>80	<9	Large	List or newsgroup
IV	>80	>9	Large	List or newsgroup

Definition 9 (Thread). A thread is a set of messages discussing a particular topic.

MIT LL mentions little about thread classification and maintenance. Although every recipient has a probability to respond to the sender, the respondence message is randomly chosen, which breaks the thread information. The difference between thread information and the others is that the thread information is not provided explicitly. It must be deduced from other data fields. There has not been much work in how to detect thread information automatically. Thus, we use a public email dataset for contents generation and thread maintenance. The Enron email dataset[17] is a corpus of email messages with threads detected and classified. There are totally 200,399 messages in Enron corpus with 101,786 threads. 71,695 of the threads were trivial threads that consist of only one message each. Other 30,091 remaining consist of 123,501 messages. Messages with empty subjects are not considered as a thread.

4.3   Other Types of Traffic Simulation

We give a short description of other types of traffic simulation because of page limitation. FTP sessions simulate inside users using FTP clients to transfer files to and from file server inside and outside. According to our analysis on sniffing data, FTP traffic is a big but not important traffic because most of the FTP traffic is ftp data traffic. Hence we make a trade-off for FTP traffic simulation. We simulate the ftp sessions of commands but omit the file transferring. Otherwise the dataset size may become too big to be portable and publicly released.

TELNET traffic simulates interactive sessions of users on remote servers. Users are simulated based on individual statistical profiles. Thousands of history commands are collected for user personalization. Different with other traffic simulation, TELNET traffic simulation needs to log every user's commands during the simulation so as to roll back to the previous state after simulation if it is necessary. Some commands don't change the state of the server (e.g. ls, cd), while some commands do. For example, if a programmer user edits programs and compiles them, and finally run the programs. Some files are created by commands (vi and cc) after simulation.

P2P traffic is a highlighted new member of dataset. The P2P applications running on reference network include file exchanging applications, instant messengers and real time video broadcasting application. The file exchanging applications and real time video broadcasting application are relatively easy to simulate because they are less interactive. Instant messengers are hardly to simulate because of too much concerned privacy. Thus we give up the simulation of instant messengers in experiment.

Since most of the users on reference network are working on windows workstations, windows GUI applications are ubiquitous. We developed *ScriptMaster* scripts specially used for GUI interactive simulation. It takes advantage of the message-driven nature of Windows and allows user automata behave as if a real user was using the applications.

5   Attack Scenarios

More than 300 instances of 62 different automated attacks are launched against victim hosts and servers. All the exploit scripts are maintained in a vulnerability database internally. Attack initiations are stored in database and scheduled by attack scheduler automata. We classify different attacker personalities into three types according to personal character and ability, each type is briefly described in table 3.

We add a lot of new attacks that were not described and implemented in MIT's dataset so as to update and extend the attack database. Table 4 shows the attack categories and new added attacks in each category. We also generate malicious emails containing worms because email has become a usual channel for attackers to compromise computers. Data confidentiality attacks involve someone (user or administrator) performing actions that they may be able to do on a given computer system, but are not allowed to do according to site policy. A "secret" attack is an attack where the attacker maliciously transfers data to a place where it doesn't belong. For example, transferring data from a classified computer/network to a non-classified computer/network would constitute a "secret" attack. We simulate these types of attacks by publishing a set of rules indicating that all files in a particular directory are not allowed to be moved out of that directory (by 'cp', 'cat', 'ftp', or whatever) . To recognize these attacks, the detection system must know which files are considered "secret", what the policies are regarding use of these files, and then look for actions carried out involving them. Naturally, such attacks are hard to detect.

Table 3. Different types of attacker personalities

Type	Description
Inexperienced beginner	Few skills. Weak motivation. Dare use any available tools from Internet.
Irritable talent	Skillful than beginner but less skillful than experienced expert. Usually scan network to quickly find out exploits of targets. Keen on trying new exploits.
Experienced expert	Scrupulous. Seldom use vertical scans. Always clean evidence after intrusion. Have strong motivation. Patient to find out target exploits. Likely to control zombies or proxies before launching attacks.

Table 4. Attack categories and new added attacks

Categories	New Added Attacks
Denial of Services	UDPFlood, SMBdie, UPNPdos, RPCNuke, IpHacker, IIS-smtp
User to Root	SU, ErunAsX, NDDE, Linux_ATM
Remote to Local	Wuftpd2600, SqlExec, AspX, WebDavX3, SQL2kUDP, Unicode, IISidq, CrackPasswd, GetAccount, Shed, SMBCrack, WMICracker, SendMail2, Re, T-Cmd, Pqwak, NtRootKit, BingHe, MIME, AckCmd, BSDTelnetd
Probes	X-Port, X-Scan, CIS, SSS, SDS, Twwwscan, ScanloOk
Worms	IIS-Worm.CodeRed, IIS-Worm.HLLW, IIS-Worm.Nimda
Data Confidentiality	Secret

6 Experiment

MIT LL claimed that the generated dataset is similar to that observed on reference network, but the statistics used to describe the real traffic and the measures used to establish similarity are not given, except for the claim that word pair statistics of email messages matching those sampled.

We bring our synthetic traffic in comparison with MIT's dataset (Monday, Week 1) and observed traffic respectively. We analyze the distribution of total HTTP connections according to the number of packets of each HTTP connection.

Figure 9(a) shows the result of MIT's dataset. We present ours in figure 9(b). A significant difference between (a) and (b) is that the distribution curve in (a) is absent when packet number is less than 8. It indicates that none of HTTP connections contains less than 8 packets. It is quite odd and not true of real traffic. For example, if a requested page doesn't exist (often caused by typo), the connection will be closed. Figure 9(c) shows the result of observed traffic on reference network. We only give the result of our reference network because MIT didn't publish their observed network traffic, neither can we repeat it. The packet number of curve in figure 9(a) mainly distributes in [10, 100] because the number of pages accessed per session is randomly chosen between 1 and 15 without user personalization. By contrast, the curve in figure 9(b), which based on user personalization, is quite similar with that in figure 9(c). It indicates that our simulated traffic keeps high fidelity to real traffic.

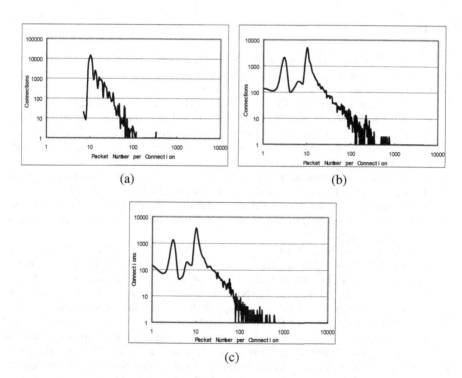

(a)

(b)

(c)

Fig. 9. Statistics of HTTP connections comparison between (a)MIT's dataset(Mon, Week 1), (b)Our dataset, (c)Observed traffic on our reference network

7 Conclusion

The off-line dataset evaluation methodology proposed by MIT LL is a practical solution in terms of evaluating the performance of IDS. Like other open project and research, continuous improvement makes it a key element to keep the dataset valuable for researchers. Network bandwidth is increasing quickly with new applications and attacks are booming. Such factors require the dataset to be updated in time.

User behavior simulation is very important in IDS evaluation. Simulating how user behaves is an immensely challenging undertaking because of the complexity and intricacy of human behaviors, but it does not mean to weaken the efforts by claiming too many difficulties for them. MIT LL models the synthetic traffic more from session level rather than from user level. We think it more reasonable to model the synthetic traffic from user level because it is the user behaviors that have effect on traffic sessions rather than the converse. In this paper we discuss our effort to improve on the modeling and simulation of evaluation dataset. It gives our model the ability to feasibly construct synthetic traffic and keep high scalability and fidelity.

References

1. R.A. Cole, J. Mariani, H. Uszkoreit, A. Zaenen and V. Zue, "Survey of the State of the Art in Human Language Technology," *Center for Spoken Language Understanding CSLU, Carnegie Mellon University*, Pittsburgh, PA, 1995.
2. R.P. Lippmann, D.J. Fried, I. Graf, J.W. Haines, K.R. Kendall, D. McClung, D. Weber, S.E. Webster, D. Wyschogrod, R.K. Cunningham and M.A. Zissman, "Evaluating Intrusion Detection Systems:The 1998 DARPA Off-Line Intrusion Detection Evaluation," *In: Proc. of the 2000 DARPA Information Survivability Conference and Exposition (DISCEX)*, Los Alamitos, CA, 2000. 2:12-26
3. R. P. Lippmann, J.W. Haines, D.J. Fried, J. Korba and K. Das, "The 1999 DARPA Offline Intrusion Detection Evaluation," *in Computer Networks*, 34(2), 2000. 579-595
4. P. Ning and Y. Cui, "An intrusion alert correlator based on prerequisites of intrusions," *Technical Report TR-2002-01, Department of Computer Science, North Carolina State University*, January 2002.
5. V. M. Matthew and K.C. Philip, "Learning nonstationary models of normal network traffic for detecting novel attacks," *In Proc. of the 8th ACM SIGKDD international conference on Knowledge discovery and data mining*, Edmonton, Alberta, Canada, July 2002.
6. R. Sekar, A. Gupta, J. Frullo, T. Shanbhag, A. Tiwari, H. Yang and S. Zhou, "Specification Based Anomaly Detection: A New Approach for Detecting Network Intrusions," *in ACM CCS'02*, Washington DC, USA, Nov. 2002.
7. W. Lee and S. Stolfo, "A Framework for Constructing Features and Models for Intrusion Detection Systems," *in ACM Transactions on Information and System Security*, 3(4), 2000.
8. K. Wang and J.S. Salvatore, "Anomalous Payload-based Network Intrusion Detection," *In Recent Advances in Intrusion Detection (RAID2004)*, September 2004.
9. J. McHugh, "Testing intrusion detection systems: A critique of the 1998 and 1999 DARPA intrusion detection system evaluations as performed by Lincoln Laboratory," *in ACM Transactions on Information and System Security*, 3(4), 2000. 262-294

10. M.V. Mahoney, P.K. Chan, "An Analysis of the 1999 DARPA/Lincoln Laboratory Evaluation Data for Network Anomaly Detection," *In Recent Advances in Intrusion Detection (RAID2003)*, Lecture Notes in Computer Science, Vol. 2820. Springer-Verlag, 2003. 220–237

11. N. Puketza, M. Chung, R.A. Olsson and B. Mukherjee, "A Software Platform for Testing Intrusion Detection Systems," *in IEEE Software*, 14(5), 1997. 43-51

12. H. Debar, M. Dacier, A. Wespi and S. Lampart, "An Experimentation Workbench for Intrusion Detection Systems," *Technical Report No.RZ2998, IBM Zurich Research Laboratory*, September 1998.

13. D. Song, G. Shaffer and M. Undy, "Nidsbench: a Network Intrusion Detection Test Suite," *In Proc. of Recent Advances in Intrusion Detection(RAID1999)*, September 1999.

14. http://osec.neohapsis.com/about.html

15. http://www.nss.co.uk/default.htm

16. Bryan Costales. Sendmail 3rd Edition. O'Reilly, December 2002. ISBN: 1-56592-839-3.

17. K. Bryan and Y. Yiming, "The Enron Corpus: A New Dataset for Email Classification Research," *In European Conference on Machine Learning*, Pisa, Italy, 2004.

Requirements of Information Reductions for Cooperating Intrusion Detection Agents[*]

Ulrich Flegel and Joachim Biskup

University of Dortmund, D-44221 Dortmund, Germany
{flegel, biskup}@ls6.cs.uni-dortmund.de

Abstract. We consider cooperating intrusion detection agents that limit the co-operation information flow with a focus on privacy and confidentiality. Generalizing our previous work on privacy respecting intrusion detection for centralized systems we propose an extended functional model for information reductions that is used for cooperation between intrusion detection agents. The reductions have the following goals: detective effectiveness of cooperation alliances, privacy of honest individuals, further organizational confidentiality requirements, and efficiency. For the reductions we outline the basic requirements, and derive the specific requirements imposed by the cooperation methods used for intrusion detection. It is shown, how our existing solutions could be adapted and what restrictions apply.

1 Introduction

When designing IT systems we not only need to take the security requirements of the providers into perspective, but also the security requirements of the users. Both, users and IT system providers are interested in the dependability, in particular the integrity and availability of the IT system. In the recent years it has been recognized that preventive safeguards need to be complemented by reactive aspects of security.

A security incident comprises the violation of the given security policy. Reacting to security incidents requires detecting them in the first place. To be able to detect violations of the security policy, one must be able to observe all activity that could potentially be part of such violations. Modern services and operating systems either already supply mechanisms for observation or can be instrumented appropriately. The observed information is denoted as *audit data* in the following. The audit data can be analyzed by an *intrusion detection system* (IDS) in order to detect security incidents. If an IDS detects a security incident, appropriate reaction should be initiated. A reaction may require to hold a user accountable for the damage caused. Therefore, audit data usually provides information to account activity to persons.

Since most audit data can be used without much effort to identify individual users, recording and sharing such data may conflict with the users' expectancy for privacy and with pertinent legislation concerning the personal data of users. In Sect. 2 we summarize existing solutions to solve the conflict between the need for audit data for intrusion

---

[*] This work has been partially funded by the German Research Council (DFG) under grant number Bi 311/10-3.

G. Müller (Ed.): ETRICS 2006, LNCS 3995, pp. 466–480, 2006.

detection and the privacy requirements. The core idea is to replace personal data in audit data with carefully chosen pseudonyms. Current technology for pseudonymizing audit data is applicable to centralized intrusion detection systems, only. In Sect. 3 we argue, that centralized intrusion detection will not be sufficient in the future. Rather, intrusion detection agents need to cooperate to sustain adequate detection facilities. Recent work on cooperating intrusion detection agents is summarized in Sect. 4.

In Sect. 5 we generalize prior concepts of pseudonymization and propose an extended functional model for information reductions. Information reductions are a prerequisite for cooperating with partially trusted agents that should not learn certain information. The basic requirements of such information reductions are outlined in Sect. 6, whereas requirements for the specific cooperation methods used by intrusion detection agents are derived in Sect. 7 and Sect. 8. The derived results are related to audit data pseudonymization and according adaptations of prior solutions are proposed. The paper discusses related work and concludes in Sect. 9. The main contribution is fivefold:

- proposing a novel *functional model for information reductions* that is used for cooperation between intrusion detection agents,
- identifying the *basic requirements* of such information reductions,
- deriving *specific requirements* based on existing work on cooperation of intrusion detection agents,
- proposing according *adaptations of existing solutions* for audit data pseudonymization, as well as identifying the *inherent limitations*, and
- identifying the major *challenges wrt. intrusion detection, inference control and cryptography* in order to achieve secure and useful information reductions for cooperating intrusion detection agents.

2   Pseudonymization for Centralized Intrusion Detection

We proposed concepts for the pseudonymization of audit data for intrusion detection while balancing the conflicting requirements for accountability and anonymity [3]. In our approach Unix *syslog audit data* is pseudonymized by a *source agent* immediately after it has been generated by an *information source*, such that users appear under pseudonyms in the audit data (see Fig. 1). The *audit data with pseudonyms* maintains the degree of linkability required for intrusion detection by the analyzing agent. The pseudonymization process also produces additional data that allows for the recovery of the original data, subject to specific conditions. The audit data with pseudonyms and the *pseudonym recovery data* are forwarded by the source agent to the analyzing agent.

The *analyzing agent* normally works in a *surveillance mode*, where merely the audit data with pseudonyms is analyzed with respect to misuse suspicions. Only if a (*threshold*) *alert* occurs, i.e., a misuse suspicion has been detected, the pseudonym recovery data can be used for *reidentification*, i.e., the original audit data can be reconstructed. In the *alert mode* the analyzing agent can employ the *reconstructed audit data* to establish accountability for legal purposes, such as damage prevention and litigation.

For the pseudonym recovery data, the approach leverages Shamir's threshold scheme for cryptographic secret sharing [4]: The misuse suspicions for intrusion detection are modeled as thresholds of secret sharing schemes. The pseudonym recovery data contains the encrypted identifying data that is replaced by the pseudonyms, and it contains shares of the respective decryption keys. As a result, the disclosure of the encrypted identifying data is enforced cryptographically, such that decryption is possible if and only if the pseudonyms are involved in a sufficient suspicion of misuse (*technical purpose binding*), i.e., the number of shares associated with the pseudonyms exceeds the threshold in the model of the misuse suspicion. Note that it may be necessary to provide the ability to recover the decryption keys independently of a priori defined models of misuse suspicion in order to investigate misuse that has not (yet) been modeled. In that case, the grounds for decryption must be scrutinized by one or more trusted parties (*organizational purpose binding*). Involving these parties can be enforced cryptographically, e.g. using threshold cryptosystems [1].

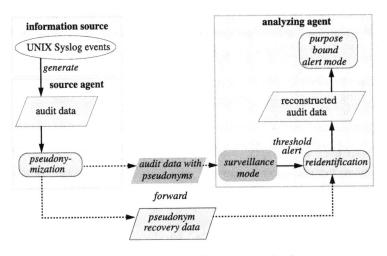

Fig. 1. Functional model for pseudonymization

For the pseudonymization approach we have implemented a suitable system design and described practical aspects of its use [2]. The evaluation has shown, that the concepts are viable in practice to handle real-world audit data volumes [2].

3   The Need for Cooperation

The approach described in Sect. 2 is suitable for centralized intrusion detection, where information sources and source agents are controlled by a single authority, such that pseudonyms and recovery data are generated consistently with respect to a central analyzing agent. We expect to see the following main problem in the future. Complex and orchestrated attacks increasingly span larger and more heterogeneous networks, and they cross organizational boundaries. From the attacker's point of view this is a logical step to conceal his attacks by breaking it down into smaller parts, which might seem innocuous, if observed isolatedly. Also by using several distributed machines an attacker can gain firepower for denial of service attacks. Complex attacks of this kind cannot be monitored by local source agents of one intrusion detection system alone. Conventional centralized approaches for intrusion detection will neither be able to collect sufficient information about complex attacks nor to support an appropriate response. Therefore, cooperation between distributed IDS agents is required.

The main problem comes along with further weaknesses of centralized systems. (1) The increasing capacity of networks and computers results in an ever increasing audit-data volume that needs to be analyzed. In the face of this development, centralized intrusion detection approaches do not scale adequately any more. (2) A single central-ized analyzing agent is a single point of failure and cannot constitute a robust solution. (3) Complex attacks implement strategies that comprise several elementary sub-attacks. Conventional intrusion detection systems merely focus on the detection of the elemen-tary attacks. As a consequence of a complex attack, security administrators are con-fronted with a multitude of alarms that only together describe the complex attack on a low level of abstraction. The recognition of attack strategies and their overall goals is left to the security administrators.

4   On Cooperating Intrusion Detection Agents

Cooperative and distributed intrusion detection agents are proposed as the solution for the sketched problems. There has been some development primarily focusing on the technical and practical issues that enable distributed intrusion detection to face problems (1) and (2). In order to move from centralized solutions to distributed IDS, algorithms for distributed audit data analysis have been proposed [5, 6, 7]. Recently, research also extends on improving the results of distributed analysis, in order to solve problem (3).

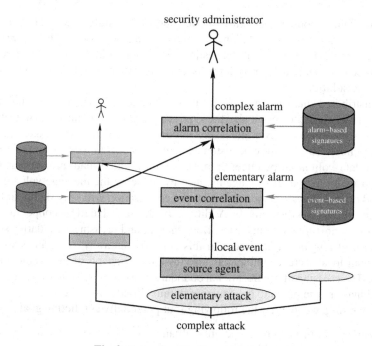

Fig. 2. Example with alarm correlation

Seminal proposals of Huang and Bass [8, 9] deal with the analysis of strategies and goals of attackers, utilizing results from the field of multisensor data fusion. Fusion or aggregation of alarms of elementary attacks that have been generated by different analyzing agents result in the reduction of the alarm volume, thereby relieving the security administrators. To do this, knowledge-based rule systems and probabilistic methods have been proposed [10, 11, 12, 13, 14, 7]. These approaches use simple heuristics based on domain knowledge about invariants of certain classes of attacks.

Knowledge-based correlation of alarms of elementary attacks can be used to recognize complex attacks in detail (see Fig. 2). The correlation can be conducted using explicit models such as signatures interpreting alarms as events, where the models can be specified by experts [15, 10, 16, 17] or learned from labeled training data based on similar heuristics as used for alarm aggregation [18]. Alarm correlation based on explicit models fails to recognize not explicitly specified variants of complex attacks. Specifying instead the pre and post conditions of alarms, all (variants of) complex attacks can be recognized wrt. these conditions [19, 20, 21, 14].

Correctly abstracting many elementary attacks into a few complex attacks has several advantages. Firstly, the alarm volume is reduced. Secondly, strategies and possible intentions of attackers can be recognized [8, 22] or extrapolated, such that target systems can possibly be protected before the complex attack is completed. This extends the use of intrusion detection to the practically more important domain of intrusion prevention. Thirdly, uncorrelated alarms can be assumed to be false alarms [21].

5   Reduction of Cooperation Data

While distributed cooperating intrusion detection is strongly needed, it also has the potential to be abused as a surveillance technology on a large scale. The arising conflict is an open problem not sufficiently investigated by the literature, as surveyed in Sect. 9. We propose to extend our approach for pseudonymization, as introduced in Sect. 2, as a promising solution.

The distributed character of future intrusion detection not only brings out the importance of privacy protection, but also the significance of *efficient* intrusion detection. We can compare analyzing an ever increasing amount of audit data with the attempt to drink from a fire hose. To put future intrusion detection systems in the position to cope with the audit data volume in practice, the results of local audit data pre-processing must be shared with other analyzing agents, thereby reducing the message volume and the workload of the analyzing agents. Successful cooperation will only be possible, if the data is not filtered too restrictively. Additionally, the data shared by cooperating agents may cross organizational boundaries. Both sharing and crossing boundaries stress the importance of *confidentiality* issues in this context. Naturally, companies would like to keep their local secrets confidential, also towards the agents of their remote business partners. The crossing of organizational boundaries also amplifies *privacy* requirements of individuals as compared to the situation within closed organizations.

Summarizing, we identify the following four potentially conflicting goals:

1. *detective effectiveness* of cooperation alliances,
2. *privacy* of honest individuals,

3. further organizational *confidentiality* requirements of local agents, and
4. *efficiency*.

Our previous solution exploits domain knowledge (about the given models of attack scenarios), as well as organization-specific knowledge (about requirements for privacy, analyzability and accountability). Accordingly, the solution for the more general problem is expected to use domain knowledge about the cooperation method to account for efficiency and cooperation effectiveness. And for considering privacy and confidentiality, again organization-specific knowledge is required. Particularly, in practice we need solutions with realistic and implementable trust requirements, because cooperating intrusion detection agents can be operated by different organizations. Our extended solution will be based on a generalization of the functional model from Sect. 2. An *information source* generates *events* or just *information*, being consumed by a source agent. The *source agent* represents the events or information using *structured data objects*. Appropriate information reductions process the structured data objects to satisfy detective effectiveness, privacy, confidentiality and efficiency. We distinguish lossless reductions and lossy reductions, depending on whether the original information from the structured data objects can be reconstructed or not, respectively:

- *Lossy reductions* remove information from structured data objects before forwarding it as *open data* to remote agents. The removed information must not be needed for further remote processing, and it should be definitely kept secret from remote agents, even under *inferences*. When information is coarsened, the detective effectiveness of the surveillance mode should not be affected unreasonably.
- *Lossless reductions* work by *splitting the information* contained in structured data objects into *open data* and *covered (masked, blinded) data* before forwarding it to remote agents (see Fig. 3).

The open data of a lossless reduction is sufficient for the normal surveillance mode of analyzing agents, possibly in conjunction with *exploiting* certain properties of the covered data, or in conjunction with some *supporting data* that must be additionally generated depending on the specific application. As an example, the covered data may be the protected input to a surveillance mode that is implemented using secure multiparty computation. If a specific detective purpose is met in the surveillance mode, a *purpose alert* is triggered. The respective open data together with the covered data allows for the reconstruction of the original information, subject to the detective purpose, e.g. sufficient suspicion. The *data with the reconstructed information* can be used in the *alert mode*, e.g. to hold perpetrators accountable. Note that lossless reductions are a generalization of the pseudonymization approach described in Sect. 2 (compare Fig. 1 and Fig. 3). The audit data with pseudonyms is open data being used in the normal surveillance mode, and the pseudonym recovery data is covered data, that can be used to reconstruct the identifying information in the original audit data, if and only if the detective purpose is met (purpose alert), i.e., a sufficient suspicion of misuse has occurred (threshold alert).

Both kinds of open data, as well as the supporting data should keep some information secret, even under inferences. In general, inference control is a highly challenging task that can only partially be solved in a purely algorithmic way, see e.g. [23, 24, 25]. Accordingly, in the context of intrusion detection, specific considerations are due.

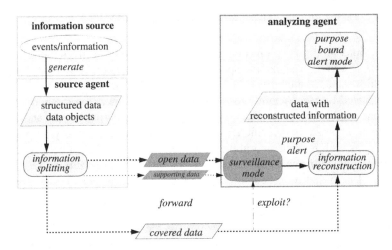

Fig. 3. Functional model for lossless reductions

6   Basic Requirements for Lossless Reductions

We summarize the required properties of the output of lossless reductions as follows:

– *Open data* in conjunction with *supporting data* must be sufficient for the normal *surveillance mode* of given kinds of analyzing agents.
– *Covered data* may possibly be exploited for the normal surveillance mode of given kinds of analyzing agents. The main use of the covered data is in the *alert mode* of given kinds of analyzing agents. For this purpose, the covered data must exhibit the following properties:
  • *correctness:* If the given purpose of the alert mode is met, the original information can be reconstructed by the analyzing agent from the open data together with the covered data. Note that this definition comprises technical and organizational purpose binding (cf. Sect. 2). However, in the following we focus on aspects of technical purpose binding.
  • *secrecy:* If the given purpose of the alert mode is not (yet) met, the original information cannot be determined by the analyzing agent from the open data, the supporting data and the covered data.
  • *verifiability:* If the analyzing agent does not trust the source agent to correctly perform the lossless reduction, the analyzing agent can recognize the covered data as useful for the surveillance mode, and for the information reconstruction for the alert mode.

7   Specific Requirements for Open Data

As required in Sect. 6 the open output data of lossless reductions must be sufficient for the normal surveillance mode of given kinds of analyzing agents. This also applies to lossy reductions. As a consequence and as mentioned in Sect. 5, accounting for the goal detective effectiveness requires domain knowledge about the cooperation method(s) used by the analyzing agent(s). Krgel et al. survey existing work on such cooperation methods and propose a straightforward model incorporating useful heuristics for reducing the number of alarms, while retaining the relevant information [7].

Identifying Requirements for the Effectiveness of Cooperation Methods

In the following, we briefly motivate the rationale of these heuristics and focus on those of the operations, which use the open output data as operands. The ability to obtain useful results via these operations must be sustained in open data. Thereby we derive concrete requirements that must be met when generating open data using lossless reductions for cooperating intrusion detection agents.

Unlike local events, which are considered atomic events with only one *timestamp*, alarms have a *start time* and an *end time*, because they may describe a set of events that occurred at possibly distinct points in time. As can be seen below, start and end times play a crucial role in alarm correlation.

Most proposed approaches use exact matches of certain common features to identify alerts to be fused. However, two approaches employ probabilistic similarity measures for IP addresses [11, 18], and one approach reasons about implications of IP network addresses and directory pathes [14]. Such constraints determine exact matches in the first p bits of the features, where p is the length of the common prefix of the features.

When aggregating/fusing a set of alarms into a complex alarm, the values of a given feature for all fused alarms are copied to the corresponding feature in the complex alarm, and the start and end time are determined from the set of alarms according to the semantics of the respective heuristic.

Firstly, alarms are mapped to a common format with common semantics and mandatory features (start time, end time, source, target), which are complemented in a best-effort manner. Then, various heuristics are applied to reduce the number of alarms by prioritizing alarms, or by fusing alarms into more complex alarms. For the names of the heuristics we follow the terminology of Krgel et. al. [7].

Alarm Fusion aims at discarding obvious duplicate alarms generated by different sensors when observing a given activity. Two given alarms are fused, if their start times fall in a configurable time interval, if they are generated by different sensors, and if for a given feature in both alarms the values are equal, if available. For alarm fusion, the distance of timestamps needs to be computed and compared to a constant value, and features are tested for equal content.

Alarm Verification aims at identifying irrelevant alarms and false alarms. As a prerequisite, a *verification database* is required, which maps each provided service to a verification method. The effect of a reported attack can be verified by determining the affected system service via the target port feature or the service identifier of the alarm and executing the associated verification method. For alarm verification, features are compared to entries in the verification database.

Attack Thread Reconstruction aims at representing subsequent alarms describing attacks from a given attacker on a given target. Two given alarms are fused, if the end time of one alarm and the start time of the other alarm fall in a configurable time interval, and they are reported for the same source and the same target. For attack thread reconstruction the distance of timestamps needs to be computed and compared to a constant value, and features are tested for equal content.

Attack Session Reconstruction aims at correlating alarms that describe events on the network and in a host. As a prerequisite, a *port-process database* is required, which (1) maps network transport protocol port numbers to the identifiers of the processes on the host, who listen on the respective ports, and which (2) describes the parent-child relationship of the processes on the host. Two given alarms are fused, if the end time of the network-based alarm falls in a configurable time interval with the start time of the host-based alarm, and the target port feature of the network-based alarm identifies a port that is listened on by the process that is identified by the process id feature of the host-based alarm. For attack session reconstruction, the distance of timestamps needs to be computed and compared to a constant value, and features are compared to entries of the port-process database.

Attack Focus Recognition aims at fusing alarms describing attacks where a given attacker attacks many targets, e.g. reconnaissance scans, or where a given target is attacked by many sources, e.g. distributed denial of service attacks. Two given alarms are fused, if their start times fall in a configurable sliding time window, and they are reported for the same source or the same target. For attack focus recognition, the distance of timestamps needs to be computed and compared to a constant value, and features are tested for equal content.

Multi Step Correlation aims at representing alarm patterns constituting complex attacks as complex alarms. This is achieved by alarm correlation. Different approaches to centralized [15, 19, 10, 20, 16, 18, 17, 21, 14] and distributed [5, 6, 7] alarm correlation have been proposed (cf. Sect. 4). The operations relevant wrt. lossless reductions are independent from the possibly distributed nature of these approaches. We have already analyzed the problem of lossless reduction by pseudonymization in depth for the centralized case [1], which also applies to the distributed case. For multi step correlation, the timestamps need to be compared wrt. to their order, and features are tested for equal content, or their features are compared to constant values.

Impact Analysis and Alarm Prioritization aim at determining the effect of an attack in order to prioritize the respective alarm accordingly. As a prerequisite, an *asset database* is required, which (1) maps provided services to the importance of the services, and which (2) models the dependencies of the services. The impact of an attack described by a given alarm can be determined by identifying the target port or service identifier feature of the alarm in the asset database and determining all services depending on that service. The identified services can then be correlated with service failures detected by service monitors.

Moreover, the asset database is used to determine the importance of the affected services and to prioritize the involved alarms accordingly. Alarms that have already been fused into more complex alarms, as well as alarms found to be irrelevant are set to a low priority, such that they are still available for review. For impact analysis and for alarm prioritization, features are compared to entries of the asset database.

Resulting Requirements for Open Data

It can be seen, that the following requirements are crucial for sustaining the functionality of the relevant operations of the above heuristics:

R1: certain alarm features (except for timestamps) need to be compared to certain alarm features for equal content, or equal prefix content
R2: certain alarm features (except for timestamps) need to be compared to values outside of the open data, e.g. constant values, entries of a database (see above)
R3: distances of alarm timestamps need to be computed and compared to values outside of the open data, i.e. a constant value
R4: the order of alarm timestamps needs to be determined

As a result, in order to sustain the effectiveness of the surveillance mode of the analyzing agent(s), lossy reductions must be designed, such that they do not remove timestamps and features that are used in the aforementioned operations (cf. Sect. 9).

Lossless reductions must be designed, such that the above operations can still be computed on the described alarm timestamps and alarm features, and such that the results of the operations are still meaningful, i.e., for an operation $\circ \in \{=_p, <, >\}$, where $=_p$ compares the features up to a suitably determined prefix p, including $=_\infty$ for the full length, and two operands op_1 and op_2 in the open data and for a lossless reduction $r()$ holds $op_1 \circ op_2 = r(op_1) \circ r(op_2)$.

Note that sustaining the ability to compare alarm features or operation results on alarm features to values outside of the open data may require to provide *supporting data*, i.e., the reduction $r_s()$ uses some parameter s, such that $op_1 \circ op_2 = r_s(op_1) \circ r_s(op_2)$ holds, where $r_s(op_1)$ is computed by the source agent and $r_s(op_2)$ is computed by the analyzing agent.

Specific Requirements for Pseudonyms in Open Data

In the following, we consider pseudonymization as a special case of lossless reductions, and we focus on the specific requirements for pseudonyms in the open data, such that the surveillance mode of the analyzing agent(s) sustains its detective effectiveness. Hence, the lossless reduction $r_s()$ replaces some feature f with an appropriate pseudonym $r_s(f)$, where s is a parameter that can be used to generate distinct pseudonyms for f. Note that $r_s(f)$ needs to preserve the comparability of feature prefixes, if required by R1, e.g. [26]. Also note that pseudonyms traditionally are used to hide personal data, such as identifiers of users, but within our generalized scope we consider pseudonyms as place-holders for arbitrary features. A pseudonym $r_s(f)$ is appropriate, if

- $r_s(f)$ respects the syntax constraints of the surveillance mode wrt. f
- $f =_p f' \Rightarrow r_s(f) =_p r_s(f')$ holds if R1 requires that f must be testable for equal content or prefix to an alarm feature f'; note that both $r_s(f)$ and $r_s(f')$ are computed by the source agent
- $f \neq_p f', s \neq s' \Rightarrow r_s(f) \neq_p r_s(f'), r_s(f) \neq_p r_{s'}(f')$ holds generally, i.e., $r_s()$ is collision-resistant, such that no unrelated alarms are correlated by accident
- $f = c \Rightarrow r_s(f) = r_s(c)$ holds if R2 requires $r_s(f)$ to be testable for equal content of a clear-text value c; note that $r_s(f)$ is computed by the source agent, who also provides s in the supporting data, such that the analyzing agent can compute $r_s(c)$

– $f \neq c \Rightarrow r_s(f) \neq r_s(c)$ holds generally, i.e. $r_s()$ is collision-resistant (see above)

Note that R2 can be required independently from R1 wrt. to f, such that R2 may be required in addition to R1. The source agent only needs to provide s in the supporting data, if R2 holds. Also note that a database lookup for a given $r_s(f)$ requires the analyzing agent to compute $r_s(c)$ for all c visited in the database, until a match is found.

In order to reduce the inferences an attacker can make on the transitive closure of a given pseudonym, it is desirable to use $r_s()$ in way, such that additionally

– $f =_p f' \Rightarrow r_s(f) \neq_p r_{s'}(f'), s \neq s'$ holds if R1 does not require that f must be testable for equal content or prefix to an alarm feature f'; note that the analyzing agent then does not need to and therefore is incapacitated to decide whether $f =_p f'$ or $f \neq_p f'$

We assume that all (source/analyzing) agents a priori know the heuristics, such that all agents know, when R1 and/or R2 are required. This assumption can be met by proper coordination of the configuration of all agents.

All source agents that pseudonymize a given f must choose s in a coordinated way, if R1 is required. Then, the analyzing agents can correlate alarms originating from distinct source agents by means of $r_s(f)$. If there is no coordination wrt. s, the following error can occur: $r_s(f) \neq_p r_{s'}(f'), s \neq s'$, despite $f =_p f'$, resulting in failure to correlate related alarms, i.e., the number of alarms is not reduced.

Depending on the given communication infrastructure it may be viable to choose s in a coordinated way. However, this seems to be impossible to achieve for simultaneously generated alarms, if there are real-time constraints to be respected, i.e., alarms cannot be buffered until s has been agreed upon by all agents. Note that a single centralized source agent can choose s randomly [1] and thus can significantly reduce the transitive closure of a given pseudonym, i.e. reduce the working surface of an attacker who reasons about pseudonyms. Assuming that a timely coordination of s with all source agents is impractical, s should be a static parameter that is known to all source agents cooperating with a given set of analyzing agents. If a source agent wants to prevent the analyzing agent from dictionary attacks yielding information about the source agent's private network, it could use a secret value s to pseudonymize all highly critical information. The down-side of this approach is, that the pseudonyms for the highly critical information cannot be correlated with alarms from other source agents. Our solutions for the centralized case need to be carefully adapted to the requirements wrt. s [1].

Regarding R3 and R4, currently no useful $r_s()$ is known, which meets these requirements in the distributed case. Thus, so far timestamps must not be pseudonymized in alarms. Note that time-shifting and enumeration can be used in the centralized case [27], but require timely coordination of all source agents in the distributed case, which we assumed to be impractical. However, timestamps could be coarsened by lossy reductions removing the more fine-grained time units (cf. [27, 28, 29] in Sect. 9), or the point in time could be hidden by removing the more coarse-grained time units [27].

8   Specific Requirements for Covered Data

In contrast to the open data the covered data is basically independent from the cooperation methods used by the analyzing agent(s). This results from the fact that the covered
data is not used in the surveillance mode. In the following, we ignore the extension that
the surveillance mode may exploit certain properties of the covered data. Rather, the
covered data is used for information reconstruction when a purpose alert is triggered in
the surveillance mode. This obviously results in fewer specific constraints for the design
of lossless reductions.

The basic requirements for lossless reductions must still be met in a distributed setup.
Regarding correctness, the lossless reduction must generate covered data that allows for
information reconstruction, even if the covered data used for information reconstruction
is generated by distinct source agents accounting for simultaneous events at different
locations of the system. As an example, a lossless reduction may provide the information, which is hidden in the open data, in several parts in masked form in the covered
data, where each *insufficient set of parts* satisfies the secrecy requirement. The information reconstruction requires a *sufficient set of parts* to enable reconstructing the hidden
information. Then, if several distinct source agents generate such parts accounting for
events at different locations of the system, the parts in the sufficient set must still "fit
together", such that the original information can be reconstructed.

Clearly, this requires the source agents to generate covered data in a coordinated way.
Note the analogy to the situation wrt. to the parameter s in Sect. 7. The same rationale
applies here, and we assume that a timely coordination of all source agents is impractical. As a result, covered data must be generated using only the original information to
be hidden and information that is known a priori to all source agents.

Extending Existing Solutions for Pseudonym Recovery Data

Considering our previous work using Shamir's threshold scheme for cryptographic secret sharing [4], we find that it is viable in the centralized case to choose keys for
encryption and decryption randomly, and that shares can be generated by using linear
sample points in an increasing order [3]. Both of these methods do not extend to the distributed case. We envision the following two solutions for the problem of distinct share
generation. First, each source agent is assigned his own interval for sample points, such
that each source agent generates distinct sample points. The downside of this approach
is, that the number of possible sample points per source agent is artificially limited
depending on the number of source agents. Second, source agents can choose sample
points pseudo-randomly, where each source agent initializes his pseudo-random number generator with a distinct secret. While this solution does not reduce the number of
possible sample points per source agent, there is a chance for collisions.

The problem of synchronized key generation in the absence of timely coordination could be solved by using cryptographic one-way functions to compute a key,
where some common secret and the feature to be encrypted are used as parameters.
Such a solution is less secure than using random keys, because the search-space is
reduced to all syntactically possible features, opening an avenue for dictionary
attacks.

9   Related Work and Conclusion

Slagell and Yurcik summarize related work in the field of audit data anonymization, analyze the problem based on a collection of attacks against anonymization schemes and propose a straightforward architecture for audit data anonymization considering merely lossy reductions [30]. However, their analysis focuses on the identifying information found within the audit data and does not sufficiently consider the linkability of features, as required by the applications using the audit data. The CANINE tool implemented by Slagell et al. is heavily geared to pseudonymization of network flows [27], merely provides for lossy reductions, and does not meet requirement R2. Similarly, Pang and Paxson turn their IDS Bro into a tool for network data anonymization [31], merely providing lossy reductions and no support for R2.

Lincoln et al. propose a solution for alarm repositories, which collect alarms from source agents and publish them for further analysis [28]. They analyze, which kinds of surveillance modes are supported by their solution with the result that they only support limited analysis capabilities. We take the other road, firstly analyzing the requirements for surveillance modes proposed by the community and then deriving requirements for designing appropriate solutions. The solution proposed by Lincoln et al. does not meet R1 wrt. prefixes and R2, and supports merely lossy reductions, it however introduces a notion of uncertainty by coarsening timestamp features. Xu and Ning propose the first solution directly aimed at supporting cooperation of intrusion detection agents [29]. They merely consider lossy information reduction by coarsening features using concept hierarchies. Obviously, coarsening features introduces uncertainty, leading to worse correlation results, which may or may not be acceptable.

Summarizing, there are currently no solutions supporting lossless reductions for cooperating distributed intrusion detection agents. Lossless reductions provide a chance for privacy protection without sacrificing the precision of surveillance mode results.

Our previous work and the proposed general model for information reduction for cooperating intrusion detection agents are aimed towards technically balancing the conflicting interests in intrusion detection. The general model brings up challenges with respect to intrusion detection, inference control and cryptography. For both, lossy and lossless information reductions, we identified the information requirements of the normal surveillance mode of the given analyzing agents. For lossless reductions we still need to identify and formalize the given purposes for the alert mode. According to these requirements we need to define appropriate data transformations and prove their effectiveness as well as their efficiency for both modes (intrusion detection). We provided first ideas, how the transformations we proposed for the centralized case [1] could be adapted to the distributed case.

For lossy reductions we need to prove that (a sufficient degree of) confidentiality is achieved with respect to remote agents (inference control) and in the case of coarsening we need to show that the detective effectiveness of the surveillance mode is only mildly affected. Finally, for lossless reductions we need to prove that they exhibit the properties correctness, secrecy preservation, verifiability and possibly further properties that are important in the context of the given analyzing agents (cryptography).

References

[1] Ulrich Flegel. *Pseudonymizing Audit Data for Privacy Respecting Misuse Detection*. PhD thesis, University of Dortmund, Dept. of Computer Science, 2005.

[2] Ulrich Flegel. Pseudonymizing Unix log files. In George Davida, Yair Frankel, and Owen Rees, editors, *Proceedings of the Infrastructure Security Conference (InfraSec2002)*, number 2437 in Lecture Notes in Computer Science, pages 162–179, Bristol, United Kingdom, October 2002. Springer.

[3] Joachim Biskup and Ulrich Flegel. Threshold-based identity recovery for privacy enhanced applications. In Sushil Jajodia and Pierangela Samarati, editors, *Proceedings of the 7th ACM Conference on Computer and Communications Security*, pages 71–79, Athens, Greece, November 2000. ACM SIGSAC, ACM Press.

[4] Adi Shamir. How to share a secret. *Communications of the ACM*, 22:612–613, 1979.

[5] Giovanni Vigna, Richard A. Kemmerer, and Per Blix. Designing a web of highly-configurable intrusion detection sensors. In Lee et al. [32], pages 69–84.

[6] Peng Ning, Sushil Jajodia, and X. Sean Wang. *Intrusion Detection in Distributed Systems*. Number 9 in Advances in Information Security. Springer, 2004.

[7] Christopher Krgel, Fredrik Valeur, and Giovanni Vigna. *Intrusion Detection and Correlation*. Number 14 in Advances in Information Security. Springer, 2005.

[8] Ming-Yuh Huang, Robert J. Jasper, and Thomas M. Wicks. A large scale distributed intrusion detection framework based on attack strategy analysis. *Computer Networks*, 31(23–24):2465–2475, 1999.

[9] Tim Bass. Intrusion detection systems and multisensor data fusion. *Communications of the ACM*, 43(4):99–105, 2000.

[10] Hervé Debar and Andreas Wespi. Aggregation and correlation of intrusion-detection alerts. In Lee et al. [32], pages 85–103.

[11] Alfonso Valdes and Keith Skinner. Probabilistic alert correlation. In Lee et al. [32], pages 54–68.

[12] Frédéric Cuppens. Managing alerts in a multi-intrusion detection environment. In *Proceedings of the 17th Annual Computer Security Applications Conference (ACSAC 2001)*, pages 22–31, New Orleans, Louisiana, USA, December 2001. IEEE Computer Society Press.

[13] Philip A. Porras, Martin W. Fong, and Alfonso Valdes. A mission-impact-based approach to INFOSEC alarm correlation. In Andreas Wespi, Giovanni Vigna, and Luca Deri, editors, *Proceedings of the Fifth International Symposium on Recent Advances in Intrusion Detection (RAID 2002)*, number 2516 in Lecture Notes in Computer Science, pages 95–114, Zurich, Switzerland, October 2002. Springer.

[14] Dingbang Xu and Peng Ning. Alert correlation through triggering events and common resources. In *Proceedings of the 20th Annual Computer Security Applications Conference (ACSAC 2004)*, pages 360–369, Tucson, Arizona, USA, December 2004. IEEE Computer Society Press.

[15] Louis Perrochon, Eunhei Jang, and David C. Luckham. Enlisting event patterns for cyber battlefield awareness. In *Proceedings of the DARPA Information Survivability Conference and Exposition (DISCEX 2000)*, pages 1411–1422, Hilton Head, South Carolina, January 2000. DARPA and the IEEE Computer Society, IEEE Press.

[16] Nathan Carey, Andrew Clark, and George Mohay. IDS interoperability and correlation using IDMEF and commodity systems. In *Proceedings of the Fourth International Conference on Information and Communications Security (ICICS 2002)*, number 2513 in Lecture Notes in Computer Science, pages 252–264, Singapore, December 2002.

[17] Benjamin Morin and Hervé Debar. Correlation of intrusion symptoms: An application of chronicles. In Giovanni Vigna, Erland Jonsson, and Christopher Krgel, editors, *Proceedings of the Sixth International Symposium on Recent Advances in Intrusion Detection (RAID 2003)*, number 2820 in Lecture Notes in Computer Science, pages 94–112, Pittsburgh, Pennsylvania, USA, September 2003. Springer.

[18] Oliver M. Dain and Robert K. Cunningham. *Applications of Data Mining in Computer Security*, chapter Fusing Heterogeneous Alert Streams into Scenarios. Kluwer, Boston, 2002.

[19] Steven J. Templeton and Karl Levitt. A requires/provides model for computer attacks. In *Proceedings of the New Security Paradigms Workshop*, pages 31–38, Cork, Ireland, September 2000. ACM, ACM Press.

[20] Frédéric Cuppens and Alexandre Miège. Alert correlation in a cooperative intrusion detection framework. In *Proceedings of the IEEE Symposium on Research in Security and Privacy*, pages 202–215, Berkeley, California, USA, May 2002. IEEE, IEEE Press.

[21] Peng Ning, Yun Cui, Douglas S. Reeves, and Dingbang Xu. Techniques and tools for analyzing intrusion alerts. *ACM Transactions on Information and System Security*, 7(2):274–318, May 2004.

[22] Peng Ning and Dingbang Xu. Learning attack strategies from intrusion alerts. In Sushil Jajodia, Vijay Atluri, and Trent Jaeger, editors, *Proceedings of the 10th ACM Conference on Computer and Communications Security*, pages 200–209, Washington, D.C., USA, October 2003. ACM SIGSAC, ACM Press.

[23] Dorothy E. Denning. *Cryptography and Data Security*. Addison-Wesley, 1982.

[24] Csilla Farkas and Sushil Jajodia. The inference problem: a survey. *ACM SIGKDD Explorations Newsletter*, 4(2):6–11, 2002.

[25] Joachim Biskup and Piero A. Bonatti. Controlled query evaluation for enforcing confidentiality in complete information systems. *International Journal of Information Security*, 3(1):14–27, 2004.

[26] Jun Xu, Jinliang Fan, Mostafa Ammar, and Sue B. Moon. Prefix-preserving IP address anonymization: Measurement-based security evaluation and a new cryptography-based scheme. In *Proceedings of the 10th IEEE International Conference on Network Protocols (ICNP)*, pages 280–289, 2002.

[27] Yifan Li, Adam Slagell, Katherine Luo, and William Yurcik. CANINE: A combined converter and anonymizer tool for processing netflows for security. In *Proceedings of the international Conference on Telecommunication Systems - Modeling and Analysis (ICTSM 2005)*, Dallas, Texas, USA, November 2005.

[28] Patrick Lincoln, Phillip Porras, and Vitaly Shmatikov. Privacy-preserving sharing and correlation of security alerts. In *Proceedings of the 13th USENIX Security Symposium*, pages 239–254, San Diego, California, USA, August 2004.

[29] Dingbang Xu and Peng Ning. Privacy-preserving alert correlation: A concept hierarchy based approach. In *Proceedings of the 21st Annual Computer Security Applications Conference (ACSAC 2005)*, pages 537–546, Tucson, Arizona, USA, December 2005. IEEE Computer Society Press.

[30] Adam Slagell and William Yurcik. Sharing computer network logs for security and privacy: A motivation for new methodologies of anonymization. In *Workshop on the Value of Security through Collaboration (SECOVAL)*, 2005.

[31] Ruoming Pang and Vern Paxson. A high-level programming environment for packet trace anonymization and transformation. In *Proceedings of the 2003 Conference on Applications, Technologies, Architectures, and Protocols for Computer Communications (SIGCOMM 2003)*, pages 339–351, Karlsruhe, Germany, August 2003. ACM, ACM Press.

[32] Wenke Lee, Ludovic Mé and Andreas Wespi, editors. *Proceedings of the Fourth International Symposium on Recent Advances in Intrusion Detection (RAID 2001)*, number 2212 in Lecture Notes in Computer Science, Davis, California, October 2001. Springer.

Quantum Algorithm for Solving the Discrete Logarithm Problem in the Class Group of an Imaginary Quadratic Field and Security Comparison of Current Cryptosystems at the Beginning of Quantum Computer Age

Arthur Schmidt*

Technische Universität Darmstadt, Fachbereich Informatik
Fachgebiet Kryptographie und Computeralgebra
Hochschulstr. 10, 64289 Darmstadt

Abstract. In this paper, we present a quantum algorithm which solves the discrete logarithm problem in the class group of an imaginary quadratic number field. We give an accurate estimation of the qubit complexity for this algorithm. Based on this result and analog results for the factoring and the discrete logarithm problem in the point group of an elliptic curve, we compare the run-times of cryptosystems which are based on problems above. Assuming that the size of quantum computers will grow slowly, we give proposals which cryptosystem should be used if middle-size quantum computers will be built.

1   Introduction

In [Sho94] Peter Shor has presented quantum algorithms which solve the factoring and the discrete logarithm problems in quantum polynomial time. These problems are very difficult in the classical computer model. Therefore they provide a basis for the security of the most currently-used public key cryptosystems. If large quantum computers are built in the future, then almost all public key cryptosystems which are used today will be broken. This threat makes cryptographers to investigate the impact of quantum computers closely. There are two possibilities to face it. The first one is to develop alternative cryptosystems which are based on other primitives (e.g lattice based cryptosystems). The second one is to increase the key sizes of current cryptosystems. As long as the size of quantum computers is not to large, the second possibility seems to be the better choice. We will analyze it in this paper.

The first quantum computer had two qubits. It was built in 1998 [CVZ+98]. In 2000 Shor's algorithm was implemented on a 5-qubit-computer [VSB+00]. One year later a 7-qubit-computer could be built [VSB+01]. The number 15 could be factorized on this computer using Shor's algorithm. The next improvement came up in 2005. A quantum register consisting of 8-qubits was constructed

---

* Research supported by the DFG.

G. Müller (Ed.): ETRICS 2006, LNCS 3995, pp. 481–493, 2006.

[HHR+05]. Building large quantum computers seems to be a difficult, maybe impossible, task. However it is important for cryptographers to assume that this task will be achieved.

In this paper, we will consider public key cryptosystems which are based on the following three problems:

- the factoring problem,
- the discrete logarithm problem in $\mathbb{F}_p^\times$, in the point group of an elliptic curve over $\mathbb{F}_p$, and in the ideal class group of imaginary quadratic fields,
- the principal ideal problem in real quadratic number fields.

Classical security of cryptosystems is based on the running time of the best attack which breaks a cryptosystem. In [LV01] Lenstra and Verheul presented heuristics for key sizes for RSA and cryptosystems based on discrete logarithms. In [HM00] and [Ham02], the security of cryptosystems based on class groups of imaginary quadratic fields is analyzed. In [Vol03], Vollmer analyzed algorithms for real quadratic number fields.

On quantum computers the runtime of attacks is polynomial. Therefore the security parameter from last paragraph becomes obsolete. Assuming that the size of quantum computers will grow slowly, we introduce a new security parameter: *the number of qubits* which are necessary to implement an attack. By the number of qubits, we mean the number of logical qubits. Due to quantum mechanics, several errors may occur on qubits. This problem can be overcame by encoding a logical qubit into many physical qubits and by applying error correcting techniques.

In algorithms below we try to reduce the number of working qubits. Sometimes this yields to a longer runtime. We accept this, as long as this time stays polynomial. Running times of Shor's algorithm can be found in [Kun].

Solving discrete logarithms on quantum computers requires quantum algorithms for computation in the underlying groups. These algorithms are well know for classical computers. In order to run them on quantum computers they must be made reversible. If there is no limit for the number of qubits, then this task can be easily done [Ben77]. However, we want to reduce the number of qubits which becomes very tricky.

Algorithms for factoring are well investigated. There were a lot of improvements of original algorithm by Shor. The best known algorithm can be found in [Bea]. Algorithms for efficient computing on elliptic curves are published in [PZ]. In our paper we will present algorithms for computing in the class group of imaginary quadratic fields.

The paper is structured as follows. In the second section, we summarize the results for factoring and solving the discrete logarithm problem in $\mathbb{F}_p^\times$ and on elliptic curves. In the third section, we give a necessary background of number theory and present quantum logarithms for solving the discrete log problem in the ideal class group of imaginary quadratic fields. In the fourth section, we compare the security of cryptosystems and describe runtime test which we carried out to determine which cryptosystem is the fastest one concerning the new security parameter. Moreover we compare the key sizes of several cryptosystems.

2   Previous Work

In this section, we collect the results of papers by Beauregard [Bea] and Proos and Zalka [PZ] in which the best currently known algorithms for factoring and for solving the discrete logarithm problem are presented.

We need these results for comparisons in Section 4.

2.1   Factoring and DL Problem in $\mathbb{F}_p^\times$

In [Bea] the author present a factoring algorithm which requires only $2n + 3$ qubits to factor a n-bit integer. This number of qubits is achieved by using the quantum addition [Dra00] and the semi-classical Fourier transform [GN].

This algorithm can be easily extended to an algorithm for solving the discrete logarithm problem in the group $\mathbb{F}_p^\times$, which can be implemented using $2 \operatorname{size}(p) + 3$ qubits.

2.2   DL Problem on Elliptic Curves

In [PZ] the authors propose an algorithm for solving the discrete logarithm problem in the point group of an elliptic curve over $\mathbb{F}_p$. They prove that a cryptosystem based on an elliptic curve in $\mathbb{F}_p^\times$ can be broken by using approx. $7 \log_2 p + 4 \log_2 \log_2 p$ qubits. Moreover, the authors reduce the number of qubits to approx. $5 \log_2 p + 8(\log_2 p)^{1/2} + \log_2 \log_2 p$ by using some unproven assumptions. These results can be further improved which we will show in a subsequent paper. One trivial improvement can be achieved by replacing the classical addition used in [PZ] by quantum addition proposed in [Dra00]. This reduces the last result by n qubits. In Section 4, we will use this improved result.

3   DL Problem IQ-NF

In [BW88] and [BW90], Buchmann and Williams propose to use the ideal class group of imaginary quadratic number fields for public key cryptosystems. The security of this proposal was considered in [HM00]. In [Ham02] Hamdy showed that there are secure and fast cryptosystems which underlying group is the group of ideal classes in an imaginary quadratic field. In this section we will describe this group and present quantum algorithms for computation in it.

3.1   Number Theory Background

Let Δ be a negative integer such that $\Delta \equiv 0, 1 \mod 4$. Then the module $\mathcal{O}_\Delta = \mathbb{Z} + \frac{\Delta + \sqrt{\Delta}}{2}\mathbb{Z}$ is the imaginary-quadratic order. The field of fractions of the order $\mathcal{O}_\Delta$ is the imaginary quadratic field $\mathcal{K} = \mathbb{Q}(\sqrt{\Delta})$. Let $\mathcal{X}$ and $\mathcal{Y}$ be two subsets of $\mathcal{K}$, then the product $\mathcal{X}\mathcal{Y}$ is the additive subgroup of $\mathcal{K}$ generated by $\{xy \mid x \in \mathcal{X}, y \in \mathcal{Y}\}$. An $\mathcal{O}_\Delta$-ideal is a module $\mathfrak{a} \subseteq \mathcal{O}_\Delta$ such that $\mathfrak{a}\mathcal{O}_\Delta \subseteq \mathfrak{a}$. An $\mathcal{O}_\Delta$-ideal

$\mathfrak{a}$ is invertible, if there exists an ideal $\mathfrak{b}$ with $\mathfrak{a}\mathfrak{b} = \mathcal{O}_\Delta$. Each $\mathcal{O}_\Delta$-ideal $\mathfrak{a}$ has the following form

$$\mathfrak{a} = q(a\mathbb{Z} + \frac{b + \sqrt{\Delta}}{2}\mathbb{Z}),$$

where $a, b \in \mathbb{Z}$, $q \in \mathbb{Q}$, $a, q > 0$, b is unique modulo $2a$, $c = (b^2 - \Delta)/(4a) \in \mathbb{Z}$, and $\gcd(a, b, c) = 1$. We denote such an ideal by (a, b). An ideal (a, b) is normal if $-a < b \leq a$. Let (a, b) be a normal representation of an ideal $\mathfrak{a}$ and $c = (b^2 - \Delta)/(4a)$. Then $\mathfrak{a}$ is reduced if $a < c$ or if $a = c$ and $b > 0$. Two $\mathcal{O}_\Delta$-ideals $\mathfrak{a}$ and $\mathfrak{b}$ are equivalent if there is $\alpha \in \mathcal{K}$ such that $\mathfrak{b} = \alpha\mathfrak{a}$. Each equivalence class contains exactly one reduced ideal. If (a, b) is reduced, then we have $|b| \leq a \leq \sqrt{|\Delta|/3}$. The set of equivalence classes of $\mathcal{O}_\Delta$-ideals forms a finite abelian group under ideal multiplication. We will denote this group by Cl_Δ. We have $|Cl_\Delta| \leq \sqrt{|\Delta|}$. We will present the group elements by reduced ideals. This is a short and unique representation. The group operation of Cl_Δ consists of two steps. The first step is the composition two ideals (a_1, b_1), (a_2, b_2) using the equations $a = a_1 a_2 / m$ and $b = (j a_2 b_1 + k a_1 b_2 + l(b_1 b_2 + \Delta)/2)/m \mod 2a$, where $j a_2 + k a_1 + l(b_1 + b_2)/2 = m = \gcd(a_1, a_2, (b_1 + b_2)/2)$. The resulting ideal is (a, b). The second step is to reduce (a, b). This can be done by applying the reduction operator

$$\rho(a, b) = (c, -b + 2sc), \quad \text{where } c = (b^2 - \Delta)/(4a) \text{ and } s \in \mathbb{Z} \quad \text{(1)}$$
$$\text{such that } -a < -b + 2sc \leq a$$

as long as (a, b) is not reduced. At most $\log_2(a/\sqrt{|\Delta|})$ reduction steps are necessary to reduce a normal ideal (a, b). We will call the number s from (1) *the normalization factor*. Let $s_1, \ldots, s_k$ be all normalization factors which occurs during the reduction of the normal ideal (a, b). Let $p_0 = 0$, $q_0 = 1$, $p_i = q_{i-1}$ and $q_i = q_{i-1} s_i - p_{i-1}$ for $1 \leq i \leq k$. Then we have $|p_i|, |q_i| \leq 2a/\sqrt{|\Delta|}$ for $0 \leq i \leq k$.

3.2   Elementary Gates and Arithmetic Operations

In our algorithms we will use the following elementary gates: the Hadamard gate, the Toffoly gate, the R_k gate, and the controlled R_k gate (see [NC00]). These gates are sufficient to perform the algorithms presented below.

Now we shortly mention the elementary arithmetical operations which we will use in the following sections. For addition and subtraction, we will use algorithms proposed in [Dra00] because they don't need working qubits. Their runtime is $O(t^2)$ for t-bit numbers. They can easily be extended to algorithms for multiplication and division which runtime is $O(t^3)$. Multiplication modulo a number is presented in [Bea]. In our algorithms, we have to perform the extended Euclidean algorithm. Such an algorithm can be found in [PZ]. It executes the following quantum operation:

$$|a\rangle, |b\rangle, |0\rangle \xrightarrow{\text{XGCD}} |g\rangle, |x\rangle, |\text{temp}\rangle,$$

where $g = \gcd(a, b)$ and $ax + by = g$ with an integer y. Its running time is $O(t^3)$, where $t = \max\{\text{size}(a), \text{size}(b)\}$. In addition to in/output, the algorithm needs approx. $3t$ qubits for internal computations.

Additionally we will use the algorithm $\textsc{Sgn}(x)$ which returns 1 if $x \geq 0$ and 0 if $x < 0$.

3.3   Algorithms for Ideal Classes

In this section, we will present algorithms for computing in the ideal class group of an imaginary-quadratic field. Based on these algorithms, we will explain how to solve the discrete logarithm problem in this group.

Since each equivalence class contains exactly one reduced ideal we can use this ideal to represent the equivalence class. This representation has the advantages of being short and unique. The uniqueness is necessary for the quantum discrete logarithm algorithm. The multiplication in the class group will be done in the classical way. First, we will compose the reduced representatives of two ideal classes. Afterwards we will reduce the resulting ideal. Thereby, it is important to rearrange the classical algorithm to reduce the number of working qubits.

In every reduction step we will obtain a normalization factor s. This factor is important for the reversibility of the reduction algorithm. We will store this factor in registers p and q (see Section 3.1 for this procedure).

In the presented algorithms we will use the following notation. We will write $|x\rangle$ for a quantum register which contains x. If x is given classically, we will write just x.

Algorithm 1. Composition

Input: $|a_1\rangle$, $|b_1\rangle$, a_2, b_2, Δ, where (a_1, b_1) and (a_2, b_2) are reduced $\mathcal{O}_\Delta$-ideals of a quadratic number field.
Output: $|a\rangle$, $|b\rangle$, $|a_1\rangle$, $|b_1\rangle$ such that $(a, b) = (a_1, b_1) \star (a_2, b_2)$ and $0 \leq b < 2a$.

1. Use XGCD, XGCD†, and XGCD to compute j_1, j_2, m_1, and m such that $j_1 a_2 + k_1 a_1 = m_1 = \gcd(a_2, a_1)$ and $j_2 m_1 + l\frac{b_1 + b_2}{2} = m = \gcd(m_1, \frac{b_1 + b_2}{2})$, where $k_1, l \in \mathbb{Z}$.
2. $a \leftarrow (a_1/m)(a_2/m)$
3. $b \leftarrow j_1 j_2 (a_2/m) b_1 \bmod 2a$
4. $b \leftarrow b + (j_2 m - j_1 j_2 a_2/m) b_2 \bmod 2a$
5. $b \leftarrow b + (b_1 b_2 + \Delta)/(2m) \cdot 2(m - j_2 m_1)/(b_1 + b_2) \bmod 2a$
6. Use XGCD†, XGCD, XGCD† to uncompute j_1, j_2, m_1, and m.
7. Return: $|a\rangle$, $|b\rangle$, $|a_1\rangle$, $|b_1\rangle$

Lemma 1. *Let Δ be a discriminant of an imaginary quadratic number field and $\mathfrak{a}$ and $\mathfrak{b}$ reduced $\mathcal{O}_\Delta$-ideals. On input $\mathfrak{a}$, $\mathfrak{b}$ and Δ, the algorithm* Composition *computes the composition of $\mathfrak{a}$ and $\mathfrak{b}$ in time $O((\log|\Delta|)^3)$. It can be implemented using approx. $6.5\log_2|\Delta| + \log_2\log_2|\Delta|$ qubits.*

Proof. Let $\mathfrak{a} = (a_1, b_1)$ and $\mathfrak{b} = (a_2, b_2)$. We first prove the correctness of the algorithm. After step one, we have

$$j_1 j_2 a_2 + k_1 j_2 a_1 + l\frac{b_1 + b_2}{2} = m = \gcd(a_1, a_2, \frac{b_1 + b_2}{2}), \tag{2}$$

where $k_1, l \in \mathbb{Z}$. After step two we obtain $a = (a_1/m)(a_2/m) = a_1 a_2/m^2$. Finally after step 5, we have

$$
b = \left(\left(j_1 j_2 \frac{a_2}{m} b_1 \mod 2a + (j_2 m - \frac{j_1 j_2 a_2}{m}) b_2 \right) \mod 2a + \right.
$$
$$
\left. + \frac{b_1 b_2 + \Delta}{2m} \frac{2(m - j_2 m_1)}{b_1 + b_2} \right) \mod 2a \equiv
$$
$$
\equiv \frac{j_1 j_2 a_2 b_1 + k_1 j_2 a_1 b_2 + l(b_1 b_2 + \Delta)/2}{m} \mod 2a.
$$

The runtime of the algorithm follows from Section 3.2.

Finally, we estimate a upper bound for the number of qubits. Since the input ideals are reduced we have $a_1, a_2, |b_1|, |b_2|, |j_1|, |j_2|, m_1, m \leq \sqrt{|\Delta|/3}$ and $a, |b| \leq |\Delta|/3$. An exact analysis shows that we need approx. $6.5 \log_2 |\Delta| + \log_2 \log_2 |\Delta|$ qubits in step 6 and that this number is sufficient for the whole algorithm. □

Now we present an algorithm which computes one reduction step.

Algorithm 2. RHO

Input: $|\text{control}\rangle$, $|a\rangle$, $|b\rangle$, Δ, where (a, b) is a $\mathcal{O}_\Delta$-ideal. If control = 1, then (a, b) is not reduced.
Output: $|\text{control}\rangle$, $|a'\rangle$, $|b'\rangle$, and $|s\rangle$. If control = 1, then $(a', b') = \rho(a, b)$ and $s = \lfloor (b + a')/(2a') \rfloor$. Otherwise, if control = 0, then $(a', b') = (a, b)$ and $s = 0$.

1: $a' \leftarrow (b^2 - \Delta)/(4a)$
2: **if** control = 0 **then** $b_{new} \leftarrow -b$, SWAP(a', a)
3: $a \leftarrow 4aa' - b^2 + \Delta$ /* $a = 0$ */
4: $s \leftarrow \lfloor (b + a')/(2a') \rfloor$
5: $b' \leftarrow -b + 2sa'$
6: **Return:** $|\text{control}\rangle$, $|a'\rangle$, $|b'\rangle$ and $|s\rangle$

The correctness of the algorithm is easy to see. Its complexity is estimated in the following lemma.

Lemma 2. *Let $t = \max\{\text{size}(a), \text{size}(b)\}$. Then the runtime of RHO is $O(t^3)$. It can be implemented using $4t$ qubits.*

Lemma 3. *The algorithm* cUNCOMPUTES *is correct. Let $t = \max\{\text{size}(p), \text{size}(q), \text{size}(s)\}$. Then the runtime of the algorithm is $O(t^3)$. It can be implemented by using $4t + 4$ qubits.*

We need the following lemmas for later considerations,

Lemma 4. *For* cUNCOMPUTES, *the following statement is true. If $|s| > 1$, then $|q'| > |p'|$.*

Proof. Let $|q| > |p|$ and $|s| > 1$, then we have $|q'| = |sq - p| \geq |s||q| - |p| \geq (|s| - 1)|q| \geq |q| = |p'|$. □

The following algorithm uncomputes s by updating p and q and producing one auxiliary qubit.

Algorithm 3. cUNCOMPUTES

Input: $|\text{control}\rangle$, $|p\rangle$, $|q\rangle$, $|s\rangle$ with $|q| > |p|$.
Output: $|\text{control}\rangle$, $|p'\rangle$, $|q'\rangle$, and $|\text{SGN}(p)\rangle$. If control $= 1$, then $p' = q$ and $q' = sq - p$. Otherwise, if control $= 0$, then $p' = p$ and $q' = q$.

1: **if** control $= 1$ **then** $t \leftarrow \text{SGN}(p)$, $p \leftarrow -p + sq$, $\text{SWAP}(p, q)$
2:
3: /* Compute $s' = s$ using new p, q, and t */
4: $s_1 \leftarrow \text{SGN}(q) \oplus \text{SGN}(p)$ /* $s_1 = 1$ iff sign(s) $= -1$ */
5: $s_2 \leftarrow \text{SGN}(q) \oplus t$
6: $s' \leftarrow (-1)^{s_1}(\lfloor |q|/|p| \rfloor + s_2)$
7:
8: **if** control $= 1$ **then** $s \leftarrow s - s'$ /* if control $= 1$, then $s \leftarrow 0$ */
9:
10: /* Uncompute s', s_1, and s_2 */
11: $s' \leftarrow s' - (-1)^{s_1}(\lfloor |q'|/|p'| \rfloor + s_2)$
12: $s_2 \leftarrow s_2 \oplus \text{SGN}(q) \oplus t$
13: $s_1 \leftarrow s_1 \oplus \text{SGN}(q) \oplus \text{SGN}(p)$
14:
15: Return: $|\text{control}\rangle$, $|p\rangle$, $|q\rangle$, $|t\rangle$

Lemma 5. *Let Δ be a discriminant of an imaginary quadratic number field, $\mathfrak{a} = (a, b)$ a normal $\mathcal{O}_\Delta$-ideal, and $c = (b^2 - \Delta)/(4a)$. Then the following statements are true:*

1. *If $a \leq \lfloor \sqrt{|\Delta|/3} \rfloor$, then $\rho(\mathfrak{a})$ is reduced.*
2. *If $a \leq \lfloor \sqrt{|\Delta|/3} \rfloor$, then $s(\mathfrak{a}) = \lfloor (b + c)/(2c) \rfloor \leq 1$.*
3. *If $c > \lfloor \sqrt{|\Delta|/3} \rfloor$, then $s(\mathfrak{a}) = \lfloor (b + c)/(2c) \rfloor > 1$.*

Proof. Let Δ, $\mathfrak{a}$, a, b, c, and $s = s(\mathfrak{a})$ be defined as in the lemma.

1. Since $a \leq \lfloor \sqrt{|\Delta|/3} \rfloor < \sqrt{|\Delta|}$, the statement is true.
2. Let $a \leq \lfloor \sqrt{|\Delta|/3} \rfloor$, then we have $c = (b^2 + |\Delta|)/(4a) \geq (\sqrt{3}/4)a$. If $b \geq 0$, then $s = \lfloor (c + b)/(2c) \rfloor \leq \lfloor (1 + a/c)/2 \rfloor \leq \lfloor (1 + 4/\sqrt{3})/2 \rfloor = 1$ and $s = \lfloor (c + b)/(2c) \rfloor \geq \lfloor c/(2c) \rfloor \geq 0$. If $b < 0$, then $s = \lfloor (c - |b|)/(2c) \rfloor \geq \lfloor (1 - 4/\sqrt{3})/2 \rfloor = -1$ and $s = \lfloor (c - |b|)/(2c) \rfloor \leq \lfloor c/(2c) \rfloor \leq 0$.
3. We prove the equivalent statement. Let (a, b) be not reduced, and $s \leq 1$, then $c \leq \lfloor \sqrt{|\Delta|/3} \rfloor$.
   If $s = 0$, then $\rho(\mathfrak{a}) = (c, -b)$ is reduced. Thus we have $c \leq \lfloor \sqrt{|\Delta|/3} \rfloor$. If $s = 1$, then $\rho(f) = (c, -b + 2c)$. If $\rho(\mathfrak{a})$ is reduced, then we have $c \leq \lfloor \sqrt{|\Delta|/3} \rfloor$. Otherwise, assume $\rho(\mathfrak{a})$ is not reduced. Then we have $c \geq c - b + a$. But since $|b| \leq a$ we have $c \leq c - b + a$. Therefore we have $b = a$ and $c = c - b + a$. It follows $c \leq \lfloor \sqrt{|\Delta|/3} \rfloor$. $\qquad\square$

Next we present the reduction algorithm.

Algorithm 4. REDUCE

Input: $|a\rangle$, $|b\rangle$, Δ, $\delta = \lfloor\sqrt{|\Delta|/3}\rfloor$, where $0 < a \leq \Delta/3$, $0 \leq b < 2a$, and (a,b) is a $\mathcal{O}_\Delta$-ideal.

Output: $|a'\rangle$, $|b'\rangle$, and $|\text{temp}\rangle$, where (a',b') is the reduced ideal in the equivalence class of (a,b) and $|\text{temp}\rangle$ contains auxiliary qubits, which are necessary for the reversibility.

1: $p \leftarrow 0$, counter $\leftarrow 0$, $q \leftarrow 1$, control $\leftarrow 0$
2:
3: /* Normalize (a,b) */
4: **if** $b > a$ **then** $s_0 \leftarrow 1$ **else** $s_0 \leftarrow 0$
5: **if** $s_0 = 1$ **then** $b \leftarrow b - 2a$
6:
7: **if** $a > \delta$ **then** control $\leftarrow$ control $\oplus 1$
8: **for** $i = 1, \ldots, \lfloor(\log|\Delta|)/2 + 1\rfloor$ **do**
9:     (control, a, b, s) $\leftarrow$ RHO(control, a, b) /* if control $= 1$, then $(a,b) \leftarrow \rho(a,b)$ */
10:     (control, p, q, t_i) $\leftarrow$ cUNCOMPUTES(control, p, q, s) /* if control $= 1$, then uncompute s */
11:     **if** counter $= 0$ and $a \leq \delta$ **then** control $\leftarrow$ control $\oplus 1$
12:     **if** control $= 0$ **then** counter $\leftarrow$ counter $+ 1$
13: **end for**
14: /* if (a,b) is not reduced, then apply RHO once more */
15: $c \leftarrow (-\Delta + b^2)/(4a)$
16: **if** $a > c$ or $(a = c$ and $b < 0)$ **then** $l \leftarrow 1$ **else** $l \leftarrow 0$
17: $c \leftarrow c - (-\Delta + b^2)/(4a)$ /* Uncompute c */
18: $(l, a, b, s) \leftarrow$ RHO(l, a, b)
19:
20: Return: $|a\rangle$, $|b\rangle$, $|p, q, \text{counter}, s_0, s, l, t_1, \ldots, t_{\lfloor(\log\Delta)/2+1\rfloor}\rangle$

Lemma 6. *Let Δ be a discriminant of an imaginary-quadratic number field and $\mathfrak{a} = (a,b)$ a $\mathcal{O}_\Delta$-ideal such that $0 < a \leq \Delta/3$ and $0 \leq b < 2a$. On input $\mathfrak{a}$, Δ and $\lfloor\sqrt{|\Delta|/3}\rfloor$, REDUCE computes the reduced ideal in the equivalence class of $\mathfrak{a}$ in time $O((\log|\Delta|)^4)$. It can be implemented using approx. $5\log_2|\Delta|$ qubits.*

Proof. We sketch the proof of Lemma 6.

Since $a \leq |\Delta|/3$, it follows from Section 3.1 that the number of reduction steps is at most $\log_2(a/\sqrt{|\Delta|}) + 2 \leq \log_2(\sqrt{|\Delta|}/3) + 2 \leq (\log_2|\Delta|)/2 + 1$. This shows that the number of iteration in line 8 is sufficient. As long as $a > \delta$, the algorithm RHO is applied and we have $s > 1$ (see Lemma 5) such that the precondition of cUNCOMPUTES is fulfilled. If $a \leq \delta$, then by Lemma 5 at most one reduction step is necessary to obtain a reduced ideal which is performed in lines 15–18. By using a control qubit $|\text{control}\rangle$, we control how many times a reduction step is executed. If a becomes less than or equal to δ at first time, then the control qubit is set to zero and no reduction steps will be executed anymore in the loop.

Finally we estimate the number of qubits. For input parameters a and b, we need $\lfloor 2\log_2|\Delta|\rfloor + 2$ qubits. Since $p, q \leq (2/3)\sqrt{|\Delta|}$, we need approx. Δ qubits to store p and q. For applying algorithms RHO and cUNCOMPUTES, $2\log_2|\Delta|$ auxiliary qubits are sufficient. Let a_{old} be the number a before a reduction step and a_{new} the number a immediately after a reduction step. Then we have $a_{new} \leq a_{old}/2$. Hence we can reduce the size of $|a\rangle$ by one qubit in each iteration and use this qubit to store $t_1, t_2, \dots$ Similarly, we can use register sharing to store counter. It follows that $5\log_2|\Delta|$ qubits are necessary to perform REDUCE.

The given runtime of the algorithms follows from Lemmas 2 and 3.   □

By combining the algorithms above, we obtain the following algorithm for multiplication in the ideal class group.

Algorithm 5. MULTIPLY

Input: A control qubit $|control\rangle$, a discriminant $\Delta < 0$, $|a_1\rangle$, $|b_1\rangle$, a_2, b_2, where (a_1, b_1) and (a_2, b_2) are reduced $\mathcal{O}_\Delta$-ideals.
Output: $|control\rangle$, $|a_{out}\rangle$, $|b_{out}\rangle$. If control = 1, then (a_{out}, b_{out}) is a reduced $\mathcal{O}_\Delta$-ideal in the equivalence class of $(a_1, b_1) \star (a_2, b_2)$. Otherwise, if control = 0, then $(a_{out}, b_{out}) = (a_1, b_1)$.

1: /* Compute a_{out}, b_{out} */
2: $(a, b, a_1, b_1) \leftarrow$ COMPOSITION$(a_1, b_1, a_2, b_2, \Delta)$
3: $(a, b, \text{temp}) \leftarrow$ REDUCE$(a, b, \Delta, \lfloor\sqrt{|\Delta|/3}\rfloor)$
4: **if** control = 1 **then** $a_{out} \leftarrow a$, $b_{out} \leftarrow b$ **else** $a_{out} \leftarrow a_1$, $b_{out} \leftarrow b_1$
5: **Uncompute** a, b, temp by executing steps 3 and 2 backwards
6:
7: /* Uncompute a_1, b_1 */
8: $(a, b, a_1, b_1) \leftarrow$ COMPOSITION$(a_1, b_1, a_2, -b_2, \Delta)$
9: $(a, b, \text{temp}) \leftarrow$ REDUCE$(a, b, \Delta, \lfloor\sqrt{|\Delta|/3}\rfloor)$
10: **if** control = 1 **then** $a_1 \leftarrow a_1 - a$, $b_1 \leftarrow b_1 - ba_1 \leftarrow a_1 - a_{out}$, $b_1 \leftarrow b_1 - b_{out}$
11: **Uncompute** a, b, temp by executing steps 9 and 8 backwards
12: Return: $|a_{out}\rangle$, $|b_{out}\rangle$

Using the results of Lemmas 1 and 6, we immediately obtain the following lemma.

Lemma 7. *The algorithms MULTIPLY is correct. It can be performed using approx. $7.5\log_2|\Delta|$ qubits. Its running time is $O((\log|\Delta|)^4)$.*

Let $\mathfrak{a}$ and $\mathfrak{b}$ be $\mathcal{O}_\Delta$-ideals, $\mathfrak{a} = \mathfrak{b}^n$, and $q \in \mathbb{Z}$ such that $2^{q-1} < |\Delta| \leq 2^q$. For computing the discrete logarithm n, we use the standard framework by Shor or Kitaev [Kit96] (see [NC00] for a good introduction). At first we compute classically ideals $\mathfrak{a}^2, \mathfrak{a}^4, \dots, \mathfrak{a}^{2^q}$ and $\mathfrak{b}^2, \mathfrak{b}^4, \dots, \mathfrak{b}^{2^q}$. Then using semi-classical quantum Fourier transform and fast exponentiation, we compute the period of the function $f(x, y) = \mathfrak{a}^x \mathfrak{b}^y$. Finally we obtain the number n by classical post-processing. We conclude the following theorem.

Theorem 1. *Let Δ be a discriminant of an imaginary quadratic field $\mathcal{K}$. The computing of discrete logarithms in the ideal class group of $\mathcal{K}$ on a quantum computer can be performed using $7.5\log_2|\Delta|$ qubits in time $O((\log|\Delta|)^5)$.*

4   The Choice of a Cryptosystem

The analysis of the quantum algorithms for the discrete logarithm problem in different groups shows that the qubit-complexity of these algorithms does not depend on the size of the logarithm. The number of qubits depends only on the size of group elements and the complexity of the group operation. On the other side, the running time of a cryptosystem which security is based on the discrete log problem in an abelian group depends linearly on the size of the logarithm. In the case of RSA, the running time depends on the size of the private and public keys.

Therefore a secure and fast cryptosystem must have the following properties:

1. the size of the group elements of the underlying group must be large,
2. the space complexity of the group operation must be large,
3. the number of group operation for encryption/decryption resp. signing/verifying must be small. [1]

The RSA cryptosystem does not fulfill these properties. Especially, it violates the 3rd statement because the size of the decryption key is in general very large. The 3rd statement is also violated by the ElGamal-scheme which executes a lot of group operations.

Examples for cryptosystems which fulfill the above properties are IES for encryption and DSA for signing. In these schemes the underlying group and the discrete logarithm can be chosen independently from each other.

4.1   Timings

The following table summarizes the above results for qubit-complexity of different problems.

Problem	Number of Qubits for Solving (approx.)
Factoring n	$2 \log_2 n$
DL in $\mathbb{F}_p^\times$	$2 \log_2 p$
DL on elliptic curve over $\mathbb{F}_p^\times$	$4 \log_2 p + 8 (\log_2 p)^{1/2}$
DL in IQ-NF of Discriminant Δ	$7.5 \log_2 \Delta$
PIP in RQ-NF of Discriminant Δ	$16.5 \log_2 \Delta$ [2]

Based on these results we have run several tests to determine which cryptosystem is the fastest one. Thereby we use the number of qubits which are necessary to break a cryptosystem as a security parameter. For the RSA cryptosystem, we have measured the time for encryption and decryption. For other cryptosystems, we have measured the time for raising a group element to the power of q, where q is a 160-bit integer. This time is important because exponentiation takes the most time in the IES or DSA scheme. Due to the heuristics by Lenstra and Verheul [LV01], we have chosen the number q to be 160-bit-integer. This size of the

---

[1] This number must not be to small to resist the classical attacks.

[2] This is rough estimation. We will give accurate bounds in a subsequent paper.

discrete logarithm should be sufficient to obtain a cryptosystem which remains secure for the next twenty years. For achieving the security for a longer time, the discrete logarithm should be increased. However due to [LV01], this increase is very slow. Therefore the timings stated below will barely change.

We have run the tests with the following libraries. For RSA and $\mathbb{F}_p^\times$ we have used GMP [GMP]. For computations in real quadratic number fields, we have used GMP and NTL [GMP], [NTL]. Finally for computations in imaginary quadratic number fields and computations on elliptic curves we have used GMP and LiDIA [GMP], [LiD].

In the following table we present the mean time which we have obtained for the exponentiation in random chosen groups with random chosen group elements and random discrete logarithms. For each entry we have performed several thousands tests[3].

Number of Qubits	2048	4096	8192	16384	32768	65536	131072
RSA encryption (ms)	0.08	0.3	0.9	2.9	8.8	27.3	89
RSA decryption	2.8 ms	18 ms	121 ms	0.95 s	5.5 s	36.3 s	218 s
Exp on elliptic curves (ms)	74	93	139	296	780		
Exp in RQ-NF (ms)	320 [4]	320 [4]	320 [4]	320 [4]	3414 [4]		
Exp in $\mathbb{F}_p^\times$ (ms)	1.5	5	20	62	197	600	1700
Exp in IQ-NF (ms)	10 [4]	10 [4]	25	48	128	348	1290

The following picture displays our results graphically.

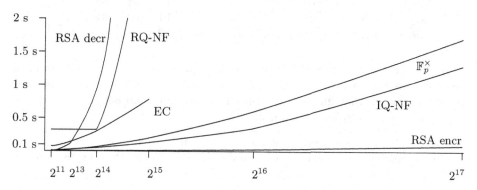

Fig. 1. X-coordinate: number of qubits (size of quantum computer). Y-coordinate: mean time for RSA en/decryption and for raising a group element to the power of q, where q is a 160-bit integer. The groups are chosen to be secure to quantum attacks on quantum computers of related size.

As we can see, the RSA cryptosystem and cryptosystems based on problems in real quadratic number fields become very slow as soon as quantum computers

---

[3] For the last two entries in the RSA decryption line we have performed only 300 resp. 10 tests.

[4] These timings correspond to classical security. On these key sizes classical attacks are more powerful than quantum attacks.

with more than eight thousand qubits can be built. Elliptic curve cryptosystems become slower than RSA even for smaller quantum computers. If quantum computers with more than a thousand qubits exist, then elliptic curve cryptosystems should not be used. Contrariwise the IES resp. DSA cryptosystems in $\mathbb{F}_p^{\times}$ and in imaginary quadratic fields stay relatively fast. The IES resp. DSA cryptosystem in $\mathbb{F}_p^{\times}$ is the fastest one as long as the size of quantum computers is less than approx. ten thousand qubits. For larger quantum computer IES/DSA in imaginary quadratic fields becomes the fastest one.

4.2   Key Sizes

Key sizes have also a relevance for the decision which cryptosystem should be used. The sizes can be derived from the first table on last side. In accordance with the last section, we will consider only the key sizes of IES/DSA cryptosystems in $\mathbb{F}_p^{\times}$ resp. in the group of ideal classes of an imaginary quadratic field. In the case of $\mathbb{F}_p^{\times}$ the public key consists of a triple (g, h, p), where p is a prime and $g \in \mathbb{F}_p^{\times}$ and $h = g^a \in \mathbb{F}_p^{\times}$, $a \in \mathbb{Z}$. It is possible to choose a small g such that the key size is approx. $2 \log_2 p$ In the case of ideal classes the key can be written as a triple (a, b, c), where (a, b) is a reduced $\mathcal{O}_{\Delta}$-ideal and $(c = b^2 - \Delta)/(4a)$. We have $a, |b| \leq \sqrt{|\Delta|/3}$ and $ac = (b^2 + |\Delta|)/4 \leq |\Delta|/3$. Therefore the public key size in this case is approx. $1.5 \operatorname{size}(|\Delta|)$.

In following table, we give some examples.

Number of qubits ($\times 1024$)	2	4	8	16	32	64	128
Key size in $\mathbb{F}_p^{\times}$ ($\times 1024$)	2	4	8	16	32	64	128
Key size in IQ-NF ($\times 1024$)	1.2^5	1.2^5	1.6	3.2	6.4	12.8	25.6

As we can see, the keys of IES and DSA cryptosystems in the group of ideal classes of an imaginary quadratic number field are always smaller than the keys in $\mathbb{F}_p^{\times}$. Assuming that quantum computers with more than 8000 qubits can be built, the key sizes differ by factor 5.

Remark 1. Note, the smallest key sizes have cryptosystems based on the principal ideal problem in a real quadratic number field. However, these cryptosystems are relative slow.

References

[Bea]   Stephane Beauregard. Circuit for Shor's algorithm using 2n+3 qubits. http://xxx.lanl.gov/abs/quant-ph/0205095.

[Ben77] C.H. Bennett. Logical Reversibility of Computation. *IBM Journal of Research and Development*, pages 525–532, November 1977.

[BW88]   Johannes Buchmann and Hugh C. Williams. A Key-Exchange System Based on Imaginary Quadratic Fields. *Journal of Cryptology*, 1(2):107–118, 1988.

---

[5] These key sizes correspond to classical security. On these key sizes classical attacks are more powerful than quantum attacks.

[BW90]   Johannes Buchmann and Hugh C. Williams. Quadratic Fields and Cryp-
            tography. In John H. Loxton, editor, *Number Theory and Cryptography*,
            volume 154 of *London Mathematical Society Lecture Note Series*, pages
            9–25. Cambridge University Press, 1990.
[CVZ+98]   I. Chuang, L. Vandersypen, X. Zhou, D. Leung, and S. Lloyd. Experimental
            Realization of a Quantum Algorithm. *Nature*, 393:143–146, 1998.
[Dra00]   Thomas   G.   Draper.   Addition   on   a   Quantum   Computer.
            http://xxx.lanl.gov/abs/quant-ph/0008033.
[GMP]   GNU multiple precision arithmetic library 4.1.4. http://swox.com/gmp/.
[GN]   Robert B. Griffiths and Chi-Sheng Niu. Semiclassical Fourier Transform
            for Quantum Computation. http://xxx.lanl.gov/abs/quant-ph/9511007.
[Ham02]   Safuat Hamdy.   *Über die Sicherheit und Effizienz kryptografis-
            cher Verfahren mit Klassengruppen imaginär-quadratischer Zahlkörper*.
            PhD thesis, Technische Universität Darmstadt, Fachbereich Infor-
            matik, Darmstadt, Germany, 2002.   http://www.cdc.informatik.tu-
            darmstadt.de/reports/reports/hamdy.diss.pdf.
[HHR+05]   H. Hfner, W. Hsel, C. F. Roos, J. Benhelm, D. Chek al kar, M. Chwalla,
            T. Kber, U. D. Rapol, M. Riebe, P. O. Schmidt, C. Becher, O. Ghne,
            W. Dr, and R. Blatt. Scalable Multiparticle Entanglement of Trapped
            Ions p643. *Nature*, 438:643 – 646, December 2005.
[HM00]   Safuat Hamdy and Bodo Möller. Security of Cryptosystems Based on Class
            Groups of Imaginary Quadratic Orders. In Tatsuaki Okamoto, editor, *Ad-
            vances in Cryptology – ASIACRYPT 2000*, volume 1976 of *Lecture Notes
            in Computer Science*, pages 234–247. Springer-Verlag, 2000.
[Kit96]   Alexei Kitaev. Quantum Measurements and the Abelian Stabilizer Problem.
            Electronic Colloquium on Computational Complexity (ECCC), 3(3), 1996.
[Kun]   N. Kunihiro. Practical Running Time of Factoring by Quantum Circuits.
            ERATO Workshop on Quantum Information Science 2003 (EQIS2003).
[LiD]   *LiDIA — A C++ Library For Computational Number Theory*.
            http://www.informatik.tu-darmstadt.de/TI/LiDIA/.
[LV01]   Arjen K. Lenstra and Eric R. Verheul. Selecting Cryptographic Key Sizes.
            Journal of Cryptology, 14(4):255–293, 2001.
[NC00]   M. A. Nielsen and I. L. Chuang. *Quantum Computation and Quantum
            Information*. Cambridge University Press, 2000.
[NTL]   NTL – a library for doing number theory. version 5.4.
            http://shoup.net/ntl/.
[PZ]   J. Proos and C. Zalka. Shor's Discrete Logarithm Quantum Algorithm for
            Elliptic Curves. http://xxx.lanl.gov/abs/quant-ph/0301141.
[Sho94]   Peter W. Shor. Algorithms for Quantum Computation: Discrete Loga-
            rithms and Factoring. In *IEEE Symposium on Foundations of Computer
            Science*, pages 124–134, 1994.
[Vol03]   Ulrich Vollmer.   *Invariant and Discrete Logarithm Computation in
            Quadratic Orders*. PhD thesis, Technische Universität Darmstadt, Fach-
            bereich Informatik, 2003. http://elib.tu-darmstadt.de/diss/000494/
[VSB+00]   L. M. K. Vandersypen, M. Steffen, G. Breyta, C. S. Yannoni, R. Cleve, and
            I. L. Chuang. Experimental Realization of an Order-Finding Algorithm
            with an NMR Quantum Computer. *Physical Review Letters*, 85:5452–5455,
            2000.
[VSB+01]   L. M. K. Vandersypen, M. Steffen, G. Breyta, C. S. Yannoni, M. H. Sherwood,
            and I. L. Chuang. Experimental Realization of Shor's Quantum Factoring
            Algorithm using Nuclear Magnetic Resonance. *Nature*, 414:883–887, 2001.

Kleptographic Attacks on E-Voting Schemes*

Marcin Gogolewski[1,**], Marek Klonowski[2,***], Przemysław Kubiak[2,†],
Mirosław Kutyłowski[2], Anna Lauks[2], and Filip Zagórski[2]

[1] Faculty of Mathematics and Computer Science,
Adam Mickiewicz University
[2] Institute of Mathematics and Computer Science,
Wrocław University of Technology
Marcin.Gogolewski@amu.edu.pl, {Marek.Klonowski,
Przemyslaw.Kubiak, Miroslaw.Kutylowski, Anna.Lauks,
Filip.Zagorski}@pwr.wroc.pl

Abstract. We analyze electronic voting schemes and show that in many cases it
is quite easy to implement a kleptographic channel, which is a profound danger
for electronic voting systems. We show serious problems with Neff's scheme. We
present also attacks on Chaum's visual voting scheme and some related schemes,
which work at least when implementation is not careful enough.

Keywords: kleptography, electronic voting, receipt voting, coercion, election integrity, verifiable pseudo-randomness.

1 Introduction

The concept of electronic elections gains popularity nowadays. Electronic voting systems contribute to decreasing costs of elections, provide more efficient procedures of counting and collecting votes and offers more flexibility than traditional voting. Due to growing interest of the topic, many new voting schemes were proposed recently. A collection of them can be found via Ronald Rivest's web page [15].

The most important goal that has to be achieved by the voting scheme is to prevent manipulation of the votes and changing the election result. At the same time, anonymity of the voters should be preserved and possibility of selling a vote by a voter must be excluded. So called *voter verifiable voting schemes* enable a voter to convince herself that her vote has been included in the final tally.

E-voting schemes become more and more sophisticated, with many wonderful tricks. Nevertheless, security analysis often disregards many dangers and does not treat the voting system as a whole. Having in mind the importance of election process and scandals

---

* partially supported by KBN grant 0 T00A 003 23.
** Author is a holder of a scholarship received from Measure 2.6 of Integrated Regional Operational Programme.
*** Author is supported in part by Domestic Grant for Young Scientists Programme from The Foundation for Polish Science.
† On a leave from Adam Mickiewicz University.

G. Müller (Ed.): ETRICS 2006, LNCS 3995, pp. 494–508, 2006.

connected with the existing voting systems [20, 19], one cannot simply assume that companies creating e-voting systems will never try to put any trapdoor in their products. Therefore a voting system should be designed in such a way that each its part can be verified.

It was observed that using randomness in e-voting schemes yields a threat of constructing a subliminal channel by a malicious voting machine. Such a machine can imperceptibly pass on its secret values by generating a random components in a cryptographic way. We point out that the actual attack on an e-voting system might be far more dangerous than a simple subliminal channel. The attack can be mounted in such a way that the information leaked can be retrieved only by a party possessing a certain secret key. Moreover, such a malicious implementation neither changes the protocol executed nor can be detected without reverse engineering of the software running on the device, and even if one reveals malicious code and data inside the device, it remains impossible to perform the same attack on other devices infected in the same way. In other words, technique called *kleptography* [22, 23, 24, 25] may favor a single party over other ones with ability to buy votes, identify its opponents, or even imperceptibly falsify the election results.

2 Previous Works and Our Contribution

Some gaps in the security of verifiable voting protocols have been noticed and described by Karlof et al. in [6]. They proposed various social engineering and subliminal channel attacks on two prominent schemes: Neff's scheme [13] and Chaum's Visual Voting [2]. These attacks enable vote coercion and changing the contents of encoded votes. They considered also denial of service attacks that can be particularly dangerous in the context of electronic voting.

Another important, recent paper about attacks on voting schemes is [17]. In this paper P. Y. A. Ryan and T. Peacock present an extended version of Prět á Voter scheme and its analysis as well as some other attacks on Chaum's and Neff's schemes not included in [6]. Authors also point to several attacks tailored for Prět á Voter scheme and design appropriate countermeasures.

In our paper we present attacks on four different verifiable voting schemes: the first one presented by M. Klonowski et al. in [7], the second one presented by D. Chaum in [2], the third one presented by C. A. Neff in [13], and the fourth one presented by P. Y. A. Ryan et al. in [3]. In some sense our work can be regarded as an extension of paper [6] of C. Karlof et. al, but we point to some aspects that seems to be far more dangerous. Namely, we prove that (pseudo) randomness can be a tool not only for creating a subliminal channel (as it was in [6]) but also for constructing a kleptographic trapdoor in the voting schemes. Such a trapdoor can be used only by a particular adversary and, as we have already noticed in the introduction, that is the cause of a huge asymmetry.

Most importantly, the possibility of implementing a kleptographic attacks in e-voting schemes is a strong argument against the point of view presented by some e-voting companies, which assure that systems are secure, since the code was written and audited according to the rigorous procedures and security standards.

Notation: In the subsequent sections Mallet is the name of an adversary and n is a number of candidates. Most systems include similar components: voting machines, registration machines, and a bulletin board, which we will denote correspondingly as VMs, RMs, and a $\mathcal{BB}$.

3   A Practical Voting Scheme with Receipts

Description of the Scheme. Below we recall the scheme from [7] (see also [21]). Besides, we took advantage of having access to the specification of a test implementation. The system consists of: VMs, RMs, and *tallying authorities*. There are also some *control servers* provided by independent watch dog organizations.

In the initialization phase, a product $\prod_{j=1}^{\lambda} y_j \bmod p$ of public keys (g, y_j, p) of λ tallying authorities is loaded to each VM, as well as the lists of the candidates. For the simplicity of a description of a protocol, we consider single elections with two candidates, namely blue party B and yellow party Y. Shortly before an election starts every VM generates two pairs of keys for signature schemes, with private keys K, K'. In the voting phase the following steps are executed:

1. A VM creates a *virtual ballot* (it exists only in the processor's memory) consisting of random numbers r, q, r_L, r_R and two sides (left and right), with $n+1$ triples on each side:

$$(B, B_1^L, B_2^L), \qquad (Y, Y_1^R, Y_2^R),$$
$$(I, I_1^L, I_2^L), \qquad (B, B_1^R, B_2^R),$$
$$(Y, Y_1^L, Y_2^L), \qquad (I, I_1^R, I_2^R).$$

   r is a random ballot identifier (according to the specification r is a 64 bit random number r_s concatenated with VM's DSA signature of r_s). The element I contained in two triples is simply the identifier r. One can see on each side of the virtual ballot there are three columns: in the leftmost one there are the names of the candidates C and identifier I, in the next two columns on each side there are so called *RE-onions*: C_1^X, C_2^X, where $X \in \{L, R\}$, for each candidate C, and RE-onions I_1^X, I_2^X encoding identifier I.

   The rows are permuted independently on each side, according to permutations π_L, π_R respectively. Each π_X is obtained deterministically from the contents of all columns on side X. RE-onions are ElGamal ciphertexts

$$(m \cdot (\textstyle\prod_{j=1}^{\lambda} y_j)^k, g^k), \tag{1}$$

   for plaintexts m defined for $X \in \{L, R\}, i \in \{1, 2\}, C \in \{B, Y\}$ as follows:

$$m = (C, r_X, \mathrm{ser}_V, \mathrm{sig}'_{K'}(C, r_X, i)) \text{ for } C_i^X, \tag{2}$$
$$m = (r, \mathrm{ser}_V, \mathrm{sig}'_{K'}(r, i, X)) \text{ for } I_i^X,$$

   (ser_V is an identifier of the VM). For each RE-onion Z_i^X, $Z \in \{C, I\}$, the exponents k are computed as follows: the VM creates a signature $\mathrm{sig}_K(q, i, X, Z)$ and uses it as a seed of a pseudo-random generator $\mathcal{R}$; then k is taken from the output of the generator. sig is a deterministic signature scheme (recall that the VM generates its keys itself, such a procedure poses a risk to RSA private keys, compare [25] and references given there).

2. The VM prints a *hash ballot* – it is a commitment to the virtual ballot that contains r, and – in a machine readable form - hashes of r, q, r_L, r_R and of all RE-onions Z_i^X, in the same order as in the virtual ballot.

3. The visualization of the virtual ballot appears on the screen of the VM.

4. The voter chooses a side (say R) and a party for which he votes (say B).

5. VM creates and prints a *voting ballot* that contains a pair (B_1^R, B_2^R) of RE-onions corresponding to the icon chosen and a pair (I_1^R, I_2^R) of RE-onions encoding the identifier I from the same side. These onions are printed in a random order, say given by a permutation π_{vb}. Additionally, the voting ballot contains a VM's signature of the values printed.

6. (Optional step) From the side X not used for voting (i.e. $X = L$ in our example) the voter may choose one column $i \in \{1, 2\}$ and some number of RE-onions Z_i^X in column i. The VM prints a *control ballot* that contains:
   - the RE-onions Z_i^X chosen for verification with their identifiers Z,
   - the signatures used to generate exponents k in these onions,
   - the string r_X,

   After getting the control ballot the voter should compare the identifiers on the control ballot with the corresponding positions on the screen.

7. The voter comes to a RM and presents the voting ballot. Four RE-onions contained in the ballot are read in and stored for counting purposes, provided that the signature of the voting machine is valid. Simultaneously, the voting ballot is marked as used, and it is retained by the voter.

The voter can control honesty of VM by checking the control, hash and voting ballots through a machine that may read the printed values.

When all ballots are registered the tallying of the votes may start. From our point of view the tallying phase has some important features: there are no intermediate bulletin boards, in particular there is no bulletin board with the onions collected by RMs. Hence it is not necessary to collect voting ballots (as a fake watch dog organization for example) to change election results.

Only the last, final tallying authority publishes the list of completely decoded onions, and the list must contain:

- pairs encoding an identifier: $(r, \text{ser}_V, \text{sig}'_{K'}(r, 1, X))$, $(r, \text{ser}_V, \text{sig}'_{K'}(r, 2, X))$,
- and the same number of pairs encoding single votes: $(C, s, \text{ser}_V, \text{sig}'_{K'}(C, s, 1))$, $(C, s, \text{ser}_V, \text{sig}'_{K'}(C, s, 2))$, where $C \in \{B, Y\}$, and s are random strings.

Having her control ballot each voter can check whether the identifier r from the ballot is on the list.

Betraying Voters Preferences via Digital Signatures. We show how a VM may betray voter's preferences, even if the ballots are built according to the protocol. Such information may be available for Mallet on the final bulletin board. The attack is possible if the signature scheme $sig'_{K'}$ used to create r from r_s is probabilistic, like DSA in the test implementation. A DSA signature (R, S) is generated as follows:

$$R = (g^\alpha \bmod p) \bmod q, \tag{3}$$

$$S = \alpha^{-1} \cdot (\mu - K' \cdot R) \bmod q, \tag{4}$$

where μ is a message to be signed, K' is the private key of the signer, and α is a random number. First, a VM can leak the signing key K' to Mallet in a kleptographic way [24] using only one signature. For this purpose, the VM must learn only the public key of Mallet. Then in every virtual ballot (except the one used for leaking K'), in all onions encoding candidates, the VM uses numbers α that betray r contained in the onions encoding identifiers. For example, let $\alpha = \alpha'\alpha''$, where

$$H(\alpha', r_s) = \alpha'', \tag{5}$$

and H is a good hash function. For each vote (2) Mallet finds α using equality (4). Then he can match the exponents α and numbers r_s by equality (5). Of course, the exponents α used in (3) as well as S have to be coprime with $\text{ord}g$. One can easily see that most α fulfill these conditions.

Betraying Voters Preferences via Ordering on the Ballot. Note that the voting ballot is constructed after a voter made her choice. We show that a kleptographic channel can be created, if an implementation allows to permute at random onions O_1, O_2, O_3, O_4 to be placed on the voting ballot. It can carry 4! messages and point, for instance, to the choice of the voter or leak secret keys of the VM (which would allow to prepare votes outside the VM).

Assume that Mallet has a public key y_M and a private key x_M such that $g^{x_M} = y_M$. Let O_1, O_2, O_3, O_4 be the list of onions for the voting ballot after sorting them lexicographically. Assume that g^k is the second component of an RE-onion O_1. Then VM computes $z = y_M^k$ and uses a few initial bits of $H(z, O_1, O_2, O_3, O_4)$ to determine a permutation π' on $\{1, 2, 3, 4\}$. Let π'' be the message–permutation on $\{1, 2, 3, 4\}$ to be hidden. Then the VM puts the onions on the voting ballot so that the ith onion gets position $\pi'(\pi''(i))$ for $i = 1, \ldots, 4$. Note that Mallet is able to recover π''. Indeed, he computes $z := (g^k)^{x_M}$, and then π' by its definition. Then finding π'' is straightforward. Note that a third party cannot find z and therefore π'' remains hidden.

Another trick is to use permutations π_L, π_R of rows on both sides of the virtual ballot. In the specification the permutation π_X depends on all columns on the side X, and thus its validity cannot be verified on the control ballot, where one column from side X is missing. Hence π_L, π_R itself might have any form convenient for Mallet. For example α from (3) might be a compressed point P^β (cf. [18]) of an elliptic curve E which is a part of Mallet's public key now defined as (E, P, Y_M), where $Y_M = P^{x_M}$. As a result Mallet might determine $\pi_X = H(X, Y_M^\beta)$ on the basis of α, and then might check with help of the hash ballot whom the vote has been cast for. Interestingly, in the above case of Diffie-Hellman protocol it suffices, instead of the point P^β, to pass only its x-coordinate (see [11]).

Selling Votes via Random Parameters. "Random" numbers r_s, q, r_L, r_R can be used in a malicious way; recall that the way of generating them is not controlled in the protocol. Let y_M, y be components of DSA public keys of Mallet and the VM respectively, with appropriate private keys x_M, K'. As a result, the key $K^* = y_M^{K'}$ for a symmetric encryption scheme might be established according to the Diffie-Hellman protocol and the numbers r_s, q, r_L, r_R might be ciphertexts addressed to Mallet. Another option to generate K^* is to use α from the previous paragraph.

Changing Votes Cast by RM. Now we assume that a RM cooperates with a malicious VM. The method taking advantage of a permutation on the voting ballot can be used to transfer the secret keys K, K' from the VM to the RM in a kleptographic way. Also, the VM may generate the parameters q through a pseudorandom generator with a secret seed. Again, the seed can be transferred to the RM in a kleptographic way.

Even if the onions on voting ballots are not permuted in step 5 of the scheme, it is still possible to transfer one bit per ballot using permutations π_L, π_R. Because $\pi_{vb} = id$ now, then the onions from each exemplary pair (B_1^R, B_2^R), (I_1^R, I_2^R) are not separated, and the order of the pairs on the voting ballot is determined by their order on the virtual ballot. Hence if bit 1 will be transmitted, each π_X, $X \in \{L, R\}$, might be determined according to ascending order of the values y_M^k for k from (1), where (1) are the second onions in consecutive rows on side X. When bit 0 need to be sent, descending order is created. Because exponents k on both sides of the virtual ballot are different, the names of candidates look to be permuted randomly and independently on each side.

Once RM got the keys it can modify the votes. It is facilitated by the fact that voting ballots are presented to the RM in about the same order as they are generated. Having appropriate q, the RM tries to "open" the onions containing the votes from the voting ballot. That is, for a given q, for each $i \in \{1, 2\}$, $X \in \{L, R\}$, $C \in \{B, Y\}$ the RM computes k used to construct an onion, Then it computes g^k and checks which onion has this number as the second component. If it is so, then the RM can retrieve the plaintext encoded by the first component by dividing it by $(\prod_{j=1}^{\lambda} y_j)^k$. Then the RM can replace the discovered onions containing a vote by a pair of new onions with a different choice – this is possible, since the RM has the necessary keys. Note that the replacement is done yet before the pools close, and without any cooperation with tallying authorities.

4   Chaum's Visual Voting Scheme

Description of the Scheme. Due to space limitation we describe this scheme only briefly (for more details see [2]). The system consists of: VMs, *tallying authorities* (mixes) and a $\mathcal{BB}$. Let us sketch the voting procedure:

1. On a VM, a voter chooses a monochrome picture with the name of the candidate chosen. This *ballot image* is encoded as a matrix B of pixels.
2. The VM deterministically computes pseudo-random binary matrices W^t and W^b based on deterministic signatures $s^t(q)$ and $s^b(q)$ respectively, where q is a ballot serial number. Then it determines L^t and L^b based on B, W^t and W^b so that $L^t \otimes L^b = B$, and it is possible to obtain an image of the vote from L^X and W^Y for $X \in \{t, b\}$, $Y \in \{t, b\} \setminus \{X\}$. Namely every second bit of L^X is from W^X, the other half of bits is denoted by R^X, and $B^X = R^X \otimes W^Y$, where B^X is composed from every second bit of B. Separately, each of L^t, L^b gives no information about B,

just like one-time-pad. Each image L^X, $X \in \{t, b\}$, will be printed on a transparent *layer*, and both layers X will be laminated together during the print.

3. The VM provides 4-tuples: $\langle L^b, q, D^t, D^b \rangle$ for the *bottom layer* and $\langle L^t, q, D^t, D^b \rangle$ for the *top layer*, where D^Y (based on $s^Y(q)$) for $Y \in \{t, b\}$, are deterministic onions containing information necessary to decrypt W^Y, and hence to obtain B^X from one layer X only (recall that B^X is a subset of pixels of $L^X \otimes W^Y$). Each 4-tuple is printed on a separate layer.

4. The voter verifies that both layers encode the ballot image $B = L^t \otimes L^b$ and the last three components of the 4-tuples are identical on both layers.

5. The voter either aborts (i.e. if verification fails), or selects the top or the bottom layer. Henceforth, the selected layer shall be denoted by X.

6. The system makes two digital signatures and provides them as a tuple:

$$\langle s^X(q), o^X(L^X, q, D^Y, D^X, s^X(q)) \rangle, \tag{6}$$

where o^X is called *overall signature*.

7. The voter separates two layers. The layer $Y \neq X$, unselected in step 5, will be shredded by a poll worker (we call him *Shredder*). Its digital counterpart in VM's memory will be destroyed as well. The layer X is a receipt for the voter. Its electronic version is used for vote counting purposes.

8. The voter can perform a consistency check to ensure that the digital signatures of the tuple are correct, i.e. $s^X(q)$ correctly determines D^X and the half of the pixels of L^X. He can also check that his vote is included in the receipt batch.

9. At the end of the election day the VM's receipt batch is transferred to the $\mathcal{BB}$ (we assume that there is no additional subliminal channel, so e.g. the ordering of receipts is deterministic).

10. Later the receipt batch is mixed and partially decoded by successive trustee-operated mixes. When the original images are revealed the election results are calculated.

Attacks on Serial Numbers. The description of the scheme [2] does not specify how the serial numbers q are created. We show that if it is admitted that the serial numbers are random, then we can install a kleptographic channel through which a VM can betray its signing key to an arbitrary party observing the first $\mathcal{BB}$. This is a threat not included in [6] in the list of potential weaknesses of the scheme.

Namely, let N_M, e_M be a public RSA key of Mallet ("public" in the sense that VM knows that it is the key of Mallet). The VM will transmit not the secret signing key k, but $z = k^{e_M} \bmod N_M$. Therefore nobody but Mallet will be able to recover k. Note that once Mallet obtains the signing keys, he will be able to buy votes (from q and (6) he can reconstruct the vote cast) or to make fake votes and claim that election results are manipulated. We assume also that VM and Mallet share a secret key s (this key will not be sufficient to recover k).

In order to create a vote the VM chooses q until it finds a proper one encoding some digit of z expressed in radix α system (for example $\alpha = 2^2$). Let $\ell = \lfloor \log_\alpha N_M \rfloor + 1$. Hence for the current q the VM takes the first $\lfloor \log_2 \ell \rfloor + 1$ bits of $H(q, s)$ as an index i of the digit z_i, where $z = (z_{\ell-1} z_{\ell-2} \ldots z_0)_\alpha$. Then the VM compares z_i with the last $\lfloor \log_2 \alpha \rfloor + 1$ bits of $H(q, s)$. If they disagree, then q is discarded. Recovering the digits of z is a random process. Each q appearing on $\mathcal{BB}$ brings information on some α-ary digit of z. Notice that the use of Mallet's key does not change the official behaviour of the VM, which is still consistent with the primary protocol.

Leaking a secret through the $\mathcal{BB}$ might be possible even if numbers q published on the $\mathcal{BB}$ after closing the polls must turn out to be consecutive. The point is that VM may use the numbers q in a non-consecutive way (at least at the beginning of the election day). Each voting ballot will carry one bit of the secret. Due to a limited number of voters perhaps only a part of the secret could be transferred in such a way, but this still poses a threat — mind the lattice attacks, which are practical, if a fraction of the RSA secret exponent is known to an attacker [1].

Let us describe the general idea. The image printed on each side depends on q and the picture B of a candidate chosen by a voter. Namely, the signature $s^Y(q)$ of VM under q determines W^Y, which together with B^X, i.e. the half of the picture B, determines R^X, i.e. the half of L^X. We shall fix some position (i, j) on R^t. It follows from the encoding scheme that on L^b a pattern of two black squares is printed - their positions at $W^b_{i,j}$ depend on q only, and not on the voter's choice. On the second layer at position $R^t_{i,j}$ VM prints the squares in exactly the same way - if the image B is white at (i, j), or the mirror image, if B is black at this place. In the second case by superimposing both transparents we get a black spot on B, while in the first case we get a spot with black and transparent pixels. We fix position (i, j) so that for about half of the votes at this point should be a black spot. Thus there are two possible configurations of the squares at the position $R^t_{i,j}$ - they encode one bit. The point is that this bit is determined by q and the choice of a candidate C. So when a voter casts a vote by choosing the picture B_c, VM takes the first number q such that the bit $q - 1 \bmod \ell$ of the ℓ bit secret is not transferred yet onto $\mathcal{BB}$, and B_c together with q encodes on $R^t_{i,j}$ the value of this bit. If we are lucky that the voter chooses the upper layer, then a bit of a secret will be transmitted. (A slight change of the protocol ensures that there will be no strategy for the voter to choose a layer that does not leak the secret.)

The attack is probabilistic in the sense that we have no control which candidates will be chosen by the voters. However, two popular candidates C would suffice (their pictures B_c must differ at some position (i, j)) to transfer onto $\mathcal{BB}$ some portion of the first bits of the secret. Moreover, the above method might be used to indicate to Mallet whether the vote is cast for some particular candidate C ($R^t_{i,j} = 1$) or not ($R^t_{i,j} = 0$).

In the next attack Mallet shall cooperate with Shredder, who observes the ordering of serial numbers q on unselected layers that he is given to shred. To make the attack more realistic we assume that Shredder is able to remember for a short time only two last digits of q (after a while he can write them down somewhere). On a voting ballot the serial number is printed over the bar-code representing it, and is expressed in base b system.

Consequently, Shredder is able to completely describe any permutation of any b^2 consecutive numbers. Thus the VM might transmit digits of z mentioned above, where z is expressed in radix $(b^2)!$ system (detailed method of coding numbers into permutations and vice versa can be found in [8]). To transfer 2048 bits in case of $b = 16$ one permutation from S_{256} and one permutation from S_{76} are enough, when for $b = 10$ three "digits" from S_{100} and one from S_{93} are needed.

Countermeasures. The attacks described above become impossible, if deterministic sequence of issuing serial numbers is guaranteed. A simple and effective solution we propose is to link subsequent receipt by "linear-linking" similar to the one used in a time-stamping system (see [5]). Let $\mathcal{L}_i$ be the ith receipt issued (6), and let the next serial number should be $q_{i+1} = h(\mathcal{L}_i)$, where h is some collision free hash function. We may start with $\mathcal{L}_0$ equal to the serial number of the VM. In this procedure VM learns the serial number q_{i+1} only after step i.

Of course, linking does not solve all problems with VMs. A user may transmit a secret code on the touch-screen or may select and cancel successive candidates from a secret sequence. This might trigger a mechanism in which the VM makes itself voter's choices and the colluding voter simply collects a valid receipt, which indicates one of $2n$ possibilities (the choice of a layer and a candidate). The set of ℓ such voters obtains one of $(2n)^\ell$ possible messages. Moreover, if a choice of a candidate is cancelled no signature is printed on the layers (so the receipt will be impossible to verify without all tallying authorities), but the printout can already contain a ciphertext of the secrets.

Note also that to prevent homomorphic attack [4] one should avoid naive implementation of a signature scheme $s^X(q)$. If for example the RSA signatures $s^t(q_1)$, $s^t(q_2)$ are available on $\mathcal{BB}$, then $s^t(q)$ for $q = q_1^{\alpha_1} q_2^{\alpha_2}$ and any $\alpha_1, \alpha_2 \in \mathbb{Z}$ can be easily calculated by an attacker. Accordingly, any receipt (6) with such a number q and $X = b$ might be opened.

5   The Neff's Scheme

Scheme Description. Below we follow a draft description [13]. The voting infrastructure includes voting machines (to be consistent with other subsections we call them VM instead of *DRE* [6] or *voting device* [13]), a $\mathcal{BB}$, and a verifiable mix-net.

The encoding techniques used are as follows: let ℓ be a security parameter ($10 \leq \ell \leq 15$), a *verifiable choice* (VC) is a $n \times \ell$ matrix of *ballot mark pairs* (BMP). Each row of VC represents a single candidate. A BMP is a pair (b_L, b_R) of ElGamal ciphertexts ($b_X = (g^{\omega_X}, m_X y^{\omega_X})$, $X \in \{L, R\}$), where pair (g, y) is a public key for the mix-net, $m_L, m_R \in \{Y, N\}$, and symbols Y, N represent, respectively, a fixed element $G \in \langle g \rangle$ and the group's $\langle g \rangle$ neutral element. Each BMP in the row representing the candidate chosen contains two ciphertexts of the same symbol - i.e. $(m_L, m_R) \in \{(Y, Y), (N, N)\}$. All other rows of VC contain BMPs with $(m_L, m_R) \in \{(N, Y), (Y, N)\}$.

Each BMP (b_L, b_R) in can be partially *opened*, according to a bit ϵ. If $\epsilon = 0$, then VM reveals the plaintext of b_L by showing the random exponent ω_L. If $\epsilon = 1$, then the right ciphertext is opened.

Finally we might describe the voting procedure:

1. VM shows a list of all candidates $C_1, C_2, \ldots, C_n$ to the voter.
2. The voter chooses a candidate C_i.
3. Let $S = \{0, 1\}^\ell$ be the set of all ℓ-bit strings. VM prepares a VC representing a vote for the candidate C_i. It chooses $x_j \in S$ for $1 \leq j \leq n$ at random. For $j \neq i$, if $(x_j)_k = 0$, then VM encrypts (N, Y) in the jth row and the kth column of VC. If $(x_j)_k = 1$, then (Y, N) are encrypted. If $(x_i)_k = 0$, then the kth BMP in the ith row contains (N, N), otherwise (Y, Y). Next the VM commits prepared VC by

printing it or it's hash on a receipt with a *ballot sequence number* BSN (BSN is present in the documentation of the *VoteHere* project based on the scheme).

4. The voter chooses strings $c_j \in S$ for $j \neq i$.
5. The VM computes *pledges* $p_j := c_j \oplus x_j$ for $j \neq i$ and $p_i := x_i$. VM commits sequences of strings $\{p_k\}_{k=1}^{n}$ in such a way that they cannot be changed but the voter gains no knowledge of the pledges.
6. The voter chooses c_i - a challenge to the row representing the candidate C_i.
7. For $j = 1, 2, \ldots, n$ and $k = 1, 2, \ldots, \ell$, VM opens BMP of VC in the jth row and the kth column according to bit $\epsilon = (c_j)_k$ as it was described before. VC with opened BMPs is called *opened verifiable choice* (OVC).
8. Values $\{(C_j, c_j)\}$ for $1 \leq j \leq n$ are printed on the receipt.
9. The voter gets the receipt containing BSN, the hash of VC, and (C_j, c_j) for $j = 1, 2, \ldots, n$.
10. After closing the polling station OVC is sent to the $\mathcal{BB}$ together with the associated BSN.

All ballots collected on the $\mathcal{BB}$ are then processed according to a *verifiable shuffle protocol* [14].

Attacks on the Scheme. Karlof et al. [6] describe a "random subliminal channel attack" on the Neff's scheme. They suggest to use the same ω for both encryptions in a given BMP. Since only one ciphertext per BMP is opened on OVC, the VM can send $n\ell \cdot \log_2(\text{ord}g)$ bits in such a channel. Of course, usage of the same ω clearly indicates that the two exponents in the BMPs are not randomly chosen. We repair this shortcoming in a kleptographic way and extend the attacks to N votes simultaneously.

According to the documentation [12] of *VoteHere* project, the numbers BSN are "unpredictably assigned to voters" (if there were no BSNs we would assume $N = 1$). The way of the BSNs assignment might be known to Mallet, hence he would be able to find on the $\mathcal{BB}$ all consecutive N-tuples of ballots issued by the VM.

Let $y_M = g^{x_M}$ is Mallet's public key. By $\text{BMP}_{t,i,j}$ we denote the BMP in the ith row of the jth column on the tth ballot. Let g^{ω_L} and g^{ω_R} be chosen at random as the first components of the ElGamal ciphertexts in the $\text{BMP}_{N,n,\ell}$ (this BMP is selected arbitrarily, e.g. $\text{BMP}_{1,2,1}$ could be taken as well). Let

$$K_X^* = h_X(y_M^{\omega_{\sigma(L)}}, y_M^{\omega_{\sigma(R)}}) \tag{7}$$

for $X \in \{L, R\}$, where $\sigma : \{L, R\} \to \{L, R\}$ is a permutation such that $g^{\omega_{\sigma(L)}} \leq g^{\omega_{\sigma(R)}}$ and h_L, h_R are some good one-way functions.

Having calculated the keys K_L^*, K_R^* the VM might prepare the exponents for creating BMPs. Let $\omega_{t,i,j}$ be a block of a message that has to be hidden kleptographically in $\text{BMP}_{t,i,j}$. Then the exponents used for creating $\text{BMP}_{t,i,j}$ are $E_{K_L^*}(\omega_{t,i,j})$, $E_{K_R^*}(\omega_{t,i,j})$, for $t = 1, \ldots, N$, $i = 1, \ldots, n$, $j = 1, \ldots, \ell$, and $(t, i, j) \neq (N, n, \ell)$, where E denotes a secure symmetric encryption scheme. To prevent repetition of the block-values $\omega_{t,i,j}$ for different triples (t, i, j), compression of the whole message can be made (note that ord$g$ is a large number).

When the OVC's are published on the $\mathcal{BB}$, Mallet can retrieve the secret messages. Namely, he reconstructs the key K_X^* from $\text{BMP}_{N,n,\ell}$ contained in OVC_N by putting

g^{ω_L}, g^{ω_R} in ascending order, raising them to power x_M and applying, respectively, h_L, h_R to the pair obtained. Since one of the exponents $E_{K_L^*}(\omega_{t,i,j})$ and $E_{K_R^*}(\omega_{t,i,j})$ is included in OVC, Mallet can decrypt it and obtain $\omega_{t,i,j}$.

If VM is forced somehow to use really random exponents for ElGamal encryption, then it is also possible to hide the choice of the voter. Namely, the strings ω_L, ω_R used for encryption in a fixed BMP are discarded until the system provides a number such that $[H(y_M^{\omega_L}, y_M^{\omega_R}) \bmod n] + 1 = i$, where C_i is the candidate chosen by the voter. Then the choice of the voter can be easily detected by Mallet, while for anybody else the information encoded in g^{ω_L}, g^{ω_R} is impossible to retrieve.

Additional kleptographic channels might be mounted thanks to BSN numbers assigned to ballots. It is reasonable to assume that each VM has some scope of at most $N_{\max}$ numbers BSN. If the method of issuing the numbers is not specified, then a VM may release BSNs in a manner that additionally hides $\omega_{t,i,j}$. Suppose that Mallet knows the BSN_1. Then BSN_t may be calculated from BSN_{t-1} as the $(r+1)$st yet unused "random" number from the scope, where

$$r = H(y_M^{E_{K_L^*}(\omega_{t-1,n,\ell})}, y_M^{E_{K_R^*}(\omega_{t-1,n,\ell})}) \bmod (N_{\max} - (t-1))$$

for some good one-way function H. Again, only Mallet would be able to recover the order of the ballots issued. Furthermore, instead of using the same pair (K_L^*, K_R^*) of keys to all $\omega_{t,i,j}$, distinct pairs of subkeys could be used: for example $K_{X,t,i,j}^* = f(K_X^*, t, i, j)$ for some function f and $X \in \{L, R\}$. Moreover, the argument t may be replaced by a kind of linear linking [5] of the values $\mathrm{BSN}_t, \mathrm{BSN}_{t-1}, \dots, \mathrm{BSN}_1$.

Another source of attacks are the numbers x_j used by the protocol. They are useful for our purposes for instance at the moment when the flaws related to random exponents become patched. Note that the numbers x_j are shown by OVC's. Indeed, if $j \neq i$ where C_i is the candidate chosen by the voter, then we can reconstruct $(x_j)_k$ for $k \leq \ell$ as follows. If the b_L is opened and it contains N, or b_R is opened and it contains Y, we have $(x_j)_k = 0$. Otherwise, $(x_j)_k = 1$. In the case of x_i the above rule provides flipped values, for the k's where b_R is opened. VM may choose all bit-strings x_j according to $H(y_M^{\omega_L}, y_M^{\omega_R})$ for some g^{ω_L}, g^{ω_R} being the first components of ElGamal ciphertexts of some BMP at established position. Then with probability $1 - 1/2^\ell$ we can detect the index i where the x_i computed according to the rule disagrees with the value obtained from $H(y_M^{\omega_L}, y_M^{\omega_R})$, and so the choice of the voter.

Let us remark that it is possible to build yet another kleptographic channel. Again, suppose that BSNs are used (if not, then take $N = 1$). VM determines the exponents ω_j in advance, for $j = 1, 2, 3, \dots, 2n\ell N$, computes g^{ω_j} and sorts them. Then VM encodes a secret message as an ordering in which permuted numbers g^{ω_j} are used in consecutive ciphertexts. So there is room for $(2n\ell N)!$ messages. To make Mallet the only addressee of the message the VM determines a permutation $\pi' = H(y_M^{\omega_1}, y_M^{\omega_2}, \dots, y_M^{\omega_{2n\ell N}})$, where the arguments of H are ordered lexicographically, and instead of a permutation π'' encoding the secret message VM can order the numbers g^{ω_j} according to the permutation $\pi = \pi' \circ \pi''$.

Finally, note that if the scope for BSNs is large enough, then the BSNs may carry messages — we may apply the same method as in Section 4.

6 Chaum, Ryan, Schneider's Scheme

Short Description of the Protocol. For the sake of simplicity, the authors of [3] illustrate a single race with v candidates. The scheme includes: RMs, $\mathcal{BB}$ and k tellers ($k \geq 3$). Each of the tellers operates two Chaum's mixes, and the ith mix, $i = 0, 1, \ldots, 2k-1$, has a pair of keys: a secret key SK_{T_i} and the corresponding public key PK_{T_i}. There is also an authority which is responsible for generating the ballots.

For each ballot the authority prepares a seed which is a random number D_0 and a sequence of $2k$ random values g_i taken from the set $\{0, 1, \ldots, 2^{32} - 1\}$. Let us define

$$D_{i+1} := \{g_i, D_i\}_{PK_{T_i}}, \qquad \theta_i := \left(\sum_{t=0}^{i} h(g_t)\right) \bmod v,$$

where h is a good hash function. In this way the authority computes an *onion* D_{2k} and a *cyclic offset* $\theta = \theta_{2k-1}$. A voting card consists of two columns: in the left column there is a list of the candidates after applying a cyclic shift by θ positions, the last cell of the column remains empty. All but the last of the cells of the right column are empty (one of them will be chosen by a voter). In the last cell of the right column the code of D_{2k} is printed.

In the voting phase a voter selects a voting card at random. She marks her candidate by making a sign $\times$ in the appropriate cell on the right side, just as for the traditional voting procedures. Let r_{2k} be the index of a cell with mark $\times$, $r_{2k} \in \{0, 1, \ldots, v-1\}$, and define $r_i := r_{i+1} - h(g_i) \bmod v$. Note that $r_0 = r_{i+1} - \theta_i \bmod v$ for any $i \in \{0, 1, \ldots, 2k-1\}$, where r_0 is the cell reflecting the voter's choice on non-shifted list of candidates. Then the voter detaches the left and the right hand side, the left hand side is destroyed, the right hand strip, containing (r_{2k}, D_{2k}), is fed into the RM. The RM marks the strip as being used and returns it to the voter as her ballot receipt.

Later, during tallying phase the ith mix transforms (r_{i+1}, D_{i+1}) into (r_i, D_i) using its private key SK_{T_i} for a deterministic encryption scheme. The input and the intermediate values of the tallying process are presented on $\mathcal{BB}$.

Attack on the Random Seed. We assume that the authority uses a secret hash function H (a hash function with a secret key) and for every ballot repeats the following procedure:

1. randomly selects D_0 and germs $g_0, \ldots, g_{2k-1}$,
2. deterministically computes onions $D_1, \ldots, D_{2k}$,

until the *Collision Condition* (CC) holds for $j = 2k - 1$:

$$CC_j : \qquad h(g_j) + \theta_{j-1} \bmod v = H(D_{j+1}) \bmod v,$$

i.e. until $H(D_{2k}) \bmod v = \theta_{2k-1} (= \theta)$.

Then the authority outputs a card with the offset θ and the onion D_{2k}. Obviously, the CC_j might be applied for any $j = 2k - 1, \ldots, 1$ (for $j = 0$ it is useless). Hence the teller who is operating the jth mix server and knows hash function H will be able to compute vote values, i.e. r_0. Accordingly, if the teller recognize partial election results as unfavorable, a DoS attack may be launched.

Note that for the attack exploiting CC_{2k-1}, everyone who knows the secret hash function H and sees a voter's ballot receipt, gets immediately knowledge about the voter's choice. Especially, it concerns members of the commission at the polling station and the RM.

As one can easily see, the expected number of tries needed to find the collision in CC_{2k-1} is equal to v. The same complexity bound applies for an attack on the extension of the scheme, where θ is a permutation, not an offset. If the authority knows the base ordering, i.e. the order of candidates on the list not permuted yet, then it is able to point out the position of the supported candidate on the list permuted according to θ_{2k-1}. The D_{2k} is accepted, when $H(D_{2k}) \bmod v$ indicates the same position as θ_{2k-1}. Hence anyone who knows H is then able to point out the cell where the sign $\times$ should be put for the candidate supported. It is easy to see that in more general case of elections which allow to vote for u out of v candidates the complexity of a single ballot preparation grows to $\frac{v!}{u!(v-u)!}$ trials on average, or to $\frac{v!}{(v-u)!}$ if a voter must rank chosen candidates, and the ranking is also important for an attacker.

Suppose now that the attack is launched on some fixed layer j, and H is a keyed hash function with secret key K^*. Then K^* might be transmitted kleptographically encoded in D_{j+1}, the same value that satisfies the condition CC_j. Namely assume that Mallet possesses a public key of ElGamal elliptic curve cryptosystem. Then the length of the ciphertext z containing K^* equals about 340 bits if the points are compressed. Let us consider a secret hash function H', which is known to Mallet, and the value $H'(D_{j+1})$. Suppose that z is expressed in radix α system and let $\ell = \lfloor \log_\alpha(2^{340} - 1) \rfloor + 1$. Then the first $\lfloor \log_2 \ell \rfloor + 1$ bits of $H'(D_{j+1})$ indicate an index i of some digit z_i, where $z = (z_{\ell-1} \ldots z_1 z_0)_\alpha$, and the last $\lfloor \log_2 \alpha \rfloor + 1$ bits of $H'(D_{j+1})$ should be equal z_i (if are not, then given D_{j+1} is discarded). On average, one out of α strings D_{j+1} properly describes one digit of z. Consequently, the average complexity of a single ballot preparation increases to $\alpha \cdot v$ trials. As one can see (cf. [9], "the occupancy problem"), for any $c > 1$ the number $c\ell \ln \ell$ of values D_{j+1} suffice to receive the complete z with probability at least $1 - (\frac{1}{\ell})^{c-1}$. Mind that the mix servers are supposed to operate much more than $2\ell \ln \ell$ ballots. Once Mallet gets z he decrypts K^* and then is able, on the basis of CC_j, read θ_j from all the D_{j+1} he obtained.

Changing Votes. The attack below seems to be problematic due to the number of co-operating parties, but fully explores the possibilities given by CC_{2k-1}.

Let us assume that a RM is cooperating with a fake or dishonest watch-dog organization (WDO) who collects receipts from voters. Let us assume that votes collected by WDO will not be checked by voters (they do not have receipts now). A WDO can pass information about onions collected to the RM and RM is now free to modify electronic vote representation, provided that the Mercuri method [10], considered as some possible extension of the scheme, is not implemented. If it is not, then spoiling election results of the most popular candidate is possible for RM even without knowing H: it may randomly change r_{2k} for votes collected by WDO.

Audit Procedure. Note that the ballots are formed properly, so the only possibility to catch cheating authority is to prove that the entropy used in the generation process is low. But let us observe that for any fixed j the sample space size for (θ_j, D_{j+1}) is larger than $\left(2^{32}\right)^{j+1}$. Instead of sampling from the space of that size, the authority mounting the attack on onions D_{j+1} chooses (still independently at random) from the space which size is larger than about $\left(2^{32}\right)^{j+1}/(\alpha \cdot v)$ (we have omitted the size of D_0). For reasonable $\alpha \cdot v$ this room is still too large to detect the fraud regarding the number of votes investigated during the audit phase.

It must be noted that to minimize the possibility of the above attacks in new, distributed procedures of ballot cards generation outlined in [17] and [16], the mixes (called *clerks*) should not be delivered from the same source.

7 Conclusions

A variety of attacks on the main election schemes have been proposed in [6, 17] and in our paper. Most of the attacks are possible because too much trust is put in a single party of the protocol, for example in a Voting Machine. We conclude that designs of schemes should try to avoid using randomness. Use of deterministic signatures and encryption schemes and Chaum's MIX like style of communication (with messages passed in lexicographic order) facilitates verification and reduces the possibility of existence of subliminal channels and kleptographic attacks.

References

1. Dan Boneh, Glenn Durfee, and Yair Frankel. An attack on RSA given a small fraction of the private key bits. In Kazuo Ohta and Dingyi Pei, editors, *ASIACRYPT*, volume 1514 of *Lecture Notes in Computer Science*, pages 25–34. Springer, 1998.
2. David Chaum. Secret-ballot receipts: True voter-verifiable elections. *IEEE Security and Privacy Magazine*, 2(1):38–47, January/February 2004.
3. David Chaum, Peter Y.A. Ryan, and Steve Schneider. A practical voter-verifiable election scheme. In *ESORICS*, volume 3679 of *Lecture Notes in Computer Science*, pages 118–139. Springer, 2005.
4. George I. Davida. Chosen signature cryptanalysis of the RSA public key cryptosystem. Technical Report TR-CS-82-2, Dept of EECS, University of Wisconsin, Milwaukee, 1982. Available from: http://www.uwm.edu/~davida/papers/chosen/.
5. Stuart Haber and W. Scott Stornetta. How to time-stamp a digital document. *Journal of Cryptology*, 3(2):99–111, 1991.
6. Chris Karlof, Naveen Sastry, and David Wagner. Cryptographic voting protocols: A systems perspective. In *USENIX Security Symposium*, pages 33–50, 2005.
7. Marek Klonowski, Miroslaw Kutyłowski, Anna Lauks, and Filip Zagórski. A practical voting scheme with receipts. In *ISC*, volume 3650 of *Lecture Notes in Computer Science*, pages 490–497. Springer, 2005.
8. Donald Ervin Knuth. *The Art of Computer Programming: Seminumerical Algorithms*, volume 2. Addison-Wesley, Reading, Massachusetts, 3rd edition, November 1998.
9. Boris Koldehofe. Simple gossiping with balls and bins. *Stud. Inform. Univ.*, 3(1):43–60, 2004.

10. Rebecca Mercuri. Government: a better ballot box? *IEEE Spectr.*, 39(10):46–50, 2002.

11. Victor S. Miller. Use of elliptic curves in cryptography. In Hugh C. Williams, editor, *CRYPTO*, volume 218 of *Lecture Notes in Computer Science*, pages 417–426. Springer, 1985.

12. C.Andrew Neff. Detecting malicious poll site voting clients. [online]. September 2003 [cited 10 January 2006]. Available from: `http://www.votehere.com/vhti/documentation`.

13. C.Andrew Neff. Practical high certainty intent verification for encrypted votes. [online]. October 2004 [cited 10 January 2006]. Available from: `http://www.votehere.com/vhti/documentation`.

14. C.Andrew Neff. Verifiable mixing (shuffling) of ElGamal pairs. [online]. April 2004 [cited 03 March 2006]. Available from: `http://www.votehere.com/vhti/documentation`.

15. Ronald L. Rivest. Voting resource page. [online, cited 10 January 2006]. Available from: `http://theory.lcs.mit.edu/~rivest/voting/index.html`.

16. Peter Ryan. Socio-technical trade-offs in cryptographic voting schemes. Workshop on Electronic Voting and e-Government in the UK, 27th–28th February 2006. Slides. Available from: `http://www.nesc.ac.uk/action/esi/contribution.cfm?Title=639`.

17. Peter Y.A. Ryan and Thea Peacock. Prêt à voter: a systems perspective. Technical Report 929, University of Newcastle upon Tyne, School of Computing Science, September 2005. Available from: `http://www.cs.ncl.ac.uk/research/pubs/trs/papers/929.pdf`.

18. Scott A. Vanstone, Ronald C. Mullin, and Gordon B. Agnew. Elliptic curve encryption systems. US patent 6141420, October 2000. Available from: `http://patft.uspto.gov/netacgi/nph-Parser?patentnumber=6,141,420`.

19. Clint Curtis affidavit. [online, cited 10 January 2006]. Available from: `http://www.buzzflash.com/alerts/04/12/images/CC_Affidavit_120604.pdf`

20. The e-voting machine fraud. [online, cited 10 January 2006]. Available from: `http://www.linkcrusader.com/vote_machines.htm`

21. The e-voting project web page. [online, cited 10 January 2006]. Available from: `http://e-voting.im.pwr.wroc.pl`.

22. Adam Young and Moti Yung. The dark side of "black-box" cryptography, or: Should we trust capstone? In *CRYPTO*, volume 1109 of *Lecture Notes in Computer Science*, pages 89–103. Springer, 1996.

23. Adam Young and Moti Yung. Kleptography: Using cryptography against cryptography. In *EUROCRYPT*, volume 1109 of *Lecture Notes in Computer Science*, pages 62–74. Springer, 1997.

24. Adam Young and Moti Yung. Bandwidth-optimal kleptographic attacks. In *CHES: International Workshop on Cryptographic Hardware and Embedded Systems, CHES, LNCS*, pages 235–250, 2001.

25. Adam Young and Moti Yung. Malicious cryptography: Kleptographic aspects. In Alfred Menezes, editor, *CT-RSA*, volume 3376 of *Lecture Notes in Computer Science*, pages 7–18. Springer, 2005.

Visual Document Authentication Using Human-Recognizable Watermarks

Igor Fischer and Thorsten Herfet

Saarland University, 66041 Saarbrcken, Germany,
{fischer, herfet}@nt.uni-saarland.de
http://www.nt.uni-saarland.de/

Abstract. Digital signatures and message authentication codes are well known methods for ensuring message integrity. However, they rely on computations which are too hard to be performed by humans and are instead done on computers. Trusting a digital signature implies trusting the computer which produced/checked it. Often, this trust cannot be taken for granted. This paper presents a method for visual authentication of large messages which relies on embedding a human-recognizable watermark and needs practically no computational power on the receiver side. Also, using a simple challenge-response mechanism is proposed to prevent attackers from obtaining signatures without author's knowledge.

1 Introduction

Paperless office has been a vision for decades and still has not come to exist. Although much – probably the vast majority – of communication today is done electronically, the most important parts are still performed in hardcopy. Most banks today offer online banking, and acquisition of a real estate can be negotiated per e-mail. However, to open a bank account, as well as to buy a property, one will have to print the documents, sign them by hand and return them by mail. The main, if not the only reason, is a legal one: for a contract to be binding, it must be provable and non-repudiable that the contracting parties have given their consent to it. This condition is actually two: (1) The contracting parties, and no-one else, have to give consent and (2) the consent has to be given to the contract, and not to anything else.

With hand-written signatures, both conditions are satisfied: a signature can be traced back to the originator (or at least the legal practice assumes so), and it may be safely assumed that the signer has read the contract before signing it. Digital signatures [1], as envisioned for the application, also fulfill the first condition: only the righteous owner should be able to apply them, because they are in his possession, e.g. on a smart card in his wallet. Furthermore, they are protected by some secret (like a PIN), so that even in the case of theft or loss, no-one else can use them. Fulfilling the second condition, however, is not that simple. Because of the computational complexity, the signing is done by a computer (e.g. the chip on the smart card). Since such devices normally do not have sufficient displaying capabilities, the user cannot actually know what exactly is being signed. To better understand the danger, consider a typical scenario:

G. Müller (Ed.): ETRICS 2006, LNCS 3995, pp. 509–521, 2006.

Alice[1] is writing a document (e.g. a contract with Bob) on her desktop computer, using some text-processing program. The computer is an ordinary, general-purpose personal computer. In addition, Alice can count on help from Trent, a trusted entity, which, for example, can be implemented as a smart card and a reader attached to the computer. Trent is the keeper of Alice's signature and signs documents Alice sends him in her name. Having written the document, Alice authenticates herself towards Trent (e.g. types in her PIN) and clicks the "Sign!" button on the computer. The computer sends the document to Trent, which signs it and returns it to Alice's computer. Alice sends the document with the accompanying signature to Bob.

Unfortunately, Mallory has installed a malicious program on Alice's computer, which changes documents to Mallory's favor without Alice's knowledge. When Alice sends the document to Trent, Mallory's program intercepts it, changes it, and passes it further to Trent. Trent, not being aware of Mallory, signs the altered document and returns it back, again through Mallory's program. Alice notices nothing. If she tries to take a look again at the document, Mallory's program would show her her original document. But when she tries to send it to Bob, the program sends the altered, signed version. Bob checks the signature and is confident that the document comes from Alice.

This is, obviously, something that must never happen and the very reason why digital signatures have been introduced in the first place. The reason why the scheme fails is, interestingly, not some weakness of the digital signature algorithm, although such weaknesses usually get much publicity. The reason for the failure is that current general purpose personal computers are inherently unsafe and cannot be trusted. As far as secure devices, such as smart cards, are concerned, they can, by definition, be trusted to perform their function correctly. But, since they lack a display, the user cannot know on which data the function is performed. The weak link is from the computer display to the trusted device.

There are basically two ways of solving the problem: making the hardware trustworthy, or empowering the user to check what is actually happening inside the computer. Attempts to pursue both approaches already exist, but have their limitations. An overview is given in the next section. In section 3, an approach belonging to the latter family, based on visual cryptography, is described. Differing from previous approaches, it uses visually recognizable watermarks to ensure the authenticity of the message. Also, using a simple challenge-response protocol is proposed to prevent the attacker from obtaining valid signatures without authors consent.

2   Related Technology

2.1   External Trusted Device with Input and Output Capabilities

One possibility to make the hardware trustworthy is to equip trusted hardware with input and output interfaces directly usable by humans, e.g. a display and a

---

[1] The actors' names try to follow the convention from [2].

keyboard. This approach is already in wide use for electronic payment, especially with debit cards. The readers for such cards include a small LCD and a numerical keypad and are certified by some authority. In Germany, for example, the authority is the Central Credit Committee (Zentraler Kreditausschuss, ZKA), which lays down the criteria which card readers have to fulfill for a certain application. The highest security level is provided by Class 3 readers, with a built-in display and a keypad.

With such readers, the user can verify the document on the display before using the keypad to initiate the signing of the document. As long as the card reader and the card can be trusted — and this is the basic assumption behind the technology — this procedure is perfectly safe. In practice, however, due to physical limitations on the display, it is useful only for very short documents: the reader's display is usually only a dozen or two characters wide with only a couple of lines. This is sufficient for displaying the price or merchant identification, but not for checking a 20-page legal document.

2.2   Trusted Computing

An opposite approach is pursued by the Trusted Computing Group (TCG), a "not-for-profit organization formed to develop, define, and promote open standards for hardware-enabled trusted computing and security technologies, including hardware building blocks and software interfaces, across multiple platforms, peripherals, and devices" [3], with AMD, Hewlett-Packard, IBM, Intel Corporation, Microsoft and Sun Microsystems, Inc. as promoters and over a hundred participants. Instead of attaching an external secure device with its own in- and output, the idea is to convert the whole user's computer, including the keyboard and display, into a "trusted platform" (TP). At the same time, the platform should remain a general purpose computer, where anyone (or at least the owner) can install software or add peripheral devices. An additional requirement is that computers must remain affordable in order to be accepted by the market. This seemingly impossible combination of goals is achieved by only a minor modification to the hardware, in which a per-definition trusted device, the so-called Trusted Platform Module (TPM), plays a central role. The TPM is a kind of cryptographic microcontroller – a processor with volatile and non-volatile memory and simple I/O bus, – much of the kind employed in smart cards.

The platform relies on the TPM to trace the state and changes to its hardware and software, so no change can pass unnoticed. The trust in the platform is achieved through the chain of trust. At power-on, the first program that runs (in common personal computers typically from the BIOS) would compute a checksum or some other hash value of the next program(s) to be performed, and compare the value with the one stored and signed by the TPM. The initial values are stored by the some trusted entity, e.g. the computer manufacturer. If the values match, the next program can be trusted and is executed. This program might perform some "measurements" of the hardware (checking the graphics adapter, the hard disk etc.) and use the same mechanism to check if the values are correct, i.e. that nothing has been changed. Again, if this test passes, the hardware can be trusted. This chain unfolds further, over the operating system loader and the operating system, up to application programs. In each step, a program checks its successor before executing it.

The security in this approach relies on the trustworthiness of the BIOS (the trust in TPM is per definition granted). As long as Mallory cannot manipulate the first program executed after power-on, she cannot plant a virus (or any other program) unnoticed. In practice this usually means that Mallory would have to have physical access to the computer. Even then, the computer might be physically protected, e.g. sealed, so that user could detect unauthorized opening. The Trusted Computing (TC) specification requires at least that the BIOS is physically marked so that removing it cannot pass unnoticed [4], at least for someone who bothers to take a look inside the computer. For even higher protection it is envisioned for the future to place the first program to be executed inside the TPM.

Leading manufacturers have announced TC products for 2006. However, the full technology will not be a part of Microsoft's new operating system [5,6], codenamed Longhorn, although it was expected to be, and the API specification has not yet been made public. The customers also seem to be reluctant about accepting it, as the technology has faced serious criticism. For example, the German Association of Insurance Industry (GDV) is decidedly against TC, for three basic reasons: lack of legal framework, lack of control possibility and high misuse potential [7]. It is feared, among other things, that through TC manufacturers might coerce users into using or not using some soft- or hardware, and that private information might be indirectly disclosed without user's knowledge. The TCG has attempted to dispel the fears [8], but their success remains unknown. That the fears are not baseless is indirectly confirmed by the TCG best-practice manual [9], which denounces such misuses of the TC technology. The manual is, however, only a recommendation, and compliance with it cannot be enforced. As experience teaches us, if something bad can be done, it usually will be done by someone. A recent example is the Sony BMG "rootkit" DRM tool, which has made computers vulnerable to virus attacks without notifying the users [10].

Notice that TC in its current form protects the cautious owner against malicious manipulations on the computer. It does not protect remote users (e.g. his communication partners) from willful abuse by the computer's owner. If the owner alters the BIOS, remote users have no way of knowing it. Therefore, to achieve the level of trust needed for legally binding documents, TC platforms will have to be complemented by technology which is unconditionally trusted, such as external smart cards.

2.3   Visual Cryptography and Authentication

Both above approaches have drawbacks, including the need to extend the trust from the personal smart card to other devices. An appealing, low-tech alternative for short messages is visual authentication [11]. The idea was originally developed for authentication of electronic payments and is based on visual cryptography [12].

Visual cryptography is a perfectly secure cryptographic method based on a visual secret key. The encryption is computationally intensive and is done by the computer, but the decryption is performed with little conscious effort by the human visual system. The method is most easily implemented for encrypting black-and-white images, and works as follows:

The image to be encoded is scaled up by an integer factor, typically a multiple of two. Thus, for each original pixel in the image there will be a square of $N \times N$ pixels in the scaled image. For a black pixel in the original image, all pixels in the corresponding $N \times N$ square (so-called "subpixels") will be made black. For white original pixels, half of the subpixels will be made black and the other half white. Visually, looking from appropriate distance, such squares appear gray. Which subpixels will be made black and which white is randomly decided for each square. This way, the whole black-and-white original image is transformed into a bigger one. Originally black areas are simply enlarged, but originally white are also transformed into a uniform distribution of black and white pixels, which appear gray to a human observer.

The next step is to split the transformed image into two "shares", so that neither of them alone reveals any information about it. A "black" square, consisting of only black subpixels, is randomly split into two complementary squares, each with half black and half white subpixels. A "white" square is split into two identical squares. It is useful to consider white subpixels to be transparent, as if printed on a transparency. Then, by superimposing the shares (laying the transparencies over each other), "black" and "white" squares, comprising the scaled image, reappear. If we denote black subpixels in the shares with 1 and white with 0, superimposing the shares corresponds to binary OR.

This is a visual implementation of the 2-out-of-2 secret sharing technique [13]. The basic idea of k-out-of-n secret sharing is to split a message into n "shares", so that none of them alone, nor any combination of less than k of them, reveal anything about the message, but k shares combined are sufficient to reconstruct the whole message. If $n = k = 2$, this is actually a one-time pad cryptography. One of the shares (transparencies in our case) is used as the cyphertext and the other as the key. But each for itself looks like a uniform distribution of black and white pixels.

Visual cryptography can be used for authentication, although not directly. Basically, the idea is for the user (Alice) and the trusted device (Trent) to share a secret key — Alice would have it in the form of a pre-printed transparency. Trent would send not only the signed document back to Alice, but also its visually encrypted version. She would visually check if it is identical to the document she sent him and only if yes, use the signed document. This simple approach, however, would not work, because Mallory knows both the plaintext and the cyphertext and, consequently, can deduce the secret key. Knowing the key, she can produce any document and properly encrypt it, and Alice would believe it comes from Trent. Therefore, Trent must expand the document with information known to Alice, but not to Mallory, before encrypting it. Several related methods have been proposed in [11]:

1. Content/Black Areas: The transparency contains two areas, denoted "black" and "content", and Mallory does not know which is which. Trent constructs the cyphertext so that the document appears in the "content" area, and the "black" area is completely black. This requires the transparency to be a one-time pad, otherwise the "black" area of the cyphertext would not change from message to message and Mallory could simply identify it

2. Position on the Screen (or, generally, output device): The transparency has a marked area in which the document has to appear. Mallory does not know where this area is positioned.

3. Black and Gray: instead of "white", "gray" is used. It is encoded by having three quarters of the subpixels in a square black and one quarter white. This increases the security even when the plaintext is known, because for a fixed share of a gray square there are many ways (four in case of $N = 2$) of constructing the other share. So, for every "gray" pixel in the original image, Mallory has only a low probability of turning it into black. It does not hold for the opposite direction, however, so Trent is required to send the document (black on gray) and its inverted version (gray on black) to Alice for checking. The other drawback is that this approach reduces the contrast, making the result difficult to visually recognize.

3   Using Watermarks for Obfuscating the Plaintext

The above visual authentication approaches require transparencies bigger than the document and possibly reduce its readability. These are not grave issues for the originally envisioned electronic payment application, where the documents would be short (like the price to pay) and displayed on a high-contrast screen. However, for documents consisting of several pages they might be impractical.

An alternative approach is presented here. Recall that the reason for not using visual cryptography directly was Mallory's knowledge of the plaintext, which allowed her to deduce the secret and, consequently, to arbitrarily modify the cyphertext, without Alice noticing it. To counter this danger, Trent can modify the document in a way known to Alice, but unknown to Mallory. On the other hand, the modified document should still allow Alice to check that the essential content arrived to Trent unaltered. Both can be achieved by incorporating a faint image, a kind of "watermark", into the document.

Watermarks have been used for centuries in paper production, presumably from the beginning for security-related purposes. They are images, visible under special circumstances, embedded into the paper. Today they are most often used on paper money as a protection against forgery. There is also an analogy for digital data, so-called digital watermarks, which are hard-to-detect and hard-to-remove pieces of information hidden among the original data. For the purpose of this text, watermarks are understood as digital, but visible, human-recognizable images. The proposed method, which is suitable for longer documents, is basically as follows:

Alice (human) and Trent (trusted device) share a secret (a physical transparency in Alice's case and its digital representation in Trent's) and, in addition, a list of images, which function as visual challenges, and simple alphanumeric responses. Such a list is just a more sophisticated variant of a Transaction Authorization Number (TAN) list, often used in Europe for online banking. It can be produced and distributed in a similar way as the TAN lists, by the entity which manufactures or distributes Trent. Alice could get her list by mail and Trent online. The distributing entity can use a mechanism similar to Alice's to authenticate Trent before sending him the encrypted list.

Alice composes the document on her ordinary, not-to-be-trusted personal computer and sends it to Trent — an external hardware device (a smart card or a USB stick), a trusted remote computer, or a tamper resistant program [14] running on the user's PC (in the latter case no additional hardware is needed). The document can be in any form Trent understands (a PDF document, LaTeXsource code etc.), but it is practical to think of it as a black-and-white image, or a sequence of images in case of multiple pages.

Trent, having received Alice's i-th document (page), superimposes it (performs logical OR) with the i-th image (watermark) from the list, splits the result into two shares, one of the shares being the secret held by Alice, and sends her the other share. Alice lays her transparency over the share (she can do it directly on her computer display or print the share) and checks if

1. the document she wrote is embedded into Trent's image unaltered, and
2. the image superimposed to it is the i-th watermark from her list

If both conditions are satisfied, Alice sends Trent the corresponding alphanumeric response. Trent checks if the response corresponds to the i-th image in the list (the one he superimposed to the document) and if yes, signs the document and returns the signed file to Alice. The workflow is depicted in Figure 1. An example for the transparency, Trent's challenge, and the superposition result are shown in the Figure 2.

The purpose of superimposing the document with a watermark is to make any tampering with the document obvious to Alice. However, it does not prevent Mallory from misleading Trent into signing a modified document and using it for his own benefit. Mallory could impersonate Alice towards Trent and make him sign any document. Since she could be in control of Alice's computer, she could send the document in Alice's name, who would not be able to prevent her, even if she would notice the fraud. Only through the challenge–response mechanism can Trent be sure that it is not Mallory asking him to sign the document and can confidently send the signed document back to Alice.

3.1   Attacks

Knowing the document, Mallory can still deduce for each transparency how the squares corresponding to black pixels in the document (but not in the whole challenge!) are encoded (split into shares). But, this would not be enough to allow her to meaningfully modify it. She would need to be able to turn black document pixels into white, and white into black, without damaging the watermark.

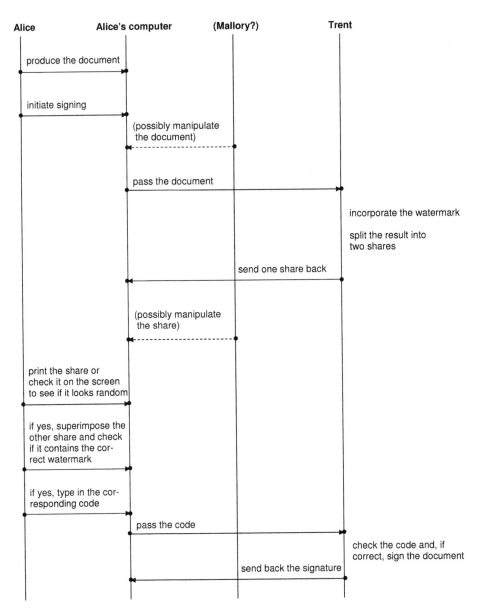

Fig. 1. Document authentication protocol with possible attack poinst for Mallory

Consider the task of turning a black document pixel $d = 1$ into white. Through the watermarking the pixel is ORed with the corresponding watermark pixel w, which is unknown to Mallory. She knows the superposition result, $d \vee w = 1$ and how it is coded in shares, but, not knowing w, cannot deduce $\overline{d} \vee w$. She can force the corresponding square to "white", by inverting its share, or throw a coin and decide whether to leave it as it is or invert it. In both cases she is guessing

Fig. 2. An example of visual authentication through watermarking: the secret key (transparency) (top), the Trent's share (middle), and the watermarked and encoded document (bottom)

the value of w and his chances depend on the distribution of white and black in the watermark. For watermarks with an equal number of black and white pixels Mallory's probability of guessing one pixel are $1/2$. In a typical document, where a character is composed of dozens of pixels, Mallory's chances of tampering with the document without distorting the watermark are negligible.

In turning a white document pixel into black, Mallory has similar problems. She knows $d = 0$, but not whether $d \vee w$ is 0 or 1. If she decides to invert the corresponding share, she again runs into the risk of distorting the watermark. What she can do is to force an illegal share, by making all subpixels in the square black, but such tampering with the cyphertext is easily spotted before overlaying it with the secret key.

Results of example attacks, where Mallory has tried to change the sum 10,000 into 100,000, are shown in Figures 3 and 4.

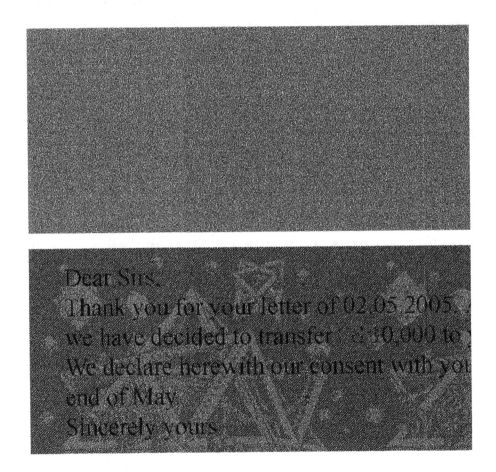

Fig. 3. An example attack with randomly inverting shares of pixels that need to be manipulated. The forged document share (top) is indistinguishable from the original one, but the superposition result clearly reveals tampering.

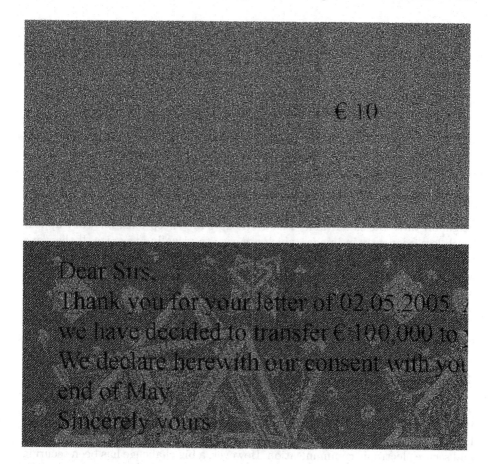

Fig. 4. An example attack, where the attacker, for the pixels he wants black, forces the complete pixel shares to be black. The result is better than in the previous example, but the forged document share (top) is clearly illegal.

3.2 Security Considerations for Repeated Use

The basic scheme above has a potential weakness. Since Trent uses logical OR to combine the watermark with the document, Mallory knows that any black square in the document will remain black in Trent's challenge image. This might not be enough to manipulate the document, because she still lacks the information corresponding to "white areas" in the document, but allows her to deduce a part of the secret key (the transparency). After a repeated use of the same transparency, the danger is that Mallory could collect enough data to reconstruct it in full.

There are several possibilities to counter this danger:

1. Instead of repeatedly using single transparency, let Alice and Trent share a whole codebook — a staple of transparencies in Alice's case. Each would be used only once, as a one-time pad.

2. Trent might use XOR instead of OR for combining the watermark and the document. This way Mallory, although knowing every document pixel d, does not know if $d \oplus w$ is 0 or 1 (white or black) for any pixel in the challenge image and, consequently, cannot meaningfully modify the document. The drawback is that the document becomes visually harder to recognize.
3. Trent introduces some simple transformation to the document before watermarking it, like inversion, slanting, rotation, or translation. The transformation can be only slight, like rotation for several degrees and translation for a couple of pixels. The document remains visually recognizable to Alice, but becomes unknown to Mallory.

The last two approaches alone are still susceptible to statistical attacks. High-resolution black-and-white images have the property that for most pixels their neighbors have the same value. Pixels on edges are exceptions, but they appear much less frequently in images which are easy to visually recognize. If the same secret key is used over and over again, Mallory could use this property to gain knowledge about it. It is therefore advisable to combine them with the first approach. For practical purposes, however, it is not necessary to use each transparency only once. Depending on the complexity of the watermarks and Mallory's assumed pattern recognition capabilities, Alice could use a transparency several times before Mallory collects enough data for an attack.

4   Conclusion

The computational complexity of "classical", non-visual cryptographic techniques implies the need for cryptographic devices. Classical cryptography offers a high level of protection for digital documents and is essential in ensuring an efficient and secure electronic communication. However, a big challenge has been securing the path from the human to the cryptographic module. This path is currently the weakest link, which limits the security of the whole cryptographic chain.

In this paper, an approach for bidirectional document authentication based on visual cryptography and watermarking was presented. It requires no additional computer hardware and is very easy to implement using the existing infrastructure. Compared to previous such approaches, this method uses the available area of the visual shared secret area (the transparency) more efficiently, which makes it much more suitable for authentication of larger documents, even consisting of a number of pages. The proposed challenge-response mechanism prevents the man-in-the-middle attacker from obtaining a signed document without author's approval. Assuming that the author would not approve a forged document, the attacker is prevented from obtaining a valid signature on a forged document.

On the user's side, the method requires a list of watermarks and a staple of transparencies. For each document page, a watermark and a transparency are needed. The watermarks, which appear only faint over the document, can in the list be printed reduced in size, so that a dozen or two fit on a sheet of paper. The transparencies, however, have to be full-sized and would probably be distributed in a form of a booklet.

The method is not inteded for to be used among arbitrary number of users and trusted devices. It essentially relies on symmetric cryptography, so the number of key sets (staples of transparencies and watermarks) increases linearly with the number of user per trusted device. However, for the envisioned application — securing the channel between a user and her trusted device — there should be only one key set per user.

References

1. Rivest, R., Shamir, A., Adleman, L.: A method for obtaining digital signatures and public-key cryptosystems. Communications of the ACM **21** (1978) 120–126
2. Schneier, B.: Applied Cryptography. John Wiley & Sons, Inc. (1996)
3. Trusted Computing Group: Home page (2005)
4. Pearson, S., ed.: Trusted Computing Platforms. Prentice Hall PTR, Upper Saddle River, New Jersey (2003)
5. Fried, I.: Microsoft: 'Trusted Windows' still coming, trust us (2005)
6. Slater, D.: Microsoft trusted computing updates (2005)
7. Chiachiarella, F., Fasting, U., Fey, T., Leppler, S., Lux, G., Lubb, P., Moser, A., Otten, G., Schlattmann, J., Schumann, S., Schweizer, L., Souren, F.J.: Das Risiko Trusted Computing für die deutsche Versicherungswirtschaft. Schriftenreihe des Betriebswirtschaftlichen Institutes des GDV **13** (2004)
8. Trusted Computing Group: Trusted Computing Group Clarifications for the German Insurance Industry Association paper "The Threat, Trusted Computing, to the German Insurance Industry" (2005)
9. TCG Best Practices Committee: Design, implementation, and usage principles for TPM-based platforms (2005)
10. Russinovich, M.: Sony, rootkits and digital rights management gone too far (2005)
11. Naor, M., Pinkas, B.: Visual authentication and identification. In: CRYPTO '97: Proceedings of the 17th Annual International Cryptology Conference on Advances in Cryptology, London, UK, Springer-Verlag (1997) 322–336
12. Naor, M., Shamir, A.: Visual cryptography. Lecture Notes in Computer Science **950** (1995) 1–12
13. Shamir, A.: How to share a secret. Communications of the ACM **22** (1979) 612–613
14. Aucsmith, D.: Tamper resistant software: An implementation. In: Proceedings of the First International Workshop on Information Hiding, London, UK, Springer-Verlag (1996) 317–333

Author Index

Lecture Notes in Computer Science

For information about Vols. 1–3908

please contact your bookseller or Springer